P9-DKE-990

CLIFFS NOTES

HARDBOUND LITERARY LIBRARIES

CLASSICS LIBRARY

Volume 3

Early Christian/European Classics

Part 1

7 Titles

ISBN 0-931013-05-4

Library distributors, hardbound editions:
Moonbeam Publications
18530 Mack Avenue
Grosse Pointe, MI 48236
(313) 884-5255

MOONBEAM PUBLICATIONS
Judith M. Tyler, President
Elizabeth Jones, Index Editor

FOREWORD

Moonbeam Publications has organized **CLIFFS NOTES**, the best-selling popular (trade) literary reference series, into a fully indexed hardbound series designed to offer a more permanent format for the series.

Hardbound volumes are available in a **BASIC LIBRARY**, a 24 volume series. The current softbound series (over 200 booklets) has been divided into five major literary libraries to help researchers, librarians, teachers, students and all readers use this series more effectively. The five major literary groupings are further subdivided into 17 literary periods or genres to enhance the use of this series as a more precise literary reference book.

Hardbound volumes are also available in an **AUTHORS LIBRARY**, a 13 volume series classified by author, covering 11 authors and over 70 Cliffs Notes titles. This series helps readers who prefer to study the works of a particular author, rather than an entire literary period.

CLIFFS NOTES HARDBOUND LITERARY LIBRARIES
1990 by
Moonbeam Publications
18530 Mack Avenue
Grosse Pointe, MI 48236
(313) 884-5255

Basic Library - 24 Volume
ISBN 0-931013-24-0

Authors Library - 13 Volume
ISBN 0-931013-65-8

Bound In U.S.A.

THE CLASSICS LIBRARY

Volume 3

Early Christian and European Classics

Part 1

CONTENTS

Beowulf

BEOWULF

NOTES

including

- *Introduction*
- *The Manuscript*
- *Terms to Remember*
- *List of Characters*
- *Genealogy*
- Beowulf: *A Synopsis*
- *Character Analyses*
- *Critical Essays*
- *Suggested Essay Topics*
- *Selected Bibliography*

by
Elaine Strong Skill, Ph.D.
University of Oregon

NEW EDITION

INCORPORATED
LINCOLN, NEBRASKA 68501

Editor

Gary Carey, M.A.
University of Colorado

Consulting Editor

James L. Roberts, Ph.D.
Department of English
University of Nebraska

ISBN 0-8220-0228-0

Printed in U.S.A.

1992 Printing

Cliffs Notes, Inc. Lincoln, Nebraska

CONTENTS

BEOWULF
Notes

INTRODUCTION

Beowulf is one of the oldest existing poems in the English language, but because it is written in Old English (Anglo-Saxon), most of us are unable to read it without a translation. Fortunately, however, there are many good translations which give us an opportunity to read this colorful, heroic poem of England's epic age.

When critics first began to study *Beowulf*, they were primarily concerned with the historical elements of the poem, and they neglected the basic value of the poem as an extraordinary piece of literature. There are, of course, historical references in the text–for example, King Hygelac's death during his war against the Franks (c. 520 A.D.), recorded by Saint Gregory of Tours in his *Historia Francorum*, but such historical references are not the most important elements in the poem.

Christian influences and biblical references are also critical to a serious understanding of the poem and have drawn considerable attention from scholars. Because these elements are combined with early folktales and heroic legends of the Germanic tribes who immigrated to England, early *Beowulf* scholars began to investigate whether or not Christian and biblical references were added later to an originally pagan poem. Since the 1939 Sutton Hoo discovery of a seventh-century ship, in which both Christian and pagan artifacts were discovered alongside one another in the burial barrow, we know that paganism did exist alongside Christianity during the approximate era in which *Beowulf* was composed. The Sutton Hoo discovery also indicates a high level of creativity during that time, as well as a genuine appreciation for works of art. The late British critic J.R.R. Tolkien was one of the first modern critics to view *Beowulf* as a unified work of art with all of its elements in harmony, and most critics today recognize the *Beowulf* poet's extraordinary ability to combine several unlikely, disparate elements in order to create a unified work of art.

We have no idea who the author of *Beowulf* was, and we have only a general idea of when the poem was written, but historical factors have helped us to establish a period of time during which the poem could have been written. This matter will be discussed more thoroughly later in these Notes, but one should recognize that, first and foremost, *Beowulf* fascinates modern readers because its themes are still valid. The motives behind Beowulf's actions and deeds are still acceptable to our society. We may look askance at the monsters and the dragon in the poem, but they are as much a part of *Beowulf* as the armor that the hero wears. Because we can still accept the noble purpose behind Beowulf's deeds, we can judge the social conduct and views of the characters in the epic in accordance with the mores of the period in which the poem is set.

THE MANUSCRIPT

Brief History The *Beowulf* manuscript has had an interesting life. Apparently, it was kept in a monastery until Henry VIII decided to dissolve all but a few of the monastic orders. Many of the monasteries' books were shipped to Europe, where butchers bought them and wrapped meat in their pages. We owe a great deal to Lawrence Nowell, a late sixteenth-century humanist who saved a number of the old manuscripts, among which was *Beowulf*. Later, Sir Robert Cotton gained possession of the poem, but the manuscript was again threatened during England's 1642–46 civil war. Puritans were burning books by the hundreds, but the Cotton collection was saved by Sheriff Bromfall of Blunham, who stored the books at Stratton, Bedfordshire. Later, in 1731, a fire at Ashburnham House, where the collection was stored, destroyed many manuscripts and charred many more, one of which was the *Beowulf* manuscript. Scorched at the upper and outer edges, the manuscript began to crumble. Prior to the fire, however, two transcripts had been made by a Danish scholar, and it is these transcribed manuscripts which have helped later scholars to reconstruct the damaged sections of the original *Beowulf* manuscript.

In 1753, the original copy of *Beowulf* was obtained by the British Museum, and, in order to preserve it, the museum encased each individual page in transparent plastic. Since then, the English Text Society has reproduced two facsimiles of the early manuscript, in 1882 and 1959.

Beowulf is sometimes referred to as the *Cotton Vitellius A.XV*, the reference indicating Sir Robert Cotton's arrangement in his personal library. Cotton arranged his collection by placing certain manuscripts under the busts of various Roman emperors and further arranging them by number under a letter of the alphabet. Thus, you would have found *Beowulf* on the shelf under the bust of Emperor Vitellius, Section A, Number 15.

Despite its harrowing history, the *Beowulf* manuscript is remarkably well-preserved and reasonably complete. Scholars believe that there are some missing lines, but these are so few that the poem's basic structure is not seriously flawed. Perhaps the greatest difficulty today in studying the manuscript comes from transcribal errors that crept in during the two and a half centuries before today's extant manuscript was copied down. Of course, however, our general ignorance of the language and the numerous words not found in other Old English manuscripts also gives us trouble. Overall, though, outside of human errors, the text itself is remarkably well-preserved, and the poem itself is rousing and filled with grandeur.

Date and Place of Origin Accurately dating *Beowulf* has been one of the most controversial issues surrounding the poem. Dates range from the eighth century for the epic's original composition to the late part of the tenth century as the period during which the manuscript which we possess today was copied down. Nearly all critics compare the poet's use of language structure and vocabulary with the works of other early authors. Christian beliefs, pagan practices, and the treatment of the Danes by the poet also enter into the dating process. Remember, too, that the events recorded in *Beowulf* happened two hundred years before the poem was written, and two hundred and fifty more years elapsed before our extant manuscript was copied down.

Linguistic tests, including syntax, grammar, vocabulary, and usage, have been employed on occasion to date the *Beowulf* manuscript, but these tests are not generally reliable. Similar linguistic usage, when compared to previous authors, simply indicates the *Beowulf* poet's familiarity with the traditional verse forms more than it determines a definite date for *Beowulf*'s creation. A better test for dating

Beowulf lies in the poet's culture and his attitudes toward the Danes in the poem.

Using the poet's cultural ideas and his attitudes toward the Danes, some critics believe that the poem was composed either in Northumbria or East Anglia. These critics usually point to the Sutton Hoo discovery in Suffolk for confirmation of the poem's being written in East Anglia. However, equally qualified scholars argue for a West Mercia origin. Neither of these arguments are substantial enough to pinpoint a definite place for the composition of *Beowulf*, but it is clear that the cultural material in *Beowulf* is of the heroic tradition. The conclusion most critics agree on is that the manuscript was probably copied either in a monastery or at the court of a nobleman.

As we said earlier, the poet's treatment of the Danes helps us date *Beowulf* more accurately than do the linguistic and cultural approaches. The Danes are treated with a measure of sympathy and given some praise at the beginning of the poem, but when Grendel makes his appearance, the poet inserts a subtle undercutting of the Danish king's ability to protect his thanes (his warriors); the poet also points out the Danes' lack of courage to challenge Grendel. Significantly, it is a Geat, Beowulf, who must finally save the Danes. In addition, the *Beowulf* poet is critical of the Danes because they are heathens and worship idols, turning to their pagan gods for help rather than to the true God.

The ultimate answer concerning the date of Beowulf's original composition and the date of the manuscript in the British Museum remains unanswered as yet, and we may never be certain of these dates. But the evidence uncovered thus far includes a probable span of three centuries – the early part of the eighth century as the date that *Beowulf* was composed and the late tenth century as the date of the manuscript that we have today.

The Poet We know nothing for certain about the life of the *Beowulf* poet, but critics have made some assumptions based upon internal evidence and a general knowledge about other poets and the oral literature of that time. Because the *Beowulf* poet was fascinated with the conventional modes of poetic utterances and the traditional poetic forms, we can assume that he was a trained poet. We also know that he lived during a time when there was a change in the subject matter of poetry – a change that occurred when wholly heroic poems lost their popularity and were replaced by religious poems. Poets were also beginning to write long stories in poetic form; one such poem is *Genesis*, based on the biblical book of Genesis. The *Beowulf* poet also uses run-on lines far more than end-stopped lines, a device common in religious poetry, but clearly he was adept in both styles and adapted them to his poem.

Some critics believe that the *Beowulf* poet was a scop—that is, a court poet who composed poems to be sung to the accompaniment of a simple harp in a sort of formal chant. The majority of critics, however, think that the *Beowulf* poet was not only an educated poet but that perhaps he was associated with a monastery. In particular, the Christian tone of *Beowulf* reveals a knowledge of the early Christian teachings of the monks who went to England. The fact that Pope Gregory advised his missionaries to England not to obliterate the pagan beliefs at one stroke, but to work through them, gives support to the idea that the *Beowulf* poet came from a monastery. Plainly, he was capable of fusing pagan and Christian ideas so that they emphasized the morals of his themes and enhanced his characterizations.

A poet leaves his mark upon his work through language, through his choice of words, among other techniques. These conventions, used in a specific way, reveal what the poet wants us to see in his work. Yet, despite the fact that a poet is effective in his use of conventions, language, and sources, these devices tell us little about the poet's own life. We can look only at internal evidence for knowledge about the poet. Realistically, the puzzle surrounding the identity of the *Beowulf* author may never be solved.

Poetry in *Beowulf* Alliteration is the repetition of initial sounds—*w*indow *w*iper, *m*ighty *m*an; it is a poetic device often used in contemporary poetry but not to the extent that it was used in Anglo-Saxon poetry. Alliterative verse is not only the repetition of initial sounds, but the repetition of certain sounds in each poetic line. The *Beowulf* poet, for instance, uses alliteration in almost every line of the poem, usually with at least one alliterating word in each half-line but frequently more than one, as in the following line:

2827 *w*yrm *w*ohbogen *w*ealdan ne moste

Note that the first half-line—*w*yrm *w*ohbogen—has two alliterating words, and the second half-line has only one alliterating word—*w*ealdan. Sometimes the poet includes double alliteration in each half-line. For example:

2431 *g*eaf me *s*inc ond *s*ymbel, *s*ibbe *g*emunde

In the first half-line, there are two alliterating *s*'s which correspond to the alliterating *s* in the second half-line, and there is also an alliterating *g* in each half-line.

This is an over-simplification of alliterative verse for the modern reader, but to explain the verse in detail would require pages of writing, dealing with the examinations of Sievers' Types A-E classification, the theories of Heusler and Pope, and Bliss' distinctions among light, normal, and heavy verse. Suffice it to say that Anglo-Saxon alliterative verse is alliteration in excess. You might also note that there is no rhyme in this verse, except some occasional, accidental inner rhyming.

Kennings are metaphorical circumlocutions, signifying a person or thing by a characteristic or quality, and they are characteristic of Anglo-Saxon poetry. In fact, some kennings in *Beowulf* are almost poetic cliches which recur throughout Anglo-Saxon poetry. It is possible that the *Beowulf* poet was the source from whom all other poets copied, but in all likelihood a good many of the kennings in *Beowulf* were part of the literary trappings of the day–that is, poetic diction common to all poets. Some examples of kennings are *banhus* (body; literally, bone house), *hronrade* (sea; literally, whale-road), *goldwine gumena* (generous prince; literally, gold-friend of men), *beaga brytta* (lord; literally, ring-giver), and *beadoleoma* (sword; literally, flashing light).

Similes are poetic devices which are not widely found in most Anglo-Saxon poems, but we do find them in *Beowulf.* According to the critic Albert H. Tolman, "Allegory is not found in *Beowulf,* but there are five similes (lines 218, 728, 986, 1572, and 1609)." Tolman accounts for the scarcity of similes by noting that the "poets were not yet sufficiently self-conscious." Actually, there is a sixth simile (lines 1223-24), unnoted by Tolman, but the main point of the matter is this: there is a scarcity of sophisticated poetic devices in *Beowulf.*

The diction in *Beowulf* is elevated, generalized like the diction of other epic poetry. It is a far cry from prose. There are a number of repetitions and circumlocutions in the poem, and a figure of speech which the poet is found of using is **litotes**, a negative expression usually in the form of an understatement. One example occurs in the story of Finn, when the poet remarks that "Hildeburh had no cause to praise the Jutes"; this is an example of heavy understatement functioning as a litotes—the Jutes have just killed Hildeburh's brother Hnaef. Of course, she wouldn't be "praising" them.

The *Beowulf* poet manages to include a great deal of variation in his poetic style, especially through the use of **thesis** and **antithesis**; he also makes good use of **balance** and **parallelism**. If there is anything that is characteristic of *Beowulf*, it is this great variety of stylistic techniques, especially in terms of his diction.

In selecting a translation of *Beowulf*, it would seem that the best choice might be one which captures the spirit of the language as well as the meaning. This does not mean that there should be a line-for-line, word-for-word alliteration. On the other hand, the total absence of alliteration or kennings would miss the essence of the *Beowulf* poet's style. The ideal translation, whether prose of poetry, would probably be one in which the story is sprinkled with as many of the fascinating poetic devices of Anglo-Saxon poetry as possible. One of the best alliterative verse translations, one which preserves the kennings and offers a superb critical introduction, is the translation of *Beowulf* by Charles W. Kennedy, available as an Oxford paperback.

TERMS TO REMEMBER

Comitatus

The concept of comitatus is important for understanding the actions and attitudes of a thane (warrior). A band of warriors pledged themselves to a feudal lord who was known for his bravery and generosity. They swore to defend him to their death, and they considered it shameful to leave the battlefield if their chief was slain. According to their code, if their leader was killed, his life must be avenged. He was their lord, and they were his loyal, proud retainers. They were known for their courage, bravery, recklessness, and, foremost, for their loyalty. In return, the lord gave them protection and shared his weapons and wealth with them.

Disaffection or exile from one's lord meant that one was without a home, friends, affection, and respect from others. Furthermore, the warrior who was exiled was without a means of livelihood. Although Ecgtheow, Beowulf's father, was exiled, he was fortunate to have Hrothgar (king of the Danes) pay his wergild (a man's individual, personal monetary "worth") and thereby gain the respect, trust, and protection of the Danish king.

Loyalty to one's lord sometimes created a conflict between loyalty to one's kin (see "The Fight at Finnsburg"). The relationship of a kinsman was close and important, and the murder (or even accidental death) of a kinsman had to be avenged. Consequently, feuds continued for generations (as a parallel, consider the Montague-Capulet feud, as well as the long-running Hatfield and McCoy feud).

Later, the code of vengeance was modified, and a man could accept wergild as payment for the murder of a kinsman. Each man had his "price," or worth, according to his station in life. A kinsman could accept this payment of wergild from his kinsman's murderer without loss of face.

The values of the comitatus and the relationship between kinsman and kinsman help us to understand the purpose of the *Beowulf* poet's including "The Fight at Finnsburg." These relationships point up the dilemma which Hrethel faces; he cannot avenge his son's (Herebeald's) accidental fratricide unless he kills his son Haethcyn, for whom he would also mourn.

Gnomic Sayings

Short sayings with a moral or ethical basis; general observations about the common concerns of life. For example, "The truth is clear,/ God rules forever the race of men"; the homily "A stitch in time saves nine" is an example of a gnomic saying still in modern use.

Lay

A short narrative poem focusing on one incident, such as "The Fight at Finnsburg."

Litotes

An understatement or negative statement creating irony, such as "Shakespeare is not a bad poet." Litotes are still used in modern poetry and are a special stylistic feature of *Beowulf*. For example, consider: "Nor ever had Cain/ Cause to boast of that deed of blood," as well as the phrase "Nor seemed his death/ A matter of sorrow to any man," and the statement "No kin of Grendel cloaked in his crime,/ Has cause to boast of that battle by night!"

Mead Hall

A large hall where the lord's thanes ate and slept. It was a place for gift-giving, entertainment, and royal festivals. Heorot is Hrothgar's mead hall.

Mead

A drink similar to beer or ale, but made by fermenting honey, instead of grain.

Scop (preferred pronunciation: "shop," or the rhyming word "skop")

The singer, or bard, for the mead hall. Sometimes the scop was attached to the court or to an aristocratic family. Sometimes he was a traveling singer who went from court to court. He was a tribal historian who remembered stories from the past and retold and recited them time after time. When the lord and his thanes listened to the valorous deeds of past heroes, their own sense of pride was strengthened. Often the scop used a contrasting story to reinforce a climactic deed–for example, "The Lay of Sigemund," which is sung after Beowulf kills Grendel in order to liken Beowulf's feat to those of the mighty Sigemund.

Thane

A warrior, or retainer, who followed his lord. As such, he was considered a member of the comitatus.

Wergild

A sum of "worth money"–the "price" of a man–based on the concept of reciprocity. According to the code of Beowulf's era, a faithful retainer received many generous gifts as a reward for his loyalty and courage. Consequently, if a thane's king were killed, the thane was duty-bound to avenge the murder. Likewise, a relative was expected to avenge the murder of a kinsman by killing a member of the tribe or family of the murderer. With the introduction of wergild, each man had a price placed on him in accordance with his position. The higher the price, the less chance of his being murdered. By the same token, paying a price after a person's death often put an end to a feud, particularly since the kinsman of the murdered man wouldn't lose face by accepting the appropriate wergild.

Wyrd

Fate. Both gods and men were subject to Wyrd. The idea behind Wyrd is that man has a choice to act or not to act a certain way. However, he had to abide by the consequences of his choice.

LIST OF CHARACTERS

DANES (also called SCYLDINGS)

Aeschere

Favorite counselor and retainer for Hrothgar.

Beowulf the Dane

Not the hero of the poem. A Danish king, son of Scyld; this "Beowulf" is sometimes called "Beow."

Ecglaf (sometimes **Ecglafing**)

Unferth's father; a Dane.

Freawaru

Hrothgar's daughter. She was married to Ingeld in order to (hopefully) end the blood feud between the Danes and the Heathobards.

Healfdene

Danish king; son of Beowulf the Dane; father of Hrothgar, Heorogar, and Halga.

Heremod

Cruel and avaricious Danish king; ruled long before the infant Scyld Sceafing was found by the Danes. Foil to Hrothgar and Beowulf.

Hrethric

Hrothgar's son; elder brother to Hrothmund. Killed when Hrothulf usurps the Danish throne after Hrothgar's death.

Hrothgar

King of the Danes; son of Healfdene and brother of Heorogar; he wishes to make peace with the Heathobards.

Hrothmund

Hrothgar's son; brother to Hrethric.

Hrothulf

Hrothgar's nephew; son of Halga.

Scyld Sceafing

Founder of Hrothgar's mighty Danish royal house; son of Sceaf.

Unferth

Son of Ecglaf; slew his brother; taunts Beowulf early in the poem, but later he lends his sword, Hrunting, to Beowulf just before Beowulf's battle with Grendel's mother.

Wealhtheow

Hrothgar's queen; mother of Hrethric and Hrothmund.

GEATS (also called WEDER-FOLK; lived in southern Sweden)

Beowulf (Bay′ o wolf)

A Geat, and the hero of the poem; son of Ecgtheow; nephew of Hygelac; later, king of the Geats.

Ecgtheow (Edge′ thay o)

Beowulf's father; married to King Hrethel's only daughter; slays a man and escapes to Denmark. Hrothgar pays his wergild.

Haethcyn (Hath′ kin)

Second son of Hrethel, king of the Geats; kills his elder brother Herebeald by accident.

Heardred (Hay′ ard red)

Geatish king; Hygelac's son. Beowulf counsels him. Slain by Swedish king Onela. Avenged by Beowulf who, with Eadgils, kills Onela.

Herebeald (Her′ ra bay ald)

Geatish prince; accidentally slain by his brother, Haethcyn.

Hrethel

Geatish king; Hygelac's father. Grandfather of Beowulf. Dies of grief after Haethcyn accidentally kills his own brother, Herebeald.

Hygd

Hygelac's queen. Mother of Heardred. Beowulf gives her the necklace which Wealhtheow gave him.

Hygelac

Geatish king and uncle to Beowulf. Historical character verified by external evidence.

Wiglaf

Helps Beowulf slay the dragon; conveys Beowulf's last message to his people.

SWEDES

Eadgils (Ay′ ad gils)

Swedish prince; son of Ohthere; brother of Eanmund. Both brothers are exiled from Sweden by King Onela, their uncle. Eadgils and Eanmund seek refuge in Heardred's court. Onela invades the Geats because Heardred gave Eadgils and Eanmund protection. Eadgils regains the Swedish throne with Beowulf's aid.

Eanmund (Ay′ an mund)

Son of Ohthere; brother of Eadgils.

Ohthere (Oht′ herra)

Swedish prince; Ongentheow's son and father of Eanmund and Eadgils. He is the elder brother of Onela.

Ongentheow (On′ gen thay o)

Swedish king; father of Ohthere and Onela. Rescues his wife from Haethcyn; slays Haethcyn. Attacks Geats at Ravenswood when Hygelac falls.

Onela

Ongentheow's son; slain by Beowulf and Eadgils in revenge for his invading the Geats.

MONSTERS

Grendel

The monster who threatens Hrothgar's kingdom. Beowulf kills him.

Grendel's Dam (mother)

Grendel's hag-like mother; sometimes called a Troll-wife. She dwells at the bottom of a mere (a large swampy pond) in a cave.

Dragon

Guarding a vast treasure, he awakens when a slave steals a cup from the treasure hoard. He ravages Beowulf's kingdom, and Beowulf, in turn, kills him but loses his own life.

Nicors, or Nickers

Water demons, or water sprites who can sometimes change themselves into horses; some sources believe that they were hippopotamuses or walruses. They function as sea-devils in *Beowulf*.

BIBLICAL CHARACTERS

Abel

Slain by his brother Cain. (See Genesis, 4:8)

Cain

Slew his brother Abel.

"THE LAY OF SIGEMUND" CHARACTERS

Fitela

Son and nephew of Sigemund; companion to Sigemund in his battles. Sometimes referred to as Sinfjotli.

Sigemund

Norse folk figure; vanquisher of a dragon; foil to Beowulf; a character from the Volsung saga.

"THE FIGHT AT FINNSBURG" CHARACTERS

Finn

Frisian king; ruler of the Jutes; son of Folcwanda; Hildeburh's husband. Finn is killed during a war with Hnaef's Danes.

Hengest

Hnaef's brother; he leads the Danes after Hnaef is slain.

Hildeburh

Finn's wife; Hnaef's sister. Directs funeral rites for her sons and Hnaef; returns to Denmark after Finn's death.

Hnaef (Hnaf)

King of the Danes; brother of Hengest and Hildeburh; slain by Finn's men; given Germanic funeral.

OTHER CHARACTERS

Breca (Brekka)

Engages in a swimming contest with Beowulf; king of the Brondings.

Eormanric (Ay′ or man ric)

Historical king of the East Goths (Ostrogoths); lived in the fourth century.

Froda

King of the Heathobards; father of Ingeld; slain while fighting the Danes.

Guthlaf (Gooth′ laf)

Danish warrior and follower of Hnaef; later, a follower of Hengest. Helps renew the feud with Finn's men.

Ingeld

Son of Froda; a prince of the Heathobards. He is involved in the Heathobard-Danish feud; married to Freawaru.

Thryth, or Modthryth

Wife of Offa; foil to Hygd; full of excessive pride, self-love, and arrogance. Female counterpart of Heremod; her marriage to Offa and assumption of womanly duties turns her into a good queen.

Weland (Way′ land)

Famous in Germanic heroic legends as a blacksmith and a magician; makes armor for Beowulf.

TRIBES

Brosings

Known in legend as owners of a magic necklace which Wealhtheow gives to Beowulf.

Geats (Gay′ ats)

Lived in southern Sweden; Beowulf belongs to this tribe.

Franks

A western Germanic people who lived in what is now France, they join the Frisians to defeat Hygelac.

Frisians

A western Germanic people living in what is now northwestern Holland.

Danes

Ruled by Hnaef; later, led by Hengest.

Waegmundings

Family related by marriage to the Geats' royal lineage; family of Wiglaf, Weohstan, and Beowulf.

Heathobards

Germanic tribe ruled by King Froda and his son Ingeld.

SWORDS

Hrunting

Unferth's ancient sword which he lends to Beowulf; used against Grendel's mother.

Naegling (Nag′ ling)

Beowulf's sword; used against the dragon.

Beowulf Genealogy

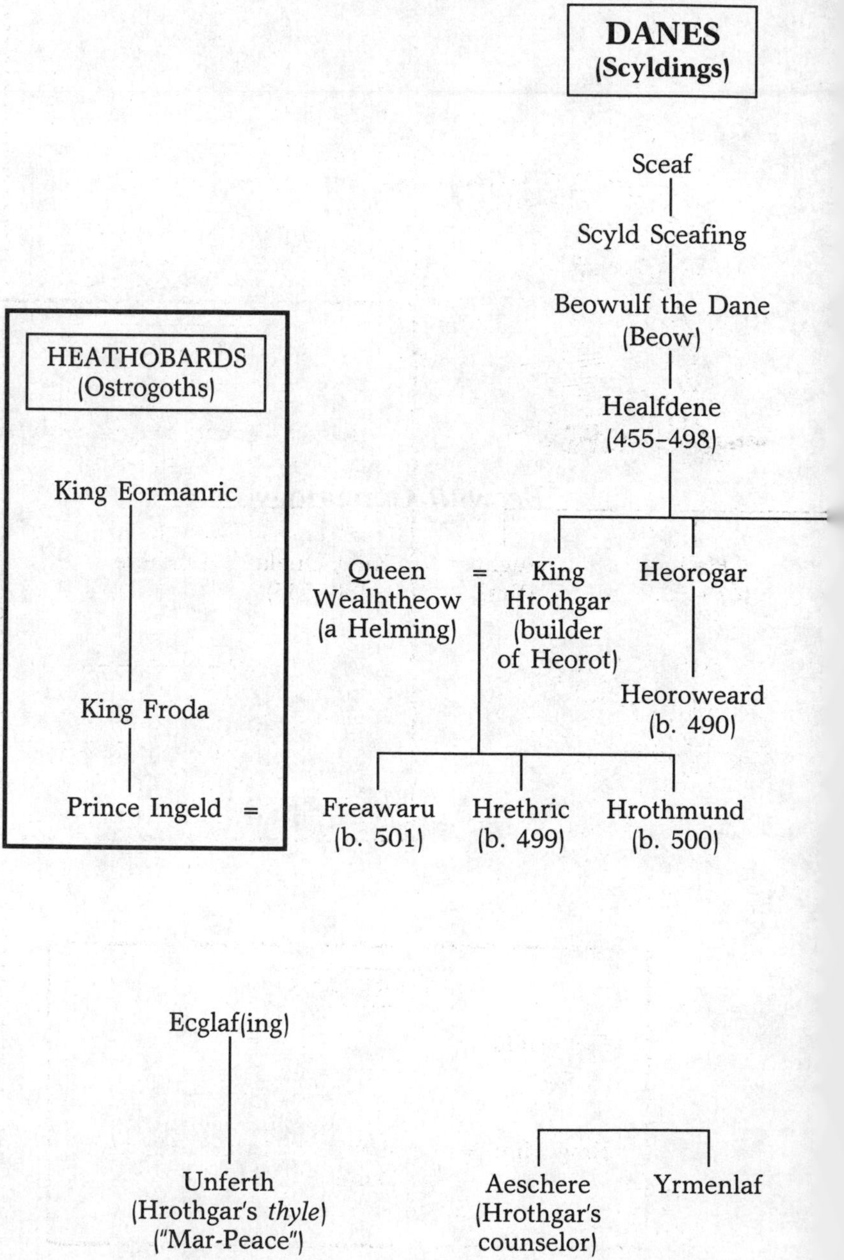

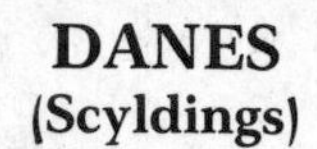

DANES
(Scyldings)
Sceaf
Scyld Sceafing
Beowulf the Dane
(Beow)
Healfdene
(455–498)
HEATHOBARDS
(Ostrogoths)
King Eormanric
King Froda
Prince Ingeld =
Queen
Wealhtheow
(a Helming)
=
King
Hrothgar
(builder
of Heorot)
Heorogar
Heoroweard
(b. 490)
Freawaru
(b. 501)
Hrethric
(b. 499)
Hrothmund
(b. 500)
Ecglaf(ing)
Unferth
(Hrothgar's *thyle*)
("Mar-Peace")
Aeschere
(Hrothgar's
counselor)
Yrmenlaf

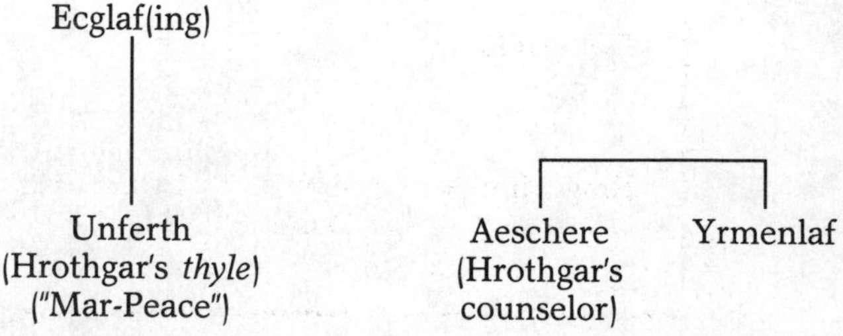

Halga
(475–503)

daughter =
(Yrs?)

King Hrothulf
(495–545)

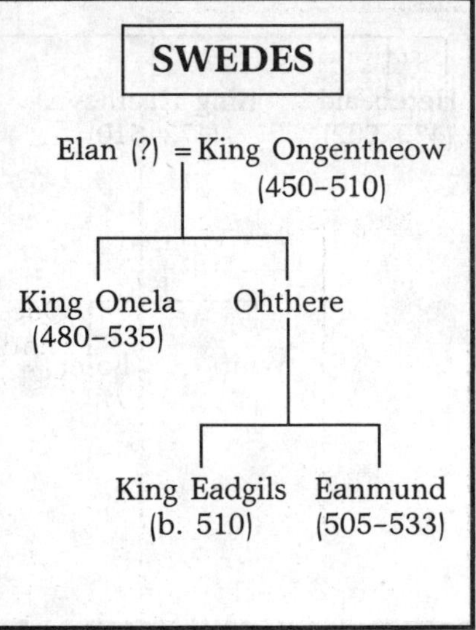

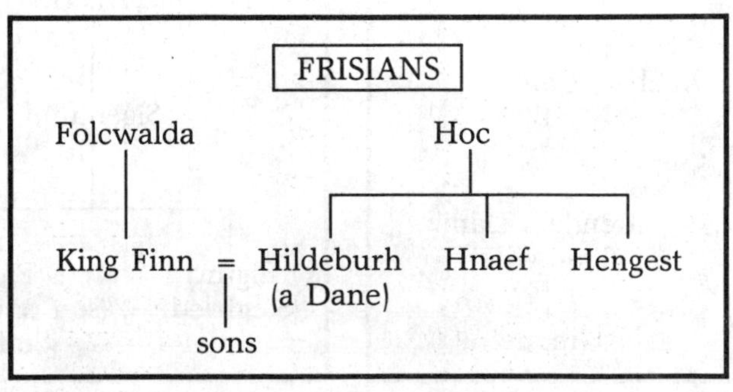

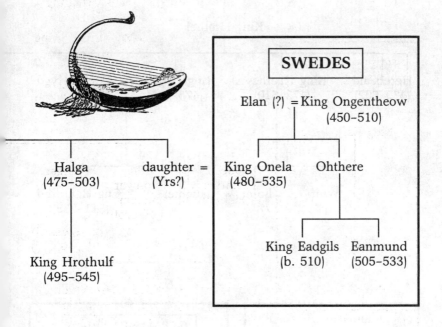

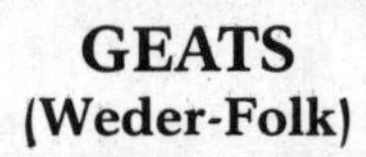
GEATS
(Weder-Folk)

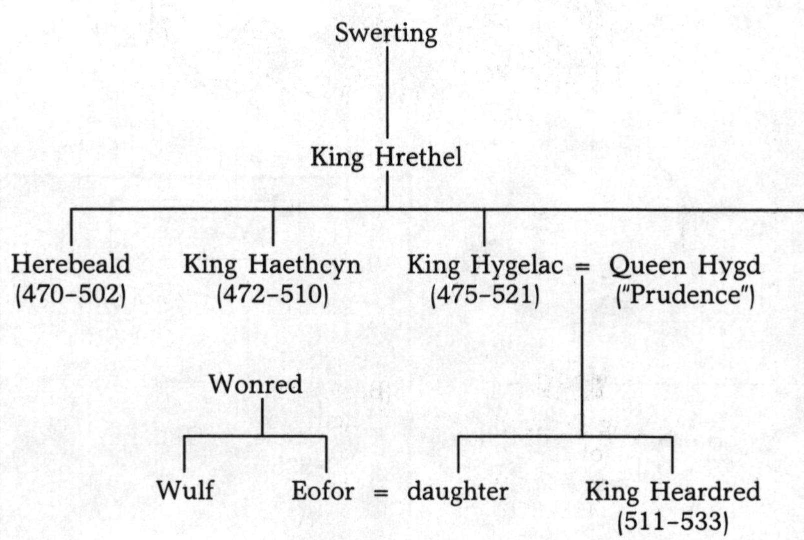
Swerting
King Hrethel
Herebeald
(470–502)
King Haethcyn
(472–510)
King Hygelac = Queen Hygd
(475–521)
("Prudence")
Wonred
Wulf
Eofor = daughter
King Heardred
(511–533)

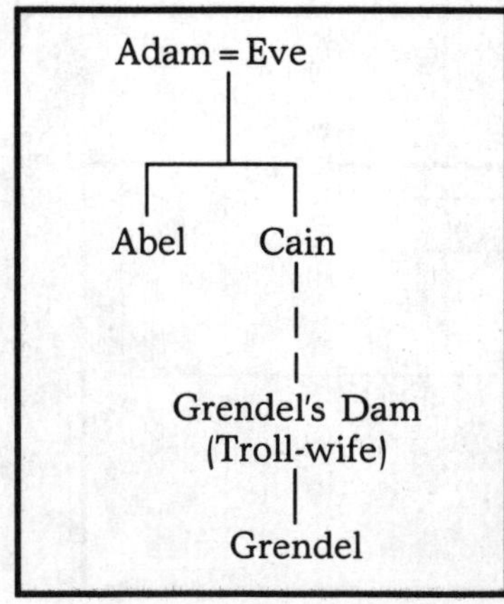
Adam = Eve
Abel
Cain
Grendel's Dam
(Troll-wife)
Grendel

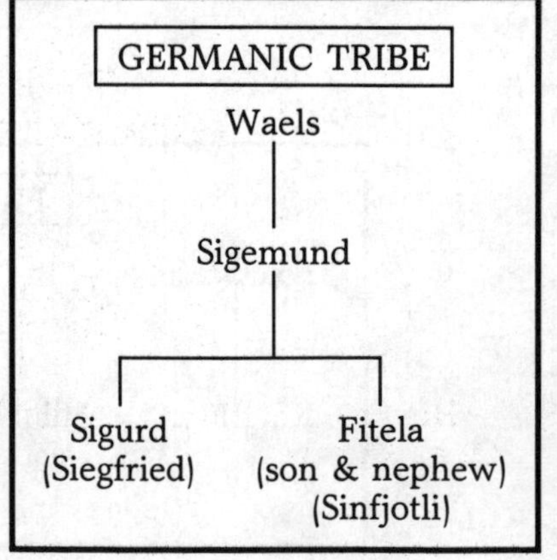
GERMANIC TRIBE
Waels
Sigemund
Sigurd
(Siegfried)
Fitela
(son & nephew)
(Sinfjotli)

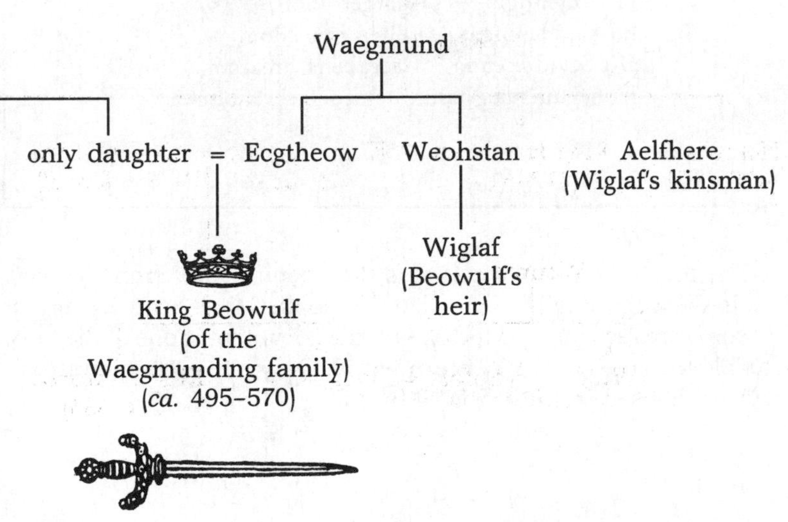

Waegmund
only daughter = Ecgtheow
Weohstan
Aelfhere
(Wiglaf's kinsman)
King Beowulf
(of the
Waegmunding family)
(*ca.* 495–570)
Wiglaf
(Beowulf's
heir)

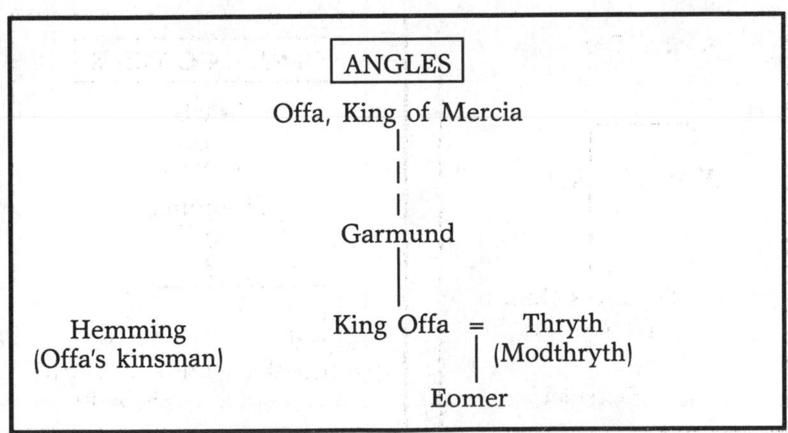

ANGLES
Offa, King of Mercia
Garmund
Hemming
(Offa's kinsman)
King Offa = Thryth
(Modthryth)
Eomer

Hwæt! we Gar-Dena   in gear-dagum
þeod cyninga   þrym gefrunon,
hu þa æþelingas   ellen fremedon.
Oft Scyld Scefing   sceaþena þreatum,
monegum mægþum   meodo-setla ofteah.

The illustration above contains the opening lines from *Beowulf.* This is what the English language first looked like. Scarcely any of the words are recognizable today, but this document is one of the most valuable treasures of the Western world. Only one early manuscript survives, housed in the British Museum.

BEOWULF: A Synopsis

Long ago, on a ship laden with many treasures, a castaway baby was rescued by a tribe of people who called themselves Danes. When the baby grew to manhood, he became an excellent king for his people; bards sang of the glory of Scyld Sceafing and of his infinite generosity to his thanes.

For many years, Scyld had no son, but God saw the misery that would befall the Danish nation if Scyld were to die and leave his country leaderless, so he provided Scyld with a son, Beowulf (not the hero of *Beowulf*), who would become ruler after Scyld's death.

In time, Scyld became ill and died, and, accordingly, his people placed him in a curved-prowed, royal ship. There also, they heaped rare treasures from distant parts, all for Scyld's journey across the sea and into the unknown.

Afterward, Beowulf rules the Danes for many years. Then his son, Healfdene, becomes ruler, and he has four sons and a daughter. One of Healfdene's sons, Hrothgar, although not the eldest, eventually becomes king of the Danes because of his courage and success in battle, and his band of warriors increases as his reputation for success and fairness grows throughout the land; eventually, he amasses a formidable army.

Hrothgar builds Heorot, the great Hall of the Hart, which becomes famous far and wide. Here, he holds great feasts and distributes his wealth among his people, and for many years, there is much joy and gladness in the hall. Then one night without warning, Grendel–a gigantic, bear-like ogre–attacks the hall, killing thirty of Hrothgar's sleeping thanes before his thirst for blood is sated. Grendel's violence soon becomes an obsession, and for twelve years, his raids continue. During these years, Hrothgar grieves for the tragic fate of his loyal thanes.

The poet tells us that Grendel attacks the hall because of jealousy. He is a descendant of Cain, a lineage which has long borne marauding monsters, trolls, goblins, and giants–all of which were banished from human society. Grendel envies the fellowship and happiness he sees; he hates living in the fens, excluded from the company of men; thus, he stalks the moors, jealous of the pleasures of mankind.

King Hrothgar is "gray and old" and is physically unable to avenge the deaths of his thanes, nor can he demand wergild (the monetary worth of a man) for his slain thanes because Grendel does not want peace. Significantly, the poet points out, Hrothgar and his throne are safe from Grendel's attacks because they are protected by God. Meanwhile, the Danish people continue to pray to heathen idols for help.

Eventually, reports of Grendel's bloodthirsty raids reach King Hygelac's court in Geatland. Soon afterward, Hygelac's nephew Beowulf announces that he will sail to Hrothgar's kingdom and offer help. He sets out immediately, sailing across the sea with fourteen carefully chosen thanes. Arriving at the Danish shore, Beowulf and his men give thanks to God for a safe journey, then wade ashore. They are greeted by Hrothgar's coastal guard, who expresses surprise at the Geats' brazenness, commenting particularly on Beowulf's formidable and princely bearing.

Beowulf tells the guard who he is and states his reasons for coming. The guard takes the Geats to Heorot, where they lean their broad battleshields along the wall and stand their spears together in a sign of friendship. Beowulf identifies himself to Wulfgar and explains that he has come to aid King Hrothgar.

Wulfgar exits and asks Hrothgar if he will see the men who have traveled so far. He says that Beowulf is a powerful and fearless leader of the Geats. Hrothgar, we learn, once protected Beowulf's father, Ecgtheow, in a time of exile, and he already knows of Beowulf's fame, for it is said that Beowulf has the strength of thirty men in his handgrip. Hrothgar feels that God has sent Beowulf to the Danes, so he dispatches his messenger to bring Beowulf forward for a king's welcome.

Beowulf tells Hrothgar that he knows about the Danes' oppression and he has come to them because he has had experience in combat against water-monsters. Using his famous handgrip, he will grapple with Grendel. He adds philosophically that "Whomever death would take must trust in God's judgment," and then he describes in gory detail what will happen to his body if he is, by chance, defeated by Grendel. If that happens, he asks Hrothgar to send his corselet to Hygelac, king of the Geats. He concludes his speech with this observation: "Fate goes as she will."

Hrothgar welcomes Beowulf to Denmark and describes Grendel's assaults against Heorot and the Danes. Many a bragging warrior, he says, has promised during a night of mead-boasting to protect the mead hall against Grendel's violence, but in the morning, the blood-stained benches and the gnawed bones of once-brave thanes are proof of Grendel's might over Hrothgar's beloved retainers.

At the banquet, Hrothgar tells Beowulf to sit and discuss the glory of victory. The welcoming celebration begins; the ale cup is passed around, and the scop begins to sing.

During the merry feast, Unferth, sitting at the feet of his Danish lord, begins to heckle Beowulf, ridiculing Beowulf's "foolhardy," week-long swimming feat with Breca, a Bronding. Unferth points out that Breca emerged the victor.

Recognizing Unferth's envy, Beowulf says that Unferth is drunk and knows little about the swimming contest because both Beowulf and Breca were young men – boys, really – when they challenged one another. Beowulf says that he lost the contest because he was attacked by a tangle of sea nicors (sea monsters); however, he adds, he saved Breca's life.

Beowulf then remarks that he has heard nothing about Unferth's glory in battle. Unferth's only battle, Beowulf recalls, was with his brother, whom he murdered, and for that, he will "endure damnation in hell." He reminds Unferth that if he were as brave as his boasts suggest, Grendel would be afraid to raid Heorot.

After Unferth's sarcastic outburst and Beowulf's firm retort, there is a return to gaiety, and the hall resounds with noise and laughter. Then the gold-adorned Wealhtheow, Hrothgar's queen, mindful of courtesy, greets the men in the hall and takes the mead cup to Hrothgar, wishing him well in his mead-drinking. She also takes the cup to other men, pausing before Beowulf to greet him and thanking God for sending help. Beowulf receives the cup and repeats his resolve to kill the Danes' terrible foe or die in the attempt. The gold-bejeweled queen, pleased with Beowulf's determination, then goes to sit by her husband.

The reveling continues until Hrothgar decides to go to bed; in a departing speech, he entrusts the mead hall to Beowulf's care, wishes him success, and leaves with his wife and band of warriors. After Hrothgar's departure, the poet comments that the most "Glorious of Kings" (God) has placed a hall-guard against Grendel; Beowulf, he says, trusts in God's will.

Beowulf removes his iron armor and puts away his ornamented sword. Before he climbs into bed, he boasts, "I do not consider myself weaker in warlike deeds than Grendel." He adds that he will not use any weapons in his combat with Grendel; he will fight Grendel on his own terms – that is, without sword or armor.

Then Beowulf lays his cheek against his pillow and falls asleep. No one in the hall believes that Beowulf will survive to return to his homeland, but, according to the poet, God supports Beowulf, and "the strength of one overcame all." The poet concludes his passage by referring to God again –"The truth is made known that almighty God rules mankind forever."

The warriors are all asleep when Grendel stalks in from the dark moor and rips open the entrance door to Heorot, ready to feast on the sleeping men. As the monster snatches up one of Beowulf's thanes, tears him apart and crunches him up in great bites, Beowulf carefully observes Grendel's method of attack.

The monster turns to grab Beowulf, but Beowulf seizes one of the monster's claws, gripping him with all his strength. Grendel realizes that he has never before met such an adversary, and he tries to escape, but Beowulf tightens his hold, and a terrible, thundering battle ensues. Soon the hall is splintered and in a shambles.

Beowulf wrestles with Grendel until he is able to crack one of the monster's arms free of its socket, ripping sinews and tearing muscles. Grendel's howls of pain echo throughout the hall, terrifying the cowering Danes; meanwhile, the Geats hold their swords in readiness to protect Beowulf. Grendel turns to run, but Beowulf holds fiercely onto the monster's arm, finally ripping it out of its socket. Leaving his arm behind and knowing that his hours are numbered, Grendel flees to his mere.

In the morning, the warriors follow Grendel's bloody trail to the desolate, darkly boiling mere. They find no trace of Grendel, so they turn back. On the way home, one of them celebrates Beowulf's victory by composing a song about Beowulf's feat and interspersing part of "The Lay of Sigemund," comparing Beowulf to Sigemund, a great warrior of ancient times who slew a dragon that guarded a rich treasure hoard.

When Hrothgar is roused from sleep, he hurries to Heorot, where he beholds a great trophy hanging from one of the rafters – Grendel's arm, claw, and shoulder. He cries aloud his thanks to God and to Beowulf for saving Heorot and the Danes from Grendel's evil raids. He promises to cherish Beowulf as a son from that day forward. (Ironically, Beowulf saves the famous mead hall from destruction by *monsters*, but what ultimately destroys Heorot is the *human* hatred of the Heathobards, led by Ingeld, Hrothgar's son-in-law.)

Beowulf humbly replies that all credit for his victory goes to God. Meantime, the usually boastful Unferth observes Grendel's bloody arm with its steel-like claw, and he too recognizes Beowulf's valor. Now he is less inclined to boast of his own deeds.

The inside of Heorot is rebuilt, redecorated, and furnished with tapestries of gold. Soon, Hrothgar holds a great feast in Beowulf's honor, and Hrothgar's thanes joyfully gather and toast one another with large mugs of mead. Hrothgar gives Beowulf a golden war banner, a helmet, and a mailshirt, as well as a jewel-studded sword and eight horses with golden bridles. He also gives him his own war saddle, studded with gems.

The harp is struck, and the court scop sings "The Fight at Finnsburg," a tale of Danish vengeance because of the murder of Hnaef, one of their kings. Hildeburh, so the saga goes, was a Danish princess who was married to Finn, a Frisian, in order to bring an end to a longstanding feud. During the Danes' visit to Finnsburg, however, Finn and his men attacked them and killed King Hnaef. A battle ensued and during a five-day skirmish, many warriors died, one of whom was Hildeburh's son. Thereupon, the two nations agreed to a truce and constructed a great funeral pyre to burn the dead. The scop concludes the funeral scene by describing in gory detail the flaming pyre with heads melting, wounds bursting open, and blood spewing forth.

Peace was not lasting. The following spring, an old Danish warrior laid a mighty sword in the lap of one of his comrades, Hengest, Hnaef's brother, the moody leader of the Danes after Hnaef's death. The sword was a potent reminder that Hnaef's death must be avenged. Hengest rose and plunged the sword into Finn's belly. Soon the hall ran with blood, and the Danes returned home, taking Hildeburh and much of Finn's treasure with them.

After the scop finishes his song, the hall again fills with the sounds of revelry. Golden-crowned Queen Wealhtheow presents a cup of mead to Beowulf, who sits between her two sons. She asks Beowulf to be a role model and mentor for her sons, and she presents him with many gifts of gold, including a necklace, the famous collar of the Brosings, the "finest golden collar in the world."

The celebration continues, and the men drink deeply. As they did before Grendel's raids, they remain in the hall tonight to sleep.

Beowulf, however, is assigned to other quarters. That night, for the first time in more than twelve years, Hrothgar's men think that they can sleep without fear.

Their peaceful slumber is short-lived. During the night, Grendel's mother comes to avenge the death of her son. As she enters the hall in a frothing rage, the men awaken and snatch up their swords and shields. The angry she-monster turns and grabs Aeschere, one of Hrothgar's most trusted thanes; then she tears down Grendel's arm and flees toward the mere.

Grieving for Aeschere, Hrothgar calls Beowulf to the hall. Unaware of what happened, Beowulf enters and asks if the night has been quiet. Sorrowfully, Hrothgar tells him about Aeschere's abduction and the ravenous fiend that now threatens their new-found peace. He says that some time ago, some of his people sighted two monsters – a male and a female – near a mere so gloomy and foreboding that even a stag hounded by dogs will die before plunging into the pool. Once more, he appeals to Beowulf for help, and Beowulf readily promises to avenge Aeschere's death.

Thanking God for Beowulf's promise, Hrothgar and his thanes lead Beowulf and his men toward the mere, a lonely and fearful lake. Their path twists through foggy fens to a mountain torrent which plunges downward upon razor-sharp crags. Twisted and gnarled roots hang over the black, frothing pool, frost-bound trees cling to the water's edge, and strange fires glow over the lake at night. No one knows the depth of the mere, but they know that fierce storms can provoke the waves until thick rains weep from heaven.

While pondering the evil that inhabits the boiling, bloody pool, the thanes suddenly see Aeschere's head on a crag overlooking the mere, and nearby, they see sea-beasts, sea-dragons, and other monsters swarming and scuttling over the rocks. Incensed by this venomous nest of evil, Beowulf aims an arrow at one of the monsters, piercing its vitals. Then he fastens on the armor which Weland, the blacksmith, made for him, and Unferth offers him his own sword, Hrunting. (The poet tells us that Unferth's offer reveals his own fear of fighting Grendel's mother; Unferth's reputation for heroism is hereby forfeited.) Prepared now to enter the mere, Beowulf asks Hrothgar to protect the Geats and – should Beowulf not return – to send Beowulf's recently earned treasures to Hygelac, king of the Geats.

Plunging deeply into the pool, Beowulf swims downward for an entire day before he sees the bottom of the mere. As he reaches the bottom, the ugly sea-beast discovers him and clutching him in her iron-clawed grip, she drags him to her den. Beowulf struggles, but he is unable to draw his sword while he remains in the monster's vice-like grip.

Inside the monster's vaulted cave, out of reach of the mere's currents, Beowulf is able to draw Unferth's sword, but he finds that it is useless against the monster's thick hide. The two foes battle fiercely, the sea-hag attempting to pierce Beowulf with her bright-bladed dagger, but the strength of Weland's armor protects the Geatish prince. Suddenly, Beowulf sees an enormous, ancient sword, one forged by giants. Although it is almost too heavy to hold, he seizes it, slashes through the hag's backbone, then drives it into her body.

Looking around the cave, Beowulf discovers Grendel's corpse stretched out on a bier. Quickly, he decapitates Grendel's head with the ancient sword, which immediately begins to melt and form "iron icicles." By this time, the sea-hag's blood has convulsed and surged to the top of the mere, convincing Hrothgar and his thanes that Beowulf is dead. The Danes turn and leave, but Beowulf's faithful Geats remain beside the blood-black mere, hoping that their king will return.

Beowulf emerges triumphant and swims ashore, carrying the hilt of the giant sword and Grendel's huge head. The Geats cluster about him, thanking God, and after impaling Grendel's heavy head on a spear, four men carry it back to Heorot. At Heorot, they drag the head across the floor for all to see, while Beowulf relates the story of his fight beneath the water, referring to Grendel's mother as the enemy of God.

Beowulf presents to Hrothgar what remains of the ancient, melted sword, and Hrothgar carefully examines the golden hilt, praising Beowulf for his great deeds and prophesying future greatness for the Geatish prince. Hrothgar warns Beowulf, though, that he must beware the temptation of bloodthirst and power, and he cites Heremod as an example of a savage, selfish king. Beowulf, he says, must always be honest, fair, and just. Again, he gives thanks to God and bids Beowulf to rejoice in the feast; more treasure awaits him tomorrow. Then the old king goes much relieved to his rest, and Beowulf also welcomes rest after a hard day.

After feasting and sleeping through an undisturbed night, the

Geats prepare to leave. Beowulf returns Hrunting to Unferth and thanks Hrothgar for his generous hospitality. He promises aid for the Danes if ever they need it again. Beowulf then speaks for the Geatish king, Hygelac, for he knows that his king would concur: if Hrethric, Hrothgar's son, should ever visit the Geatish court, he will be treated with honor.

Hrothgar praises Beowulf's wisdom and states that surely it is God-given; he says that if Hrethel's son Hygelac were ever taken in battle, the Geats could choose no better leader than Beowulf. (Hrothgar's comment is a foreshadowing of future events.) Hrothgar recognizes that the bond which Beowulf has sealed with the Danes can never be broken; Beowulf has insured a lasting peace between the Danes and the Geats. Hrothgar weeps as he bids goodby to Beowulf, for he fears that they will never see one another again.

The Geats load their ship with the golden treasures that Hrothgar gives them and set sail for Geatland. At home, the Geatish harbormaster greets the seafarers, helps them anchor their wide-bosomed ship, and watches them as they carry their treasures across the sandy beaches to Hygelac's home near the sea.

Hygelac greets Beowulf in the banqueting hall and gives thanks to God for Beowulf's safe return. He asks about Beowulf's success in saving Heorot, and Beowulf tells him about his battles with Grendel and Grendel's sea-monster mother. He also reports the proposed marriage of Freawaru, Hrothgar's daughter, to Ingeld of the Heathobards in an attempt to end the long-standing feud between the Danes and the Heathobards. Beowulf, however, fears that the marriage will not end the feud, and he predicts trouble.

Returning to the story of his battles with Grendel and his sea-monster mother, Beowulf recounts Hrothgar's generosity for Beowulf's courageous deeds. Then he tells his men to bring in Hrothgar's gifts, including four matched bay horses. In return, Hygelac gives Beowulf Hrethel's battlesword, 7000 "hides of land," and his own hall. To Hygd, Beowulf gives the necklace which Wealhtheow gave him, as well as three graceful horses.

At the close of this section, the poet commends Beowulf's recent behavior and notes that previously the Geats did not consider Beowulf to be particularly heroic. In fact, they considered him to be sluggish and rather slack. Fortunately, he proved the reverse.

Years pass, and Hygelac eventually falls in battle, as does his son,

Heardred. Thus, the kingdom of the Geats comes to be ruled by Beowulf. For fifty winters, Beowulf rules as a good and beloved king. His reign is harmonious and peaceful until one of the Geats steals an ornamented cup from the hoard of a dragon who has peacefully, but zealously, protected his vast treasure for three hundred years.

The poet explains that the thief did not steal the cup underhandedly; he stole it because of necessity. He was a servant fleeing the hostile blows of his master and thought that the ornamented cup might help make amends with his master. At any rate, even though the thief himself escaped the dragon's fury, the dragon now seeks vengeance, marauding the countryside and spewing fire, burning everything before him, including Beowulf's home, the throne of the Geats. At first, Beowulf is saddened. He wonders if he has unknowingly angered God in some way. After brooding, Beowulf begins to make his own plans for vengeance, deciding to fight the dragon alone.

The poet predicts here that both Beowulf and the dragon will die, but Beowulf, recalling his long-ago victory over Grendel and the cleansing of Hrothgar's hall, believes that he can defeat the fire dragon.

Filled with righteous and heroic anger, Beowulf takes the thief who stole the dragon's cup, along with eleven other comrades, to the dragon's cave. There, he bids a formal farewell to the men as he readies himself to do single combat with the dragon. He is sad and restless, and there is a hint of impending death in the tone of his voice as he recites the story of his life. He recalls how, at the age of seven, he arrived at the Geatish court to live with his grandfather, Hrethel. Then he speaks of the tragedy of Hrethel's life–when his son Haethcyn accidentally shot his own brother, placing Hrethel in a dilemma: should he adhere to the code of his people and take revenge for the death of his son? If so, he would have to kill his sole, remaining son. The sorrow weighed so heavily on Hrethel that he abandoned all hope of happiness and died.

Beowulf then speaks of the continuing feud between the Geats and the Swedes; he warns his thanes what to expect if he is killed by the dragon. He recalls his past battles and tells his thanes to wait and watch and see which one survives–Beowulf or the dragon.

Hearing Beowulf's fierce challenge, the dragon emerges from his cave. Beowulf tries to fend off the dragon's scorching breath, but his shield is little protection. He strikes at the dragon with his sword, but he miscalculates and fails to pierce the dragon's vital innards and spews such intense flames that Beowulf winces at the searing heat.

When Beowulf's thanes see the dragon spouting streams of flame at Beowulf, they flee – despite young Wiglaf's plea for them to remain beside their king in his time of danger. Wiglaf alone, of all of Beowulf's thanes, plunges into the battle, and immediately, the dragon turns and sears Wiglaf's shield to cinders.

Beowulf, encouraged by memories of his past success in battle, swings his sword, Naegling, with so much force that it shatters against the dragon's body. The dragon coils and strikes, sinking his fangs into Beowulf's neck. The king of the Geats is spattered with his own blood, but he continues to fight. Wiglaf strikes a blow to the dragon in the belly, and Beowulf pulls out a razor-sharp dagger and delivers the death blow, ripping open the dragon's entrails.

Afterward, Wiglaf bathes Beowulf's fatal wound, while Beowulf bemoans the fact that he has no son to whom he can give his inheritance. He reviews his life again and thanks God that he has been such a good king and that he has never murdered a kinsman, even under the influence of strong drink.

Beowulf orders Wiglaf to look after the Geats and, after the funeral fire is extinguished, build a high tomb at the sea's edge and call it "Beowulf's Barrow"; it will be a reminder of Beowulf's fearless courage, an inspiration for future mariners as they set out across the misty seas. Then he removes a golden collar from his neck and hands it and his golden helmet to Wiglaf, signifying that Wiglaf is now leader of the Geats.

Wiglaf observes his beloved lord, lying not far from the slaughtered dragon, and he bitterly mourns the loss of his king. Not long afterward, Beowulf's other companions return and see the battle-weary Wiglaf trying to revive their leader with water. He reproaches the cowards: ". . . little did I help . . . but at least I tried." He predicts that for the men who fled, there will be no treasure, land-right, or home – "Death would be better . . . than shameful life!"

Wiglaf then tells the men to inspect the scene of their lord's destruction, reminding them that no one could talk Beowulf out of fighting the fire dragon; perhaps the pull of destiny was too strong. Wiglaf describes his entry into the barrow and his gathering of treasure to display before the dying Beowulf. He relays Beowulf's request to have a funeral pyre and a high barrow, and he recommends immediate preparation of the pyre in order to place their lord "where long he shall abide in God's keeping."

Wiglaf calls for pyre wood to be brought to Beowulf's final resting place, pointing out that Beowulf, who often endured iron showers of enemy arrows, shall now be devoured by fire. Wiglaf chooses seven thanes to accompany him inside the cavern, where they appropriate the unguarded treasure, drag the fire dragon out, and shove his dead body over a cliff and into the sea.

Beowulf's body is loaded on a wagon and transported to the Whale's Headland. The Geats construct a splendid pyre, hung with helmets and shields, and as Beowulf requested, they lay their lord on the pyre. They ignite the greatest of funeral fires, wood smoke mounts up darkly above the flames, and soon the body is consumed, even the heart. There is much wailing and mourning and singing of sad songs. A Geatish woman with braided hair laments the loss of her king.

The Geats take ten days to prepare the memorial tower-barrow in which to store the ashes of Beowulf and the treasure hoard—"as useless as it ever was." Then the battle-brave sons of earls ride around the barrow, twelve at a time, chanting their laments. They exalt Beowulf's heroic deeds and valorous works, as the poet comments that it is fitting to thus praise a great lord when he dies. As for the treasure—like Beowulf's ashes, it lies buried in the earth, even now.

CHARACTER ANALYSES

HUMAN BEINGS

BEOWULF

An analysis of Beowulf reveals little or no character development, as we understand the term today. Beowulf performs great deeds of valor, and things happen to him, but we see no psychological change—other than a normal, chronological development from youth to adult. We see no emotional or intellectual growth—no inner, psychological change. The poet reveals narrative information through flashbacks and digressions, but from the time we first see Beowulf at Hrothgar's court, his character remains static.

Foremost, we see Beowulf behaving according to appropriate expectations for each chronological stage of his life. He represents the "ideal hero" in Nordic-Germanic society with Christian elements superimposed upon him by the poet. He represents the best of both worlds–pagan and Christian.

Perhaps the best way to understand Beowulf is to study the various periods in his life, and critics who take this approach usually refer to five basic periods: (1) the youthful, or "sluggish youth" period; (2) the period of adventure and testing; (3) the early manhood period; (4) the period of adulthood, and, finally, (5) old age. These periods of growing maturity do not appear in the order of their occurrence; instead, we see them through the poet's revelation of the past or through his foreshadowing of the future. Foils also serve to reveal character traits–for example, Unferth's actions and the deeds of Heremod and Sigemund in the digressions are used as contrasts and comparisons to Beowulf's actions.

In addition, the unpromising, early years of the old Danish hero Scyld Sceafing serve as a comparison with Beowulf's own uncertain Geatish beginnings. As a boy, Beowulf was abandoned by his father, Ecgtheow, who fled to Hrothgar's court, and Beowulf was raised by his maternal grandfather, King Hrethel. He seems to have been a lazy boy, but he listened and learned. Accordingly, just as Scyld became a great Danish king, Beowulf later becomes a great Geatish king. (The abandoned youth who becomes a future hero and leader is a very old literary convention; examples are Moses, King Sargon of Agade, Chandragupta, and Pope Gregory the Great.)

We learn of Beowulf's adventure-and-testing period when he relates stories about his past to Hrothgar. Beowulf had a reputation for heroic success, and even his defeats were seemingly common knowledge. Unferth, remember, challenges Beowulf to defend a youthful, "foolhardy" swimming contest with Breca.

Beowulf does not deny that it was foolish pride on his and Breca's part, but he emphasizes that they were both young when the event occurred. He vividly relates the story of his swim through a windswept sea and his battle with sea monsters. In his verbal confrontation with Unferth, Beowulf reveals his ability to think quickly and reason well; he reminds Unferth that he has never heard of any of Unferth's daring deeds.

Beowulf's prowess during his adventure-and-testing period proves that he has great strength; now he must use that strength to cleanse Hrothgar's court of Grendel's violence. Beowulf goes to the Danes not in a cavalier fashion, but because of a great generosity of spirit.

As a young man, Beowulf manifests a fast adherence to heroic ideals. He is virtuous, loyal to his lord, honest with others and with himself. He is high-minded; he faces danger courageously, and although he follows the Nordic-Germanic code of heroism, he is as close to being a Christian man as any pagan can be. As a Nordic-Germanic hero, he believes in avenging the death of a friend or kinsman, and he especially believes in a lord's responsibility to reward his loyal thanes with gifts.

If we believe the *Beowulf* poet, Beowulf's strength seems to be a gift from God; thus, his expedition to the Danes is both generous and heroic, a lucky combination of physical strength, virtue, and God's divine power; it is through God's power that he overcomes God's foe: Grendel. Note, too, that Beowulf credits God with the outcome of the battle, and, in addition, note that before Beowulf does battle with Grendel, he exhibits a sense of fairness; he refuses to use weapons against the monster, who knows nothing about "noble fighting." Beowulf exhibits altruism by fighting without a promise of reward; he does battle with Grendel without knowing Hrothgar's intention to reward him.

Other than Beowulf's encounter with the dragon, we hear very little about Beowulf as an adult, but the poet does tell us that Beowulf is loyal to King Hygelac and that he uses his great strength in many battles for his lord. The poet mentions Beowulf's physical feats in war, and he also gives evidence of Beowulf's spiritual strength. Beowulf refuses the throne which Queen Hygd offers him after King Hygelac's death, preferring to act as counselor to the new king, Heardred. Beowulf demonstrates his future, kingly qualities, as well as the other noble characteristics which we saw in his early youth.

Beowulf's moral greatness is enhanced by contrasting his refusal of the throne to Hrothulf's display of ingratitude to Hrothgar's kindness when he later usurps the Danish throne. Onela, who deprives his brother's sons of their rightful claim to the Swedish throne, is a foil to Beowulf, who refuses to claim the Geatish throne until Heardred's death.

Beowulf rules wisely for fifty years without war or disruption of peace. As a warrior, he is "incredibly gentle," "the mildest of men," and "most civil." The peace of the kingdom is destroyed only when the enraged dragon roars through the Geats' homeland, burning homes and destroying their mead hall. Beowulf's first thought is that he himself may have sinned, or broken an ancient law, and the dragon has been sent as God's punishment.

Before Beowulf battles the dragon, he reviews his life with no feelings of regret or guilt. He knows that he has followed the laws of his society. We never feel that Beowulf is obsessed with his own omnipotence, or that he is aggressively willful. Nowhere do we find Beowulf acting contrary to the ideals of a loyal thane or wise king. Fighting the dragon does not show a loss of wisdom; the scourge of the dragon must be stopped. A king must protect his people even if—as in Beowulf's case—he dies in battle.

HROTHGAR

Hrothgar, king of the Danes, is an aging, proud king who is physically unable to save his people from Grendel's violence. In his early years, Hrothgar was a strong king who attracted many warriors to his court because of his glory in battle and his generous gift-giving. Hrothgar's Danish subjects looked upon him as a "guardian of the people," and the poet depicts him as being much like the "shepherd patriarchs," the early kings of Israel. To the Danes, all good things came from Hrothgar, a wise and noble monotheist who firmly believed in the code of comitatus.

Hrothgar's success and fame leads him to build Heorot, a great hall where he can share his success and treasure with his retainers. He lives by the code of the comitatus, the *ealde riht*, or the natural law of sharing, a code which pagans followed as a matter of social necessity.

Life at Heorot is joyful and untroubled until the monster Grendel lays siege to the mead hall. Hrothgar believes that Grendel's attacks are God's punishment for his pride in power and wealth; such pride, he fears, has caused him to fail to be an inspiration for his warriors.

One generally accepted interpretation of Hrothgar's character focuses on his loss of strength because of old age, which causes him to become too introspective and contemplative. Some of the decisions which Hrothgar must make require physical strength to carry out; thus, when Beowulf comes to court, Hrothgar is at a crossroads—he knows that something must be done to stop Grendel, but he knows that he himself lacks the physical ability to successfully retaliate.

Violence in itself no longer holds a compelling interest for Hrothgar; he would rather settle his problems through counsel, diplomacy, gift-giving, or endurance. These solutions, of course, may be admirable ways of solving some problems, but they cannot solve the problem of Grendel's violent visitations. When Beowulf arrives at Hrothgar's court, Hrothgar's kingly wisdom is weakened to the point where he is unable to see the folly of marrying his daughter to Ingeld; nor can he envision Hrothulf's threat to his (Hrothgar's) sons. And although he knows of the existence of a female monster (Grendel's mother), he hasn't considered her mad desire for vengeance–should Beowulf succeed in killing her son.

It is important here not to lose sight of the poet's care in contrasting Beowulf's youth and Hrothgar's age. Beowulf's youthful, virile strength is set against the aging, weakened strength of Hrothgar. As far as we know, Hrothgar was a king without fault until old age overcame him, and the poet warns us that old age will come to us all. The problems of Hrothgar will similarly assault Beowulf in his old age; just as Hrothgar asks Beowulf to save Heorot, one day Beowulf will speak similarly to Wiglaf. Age limits strength, and without strength, Hrothgar can see no way to stop Grendel's marauding violence.

HYGELAC

Hygelac, king of the Geats, makes one speech in the poem; otherwise, he does little to indicate that he is anything other than a set character. Four times, the poet refers to the expedition that ends Hygelac's life, but he does not make an episode out of Hygelac's last battle. We know that Hygelac is a historical figure and that he was of great stature. We also know that he feared for Beowulf's life when Beowulf went to the Danish court; he apparently allowed Beowulf to go to Hrothgar's aid against his better judgment. What, then, is the poet's purpose in inserting Hygelac into the poem?

Without Hygelac's consent, Beowulf, as a loyal thane to the Geatish crown, would never have gone to fight Grendel–particularly since his lord who raised him was also his uncle. In essence, Hygelac is the catalyst who sets in motion Beowulf's opportunity to infuse his life with adventure, honor, and bravery. Beowulf's adventures among the Danes are in stark contrast to his early life as a slothful Geatish boy; even Hygelac, we hear, "held him [Beowulf] not high among the heroes in the hall." Yet, Hygelac's consent for Beowulf to sail to Hrothgar's kingdom gives Beowulf his opportunity to prove his mettle.

Upon Beowulf's return to Hygelac's court, he tells the story of his great adventure against Grendel, and he places magnificent gifts at Hygelac's feet. Recognizing Beowulf's heroism, Hygelac gives him a valuable sword, the heirloom of Hrethel, Beowulf's grandfather. Giving the sword to Beowulf is ominous, possibly a recognition of Beowulf's being the heir presumptive to the throne. It is also, of course, a recognition of Beowulf's performance and Hygelac's previous misjudgment of Beowulf's qualities.

Hygelac is known for his strength, but the poet never refers to his wisdom. In this sense, Hygelac is a contrast to Hrothgar, who has been great in both wisdom and physical strength. In addition, Hygelac is also a foil for his wife, Hygd, who is wise, but unable to ward off the inevitable results of Hygelac's lack of wisdom. Hygelac is not wise when he attacks the Swedes; as a result, Haethcyn (a Geat) and Ongentheow (a Swedish king) both lose their lives. The raid on the Swedes merely sows the seeds for further raids, which eventually lead to Heardred's death and to the eventual extinction of the Geats.

Because of Hygelac's feuding, the poet is able to underscore his thesis that life reaches a certain glory and then fades into oblivion; life never remains the same. Men die and nations fall.

WIGLAF

Wiglaf, along with Beowulf's other thanes, watches Beowulf initiate his battle against the dragon. When the fight seems to be turning against Beowulf, however, all of the thanes – except Wiglaf – flee. Wiglaf's purpose in the poem, however, is more than being simply someone to help Beowulf. Wiglaf is the model of a good thane, and as a good thane, Wiglaf demonstrates the importance of heroism to society and the necessity of loyalty to one's kinsman and lord. He is willing to sacrifice his life to reciprocate the gifts which he received from his lord, but even more important, he symbolizes the need for cooperation between thane and lord in order to preserve society against overwhelming odds. Wiglaf also demonstrates the responsibility of the good thane, a contrast to the cowardly thanes, who represent all that society should not emulate.

After Beowulf's battle with the dragon, Wiglaf reprimands the thanes who fled. Such cowardice, he says, reveals a national weakness and is an invitation for their enemies to attack. Wiglaf reminds them that the loss of Beowulf means no more gifts, a loss of land-rights and everything that makes life joyous. Wiglaf emphasizes that death is preferable to a life without a lord; without a lord, man is adrift in a hostile world.

During Beowulf's battle with the dragon, the poet tells us that Beowulf is not "undoomed," and after the battle, during Wiglaf's attempt to revive the old warrior, the poet reminds us that God not only has the power to preserve heroes in battle, but also to take life from them. He is saying that, at times, God dispenses victories and, at other times, heroes lose their lives. Here, Beowulf loses his life. God allows Beowulf to avenge himself against the dragon and fight the good fight, but we must always remember a key idea of the heroic code: a hero must fight—even though he knows that he fights against fate.

Although Wiglaf is only a young thane when he inherits the kingdom, he knows that the cowardice of the Geats will lead to their downfall. Other tribes who hear about the thanes' failure to protect their king will surely swarm down upon them, hoping to take revenge for past hostilities. In short, Wiglaf is a doomed man. He has inherited a longstanding feud, and he must lead a people who seem unable or unwilling to fight. He also faces a hostile world, leading a people who fail to recognize the necessity of a do-or-die loyalty to the code of their clan.

Wiglaf may appear only momentarily in the poem, but, without a doubt, he is more important than being simply a deus ex machina who aids Beowulf in his battle with the dragon. Wiglaf explains the seething enmity between the Swedes and the Geats, a feud which will eventually lead to the Geats' downfall. We can see only a bleak future for Wiglaf—a thane without a lord, a king without a stable kingdom, a man struggling valiantly against a hostile and ever-changing world.

UNFERTH

Unferth's name has initiated a number of critical essays attempting to associate some appropriate meaning to his character. A general, critical consensus seems to be that the name "Unferth" means "folly" or "strife"—neither of which fully depicts his character. Remember that Unferth is a *thyle,* Hrothgar's official spokesman. The poet gives Unferth prominence by positioning him at Hrothgar's side, and the fact that he is the only member of Hrothgar's court who challenges Beowulf is further evidence that he is a man of some importance.

Unferth's position at court raises some other questions. How can he hold such a high position in the court when he is a known fratricide? Furthermore, if he is not a Dane, but a Frisian (as some critics believe), how did he obtain such a high position at court? The answer lies in the conjecture that "Unferth" is a form of "Hunferth," a warrior whose father was Ecglaf(ing). Therefore, Unferth would be called "Hunferth Ecglafing," a name which would be compounded to "Hunlafing," the Frisian in Finn's court (in "The Fight at Finnsburg") who caused the slaughter of the Finns and the deaths of his brothers.

Accordingly, then, when the early audience heard that Hrothgar's thyle was named Unferth, they would have felt dark forebodings, a sense of impending doom. Then, when they learned that Unferth was a fratricide, they almost certainly would have feared that he might betray Hrothgar.

As a foil for Beowulf, Unferth can be viewed as a kind of antihero. Because he has killed his own brother, he is clearly an archetypal kinsman of Cain; he has aligned himself with those who would divide families and disrupt society itself. He has violated the social laws of the comitatus; he has joined the brotherhood of monsters. He is arrogant and envious, traits of Grendel. In Unferth, we can sense latent monster-like violence within a human being.

WEALHTHEOW

Despite the fact that Queen Wealhtheow's name means "foreign captive" and that her origins were probably Celtic, she gives us a wealth of details about the courtly manners and behavior of the Danish court. Gracious, intelligent, and of fine bearing, she meets the qualifications of being a fine queen in every respect. She is beloved by her people, cheerful, generous, and keenly observant of court procedure. At the banquet, she offers a cup of mead to Hrothgar first, then offers the cup to Beowulf as an expression of the Danes' trust in him. Accordingly, when Beowulf accepts the cup, he accepts it as a symbol of his obligation to aid Hrothgar.

Wealhtheow's speech following close after the conclusion to "The Fight at Finnsburg" sets up a fine piece of dramatic irony as we compare her with Hildeburh, the heroine of the poem. In this scene, Wealhtheow is subtly urging Hrothgar to bequeath the kingdom to their sons; in choosing a successor to the throne, kinship, she says, is more important than gratitude to a foreign warrior – even if he did save the kingdom. Ironically, as several critics have noted, Hrothulf may already be plotting with Unferth to usurp the throne at a propitious time. In that case, Wealhtheow's daughter, Freawaru, would find herself in the same position as Hildeburh – whereas, if Beowulf were to assume the throne, it would be theoretically safe from Hrothulf's crafty machinations.

Wealhtheow places great emphasis on gift-giving, an act which kings and lords must perform for their thanes in return for their loyalty. Ironically, gifts to Hrothulf will probably not save the kingdom from destruction. And there is yet another irony in Wealhtheow's speech. Her veiled plea to Hrothgar to bequeath the kingdom to their sons rather than to Beowulf, whom he has just taken as a "son," may result in disaster. Even if Beowulf were offered the crown, he would probably refuse it; when Queen Hygd offers the Geats' kingdom to him, he refuses it.

Some critics seem to think that Wealhtheow's speech is in poor taste because it reminds Hrothgar of his age and his approaching demise. It seems more likely, however, that Wealhtheow fears the possibility of the Danes' being without a definite heir to the throne, a situation much like the one when Scyld had no heir. If there is any fault in Wealhtheow's speech, it is probably her over-concern for her sons' inheriting the kingdom, but even the wisest of men cannot see into the future. Experience has taught the Danes what it is like to be without a strong leader, and while Wealhtheow may suspect Hrothulf of ambition, she attempts to manipulate him by over-honoring him with public praise of his loyalty and the "many honors and marks of love."

As Wealhtheow presents Beowulf with a precious collar, the Brosing necklace, and she wishes him prosperity and asks him to protect her sons. She seems to stress too much that everyone in the Danish court is true to one another and loyal to their lord. All is well in the Danish court, she seems to emphasize. But all is *not* well: Grendel's mother will wreak vengeance this very night. Gifts do not buy safety from evil or treachery; nor do fame and wealth save lives. Fame and wealth, the poet says, are transitory – as is man, who walks upon this earth but once.

HYGD

Like Wealhtheow, Hygd is a model of the courtly queen. Despite her youth, she is "wise and well-born"–"noble of spirit" and "not sparing of gifts." She continues the theme of the "peace-weaving queen," a theme which began with Wealhtheow. Unlike Wealhtheow, though, Hygd seems more concerned about her people's welfare after the king's death than does Wealhtheow. Hygd offers the throne to Beowulf, and, in contrast, Wealhtheow advises Hrothgar to think of his sons first – a decision which leads to the eventual destruction of the Danish court.

Hygd is also a contrast to Hygelac, who risks his life in a raid for more plunder. Hygelac clearly displays an arrogant obsession for conquest, a characteristic which we do not find in Hygd. Hygelac places Hygd in a position where she can do nothing, even though she is wiser than he is.

Immediately following the poet's introduction of Hygd, he begins a digression about Thryth, a woman who is a thorough contrast to Hygd. Thryth is a cruel, arrogant, and selfish – a prime example of the misuse of power. The poet uses her as a foil for Hygd, who is good, modest, and wise.

MONSTERS

Early critical studies of *Beowulf* focused on the poem's history, the archeology associated with it, its heroic legends, mythology, folklore, and its literary history. For a long time, no one questioned the purpose of the monsters in the poem; they were simply there because the poem was "a wild folk tale." Critics could not see that the *Beowulf* poet had created an "illusion of historical truth and perspective" in order to produce a poem using ancient and traditional material. They did not recognize the beauty of the language, the powerful use of words, or the poem's lofty themes.

More often than not, early critics complained about the disgusting presence of the monsters – that is, until J.R.R. Tolkien focused attention on the purpose of the monsters. Later, another critic pointed out that it was far better for Beowulf to fight non-human foes than for him to rise to fame by fighting "typical foes" or engaging in "commonplace wars." To fight non-human foes was to "glimpse the cosmic and move with the thought of all men concerning the fate of human life and efforts." Beowulf's battles, it is said, are above the "petty wars of princes"; they surpass the "dates and limits of historical periods." Beowulf's taking on the monster foes, who are adversaries of God, allows the poet to develop the mutability theme, the idea that man lives in an ever-changing, hostile world of change and decay. Temporal battles are less important than the metaphorical battles of the cosmos.

GRENDEL

Most discussions about the monsters focus on Grendel and give short shrift to the "nicors," the sea monsters that Beowulf battled and killed during his youthful swimming escapade with Breca. Beowulf's struggle with the nicors began at night in a storm-lashed sea, and it was only later that Beowulf fully realized the terrible dangers he had encountered. Afterward, Beowulf gained enormous confidence, and when he relates the incident to the Danish court, they are clearly impressed with his courage. Hrothgar accepts Beowulf's offer to put an end to Grendel's savagery because of Beowulf's previous success with sea monsters. Thus, Beowulf's early confrontation with the sea monsters was a test of his valor, long before he meets the fiendish creature called Grendel.

Grendel is not only a "monster" in human-like shape; he is a descendant of Cain. He lives under an inherited curse and is denied God's presence. The poet refers to him as "the guardian of sins." Grendel is a heathen, the physical image of man estranged from God. His superhuman size and strength and his hostility to man and his joys resemble the early descriptions of Satan. However, Grendel is not Satan; he does not deceive man or destroy men's souls. He is not even an apparition of "soul-destroying evil" that would attempt to bring eternal death to man. Basically, Grendel is a physical monster, an ogre who is hostile to humanity. He devours men and takes away their "temporal" lives. This is the key difference between Grendel-as-Satan and Grendel-as-"the guardian of sins."

Grendel's hideous and repugnant body reflects the inner perversion of his spirit. Figuratively, he is the repellant image of man fallen from grace through sin. Grendel has no fear or foreboding as he approaches Hrothgar's mead hall on the night that Beowulf lies in wait for him. He assumes that his nights of bloody devouring will continue, and, unlike Beowulf, he gives no attention to his method of attack. He acts without thinking. Because he has no knowledge of weapons, he depends upon his extraordinary strength and violence to destroy what he hates and envies.

As an adversary of God, Grendel is a greater challenge for Beowulf than are the nicors. With his human-like features, Grendel is the least primitive of all the monsters in the poem; it is in Beowulf's best interests as a hero to fight a sub-human, primitive creature who is God's own adversary. This fight with Grendel will prepare Beowulf for his next two climactic battles.

GRENDEL'S MOTHER

The coming of Grendel's mother, or dam, to Hrothgar's mead hall is a departure from the normal actions of this she-monster. Grendel's mother is weaker than Beowulf, but her fight with him will be more treacherous and more dangerous because Beowulf will be entering a strange new territory to seek her out. The poet builds up the horror of the monster's territory through the ominous, eerie description of the mere.

When the she-monster seizes Beowulf and drags him to her lair, she places him at a distinct disadvantage. However, it is essential that Beowulf's second fight must seem to be more difficult, as a preparation for his final battle, his contest with the dragon.

Grendel's mother is described as a "she-monster of the deep," a "water-woman," and a "she-wolf." The reference to her as a "troll-wife" (a term used often in Nordic-Germanic fairy tales) renders her inhuman and even more primitive than Grendel. Clearly, she is less of an adversary of God than Grendel is, and she attacks only because of provocation and a desire for revenge. Remember that her desire for revenge is in keeping with the theme of revenge in this poem; the perpetuation of a feud between tribes and nations accounts for the enmity inherent in this epic. Violence begets violence and continues until a man can accept wergild without a loss of face. The monsters, of course, do not recognize the code which includes the wergild option.

THE DRAGON

The dragon is more fierce than either Grendel or his mother; he has no human qualities. He does not stem from the race of Cain, nor is he a troll. As a frightening, fire-breathing beast, he is a powerful adversary–the stuff of many legends. Tolkien points out, however, that if there is any negative criticism about the dragon, it results from his being not so much a literal dragon as he is a "sense of dragonness." Yet there are places in the poem where he is indeed a real "worm" with a terrifyingly vivid presence.

Tolkien sees the dragon as a "personification of malice, greed, destruction (the evil side of heroic life), and of the undiscriminating cruelty of fortune that does not distinguish between good and evil." The poet's symbolism concerning the dragon is close to the surface, but it never breaks into blatant allegory. The dragon represents a timeless foe of man. Accordingly, Beowulf's fighting a "timeless" creature who exists in heroic history is more significant than his fighting a monster-in-human-shape.

Christian allegorists see the dragon as a symbol of the power of Satan; for them, allegory is always close to the surface of this poem. Beowulf's fight with Grendel allegorizes the essential facts of the story–"the need of a Savior and His advent." His fight with Grendel's mother retells the basic story with an emphasis upon the continuing need of a savior to protect man from the powers of evil, emphasizing the "effects of redemption" when Beowulf enters the mere and purifies it of the evil creatures. Finally, his fight with the dragon is a culmination of the story of salvation, wherein Beowulf, like Christ the Savior, gives his life for his people.

CRITICAL ESSAYS

SOURCES AND INGREDIENTS

Nordic-Germanic Elements The *Beowulf* poet found most of his material in Nordic-Germanic folklore, heroic legends, historical traditions and biblical sources. Folklore is the source for the action–that is, Beowulf's three battles: with Grendel, Grendel's mother, and the dragon. Folklore is also the poet's source for the story of Beowulf and Breca, a tale told to illuminate Beowulf's physical and emotional characteristics.

The Old Norse *Elder Edda* contains stories similar to those we find in *Beowulf*, and the *Grettissaga*, in particular, tells of Grettir the Strong fighting two monsters such as Grendel and his mother. Since these sagas were written after the tenth century, scholars believe that because of their similarity to *Beowulf* in parts, these episodes in *Beowulf* come from a common ancestry–folklore. Scholars also believe that the poets of the above Nordic-Germanic poems were not familiar with *Beowulf*, and, in fact, *Beowulf* was not known in Iceland at the time that the *Grettissaga* was written. However, in both works, the "she-troll" is a formidable adversary, and although the terrain in the *Grettisaga* is rough, it is not as fearful as Grendel's mere.

Beowulf's youth is typical of the folklore hero; he seems slothful, wanton, and foolhardy. Most people in Denmark are familiar with Holger the Dane, who is pictured as sleeping until his countrymen need him. Only then will he use his unusual strength to protect them and save his country.

The strange light in the cave of Grendel's mother is a phenomenon often found in folk literature, as is the light in the dragon's barrow. A similar light appears in the hall where Grettir fights a monster. Even place names in Medieval England point to a strong, widespread belief in the old folktales.

The figure of Scyld Sceafing in *Beowulf* hovers between being a historical figure and being a part of folklore and mythology. Breca is thought to be either a folktale character or a king, the consensus of opinion being that his name is metaphorically a synonym for royal names. Obviously, folklore provides the main foes for Beowulf and for the background of the poem itself.

Another indication of the Nordic-Germanic tradition is the alliterative verse form which continued in use for many centuries until the Battle of Hastings in 1066. The alliterative verse form is a peculiar phenomenon of Germanic poetry; Germans are the only Indo-European-speaking people who used it, as well as the only people who placed the stress of a word on the root syllable. Anglo-Saxon poets were slow to give up the form, but with the conquest of England, French *jongleurs*, or minstrels came, and the Anglo-Saxon aristocracy were unable to patronize the poets since the transfer of power and money was held by the Normans.

Heroic Legends In *Beowulf*, these legends are sometimes fused with historical elements and folklore. In some instances, there is only the mention of a figure, such as Weland, or an artifact, such as the Brosing necklace, which Wealhtheow gives to Beowulf. Swords with names are also the stuff of folklore. Here, Beowulf's sword is called

Naegling, and Unferth's sword, which he gives to Beowulf, is called Hrunting.

Sometimes a historical figure is cloaked in legends which the *Beowulf* poet uses to set off a character, as is the case with Heremod. Eormanric and Hama are also derived from the legendary stock of tales.

After Beowulf kills Grendel, the scop reflects the Danes' joy by singing about Beowulf's victory. In order to relate Beowulf's bravery and glory to an earlier hero, a singer recites "The Lay of Sigemund," a song about a famous, legendary hero who, like Beowulf, also slew a monster. That same evening, the scop sings about Heremod, setting him up as a foil to Beowulf and Hrothgar. Heremod was an evil king who apparently failed to care for his thanes and to share his treasures with them. The scop tells us that the "stain of sin" sank deep in Heremod's heart. We know little else about him except that he is possibly an early ancestor of Scyld, founder of the Scylding line of kings. Whether he is truly historical, we do not know; possibly, he is only a traditional figure. The poet's reference to him leads us to believe that legends accumulated about him, and the audience would remember and recognize stories about him.

The poet also introduces the legend of Scyld himself, supposedly the founder of the Danish throne, a hero who established an example of the strong king who consolidated the Danish state and followed the requirements of a good king. His name is associated with the legend of a child arriving in a boat with a sheaf of corn. The child's arrival, it was believed, would bring prosperity to the kingdom. Both Scyld and his son Beo(wulf) have no historical ties and are seemingly introduced merely to account for the name "Scylding" in the Danish dynasty.

Historical Elements The names of Hrothgar and Hrothulf are both recorded in the *Danish Chronicles* (written in Latin) and mentioned by other poets of later dates. The civil war, alluded to by Beowulf, was well known to the *Beowulf* audience, who also knew about the attack on Heorot by the Heathobards under Ingeld.

Gregory of Tours, in his *Historia Francorum*, records Hygelac's obsessive raiding. The troubles to come after Beowulf's death are also recorded as part of historical record, and history corroborates the Geats' fear of being annihilated by the fact that they seem to disappear from history during the sixth century.

Eormanric, an Ostragoth king, probably lived in the fourth century. Like Heremod, he was ruthless, mighty, and wealthy. His function in the poem is to account for the Brosing collar, the magic necklace, which Hama stole.

Ongentheow, Onela, Ohthere, and Eadgils are historic figures whose authenticity has been proven by archeological finds and other records. Events in *Beowulf* surrounding these figures are generally taken to be historical and would be familiar to the *Beowulf* audience.

Scholars view Ingeld as probably historical because of the political and personal motives surrounding his relationship with Hrothgar. The Hrothgar-Ingeld relationship exists because Hrothgar hoped to cement relationships between the two kingdoms by marrying his daughter, Freawaru, to Ingeld. Strained relations resulted from a feud beginning with the death of Froda, Ingeld's father. Hrothgar hoped to avoid a war which threatened to erupt. Freawaru's marriage to Ingeld would supposedly be a *wergild,* sufficient payment for Froda's death, but such a marriage would, by its very nature, include the problem of bringing a Danish queen into Ingeld's court. Beowulf sees the dilemma which Ingeld faces because his father's death is still unrevenged and he must fight his beloved wife's kin in order to satisfy his father's death.

Offa, whose wife, Thryth, is a foil to Hygd, was a historical king in England. Finn, of "The Fight at Finnsburg," is also historical, as is Hengest, who appears in the same poem.

There is always a thin, blurred line between what is legendary and what is strictly historical material. Legends are usually based upon some historical figure or incident, and after years of stories have accumulated about the figure or incident, it is difficult to determine what is factual and what is legendary.

Christian Elements Seemingly all critics recognize the Christian and biblical elements in *Beowulf,* but few seem to believe that the poem was originally pagan and that Christian ideas were incorporated at a later date. Many critics tend to think that the original *Beowulf* poet was a Christian who included both Christian and pagan elements at the time of writing and that the Christian elements are not the work of a reviser or interpolator. It is important to note that not all of the ideas of right living, of loyalty and of good kingship can be attributed to Christian ideals, for these ideas were also ingrained in the early Germanic and pagan societies. In fact, many of them were derived from the concept of comitatus, a creed of great importance to the early pagans.

The *Beowulf* poet speaks often of praise, but "praise" does not have the Christian connotation, which suggests "heavenly praise." The *Beowulf* poet is speaking about the praise of one's peers, praise which the warrior must gain in order to be remembered by future generations.

In *Beowulf,* there is hell, for hell was a concept known to the pagans, and Beowulf makes reference to hell as the destiny of both Unferth and Grendel. However, there is no reference in the poem to heaven, as Christians today think of it.

Fate, or Wyrd, is an important concept in Beowulf, and scholars have discussed it from pagan and Christian points of view. To understand the concept of Wyrd, it is important to review two key concepts: (1) Christianity and paganism existed simultaneously in the Anglo-Saxon world, and some of the moral virtues of Christianity were consistent with the ideas of the traditional code of comitatus; (2) in the Old English vocabulary, there were only pagan terms with which Anglo-Saxons would embody Christian concepts. The Old English words *frea* and *dryten* mean prince and lord, and superimposing the idea of God on these words was not inconsistent with the poet's purpose to fuse paganism and Christianity.

The same is true of Wyrd. Wyrd is sometimes equated with Divine Providence, except that Divine Providence refers more to eternal matters and Wyrd applies to situations *where the individual can make a choice.* Divine Providence controls the functions of the universe – the constellation of stars remaining in order and the seasons returning at regular intervals. Wyrd gives man a choice. Beowulf did not have to challenge Grendel, Grendel's mother, or the dragon, yet he did and he relied upon Wyrd to determine the outcome. It was Wyrd which controlled the outcome of his battles.

The *Beowulf* poet knew much about Christianity's early days and pagan beliefs. He knew that a people do not accept a new religion all at once, but that they begin to look at the old beliefs in a different perspective. He did not include dogma in his poem, but neither did he include the old gods in preference to the Christian God. Monsters have always been the foes of the gods, just as they are the foes of the Christian God. The early pagan was a mortal hemmed in by a hostile world – as was the early Christian.

The fusion of pagan and Christian ideals presents a new perspective to the idea of man's mutability. It also points to the question of "pietas" (responsible mercy) concerning the treatment of pious pagans. Do we consign the pious pagan to perdition? How do we treat him? As we can see, the fusion of pagan and Christian ideas is an important facet to understanding *Beowulf.*

Allegorical Elements Christian elements in *Beowulf* have led many critics to view the poem as an allegory of salvation. These critics cite numerous references to the liturgy of the Church, seeking parallels to Christian dogma and to Christ's life. The scene at Grendel's mere, when Beowulf prepares to descend into its watery depths particularly excites the interest of these allegorists. The poet, they say, refers to the mere as hell, but in the dark and misty atmosphere, the pagan too would see the place as hell, for he too knew about hell. The allegorists point to Beowulf's preparation for descent as though he were preparing for death, forgiving his enemies before descending, and not mourning for life. The descent is very much like a military campaign against the Powers Below, and upon Beowulf's victory, a light penetrates the scene beneath the waters. Significantly, all the thanes except Wiglaf give up hope and leave at the ninth hour of the day—the hour of Christ's death on the cross.

Beowulf returns with his trophies, and the atmosphere signals the end of winter and the return of spring. Some critics interpret this episode as containing parallels to the death of Christ, his harrowing of hell, and his resurrection.

Probably the most common referent for the allegorists is the Christian story of salvation. These critics see Beowulf as the savior of the Danes, who are being harassed by Grendel. Like Satan, jealous of Adam and Eve in the Garden of Eden, Grendel is jealous of the joy and happiness in Heorot. Because Grendel is associated with the powers of darkness and evil and because Beowulf has many of the attributes of Christ, the allegorists see him as an allegorical Christ, bringing salvation to the world.

Some critics see Grendel as an ogre having kinship with the devil, but he nonetheless remains an ogre, not a "soul-destroying monster." Still others see Grendel strictly as an ogre whom the author makes no attempt to use as a symbol for evil; he is simply a descendant of the race of Cain. Those critics who see Grendel as a real monster, in whom the Anglo-Saxons fully believed, see Beowulf as a real man come to save Heorot from Grendel.

Allegorists see the salvation story repeated three times after the battle with Grendel, the second being the descent into the mere, and the third being Beowulf's confrontation with the dragon. In the dragon episode, Beowulf gives his life for his people, just as Christ gave his life for humanity. Opposing critics argue that if killing the dragon symbolizes evil, or Satan, to the allegorists, then Beowulf's death indicates that evil, or Satan, is victorious because Beowulf dies.

Looking at the poem allegorically presents numerous knotty problems involving interpretations of the Bible and the patristic literature of the times. Both sides of the allegory debate present convincing arguments, but neither side seems to settle the question.

STRUCTURE OF THE POEM

A study of the poem's structure involves questions of the author's choice of materials, strategic placement of them, and the conventions, figures of speech, symbols, and images he uses. As most authors do, the *Beowulf* poet synthesized his materials into one artistic whole to achieve the effect he desired. We must ask why the poet juxtaposed "The Lay of Sigemund," "The Fight at Finnsburg" and other legends with Beowulf's slaying of Grendel and the celebration at Heorot. Why also do we find gnomic verse, kennings, metaphors, litotes, and other conventions used in particular positions? To understand and explain all of these usages goes beyond the scope of this study, but they contain several points for the student to consider during the study of *Beowulf*.

Nearly all critics agree that the poem is divided into two parts. Some see three parts, but this division doesn't seem to work well, and most critics reject the idea of three parts. Still others believe that *Beowulf* contains a prologue, is divided into two parts, and that each part contains three separate episodes. This division, however, sets aside the Scylding story from the main poem, and some critics see this story as being a crucial part of the poem because it sets up comparisons and contrasts for the author's later development of characters and events.

Critics who set up these types of divisions do so to show the author's design for the poem and to further the argument that a single author organized and wrote *Beowulf.* In addition, these critics present a reasonable premise for viewing the poem as a complete and structurally strong poem, as opposed to those who consider the work as a two-part structure, loosely connected by one central character.

Beowulf is obviously a complicated poem which draws from traditional material, heroic legends, historical episodes and allusions, pagan and Christian sources, and fuses these elements into a work of art.

BEOWULF AS AN EPIC POEM

Beowulf was usually regarded as an epic until J.R.R. Tolkien, an astute scholar and author of the Hobbit books, declared that the poem was a "heroic-elegaic poem." While not all scholars agree with Tolkien, many agree with him in varying degrees. For example, nearly everyone agrees that *Beowulf* is an adventure – but not all adventures are epics. To study the problem, it is necessary to know (1) the characteristics of an epic; (2) know what a heroic-elegaic poem is; (3) what is meant by a lay, and (3) study the qualities of a hero in these different types of poems. After all, it is the hero who determines the direction that the poem will take.

Tolkien bases his premise for calling *Beowulf* a heroic-elegaic poem on the idea that the poet takes a hero who is larger than life and uses folktales, legends, and other episodes, possibly historical, to bring out the heroic qualities of the hero. He also tells us that the poem is not a narrative poem because it does not tell a tale sequentially. He further argues that *Beowulf* is not a romantic tale, nor is it a lay. Tolkien chooses to call *Beowulf* a heroic-elegy because the first part of the poem, which is heroic, builds up to the second part, which ends in tragedy. Without a background of Beowulf's earlier heroic deeds, the last part would be meaningless.

Other critics point out that *Beowulf* is not a lay since a heroic lay focuses on only one episode of a well-known story from the past. In addition, the lay moves more swiftly to its conclusion, and the main interest is on the heroic deeds of men who "act out their fates" in accordance with their concepts of justice – no matter what the consequences may be. The lay is meant to bring the audience to emulate the courage of the hero.

Both the epic and the lay tell stories of great heroes, but there are significant differences. The epic moves at a more leisurely pace and amplifies the stories which the poet incorporated from older lays. In contrast to *Beowulf*, "The Fight at Finnsburg" is a lay and tells the story of a five-day battle in fifteen lines. The *Beowulf* poet takes eighty lines to describe Beowulf's battle with Grendel, which lasts only a few minutes.

Regardless of Tolkien's views, *Beowulf* clearly contains many epic characteristics. For example, the *Beowulf* poet describes (in two of many relative clauses in the poem) a coat of mail "that knew how to defend the bone-cage," and a coat of mail that protects the hero "so that no attack could injure his vital parts." The appositive is also characteristic of the epic style; note such phrases as "the war shirt *woven by hands, broad and expertly wrought*, was soon to explore the waves." Other types of diction are also typical of the epic style: (1) metaphors such as the "swan-road," "wielder of glory," "shafts of slaughter," and "cage of bones"; and (2) compounds words such as "battle-sweat" (meaning *blood*), "breast-clothing," "battle clothing," or "battle byrnie." The epic poet also makes use of kennings, figurative phrases used as synonyms, and litotes, or understatements. These figures of speech are, of course, also found in other Anglo-Saxon poetry. The language of the epic style is, therefore, an elevated language, a rather formal language.

Nearly all epics also use set forms, or set pieces, which are cues for the scop's memory. The Anglo-Saxon poets used these cues to insert stories of historical heroes into the main subject of their story.

In Greek epics, the poet calls upon the Muse to speak through him, but there is no Muse in *Beowulf*. The scop calls upon his memory of stories heard in the past. In *Beowulf*, the poet begins the poem with "We have heard it said," indicating that he relies on well-known tales, or legends.

Most epics begin *in media res* (in the middle of things), but this is not the case in *Beowulf*. The poet goes back to the early history of the Scyldings and leads up to Hrothgar's reign.

Epic characters hold high positions – kings, princes, noblemen and members of the aristocracy – but the epic hero must be more than that. He must be able to perform outstanding deeds, be greater than the average epic character, and be of heroic proportions. Most of all, he must have super-human courage.

Epic characters generally deliver numerous speeches, all of which move the action forward, tell something about the past, or reveal the speaker's character traits. Sometimes the hero's character traits are revealed in speeches by other characters. Beowulf does not give many speeches, but from those he gives, we learn about his character traits.

Warriors in epics frequently deliver boasts before attacking an enemy, and we hear Beowulf's boast to Hrothgar that he will rid Heorot of Grendel. His boast includes a mention of earlier heroic deeds, and Beowulf also refers to his reputation as a brave man who has extraordinary strength. Unferth accuses him of being cowardly, but Beowulf's accomplishments prove otherwise. Later, Beowulf boasts before confronting Grendel's mother, but he does not boast before he confronts the dragon. In fact, he says, "I forego boasting."

Genealogy is also important to the epic warrior, for he wants us (and his enemies, as well) to know that he comes from a long line of warriors. Beowulf relates his genealogy to Hrothgar when he introduces himself to the king. Hrothgar, of course, already knows Beowulf's father from Ecgtheow's years of exile in Hrothgar's court.

The taunting of the hero is also a common feature of epics, especially before a battle. Here, the *Beowulf* poet uses the taunt to expose Unferth's unsavory character traits. Unferth manifests his jealousy when he taunts Beowulf about his youthful instability, but Beowulf turns the tables on Unferth and taunts him about his lack of courage. Beowulf reminds Unferth that Grendel would not be ravaging Heorot if Unferth were as brave as he "would have men think." Beowulf also reminds Unferth of his sin against society (killing a kinsman). Interesting, the *Beowulf* poet does not use the taunt-device before Beowulf fights Grendel, Grendel's mother, or the dragon, and these are the only three battles we witness in the poem.

The usual setting for an epic is vast – usually encompassing stories about great nations, or even the universe. Although *Beowulf* is about a noble hero and his relationship with two nations, the concept of a "vast scope" is present: Beowulf's enemies are not human. The non-human enemies raise the notion of a king's fall to a fall of cosmic dimensions, a struggle with universal evil, the fate of human life and man's efforts. Beowulf's fate rises above time and history.

Supernatural "forces" are usually evident in an epic, but these do not appear in *Beowulf*. There is some reference to the Will of God and His control of Man's Fate (Wyrd), but there is no direct super-human force, such as we see in the Homeric epics. The moral or religious code seems less dependent upon superhuman beings than upon social codes. Social codes are moral because, if adhered to, they produce right action and an ordered society.

THE EPIC HERO

The meat of an epic is usually derived from violent and social chaos – a central conflict, often pitting the hero versus an unjust king, or ruler. Traditionally, the hero is brave, of course. He is almost superhuman in strength, successful in battle, and contemptuous of his wounds – even of death. In addition, the hero is of noble stock or, sometimes, he may be even semi-divine. Without these qualities, a man would never be recognized as a hero. Yet, within this traditional context, a hero becomes infinitely more interesting as a literary character when he deviates from the usual heroic pattern.

One characteristic of Beowulf that individualizes him from other early heroes is his extraordinary "quality of loyalty" to his lord, or king. Beowulf is fiercely loyal to his lord and to the lord's family, just as he is to Hrothgar, who is only a "temporary" lord for him.

In many epics, a period of turmoil exiles the hero from his homeland, or else he realizes that he can achieve heroic status only if he goes to another kingdom where there is a chaotic, disintegrating breakdown of tribal organization. Beowulf, however, is not an exile from his homeland; he leaves voluntarily with the consent of Hygelac, his lord. All of his heroic and famed exploits are performed in another country before he returns home to eventually become a lord, or king himself.

Beowulf has no responsibility to protect the Danes from Grendel, but Hrothgar, the Danish king, does have just such a responsibility. Some critics view Beowulf's purpose for taking over the duties of Hrothgar as purely personal – to establish his own reputation as a hero. However, other critics view Beowulf's contributions to the Danes as altruistic.

When Beowulf arrives at the land of the Scyldings, the coast guard asks him to identify himself and give the details of his visit. Beowulf says that he does not come to challenge Hrothgar's power, but to perform a task for the lord. Resentment is often evident at court – particularly in Unferth, who ridicules Beowulf's early feats of daring. Unferth also questions Beowulf's ability to accomplish the deed that he has come to perform.

Frequently in an epic, as a foil for the hero, we see a king who is weakened by a flaw. He may be temporarily weakened, or he may be too old to function in a protective capacity for his nation. A king's weakened position often creates chaos, for his society fears his inability to rule adequately. They fear that an outsider might invade and replace the king, thereby imposing foreign ideas on the community. This problem of a weak king exists in *Beowulf*, and had Beowulf been another type of hero, the plot of the poem would have taken another turn. A key to understanding this poem lies in an understanding of how the poet handled the problem of kingship in both the courts of the Danes and the Geats.

Beowulf differs from the usual intruder-hero in that he respects the legitimacy of the Danish kingship. He has no intention of usurping Hrothgar's kingship, and he performs in the same honorable manner when he refuses the kingship after Hygelac's death. He accepts the crown only after Hygelac's son is killed in battle.

THE SCOP

After Julius Caesar lay claim to English soil, the Britons were subject to numerous invasions, mostly from the Scandanavian tribes to the north of England. Many Scandanavian tribes who raided the northern coasts remained to become settlers and tillers of the soil, and Anglo-Saxon society continued to be reasonably well-organized, aristocratic, and rather conservative. Because of these Scandanavian invaders, many Scandinavian folktales from the Baltic region became a part of the Anglo-Saxon body of folklore and legend, and it was not long until various warrior-kings had a "singer," or scop attached to their courts who could recite and sing a body of oral literature – particularly about the warrior-king's glorious deeds.

In the late sixth century, Augustine came to England at the request of Pope Gregory. Gregory advised his monks not to disrupt England's pagan customs, but to proceed with conversion gradually. Consequently, the question arises concerning whether *Beowulf* resulted from the traditions handed down by the scops, or whether the poem was a product of the monasteries. Some critics claim that it is an amalgam of both elements.

Since the poet gives us a valuable portrait of the scop in Hrothgar's court, and because of other internal evidence, some critics believe that the poem originated in an oral tradition – that is, it is the product of a scop. After all, they reason, the scop had a storehouse of old folktales, legends, and heroic deeds performed by great heroes of the past. Hrothgar's scop was able to sing Beowulf's praises the day following his defeat of Grendel, and in the song, he includes the older "Lay of Sigemund."

The scop's purpose was to honor his noble patron or others who performed great deeds and to give praise and blame where applicable. More than this, though, the scop was a tribal historian; he was expected to remember stories from the past and be able to sing them at any time. His job was to mentally and musically recall and perform these stories because the pride of the tribe depended upon a long genealogy of heroes. Additionally, the scop defined the moral values of his society by singing about heroes and about those who acted in non-heroic ways. His songs endorsed models of behavior. By example, he taught that certain actions were profitable to the group, and wrong actions dealt serious blows to the unity of the tribe. His many stories of gift-giving by kings indicated that the good king appreciated his thanes and rewarded their loyalty with gifts. In contrast, the wicked or greedy king would offer few or no rewards. The scop defined his society's code of heroic behavior; he praised those who lived according to accepted social codes and criticized those who failed to perform according to the expectations of the group.

MAN AND COMMUNITY

If we are to consider *Beowulf* a unified poem written by a single author, as most critics today agree that it is, then it is important to look at one of its main themes and consider how it is related to the poem as a whole. One of the poem's central themes is the notion of "community." Such a theme is infused throughout the poem and accounts for the tribal history, the rise and fall of a nation, and themes – mutability, wisdom and strength, Christianity and paganism, and pride and heroism. All of the deeds that define Beowulf's heroism are done to ensure a peaceful community; Beowulf does not act heroically simply for the sake of his own fame. Similarly, Scyld comes almost by accident, it seems, to a Danish tribe who suffered under a malevolent king. Eventually Scyld set an example for his people; he was a king who was courageous, munificent, faithful to his oath and loyal to his kin. These are all factors which contribute to a peaceful community, and the *Beowulf* poet refers to these factors throughout the poem.

The poet then dovetails Scyld's goodness into his description of Hrothgar's sterling, kingly qualities. As a contrast, he introduces Grendel, a monster who stands outside the social realm and cannot share in the joys and the gift-giving in Heorot. Like Cain, Grendel represents a figure who is denied a place within the community.

Beowulf goes to Hrothgar because he owes Hrothgar a familial debt and because his own nation urges him to use his strength to help the Danes triumph over Grendel's malevolence. Beowulf battles with Grendel because of social reciprocity and because Grendel has attempted to tear asunder the fabric of Hrothgar's community. Later, Beowulf frees the Danes from the devastation wrought by Grendel's mother. He fights the creature not to prove himself a hero, but to assume his social obligation and restore the Danish society to its former peace. In both these battles, we see how a community functions and what is necessary if it is to retain its framework.

The dragon is yet another creature outside of the community. He is a threat to the Geatish community because he has been disturbed by a thief. He devastates the land, and Beowulf decides to fight the dragon because, again, there is a social need to do so if the community is to survive. The dragon destroys Beowulf's dwelling place and the throne of the Geats, while guarding a treasure that could have been used to hold a community more securely together. Beowulf fights to save his country, to secure the treasure, and to restore peace. The irony in this battle is that Beowulf is buried with the treasure and society is in greater danger than before Beowulf killed the dragon. However, it is partially the community's fault since one of its members broke a social law.

ALLEGORY IN *BEOWULF*

Is *Beowulf* an allegory? Is so, what kind of an allegory is it? All critics agree that the poet never refers to any singular pagan god by name, but many strongly contend that the "God" to which Beowulf and Hrothgar refer is the Christian God. Thus, some critics see the poem as lending itself to Christian allegory, and others see it as an allegory of salvation, drawing upon church liturgy and New Testament theology. There is also a critical tradition that *Beowulf* is not a Christian allegory at all, but that it is a secular allegory.

Most of us recognize the poet's references to the Old Testament, but few of us are able to find *direct* references to the New Testament. However, those scholars who see the poem as an allegory of salvation usually support the concept that man is fallen from grace and must be redeemed, which is a creed as much a part of the New Testament as the story of creation is of the Old Testament.

Christian allegorists see the Danes as fallen from grace and in the clutches of Grendel, a demon whom they compare to Satan because the poem says that Grendel is of the race of Cain. To free themselves from this monster, the Danes need a savior, and Beowulf, through his desire to alleviate their suffering, comes to save them. With his great strength and God's help, he is successful.

Beowulf's humility and charity are similar to that of Christ, and even those who do not see the poem as a Christian allegory can see why some critics parallel Beowulf with Christ. As a savior of the Danes, Beowulf destroys Grendel (Evil). Later, when Grendel's mother threatens the Danes, Beowulf promises to save them from this new evil demon. Later, Beowulf gives his life to save the Geats from the fierce, destructive dragon.

Christian allegorists also view Beowulf's descent into the mere as a baptismal rite involving both death and resurrection, and they parallel Beowulf's descent into the mere with Christ's Harrowing of Hell. Beowulf's immersion purifies him, and he overcomes these evil powers. He rises from the waters a redeemed man, purified by the death and burial of sin.

Those disagreeing with the allegorical treatment point out that baptism represents the death of one's sinful life and the birth of a new life in grace. However, Beowulf is not changed after he rises from the mere. He does not walk in a "newness of life." He holds the same social ideas and the same belief in Fate (Wyrd) and God. He remains the model of a good warrior and a faithful thane to Hygelac, still very much a warrior who is faithful to the ideals of the comitatus.

Allegorists usually ignore the importance of kinship ties, courtly behavior, loyalty and revenge. These elements involve moral and ethical behaviors, but they do not fit well into an allegory of salvation.

Critics favoring strong Christian elements in the poem assume that the poet was a Christian, which he may well have been. They point to the various Church writers of the period as sources for the poet's Christian perspectives, and they point out that the poem reveals the poet's views about man and the universe and his concept of reality. He is aware of man's weakness and imperfections, and he knows that strength and wealth are transient. Such a poet would logically believe that alienation from God begets envy and hatred of the good; therefore, we see an emphasis on the story of Cain. When the poet writes about pride and covetousness and envy and hatred, he is simply writing about how he, as a Christian, views the human tragedy.

There is no argument from the Christian allegorists that biblical, Christian, and pagan references all appear in *Beowulf*. The question is whether any of these references is pervasive enough to develop a controlling theme. Any assessment of *Beowulf* must deal with its treatment of the pagan references in the poem itself, in the social context of the era, and in the digressions. These are all part of the poem, and no part may be ignored when interpreting the poet's desired effect.

SUGGESTED ESSAY TOPICS

1. The purpose of the Scylding digression
2. Elements of Christianity in *Beowulf*
3. Beowulf–a tragic figure?
4. The heroic code in *Beowulf*
5. Hygelac and Thryth, foils to Hygd
6. The scop's role in *Beowulf*
7. An analysis of Hrothgar's homilies
8. Grendel, a descendant of Cain
9. Beowulf's three battles
10. Hrothgar as king
11. Unferth as anti-hero

12. Beowulf, the ideal Nordic-Germanic hero

13. The problem of evil in *Beowulf*

14. The battle with Grendel's mother

15. The place of women in Nordic-Germanic courts

16. Wyrd and Divine Providence

17. Grendel–in *Beowulf* and in John Gardner's *Grendel*

18. The monsters in *Beowulf*

19. German society in *Beowulf*

20. Wealhtheow, Hygd, and Thryth

SELECTED BIBLIOGRAPHY

Translations

CHICKERING, HOWARD D., JR., TRANS. *Beowulf: A Dual-Language Edition.* Garden City, New York: Anchor Press/Doubleday, 1977.

DONALDSON, E. TALBOT, TRANS. *Beowulf: A New Prose Translation.* New York: W. W. Norton & Company, 1966.

KENNEDY, CHARLES W., TRANS. *Beowulf: The Oldest English Epic.* New York: Oxford University Press, 1940.

RAFFEL, BURTON, TRANS. *Beowulf.* New York: A Mentor Book, 1963.

Works Cited and Consulted

BONJOUR, ADRIEN. *The Digressions in* Beowulf. Oxford: Blackwell, 1950.

BRODEUR, ARTHUR GILCHRIST. *The Art of* Beowulf. Berkeley: University of California Press, 1959.

GIRVAN, RITCHIE. Beowulf *and the Seventh Century: Language and Content.* Norwood, Pa.: Norwood Editions, 1975.

HUPPE, BERNARD FELIX. *The Hero in the Earthly City: a Reading of* Beowulf. Binghamton, N.Y.: Medieval & Renaissance Texts and Studies, State University of New York, 1984.

JACKSON, W.T.H. *The Hero and the King: An Epic Theme.* New York: Columbia Press, 1982.

NICHOLSON, LEWIS E. *An Anthology of* Beowulf *Criticism*. Notre Dame, Ind.: University of Notre Dame Press, 1963.

NILES, JOHN D. Beowulf: *the Poem and its Tradition.* Cambridge: Harvard University Press, 1983.

NIST, JOHN A. *The Structure and Texture of* Beowulf. Norwood, Pa.: Norwood Editions, 1977.

WILLIAMS, DAVID. *Cain and* Beowulf: *A Study in Secular Allegory.* Toronto: University of Toronto Press, 1982.

WRENN, CHARLES LESLIE, ED. Beowulf *and the Finnsburg Fragment.* 3rd ed. Revised by W. F. Bolton. London: Harrop Limited, 1953. Rev. 1982.

Additional Works

CHAMBERS, R. W. Beowulf: *An Introduction*. 3rd ed., with supplement by C. L. Wrenn. London: Cambridge University Press, 1959.

GREENFIELD, STANLEY. *Studies in Old English Literature in Honor of Arthur G. Brodeur.* Eugene: University of Oregon Press, 1963.

Canterbury Tales

CANTERBURY TALES

NOTES

including

- *Biographical and Historical Introduction*
- *Chaucer's Language*
- *Summaries and Commentaries*
- *Principal Characters*
- *Critical Analysis*
- *Questions for Examination and Review*
- *Select Bibliography*

by
Bruce Nicoll
University of Nebraska

INCORPORATED
LINCOLN, NEBRASKA 68501

ISBN 0-8220-0292-2

Printed in U.S.A.

1992 Printing

Cliffs Notes, Inc. Lincoln, Nebraska

CONTENTS

CHRONOLOGY OF CHAUCER'S LIFE AND WORKS

c. 1340 – Chaucer born in London.

1357 – Became page to Countess of Ulster.

1359 – Captured by French while serving in English army and later ransomed.

(1360-72?) – Completed translation of *Roman de la Rose,* and wrote *The Book of the Duchess* and *Legend of Good Women.*

1374 – Became controller of customs in London.

(1374-1380?) – Completed *The House of Fame, Parliament of Fowls,* and several of the *Canterbury Tales.*

1386 – Appointed Knight of the Shire and became member of Parliament; Richard II removed him for his customs offices.

(1380-1390) – Translated *Troilus and Criseyde* and resumed work on the *Canterbury Tales.*

1390 – Appointed Clerk of King's Works at Windsor.

1399 – Pension increased by Henry IV.

(1390-1399) – Completed *Treatise on the Astrolabe, Envoy to Scogan, Envoy to Bukton,* and *To His Empty Purse.*

1400 – Chaucer died and buried in Westminster Abbey.

GEOFFREY CHAUCER

A SKETCH OF HIS LIFE AND TIMES

England in the fourteenth century had a population of about 2,500,000. London was the capital city which a contemporary writer described as "clean, white, and small," encompassing an area of about one square mile.

The English countryside was dotted with small market towns seldom populated by more than 150 persons, monasteries, churches, and manor houses. Between these landmarks were open fields and in some instances native forests. Travel was common and not too difficult because the cities were connected by stone-paved highways constructed during Roman times.

England, in Chaucer's time, was a nation in social ferment. Medievalism still was a dominant influence in the lives of Englishmen, but the renaissance had assumed definite form and the country stood on the threshold of the modern world. These were the forces which stood face to face: the medievalist believed in the spiritual and the abstract, that the community, not the individual, was the great ideal. Man, the medievalist asserted, had no right to think for himself or to make judgments, for man was a member of a great spiritual community, the church catholic and universal. The early renaissance man believed in developing his own social groups, and national interests, as opposed to a united Christendom.

In Chaucer's time there were many manifestations of rebellion against the old order of things. Wycliffe and his followers were sowing the seeds of the Protestant Reformation which placed the emphasis on the individual. Chaucer's countrymen began thinking of themselves as Englishmen, and national patriotism showed in the battles with France which ushered in the Hundred Years' War. The growth of manufacturing and commerce gave rise to a middle class which speeded the end of the feudal system. The people demanded more voice in the affairs of their government. The church became corrupt; this corruption in turn invited corruption among the people. And, in the midst of this social ferment, England was three times swept by the Black Plague which reduced its population by one half and dealt an almost mortal blow to its industry.

This great century of social, political, literary, and religious ferment was nearly half over when Geoffrey Chaucer was born in 1340. His father was a successful wine maker in London, and his mother, Agnes de Compton, a member of the Court. Chaucer was sent to the Inner Court at St. Paul's Almonry where he received an excellent education.

In 1357 Chaucer became page to the Countess of Ulster; he met some of the greatest men in England, among them John of Gaunt, Duke of Lancaster. Two years later Chaucer, as a soldier, went to France on an invasion excursion which was doomed to failure. He was captured, and in 1360 was successfully ransomed. No information is available about Chaucer again until 1366. By that time Chaucer's father was dead, his mother was remarried, and Chaucer was married to a woman named Philippa de Roet. Whether this was a marriage of love or convenience is not known. Philippa was a woman of high rank in the service of the Queen. In 1367 Chaucer was in the service of the King and was granted a life pension as a valet.

In 1370, Chaucer was employed by the King for diplomatic errands, and during the next ten years made seven trips abroad. In 1374 he was appointed controller of the customs in London. That same year he was given permission to quit the royal residence, and he leased a home in the city of London. Chaucer received other appointments from the King, the most important coming in 1386 when he became a Knight of the Shire.

That same year John of Gaunt, Chaucer's life-long benefactor, left England for a military foray in Spain. King Richard II promptly stripped Chaucer of all his customs appointments. When John of Gaunt returned in 1389, however, Chaucer was restored to his previous offices.

In the following eleven years Chaucer managed to retain royal favors and lived comfortably until his death on October 25, 1400. He was buried in Westminster Abbey. His grave there was the first in what has become known as the Poet's Corner.

There is some reliable evidence, therefore, which traces Chaucer's life as a civil servant. Very little evidence exists, however, to pinpoint the life of Chaucer as a poet.

It is now believed that Chaucer began writing about 1360, and by 1372 he completed most of the translation of *Roman de la Rose* and wrote The *Book of the Duchess* and the *Legend of Good Women.* By 1380 he completed *The House of Fame,* the *Paliament of Fowls,* and some of the stories which later appeared in the *Canterbury Tales.*

By 1385 he translated *Troilus and Criseyde.* About this time he began the *Canterbury Tales.* (They were never finished, and scholars in later centuries arranged them in the order thought most likely.) In 1391 he wrote *Treatise on the Astrolabe* and the following year *Envoy to Scogan.* Just before his death he wrote *Envoy to Bukton* and *To His Empty Purse.*

CHAUCER'S PUBLIC

The public for which Chaucer wrote his tales is important to their understanding. As noted above, Chaucer moved in a high society and among the learned members of the Court. His audience, therefore, would have been a highly educated, sophisticated, and worldly audience. Chaucer probably read his tales aloud to this audience. Thus, his hearers would have had a knowledge of French, Latin, and English. They would also be familiar with the many types of stories, tales, and fabliaus that Chaucer imitated. Therefore, Chaucer could easily utilize various types of classical allusions, subtle satire, and irony, all of which would have been fully understood by his audience.

Chaucer's tales, of course, were not published or read by a general public, but many students of the English language think that they became so popular that the entire course of the English language was affected by them. At the time Chaucer wrote, there were five different accents spoken in English. These accents varied so much that a person of one section could understand another not at all or only with great difficulty.

CHAUCER'S LANGUAGE

The language of Chaucer is Middle English, which, roughly speaking, extends from about 1100 to 1500 A.D. The following explanation may help clarify the linguistic divisions of English for the beginning student of English literature:

OLD ENGLISH *(or Anglo-Saxon)–597 A.D. to 1100 A.D.*

Beowulf, the most famous literary work of the period, is an epic poem in alliterative verse. The author is unknown, but the manuscript (Cotton Vitellius A xv) dates from 1000 A.D.
Example of an Old English half-line from *Beowulf:*
Hwæt we gardena in geardagum–Old English
La. we the spear-Danes in the days of yore–Modern English
(Notice the Germanic quality of the Old English.)
787 A.D.–Danish influence on Old English

MIDDLE ENGLISH–*1100 A.D. to 1500 A.D.*

Geoffrey Chaucer (*1340-1400 A.D.*) is the acknowledged literary master of the period, and the *Canterbury Tales* is his most famous work.
Example of Chaucer's poetry in Middle English:
At mortal batailles hadde he been fiftene–Middle English
Of mortal battles he had fought fifteen–Modern English
(Notice the French influence on Middle English; also, notice how much closer, linguistically, Middle English is to Modern English than Old English is to Modern English.)

MODERN ENGLISH–*1500 A.D. to the present*

Some famous English writers of this period–Shakespeare, Milton, Swift, Wordsworth, Dickens, Shaw
Some famous American writers of this period–Poe, Hawthorne, Twain, O'Neill, Faulkner

There is some argument among scholars about the dates for the linguistic periods, particularly regarding the shift from Old English to Middle English. Naturally there was no overnight change from Old to Middle English, but the action which triggered the greatest change was the Norman Conquest of England in 1066 A.D.–thereafter, the English language exhibited a French influence. Typical of the scholarly controversy which centers upon the assignment of an initial date to Middle English is an excellent twentieth-century article by Kemp Malone entitled "When Did Middle English Begin?" (*See Curme Linguistic Studies.*)

TEXTS AND TRANSLATIONS

In many ways, the Middle English of the *Canterbury Tales* is much like

Modern English (unlike the almost foreign language of the Old English in *Beowulf),* and the student of Chaucer should read the Middle English text for full appreciation of Chaucer's poetry. Three excellent books which offer the original text are Vincent F. Hopper's interlinear edition of the *Canterbury Tales* (with selections only, in both Middle and Modern English, line by line), the John Matthews Manly expurgated edition of the *Canterbury Tales* (with helpful commentary and glossary), and the F. N. Robinson complete edition of *The Poetic Works of Chaucer* (including bibliography along with helpful introduction and glossary).

If the student is, for some reason, unable to read the original text of the poem, he should by all means get one of the good modern translations – for example, the poetic translations of J. U. Nicolson or Nevil Coghill. Nevil Coghill points out the variety of meaning which the translator encounters with Chaucerian words. Here is a Middle English line from the General Prologue, for example:

He was a verray parfit gentil knyght

Now according to Coghill, "verray" does not mean "very" but "true," "gentil" means "gentle" but also, and more importantly, of "high breeding" and "good birth." So, to render Chaucer meaningfully and rhythmically into one line, Coghill writes:

He was a true, a perfect gentle-knight.

CHAUCER'S POETRY

Both Manly's and Robinson's explanations of Chaucer's versification are so good that the student or teacher ought to take time to read them. If these texts are not available, however, in the school or local library, the present summary should suffice temporarily.

1. "All of Chaucer's narrative verse, except the 'Monk's Tale,' is written either in rhymed couplets or in stanzas of seven lines."[1]

2. "There is...a difference between Chaucer's English and Present English which is of much importance to the versification. This consists in the fact that a majority of the words in Chaucer's English ended in an unstressed final *e* or *en* or *es*."[2]

3. "The general character of the verse was also affected by the fact that a large number of lines ended in so-called feminine rhymes."[3]

[1]John Matthews Manly, editor, the *Canterbury Tales,* p. 131.
[2]*Ibid.,* p. 123.
[3]*Ibid.,* p. 123.

4. Chaucer used iambic pentameter a great deal (with couplets)—his usage was forerunner of the heroic couplet brought to perfection by Alexander Pope. There were, of course, variations. The heroic couplet is an effective poetic form for satire.

5. The "Tale of Melibeus" and the "Parson's Tale" are the only tales written in prose; the rest of Chaucer's tales are poetic.

A GUIDE TO PRONUNCIATION

Much is lost if Chaucer's poetry is read in translation. It is close enough to modern English so that the student with only a little practice can easily overcome the language barrier. The following brief list of aids will help with the basic differences.

Essentially, the vowels in Chaucer's poetry resemble the modern continental sounds more than they do modern English. The following basic guide is not meant to be a complete pronunciation guide, but functions as a simplified approach to reading the poetry.

1) The *"A"* is always pronounced like the "a" in *father*. In words like "that" or "whan" the "a" sound is shorter than in words like "bathed." See lines 1-3 of the general prologue.

2) The long "i" and "y" are both pronounced like the long "ee" sound found in such modern words as *machine*.

3) The long "e" has the sound of the "a" in such words as *late, hate, mate,* etc. If the "e" is short, give it the modern English pronunciation.

4) The "o" sounds are similar to those of modern English, that is, the majority take the "oh" sound.

5) The "u" is also pronounced approximately the same as in modern English.

6) The following three dipthongs are the most frequent:

A) the "ei," "ey," and "ay" all take the modern "ay" sound found in words like *day, way, pay*.

B) The "au" and "aw" are the "ou" sounds found in *house, mouse,* and *louse*.

C) The "ou" is something in between the "ou" of *you* and the "ew" sound of *few*.

7) The final "e", "es" and "ed"; the final "e" is always pronounced *except* when the next word begins with a vowel (or "h") and except when the rhythm would be violated in which case it resembles the "uh" and is never stressed.

8) The consonants are essentially the same as in modern English but with more emphasis.

MIDDLE ENGLISH GENRES

According to Baugh's *A Literary History of England,* the *Canterbury Tales* in its extent and variety offers a remarkable anthology of medieval literature." Baugh then goes on to label the tales according to genre (or literary type); the following is a simplification of his discussion:

Courtly Romance – Knight's Tale
Man of Law's Tale (of Constance)
Squire's Tale (fragmentary)

Breton Lay[1] – Franklin's Tale
Fabliaux[2] – Miller's Tale
Reeve's Tale
Merchant's Tale
Saint's Legend – Prioress' Tale
Tragedy (through medieval eyes, at least) – the Monk's Tale
Exemplum[3] – Pardoner's Tale
Sermon (or didactic treatise) – Tale of Melibeus
Parson's Tale
Beast Fable – the Nun's Priest's Tale

THE GENERAL PROLOGUE

In April the gentle rain, warming sun, and gentle winds, awakened nature from its winter sleep. Then man yearned to travel. In this season in England, from every corner of the land, people made their way to Canterbury to receive the blessings of "the holy blissful martyr" – St. Thomas á Becket.

One spring day in Southwark at the Tabard Inn, the narrator (Chaucer) awaited the next day when he would commence his journey to Canterbury. That evening a company of twenty-nine persons arrived at the inn, all of whom were Canterbury pilgrims. Chaucer was admitted to their

[1]A *lay,* in this case, is a short romantic poem, not a song.
[2]A *fabliau* is a short story with a snappy ending.
[3]The *exemplum* was one section of the medieval sermon – the part which set forth examples to illustrate the theme of text of the sermon.

company. Before the pilgrimage began, Chaucer took time to describe his companions.

The Knight

The Knight is the perfect and genteel man who loved truth, freedom, chivalry and honor. He was truly a distinguished man. He had ridden into battle in both Christian and heathen lands and in every instance served his king well. Despite his valorous deeds, the Knight never boasted of his actions nor bored his listeners with his feats.

Commentary

The Knight is the most socially prominent person on the journey, and certain *obeisances* are paid to him throughout the journey. He tells the first story and many pilgrims offer him compliments. One fact that Chaucer's audience would be aware of is that of all the battles the Knight fought in, *none* were in the King's secular wars. They were all religious wars of some nature.

The Squire

The Squire would be a candidate for knighthood. When not in battle, he thinks of himself as quite a lady's man. He takes meticulous care of his curly locks (hair) and is somewhat proud of his appearance. He could also sing lusty songs, compose melodies, write poetry and could ride a horse with distinction.

The Yeoman

The Yeoman was a servant to the Knight and Squire. He dressed all in green and was known as an expert woodsman and an excellent shot with the bow and arrow.

The Prioress

A Prioress named Madame Eglantine was also among the pilgrims. She was a gentle lady whose greatest oath was "by Sainte Loy." She was rather well educated, even though her French was not the accepted Parisian French. She was very coy and delicate. When she ate, she took great care that no morsel fell from her lips and that no stains were on her clothes. She was very courteous and amiable and tried to imitate the manners of the Court. She could not stand pain and would weep to see a mouse caught in a trap. She had three small hounds with her which she treated very gently and tenderly. Her dress was very neat and tidy and she wore a gold brooch with the inscription *"amor vincit omnia."*

Commentary

Chaucer's depiction of the Prioress is filled with gentle and subtle irony. Here is a picture of a lady who happens to be a nun, but she never forgets that she is a lady first. Her oath, "by Sainte Loy," implies that she has chosen the most fashionable and handsome saint who was also famous for his great courtesy. Her emphasis on her appearance and her possessions (including her three dogs) suggest that she secretly longs for a more worldly life. Even the inscription "*amor vincit omnia* (love conquers all) is a phrase that was used both in religion and also in the many courtly romances. And the brooch *is* a piece of lovely jewelry. In general she would be the ideal head of a girl's finishing school in nineteenth century America.

Associates of the Prioress

The Prioress had another nun with her who functioned as her secretary and also three priests.

Commentary

Two of the three priests will relate tales, and one of these tales (The tale of Chaunticleer) will prove to be one of the most popular of all the tales.

The Monk

The Monk was an outrider for his monastery (that is, he was in charge of the outlying property). He owned several horses furnished with the finest saddles and bridles. He loved hunting, fine foods and lots of it; he had several good hunting dogs of which he was very proud. He dressed in fine clothes, some were even trimmed in fur. He was rather fat, very jolly and bald headed. His favorite food was a roasted swan. In general, he favored an outdoor life to that of a closed, indoor existence.

Commentary

Chaucer's art is here demonstrated through his use of irony. While Chaucer never makes a comment about his characters, he arranges and selects his material so that the reader can come to a conclusion about the character. When the monk says that he doesn't approve of the solitary prayerful existence in a monastery, Chaucer pretends to be convinced that the Monk's argument is right. But we see that it is right only because this particular monk tries to justify his non-monastic activities and for this monk, it is the right existence. Everything that the Monk does is a violation of his monastic orders. His love of the worldly goods, food, and pleasures, and his dislike of the quiet monastery contradict his religious vows.

The Friar

The Friar was a wanton and merry man who had helped many girls get married after he got them in trouble. When he heard confessions, he worked under the principle that the penance is best executed by money rather than by prayers. So the person contributing the most money received the quickest and best pardon. The Friar was the type who knew the taverns and inns better than he knew the leper houses and the almshouses. Chaucer says that there was no better man than the Friar when it comes to the practice of his profession. He was always able to get money from people. His name was Hubert.

Commentary

The Friar was a person licensed to hear confessions and to beg for money. This Friar used every vicious and immoral method to extract money from the parishioners, so when Chaucer says there were none so good as Hubert in his profession, he is being ironical. That is, if we judge the Friar by how much money he extorted from people, then he is a great success. But essentially, this Friar is notoriously evil and cunning.

The Merchant

The Merchant was a member of the rich and powerful rising middle class. He is shrewd and knows a good bargain. He talks and looks so solemn and impressive, and transacts his business in such a stately manner that few knew that he was deeply in debt.

The Clerk

The Clerk, who was a student at Oxford, was extremely thin, rode a very thin horse, and his clothes were threadbare because he preferred to buy books rather than clothes and food. He did not talk often, but when he did, it was with great dignity and moral virtue.

Commentary

The Clerk was probably working on his M.A. degree with the idea of attaining some type of ecclesiastical position. Next to the Knight, he is one of the most admired people on the pilgrimage.

The Sergeant of Law

The Sergeant of Law was an able attorney who could recall every word and comma of every judgment, a feat which earned him high distinction and handsome fees. But he makes people think that he is busier and wiser than he really is. There is an implication that he has perhaps used his position to attain wealth without ever actually violating the letter of the law.

The Franklin

The Franklin was a large landowner with a certain amount of wealth, but he was not of noble birth. He spent his money freely, enjoying good food, wine, and company. His house was always open and he was a true epicurean, devoting his energies to fine living and was generally liked by the other pilgrims.

The Haberdasher, The Dyer, The Carpenter, The Weaver, and The Carpet Maker

These were men who belonged to a gild, an organization similiar to a fraternity and labor union. Each was luxuriously dressed in the manner of his calling, and each was impressed with his membership in the gild to which he belonged. The gildsmen had a cook who was one of the best.

The Cook

The Cook was a master of his trade. He knew how to boil, bake, roast and fry. But Chaucer thinks it a shame that he had a running sore on his shin, because his best dish was a creamed chicken pie whose white sauce might be the same color as the pus from the running sore.

The Shipman

The Shipman was a huge man and somewhat uncouth. He was the master of a vessel and knew all the ports from the Mediterranean to the Baltic. He could read the stars and knew how to fight well. But he did not ride a horse well. He looked like a fish out of water as he sat on his horse.

The Doctor of Physic

There was no one who could speak so well about medicine as this doctor. He knew astronomy (astrology) and something of nature and could tell what humour was responsible for a sickness. But everyone thought he was in league with the druggist. He could quote all the medical authorities, but knew nothing of the Bible. He had apparently made a lot of money during the plague, but doesn't seem to spend it very readily. Since he prescribes gold for cures, he has a special love for this metal.

The Wife of Bath

The Wife of Bath was somewhat deaf, but was an excellent seamstress and weaver. She made a point of being first at the altar or offering in church. Her kerchiefs must have weighed ten pounds and she wore scarlet red stockings. She has been married five times and has been on pilgrimages to Jerusalem, Rome, Bologna, Galice, and Cologne. She was gap-toothed and rode a horse easily. She enjoyed good fellowship and would readily laugh and joke. Her special talent was her knowledge of all the remedies of love.

The Parson

The Parson was very poor, but was rich in holy thoughts and works. He would rather give his own scarce money to his poor parishioners than to demand tithes from them. His principle was to live the perfect life first, and then to teach it. His life was a perfect example of the true Christian priest, and by his good example, he taught, but first followed it himself.

Commentary

Amid the worldly clerics and the false and superficial religious adherents, the poor Parson stands out as the *ideal* portrait of what a parish priest should be. The same can be said of the following portrait of the plowman. He is the *ideal* Christian man.

The Plowman

The Plowman was a small tenant farmer who lived in perfect peace and charity. He loved God with all his heart. He was always honest with his neighbors and promptly paid his tithes to the church.

The Miller

The Miller was a big brawny man who could outwrestle any man (and even a ram). He was short shouldered, broad and thick set. His red beard and a wart on his nose from which bristly red hairs protruded made him look fearful. He played the bagpipes as the pilgrims left the town.

The Manciple

The Manciple was a steward for a law school (or dormitory for lawyers) in London and was in charge of purchasing the food. He was not as learned as the lawyers, but was so shrewd in buying that he had been able to put aside a tidy little sum for himself.

The Reeve

The Reeve was the manager of a large estate. He was a skinny man with a bad temper. His close cut beard and his short haircut accentuates his thinness and long legs. He was an able, efficient, and shrewd man who had reaped rich rewards from his master. The serfs, herdsmen, and workers feared him dreadfully because of his unrelenting perseverance. Like the Manciple, he had reaped profits for himself by being so shrewd at buying. He was once a carpenter and rode last among the group.

Commentary

It is not important to the Reeve's characterization that he is a carpenter, but Chaucer is anticipating *The Reeve's Tale* later on. The Miller will tell a dirty story about a carpenter, and since the Reeve was once a carpenter, he feels the need for revenge by telling a dirty story about a miller.

The Summoner

The Summoner (a man paid to summon sinners for a trial before a church court) had a fire-red complexion, pimples and boils, a scaly infection around the eyebrows, and a moth-eaten beard. Children were afraid of his looks. He treats his sores as leprosy. To make matters worse, he loved to eat garlic, onions, leeks, and drink strong wine. He could quote a few lines of Latin which he used to impress people. Chaucer calls him a gentil harlot (genteel fellow) and implies it would be difficult to find a better fellow, because for a bottle of wine, the Summoner would often turn his back and let a sinner continue living in sin. He was also well acquainted with "ladies of questionable reputation."

Commentary

The physical appearance of the Summoner fits his profession well. He is so ugly and so gruesome looking that a summons from him is in itself a horrible experience. Thus, Chaucer ironically implies that he is a good fellow. But furthermore, he is a good fellow because sinners could easily bribe him. The reader should be aware of these subtle ironic statements which are often made in paradoxical situations.

The Pardoner

The Pardoner was a church official who had authority from Rome to sell pardons and indulgences to those charged with sins. He had just returned from Rome with a bagful of pardons which he planned to sell to the ignorant at a great profit to himself. He had a loud, high-pitched voice, yellow, flowing hair, was beardless and furthermore would never have a beard. Chaucer believes he was a "gelding or a mare." But there was no one so good at his profession as was this Pardoner. He knew how to sing and preach so as to frighten everyone into buying his pardons at a great price.

Commentary

The Pardoner seems to be one of the most corrupt of the churchmen. In the prologue to his tale, he confesses to his hypocrisy. And furthermore, Chaucer implies that he is not really a man, that is, that he is either sexually impotent or perverted.

The Host

The Host, whose name is Harry Bailey, was a merry man who liked good company and good stories. He was a large jovial person and was well liked by the pilgrims.

These, then, were the principal members of the party about to leave for Canterbury. That evening the Host of Tabard Inn served the company an excellent dinner after which he suggested that, to make the trip pass more pleasantly, each member of the party should tell two tales on the way to Canterbury. On the return trip each member of the company should tell two more tales. The man who told his story best was to be given a sumptuous dinner by the other members of the party. The Host added that, to keep the journey bright and merry, he would accompany them to Canterbury, and in all things he was to be the judge of what was best for the group. All members of the company agreed to his proposal to act as governor of the journey.

Early the next morning the party departed. Two miles away at St. Thomas-a-Watering, the Host silenced the group and announced that they would draw straws to see in which order the tales would be told. The Knight drew the shortest straw. The Knight agrees to tell the first tale, and here ends the prologue and begins the first tale.

Commentary

If Chaucer had completed his original plans, that of each pilgrim telling two tales going and two coming back, there would have been approximately 120 tales in all.

The Prologue gives an admirable description of the uncomplicated life of England in the Middle Ages. Here are portraits of all levels of English life. In this group Chaucer brings together all of the foibles and virtues of man and the manners and morals of his time with remarkable clarity.

Throughout *The Prologue,* Chaucer alternately praises or chides the travelers with deftly drawn word portraits which provide insights into the life of his time.

Before Chaucer, there were other groups of tales such as Boccacio's *Decameron,* but never was there such a diversity of people within the same group. It is then a stroke of genius that Chaucer uses the device of the religious pilgrimage to bring together such a diverse group.

The shrine of St. Thomas á Becket to which the pilgrims are going was reputed to have great healing qualities. Thus, some of the pilgrims are undoubtedly going for health rather than religious reasons. For example, The Wife of Bath was somewhat deaf, The Pardoner was beardless, The Cook had a sore, The Summoner had boils and other skin trouble, The Miller had an awful wart on his nose, The Reeve was choleric, etc.

THE KNIGHT'S TALE

Summary

PART I

Long ago there was once a Duke called Theseus who was the Lord and Governor of Athens. He was also a great soldier who vanquished every foe he met. Among his victims was a realm once known as Scythia, ruled by women called Amazons. Returning home with his amazon wife Hippolyta and her sister, Emelye, Theseus met a group of women dressed in black who were weeping and wailing. They told how each had been a queen or duchess, but had lost their husbands during the siege of Thebes. The cruel tyrant Creon now plans to dishonor the dead bodies.

The Duke, smitten with rage and pity, ordered Queen Hippolyta and her beautiful sister Emelye to return to Athens where they were to dwell in peace. Then, in anger, the Duke and his army marched on Thebes. There, on a chosen field of battle, King Creon was slain and the bones of their dead husbands were restored to the mourning ladies.

After the battle was over, two young warriors of Thebes, fearfully wounded, were brought before Theseus. He recognized them as young men of noble birth and was informed they were royal knights named Arcite and Palamon. In appearance, the two knights were very similar, being the sons of two sisters. Theseus ordered that they be returned to Athens as prisoners who could not be ransomed for any sum. They were, he said, to be his prisoners in perpetuity.

Several years passed by, and Arcite and Palamon lay in the prison tower in grief and anguish. On a fair morning in May, however, the beautiful Emelye arose and wandered happily about in her garden, which was adjacent to the prison tower.

At that moment, Palamon, the sorrowful prisoner, glanced down through the prison bars and saw the beautiful Emelye. He cried out in pain.

Arcite, alarmed, asked him what evil had befallen him. Palamon replied that the beauty of the young lady had caused him to cry out. Arcite's curiosity was aroused and he peered from the tower window. When he saw the fair Emelye, he cried out that unless he could see her everyday he would die.

When Palamon heard this, he was enraged. After all, he cried to Arcite, I found her first. To counter his argument, Arcite maintains that he *loved* her first. Thus, even though they are kin and had sworn eternal friendship, they decide that in love it is every man for himself. And so the argument continued until their friendship gave way to hostility.

About this time, a famous Duke called Perotheus, a friend of both Theseus and Arcite, arrived in Athens. He implored Duke Theseus to release Arcite on the condition that Arcite would leave Athens forever, and if he happened to return, he would be immediately beheaded.

Arcite then bemoans his fate. Even though he is now in prison, he can catch a glimpse of his beloved, but in banishment, he will never again see the fair Emelye. He acknowledges that Palamon is the winner since he can remain in prison and near to Emelye. But Palamon is equally disturbed because he thinks that Arcite can raise an army in exile, return to Athens and capture the fair Emelye. Chaucer then asks the reader which position is worse, that of Arcite or Palamon.

PART II

Arcite returned to Thebes where he lived for two years moaning his hard fate. His lamenting began to change his physical appearance. One night a vision appeared before him and urged him to return to Athens and the fair Emelye. Acrite arose and looked at himself in the mirror and realized that his grief had drastically changed his appearance. So he took the name of Philostrate and returned to Athens where he was employed as a page in the house of Emelye. Several years passed, and Philostrate rose to a high and well-to-do position in the Court of Theseus, even becoming a trusted friend of Theseus himself.

Meanwhile, Palamon languished in the prison tower. One night, however, he escaped. He hid in a field the next morning to escape detection. That same day, by chance, Arcite arrived at the same field. Arcite was so changed in appearance that Palamon did not recognize him. Arcite, thinking himself alone, began to recite his entire history aloud. Palamon, hearing the confession, jumped out of hiding and cursed Arcite as a traitor.

Arcite admitted his identity and challenged Palamon to a duel. The winner was to have Emelye. The next morning Arcite brought armor, food, and sword to Palamon. The duel began, and they fought fiercely. At this time, Theseus and his entourage arrived upon the bloody scene.

Palamon explained who they were and why they were fighting. The King, in a rage, condemmed them to death. The ladies of the Court, including Emelye, cried bitterly. Theseus finally agreed to give both of them their freedom on this condition: they should return to Athens in a year, each with one hundred knights. A joust would be held, and the winner would get the hand of Emelye. Arcite and Palamon returned to Thebes.

PART III

During the year, Theseus spent his time building a magnificant stadium in which the fight was to take place. He built an altar to Venus (goddess of love), to Mars (god of war) and to Diana, (goddess of chastity). These altars and the entire stadium were richly decorated with elegant details which the Knight enjoys describing. At the end of the year, Arcite and Palamon, each at the head of one hundred knights, returned to Athens for the joust. Theseus welcomed them all and entertained them in high fashion with wine, foods, singing, dancing and other forms of entertainment. Again, the Knight enjoys relating all aspects of this magnificent feast.

Before the battle, Palamon goes to the altar of Venus and prays that he be granted possession of the fair Emelye. If he can't have his beloved one, he would rather die by Arcite's spear. Emelye also prays before the altar of Diana. She asks that Arcite and Palamon's love be extinguished, and if not, that she be given the one who loves her the most. Diana tells her that it is destined that she marry one of the young knights, but she was not free to tell which one. Finally, Arcite appears and asks Mars for victory in the battle. Mars appears and assures Arcite that he will be victorious.

The three prayers and promises caused some confusion in heaven until Saturn, god of destiny, promised that Palamon would win his love and Arcite would win the battle.

PART IV

The great day for the joust dawned bright and beautiful. The entire populace of Athens swarmed excitedly into the ampitheater. The contestants, on excited steeds, gathered at the ends of the arena facing each other. The great King Theseus arrived and announced that once a warrior was badly wounded he would be removed from the field of battle by the King's marshal, in order to determine the winner without needless loss of life. The milling battle began. Finally, Palamon was badly wounded. Although he resisted the marshals, he was taken from the field.

The victorious Arcite, in his blood-spattered uniform, rode his horse triumphantly around the arena to receive the plaudits of the multitude and the smiles of the fair Emelye. But all of a sudden a fury arose from the ground and so frightened Arcite's horse that the victorous warrior was plunged to the earth. Arcite was badly hurt.

The King returned to his Court, and the populace was happy because in all the spectacle of the arena not one man was killed. Even Arcite, it was thought, would survive his injury.

The Duke of Theseus summoned his physicians to attend Arcite. But Arcite was dying. Gasping for breath, Arcite protested an eternal love for Emelye and then adds that he knows no person better than Palamon and begs her to think about accepting Palamon in marriage.

Arcite died. His earthly remains were reduced to ashes in a great funeral pyre. After a long period of mourning, Theseus summoned Palamon to Athens. Then in the presence of Emelye and the court, Theseus declared that Jupiter, " 'the King, The Prince and Cause of all and everything,' " had decreed that Thebes and Athens should live in peace and that Palamon and Emelye should be joined in marriage. They were wed and lived out their lives in "a love unbroken."

Commentary

The Knight tells a tale of ideal love and chivalry. This type of tale might seem somewhat tedious to the modern reader, but would have been very popular in Chaucer's day. The reader should notice how well the story fits the character of the Knight. He chooses a story filled with knights, love, honor, chivalry, and adventure. Furthermore, fitting the Knight's character, there are no episodes bordering on the vulgar and no coarseness. The love is an ideal love in which there is no hint of sensuality. The love exists on a high, ideal, platonic plane. The emphasis in the story is upon rules of honor and proper conduct. It is befitting the qualities of a knight that he would bring armor to his opponent before they begin to fight. The sense of honor is central to the story and the purity of the love each knight feels for Emelye tends to ennoble the character.

It is also typical of the Knight that he would love to describe the richness of the banquet and the elaborate decorations of the stadium and the rituals connected with the funeral. This type of richness and magnificence would appeal to a man of such distinction as the Knight. Furthermore, the extreme emphasis on form, ritual, and code of behavior are elements of the knighthood.

The modern reader might find it strange that so many elements of *chance* enter into the story. Chaucer himself comments on the role which Chance (or Fortune or Destiny) plays during the narrative. The women at the beginning are bemoaning the harshness of Fortune. It is by chance that Emelye walks beneath the prison. Later it is by chance that the Duke Perotheus knew Arcite. Again, it is chance that Arcite is employed by Emelye and later accidentaly meets Palamon. Chance brings Theseus to the same spot where Arcite and Palamon are fighting. And finally, it is the God of Chance or Destiny who determines how the story will be solved. In other words, Chaucer or the Knight seems to be implying that the lives of men are influenced by what seems to be chance, but in the long run and in terms of a total world picture, there is a god who is controlling the seemingly chance occurrences of the world. The universe, then, is not as incoherent and unorderly as might first be expected. There is a *logic* or controlling purpose behind all the acts of the universe even though man might not understand it.

Any reader the least familiar with ancient Greece will be a little surprised to discover that the medieval custom of knights in armor jousting for the hand of a maiden was an attribute of Athenian life. Of course it was not. Yet, we may forgive Chaucer this anachronism. After all, what better way to begin his tales than with the Knight, and a tale of chivalry and romance which a knight would be expected to tell? The Knight does not tell of his own deeds of valor in foreign lands. His tale is about men and women of ages past who lived in dream and fancy. The story could have happended in Greece, of course, but hardly in the trappings of medieval chivalry.

THE MILLER'S TALE: PROLOGUE

Summary

When the Knight had finished his story, everyone said it was a fine story and worthy to be remembered. The Host then calls upon the Monk to tell a tale that will match the Knight's for nobility. But the Miller, who was drunk, shouted that he had a noble tale, and he would match the Knight's tale with his. The Host tried to stop the Miller because of the Miller's drunkenness, but the Miller insisted. He announced that he was going to tell a story about a carpenter, and the Reeve objects. The Miller, however, insists. Chaucer then warns the reader that this story might be a bit vulgar, but it is his duty to tell all the stories because a prize is at stake.

THE MILLER'S TALE

Summary

Some time ago, the Miller said, there was a rich, old carpenter who lived in Oxford and who took in a lodger named Nicholas. Nicholas was a clerk and was also a student of astrology who, among other things, was able to forecast the likelihood of drought or showers, Nicholas was also a clever young man, neat-appearing, a marvelous harp player and singer, and a lover whose passions were carefully clocked beneath a shy boyish manner and appearance.

Now it happened that the carpenter was married to an eighteen-year-old girl named Alison, and many years younger than the carpenter. Alison was a bright, lively, pretty girl. It was not long before Nicholas fell in love with her. One day he grasped her and cried, "O love-me-all-at-once or I shall die!" At first, Alison made a pretense of objecting, but the young clerk soon overcame her objections. They worked out a plan whereby they would play a trick on her husband, Old John the carpenter. Alison, however, warned Nicholas that John was very jealous.

It happened that sometime later, Alison went to church and there another young clerk saw her, and he was immediately smitten with her beauty as he passed the collection plate. He was the parish clerk and was named Absalon. Chaucer describes this clerk as being very dainty and particular. He is even somewhat effeminate. The final touch to his personality is that he is so dainty that the one thing he could not tolerate was people who expelled gas in public.

That evening with guitar in hand he strolled the streets looking for tarts when he came to the carpenter's abode. Beneath Alison's window he softly sang, "Now dearest lady, if thy pleasure be in thoughts of love, think tenderly of me." The carpenter was awakened but discovered his wife unimpressed with the youth's entreaties.

One day, when the ignorant carpenter had gone to work at a nearby town, Nicholas and Alison agreed that something must be done to get the carpenter out of the house for a night. Nicholas agreed to devise a plan.

And so it happened that Nicholas, gathering plenty of food and ale, locked himself in his room. After several days the carpenter missed the youth's presence. When told Nicholas might be dead in his room, the carpenter and his serving boy went to Nicholas' room and pounded on the door. When there was no answer, they knocked down the door and found the yought lying on his bed, gaping as though dead, at the ceiling. The carpenter aroused the youth who then told of a vision seen in his trance that Oxford was soon to be visited with a rain and flood not unlike the one experienced by Noah. The alarmed carpenter wondered what could be done to escape the flood. Nicholas counseled him to fasten three boat-like tubs to the ceiling of the house, provision each with food and drink enough to last one day after which the flood would subside, and also include an axe with which they could cut the ropes and allow the tubs to float. And finally, the three tubs should be hung some distance apart.

The tub-like boats were hung in place by the stupid carpenter and the evening before the predicted flood all three entered their boats and prayed, When the carpenter fell into troubled sleep, Alison and Nicholas descended the ladder from their boats and sped downstairs, without a word, to bed.

Meanwhile, later that night the young parish clerk Absalon, having heard the carpenter was away from the city, stole beneath Alison's window and begged her for a kiss. "'Go away,'" she cried, "'there's no come-up-and-kiss-me-here for you.'" But he entreated her and Alison, afraid the youth would arouse the neighbors, agreed to give him a kiss. But deciding to play a trick on this bothersome clerk, she extended her rear end out the window which the young clerk kissed most savorously.

When he discovered how Alison had tricked him, young Absalon strode away in anger. He was not completely cured of his lovesickness. He therefore plans revenge. He goes across the street and arouses the blacksmith and borrows a red-hot poker. Returning to the carpenter's house, Absalon knocked at the window again and pleaded for one more kiss. Nicholas decided that Alison's trick was so good that he would now try the same thing, so he presents his rear to be kissed. When Absalon called for Alison to speak to him, Nicholas expelled gas which, as Chaucer says, was like a stroke of thunder. It almost knocked poor dainty Absalon off his feet, but recovering rapidly, Absalon applied the hot poker to Nicholas' arse.

"'Help! Water! Water! Help!'" shouted Nicholas. The carpenter was startled from his sleep, "'Heaven help us,'"he thought, "'here comes Nowel's Flood!'" With an axe, he cut the ropes which held his boat to the eaves of the house. Down he crashed. Alison and Nicholas shouted "'Help!'" and "'Murder!'" and the neighbors rushed to the house. Nicholas told them of the carpenter's preparation for a flood. All laughed at this lunacy, and none would help him for they considered him mad. And to conclude it all, the carpenter received a broken arm from the fall.

Commentary

Many who like Chaucer do not like *The Miller's Tale* and choose to skip it. Yet, it is reasonable to assume that stories such as this were rather common in the inns of Chaucer's time. The point here is not that the tale has its bawdy moments, but rather that the reader has enjoyed an expert telling of a practical joke. Is not the point here the stupidity of the jealous carpenter in falling for Nicholas' preposterous flood, rather than the ends for which the trick was devised? With great economy of words, Chaucer's writing here exhibits the deft, concentrated portraiture found in the Prologue to the book.

The reader should also remember that one story is often told in relationship to the story (or Prologue) which has preceded it. Therefore, we should see if *The Miller's Tale* has any relationship with *The Knight's Tale*. We must remember that in the Prologue to the tale, the Miller had promised to tell something which would *match The Knight's Tale*. Consequently, upon reflection, we see that both the Knight's and Miller's tales are involved with a three-way love triangle. In both tales, two men are seeking the love of the same woman. In both tales, the woman remains the more-or-less passive bystander while the men struggle for her. Furthermore, both tales involve destiny or getting-what-comes-to-you. As destiny entered in to solve the dilemma between Palamon and Arcite, so in *The Miller's Tale* there is the sense of every man getting his just desserts. The Carpenter is cuckolded and has a broken arm because of his extreme jealousy. Nicholas has a severly burned rear end. Absalon has been mistreated in another way. One might therefore say that destiny or poetic justice played an important role in both tales. Visions and astrology play a role in both stories. The duel in *The Knight's Tale* is replaced by the window episode in *The Miller's Tale*. The analogies here suggest Chaucer's awareness of the difference between the two narrators. The contrast between the noble Knight and the burly Miller is made more prominent by the type of story each chose to relate. And finally, the type of story the Miller tells is still popular today. Any time a very old man marries a young girl, there will naturally be jealousy and sooner or later, the young wife usually takes on a lover.

THE REEVE'S TALE: PROLOGUE

Summary

After everyone has laughed at the Miller's tale, the Reeve becomes sullen because the tale was unfavorable to a carpenter. The Reeve, whose name is Osewold, promises to repay the Miller with a story. He then tells how he resents the carpenter's advanced age because he is also somewhat advanced in age and can enjoy only a limited amount of things. He points out that in old age, man can only boast or lie or covet. The Host interrupts him and tells him to get on with the tale. Osewold warns the group that his tale will employ the same rough language as was found in *The Miller's Tale*.

Commentary

Once again, the reader should keep in mind the idea that one tale is often told to repay another. Thus since the Reeve is upset over the Miller's Tale, he is now going to tell a tale whereby a miller is ridiculed.

THE REEVE'S TALE

Summary

At Trumpington, not far from Cambridge, there lived a Miller. He was a heavy-set man, a bully, who carried several knives and knew how to use them. No one dared lay a hand on the man for fear of their lives. He was also a thief and always stole corn or meal brought to his mill for grinding. His wife was a portly creature who was the daughter of the town clergyman. She has been raised in a nunnery. The Miller wed her because he was something of a social climber and wanted a refined wife. But Chaucer implies that being the daughter of the town clergyman, she was probably illegitimate. But both of them were proud of their twenty-year old daughter and six-month baby boy.

The Miller levied excessive charges for his work, in addition to stealing what he could. This was particularly true of the corn brought to him for grinding from a large-sized college at Cambridge. One day when the manciple (steward) was too ill to go to the mill to watch the Miller grind his corn, the man sent to the mill was duped and robbed outrageously.

Two students at the college, John and Alan, were enraged when news of the theft reached them. They volunteered to take a sack of corn to the mill for grinding and beat the Miller at his own game. They arrived and announced they would watch the milling. The Miller sensed the students would try to prevent him from stealing some of the grain. He decided therefore that he would take even more than usual so as to prove that the greatest scholar is not always the wisest or cleverest man.

When he had a chance, the Miller slipped out to the students' horse, untied it, and away it ran to the wild horses in the fen. The Miller returned and ground and sacked the corn. The students discovered their horse was missing and chased the spirited animal until dark before catching it. While they were gone, the Miller emptied half the flour from the sack and gave it to his wife.

When John and Alan returned from catching their horse, it was already dark. They asked the Miller to put them up for the night and offered to pay for food and lodging. The Miller sarcastically said to them that his house was small, but that college men could always make things seem to be what they aren't. He challenges them to make his one bedroom into a grand chamber. But he agrees to put them up and sends his daughter for food and drink. Meanwhile, he makes a space in his only bedroom for John and Alan, thus all slept in the same room but in three separate beds: the Miller and his wife in one, John and Alan in another and the daughter in the third. The baby's cradle was at the foot of the Miller's bed.

After drinking for a long time, everyone went to bed and soon the Miller and his family were asleep. But John and Alan lay awake thinking of ways in which to get revenge. Suddenly, Alan gets up and goes over to the daughter's bed. Apparently, they got along just fine. But John stayed in his bed and grumbled about his fate. He then got up and moved the cradle next to his bed. Shortly after that, the Wife had to relieve herself of all the wine she had drunk. Returning to her bed, she felt for the baby's cradle and couldn't find it. She felt in the next bed and discovered the cradle and climbed in bed beside John. He immediately "tumbled" on her, "and on this goode wyf he" layed it on well.

As dawn neared Alan said goodbye to the daughter who suggested that as they left the mill, they look behind the main door and find the half sack of flour her father had stolen. Alan walked over to wake John and, discovering the cradle, assumed he was mixed up and went to the Miller's bed and hopped in. He shook the pillow and told John to wake up. Alan immediately told how he had already had the Miller's daughter three times in this one short night. The Miller rose from his bed in a fury and started cursing. The Miller's wife, thinking she was in bed with the Miller, grabbed a club, and mistaking her husband for one of the clerks, struck him down. Then Alan and John fled the premises.

Commentary

Chaucer has again given us a tale of immorality—not for the sake of immorality but for the sake of a joke. Like *The Miller's Tale,* there is here a rough sort of poetic justice meted out. The Miller had intended to cheat the students, and had ridiculed them when telling them to try to make a hotel out of his small bedroom. During the course of the night, the students had indeed made a type of hotel (house of prostitution) out of his house.

The nature of the two stories (the Miller's and the Reeve's) again testify to the differences in their personality. The Reeve, it will be remembered, is sullen and choleric. His tale is more bitter and somewhat less funny than the Miller's. But on the contrary, the Miller was a boisterous and jolly person, and his tale was the more comic of the two.

THE COOK'S TALE: PROLOGUE

Summary

The Cook, Roger, is laughing over *The Reeve's Tale.* He thought the Miller was well repaid for arguing that his house was too small. He promises to tell a tale that really happened in his town. The Host interrupts and tells him he will have to tell a good one to repay the company for all the stale pies he has sold to them. Then the Host tells that he is only joking. Roger then turns to his tale.

Commentary

Here the Host is playing with words when he tells Roger to tell a good tale to repay the pilgrims for the stale pies. Actually the tale is to repay the earlier narrators.

THE COOK'S TALE

Summary

There was an apprentice cook working in London named Perkin Reveler who was as full of love as he was full of sin. At every wedding he would dance and sing rather than tend the shop. And when he wasn't dancing or singing or drinking, he was gambling. His master finally decided that one rotten apple could spoil the whole barrel. Thus, the master dismissed Perkin. The young man, obeying another proverb, "birds of a feather flock together," joined another young man of the same habits as his. The friend's wife kept a shop, but this shop was just a front to her loose and immoral activities.

Commentary

Most authorities agree that *The Cook's Tale* is only a fragment. Perhaps Chaucer came to feel that three "merry" tales was too much of a dose of humor, thus abandoned it. Nonetheless, we are given a wonderful portrait of a careless young man, even though the ultimate fate he may have suffered for his folly will never be known.

THE MAN OF LAW'S INTRODUCTION

Summary

The Host, noting the rapidly passing day, reminds the company that they must proceed with the tales. Then addressing himself to the Man of Law in what he considers the best of legal language, the Host exhorts the Man of Law to acquit himself by fulfilling his contract to tell a tale. The Man of Law protests that Chaucer has already written about all the good stories of the world and has left nothing else to be told. He also protests that he will not tell his story in rhyme. I am not a poet, he said, but a plain spoken man who will tell a story plainly.

THE MAN OF LAW'S TALE

Summary

PART I

There once dwelt in Syria a company of wise, honest, and prosperous merchants. Their trade in spices, gold, satins, and many other articles was far-flung. It happened that some of these merchants decided to go to Rome to determine if there were opportunities for trade.

During their sojourn in Rome, they heard of Constance, the daughter of the emperor. She was praised for her beauty, her goodness, and her innocence. She was reputed to be the perfect woman, untainted by any of the frivolity of life.

Upon the return of these merchants to Syria, the young Syrian Sultan was, as always, anxious to hear of their good fortune in trading. As the merchants spoke of the wonders they had seen in Rome, they also made special mention of the Lady Constance.

The young Sultan was enraptured with their description of her, and soon his heart was set upon having her as his wife. No one else would do. He took the matter before his council and told them that he must perish if he could not win her hand.

The councilors saw great difficulties. For one thing, the Emperor of a Christian land would not find it convenient to form such an alliance with a nation which worshipped Mahomet. The Sultan cried: " 'Rather than that I lose/ The Lady Constance, I will be baptized.' " Brushing aside objections it was arranged that all of his subjects should become Christians.

All was made ready in Rome for the voyage to Syria. But on the day of departure Lady Constance arose pale and sorrowful for she sorely regretted leaving her homeland and friends.

As plans were being made for the big wedding, the mother of the Sultan was conspiring against Constance and her son. She was angry that her son was making her give up her old religion for the sake of this foreign girl. She called together certain of the councilors and protested that she would rather die than depart from the holy teachings of Mahomet. They all agreed that they would pretend to accept the new religion, but at the climax of the feast, would attack the group and slay them all. The first part ends with the Man of Law attacking the baseness and falseness of the Sultan's mother.

PART II

The Christians arrived in Syria and, amid great pomp, journeyed to the Sultan's palace where he and Lady Constance were overcome with great joy. The wedding ceremony was completed and the dazzling array of dignitaries sat down to a sumptuous feast. At that moment the confederates of the Sultan's mother swept into the banquet hall and all of the Christians including the young Sultan were slain—all, that is, except Lady Constance. She was put aboard a sailing vessel, well provisioned, and cast upon the sea. For days on end her little ship roamed the seas. Finally, one day, the ship beached in the northern isle of Northumberland.

There she was found by the Constable and his wife who took her in and cared for her. This was a pagan land but Constance secretly kept her faith with Jesus Christ. Soon Hermengild, the Constable's wife, became a Christian and then the Constable himself.

Then one night Satan (in the person of a Knight) entered the Constable's home and slit the throat of Hermengild, and when the Constable returned he found the murder weapon in Constance's bed. Forthwith, the Constable took Constance before his king—Alla—who ruled with a wise and powerful hand. The King sentenced her to death but there was such a wailing among the women of the Court, the Knight was asked again if he had killed Hermengild. No, he cried, it was Constance. At that moment he was stricken dead, and a voice was heard to say that the King had unjustly judged a disciple of Christ.

The court was awe-stricken, and soon all were converted to Christianity. All rejoiced at this but Donegild, mother of the King. The King and Constance fell in love and were soon wed. While the King was away at war with the Scots, a beautiful son was born to Constance. But Donegild intercepted the message and wrote a false letter saying the child was terribly disfigured. But the King said if this was God's will, let it be done. Enraged, Donegild intercepted the King's message and wrote a false message that it was the King's will to have the son destroyed. The embittered Constance, aided by the Constable, was taken to a sailing ship and she and her beloved son sailed beyond the horizon.

PART III

King Alla returned from the war, dismayed with the news of his falsified messages and grief-stricken at the loss of his son and wife. Donegild was soon discovered responsible, and she was put to death.

In the meantime, the Emperor of Rome heard of the tragic news of the death of the Christians and sent an army to Syria; the culprits were put to death. As the Romans were returning they saw the vessel steered by Constance. Not recognizing her, they took her to Rome where she lived in obscurity, for she had lost her memory and she did not recognize her homeland.

The grief-stricken Alla decided to make a pilgrimage to Rome to seek penance for the foul play which befell his beloved Constance. There, while in the company of a Senator, he chanced to see a child whose face strongly resembled that of Constance. Upon inquiring, he learned of the circumstances. When led to the dwelling place of Constance, Alla told her how his true feeling for their son had been distorted by his mother.

A joyous reunion followed, and then Constance went before the Emperor and acknowledged that she was his daughter. There was great joy in the land. Alla and Constance returned to Northumberland, but within a year the King died. Constance and her son, Maurice, returned to Rome where he later became Emperor.

Commentary

The pilgrims completed their first day's journey to Canterbury, spent the night at Dartford and apparently started late on the second day's journey. The Host suddenly confronted the company and told them a fourth of the day had passed. He called upon the Man of the Law to tell his story. The lawyer, all too familiar with contracts, said he would fulfill his obligation.

Chaucer wrote *The Man of the Law's Tale* from an earlier chronicle by Nicholas Trivet, an English scholar and historian who lived in the first half of the fourteenth century. Chaucer considerably condensed Trivet's story.

This story of Constance Chaucer converted from ordinary legend to a great work of art. The author produced his work – we must remember – in the spirit of the Christian Middle Ages when man loved the perfect, the universal, as opposed to the Renaissance which focused its attention on the imperfect individual.

Constance, the beautiful, is the perfect and the universal. We see her in poverty and prosperity, in joy and sorrow, in defeat and in victory. Throughout the story Constance is unmoved, unshaken, from the great Christian virtues of humility, faith, hope, and charity. She moves from one improbable situation to another and always, in the end, is miraculously saved. Chaucer does not explain away these events. He accepts them joyously.

THE EPILOGUE OF THE MAN OF LAW'S TALE

Summary

The Host breaks in and congratulates the Man of Law for the excellence of his tale. He then calls upon the Parson to deliver something equally good. But the Parson rebukes the Host for swearing. In turn the Host mildly ridicules the Parson for prudery. Here the Shipman breaks in and maintains that they need a lively story.

Commentary

This fragment is incomplete. It implies that perhaps the Shipman will tell a tale next. But there is much to suggest that Chaucer meant to remove this epilogue from the total picture. Therefore, most scholars prefer the arrangement wherein the so-called Marriage group follows next.

THE WIFE OF BATH'S PROLOGUE

Summary

The Wife of Bath begins her prologue by announcing that she has always followed the rule of experience rather than authority. And since she has had five husbands at the church door, she has had a great amount of experience. She sees nothing wrong with having had five husbands, and cannot understand Jesus' rebuke to the woman at the well who had also had five husbands. She prefers the biblical injunction to "increase and multiply." She reminds the pilgrims of several biblical incidents: Solomon and his many wives, the command that a husband must leave his family and join with his wife, and St. Paul's warning that it is better to marry than to burn. Having shown herself to have a knowledge of the Bible, she asks where it is that virginity is commanded. It is, she admits, *advised* for those who want to live a perfect life, but she admits that she is not perfect. Moreover, she asks, what is the purpose of the sex organs. They were made for both functional purposes and for pleasure. And unlike many cold and bashful women, she was always *willing* to have sex whenever her husband wanted to. The Pardoner interrupts and says that he was thinking of getting married, but having heard the Wife of Bath, he is glad that he is single. She responds that she could tell more, and the Pardoner encourages her to do so.

The Wife then relates stories concerning her five husbands. She recalled that three of them were very old and good and rich. And she will now reveal how she was able to control each one. Her techniques were very simple. She accused her husbands (the first three) of being at fault. She scolded them when they accused her of being extravagant with clothes and jewelry when her only purpose was to please her husband. She railed at her husband when he refused to disclose the worth of his land and the value of his coffers. She derided the husband who considered her as property. She denounced men who refused her the liberty of visiting her friends for women, like men, like freedom. She decried the husband who suspected her chastity was in danger every time she smiled at another gentleman to whom she wished only to be courteous. She denounced the husband who hired spies to determine if she was unfaithful, and indeed, hired her own witnesses to testify to her faithfulness to her marriage bed.

Each time she gained complete mastery over one of her husbands, he would then die. But her fourth husband was different. He kept a mistress, and this bothered her because she was in the prime of life and full of passion. Thus, while not being actually unfaithful to her fourth husband, she made him think so. Thus "in his own greece I made him fry." But now he is dead, and when she was burying him, she could hardly keep her eyes off a young clerk named Jankyn whom she had already admired. Thus, at the month's end, she married for a fifth time even though she was twice the clerk's age. And this time she married for love and not riches. But as soon as the honeymoon was over, she was disturbed to find that the clerk spent all of his time reading books, especially books which disparaged women. In fact, he collected all the books he could which told unfavorable stories about women and he spent all his time reading from these collections.

One night, he began to read aloud from his collection. He began with the story of Eve and read about all the unfaithful women, murderesses, prostitutes, etc., which he could find. The Wife of Bath could not stand this any more, so she grabbed the book and hit Jankyn so hard that he fell over backwards into the fire. He jumped up and hit her with his fist. She fell to the floor and pretended to be dead. When he kneeled over her, she hit him once more and pretended to die. He was so upset that he promised her anything if she would live. And this is how she gained "sovereignty" over her fifth husband. And from that day on, she was a true and faithful wife for him.

Commentary

The Wife of Bath's Prologue occupies a unique position in that it is longer than the tale. It functions to justify her five marriages and to suggest that the thing women most desire is complete control over their husbands. But in addition to being a defense of her marriages, it is also a confession of her techniques and subtly speaking, a plea for certain reforms for women. She uses two basic arguments: if women remained virgins, there would be no one left to give birth to more virgins, and that the sex organs are to be used for pleasure as well as function. And like the Devil who can quote scripture to prove a point, the Wife of Bath also uses this same technique. Her prologue then refutes the popular theory that women should be submissive, especially in matters of sex. And we should remember that her argument is against the authorities of the church and state and that she is a woman who prefers experience to scholarly arguments.

WORDS BETWEEN THE SUMMONER AND THE FRIAR

Summary

The Friar thinks that this was a rather long preamble for a tale. The Summoner reminds the Friar that he is rather long-winded. The Summoner and the Friar then exchange a few words.

Commentary

This exchange between the Summoner and the Friar anticipate their tales which follow *The Wife of Bath's Tale.*

THE WIFE OF BATH'S TALE

Summary

Once, long ago, a knight was returning to King Arthur's Court when he saw a fair young maiden all alone, and raped her.

The countryside was revolted by the knight's act, and King Arthur was petitioned to bring the knight to justice. The king condemned the knight to death. The queen, however, begged the king to permit her to pass judgment on the knight. When brought before her, the queen informed him he would live or die depending upon how successfully he answered this question: "What is the thing that women most desire?" The knight confessed he did not have a ready answer; so the gracious queen bade him return within one year.

The knight roamed from place to place. Some women said they wanted wealth and treasure. Others said jollity and pleasure. Others said it was to be gratified and flattered. And so it went. At each place he heard a different answer.

He rode toward King Arthur's court in a dejected mood. Suddenly, in a clearing in the wood, he saw twenty-four maidens dancing and singing. But as he approached them they disappeared, as if by magic. There was not a living creature to be seen save an old woman, whose foul looks exceeded anything the knight had ever seen before.

The old woman approached the knight and asked what he was seeking. She reminded him that old women often know quite a bit.

The knight explained his problem. The old woman said she could provide the answer, provided that he would do what she would require for saving his life. The knight agreed, and they journeyed to the Court.

Before the queen the knight said he had the answer to what women desired most, and the queen bade him speak.

The knight responded that women most desire sovereignty over their husbands. None of the women of the Court could deny the validity of this answer.

The knight was acquitted. Then the old crone told the Court she had supplied the knight's answer. In exchange the knight had, upon his honor, agreed to honor any request she made of him. She said that she would settle for nothing less than to be his very wife and love. The knight, in agony, agreed to wed her.

On their wedding night the knight turned restlessly paying no heed to the foul woman lying next to him in bed. She said, "Is this how knights treat their wives upon the whole?' " Then the knight confessed that her age, ugliness, and low breeding were repulsive to him.

The old hag then gives the knight a long lecture in which she reminds him that true gentility is not a matter of appearances but rather virtue is the true mark of the gentle and noble. And poverty is not to be spurned because Christ Himself was a poor man as were many of the fathers of the church and all saints. All the Christian and even pagan authorities say that poverty can lead a person to salvation. Then she reminds him that her looks can be viewed as an asset. If she were beautiful, there would be many men who would desire her; so as long as she is old and ugly, he can be assured that he has a virtuous wife. She offers him a choice: an old ugly hag such as she, but still a loyal, true and humble wife, or a beautiful woman with whom he must take his chances in the covetousness of handsome men who would visit their home because of her and not him.

The knight groaned and said the choice was hers. " 'And have I won the mastery?' " she said. " 'Since I'm to choose and rule as I think fit?' " " 'Certainly, wife,' " the knight answered. " 'Kiss me,' " she said. " '...On my honor you shall find me both...fair and faithful as a wife... Look at me' " she said. The knight turned, and she was indeed now a young and lovely woman. And so, the Wife concluded, they lived blissfully ever after.

Commentary

The Wife of Bath's Prologue and *Tale* is one of Chaucer's most original stories. Yet even here he confesses that he has depended upon "old books." Two are of principal interest, *Roman de la Rose* as elaborated by Jean de Meun, and St. Jerome's statement upholding celibacy *Hieronymous contra Jovinianum*. Yet, Chaucer has created here a work of literary art and good story telling that goes far beyond his source material. The tale is, of course, an *exemplum,* that is, a tale told to prove a point. And the reader should remember that the narrator is an old hag telling a story about an old hag who gained sovereignty over her husband.

In Chaucer's time, the literature was filled with the favorite theme of vilifying the frailty of woman. Chaucer's tale, however, is not a moral diatribe for or against woman. He has created a woman in the person of the Wife of Bath who both exemplifies all that has been charged against women but openly glories in the possession of these qualities. Chaucer goes further. He asks the reader to accept woman's point of view and, perhaps, even feel some sympathy for her.

Chaucer does not make it clear whether he sympathizes with the Wife's opinion of marriage and celibacy, but it is obvious that he did not agree with the prevailing notions of his time about celibacy.

In Chaucer's time, as in a lesser degree today, a second marriage was considered sinful. *The Wife's Prologue* has been described, therefore, as a revolutionary document. This is why Chaucer has the Wife so carefully review the words of God as revealed in scripture. Nowhere, she confesses, can she find a stricture against more than one marriage save the rebuke Jesus gave the woman of Samaria about her five husbands. But this, she confesses, she cannot understand.

There was also, in Chaucer's time, considerable praise for perpetual virginity. The Wife now departs from holy writ and appeals to common sense. If everyone should practice virginity, who is to beget more virgins?

The truly remarkable aspect of *The Wife of Bath's Prologue* however, is not her argument with the mores of her time, but the very wonderful portrait of a human being. She tells the company she married her first three husbands for their money, and each of them died in an effort to satisfy her lust. Her fourth was a reveler who made her jealous and the fifth a young man who tried to lord it over her and when she had mastered him, he ungraciously died. Surely, she moralizes, is this not the tribulation of marriage?

Despite her brash accounting of marriage, one gets the impression she is not sure of herself when she exclaims, "Alas, that every love was sin!" Chaucer has given us a portrait of an immoral woman, a coarse creature to shock her age. But the author does not apologize for her. He leaves the moral arguments in balance. One can only conclude that he believes that unbridled sensuousness is not the key to happiness.

The Wife of Bath's Tale simply underscores the *Prologue*. Here she again pleads for the emancipation of women in the Middle Ages. Many authorities believe that it was not Chaucer's intention to change the filthy hag literally into a beautiful woman. Rather it is a change from a *kind* of ugliness into a *kind* of beauty. Similar tales were widespread in Chaucer's time and he has done little to disguise the fact that he borrowed heavily from them in devising his story.

THE FRIAR'S TALE: PROLOGUE

Summary

When the Wife of Bath had finished her tale, the Friar wonders if such academic problems shouldn't be left to the authorities. He now offers to tell a tale about a summoner, but the Host admonishes him to let the Summoner alone and tell something else. But the Summoner interrupts and says the Friar can do as he likes and will be repaid for a tale about a summoner by one about a friar.

THE FRIAR'S TALE

Summary

There was once a summoner for a bishop who had developed his craft to a very high degree. He had a crew of spies, including harlots, who would seek out information on all of the persons living in the parish and such information was to be used against them by the church. Once the derogatory information was in hand, he called upon the miscreants and squeezed exorbitant tribute from them so that their names would not be entered among those doing evil.

Then one day the Summoner, as he made his rounds blackmailing the rich and poor alike, met a gay young yeoman bearing bows and arrows and wearing a jacket of bright green and a black hat. The yeoman inquired of his calling, and the Summoner replied that he was a bailiff. " 'Well, I'll be damned!' the yeoman said. 'Dear brother,/ You say you are a bailiff? I'm another.' "

The yeoman said he lived in the far north country and was on his way there. Soon the conversation turned to their vocation of bailiff. " 'From year to year I cover my expenses,' " the yeoman said. " 'I can't say better, speaking truthfully.' " " 'It's just the same with me,' " the Summoner said. " 'I'm ready to take anything.' " They agreed to enter into a partnership.

The Summoner then suggested a swapping of their names.

" 'Brother,' " the smiling yeoman replied, "would you have me tell? I am a fiend, my dwelling is in Hell.' "

The surprised Summoner then asked the fiend how he could appear in various shapes. But the fiend said in effect that the Summoner was too ignorant to understand. Nonetheless the Summoner said he had made a bargain to join forces with the yeoman, even if he was Lucifer himself, and he would honor his word. The bargain was sealed, and they began the journey to the next village.

Somewhat further on, they came upon a farmer whose cart full of hay was stuck in the mud. No matter how he whipped his horses the cart would not move. In exasperation he shouted for the Devil to take all—cart, horse, hay and all. The Summoner urged the fiend to do as he was bid, but the Devil explained that since the curse was not uttered from the heart and in sincerity, he had no power to do so.

Later they went to the home of a rich widow who had consistently refused to pay the Summoner bribes. The Summoner demanded twelve pence, but she again refused. Then he threatened to take her new frying pan. She then became so exasperated at the Summoner's continued threats, she cried "the Devil take you and the frying pan." The Devil asked her if she really meant these words and she said yes, unless the Summoner repented. The Summoner refused. The fiend thereupon dragged the Summoner, body and soul, off to Hell where summoners have very special places. The Friar ends his tale by hoping that summoners can someday repent and become good men.

Commentary

The Wife of Bath began discussing some academic problems. The Friar continues by alluding to the qualities and powers of demons in this world. Since the fiend cannot take the horse, cart and hay, we see that the power of demons is limited.

The height of the irony is that the Summoner thinks the Devil looks enough like him to be his brother. This is the indirect method of commenting on the Summoner's character and occupation.

While reading *The Friar's Tale,* remember that no personal quarrel takes place between the Friar and the Summoner, but rather a quarrel about their professions. The Summoner belongs to the secular clergy which includes parish priests, arch-deacons, and bishops. The Friar, as a member of a mendicant order, belongs to world-wide organizations, holding authority directly from the Pope, and independent of the jurisdiction of the national church. This coexistence often leads to conflict. Thus, the Friar boasts that he is beyond the authority of the Summoner.

Chaucer has relied here on similar stories, but he has given it form and structure which raises it to the level of good literature. The conversation between the fiend and the Summoner is a classic. The shameless Summoner refuses to acknowledge his calling, and even after he learns the yeoman is a fiend, refuses to break the partnership agreement because he finds the fiend such charming if not evil company.

THE SUMMONER'S TALE: PROLOGUE

Summary

After hearing *The Friar's Tale,* the Summoner arose in his stirrups and was so angry that he shook like an aspen leaf. He suggests that the Friar told a well-documented story since Friars and fiends are always good friends. He then recalls the story of the Friar who once had a vision of hell. He had an angel guiding him through hell, but he saw no friars. He then inquired if there were no friars in hell. The angel then asked Satan to lift up his tail, and suddenly millions of friars were seen swarming around Satan's arse-hole. The Friar awoke from his dream, quaking with fear over the very thought of his future home.

THE SUMMONER'S TALE

Summary

In Yorkshire, in a marshy district known as Holderness, there was a Friar who went about praying for his parishioners, and casting a spell over them so that they would contribute money to the Friars. But despite his obvious piety, this priest would go from door to door promising prayers and supplications to the Lord in exchange for anything his parishioners could give him. Following him from door to door was a servant carrying a large sack into which the gifts were poured. Once back to the convent, the priest promptly forgot to make his prayers.

One day he came to the home of Thomas who had been ill abed for many days. The old man reproached the Friar for not having called upon him for a fortnight. The Friar replied that he had spent his entire time praying in Thomas' behalf.

At this moment, the old man's wife entered the house and the Friar greeted her excitedly and kissed her sweetly, chirping like a sparrow. He tells her he came to preach a little to Thomas. She asks him to talk about anger, because Thomas is always so crabbed and unpleasant. But before she goes, she offers the Friar some dinner. The Friar accepted and then suggested that since he lived a life of poverty, he needed little food, but then he suggested a menu sumptuous enough for a king.

The wife adds one more word before she goes. She reminds the Friar that her baby had died very recently and the Friar quickly acknowledged (or pretends) that he knows it because he and the other Friars had seen the child being lofted upward in angelic flight, and they had offered a *Te Deum,* and they had also fasted. He then gives the wife a long sermon or lecture on the virtues of fasting and on the sin of gluttony. He quotes the examples of Moses' forty-day fast, the fast of Aaron and other priests in the temple, and even suggested that Eve was gluttonous.

The Friar then turns to Thomas and embarks upon a long sermon on the necessity of avoiding excessive wealth and the blessings to be received by the "poor in spirit." He recited how those at the convent lived a life of poverty, carefully avoiding excesses of gluttony, wealth, and drink. He ends by telling Thomas how the entire convent prays for him every night, and Thomas should repay him for his prayers by donating a portion of his gold for an improvement in the convent.

Thomas responds that he has given quite a bit to the friars in the past and he can't see that it has helped very much. The Friar then points out that he has diversified his gifts too much by giving a bushel of oats to one convent, some groats to another, and a penny to this and that Friar. What Thomas should do is concentrate his gifts and give everything to the Friars who then would be the sole authority for Thomas' betterment.

The Friar then returns to his sermon on anger, quoting many authorities connecting the sin of anger with satan and vengeful women. Once Seneca pointed out how a ruler brought about the death of three innocent men because of anger; angry Cambyses, who was also a drunkard, once slew an innocent man, so beware of both anger and drink; and angry Cyrus of Persia once destroyed a river because his horse had drowned in the river. The Friar then tells Thomas to leave off his anger, and instead give of his gold to the Friars. Thomas says that he has given enough, but the Friar insists on something for his cloister. But the sermon on anger and the Friar's insistence only made Thomas angrier.

Thomas then thought a moment and said he had a gift for the Friar if it would be equally shared by all the Friars at the convent. But the Friar would have to swear to share it. He quickly agreed. " 'Reach down...Beneath my buttocks,' " said Thomas, and there " 'you are sure to find/Something I've hidden there.' " Hurriedly the Friar placed his hand on the old man's buttocks. At that moment, the old man let an enormous fart. The enraged priest stomped from the house and made his way to a wealthy lord's house. There, shaking with anger, he told how the old man had offended him. " 'I'll pay him out for it,' " the Friar shouted. " 'I can defame him! I won't be...bidden divide what cannot be divided/ In equal parts.' "

The lord's valet, standing nearby, suggested a way the fart could be equally divided. He suggested that a thirteen-spoke wheel be secured. At the end of each spoke should kneel a friar. Strapped to the hub of the wheel would be the old man. When he passed his gas, the wheel could be turned and thus each Friar could share equally. The lord and lady, all except the Friar, thought the valet's answer all they could desire.

Commentary

The reader should note some of the subtle irony employed in this story. The Friar gives a sermon on fasting and gluttony, but at the same time orders a meal that would be rather gluttonous. He speaks about anger, but in doing so, gets very angry himself. He sermonizes on the value of the "poor in spirit" and poverty, but is openly insistent that money be given to him. And while supposedly chaste, he is somewhat overly familiar with Thomas' wife. Finally from a large view, the story is filled with academic references which seem ironically misplaced in a story which deals with a rather vulgar joke.

The coarseness of *The Summoner's Tale* may offend some readers, particularly the final part. Yet when considered in the context of the Summoner's vicious story of the wretched hypocrisy of the Friar, the coarse insult suffered is perhaps suitable discipline.

Chaucer has, with outspoken frankness, revealed the Friar for what he is. It is this, and not the plot, which gives the work literary value.

On the face of it, this is a humorous story. Inherent in the tale, however, is a greater moral. Anyone who knows of the sacrifice, nobility, poverty, and purity of the early orders of the church makes this tale a tragedy rather than a comedy. It was inevitable that the nobility of the early Friars would be turned into the instrument for positive evil at a later time. The Friar in Chaucer's story even parrots the precepts of his pious founder. They become a hollow mockery.

The reader should, perhaps, compare the two sets of tales which were told to *repay* someone else. The Reeve told a tale to repay the Miller. The Summoner tells a tale to repay the Friar. In both cases, the latter tale tends to be the coarser of the two and each time, the last of the two tales has less wit and less subtlety, It seems as though the Reeve and Summoner both rely upon excessive vulgarity in order to repay the previous narrator with viciousness.

THE CLERK'S TALE: PROLOGUE

Summary

After the Summoner concluded his story, the Host turned to the Clerk from Oxford. "'You haven't said a word since we left the stable,'" the Host said. "'For goodness' sake cheer up...this is no time for abstruse meditation./ Tell us a lively tale.'" The Clerk bestirred himself and agreed to tell his story, which he said was told to him by a learned gentleman of Italy named Petrarch.

THE CLERK'S TALE

Summary

PART I

In the region of Saluzzo in Italy, there lived a noble and gracious king named Walter. His subjects held him in high esteem. Yet there was one thing that concerned him. Walter enjoyed his freedom to roam the countryside and refused to be bound by marriage.

One day a delegation of the lords of the kingdom called upon him and humbly beseeched him to seek a woman whom he would wed. The king was so impressed with their petition that he agreed to marry. Concerned lest he did not mean it, they asked him to set a date and this was done.

The lords even offered to find a suitable bride. To this the king demurred. He would choose the woman and would marry her if they would agree to be subservient to her forever. The lords agreed.

PART II

The day of the wedding arrived and all preparations were completed. The populace was puzzled, for the king had not selected his bride. It happened, however, that nearby there lived the poorest man, named Janicula. He had a beautiful and virtuous daughter named Griselda. The king often saw her as he traveled about and looked upon her form and beauty with a virtuous eye.

Shortly before the wedding was to take place, Walter went to Janicula and asked for permission to marry his daughter. The old man agreed and then Walter sought out Griselda and won her consent. Walter, however, made one condition: he made Griselda promise to always obey his will and to do so cheerfully even if it caused her pain. And furthermore, she is never to balk or complain about any of his commands. Griselda assented to these conditions and they were married.

In marriage, those qualities of patience, virtue, and kindness which Griselda had always possessed began to increase so that her fame spread to all the lands far and wide. People came from great distances simply to behold this paragon of virtue. Shortly afterwards, Griselda bore her husband a daughter. There was great rejoicing because now the people knew that she was not barren and would perhaps bear him a son.

PART III

While the baby was still suckling at her mother's breasts, the king resolved to banish any doubt about his wife's steadfastness to him. He called her to him and told her that one of his courtiers would soon call for the child. He expressed the hope that taking the child from her would in no way change her love for him. She said it would not.

The king's agent arrived and took the child. Griselda did not utter one word which indicated hate for her husband. Time passed, and never in any way did Griselda show loss of love for her husband.

PART IV

Four years passed and then Griselda bore her husband a son, and the people were happy that an heir to the throne had been born. When the son was two years old Walter again decided to test his wife's patience and fidelity. He went to her and told her that she must give up her son. Again she took the news patiently and said that if this was her husband's wish she would abide by his decision in good grace.

When Walter's daughter was twelve years old and the son ten, he decided to put Griselda to one final test. He had a Papal Bull forged declaring Walter free of Griselda and giving him permission to marry another woman. Then he ordered his sister, with whom the children had been placed, to bring his daughter and son home. Plans were then set in motion for another wedding.

PART V

Walter now decided to put Griselda to her greatest test. He called her before him and showed her the counterfeit Papal permission and told her of his intent to marry again. He explained that his subjects thought Griselda of too low a birth and he must take a woman of higher birth. Griselda took the news with a sad heart, but again with great patience and humility, she said that she would abide by her husband's decision and would return to her father's house. She takes nothing with her and explains to Walter that she came naked from her father's house and will return the same, but asks for permission to wear an old smock to cover her nakedness. So she returned to her father who received her with sadness, and there she remained for a short time.

PART VI

Through it all, Griselda went patiently and in good grace about her work helping to prepare the beautiful young girl, whom she did not recognize as her daughter, for the wedding. But Walter could stand his cruelty no longer. He went to Griselda and confessed that the beautiful young girl and the handsome boy were their children and that they had been given loving care in Bologna. He confessed that the cruel tests had been perfectly met by Griselda and that he could find no more patient and steadfast woman. They lived in bliss and when Walter died, his son succeeded to the throne.

The Clerk ends by saying that women should not follow so completely Griselda's example, but everyone should be constant in the face of adversity. And then, addressing the Wife of Bath, he says he will sing a song praising the gentle virtues of Griselda.

Commentary

The reader should remember that this story is told as a result of the Wife of Bath's story about women who desire sovereignty over their husbands. Thus the Clerk tells a story with the opposite view: that of a woman who is completely submissive to her husband.

It is apparent that the Clerk, a student at Oxford, was no grind. The Host's warning against too lofty and pedantic style was not necessary. After the Clerk concluded, the Host declared enthusiastically that the student had told his story in an "honest method, as wholesome as sweet."

The tale was not an original one with Chaucer. As he has the Clerk declare at the outset, Chaucer relied upon Petrarch's *Fable of Obedience and Wifely Faith* which was a considerably shortened translation from Boccaccio's *Decameron*.

What can one possibly conclude from this tale of a virtuous young peasant girl suddenly lifted from poverty and placed among the riches of the palace? Her sweet nobility, however, overcomes both sudden prosperity and also adversity created by her husband.

Is it possible for a woman to possess this overwhelming patience and unquestioning obedience? Perhaps many modern women would consider Griselda a rather ridiculous creature. Chaucer's portrait of this tender maiden may tax one's imagination, yet history is full of actual people and situations which match or surpass the seeming peculiarity of *The Clerk's Tale*.

There is also the question of one's moral duties. Griselda simply did what was common practice at the time she was created by Petrarch: She was a wife, a mother, and a subject of the king. We have little to judge Chaucer's feelings about Griselda.

The character of Walter is another matter. The man is selfish, spoiled, and wantonly cruel. Yet, Chaucer coats this bitter pill by telling us that he is young, handsome, good-natured, and loved by his people. He revels in his eccentric choices of Griselda as his queen and seems to take some pleasure in being cruel to her. It must be said that Walter is thorough. Twelve years of misery for his wife, and seldom do we witness the slightest spark of remorse!

The structure of this story, therefore, grows out of the nature of the two main characters. Walter seems to be as determined to be wanton in his testing of Griselda as Griselda is in being submissive to Walter's perverted demands. Each then possesses a single quality and these are seen pitted against each other.

THE MERCHANT'S TALE: PROLOGUE

Summary

The Merchant begins by saying he has no such wife as Griselda. He makes it clear that his story will characterize wives of a different sort. The Merchant, who is very old and only recently married, says he got a wife who has put him through hell in only two short months of marriage. His intolerable wife makes his life miserable. The Host begs him to impart a portion of his sorrow.

THE MERCHANT'S TALE

Summary

In Lombardy, in the town of Pavia, the Merchant began, there lived a prosperous knight named January. When he passed his sixtieth year, the knight decided to abandon a life of wanton lust and marry a beautiful young maiden who lived in the city. His reasons were clear enough. He wished to fulfill God's wish that man and woman should marry. He also wished to have a son to inherit his estates.

The Merchant offers such high praise of marriage and such praise of the role of the wife that it becomes apparent that he is being sarcastic. He then provides many examples of good women—women like Rebecca, Judith, Abigail, Esther, and quotes freely from Seneca, Cato and the Bible. (In actuality, the examples of the good woman are cases where the woman had been the cause of the destruction of a man.)

The matter was discussed with his brother Justinius, and with Placebo. Justinius argued vehemently against marriage, pointing out the faithfulness of women as a major pitfall. Placebo, however, argued the other way and counseled January to make up his own mind, for this was not a matter on which to seek advice.

January finally decided to marry. He looked over the crop of young maidens and chose the beautiful young girl named May. He then called his friends together in order to announce his wedding and ask help in solving a dilemma. He wants to know about the old saying that marriage is heaven on earth. And if he is supposed to have heaven on earth, how can he be sure of choosing the right wife. His friend, Justinius, said that perhaps his wife would be more of a purgatory than a heaven. But January went ahead with the wedding plans. The wedding feast was a sumptuous affair, but it lasted so long that January became impatient for the guests to leave so that he might enjoy his wedding bed. Finally, he was obliged to ask his guests to leave, and when the priest had blessed the marriage bed, he fulfilled his role as husband. The next morning, he sat up and sang like a bird in bed, and his loose skin around his neck also shook like a bird's neck.

It happened that one of January's serving men was a handsome youth named Damian who was smitted with love the moment he first saw the fair May. So remorseful was his unrequited love that he was taken to bed. Upon learning of this, January sent his wife and other women of the Court to Damian's bedside to comfort him. Damian found this an opportunity to pass a note to May in which he professed an undying love for her. Later May responded with a note to Damian acknowledging his desires.

One day January was suddenly stricken with blindness. His heart was sad and as the blindness continued, his evil thoughts of jealousy toward his wife could hardly be contained. He now insisted that May remain by him all the time. He would not let her to go anywhere unless he had hold of her hand. She was nevertheless able to send messages to Damian. By prearrangement, May admitted Damian to the Knight's garden which was kept under lock and key for his personal use. Later that day, May led January into the garden and signalled for Damian to climb up a pear tree.

We leave Damian in the pear tree and visit the gods. Pluto and his wife were discussing the situation involving January and May. Pluto said that he was going to restore January's sight because women are so deceitful, but he will wait till just the right moment to do so. But his wife, Proserpina, said men are so lecherous that she will provide May with a believable excuse.

Later, May led January to a pear tree where Damian was perched. Then she offered to climb up into the pear tree, beneath which they sat, and pluck a ripe pear for his enjoyment. In the tree above, of course, sat Damian. Soon the young couple was locked in amorous bliss. At that moment, January's sight was miraculously restored. He looked up and saw the young couple in an embrace. He bellowed with rage. May, however, was equal to the occasion. His sight was faulty; it was the same thing as awakening from a deep sleep when the eyes are not yet accustomed to the bright light and see strange things dimly. She then jumped down from the tree, and January clasped her in a fond embrace.

Commentary

This is the second tale handling the cuckolding of an old husband by a young bride. The first was *The Miller's Tale*. The difference between the character of the Miller and the Merchant can be seen by comparing the manner in which each tells a similar story.

The choice of names supports the story. January (the old man) marries May (the young woman) after rejecting the advice of Justinius (the just or righteous man) and following the advice of Placebo (the flattering man).

Some have condemned *The Merchant's Tale* as a senseless story of harlotry. There is much more to be said for it. Chaucer has given us one of his finest character sketches in this tale. Old January, now in his dotage, simply bargained for more than he was capable of. Throughout the story, Chaucer's point of view occupies our attention. It is not her faithlessness that concerns us but her very clever intrigue and her supreme audacity of escaping when she is caught. It would have been a simple matter for Chaucer to give the story a tragic ending. The element of tragedy is surely there, yet Chaucer chooses to put his hero into a fool's paradise. The spirit of the story is comedy, not immorality.

THE SQUIRE'S TALE: PROLOGUE

Summary

The Host turns to the Squire and requests another tale of love. The Squire says he will not tell a tale of love but a tale of something else, requesting that he be excused if he says anything amiss.

THE SQUIRE'S TALE

Summary

At Tzarev in the land of Tartary there lived a noble king named Cambuskan. He was excellent in everything and his subjects held him in high esteem. This compassionate monarch begat two sons of his wife Elpheta. They were Algarsyf and Cambalo. Another child, a daughter, was named Canace and no fairer creature ever graced this earth.

At the time of his twentieth anniversary as king, Cambuskan ordered that a lavish celebration be held. In the banquet hall, as the revelry was at its height, there suddenly appeared at the doorway a knight unknown to the people of Tzarev. With humility and grace, this knight named Gawain announced that he had come to the celebration bearing gifts from his sovereign lord, the king of India and Araby.

One gift was a brass horse which could fly faster and farther than any known creature. By pressing a magic lever in the horse's ear, the animal would transform itself from a rigid piece of statuary into a lively yet gentle horse.

The second gift was a mirror which could inform the owner of the innermost thoughts of friends and enemies, and recount the past, and foretell the future.

The third gift was a ring which would enable the wearer to understand the language of any living thing, be it bush or bird; further, the ring enabled the wearer to speak in the language of all these living things.

The fourth gift was a sword which would slay any beast, known or unknown, and cut through even the hardest rock.

The knight was thanked profusely for his gifts and bidden to join the feast. The king, meanwhile, gave the ring to his beautiful daughter. Early the next morning she arose, dressed, slipped on the ring, and entered the palace garden. In a nearby tree sat a female hawk crying piteously. Smitten with compassion, Canace climbed into the tree and, through the power of the ring, inquired of the hawk what had caused her unhappiness. The hawk related the story of how a handsome young male hawk had wooed and won her in marriage and how he tired of her and took up with a beautiful kite. So remorsefull was the jilted female hawk that she left her homeland and wandered aimlessly about the earth. Canace took her to the palace and restored the hawk back to health.

The Squire said he would also tell of how the mirror, horse, and sword profoundly affected the lives of the king and his sons. At this moment, the Franklin breaks in and insists on telling his story.

Commentary

Virtually everything about *The Squire's Tale* resembles countless similar stories found in Oriental literature. Why Chaucer never finished his tale has never been discovered. Scholars have long puzzled over *The Squire's Tale,* perhaps because it is less than half told.

The tale aptly fits the character of the Squire. He had been to strange lands, and had perhaps heard of strange magical events. And similar to *The Knight's Tale, The Squire's Tale* is filled with much elaborate description.

WORDS OF THE FRANKLIN TO THE SQUIRE

Summary

The Franklin interrupts the Squire's tale to compliment him on his eloquence and gentility. He wishes that his own son were more like the Squire or would imitate the Squire's manners and virtues. But the Host is not concerned with gentility, and he instructs the Franklin to tell a tale.

THE FRANKLIN'S TALE: PROLOGUE

Summary

The Franklin interrupts *The Squire's Tale* to compliment him on his eloquence, and he says he will repeat this tale to the pilgrims, but they must forgive him for his rude and plain speech because he never learned rhetoric and never studied the classic orators. And the only colors he can use to enrich his tale are those he has noticed in the meadows.

THE FRANKLIN'S TALE

Summary

In the land of Brittany, in France, there lived a knight named Arveragus. He was noble, prosperous, and courageous. Yet with all these blesssings he wished to take a wife. He found a beautiful maiden named Dorigen. They vowed that they would always respect each other and practice the strictest forbearance towards each other's words and actions. Thus solemnly pledged, they were wed.

Soon after the marriage, Arveragus had to go to a distant land for two years to replenish his wealth. While he was absent, Dorigen was so unhappy, forlorn, and grief stricken with her husband's absence that she sat and mourned and refused to join her neighbors in revelry.

Nearby to Dorigen's Castle was the rocky coast of France. In her grief, she often sat on the shore, observed the rocks, and meditated on the reason of existence. The sight of the grisly bare rocks made her apprehensive for her husband's safety because many men had lost their lives upon these dreadful rocks. She even wonders why God allowed so many men to be killed on these rocks, and wishes they would disappear into hell.

One day in May, however, she attended a gay picnic. Also present was Aurelius who had been secretly and madly in love with Dorigen. He mustered enough courage to approach and tell her of his love for her. She repudiated his advances. He became so despondent she believed she must do something to raise him from his depths of despair. She said, half-jokingly, that she'd agree to his embraces if he would remove all the rocks from the coast of Brittany. But this was impossible, he cried. Aurelius returned home where he prayed to Apollo to send a flood which would cover the rocks so that he might then hold Dorigen to her promise. He went into a spell of complete despondency and was cared for by his brother.

Meanwhile Arveragus returned home and was joyfully reunited with Dorigen. But to return to Aurelius; for two years he lay sick because of his unrequited love for Dorigen. During this time, his brother cared for him and was told of his love. Then the brother thought of a way to solve the dilemma. He knew of a student in southern France who claimed to have deciphered the secret codes of magic found in rare books. Aurelius went to him and promised payment of 1,000 pounds if his magic would clear the coast of rocks. The student agreed and the deed was performed. Aurelius then asked Dorigen to keep her promise. When Arveragus returned, he found his wife prostrate with grief. She told him the story of her bargain and he said she must keep her promise, although it would grieve him deeply. Dorigen presented herself to Aurelius. When he learned of the nobility and sacrifice of Arveragus, he could not force himself to possess Dorigen and sent the relieved woman back to her husband. Aurelius gathered all of his gold together and found he could only pay half of his fee owed the student. The student, when told that Dorigen was relieved of her part of the bargain, acquired a noble demeanor and forgave Aurelius of his debt. The Franklin concluded, "Which seemed the finest gentleman to you?"

Commentary

The Franklin is somewhat subservient in the way he insists upon paying compliments to the Squire and in the way he sides with the Clerk in emphasizing the need of patience in marriage. In fact this tale is connected with many that precede it. The Knight's and Miller's Tales involve a three-way love affair. The Franklin is also striving for something in between the complete sovereignty advocated by the Wife of Bath and the patience suggested by the Clerk. The Franklin's couple base their marriage on mutual trust and faith in each other.

The chief virtue of *The Franklin's Tale* is the noble spirit which pervades it. Here we have the beautiful Dorigen who refuses to be unfaithful while her husband is away; the duty to keep a promise even though it may be spoken in jest. Indeed, so powerful are the words of good here that the lover and the poor student are obliged to accept a degree of nobility. Supporting all this is Chaucer's main theme that love and force are antithetical, and patience and forbearance are the essence of love. Chaucer is not one, however, to let a story become overly sentimental, and throughout the tale sly humor makes its appearance.

The Franklin's question—which of the three seemed to be the finest gentleman—probably cannot be answered. This literary device, however, surely provokes a picture of heated debate between the members of the company. Perhaps many of us will agree that Arveragus erred when he demanded that his wife make a sacrifice for a pledge made in jest. Nonetheless, his noble deed begets nobility from the other two, demonstrating that is is possible for good to overcome evil.

THE PHYSICIAN'S TALE

Summary

There was once a knight named Virginius who was rich, kindly, and honorable. The knight had only one child, a beautiful fourteen-year old daughter. Her beauty was beyond compare, and she was endowed with all the other noble virtues: patience, kindness, humility, abstinence and temperance. The Physician then departs from his story and addresses all people who are involved with bringing up children, telling them that they must set the example for the child.

Returning to his story, the Physician said the girl and her mother went to the town one morning. On the street a judge named Appius saw her. He was taken by her beauty and was determined to have her. After pondering on a scheme, he sent for the town's worst blackguard, called Claudius and paid him well to take part in the plan.

Claudius then accused the noble knight of having stolen a servant girl from his house many years ago and has kept her all these years pretending that she is his daughter. Before the knight had a chance to call witnesses, Appius the judge ruled that the child must be brought to him immediately as a ward of the court.

Virginius returned home and called his daughter into his presence. She must, he said, accept death, or shame at the hands of Claudius. Since the knight could never accept the shame, he withdrew his sword and cut off his daughter's head. Holding it by the hair, he went to the judge and handed it to him. The judge ordered the knight hung for murder. At that moment a throng of citizens, aroused by the judge's treachery, threw the judge into prison. Claudius was to be hung but the knight pleaded for his life and suggested only exile, which was done. "Here," said the Physician, "one can see how sin is paid its wages."

Commentary

The Physician's Tale begins, "Livy has handed down a tale to us..." There is no doubt that Titus Livius' history is the source of Chaucer's tale, but there is a substantial difference between them. Indeed, students of Chaucer now believe that Chaucer never consulted Livy at all but borrowed this story from Jean de Meun's *Roman de la Rose*. Chaucer's tale puts the emphasis on the loveliness and chastity of the girl, whereas the French version places the most emphasis on the unjust judge and the punishment meted out to him.

Chaucer's story, however, is made much more interesting by added description and the introduction of dialogue, particularly between Virginius and his daughter.

THE PARDONER'S TALE

WORDS OF THE HOST TO THE PHYSICIAN AND THE PARDONER

Summary

The Host was terribly upset by *The Physician's Tale*. He called the judge a low blackguard and treacherous man. The Host thinks that the pilgrims need a merry tale to follow and turns to the Pardoner who agrees to tell a merry tale. The more genteel members of the company fear that the Pardoner will tell a ribald story and ask for something with a moral. The Pardoner asks for something to drink, and he will tell a moral tale.

THE PARDONER'S PROLOGUE

Summary

The Pardoner explains to the pilgrims his methods used in preaching. He always takes as his text *Radix malorum est* (Love of money is the root of all evil). His technique is as follows: first, he shows all of his official documents, then he uses some latin; following that he shows his relics which include a sheep bone for good luck in preventing diseases in animals and will bring a man wealth and cure jèalousy; a mitten which will bring more money when the Pardoner receives his money for the relic. Addressing himself to the audience, he announces that he can do nothing for the really bad sinners, but if all the good people will come forward, he will sell them relics which will absolve them from sins. In this way he had won a hundred marks in a year. Next, he stands in the pulpit and preaches very rapidly over the sin of avarice so as to intimidate the members into donating money to him. He acknowledges that many sermons are the result of selfish and evil intentions, and he even admits that he spits out venom under the guise of holiness; and even though he is guilty of the same sins he is preaching against, he can still make other people repent.

The Pardoner then admits that he likes money, rich food, and fine living. And even if he is not a moral man, he can tell a good moral tale.

Commentary

The Pardoner's Prologue is in the form of a confession. Even though he is essentially a hypocrite in his profession, he is at least being honest here as he makes his confession.

Notice that he takes as his text that "Love of money is the root of all evil," but with each relic, he emphasizes how it will bring the purchaser more money. And in emphasizing this, he sells more, and gains more money for himself. Thus there is the double irony in his text, since his love for money is the root of his evil, and his sales depend upon the purchaser's love for money. Furthermore, his technique of relying upon basic psychology by selling only to the good people brings him more money. His sermon on avarice is given because the Pardoner is filled with avarice, and this sermon fills his purse with money.

THE PARDONER'S TALE

Summary

In Flanders, three young men sat in an inn after drinking, gambling, and swearing all night long. The Pardoner now stops his tale and gives a rather long sermon directed against drinking, gambling, and swearing, and gluttony. He suggests that gluttony was the cause of Lot's incest, it caused Herod to have John the Baptist beheaded, and it caused Eve to eat the fruit. He quotes St. Paul and elaborates more on the sin of eating and drinking to excess. He then attacks cooks who contribute to gluttony by preparing dishes too succulently. He turns to wine and drunkenness and quotes authorities and examples to affirm the evil of drinking. This leads him into saying how evil gambling is since it leads to lying, swearing and waste of property. He cites again the history of gambling. He closes his sermon with a long diatribe against swearing.

He returns to these three rioters "of whiche I telle" who were drinking when they heard bells sounding which signified that a coffin was passing the inn. The young men asked the servant to go and find out who had died. The lad told them it was not necessary since he already knew. The dead men was a friend of theirs who was stabbed in the back the night before by some sneaky thief called Death—the same thief who took so many lives in the neighboring town recently. The young rioters thought that Death might still be in the next town, and they decided to seek him out and slay him. On the way, they met an extremely old man dressed rather poorly. The rioters comment on his advanced age. He explains that he must wander the earth until he can find someone who will be willing to exchange youth for age. He says that not even Death will take his life. Hearing him speak of Death, the three young rioters ask the old man if he knows where they can find Death. He told the three men that he had last seen Death under a tree at the end of the lane. The rioters rush to the tree and find instead eight bushels of gold. They decide to keep the gold for themselves, but are afraid to move it in the daytime. They decide to wait for the night, and they draw straws to see which one will go into town to get food and wine to hold them over. The youngest of the three drew the shortest straw and started for town. As soon as he had left, the two decided to kill the youngest and split the money between them. But the youngest decided that he wanted all of the money. He goes to the druggist and buys poison that will kill rats quickly. He buys three bottles of wine and pours the poison into two of them. When he approaches the tree, the two immediately stab him and then they sit down and drink all of the wine. Thus ended these homicides.

The Pardoner now decries against sin and reminds the pilgrims that he has pardons that they can buy. He invites them to buy from him and he will immediately record their names as purchasers. He suggests that the Host should begin since the Host is the most sinful. But in turn, the Host attacks the Pardoner, intimating that the Pardoner is not a full man. The Pardoner became so angry he could not speak. The Knight restored peace and they rode forth on their way.

Commentary

The Pardoner is one of the most complex figures in the entire pilgrimage. He is certainly an intellectual figure; his references and knowledge and use of psychology attest to his intellect. But in making his confessions to the pilgrims about his hypocrisy, he seems to be saying that he wished he could be more sincere in his ways, except that he does love money and power too much.

His tale is told to illustrate his preaching methods. It is often considered one of the finest examples of the short story. Its brevity and use of dialogue and its quick denouement fufill the standards for a good short story.

There has been much argument as to the meaning of the old man. Perhaps he is death itself, or perhaps a mystic figure like the "Wandering Jew." But his function in the story is clear. He is the instrument by which the three rioters find Death. And for the Pardoner, a conscious practitioner of hyprocrisy, this old man is a splendid example of hyprocrisy in the way he deceived the three rioters.

Note that at the end, the host implies that the Pardoner is not a full man. We know from *The General Prologue* that he has no beard, and now it is implied that he is perhaps impotent or perverted. Perhaps it is this condition which causes the Pardoner to be so cynical, and yet there are suggestions that he would like to be different.

The popularity of this tale is easy to understand. It is a tragic story, or at least an ironic tragedy. It is the Pardoner's own lesson: the love of money is the root of all evil, and those who covet money covet death and find it.

The Pardoner's Tale, however, is Chaucer's adaptation of a popular fable thought to have its origins in the Orient. It is not possible to determine the exact source of Chaucer's story. Here again, however, the artistry of Chaucer is evident. No known fable bearing this plot employs the dark background of the Plague or the sinister figure which the three drunken men meet in their search for Death.

THE SHIPMAN'S TALE

Summary

There once was a merchant in St. Denys, the Shipman began, who was rich and had an uncommonly beautiful wife. They lived in a splendid house which, more often than not, was filled with guests.

Among these guests was a handsome young monk about thirty years old. The young monk was on the best of terms with the kind hearted merchant. Indeed, to avail himself of the merchant's hospitality the young monk stated that they were cousins, or very nearly related, since both were born in the same town. So happy was the merchant about this relationship he vowed he would always regard the monk as a brother.

It happened that the merchant, as was the custom in those days, planned to go to Brussels to purchase wares. He invited the young monk to his home for a few days before he left. The monk gladly accepted.

On the third day of the monk's visit the merchant went to his counting room to total up his debts and money to see where he stood financially before he left for Brussels. While the merchant was thus engaged, the monk was in the garden. Soon the merchant's wife entered the garden. The monk remarked that she looked quite pale and suggested wryly that perhaps her husband had kept her awake all night at play. " 'No, cousin mine,' " the merchant's wife protested, " 'things aren't like that with me.' " She then said she could kill herself because things had gone so badly with her.

The monk then said, " 'God forbid...Unfold your grief...' ." She agreed to tell him her problem of marital neglect if both swore themselves to secrecy. They took a solemn vow, and she told the story, and apologized for berating the monk's cousin. " 'Cousin indeed!' " the monk cried, " 'He's no more cousin to me/ Than is this leaf, here, hanging on the tree.' "

Finally, the merchant's wife begged the monk to loan her one hundred francs to buy some things her frugal husband had denied her. The monk agreed to bring her the money as soon as the merchant left for Brussels. Then he drew the wife to him and kissed her madly.

After dinner that night, the monk drew the merchant aside and begged him for a loan of one hundred francs to purchase some cattle. The merchant gladly gave him the money.

The next day the merchant left for Brussels. Soon after, the monk arrived at the merchant's home and, as agreed, in exchange for the money, the wife agreed to spend the night in bed with the monk.

Some time later the merchant made another business trip and on his way stopped by the monk's abbey to pay a social call, but not to collect the loan. The monk, however, said he had paid the money to the merchant's wife only a day or two after it had been loaned.

When the merchant returned home, he chided his wife for not having told him the loan had been repaid. Then she explained that she had used the money to buy fine clothes. The merchant saw that there was no point in scolding her further and concluded, " '...Well, I forgave you what you spent,/But don't be so extravagant again.' "

Commentary

This tale fits the personality of the Shipman. A thief and a pirate, he tells a grossly immoral story. The monk not only betrayed his vows as a man of God, but also had a deliberate disregard for common decency toward a man who had opened his home to him. Indeed, he falsely cultivated the merchant's friendship by professing that they were in some way related. The monk then went further by betraying the merchant's wife. Finally, the monk left her in an embarrassing situation about the loan.

The laugh is on the merchant and his wife. The moral of the story is, perhaps, that adultery can be very amusing and profitable, provided that it is not found out. Chaucer's tale has a fine sense of narrative and the characters are well-designed but yet there remains the rather distasteful portrait of lust and treachery.

This story is presumed to have been originally told as a French fable. There is a question, however, about why Chaucer assigned this tale to the Shipman. At the beginning of the tale, the narrator says our husbands want us to be hardy, wise and good in bed. The use of the pronoun suggests that Chaucer intended to assign this story to one of the female members of the party, and probably by the nature of the tale, intended it for the Wife of Bath. When he changed his mind, Chaucer apparently forgot to eliminate this inconsistency.

THE PRIORESS' TALE: PROLOGUE

Summary

The Prioress begins by addressing the Virgin Mary and extolling the praises of Mary. The prologue is thus a hymn of praise, in which the virtues of the Virgin are praised.

THE PRIORESS' TALE

Summary

In a Christian town in Asia, there was one quarter of the town where Jews lived. They were kept by the lord of the town for usurious purposes.

At the far end of the street through the ghetto stood a school for young Christian children. The children were free to walk through the street to and from school.

One of the pupils was a mere child who had not learned to read and was only beginning to recognize the Latin of his prayers. At school he heard the older children singing *O Alma Redemptoris*. Day after day he drew near as they sang and listened carefully. Soon he had memorized the first verse even though he had no notion of what the Latin meant. One day he begged another lad to tell him what the song meant and the older lad said:

> "...This song, I have herd seye,
> Was maked of our blisful Lady free,
> Hire to salue, and eek hire for to preye..."

Thus when the child learned that the song was in praise of the Virgin Mary, he was delighted and decided to learn the entire song so that on Christmas day he would pay reverence to Christ's mother.

So every day the child would go along the Jewish street singing the song boldly and clearly. At about this time the Serpent Satan whispered to the Jews that this singing boy was a disgrace to them and the singing was being done to spite the Jewish Holy Laws.

The Jews then began conspiring. A murderer was hired and one day he grasped the child, slit his throat, and tossed his body in a cesspool.

The child's mother, a widow, waited all that night. When the sun rose, she went to the school where she got the news her son was last seen in the street of the Jews. She made inquiry of the Jews from house to house, and all said they knew nothing of the child. Then Jesus put in her thoughts the direction to the alley where he had been murdered and the pit where her boy was cast.

As the widow neared the place, the child's voice broke forth singing *O Alma.* The Christian people gathered around in astonishment. The Provost of the city was called, and upon seeing the child, bade all Jews be fettered and confined. They were later drawn by wild horses and then hanged.

The child was taken to a neighboring abbey. As the burial mass drew near, the child continued to sing *O Alma* loud and clear. He then told the abbots that Christ had commanded him to sing until his time for burial and that, at the same moment, the Virgin Mary laid a grain upon his tongue.

" 'And...I must sing,' " the child said, " 'For love of her,.../ Till from my tongue you take away the grain.' " The monk took away the grain, and the child "gave up the ghost...peacefully." Later a tomb of marble was erected as a memorial to the young boy.

Commentary

The Prioress' Prologue is aptly fitted to her character and position. She is a nun whose order relies heavily upon the patronage of the Virgin Mary. Furthermore, her hymn to the Virgin Mary acts as a preview to the tale which concerns the same type of hymn of praise sung for the Virgin.

To understand *The Prioress' Tale,* one must first understand the background for tales such as these. In medieval England, the Christian hatred for the Jews took the form of a religious passion. This passion was periodically renewed by stories such as this one and passed along as true.

The first story of this sort was written by Socrates in the fifth century. The story was "localized" in 1144 when St. William of Norwich was supposed to have been murdered by Jews. The number of these martyrdoms has never been accurately accounted for, but one authority in 1745 recounted fifty-two. The belief persists in some parts of Europe today.

A legend so widespread as this could not fail to appear in the literature of Chaucer's time, although the particular source of his story has never been discovered.

In this tale, as in so many of Chaucer's, the author lays most of the emphasis on the human aspects of the tale rather than the supernatural. Chaucer, of course, has not slighted the glories of the Virgin Mary nor the wickedness of the Jews. But his chief interest centers on the child and his mother.

SIR TOPAS: PROLOGUE

Summary

The Prioress' Tale of the miracle of the child naturally sobered the pilgrims. But soon the Host told jokes to liven the group and then turned to Chaucer. He asks "what kind of man are you since you are always looking at the ground." The Host then comments on Chaucer's physical appearance and tells him to come forth with a tale. Chaucer explains that he knows only one story; it is in rhyme and he heard it a long time ago.

CHAUCER'S TALE OF SIR TOPAS

Summary

The Prioress' tale of the miracle of the child naturally sobered the pilgrims. But soon the Host told jokes to liven the group and then turned to Chaucer. " 'Who might this fellow be?" He inquired, and then suggested that Chaucer tell his story.

Far across the sea, in Flanders, there lived a young knight by the name of Sir Topas. His father was a titled nobleman who possessed much wealth.

Sir Topas was a handsome man. He was a great hunter, an accomplished archer, and a skilled wrestler. Every maiden in the land spent restless nights pining for his love. But Sir Topas took little interest in these maidens.

So, one day, he rode away to the forest and after an exhausting ride, he paused at nightfall beside a watering place. When he fell asleep he dreamed that an Elf Queen had slept beneath his cloak. When he awoke he was determined that he would ride to the ends of the earth in search of an Elf Queen. Nothing would requite his love.

He rode on. Soon he met a three-headed giant who bade him depart this part of the forest, for it was the kingdom of the Elf Queen. The Giant threatened death should Sir Topas fail to leave. The knight accepted the challenge and then rode away to his home to secure his armor and prepare for the great battle with the giant.

At his father's castle he feasted elegantly and prepared for the battle with the finest armor and weapons.

HERE THE HOST STINTETH CHAUCER OF HIS TALE OF TOPAS

Summary

The Host interrupts Chaucer crying "For God's sake, no more of this." And he added, "I am exhausted by these illiterate rhymes." He then asks Chaucer to leave off the rhymes and tell something in prose. Chaucer agrees to tell a *little* thing in prose, but warns that he might repeat some of the proverbs that the pilgrims have heard before.

Commentary

It is, of course, ironic that Chaucer says to the Host that these are the best rhymes that he can do. Each stanza is filled with traditional clichés and absurd speech. Chaucer was making fun of himself, ridiculing this type of literature, and belittling the people who read this type of poetry. And most ironic of all is that Chaucer assigns this silly tale to himself.

Furthermore, when the Host interrupts Chaucer, he pretends to be a little offended saying that these are his best rhymes. And then Chaucer promises a *little* thing in prose with a few familiar proverbs, but he proceeds to write a long, dull tale that rambles on forever and is filled with many proverbs.

The Tale of Sir Topas has long puzzled scholars. At the time Chaucer wrote it, there were already in existence scores of tales of handsome knights in search of adventure and fair maidens. All of them were naively simple, long-winded, larded with minute descriptions, and plotted with improbability.

CHAUCER'S TALE OF MELIBEE

Summary

The principal character in the tedious debate is Dame Prudence, the wife of Melibee. The principal subject is whether we should avenge a violent injury by further violence. It so happened that when Melibee and his wife were away three burglars entered their home and seriously injured their daughter Sophia. The question was: Should they take revenge upon the burglars?

In the course of the argument a variety of subjects arise and are dealt with in a learned manner by doctors, lawyers, clerics and many others. These subjects included the importance of not making God an enemy, whether women are to be trusted, and whether private revenge is dangerous, or morally justifiable, or expedient.

Finally, the three burglars are found and brought before Dame Prudence who astonished and delighted the ruffians by her suggestion of a peaceful settlement. Her husband, Melibee, decided to let them off with a fine, but Dame Prudence vetoed this. Melibee then forgave the burglars, rebuked them, and extolled his own magnanimity. What happened to Sophia was never learned.

Commentary

The Tale of Melibee is, as one authority describes it, a prime example of a literary vice of the Middle Ages—an essay abounding in dull commonplaceness, forced allegory, and spiritless and interminable moralizing. Some think this tale is a mischievous companion to Chaucer's *Tale of Sir Topas*. At any rate, the tale was not Chaucer's own but a translation of a French tale, *Le Livre de Melibee et de Dame Prudence,* which in turn had been translated from the Latin work, *Liber Consolationis et Consilli* by Albertano.

THE MONK'S TALE: PROLOGUE

Summary

The Host, true to his middle-class upbringing in medieval England, was delighted with the marvelous tale of Dame Prudence, the benign, gentle, and understanding woman. Crowed he: " 'As I'm an honest man...I'd rather have had my wife hear this tale....' " His wife, he explained, drove him continually to acts of dishonesty and violence.

Then the Host turned to the Monk and demanded a story which he confidently expects to be a merry tale, But he is disappointed, for the Monk began a series of tales in which tragedy was the theme. Some of the stories he warned might be familiar to his hearers and some might not.

THE MONK'S TALE

Summary

After reciting briefly the fall of *Adam* and *Lucifer,* the Monk told the story of *Samson* whose great feats of strength made him ruler of Israel. But tragedy befell him when he married Delilah and told her one night that his strength was in his hair. To his enemies Delilah sold the secret. They clipped away his hair, put out his eyes, and threw him in a cave where he was the subject of jeers. One day he was asked to show his feats of strength and, his power restored, he destroyed the temple of his enemies and its 3,000 inhabitants. The monk moralized that men should not tell their wives secrets that should remain secret.

Next the Monk related the story of *Hercules* and how his great feats of strength and bravery led him into all the regions of the earth where he slew an infinite variety of monsters. Hercules fell in love with the beautiful

Deianira and soon she fashioned him a gay shirt, But its fabric was poisoned and when he donned it his life ebbed. Disdaining death by poison, Hercules threw himself into a fire. Let all successful men, the Monk moralized, beware how Fortune elects to plot their overthrow.

The Monk continued with the stories of *Nebuchadnezzar* who was turned into an animal until he repented his idolatrous sins, and of *Balthasar* who refused to abandon the ways of the wicked, despite God's warning, and ultimately lost his kingdom.

The Monk's seventh story was of *Zenobia,* a Persian woman who was not only beautiful but of great strength and courage. She feared neither man nor beast. One day she met and fell in love with Prince Idenathus, also a great warrior. They were wed and she bore him two sons. Zenobia and her husband swept all foes before them and ruled a vast region as far away as the Orient. The Prince died but Zenobia and her sons continued to rule and showed their captive nations no mercy. Then one year Aurelius, the great Roman emperor, invaded Zenobia's kingdom, took her and her sons captive, and in Rome they were jeered and gaped at.

The Monk then said that the mighty must always be on guard against treachery. He related briefly stories to prove his point. *King Peter of Spain* was betrayed and slain by his own brother. *King Peter of Cyprus* was slain by his own companions. *Bernabo of Lombardy* was killed in prison at the instigation of his nephew. *Count Ugolino of Pisa* was imprisoned with his three children and left to starve. After some time, the children began to cry out for bread. Then the youngest died. The count began to gnaw his own arm and one of the children offered his own flesh. Finally the other children starved and later the Count also died from starvation. Thus many of the mighty, after reaching the height of power, are betrayed and brought low.

Men who rise to power and fame are also dangerous to themselves. *Nero* rose to great fame. He loved all the fine and delicate things in the world. To satisfy his imagination, he had Rome burned, he killed people simply to hear the sounds of weeping and he even killed his mother so as to cut open her womb and observe his place of birth. But when his time was up, he could find no person who would shelter him or even kill him. He finally had to kill himself.

Holofernes was once so powerful that he made the entire world give up worship of individual gods and pay homage to Nebuchadnezzar. But as he lay drunk in his tent one night, Judith slipped in and cut off his head.

Good fortune smiled so readily upon *Antiochus* that he considered it possible for him to reach the stars. Out of his hatred for the Jews, he attempted to destroy them, but God sent down invisible pains upon him. In spite of the pain, he still proceeded to execute his plans. God then caused him to be crippled and made his body stink so badly that all people avoided him. Finally, he died a wretched and lonely death.

Alexander was so courageous that nothing could keep him from great deeds of valor and heroism. But eventually his own people turned against him and poisoned him.

Julius Caesar rose from a simple birth to become the mightiest man in the world. He was indeed blest with good fortune for a long time. But finally, even fickle fortune turned against him. Brutus and his cohorts stabbed Caesar to death, but even in death, Caesar remained a man as indicated by the way he covered himself with his cloak when he was dying.

The king of Lydia, *Croesus,* considered himself lucky after he was sentenced to death by fire and a heavy rain came and put out the fire. From there on, he thought himself immune to death. But he had a dream which was explained by his daughter as meaning that he would soon die by hanging.

Here the Knight interrupts the Monk.

Commentary

The Monk, unlike the Pardoner, will not permit himself the luxury of jest nor the undignified tale. Each of the Monk's stories is much like the others. It is not clear why Chaucer wrote these stories for the Monk. They are monotonous, and the inevitable moral of each comes as no surprise to the reader. Some authorities believe that Chaucer at one time considered writing a book of tragedies in the manner of Boccaccio. Indeed, Chaucer depended upon Boccaccio's work for his stories of Adam, Samson, Balthasar, Zenobia, Nero, and Croesus. Biblical narrative provided him with several of the other stories. His stories were sometimes incomplete, and Chaucer did not arrange them in chronological sequence; this perhaps accounts for the sense of whim and spontaneity of *The Monk's Tale*. Since Chaucer never completed his book of tragedies, it is believed that they are used in the *Canterbury Tales* simply because they were available and seemed suitable for the Monk to relate.

THE NUN'S PRIEST'S TALE: PROLOGUE

Summary

The Knight interrupts the Monk crying that his tales of woe are too much to bear. He asks the monk to tell a tale about a poor man who rises to good fortune. The Host agrees with the Knight and adds that the stories were so boring that he almost went to sleep. He entreats the Monk to tell a merry tale, but the Monk wants someone else to take a turn. The Host turns to the Nun's Priest and calls for a tale.

THE NUN'S PRIEST'S TALE

Summary

Once long ago in a small cottage near a meadow, the Nun's Priest began, there lived a widow and her two daughters. They had barely enough to keep them comfortable. Among her possessions was a cock called Chaunticleer. This rooster was a beautiful sight to behold, and nowhere in the land was there a cock who could match him in crowing. Chaunticleer was the master in some measure of seven hens. The loveliest of these was a beautiful and gracious hen named Lady Pertelote. She held the heart of Chaunticleer.

Now it so happened that one spring dawn as these birds sat on their perch, Chaunticleer began to groan and lurch. "'O dearest heart,/ What's ailing you?'" said Pertelote. Chaunticleer then recounted a terrible dream he had of a kind of beast or hound roaming in the yard trying to seize him. His color and marking were much the same as a fox.

"For Same," Pertelote said, "fye on you." She told him that it was cowardly to be afraid of dreams, and by showing such fear he has lost her love. She told him he dreamed because he ate too much and that no one should be afraid of dreams. It is well known that dreams have no meaning. She quotes Cato who says that dreams have no significance. Thus, she recommends a good laxative for Chaunticleer, and explains the relative value of each laxative. She even offers to prepare the cathartic, to be followed by a feast of choice worms.

Chaunticleer graciously thanks Pertelote, but he will quote a few authors who maintain that dreams have a very definite meaning. He recalled the story of two pilgrims who arrived in a busy town. There was a large crowd so they could not find lodging together. The first pilgrim found one room in an inn, but the second had to sleep in a nearby barn. During the night, the second pilgrim appeared to the first in a dream, saying that he was being murdered and crying for help. But the first pilgrim put this dream out of his mind and went back to sleep. Then in a second dream, the companion appeared again and said that the murderer was tossing his body in a dung cart which would be found at the city's gate the next morning. The next morning the companion arose and sought his friend in the barn. He was told that his friend was gone. The first pilgrim searched for the dung cart, and sure enough there was the body of his friend.

Chaunticleer then moralizes on murder, and is very pleased with his story, so pleased that he tells another one. Two men were to set sail the next day, but one dreamed that they were sure to be drowned and refused to go. His companion laughed at him for believing in dreams and went by himself. But as the ship was just a short distance out to sea, it sank and everyone was drowned.

Chaunticleer sees that his narration is affecting Pertelote, so he quotes several more authorities. He reminds her of St. Kenelm who saw his own murder in a dream. Furthermore, the *Dream of Scipio,* Daniel and Joseph's interpretation of dreams, and Andromache's dream should be remembered. And thus he ends his long speech with the conclusions that he needs no laxative.

Chaunticleer then felt that he had perhaps been too harsh on dear Pertelote, and he turns and compliments her on her looks and quotes to her the Latin phrase "In principio, mulier est hominis confusio" which he translates as "Woman is man's sole joy and bliss."

The Nun's Priest leaves Chaunticleer in his victory and pride with his seven ladies, and turns to the fox. This fox named Daun Russel has been hiding near the farmyard. The Nun's Priest now comments on traitors such as this fox, and compares him with such traitors as Judas and Ganelon. He follows this with a discussion of divine foreknowledge.

Returning to the plot, the Nun's Priest relates how Chaunticleer was watching a butterfly when he caught sight of the fox. He began immediately to run, but the fox called out in a gentle voice for Chaunticleer not to be afraid of a friend. He explains that he only came to hear Chaunticleer's beautiful voice. He maintains that he has only once before heard such a fine voice and that belonged to Chaunticleer's father. Now the fox wants to see if Chaunticleer can sing as well as his father could.

Thus, the vain cock shut his eyes and burst into song. At that moment the fox raced to the cock, grasped him about the neck, and made off with him. The hens in the barnyard made such a terrible commotion that they aroused the entire household. Soon the Widow, her two daughters, the dogs, hens, geese, ducks and even the bees were chasing the fox. It was so noisy that one would think the heavens were falling down.

Chaunticleer then says to the fox, "Why don't you turn around and throw a few insults at them." The fox thought this a good idea and as soon as he opened his mouth, Chaunticleer escaped and flew to a tree top. The fox tried to lure Chaunticleer down by compliments and sweet talk, but Chaunticleer had learned his lesson.

The Nun's Priest closes his tale by suggesting that his tale does have a moral.

Commentary

In *The Nun's Priest's Tale,* we have Chaucer at his best. Now, of course, animal stories are commonplace, and they have been a part of man's literature since earliest times. Perhaps Chaucer drew upon two similar fables, the French *Roman de Renard* and the German *Reinhart Fuchs.*

Nonetheless he improved upon these earlier stories by making his version much more real and much more interesting.

He did this by simply humanizing the rooster. Both the rooster and man have the same quality in common—vanity. The fox practices obvious flattery which is preeminently the quality of a tyrant.

Now if animals can talk, as indeed they do here, then they can dream and finally can discuss with great erudition the plausibility of dreams. Chaucer leads us charmingly through these stages in developing Chaunticleer, Pertelote, and the Fox into individuals suffering all the foibles of human nature. Yet never does Chaucer let us forget that these characters are but a cock, a hen, and a fox. For if we were to forget, the delicious humor of the story would be lost.

The reader should also remember that as the Priest is telling his story of Chaunticleer and his seven hens, the Priest is in a similar situation himself since he is the confessor to a group of nuns.

This tale is filled with many types of ironies. The reader should be aware of the human aspects of these barnyard creatures. Pertelote even refers to Chaunticleer's beard; yet in spite of their humanity they are nevertheless barnyard creatures. That they thus speak so learnedly and so nobly is an indirect comment on the absurdity of human aspirations.

The mock heroic tone should also be noted. The story is filled with classical allusions, with discussions about divine foreknowledge, and with a high moral tone. To offer a discussion of divine foreknowledge in the context of a barnyard chicken is the height of comic irony; that is, to have a foolish rooster being caught by a fox used as proof of divine foreknowledge is absurd. And to compare the plight of Chaunticleer to that of Homer's Hector and to suggest that the chase of the fox is an epic chase similar to classical epics indicates the absurdity of this situation.

It is likewise comic that Chaunticleer translates the Latin phrase incorrectly. He translates it as meaning that "woman is man's joy and bliss." But it actually means that woman is the downfall of man. And since Pertelote does not want to believe in Chaunticleer's dream, she is ironically contributing to his and ultimately her downfall.

THE SECOND NUN'S TALE: PROLOGUE

Summary

Idleness is a fiend that encourages vice and that fiend is forever laying a trap to catch people in his snare. Since Idleness is so dreadful, the Second Nun says she will follow her advice and get immediately down to the business of telling a tale. She offers to translate the life of St. Cecilia for the pilgrims.

The Second Nun offers an invocation to Mary. She asks for help in rendering accurately this tale of a maiden who remained true to her faith and conquered over the Devil. The Second Nun then praises the glories of Mary, the maid and mother. She asks forgiveness for possessing no more artistry with which to tell her tale.

The Second Nun now offers an *Interpretation of the Name Cecilia.* It means 1) heavenly lily for her chaste virginity; 2) the way for the blind by the example of her teachings; 3) holiness and busy-ness because of the derivation of the name from Latin; 4) wanting in blindness because of her clear virtues; and 5) heavenly because of the brightness of her works of excellence.

Commentary

Since Nuns in Chaucer's day were compelled to read stories of the saints, this is an apt selection for the Second Nun simply because she is a nun. Her invocation to Mary is typical for all stories, but more so here since the story of St. Cecilia is a story of chastity. And the interpretation of the name was a favorite device during Chaucer's day. Let it suffice here to say that the interpretation is not correct from an etymological viewpoint.

THE SECOND NUN'S TALE

Summary

There was once a noble young woman of Rome who loved chastity so much that she wanted to remain a virgin forever. But in time, she was given to a young man named Valerian in marriage. While the chapel bells were ringing for her wedding, she was praying to God to keep her chaste. That night after the wedding, she told her new husband that she had a guardian angel who would slay anyone who violated her body. Valerian asked to see the angel if he were to believe her. Cecilia tells him that he must first go to the Appian Way and there be baptised by Holy Urban.

Valerian went to Urban who rejoiced to see what power Cecilia had that she could convince a young man to be baptised. He praised God for Cecilia's chaste counsel. Suddenly, an old man appeared to them in a vision saying that there is one God and one faith and no more. Then the vision disappeared. But Valerian now believed and allowed himself to be baptized.

When he returned home, he found Cecilia with an angel holding a crown of lilies and a crown of roses. The angel said the crowns came from paradise, and no one will ever be able to see them unless he is chaste and hates villainy. The angel then grants Valerian a wish. Valerian explains that he has a brother whom he would like baptized into this great truth. But the brother, Tiburce, had objections. He did not want to be hunted for an outlaw as is Pope Urban. But when Cecilia explains that this life is not so important as the next, he asks other questions about the Christian faith which Cecilia carefully explained. Then Tiburce allowed himself to be baptized.

Later, an official named Almachius discovered the Christians, had them arrested and ordered them to sacrifice to the pagan gods. Supported by Cecilia, Valerian and Tiburce refused and were sentenced to death. Another official was so moved by their refusal that he became a Christian and was also executed.

When Cecilia was brought before the judge, he asked her many questions which she answered cleverly and wittily. She insults the pagan gods, and infers that Almachius is rather vain and ignorant. She is sentenced to death by being placed in heated water, but this fails. Then an executioner with a sword appeared and tried three times to cut off her head and did not completely succeed. Cecilia continued to live for three more days, converted more people to the church and finally died after willing her house to be made into a church. Pope Urban buried her body and proclaimed the house to be that of Saint Cecilia.

Commentary

Chaucer has repeated in *The Second Nun's Tale* an almost verbatim translation of an earlier and familiar Latin version. Despite the legend's improbabilities and use of the supernatural, the tale is filled with the noble spirit of high religion. Little is known of the historical Cecilia. Her martyrdom is assigned to the reign of Severus (A.D. 222-235).

THE CANON'S YEOMAN'S TALE: PROLOGUE

Summary

After the tale of Saint Cecilia, two men rode rapidly up to the pilgrims. One was judged to be a Canon by his black dress. The other was the Canon's Yeoman. Both seemed polite and the Host welcomed them and asked if either had a tale he could tell. The Yeoman answered immediately that his master knew lots about mirth and jollity. He then proceeded to tell about the Canon. They lived on the edges of towns and avoid the main roads. When asked why his face is so discolored, the Yeoman explained how he had to work with furnaces and fires, and his color is from his continually blowing. The Yeoman begins to tell the secrets of their trade, and all he knows about alchemy. The Canon attempts to stop him, but the Host will allow no threats. When the Canon sees that the Yeoman is going to tell everything, the Canon slips away in shame.

THE CANON'S YEOMAN'S TALE

Summary

PART I

Part one is actually a type of prologue where the Canon's Yeoman explains about their occupation and attempts at alchemy. He says that he is so deep in debt now that he will never be able to repay it all, and as a result of all his labors he has received this complexion and weak eyes. He explains about the various objects and equipment that they use in the practice of their craft. And everytime an experiment fails, the master tells him to begin again.

PART II

Once a Canon lived in London and practiced alchemy. He once borrowed a mark from a priest who reportedly had plenty of silver, and promised to return the mark in three days. The priest agreed but didn't expect to see his mark again. Therefore, he was very pleased when it was returned in three days. Furthermore, the Canon offered to reveal a couple of his discoveries. He sent for some quicksilver, and by tricks made the priest think that the quicksilver had been turned into real silver. The priest, not noticing the trick, was very pleased. The Canon then pretended to put an ingot of chalk into the fires, but he slipped a real ingot of silver in when the priest looked away. Again, the priest thought the chalk had been turned into silver. For a third time, the Canon filled a hollow stick with silver and plugged it with wax. When he placed it in the fire, the wax melted and silver poured forth. The beguiled priest wanted to buy the secret. The Canon asked for forty pounds and made the priest promise not to reveal the secrets to anyone. The Canon then promptly disappeared.

The remainder of the tale is an attack on the subject of alchemy and a conglomeration of all the ridiculous terms used by alchemists.

Commentary

The basic belief of alchemy involves the idea that certain baser metals lay in the ground for many years and ultimately become purer higher metals. The alchemist maintained that he could accelerate this process, and in a few moments time turn a base metal into a precious metal. This tale is not very popular with modern audiences because the entire concept of alchemy ceased to exist within a short period of time. But the alchemist made himself seem important by creating and using a very special set of terms. Then for the modern reader who does not know these terms and is not interested in learning them, the appeal of the story is limited.

THE MANCIPLE'S TALE: PROLOGUE

Summary

As the party moved on towards Canterbury, the Host noticed the Cook swaying in his saddle. The Cook was drunk and despite the Host's efforts to rouse him, he fell from his horse. The party of pilgrims halted and with great effort, the Cook was restored to his saddle. Then the Host turned to the Manciple and demanded a story.

THE MANCIPLE'S TALE

Summary

In a faraway land there lived a man named Phoebus. He was a great warrior, a skilled musician, very handsome, and kind. Phoebus had a wife whom he loved more than life itself. He bestowed upon her all the kindness and love at his command. But there was another side to Phoebus' character. He was extremely jealous.

Phoebus also kept in his house a marvelous, white-feathered crow which could repeat the words of anything he heard. Now it happened that Phoebus was called out of town. While he was gone, his wife's secret lover came to the home and made passionate love to her.

When Phoebus returned, the crow told him the scandalous sight he had seen. In a rage, Phoebus killed his wife. As his rage cooled, the sight of his wife's dead body brought on great remorse. In anger he turned to the crow and pulled all of its white feathers out and replaced them with black ones. And before throwing him out, he removed the crow's ability to sing and speak. The Manciple ends his tale by admonishing all people to restrain their tongues.

Commentary

The tale of the Manciple was short and simple. Its moral is clear: repeating scandal is a dangerous business. Chaucer also adds his own reflections on the futility of trying to restrain a wife. The author has simply retold here the long familiar tale of Apollo and Coronis in Ovid's *Metamorphoses.*

THE PARSON'S TALE: PROLOGUE

Summary

It was dusk and the pilgrims neared a small village. The Host turned to the last of the group, the Parson, and bid him tell his story and to be quick about it since it would soon be dark. The Parson said he was no rhymester, nor would he have a story that would amuse and entertain. Rather, he said, he had a sermon designed for those who wished to make the final mortal pilgrimage to the Heavenly Jerusalem.

THE PARSON'S TALE

Summary

God desires no man to perish, the Parson said, and there are many spiritual ways to the celestial city. One noble way is *Penitence,* the lamenting for sin, and the will to sin no more. The root of the tree of *Penitence* is *contrition;* the branches and the leaves are *confession;* the fruit, is *satisfaction;* the seed, is *grace;* and the heat in that seed is the *Love of God.*

Contrition, the Parson continued, is the heart's sorrow for sin. There are seven deadly sins, the first of which is *pride*. *Pride* takes many forms: arrogance, impudence, boasting, hypocrisy, and joy at having done someone harm. The remedy for *pride* is *humility*.

Envy is sorrow at the prosperity of others and joy in their hurt. The remedy for *envy* is to love God, your neighbor, your enemy.

Anger is the wicked will to vengeance. The remedy for *anger* is *patience*.

Sloth does all tasks with vexation, slackly, and without joy. The remedy is *fortitude*.

Avarice is the lecherous desire for earthy things. The remedy is *mercy*.

Gluttony is an immeasureable appetite for food and drink. The remedy is *abstinence, temperance,* and *sobriety*.

Lechery is theft. The remedy is *chastity* and *continence*.

Confession must be freely willed and made in good faith. It must be considered, and frequent.

Satisfaction consists in alms-giving, penance, fastings, and bodily pains. Its fruit is endless bliss in Heaven.

Commentary

It is rather obvious from the tales told by the pilgrims, and particularly by the eleven connected with the ecclesiastical organization, that the church of Chaucer's time had fallen upon evil days. It is fitting, therefore, that the tales should end on the high moral tone of the Parson's sermon. The original sermon, however, is a dreary and tiresome tract on the seven deadly sins that would have driven the ordinary parishioner from a church.

Scholars originally believed that *The Parson's Tale* was written by Chaucer. However, later research revealed that it was written from the work of two thirteenth-century Dominican friars. Indeed, so inartistic is Chaucer's writing here that some scholars believe that it was not Chaucer's work at all.

CHAUCER'S RETRACTIONS

The Maker of this Book here takes his Leave

Chaucer concluded his *Canterbury Tales* with a series of retractions. And if there be anything that displeases them, I beg them also to impute it to the fault of my want of ability, and not to my will, who would very gladly have said better if I had had the power. For our Books say 'all that is written is written for our doctrine'; and that is my intention. Wherefore I beseech you meekly for the mercy of God to pray for me, that Christ have mercy on me and forgive me for my sins: and especially for my translations and indictings of worldly vanities, which I revoke in my retractions: as are the book of *Troilus;* also the book of *Fame;* the book of *The Nineteen Ladies;* the book of *The Duchess;* the book of *St. Valentine's Day of the Parliament of Fowls; The Tales of Canterbury,*...and many another book, if they were in my memory; and many a song and many a lecherous lay; that Christ in his great mercy forgive me the sin.

Commentary

It is not clear why Chaucer wrote his retractions. Many wish that he had not. Perhaps the reason is that much of the *Canterbury Tales* was written at the zenith of his power and, in his latter days of sadness, he was seized by a poet's conscience. Scholars have puzzled over the retractions and conclude that perhaps we should not pry further into Chaucer's intentions here.

THE PRINCIPAL CHARACTERS

The principal characters of *The Canterbury Tales* are, of course, the twenty-nine members of the party of pilgrims who journeyed from London to the shrine of St. Thomas á Becket in Canterbury. While some of the tales told during the four-day journey certainly offer glimpses of Chaucer's life and times, the story tellers give an admirable view of fourteenth-century England as seen through the eyes of Chaucer.

A somewhat detailed description of each of the pilgrims is given in the Prologue (see its synopsis), but a complete listing will be repeated here.

Chaucer

The author (and our observer during the pilgrimage), who finally identifies himself.

The Knight

A distinguished soldier, gentleman, and idealist.

The Squire

The Knight's son, also a soldier of great valor, and a handsome young man filled with fire and enthusiasm.

The Yeoman

The servant of the Knight and the Squire, and also an expert bowsman.

The Nun

A graceful and mannerly Prioress who was "all sentiment and tender heart."

The Second Nun

Chaplain to the Prioress.

The Monk

An affluent priest who combined godliness and worldliness into a profitable and comfortable living.

The Friar

He was a Limiter which restricted his alms-begging to a certain district.

The Merchant

His forking beard and handsome dress, and his austere speech led all to believe him successful – which he was not.

The Oxford Cleric

Making a decent living was much less important to him than his study of books.

The Sergeant at the Law

An able lawyer who commanded good fees.

The Franklin

A land-owning Free Man, an epicure with adequate means to enjoy it.

The Haberdasher, Dyer, Carpenter, Weaver, and Carpet-maker

All guildsmen, impressively dressed, and obviously proud of their callings.

The Cook

He was the servant to the guildsmen and capable of making the finest dishes.

The Skipper

A good seaman, but a ruthless one.

The Doctor

Ably attended upon the sick, but not reluctant about charging a good fee.

The Woman of Bath
An excellent weaver, and a skilled wife who outlived her five husbands.

The Parson
A poor but honest cleric.

The Plowman
Honest workmen, faithful Christians, and unseemly charitable.

The Miller
A "great stout fellow" famous for his store of off-color stories but not noted for his honesty.

The Manciple
A steward for a college, noted as a shrewd buyer and running a debt-free school.

The Reeve
The successful manager of an estate, admired by his employers but feared by his employees.

The Summoner
His job—to summon sinners before the church court—condoned sin for a handsome bribe.

The Pardoner
His position (to offer indulgences or pardons of the Pope to sinners) were most often sold at handsome prices.

CRITICAL ANALYSIS

Geoffrey Chaucer is generally considered the Father of English poetry, and thus, one of the truly great men in our literature.

John Dyrden called him "the father of English poetry" and regarded him thusly:

> [with the] same degree of veneration as the Grecians held Homer or the Romans held Virgil. He is a perpetual fountain of good sense, learned in all the sciences, and therefore speaks properly on all subjects: as he knew what to say, so he knows also to leave off, a habit which is practiced by few writers....

Coleridge looked at the poet this way:

> I take unceasing delight in Chaucer. His cheerfulness is especially delicious to me in my old age. How exquisitely tender he is, and yet how perfectly free from the least touch of sickly melancholy or morbid drooping. The sympathy of the poet with the subjects of his poetry is particularly remarkable in Shakespeare and Chaucer; but what Shakespeare effects by a strong act of imagination and mental changing, Chaucer does without any effort, merely by the inborn kindly joyousness of his nature. How well we seem to know Chaucer! How absolutely nothing do we know of Shakespeare!

Yet it is a fact that somehow we have not realized the greatness of Chaucer, nor his genius. Perhaps a reason for this neglect lies in the difficulty and antiquity of his language. Yet an increasing number of modernized versions of his *Canterbury Tales* appear, and many of them preserve the essence of Chaucer's great art. There are, of course, many purists who believe there is no substitute for the original.

The student will note that in the commentary following each of the tales the origins of Chaucer's writings are attributed to other authors. It is indeed a fact that Chaucer owed a great debt to authors who went before him. Since virtually all of the tales are borrowed, what, one might ask, is properly Chaucer's own genius? The answer might be that nothing is left to Chaucer. Or the question might be answered that all is left to Chaucer!

Authors are seldom original. It is not the function of writers such as Chaucer to turn up something new under the sun. Rather, it is Chaucer's task to reassemble his material, give it fresh meaning, reveal new truths, commend new insights to his reader. In this sense, then, Chaucer was a remarkably original man.

Since Chaucer did give new meanings to twice-told tales, what was his purpose? Was he a great moral crusader? Do the *Canterbury Tales* offer new philosophic vistas?

Chaucer was a learned man. It is known that he read widely in French, Latin, and Italian. Yet it is rather remarkable that he did not write in the highly moralistic sense of the literary models he studied. He did not write in an abstract manner. He did not urge upon his readers new moralistic directions. *The Canterbury Tales* does not waft the reader to an exotic Oriental kingdom. He chose, instead, to set his story in the commonest sight of his time—a pilgrimmage to Canterbury. If Chaucer wished to create an illusion it was not of an imaginary world but of a real one. The tales of some of the pilgrims themselves *are* artificial forms but his real-life setting simply heightens the tales of some of the pilgrims.

When one considers the great scope of the *Tales,* perhaps the most consistent aspect of Chaucer's writing is its tremendous variety. Consider for a moment the brutally frank realism of *The Wife of Bath's Tale,* or the romance of *The Knight's Tale,* or the idealism of *The Prioress' Tale,* or the bawdiness of the Miller's Tale. But beyond the variety of Chaucer's tales, one is constantly reminded of Chaucer's humor. At one moment it is sly, at another moment, pure slapstick. But through it all, there is freshness and kindliness.

Chaucer, however, is capable of pathos and irony which sometimes blend as tragedy, sometimes as melodrama. As one reads Chaucer, the inescapable conclusion comes again and again that the great poet was forever concerned with the essential irony of human existence, with the rather ludicrous mockery arising from joy and ambition dashed unexpectedly by frustration and despair.

Chaucer's style is characterized chiefly by simplicity. Except in those cases where the author uses archaic form to preserve the rhyme effect, his words are commonplaces of ordinary people in ordinary circumstances. His sentences are simple in form and structure and noticeably free of studied balance. Indeed his writing is singularly free of the far-fetched puns and metaphors which characterize Shakespeare. To read Chaucer, then, is much like listening to a cultured and accomplished story teller. The tales tell themselves without effort or delay.

The device of a springtime pilgrimage, the diverse group of persons making up the company, and the adventures one can reasonably expect on such a journey, provided Chaucer with a wide range of characters and experiences. The setting does not permit boredom. We are told in the Prologue that each member of the company was to tell two stories. This would have amounted to sixty tales, plus the author's account of the stay in Canterbury. All of which brings us around to another aspect of *The Canterbury Tales.*

What we have today are, in reality, fragments. Chaucer had intended a much more ambitious undertaking which surely would have exceeded in length Boccaccio's famous *Decameron.* Chaucer's scheme never materialized and what survives is one fourth of his original proposal. There is not even one tale from each pilgrim, nor are there connecting links (between many of the tales) which would have given greater unity to Chaucer's work. Chaucer did not leave for posterity the order in which the tales were to be told beyond *The Prologue* and *The Knight's Tale,* at the beginning, and *The Parson's Tale* at the close.

Of all of the tales in this work, surely the greatest of them is *The Prologue.* Here Chaucer gives an accounting of human life as he viewed it in medieval England. Every phase of life in England is represented, except royalty. This, it may be added, is the truly original work of Chaucer, for nothing like it prior to Chaucer's time has ever been discovered.

The gay, bouyant, good-natured *Prologue,* however, contrasts sharply with the ending of the tales. In *The Prologue* and throughout the telling of the tales, the members of the company are repeatedly urged by the Host to tell humorous and interesting tales. But *The Parson's Tale,* and more strikingly, Chaucer's Retractions, offer the totally new note of disavowing pleasure, story-telling, and sensuousness. "Let us repent," Chaucer cries, "and beg the mercy of God."

Chaucer must have been a good churchman or he would have lost his favors from the Court. His writings, it must be remembered, were aimed at satirizing or exposing only individuals. Matters of doctrine were never attacked by Chaucer. And so Chaucer, who had composed one of the great classics of English literature in a largely playful mood, embracing and enjoying all the foibles of human nature, closes his great work with a grim supplication for heavenly forbearance.

QUESTIONS FOR EXAMINATION AND REVIEW

Note: The section or sections indicated in parenthesis following each question contain information which will help you answer the question.

1. How did Geoffrey Chaucer differ from other writers of his time in the English Middle Ages? (See Sketch of Chaucer's Life and Times.)

2. What in your opinion was the underlying motive for the tale told by the Wife of Bath? (See Synopsis.)

3. If you were asked to single out the most persistent aspect of Chaucer's style in the *Canterbury Tales,* what in your opinion would it be? Why? (See Critical Analysis.) What is the major strength of his style?

4. Some critics have held that Chaucer had embraced the early spirit of Wycliffe's Reformation and therefore was against the established Roman Church. Do you agree? (See Critical Analysis, and Synopsis of the Author's Retractions.)

5. Many believe that the most important single part of *The Canterbury Tales* is *The Prologue*. What is the basis for this judgment? (See Critical Analysis.)

6. When is it assumed that Chaucer began writing his *Canterbury Tales* and when did he stop work on them? (See Sketch of the Author's Life and Times.)

7. How many pilgrims started the journey to Canterbury? How was it determined who should tell stories while the party was enroute? (See Synopsis of *Prologue*.)

8. What is the importance of *The Canterbury Tales* to the social historian? (See Critical Analysis.)

9. Which character occupies the central position among the pilgrims as they near their destination? (See Synopsis, *The Parson's Tale*.)

10. Define and illustrate at least five literary forms used by Chaucer in the *Tales*. (See Middle English Literary Genres.)

11. What is the function of the final chapter of the Book? (See Critical Analysis and Synopsis.)

12. How complete is Chaucer's description of England in the Fourteenth Century? (See Sketch of Author's Life and Times, and the Critical Analysis.)

13. Who are the chief characters in the Pilgrimage? Identify and briefly characterize each. (See Synopsis of the *Prologue*, and the Characters.)

14. If you were asked to select the best tale told during the journey to Canterbury which would it be? Why?

15. What reason is advanced for the fact that Chaucer's *Canterbury Tales* has not been as widely read as, for example, some of Shakespeare's plays? (See Critical Analysis.)

16. What position has Chaucer been assigned in the history of English literature? (See Introduction.)

17. What role does realism play in Chaucer's writings? (See Critical Analysis.)

18. Critics claim that precious little of Chaucer's writings were original; that is, that he borrowed from others for his tales. Discuss. (See Critical Analysis.)

19. Describe briefly life in England during Chaucer's time. (See Sketch of Author's Life and Times.)

20. Discuss Chaucer as a humorist or a satirist. Is he obvious or subtle? Is he kind or critical? Is he coarse? Is he merry? (Develop your own ideas here.)

21. Select your favorite person on the journey to Canterbury. Describe him or her in detail. Select and describe your favorite character from one of the tales. (Develop your own ideas here.)

22. Which of the Tales interested you the most? Which Tale seemed the most artistically conceived of the whole group? (Again develop your own ideas.)

FOR FURTHER READING: A SELECT BIBLIOGRAPHY

Bowden, Muriel, *A Commentary on the General Prologue to The Canterbury Tales,* New York: Macmillan Co., 1948.

Chute, Marchette G., *Geoffrey Chaucer of England,* New York: Dutton, 1946.

Coghill, Nevill, *The Canterbury Tales,* Baltimore: Penguin Books, 1952.

Coghill, Nevill, *The Poet Chaucer,* Oxford: Oxford University Press, 1949.

French, Robert D., *A Chaucer Handbook,* New York: Appleton-Century-Crofts, 1947.

Hitchins, H. L., *The Canterbury Tales,* London: John Murray, 1947.

Kennedy's *Concordance of Chaucer.*

Kluge, Freidrich, *The Language and Meter of Chaucer,* New York: Macmillan Co., 1915.

Kittredge, G. L., *Chaucer and His Poetry,* Cambridge: Harvard University Press, 1901.

Lloyd, J. L., *A Chaucer Selection,* London: George C. Harrop, 1952.

Lowes, John Livingston, *Geoffrey Chaucer and the Development of His Genius,* Boston: Houghton-Mifflin Co., 1934.

Lumiensky, M. R., *The Canterbury Tales,* London: John Murray Ltd, 1948.

Malone, Kemp, *Chapters on Chaucer,* Baltimore: Johns Hopkins University Press, 1951.

Manly, J. M., *Canterbury Tales,* New York: Holt, 1930.

Moody, William Vaughn, and Lovett, Robert Morss, *A History of English Literature,* New, York: Charles Scribner's Sons, 1946.

Morrison, Theodore, *The Portable Chaucer,* New York: The Viking Press, 1949.

Owens, Charles A. Jr., *Discussions of the Canterbury Tales,* Boston: D. C. Heath, 1961.

Spurgeon, C. F. E., *Five Hundred Years of Chaucer Criticism and Allusion, 1357-1900.* Chaucer Society, 7 parts, 1914-1924; also 3 volumes, Cambridge, 1925; Supplement, London, 1920.

Vickers, K. H., *England in the Later Middle Ages,* New York: Putnam, 1919.

Divine Comedy - I. Inferno

THE DIVINE COMEDY: THE INFERNO

NOTES

including

- *Life and Background*
- *Dante's World*
- *The Figure of Virgil*
- *Structure of the* Comedy
- *Interpretation*
- *General Synopsis*
- *Summaries and Commentaries*
- *List of Characters*
- *Review Questions and Essay Topics*
- *Selected Bibliography*

by
Luisa Vergani, Ph.D.
University of San Diego
College for Women

NEW EDITION

INCORPORATED
LINCOLN, NEBRASKA 68501

Editor

Gary Carey, M.A.
University of Colorado

Consulting Editor

James L. Roberts, Ph.D.
Department of English
University of Nebraska

ISBN 0-8220-0391-0

Printed in U.S.A.

1992 Printing

Cliffs Notes, Inc. Lincoln, Nebraska

CONTENTS

The Inferno Notes

LIFE AND BACKGROUND

Dante Alighieri was born in Florence in May, 1265, of an old family, of noble origin but no longer wealthy. His education was probably typical of any youth of his time and station: he studied the *trivium* and *quadrivium,* probably spent a year, or part of a year, at the University of Bologna, and came under the influence of some of the learned men of his day. Most notable of these was Ser Brunetto Latini, whose influence Dante records in his poem *(Inferno* 15).

In accordance with custom, Dante was betrothed in his youth to Gemma Donati, daughter of Manetto Donati. These betrothals and marriages were matters of family alliance, and Gemma's dowry was fixed as early as 1277, when Dante was twelve years old. There were at least three children: sons Pietro and Jacopo, and a daughter Antonia, who later entered a convent at Ravenna and took the name of Sister Beatrice. A third son, Giovanni, is sometimes mentioned.

There can be no doubt that the great love of Dante's life, and the greatest single influence on his work, was his beloved Beatrice. He first met her when he was nine years old and she was eight. The meeting took place in her father's home, probably at a May Day festival. Dante has described this meeting in his *Vita Nuova.* He tells of seeing the child Beatrice, wearing a crimson gown and looking like an angel. From that day on, his life and work was dedicated to her. He mentions no other meeting with her until nine years later, when he saw her on the street, dressed in white, accompanied by two other girls. She greeted him sweetly by name, and he was in raptures. A short time later, having heard gossip linking his name with another young woman, she passed him without speaking, and Dante mourned for days, determining to mend his ways.

If all this seems slightly preposterous, it is necessary to remember two things: that the young women of marriageable age were so strictly chaperoned that it was virtually impossible to have even a speaking acquaintance with them and that Dante's love for Beatrice was in the strictest tradition of courtly love, wherein the lover addressed his beloved as being completely out of his reach, and which viewed marriage between the lovers as impossible, in fact undesirable.

To what extent this was, at first, a true and lasting love cannot be determined. There is little doubt that Dante enjoyed the sweet misery of his situation and the sympathy of other ladies for his plight. After the death of Beatrice, and particularly after his exile, he put away his adolescent fancies, and Beatrice became a true inspiration.

Beatrice was married in about 1287 to Simone de' Bardi, a wealthy banker of Florence, a marriage of alliance of the two houses and one completely immaterial to Dante and his work.

Dante wrote many poems in praise of his lady during her lifetime, and when she died in 1290, at the age of twenty-five, he was inconsolable. He had had a dream of her death, and in her honor collected the poems he had written about her, which are included in the *Vita Nuova*. The later *Comedy* was also inspired by her memory.

Dante's public life began in 1289, when he fought against Arezzo at Campaldino. In 1295 he was one of the council for the election of priors of Florence, and in May, 1300, went as ambassador to San Gemignano to invite that commune to an assembly of the Guelph cities of Tuscany. From June 15 to August of the same year, he was one of the priors of Florence, and it was during that year that his best friend, Guido Cavalcanti *(Inferno,* Canto 22), caused a street riot on May Day. Guido was exiled to Sarzana by the officers of the city, one of whom was Dante. Sarzana proved so unhealthful that Guido petitioned to return to Florence, and was allowed to do so. He died of malaria, contracted in Sarzana, in August, 1300.

Dante was vigorously opposed to the interference of the pope in secular affairs, and was induced to take a stand with the Whites when the Blacks favored the intrigues of the pope. Charles of Valois was coming to Florence, ostensibly as a peacemaker between the two factions but in reality as a partisan of the Blacks and supporter of the pope. In October, 1301, Dante and two other men were chosen as ambassadors on a mission to Rome, rightly suspecting the motives of Charles as peacemaker. After they had left Florence, the Blacks easily took over control of the city with the help of Charles, and Dante was exiled from his native city, never to return.

The terms of exile were harsh: Dante was charged with graft, with intrigue against the peace of the city, and with hostility against the pope, among other things. The list of charges is so long that it is reminiscent of those brought against the political enemies of any party in power today. In addition, a heavy fine was imposed, and Dante was forbidden to hold public office in Florence for the rest of his life.

Dante did not appear to answer the charges—it probably would not have been safe to do so—and a heavier penalty was imposed: in addition to confiscation of his property, he was sentenced to be burnt alive if caught. Also, his sons, when they reached their legal majority at age fourteen, were compelled to join him in exile.

Thus began Dante's wanderings. At first he joined in the political intrigues of his fellow exiles, but, disgusted by what he considered their wickedness and stupidity, he formed a party by himself. It is not known exactly where he spent the years of his exile, though part of the time he was with the Malaspini, and he also spent time at the court of Can Grande della Scala in Verona, with whom he remained on good terms for the rest of his life.

Once during the years of his banishment his hopes for peace in Italy, and his own return to Florence, were revived. This was in the reign of Henry VII of Luxemburg, who announced his intention of coming to Italy to be crowned. Dante addressed a letter to his fellow citizens urging them to welcome Henry as emperor. When Henry was met by strong opposition, Dante in great bitterness sent a letter to him, urging him to put down the rebellion quickly; he also addressed a letter in similar vein to Florence, using abusive terms which could not be forgiven. When Henry's expedition failed, and the hopes of empire died with him, Dante was not included in the amnesty granted certain exiles. Later, amnesty was extended to him on the condition that he admit his guilt and ask forgiveness publicly, which the poet refused to do. His sentence of death was renewed.

Dante's last years were spent in Ravenna, under the protection of Guido Novello da Polenta. They seem to have been years of relative contentment in compatible company—but Ravenna was not Florence. One final mission was entrusted to Dante: he was sent to Venice in the summer of 1321 by his patron in an unsuccessful attempt to avert a war between Ravenna and Venice. On his return trip, he fell ill, possibly of malaria. He reached Ravenna and died there on the night of September 13, 1321.

He was buried with the honors due him. Several times during the following centuries, the city of Florence sought to have his body interred with honor in the place of his birth, but even the intercession of popes could not bring this about. His opinion of the citizens of his city was clearly stated in the full title of his great work: *The Comedy of Dante Alighieri, Florentine by Citizenship, Not by Morals.*

Dante still lies in the monastery of the Franciscan friars in Ravenna.

DANTE'S WORLD

Dante's world was threefold: the world of politics, the world of theology, and the world of learning. His *Comedy* encompasses and builds upon all of these, and so interdependent were they that it would be impossible to say that any one was the most important.

Throughout the Middle Ages, politics was dominated by the struggle between the two greatest powers of that age: the papacy and the empire. Each believed itself to be of divine origin and to be indispensable to the welfare of mankind. The cause of this struggle was the papal claim to temporal power, supported and justified by the spurious "Donation of Constantine." This document, which was a forgery of the eighth century, maintained that Emperor Constantine, before leaving for Byzantium, had transferred to the Bishop of Rome, Pope Sylvester I, political dominion over Italy and the western empire.

Dante lived in an era of virtually autonomous communes, ruled by either an autocratic hereditary count or a council elected from an aristocratic—and exclusive—few. The political situation was never stable, and the vendettas went on forever, family against family, party against party, city against city.

The strife began in the tenth century with Otto I, the emperor who laid the foundation for the power which was to transform Germany into the mightiest state in Europe and who dreamed of restoring the Holy Roman Empire. At the beginning of the eleventh century, the situation worsened, with Henry IV humiliated at Canossa by an aggressive opponent, autocratic Pope Gregory VII (Hildebrand).

In the first part of the thirteenth century, the growing conflict was headed by two outstanding antagonists: Innocent III, the most powerful of all the popes, and the brilliant Frederick II, King of Germany, Emperor of Rome, and King of Naples and Sicily, the most gifted of all the monarchs of the Middle Ages. The enmity of the pope, who was firmly resolved to free Italy from German authority, shook the stability of the empire, which was already undermined by the insubordination of the princes in Germany and the rebellion of some of the city-states of northern Italy.

When Frederick died in 1250, he left a very unstable situation to be handled by his successors, especially in Italy. There, in 1266, his illegitimate son Manfred was defeated and killed in the battle fought at Benevento against Charles of Anjou, who had been summoned to Italy by the pope. Two years later, this same Charles defeated Corradino, Frederick's grandson, at Tagliacozzo, and put him to death. Thus the line of the descendants of the great emperor was extinguished and Italy was lost to the empire.

In reading Dante, indeed throughout medieval history, one hears much about two major political factions, the Guelphs and the Ghibellines. In Italy the party lines were originally drawn over the dispute between the papacy and the emperor for temporal authority. The Ghibellines, representing the feudal aristocracy, wished to retain the power of the emperor in Italy as well as in Germany. The Guelphs were mainly supported by the rising middle-class merchant society, who hoped to rid Italy of foreign influence and maintain the control of governments in their independent communes. They espoused the cause of the papacy in opposition to the emperor.

The rivalry between the two parties not only set one city against another but also divided the same city and the same family into factions. In time the original alliances and allegiances became confused in strange ways. For example, Dante, who was a Guelph, was a passionate supporter of imperial authority all his life.

In Florence the Guelphs and Ghibellines succeeded each other, alternately ruling the city. During the rein of Frederick II, the Ghibellines, supported by the emperor, gained the upper hand and drove the Guelphs out of the city. But at the death of Frederick II, in 1250, the Guelphs were recalled to Florence for a temporary reconciliation and later gained control of the city.

The Ghibellines again returned to power in 1260, and ruled the city until 1266, but the next year the Guelphs, aided by French forces, gained supremacy in the city, and the Ghibellines left Florence, never to return.

Dante was an ardent White Guelph, putting his hopes for Italy's future in the restoration of the empire, and to the end of his days was politically active, though ultimately he was forced by the violence of his views to form a party "by himself," and, as a White, was actually allied to the Ghibellines.

Not even the supremacy of the Guelphs, however, endowed Florence with a peaceful and stable government, for in 1300 the Guelph party split into two factions: the Whites and the Blacks, led respectively by the families of the Cerchi and the Donati. The basis of this split was the usual blood-feud between two families. In nearby Pistoia, a family quarrel existed between two branches of the Cancelliere family. The first wife of the original Cancelliere was named Bianca, and her descendants called themselves Whites in her honor. The name of the second wife is not known, but her descendants, in opposition to the Whites, called themselves Blacks. The quarrel erupted into open violence after a murder committed by one Foccaccia (mentioned by Dante in Canto 32 of the *Inferno*).

The Guelphs of Florence, in the interests of maintaining the precarious peace of the district, intervened in the hostilities, and in so doing furthered the jealous rivalry of the Cerchi and the Donati families, who naturally took opposite sides. The city was torn by strife; personal ambitions, feuds, and the arrogance of individuals and families further agitated the situation.

At this point, the Blacks secretly enlisted the aid of Pope Boniface VIII, who intervened in the affairs of the city, largely in his own interest. The pope considered the throne of the empire still vacant, since Albert I had not received his crown in Rome. In his assumed capacity as vicar of the emperor, Boniface plotted to extend the rule of the church over the territory of Tuscany. To accomplish this, he first obtained the favor of the Blacks, then dispatched Charles of Valois, brother of the King of France, to Florence, ostensibly as a peacemaker, but actually as a supporter of the Blacks. In 1302, with the help of Charles of Valois, the Blacks gained control of the city. In the list of some six hundred Whites banished from Florence was the name of the citizen Dante Alighieri.

While the rest of Italy, like Florence, was troubled by rivalries between parties, or by wars of city against city, in Germany the emperor's throne was vacant, first because of an interregnum, then because of a conflict between two rival claimants. The emperor's position was still regarded as vacant by the Italians when the two emperors who followed, Rudolph of Hapsburg and Albert I, failed to come to Italy to be crowned and paid no attention to Italian affairs. Therefore when the news came that Henry of Luxemburg, who succeeded Albert I in 1308, was coming to Italy to oppose King Robert of Sicily, many Italians, for whom Dante was the most eloquent and fervent spokesman, welcomed the prospect with feverish enthusiasm. They saw in the figure of Henry the end of all the woes which had wracked the peninsula.

Henry was crowned at Milan early in 1311. Very soon after, he faced the armed hostility of the opposing party, which had Florence as its leader. Henry, nevertheless, was able to reach Rome and be crowned there in 1312. The coronation took place in the church of St. John Lateran rather than in St. Peter's because the latter was being held by the forces of King Robert of Sicily. The emperor was still fighting to unite the empire when he died in the summer of 1313, succumbing to a fever with suspicious suddenness. The death of Henry put an end forever to the expectations of Dante and all other Italians who had longed for the restoration of the imperial power in Italy.

Dante's theological ideas were strictly orthodox, that is, those of medieval Catholicism. He accepted church dogma without reservation. His best authorities for insight into the more complex problems confronting the medieval thinkers were Augustine, Albertus Magnus, and Thomas Aquinas. He followed the Pauline doctrine of predestination and grace as presented by Augustine, but he managed to bring this into a kind of conformity with free will, to which he firmly adhered. Man has inherited sin and death through Adam's fall, but also hope of salvation through Christ's redemption. God in his love created humans with the power of perceiving good and evil and the opportunity of choosing. On the basis of their choice depended their eternal bliss or damnation. Those who set their will against the divine law were sentenced to Inferno and everlasting torment. Those who sinned but confessed and repented were given their reward in heaven after a period of purifying atonement in Purgatory. Thus repentance, the acceptance of divine law, was the crux of judgment in the afterlife.

Among the familiar tenets of medieval theology, we recognize such concepts as the "seven deadly sins" in Purgatory and the corresponding seven virtues in Paradise. The doctrine that only those persons who had been baptized as worshipers of Christ were to be admitted to Paradise is expressed in the treatment of the souls in Limbo (*Inferno* 4). Of the many more complex theological concepts expounded through the *Commedia,* explanations will be offered in the textual commentaries.

In castigating the individual popes (and particularly his bitter enemy, Boniface VIII), he was in no way showing disrespect for the *office* of the papacy, for which he held the greatest reverence. He was, in fact, following the long tradition of critics, many of them in high places in the church, who had not hesitated to recall popes to the duties and responsibilities of the chair of Peter. Dante held to the ideal of the papacy and the empire as the dual guardians of the welfare of man, spiritual and secular, each deriving its separate powers directly from God.

Readers cannot fail to recognize Dante's erudition. He appears to have taken all learning for his province, or what passed for learning then. The fact that much of the scientific teaching was hopelessly in error is not Dante's responsibility. The fact that he displayed extraordinary curiosity and avid interest in all branches of scientific learning (geography, geology, astronomy, astrology, natural history, and optics) reveals something important about the poet's mind.

Among the concepts that influenced the plan of the *Commedia* was the belief that only the northern hemisphere of the earth was inhabited, that the southern hemisphere was covered with water except for the mount of Purgatory. The scheme of the heavens was dictated by the Ptolemaic, or geocentric, system of astronomy, upon which Dante based the entire plan of *Paradiso*.

THE FIGURE OF VIRGIL

In the Middle Ages, Virgil had come to be regarded as a sage and necromancer. Virgil's poems were used in the type of divination called *sortes,* in which the book is opened at random and a verse selected in the same manner, as an answer to a problem or question. The Bible has been, and still is, used in the same manner.

Virgil's *Aeneid* offered the pattern for the structure of Dante's Hell, but this alone is not the reason why Virgil was chosen as the guide through Hell. Dante himself salutes Virgil as his master and the inspiration for his poetic style; further, Virgil is revered by Dante as the poet of the Roman Empire, since his *Aeneid* tells the story of the empire's founding. Finally, in his fourth eclogue, Virgil writes symbolically of the coming of a Wonder Child who will bring the Golden Age to the world, and in the Middle Ages this was interpreted as being prophetic of the coming of Christ. Thus, in the figure of Virgil, Dante found symbolically represented the two institutions, church and empire, destined by God to save mankind.

STRUCTURE OF THE "COMEDY"

Dante lived in a world that believed in mystical correspondences, in which numbers—like stars, stones, and even the events of history—had a mystical significance. In planning the structure of the *Divine Comedy,* therefore, Dante had in mind a series of symbolic numbers: three, a symbol of the Holy Trinity; nine, three times three; thirty-three, a multiple of three; seven, the days of creation; ten, considered during the Middle Ages a symbol of perfection; and one hundred, the multiple of ten.

The plan was carried out with consummate precision. We find three *cantiche,* each formed by thirty-three cantos, totaling ninety-nine. The introductory first canto of the *Inferno* makes one hundred cantos in all. The entire poem is written in the difficult *terza rima,* a verse form of three-line stanzas, or tercets. The first and third lines rhyme, and the second line rhymes with the beginning line of the next stanza – again, three, and three.

Hell is divided into nine circles (in three divisions), the vestibule making the tenth; Purgatory is separated into nine levels, the terrestrial paradise making ten; and Paradise is formed by nine heavens, plus the Empyrean. The celestial hierarchies are nine and are divided into triads. The sinners in Hell are arranged according to three capital vices: incontinence, violence, and fraud. The distribution of the penitents in Purgatory is based on the threefold nature of their rational love. The partition of the blessed in Paradise is made according to the secular, active, or contemplative nature of their love for God. The very fact that each *cantica* ends with the word "stars" helps to demonstrate the studied plan of the whole work.

Inferno is a huge, funnel-shaped pit located with its center beneath Jerusalem, its regions arranged in a series of circular stairsteps, or terraces, diminishing in circumference as they descend. Each of the nine regions is designated for a particular sin, and the order of the sins is according to their wickedness, the lightest near the top of the pit and the most heinous at the bottom.

The punishments in Inferno are regulated by the law of retribution; therefore, they correspond to the sins either by analogy or by antithesis. Thus, for example, the carnal sinners, who abandoned themselves to the tempests of passion, are tossed about incessantly by a fierce storm. The violent, who were bloodthirsty and vicious during their lives, are drowned in a river of blood. The sowers of dissension, who promoted social and domestic separations, are wounded and mutilated according to the nature of their crimes.

INTERPRETATION

The *Divine Comedy* has had many interpreters. Some have followed Dante's own thought, as outlined so clearly in his letter to Can Grande; others appear to ignore it.

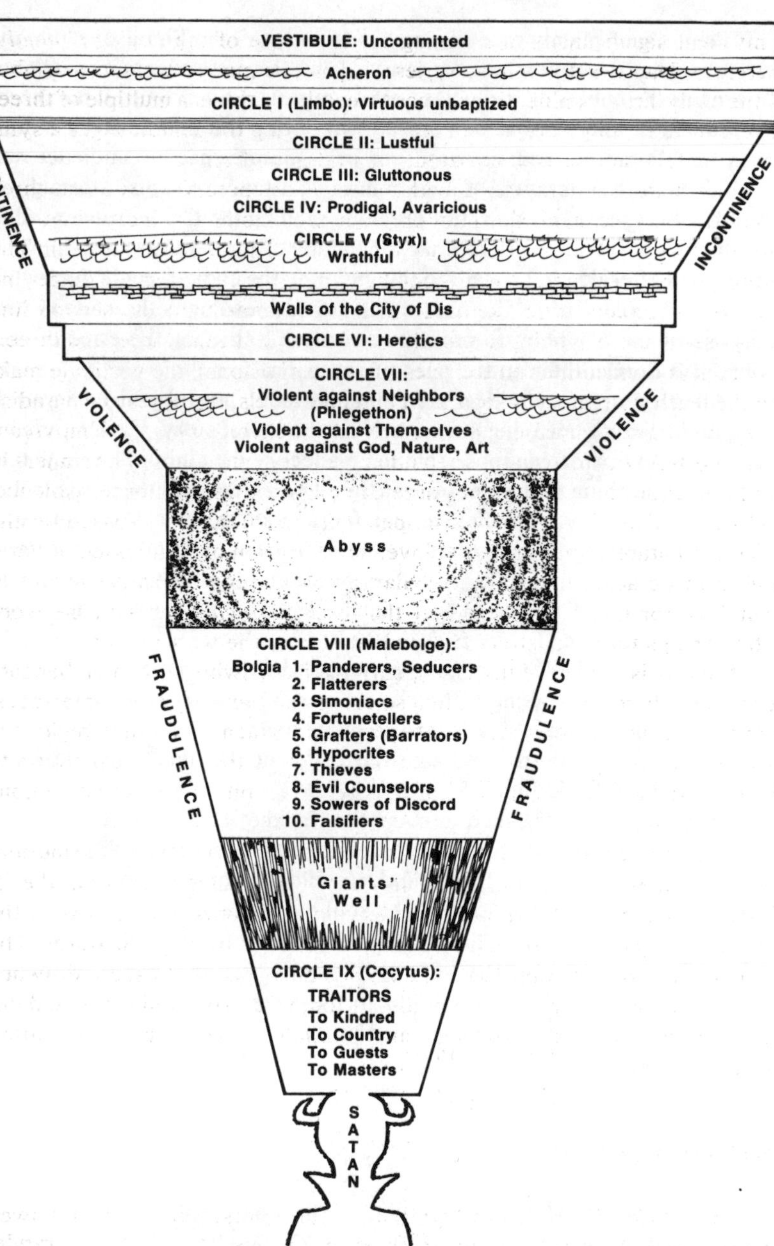

PLAN OF DANTE'S INFERNO

Dante said plainly that the first meaning was the literal one. By this he meant that the cantos tell the story of the state of souls after death, according to the beliefs of medieval Christianity. He did *not* mean, nor intend his readers to infer, that it was a literal story of a trip through Hell, Purgatory, and Paradise; and he was safe in assuming that his audience was familiar with the literature of such journeys, a favorite subject throughout the Middle Ages. (This does not preclude reading the *Comedy* as excellent science fiction.) Hell (or Purgatory, or Paradise) is, therefore, the *condition* of the soul after death, brought to that point by the choices made during life.

Closely allied to its literal and allegorical meaning is the stated moral purpose of the *Comedy:* to point out to those yet living the error of their ways, and to turn them to the path of salvation.

Allegory is, by definition, an extended metaphor, organized in a pattern, and having a meaning separate from the literal story. C. S. Lewis has said "It is an error to suppose that in an allegory the author is 'really' talking about the thing that symbolizes; the very essence of the art is to talk about both." Aristotle believed that for a poet to have a command of metaphor was the mark of genius because it indicated a gift for seeing resemblances. This implies the gift of imagination, the ability to set down not only the images of vision, but, particularly in Dante's case, vivid images of noise and odor.

Dante wanted his reader to experience what he experienced, and from the beginning of the poem to the end he grows in power and mastery. His language is deceptively simple and so is his method. He writes in the vernacular, using all its force and directness; it is not the high poetic language of tragedy, as he said himself.

The imagery is designed to make the world of Dante's Hell intelligible to the reader. His world is the world of the thirteenth-century church, but his Hell is the creation of his mind, an allegory of redemption in which Dante seeks to show the state of the soul after death.

The poem is a demanding one. The reader must enter Dante's world without prejudice, and perhaps T. S. Eliot was right in recommending that the *Comedy* should be read straight through the first time, without giving too much attention to the background of the times, and without examining the more complex symbols.

GENERAL SYNOPSIS

On the night before Good Friday in the year 1300, Dante, at the age of thirty-five, finds himself astray in a dark wood. The morning sun reveals a beautiful mountain toward which he makes his way, but his ascent is checked by three beasts: a leopard, a lion, and a she-wolf. Dante, therefore, is forced to return to the forest, where he is met by the shadow of Virgil, who promises to rescue him and take him on a journey through Hell, Purgatory, and Paradise (Canto 1). In undertaking the journey, Dante is troubled by fear; however, this is overcome when Virgil explains that he has been sent to his aid by Beatrice, who descended into Limbo to ask for his help. Moreover, Beatrice was sent by the Virgin Mary through her messenger, St. Lucia. Comforted by this, Dante follows Virgil as his guide and master (Canto 2).

After reading the dreadful inscription written on the gate of Hell, the two poets pass into the Vestibule where the uncommitted are tormented and then reach the bank of the river Acheron. Here the lost souls wait their turn to be carried across the river by Charon, an ancient boatman with flaming eyes who agrees only reluctantly to take Dante on his boat (Canto 3). In Limbo, the first circle of Hell, Dante is received by the great poets of the ages, Homer, Horace, Ovid, and Lucan. In the Palace of Wisdom he is also privileged to see the sages of antiquity, whose only punishment is being deprived of the vision of God (Canto 4).

Then Dante and Virgil enter Hell proper, which may be said to begin with the second circle. There the hideous Minos is seated as a judge, and the carnal sinners are tossed about by an incessant storm. The poets meet Paolo and Francesca and listen to their story of love and death (Canto 5). Among the gluttonous, guarded by the monster Cerberus and buried in mud in the third circle, Dante recognizes the Florentine Ciacco and receives from him a gloomy political prophecy. Then, as they talk about the resurrection of the body, Dante and Virgil move to the fourth circle (Canto 6), where Plutus reigns over the nameless mass of the prodigals and the avaricious, condemned to roll heavy stones against one another. This sight gives occasion for a disquisition upon Fortune. When Dante's doubts have been resolved, the two poets reach the fifth circle, the marsh of Styx, where the souls of the wrathful and sullen are condemned (Canto 7). The Florentine Filippo Argenti, one of the wrathful, tries to overturn the boat on which Dante is carried by the demon Phlegyas, but to Dante's satisfaction, Argenti is ferociously attacked by his companions.

Meanwhile Dante and Virgil come under the walls of the City of Dis, the sixth circle, to which, however, the fallen angels deny access (Canto 8). This is obtained only with the help of a heavenly messenger. Inside the City of Dis, the poets see the burning tombs in which the heretics are confined (Canto 9). Dante stops to speak with a great enemy, the Ghibelline Farinata degli Uberti, and also meets Cavalcante dei Cavalcanti, the father of his friend Guido (Canto 10).

When the poets approach the seventh circle, the air becomes so fetid that they have to halt for a while behind a tomb. While waiting to grow accustomed to the stench, they take advantage of the pause to discuss the division of the lower part of Hell (Canto 11). Finally the poets begin to descend through a deep valley and first meet the monstrous Minotaur, then reach a river of boiling blood, the Phlegethon, which forms the first section of the seventh circle. Here are plunged those violent against their neighbors, tyrants, and warmakers like Attila and Alexander the Great, watched over by the centaurs (Canto 12).

After being carried across the river by the centaur Nessus, Dante and Virgil enter the second round of the seventh circle, where the souls of the suicides grow like plants in a dreadful wood ruled by the hideous harpies. One of these plants is the soul of Pier delle Vigne, who narrates his sad story. In the same wood the reckless squanderers are seen by the poets being chased and torn to pieces by hounds (Canto 13).

The third round is formed by a desert of burning sand on which the blasphemers, sodomites, and usurers are exposed to a rain of fire. Among the blasphemers, Dante recognizes Capaneus (Canto 14); among the sodomites he encounters his master Brunetto Latini (Canto 15) and listens to the considerations of some famous men of ancient Florence in regard to the sad state of their city (Canto 16).

Then, after a contemptuous exchange with the usurers, Dante and his guide fly down to Malebolge, the eighth circle, on the back of the huge and repugnant monster, Geryon (Canto 17). Malebolge is the circle where the sinners of simple fraud are condemned. In the first bolgia the poets see the panderers and seducers, beaten with lashes; in the second the flatterers, plunged in a canal of excrement (Canto 18). In the third the simoniacs are sunk upside down in round holes, and from each hole protrudes a pair of feet with the soles ablaze. Dante approaches Pope Nicholas III and speaks to him (Canto 19). Then he reaches the fourth bolgia and, standing on the bridge overlooking it, watches the fortunetellers and the diviners who pace slowly and weep silently with their heads reversed on their bodies, so that they are obliged to walk backward (Canto 20).

Thence Dante and Virgil pass to the bridge overlooking the fifth bolgia, where the grafters are plunged into boiling pitch and tormented by black devils. The poets arrive just in time to see a senator of Lucca thrown into the pitch and torn to pieces by the hooks of the demons. At this point, since the bridge across the sixth bolgia lies broken, they have to seek help from the demons, and from their leader, Malacoda, obtain an escort to the next bridge (Canto 21). Walking along the bank of the canal, Dante and Virgil see the sinners lying in the pitch. One is hooked by the demons and pulled out to speak briefly with the poets. The unidentified Navarrese, after furnishing some information to the travelers, plays a trick on the demons who claw him. He escapes into the pitch, and the trick is immediately followed by a brawl in which the black creatures fall into the pitch themselves. The two poets take advantage of the incident and escape from the dangerous company (Canto 22).

After their flight, Dante and Virgil find themselves at the bottom of the sixth bolgia, where the hypocrites are punished by walking slowly and wearing heavy leaden friars' robes. At a certain point of their walk, the sinners step upon Caiaphas crucified on the ground. Two Jovial Friars talk to the poets and show them the way to climb to the seventh bolgia (Canto 23). This appears as a pit full of monstrous snakes and of naked men rushing in terror among them. They are the thieves. One of them, Vanni Fucci, relates to Dante a political prophecy (Canto 24); then the poet recognizes five noble Florentines and witnesses their endless and painful transformation from men into reptiles and vice versa (Canto 25).

Afterward, while addressing a lament to Florence, which has so many representatives in Hell, Dante reaches the bridge overlooking the eighth bolgia. The valley twinkles with innumerable little flames which conceal the souls of the evil counselors. One of them, Ulysses, gives Dante an account of his last journey and of his death (Canto 26) and another, Guido, Count of Montefeltro, inquires about the state of Romagna, and tells the story of his life (Canto 27).

When the poets come to the ninth bolgia they see a mass of bodies horribly mutilated. They are sowers of religious, political, and family discord, and are mutilated in different degrees. Pier da Medicina, Mosca dei Lamberti, and Bertrand de Born ask to be remembered in this world (Canto 28).

Dante would like to linger, hoping to see one of his kinsmen, Geri del Bello, but Virgil hurries him to the tenth bolgia, where the falsifiers are punished, all afflicted with horrible plagues and diseases. They are divided into four classes. Two of the alchemists, Griffolino d'Arezzo and Capocchio, speak to Dante (Canto 29). Later, Gianni Schicchi and Myrrha are identified among the evil impersonators, and Master Adam among the counterfeiters. Dante then watches a fight between Master Adam and Simon the Greek who belongs to the fourth class of sinners, the falsifiers of words, but being too attentive to the scene, is reproached by Virgil (Canto 30) and moves toward the ninth circle, the prison of traitors.

The ninth circle is a well, the bottom of which is a great frozen lake, Cocytus, formed by the infernal rivers that are draining there. Through the dusk it seems to Dante that he discerns the great towers of a city, but as he approaches them, he discovers that they are giants and Titans visible from the waist up. A giant, Antaeus, takes the travelers in his palm and places them on the ice at the bottom of the well (Canto 31). The traitors who are punished here are confined in four concentric rounds. In the first round (Caina) are the traitors to kindred, fixed in the ice except for their heads. Dante speaks to Camicion dei Pazzi, who identifies, among the others, Alessandro and Napoleone degli Alberti. In the second round (Antenora) are the traitors to country. Here Dante kicks Bocca degli Abati in the face and treats him savagely, then comes upon a sinner gnawing another traitor's skull and asks him to explain the reason why he is acting in such a bestial manner (Canto 32). The sinner, who is Count Ugolino della Gherardesca, answers that the head he is gnawing is that of Archbishop Ruggieri and tells Dante how he and his sons died of starvation. Then Dante visits the third round (Ptolomea), where are the traitors to friends and guests, among whom he meets Friar Alberigo and Branca d'Oria (Canto 33). Finally the poets reach Judecca, the fourth round, where the traitors to their masters and benefactors are completely covered with ice. In the center of the round they see Lucifer, who has three faces and is crushing Judas, Brutus, and Cassius in his three mouths. They climb down the thick hair of the demon's side, pass by the center of gravity and, through a natural dark passage, ascend once more to the upper world before daybreak on the morning of Easter Sunday (Canto 34), look up, and see the stars.

SUMMARIES AND COMMENTARIES

CANTO 1

Summary

At the midpoint of his life, Dante finds himself in a dark wood where there is no path. It is a fearful place, impenetrable and wild. Dante is unable to recall how he got here, and knows only that he has wandered from the path he should be following. He goes along the dismal valley of the wood to the foot of a hill, looks up, and to his joy sees the sun shining on the hilltop. The fears of the night are ended, and he looks back at the valley which no one leaves alive.

Dante rests for a time, then begins to climb the hill. He has barely started when he is confronted by a leopard, which blocks his path. Dante turns this way and that to evade it. This beast has not particularly frightened Dante, but it is soon joined by a hungry lion, more fearful in its aspect, and then by a she-wolf, which so terrifies Dante that he gives up the attempt to climb the hill. The she-wolf drives him back down into the darkness of the valley.

As Dante rushes headlong to escape the beast, a figure appears before him. It has difficulty in speaking, as though it had not spoken for a long time. Dante implores its help, whether it is spirit or man. The reply is given: it is the spirit of a man born in Mantua. He was born late in the reign of Julius Caesar and lived in the time of Augustus; he was a poet and wrote of Aeneas, son of Anchises of Troy. The shade asks why Dante has come back to this dark valley and why he did not continue his climb up the sunlit mountain.

Dante of course recognizes that this is Virgil, and hailing him as his master and his inspiration, points out the she-wolf which has driven him back. Virgil tells him that he must go another way, for this beast will not allow men to pass. She snares and kills them, and is so greedy she is never filled, but is always ravenous. Many are the animals with which she mates, but one day a hound will come that will cause her painful death. Virgil prophesies that this greyhound, whose food is wisdom, love, and courage, will come from the nation "between Feltro and Feltro," and will save Italy, chasing the she-wolf back to Hell.

Virgil commands Dante to follow him and see the harrowing sights of the damned, the hope of those doing penance, and, if he so desires, the realm of the blessed. Another guide will take him to this last realm, which Virgil may not enter.

Dante eagerly consents, and the two poets begin their long journey.

Commentary

Without preliminaries, Dante plunges into the story of his journey to salvation. He stands at the midpoint of his life – half the biblical three score and ten – and has lost his way: "I came to myself . . . ," he says – I found myself – I came to my senses. He has strayed from the true faith without realizing it, not knowing exactly how it came about, and is seeking to return. Through the allegory, he is saying that human reason can guide him back to faith – up to a point.

When Dante speaks of having strayed from the right path the reader should not assume that Dante has committed any specific sin or crime. Throughout the poem Dante is advocating that man must *consciously* strive for righteousness and morality. Man can often become so involved with the day-to-day affairs of living that he will gradually relapse into a sort of lethargy in which he strays from the very strict paths of morality.

For Dante, man must always be aware intellectually of his own need to perform the righteous act. Sin, therefore, is a perversion of the intellect. When Dante says he has strayed and that he does not know how he came to such a position, it simply means that by gradual degrees he has lapsed into a type of indifference and now this must be corrected. Thus the dark wood typifies a human life where every waking moment is not consciously devoted to morality.

Virgil stands for human reason, upon which Dante must depend for his return to grace, and explains that he was sent by another (Beatrice, symbolizing Revelation), though he does not name her until later. The figure of Virgil is not merely that of guide and master. In Dante's time Virgil was viewed as a "white magician," as his prophecy of the greyhound shows, and in the *Inferno,* he uses formal incantations to command the spirits and demons of Hell. In later cantos he becomes a superhuman figure, fearing nothing.

A typically Dantean touch is the hoarseness of Virgil; it may be interpreted in several ways: that Virgil was not much read in Dante's time; that he has not spoken to a mortal since he was first conjured to make a descent into Hell, a journey he tells Dante about in Canto 9; or, what is most likely, that, as the voice of the empire, he has not been heard or heeded for a very long time. Note also that Virgil's spirit cannot speak until it is spoken to: a widely held belief in Dante's superstitious age, and one used by Shakespeare in *Hamlet*.

The three beasts, referred to in Jeremiah 5:6, are sometimes considered to have a double symbolism. Allegorically, the leopard is worldly pleasure, politically it is the city of Florence, so given to worldly pursuits; the lion is ambition, politically the royal house of France, which sought to rule Italy; finally, the she-wolf symbolizes avarice, and politically is the papacy, which Dante viewed as an avaricious religious entity seeking more and more secular power. There are, of course, many other interpretations, among them that the beasts symbolize lechery, pride, and covetousness; or the sins of incontinence, violence, and fraud, which are punished in the three divisions of Hell. Whatever they are, they stand firmly in the way of Dante's salvation.

The hound referred to has been the subject of controversy, but by some commentators has been taken to refer to Dante's friend and protector, Can Grande della Scala, the great Ghibelline leader. (Note: Can Grande means "great dog" in Italian.) His "nation" – the land where he ruled – was between Feltre and Montefeltro; Dante believed that Can Grande was one of the few leaders capable of driving the avaricious popes out of the affairs of the empire and back into their proper sphere of religious rule. It has also been considered that the greyhound symbolizes the eventual reign of the church on earth, conquering the vices symbolized by the beasts on the mountain.

The entire canto is characterized by a note of fear: Dante's natural fear of the dark wood, his superstitious fear of the three beasts, and the apprehension caused by Virgil's description of the journey through Hell. This is counterbalanced in some measure by Dante's view of the sunlight on the mountain, his equally superstitious hope that he will be saved from the beasts because the sun is in the sign of Aries, believed to be its location at the time of Creation, and by the promise of Virgil that he will see Heaven.

The *Comedy* is a long poem of 100 cantos, and each of the three divisions has 33 cantos. Therefore we must view the first canto as the introduction to the entire *Comedy,* not just to the *Inferno*. It sets the scene and starts the poets on their long, long journey.

CANTO 2

Summary

It is near the end of the day. Dante gives a short invocation to the Muses, then asks Virgil if he considers him worthy of making the long and arduous journey. Dante recalls others who, while living, have been permitted to visit the realms of the dead–Aeneas, St. Paul–and compares himself unfavorably with them.

Virgil replies by telling him of the great concern for him of a certain angelic spirit, namely Beatrice; and Virgil relates the conversation between them when she descended to Limbo. Beatrice, he says, had been sent by the Virgin Mary, through her messenger St. Lucia, to ask Virgil's help in bringing Dante back from his wanderings. Beatrice wept as she spoke, and Virgil eagerly rescued Dante and began the journey with him for her sake.

Virgil tells Dante to have courage, because the three ladies of Heaven care for him. Dante immediately puts his fears behind him and tells Virgil that he has inspired him to continue on the way. Virgil moves off, and Dante follows.

Commentary

If the first canto acts as an introduction to the entire poem, then Canto 2 is the introduction to the *Inferno* proper. It begins with an invocation; in all of the classic epics–the *Iliad,* the *Odyssey,* and the *Aeneid*–the poem begins with an invocation to the Muses or to some other type of deity. Thus Dante in the *Inferno* uses an invocation to the Muses, to Genius, and to Memory. One might ask why, in a poem that is obviously Christian, Dante does not invoke the aid of Christian deities. The answer should be obvious: he *does* invoke Christian deities in *Purgatorio* and *Paradiso*. But in an invocation concerning Hell, one does not invoke Christian aid.

Dante's traditional invocation to the Muses is very brief indeed; his references to Memory almost seem a longer invocation. The background of the action is given, and Dante portrays himself as a frightened and humble man. The two others he mentions as going before him through Hell are symbolic of his two great concerns: the church and the empire.

The Chosen Vessel is St. Paul, and the reference is to his vision of Hell, as recorded in a widely circulated work of the Middle Ages. The father of Sylvius was Aeneas, who descended into Hell to consult his father Anchises and learn of the future greatness of his people, the Romans. This preoccupation with the church and the empire will continue through the entire *cantica.*

Virgil's account of Beatrice is an interesting one. This is the only canto in the *Inferno* where she is mentioned by name; nor is Jesus *ever* mentioned by name in this unholy place—only by allusion. This indeed is one of the punishments of Hell: that the condemned know God, but have forfeited the right to call upon Jesus as their redeemer.

CANTO 3

Summary

The inscription over the Gate of Hell moves Dante to comment on it. Virgil answers, reminding Dante to have courage and telling him that this is the place he had spoken of earlier. He takes Dante's hand and leads him in to a dark and starless place of such terrible noise that it makes Dante weep.

The unending cries make Dante ask where they come from, and Virgil replies that these are the souls of the uncommitted, who lived for themselves alone, and of the angels who were not rebellious against God, but neither were they faithful to Satan. Neither Heaven nor Hell would have them, and so they must remain here with the selfish, forever running behind a banner, eternally stung by hornets and wasps. Worms at their feet are fed by the blood and tears of these beings.

Dante sees the shore of a river ahead, with people standing and eagerly awaiting passage, and he questions Virgil. Virgil replies that Dante will know the answers when they reach the shore, and Dante remains silent, believing he has offended Virgil with his questions.

As they reach the stream Acheron, they see the boatman, who shouts at the spirits. He tells them that he is to take them to a place from which they can never escape, but he orders Dante to leave because Dante is still living. Virgil answers Charon, saying it had been willed in Heaven that Dante should make this journey.

Charon remains silent, but the cursing, weeping spirits are ordered aboard by the boatman, who strikes with his oars any soul who hesitates. The boat crosses, but before it has landed, the opposite shore is again crowded with condemned souls. Virgil gently explains to Dante (calling him "my son") that the condemned souls come here from every country and that they are impelled by Divine Justice to cross the river into Hell, where, as in life, their fear of retribution is stilled by their desire for their particular sin. He says, also, that Dante can be comforted by Charon's first refusal to carry him on the boat, for only condemned spirits come this way.

As Virgil finishes his explanation, a sudden earthquake, accompanied by wind and flashing fire from the ground, so terrifies Dante that he faints.

Commentary

The inscription over the gate of Hell has a powerful impact: "Abandon hope, all ye who enter here." Dante naturally thinks this applies also to him, and, in the first of many passages which bring a breath of life to the figures of the poets, Virgil smiles and reassures him.

The inscription implies the horror of total despair. It suggests that anyone may enter into Hell at any time—and then all hope is lost. Dante cries out that this sentence is difficult for him to bear. He is using the word in two senses: first, the sentence (with subject and verb) whose meaning is unnerving to him and, second, the sentence as of a judge who has condemned him to abandon all hope. This condemnation does not apply to Dante because allegorically it is still possible for him to achieve salvation, and realistically he is not yet dead so it will not (necessarily) apply to him at all.

Beginning with this canto Dante is setting up the intellectual structure of Hell. Hell is the place for those who deliberately, intellectually, and consciously chose an evil way of life, whereas Paradise is a place of reward for those who consciously chose a righteous way of life. If Hell, then, is a place for the man who made a deliberate and intentional choice of the wrong way, there must be a place for those people who refused to choose either evil or good. Therefore the vestibule of Hell is for those people who refused to make a choice. They are the uncommitted of the world, and having been indecisive in life, that is, never coming to make a choice for themselves, they are constantly stung into movement.

This is the first example of the law of retribution as applied by Dante, where the uncommitted race endlessly after a wavering (and blank) banner. Because they were unwilling to shed their blood for any worthy cause in life, now it is shed unwillingly, to fall to the ground as food for worms. Dante is terrified by the overpowering noise of this dark and starless place. Again and again he will mention noise, as though it were a part, rather than a result, of the punishment of Hell.

Among the sinners are the fallen angels who supported neither God nor Lucifer, but refused to commit themselves and stayed neutral. A refusal to choose is in itself a choice, an idea used by Dante which has since become central in the existentialist philosophy of Jean Paul Sartre.

Dante spies Pope Celestine V, who "made the great refusal" of giving up the chair of Peter after only five months, thereby clearing the way for Boniface VIII, to whom Dante was an implacable enemy. Celestine preferred to return to the obscurity of noncommitment rather than face the problems of the papacy.

The abrupt opening of the canto, with the poets just outside the gate of Hell, brings up the question of how they got there, but there is no answer. After revealing an almost feminine weakness here, Dante gains courage later, in the face of unknown horrors, until he can face even Satan with something like equanimity.

In this early canto, Dante has given examples of two other themes which will continue through the story: the mythological character and the formal incantation of Virgil, the white magician. Charon is a familiar figure in this aspect of ferryman, although in mythology his domain is sometimes the Styx, which in the *Inferno* does not appear until Canto 7, and with a different boatman. When Charon refuses to take Dante across the river it is because his job is to take only the dead who have no chance of salvation. Dante, however, is both a living man and one who still has the possibility of achieving salvation. In some of the later cantos the mythological figures, and even the figure of Satan, are much changed from the usual concept of them.

Virgil's incantation, "Thus it is willed there, where what is willed can be done," is a circumlocution to avoid the word "Heaven," and is repeated in Canto 5. In later cantos other periphrases of various kinds are used.

The shore of the river Acheron (river of Sorrows) is crowded with more souls than Dante believed possible, souls propelled not alone by the anger of Charon but by the sharp prod of divine justice, until they desire to make the crossing; actually this is their final choice, for their desire for sin on earth was also of their own choosing.

In lines 121-25, Dante again emphasizes that Hell is for those who chose it. Only once in the poem (Canto 33) does Dante ever suggest that the choice is irrevocable, and that if you commit an act of sin you will be automatically condemned to Hell. The entire theological basis of Hell is that it is for those who died unrepentant of their sins. As the poet says, it is for those who have died in the wrath of God. Dante leaves room for men to repent of their sins, enter into Purgatory, and later achieve salvation. Hell is filled with people who at the moment of death were either unrepentant or were still committing the same sins. This suggests that the sinners in Hell seem to long for the punishment that is reserved for them.

When Dante looks upon the number of people he sees in the vestibule, he makes the statement that he had not known that Death had undone so many people. In other words, Dante sees many irresolute, indecisive, uncommitted people in the vestibule, and had not realized that so many people had even lived, much less died, without choosing the path of righteousness, or any path at all. The line is interesting because in T. S. Eliot's modern poem *The Wasteland,* Eliot has a character walking through one of the streets in the Wasteland, repeating the same thought.

CANTO 4

Summary

Dante is awakened by loud thunder. He has been in a deep sleep for some time: his eyes are rested, and he finds himself in a strange place, on the brink of an abyss so deep he cannot see the bottom. Virgil says it is time to descend, but Dante notices his pallor and believes that Virgil is afraid. If he, who has been a source of strength to Dante, fears the descent, how can he expect Dante to follow?

Virgil explains that he is pale, not from fear, but from pity for those who are below them. He urges Dante to hurry, for the way is long. They move to the first circle.

Dante hears no sound but the quiet sighs of sadness from those confined in this circle. His guide explains that these are the souls of those who had led blameless lives, but were not baptized. Virgil himself is one of this group, those who lived before Christianity, and whose sadness comes only from being unable to see God. Dante expresses his sorrow, for he knows good men who are confined in Limbo. He asks Virgil if any soul had ever gone out from this place to the realm of the blessed, and Virgil enumerates those liberated by Jesus when he descended into Hell.

The two poets have been walking during this conversation, and pass by the wood of Limbo. Dante sees a fire ahead and realizes that figures of honor rest near it. He asks Virgil why these are honored by separation from the other spirits, and Virgil replies that their fame on earth has gained them this place.

A voice hails Virgil's return, and the two poets are approached by the shades of Homer, Horace, Ovid, and Lucan. Virgil tells Dante their names, then turns away to talk with them. After a time, the group salutes Dante, saying they regard him as one of their number. The entire group moves ahead, talking of subjects which Dante will not disclose, and they come to a castle with seven walls surrounded by a small stream.

They pass over the stream and through the seven gates and reach a green meadow. Dante recognizes the figures of authority dwelling there, and as the poets stand on a small hill, he gives the names of rulers, philosophers, and others who are there, and regrets that he does not have time to name them all. Prominent among the philosophers are Socrates, Plato, Cicero, Seneca, and "the master of those who know" (Aristotle). Now Dante and Virgil leave this quiet place and come to one where there is no light.

Commentary

Dante again underlines the human Virgil, who turns pale with pity. Virgil has made this journey once before, so he knows the torments which are taking place below. More important, he is approaching the place where he himself dwells and will remain through all eternity, and Dante echoes the sadness of the place – which Virgil knows only too well – when he says he knows many good men who dwell here in Limbo.

When Dante states that he is awakened from his swoon by a heavy peal of thunder, we should be aware that it is not really thunder but instead is the horrible cry emerging from the great pit of Hell–the cry of all the damned souls heard as one. This is the only time that Dante is able to see Hell in its entirety. In the future cantos, and later in this canto, he will hear only the cries and sounds of the sinners who are confined to each individual circle of Hell, but here he is awakened by the hopeless sounds of all Hell emerging, and sounding like terrible peals of thunder. In contrast to this, when Dante reaches this first circle of Hell there is silence–total silence. No sound comes from this circle. This is because those who are confined to Limbo are not being punished, and the silence is a silence of dignity.

Between Hell proper, that is, the place of punishment, and the vestibule, Dante places the circle of Limbo, devoted to those people who had no opportunity to choose either good or evil in terms of having faith in Christ. This circle is occupied by the virtuous pagans, those who lived before Christ was born, and by the unbaptized.

The virtuous pagans had lived blameless lives, and they are judged and honored according to their virtue. They exist here according to what they had themselves envisioned as a life after death. This may be illustrated by turning to one of the dialogues of Socrates. At the end of the *Apology,* Socrates speaks of the afterlife in which he envisions the migration of the soul to a place where that soul can spend an eternity talking with great people who have gone before him or who live at the present moment.

Thus we see Socrates in Limbo discussing philosophy and ethics with the great souls who are there. In other words, Socrates has attained the kind of afterlife which he, as a wise man, envisioned as the perfect one. It is not a punishment; it is the failure of the imagination to envision the coming of the Christ and the faith that man should have in the coming of a Messiah. Thus when Virgil was just dead, he records that someone "in power crowned" appeared in Hell and took from there the shades of all the ancient patriarchs of the Old Testament, who had faith that the Messiah would some day come.

On the allegorical level, the fact that these pagans in Limbo lived a highly virtuous, or ethical, or moral life, and are still in Limbo, implies that no amount of humanistic endeavor, no amount of virtue or knowledge, ethics or morality, can save or redeem one who has not had faith in Christ, and, having faith in Christ, has been openly baptized and is in a state of grace. For Dante, good works, virtue, or morality count for nothing if one has not acknowledged Christ as the redeemer.

Note, finally, that Hell is a place where the person is given no further opportunity to choose. He has made the choice long before.

CANTO 5

Summary

Dante has moved down to the second circle, smaller than the first, which forms the real beginning of Hell. The grinning Minos sits at the entrance judging condemned souls, and the circles of his tail around his body indicate the place in Hell where a spirit is to go for punishment. There is a constant crowd of spirits around him, coming to him for judgment and being carried down the circles of Hell.

Minos cautions Dante against entering, but Virgil silences him, first by asking him why he too questions Dante (as Charon did), then by telling him, in the same words he used to Charon, that it had been willed in Heaven that Dante should make this journey. (The word "Heaven" is not used, here or anywhere else in Hell.)

Dante beholds a place completely dark, in which there is noise worse than that of a storm at sea. Lamenting, moaning, shrieking, the spirits are whirled and swept by an unceasing storm; Dante learns that these are the spirits doomed by carnal lust. He asks the names of some who are blown past, and Virgil answers with their names and something of their stories.

Then Dante asks particularly to speak to two who are together, and Virgil tells him to call them to him in the name of love. They come, and one thanks Dante for his pity and wishes him peace, then tells their story. She reveals first that a lower circle of Hell waits for the man who murdered them. With bowed head, Dante tells Virgil he is thinking of the "sweet thoughts and desires" that had brought the lovers to this place. Calling Francesca by name, he asks her to explain how she and her lover were lured into sin.

Francesca replies that it was a book of the romance of Lancelot that caused their downfall. They were alone, reading it aloud, and so many parts of the book seemed to tell of their own love. They kissed, and the book was forgotten. During her story, the other spirit has been weeping bitterly, and Dante is so moved by pity, he also weeps—and faints.

Commentary

This second circle is the true beginning of Hell. Here Minos sits as judge, but unlike Charon, this grotesque creature is not the Minos of mythology, the great king (or line of kings) who ruled the fabled isle of Crete. The formal incantation of Canto 3 is repeated here and silences the protests of Minos.

This is the circle of carnal lust, first of the four circles of incontinence. The sinners are tossed and whirled by the winds, as in life they felt themselves helpless in the tempests of passion. This canto begins the circles devoted to the sins of incontinence: the sins of the appetite, the sins of self-indulgence, the sins of passion. These are also the sins of the person who has a weakness of will: here are those who did not make a "resolute choice" for good; those who yielded too easily to temptation; and those who did not remain steadfast in searching out goodness.

Before Dante sees the sinners, he first comes upon the judge of all Hell, Minos, before whom all of the condemned spirits come. When a new spirit arrives in Hell, it immediately confesses all of its past sins and by this confession gains a self-knowledge of the sin. In Hell there can be no more self-deception. But the irony is that these souls, being damned, can no longer benefit from the knowledge of their sins. Thus their confession is also a kind of damnation for them.

Minos, like the other guardians of Hell, does not want to admit Dante, a living being still capable of redemption. But he is forced to do so by Virgil. Among those whom Dante sees in this circle are people like Cleopatra, Dido, and Helen. Some of these women, besides being adulteresses, have also committed suicide. The question immediately arises as to why they are not deeper down in Hell in the circle reserved for suicides. We must remember that in Dante's Hell a person is judged by his own standards, that is, by the standards of the society in which he lived. For example, in classical times suicide was not considered a sin, but adultery was. Therefore the spirit is judged by the ethics by which he lived and is condemned for adultery, not suicide.

One of the loveliest of images is given in Dante's simile of the cranes, and Francesca's gentle words, beginning with line 100, are touching with their repetition of "love . . . love . . . love. . . ." However, Dante still retains some of the artificial, posturing attitude of the poet of courtly love. As his technique grows more sure in later cantos, it will be seen that the language and style of the spirits' stories becomes more definitely their own and not Dante's. In telling the tale of Paolo and Francesca, Dante is following the tradition of the poets of courtly love, and the language reveals it. He has, however, given the story the human, individual touch of his "sweet new style," which has made it one of the best-known episodes of the *Comedy*.

Dante sees Paolo and Francesca, and calls them to him in the name of love—a mild conjuration at Virgil's insistence. Francesca tells their story; Paolo can only weep. Francesca da Rimini was the wife of Gianciotto, the deformed older brother of Paolo, who was a beautiful youth. The marriage had been one of alliance and had continued for some ten years when Paolo and Francesca were surprised in the compromising situation described in the poem. Gianciotto promptly murdered them both, for which he will be confined in the lowest circle of Hell.

For modern readers, it is sometimes difficult to understand why Dante considered adultery, or lustfulness, the least hateful of the sins of incontinence. It is important to understand Dante's reasoning: as the intellectual basis of Hell, Dante conceived of Hell as a place where the sinner deliberately chose his sin and failed to repent of it. This is particularly true of the lower circles of malice and fraud. Here, however, Francesca did not *deliberately* choose adultery; hers was a gentle lapsing into love for Paolo; a matter of incontinence, of weakness of will. Only the fact that she was killed by her husband in the moment of adultery allowed her no opportunity to repent, and for this reason she is condemned to Hell.

By this means, Dante seeks to show the difference in the enormity of the sins and therefore the placing of these adulterers in this higher circle. The sin of adultery committed over and over in deliberate assignations would be placed in the lower part of Hell, in the circle reserved for sexual perverts. It would then properly be called concupiscence. But Francesca's sin is not of this type. She is passionate, certainly she is capable of sin and she is certainly guilty of sin, but she represents the woman whose only concern is the man she loves, not her immortal soul. She found her only happiness in his love, and of course, now her misery. Her love had been her heaven; it is now her hell.

Francesca feels that love is something that does not need to be justified. It is a case, not of depravity or concupiscence, not of some vulgar sexual sin, but of a woman who has drifted helplessly—though willingly—into love. Someone like Francesca, who even in Hell retains those essential characteristics of the feminine being—her modesty, her delicate expression of feeling—arouses in us nothing but sympathy for her plight. She is kind, she is graceful, she is gentle, and in spite of her being in Hell, there is still a sense of modesty and of charm. It is these qualities which cause Dante to faint at the end of the canto after hearing her story.

In this love of Paolo and Francesca there is desire, delicate fancy, tenderness, and human frailty—and there is the mark of tragedy. And Dante, who has entered the realm of eternity carrying with him the whole of his humanity, as a Christian must indeed condemn the sinners, but as a man is captivated and saddened, and his eyes fill with tears when Francesca says quietly, "We read no more." One cannot help being moved by the lovers, particularly Francesca, who cannot bless Dante, but can only wish him peace—a peace she and her lover will never know in this tempestuous place, though they are together forever. No bitterness is greater than this, to remember happiness when one is in a state of wretchedness, so that remembering causes bitter torment.

In Hell the sinners retain all of those qualities for which they were damned, and they remain the same throughout eternity, that is, the soul is depicted in Hell with those exact characteristics which condemned him to Hell in the first place. Consequently, as Francesca loved Paolo in this world, throughout eternity she will love him in Hell. But they are damned, they will not change, they will never cease to love, and they can never be redeemed. And this is represented metaphorically by placing Paolo close to Francesca and by having the two of them being buffeted about together through this circle of Hell for eternity.

By reading the story of Francesca, we can perhaps understand better the intellectual basis by which Dante depicts the other sins in Hell. He chooses a character who represents a sin; then he expresses poetically the person who committed the sin. Francesca is not perhaps truly representative of the sin of this circle, and "carnal lust" seems a harsh term for her feelings, but Dante has chosen her story to make his point: that the sin here is a sin of incontinence, of weakness of the will, of falling from grace through inaction of conscience. Many times in Hell Dante will respond sympathetically, or with pity, to some of these lost souls.

CANTO 6

Summary

Dante regains consciousness, to find himself in the third circle, witnessing a new torment: endless cold rain mixed with hail and snow, falling on the ground which gives off a terrible stench.

Cerberus, the three-headed monster, stands over those sunk deep in the slush. He barks furiously, and claws and bites all within reach. These spirits howl in the rain and attempt to evade the monster. Seeing the two travelers, Cerberus turns on them and is silenced only when Virgil throws handfuls of the reeking dirt into his three mouths.

Dante and Virgil pass by him, walking on the shades who lie on the ground and who seem to Dante to have physical bodies. Only one spirit is not on the ground, and it speaks to Dante as one who knew him in life. Dante, however, cannot recognize him and asks him to tell his name and why he is here. The shade says he was a citizen of Florence, a city full of envy, and was known to Dante as Ciacco (the Hog). For his well-known gluttony, he was doomed to his third circle of Hell.

Dante expresses his sympathy, and then asks the fate of Florence and why it is so divided now. Ciacco foretells a future war and the defeat and expulsion of one party. He concludes his prophecy, and Dante asks where certain good citizens of Florence can now be found. Ciacco tells him that they are much further down in Hell, for worse crimes than his, and that Dante will see them if he travels that far. He also asks Dante to speak of him when he returns to earth, then, refusing to say more, he looks sideways at Dante and falls to the ground.

Virgil tells Dante that Ciacco will now remain as he is until the Last Judgment, and they talk of the future life. Dante questions Virgil concerning the Last Judgment, and Virgil answers that, although these souls will never reach perfection, they will be nearer to it after the Last Judgment than before and therefore will feel more pain as well as more pleasure.

Commentary

Dante awakens in the third circle, that of the gluttons. Again, he has been borne unconscious to this place, still in the region of the incontinent.

Cerberus guards the place, and as in mythology, he requires a sop for each of his three mouths (this time the foul mud of the circle will suffice) before he will permit passage. With this constant hunger, he is a fitting guardian for the circle of gluttons, who transformed their lives into a continual feast and did nothing but eat and drink and now lie like pigs in the mire.

In the intellectual progression down through Hell we move from the circle of lust, a type of sin that was mutual or shared, to the third circle, that of sin performed in isolation. The glutton is one of uncontrolled appetite, one who deliberately, in his own solitary way, converted natural foods into a sort of god, or at least an object of worship. So now his punishment is a reversal, and instead of eating the fine delicate foods and wines of the world, he is forced to eat filth and mud. Instead of sitting in his comfortable house relishing all of the sensual aspects of good food and good wine and good surroundings, he lies in the foul rain.

Aside from brief mention in earlier cantos, this is Dante's first political allusion, and it takes the form of an outburst from Ciacco. The voice is Ciacco's, but the words are Dante's. Ciacco's prophecies are the first of many political predictions which recur in the *Divine Comedy* and especially in the *Inferno.* Since the imaginary journey takes place in 1300, Dante relates, as prophecies, events which had already occurred at the time the poem was being composed.

Curiously, Ciacco falls into what might be called unconsciousness, from which he will not awaken, Virgil says, until Judgment Day. One wonders why this privilege of release from torment is given him; surely not for his political harangue, which is surpassed in bitterness by other spirits in the cantica. Perhaps Dante's acquaintance with Ciacco in life, as a jolly companion, would be enough to permit poetic license, but not to permit his exclusion from Hell.

Another note may be useful. The souls in this upper part of Hell often wish to be remembered to people in the world. But as we descend deeper into Hell the souls wish to conceal the fact that they are in Hell and have no desire to be remembered on earth. For example, the glutton is often depicted as a happy-go-lucky, charming person whom it is a pleasure to be around. Thus Ciacco wishes Dante to speak of him to his friends when he returns to earth. But the sins of those lower in Hell are more vicious, and these souls do *not* wish to be remembered in the world.

The conversation between Dante and Virgil concerning the day of judgment is based upon the philosophy of Aristotle as expounded by St.

Thomas Aquinas, who wrote that "The soul without the body hath not the perfection of its nature." Virgil explains that after the day of judgment the shades will be *nearer* perfection because their souls will be reunited with their bodies. They will not, however, *achieve* perfection—that is, salvation—and will, according to the doctrine of Aquinas, feel more pain after Judgment Day, as well as more pleasure: "The more a thing is perfect, the more it feels pleasure and likewise pain."

CANTO 7

Summary

Plutus challenges the travelers with unintelligible words, but Virgil tells Dante to keep up his courage; nothing can stop them from descending. Plutus has swelled to terrifying size. However, when Virgil tells him their journey is willed in Heaven, he falls limply to the ground, and the poets descend to the fourth circle, where Dante witnesses new torments.

Comparing the actions of these souls to the whirlpool Charybdis, Dante watches as the two groups roll great weights halfway around the circle, where they crash into one another and, each blaming the other, turn back only to clash again on the other side of the circle, one group crying, "Why grasp?" and the other, "Why squander?"

Dante asks the identity of the many tonsured spirits, and Virgil replies that they were priests and popes and cardinals, who sinned greatly either in avarice or prodigality, the opposite vices in the management of worldly goods.

Dante is surprised that he cannot recognize any of the figures, but Virgil explains that as in life they showed no discernment, so now the distinction of their features is dimmed beyond recognition. He adds a warning against greed for gold, the goods of Fortune, since no amount of gold can now stop the punishment of these spirits.

Dante asks what Fortune is, that she should hold all the good things of the world, and Virgil, disgusted at the foolishness of greedy men, delivers his judgment of her: Fortune (Luck) was ordained by Heaven as guardian or overseer of the wealth of the world. Some persons and nations have a greater share of this wealth, others a lesser one, but the balance is changing constantly. Fortune is the maker of her own laws in her own realm, as the other gods are in theirs; she cannot be understood and does not hear those who curse her, but goes her own way.

Virgil then reminds Dante that time has passed quickly, and they must descend to another circle. They cross to the other bank and find a fountain of strange, dark water which flows in a stream down through a crack in the rock. Following this to the foot of the rocks, they come to the marsh called Styx.

Here Dante finds people immersed in mud, striking at one another with hands, feet, and head, and biting one another. Virgil tells him that he is looking at souls destroyed by anger and that more lie under the waters of Styx, making bubbles with each cry. Virgil repeats their words, which cannot be fully understood. They are telling of the sullenness of their lives, when they should have been happy in the light of the sun, and now they live sullen forever.

The two poets circle the edge of the marsh and finally reach the base of a tower.

Commentary

Plutus, legendary god of riches, appropriately guards the fourth circle, the abode of the prodigal (the spendthrifts) and of the avaricious (the misers). Although his words are commonly held to be gibberish, a little stretch of the imagination can translate them into a cry for Satan's assistance. Plutus swells with rage (perhaps symbolic of the overinflated importance given to riches?) but promptly collapses when Virgil repeats a variation of the incantation he used in Canto 3 and again in Canto 5.

Dante compares the action of the sinners in the circle to the dreaded whirlpool Charybdis and its surrounding waters. The useless efforts with which the sinners push the huge stones represent the futile persistence they practiced in gathering worldly goods during their lives.

The question immediately arises as to why Dante places hoarders and spendthrifts in a circle lower than the gluttons. That is, why is hoarding and spending more horrible than mere gluttony? The gluttons misused the natural products of the world, which, for Dante, was not so bad as the misers and spendthrifts, who hoarded and had no respect for the man-made objects of this world, that is, money and property. The distinction, however, is not vitally important. What is poetically significant is that these two types of people were opposites in life, thus the punishment for them in Hell is the mutual antagonism that they have after death. A miser could not understand someone who spent money wildly, so in Hell these people are pitted against each other.

The Styx is called a marsh; in mythology it was a river (the river of Hate), one of the five rivers of Hades, and its boatman was Charon. The source of the Styx is described rather fully by Dante. The Styx serves a double purpose. It separates the upper Hell from the nether Hell, and it also functions as the circle for the wrathful. As the wrathful people were hateful during their lifetime, they are now in a river of hate. These people are divided into two categories. First is the open and violent hatred, and the punishment is that they strike out at each other in almost any fashion; the second type of hatred is the slow, sullen hatred. The punishment for this type is that they are choking on their own rage, gurgling in the filth of Styx, unable to express themselves as they become choked on their own malevolent hatred. Virgil's words quoting the lament of the sullen comprise one of the brief passages that come through beautifully in translation.

Thus with the end of the sins of the incontinent we have completed a pattern, beginning where adultery is a weakness of the will and therefore not intended to hurt another, through the circle of gluttony, miserliness, and waste—types of sins committed in isolation—and finally approaching the worst of the sins of the incontinent, the wrathful, who by their hatred *can* possibly harm someone.

CANTOS 8-9

Summary

As Dante and Virgil were approaching the tower, they saw two fires, which were answered by a signal flame in the far distance. Dante now asks the reason for the beacons and who made them. Virgil tells him to look into the mist and he will see the answer. Dante sees a little boat coming swiftly toward them, with only one oarsman, who challenges them. Virgil replies that he, Phlegyas, complains for nothing, since he must only carry them across the water.

Although Phlegyas is in a towering rage, Virgil enters the boat. Dante follows, noting that he alone has any weight and that this causes the prow of the boat to dip as they cross the water.

Before they reach the shore, a muddy figure rises up and tries to attack Dante, asking why he is here when he is not yet dead. There is an exchange of words between the spirit and Dante, who at first does not know him. The shade informs Dante that he weeps endlessly here in the mud, and Dante, in sudden recognition, wishes that he may remain so and curses him.

Virgil praises Dante for his action, and tells him that others now alive think themselves great will come to the same end as this spirit. Dante expresses a wish to see the spirit sink into the Stygian marsh, and is told that this will happen before they reach the shore. He looks back, and to his satisfaction Filippo Argenti is attacked by others in the circle of the wrathful.

Virgil tells Dante that ahead is the city of Dis, with many inhabitants, and when Dante remarks on the red glow of its structures, Virgil tells him this is the eternal fire of Hell.

The boat circles the walls, which seem to be made of iron, and the boatman orders them out at the entrance. Above the gates, Dante sees the rebellious angels, who angrily ask why he is in the realm of the dead. Virgil quiets them by indicating he wishes to talk with them. They reply that they will speak only with him and that Dante must return the way he came, if he can find the way alone.

Dante realizes he can never return without a guide and begs Virgil, who has saved him so often, to end their journey here if they are not allowed to go on together and to return with him by the same path.

Virgil reassures him, again, that no one can stop their journey and asks him to remain where he is, for Virgil will surely not abandon him. Dante is left behind in a very doubtful state of mind, for he cannot hear the conversation. It is a short one, however, for the angels rush back and slam the gates shut. Virgil returns to Dante, sighing because the fallen angels bar the way. However, he tells Dante of the approach of one who will open the gates.

Virgil listens intently, because he cannot see through the heavy mist. He regrets they could not enter the gates by themselves, but help has been promised, though it seems long delayed. Dante is much alarmed and asks his guide, in a roundabout way, if anyone from the upper circles has ever made this descent. Virgil answers that he himself had once been sent to summon a shade from the circle of Judas, far below here, so he knows the way well.

Dante's attention turns to the tower, where three bloody Furies now stand. Their heads are covered with snakes instead of hair, and Virgil gives their names. Dante cowers near his master as the Furies call for Medusa, so that the sight of her will turn Dante to stone.

Because Dante is still mortal, and Medusa *can* petrify him (literally), Virgil turns him around with his back to the wall and tells him to cover his eyes and then puts his own hands over Dante's. Dante comments briefly upon the hidden meaning of what has happened, and of what is to come.

A noise like a hurricane causes the poets to look toward Styx, and they see a figure crossing without touching the marsh. Spirits rush away from him, and he moves his left hand before him to dispel the fog of the marsh.

Dante recognizes the heavenly messenger, and Virgil asks him to remain quiet and bow down. The angry messenger reaches the gate, which opens at the touch of his wand. He then reproves the insolent angels for trying to stop what is willed in Heaven and reminds them of the injuries suffered by Cerberus when he was dragged to the upper world.

The messenger turns, and without speaking, goes back across the marsh, intent upon other cares. The two poets enter the city, and Dante sees a wide plain covered with sepulchers. They are red hot, and flames come from their open tops. Dante hears terrible cries and asks their source, and Virgil replies that these are the tombs of the numerous arch-heretics. They turn to the right, and walk between the wall and the tombs.

Commentary

The first stanza of Canto 8 is probably the source for the tradition that Dante wrote the first seven cantos of the *Comedy* before his exile.

This appears to be almost the only evidence. There is, however, little unity in the canto. It is weak in construction; too much happens: there is a signal given, a boat appears, Virgil has a short argument with the boatman, and Dante a fierce one with Filippo Argenti, and so on. Why Argenti should be singled out for mention remains an enigma, but he was apparently a bitter enemy of Dante's and reveals himself as a man marked by all the passions, hatreds, and loves of his time.

The marsh of Styx is the fifth circle. When Dante enters the boat to cross it, he mentions for the first time the fact of his physical weight. Later this causes the spirits of other circles to realize that Dante is still alive.

The marsh is crossed with unseemly haste, and the city of Dis looms ahead. As they approach the city, they are leaving the first division of Hell, that of incontinence, and entering the realm of malice, the sins of the will. Dante uses the word "mosques" to describe the towers of the city because the teachings of Mohammed were considered a Christian heresy rather than a separate religion. The fallen angels who oppose the poets' entrance to the city are said by Virgil to be the same ones who tried to prevent Jesus from entering the gate of Hell.

As Dante descends in the circles of Hell, he will gradually lose his sympathy and his pity, and as one of the spirits of the damned provokes him he will retaliate with a certain degree of violence. The first indication of this is in Canto 8 when Dante turns on Filippo Argenti in such a furious manner. This does not mean that Dante cannot respond with sympathy to some of the spirits, but in Hell the sin of the person evokes from Dante a certain righteous indignation, and he responds sometimes with violence.

In Canto 9, Dante returns to his customary style and grasp of his material. There is a short passage of dramatic impact: Virgil, the fearless guide, stands pale and helpless, speaking brokenly to himself. His incantations, and his reason, are useless against those who willfully dared to oppose Jesus himself, and Virgil is forced to ask for the help which has been promised. Allegorically, this is another reminder that human reason cannot achieve salvation without divine aid. Virgil, as reason, cannot understand sin committed in full knowledge and with deliberate will.

Dante, in a touching manner, asks a diplomatic question designed to change his master's train of thought—and perhaps quiet his own fears. Virgil relates the story of his earlier journey down to the circle of Judecca. This took place not long after Virgil's death, he says, when Erichtho, the sorceress, at the insistence of Sextius Pompeius, summoned Virgil to bring a spirit from the circle of Judecca to foretell the outcome of a battle.

The story of Erichtho's sorcery was related by Lucan and concerns the battle of Pharsalia, between Julius Caesar and Pompey the Great, which was fought in 48 B.C. Lucan of course did not mention Virgil's name in this connection, and no doubt medieval legend added the name of Virgil because he had told the story of the descent of Aeneas into Hell. A curious discrepancy arises from Dante's use of the tale, however, because Virgil was still alive at the time of the battle of Pharsalia.

Dante's attention has been diverted to the activity on the city walls. The figures of the Furies are the same as found in the myths, and the threat of showing Medusa to Dante is a strong reminder that Dante is still alive. There is an obscure reference to the lesson to be learned from this episode. Its general meaning is that a guilty conscience (the Furies) and a hard heart (Medusa) stand in the way of salvation; that reason (Virgil) may be of help but only if joined by divine aid (the Heavenly Messenger). The complex and dramatic action of Canto 9 is expressed with a more mature art which transforms the symbols into concrete and realistic images. We experience with Dante his tension and his expectation of divine help, his confidence and his anxiety, and finally his relief at the arrival of the messenger from Heaven.

The figure of the angelic messenger is not described as we should expect, a resplendent, winged creature. His physical attributes are purposely left undefined. The impression of his approach is conveyed through two dramatic figures of speech. His bursting open the barred gates with a light touch is impressive. His haughty speech to the fiends and his abrupt departure are expressive of his hatred for the abhorrent place.

CANTO 10

Summary

As the poets travel the secret path, Dante asks if he may speak with one of the spirits, since all the tombs are open. Virgil replies that they will be closed forever after the Last Judgment, but that Dante's wish will be granted and so will the wish he has not expressed. Dante answers that he did not want to conceal anything but only wanted to stop asking so many questions, since his master had indicated that this questioning troubled him.

Dante is startled by a voice, identified by Virgil as that of Farinata, which tells them to turn and they will see him. Dante looks, and Virgil urges him forward to the edge of Farinata's tomb and tells him to be brief in his conversation.

The haughty Farinata is sitting upright and inquires about Dante's ancestors. The poet answers. The shade then says that he was their enemy and twice defeated them, but Dante replies that they returned both times, which was more than Farinata's party had been able to do.

The argument is interrupted by a spirit in another tomb, who recognizes Dante and believes he is making the journey because of the greatness of his poetry. If this is so, he asks, where is his own son and why isn't he on this journey also? Dante replies that he himself is being led by another, whom the poet Guido (the spirit's son) may have disdained. Because Dante has spoken in the past tense, the shade believes his son is dead, and before Dante can answer, it falls back into the tomb.

Farinata's shade resumes the argument exactly where it left off, telling Dante that if his party has not yet returned to power, it is more torture to him than his fiery tomb. He also warns Dante that before the full moon has risen fifty times (that is, within fifty months), his party will return. Then he asks Dante a question: why is the other party so bitterly opposed to his own? And Dante replies that it is because of the fierce battle [at Montaperti] which caused the other party to issue decrees of exile. Farinata says that he was not the only leader in the battles against Florence, but he *was* alone in saving the city from destruction after it was defeated.

Dante, in turn, asks a question. He has noticed that the spirits can look back into the past, or ahead into the future, and tell of what has happened and of what will come to pass; but they do not know what is happening on earth at the present moment, and he wishes to know why this is so. The spirit replies that they are like a person whose sight is defective; they can see only at a distance—God has given them this much light—and they know nothing of the present world.

Dante asks Farinata to tell the spirit of Guido's father that his son still lives; then hearing Virgil call him, he quickly asks the identity of the other spirits who lie nearby. Farinata answers only that Frederick II and "the cardinal" are here and refuses to speak again. Dante is bewildered by this knowledge of the spirits concerning the past and the future. He returns to his guide, and as they move away, Virgil asks why he is so puzzled. Dante tells him, and his master replies that he should remember this, for when they reach the blessed lady she will reveal all of Dante's life, past and future.

They turn to the left, go across the walled city, following a path which goes down into a fetid valley.

Commentary

The city of Dis generally considered as including all of the rest of Hell, from the wall to the pit of Cocytus. It is indeed Satan's own. Here again, there is a difference of opinion among critics, some considering that only this circle of Hell is the city of Dis. Dante's words, beginning with line 70, would seem to confirm this. However, since the heretics are confined here, it seems more probable that Dante's intention was for the city to include all the rest of Hell; otherwise the heretics, whom Dante would consider as devoted to Satan, would be confined in a place much closer to Satan. Dante recognizes many of the figures here but does not disclose the nature of their heresy.

Dante wonders if the tombs are not empty; therefore when Farinata speaks to Dante, Dante cringes partly in fright and and in awe of the great man, and partly because he had not expected a voice to come from these supposedly empty sepulchers. The first words that Farinata speaks inspire a certain amount of sympathy and affection for him. In a fiery bed enclosed in a dreadful tomb, he can still be touched by once again hearing the beloved Tuscan speech, recalling to him cherished memories of his country.

Since Farinata is depicted ultimately as having a very haughty and proud nature, his sentimentality and his love for his country create in our minds a sympathetic feeling for this proud man. At the end of his speech he even suggests that perhaps he, Farinata, caused too much trouble in his own land, that famed country which he says he perhaps "tested too much."

Historically speaking, Farinata was a powerful personality of the preceding generation. He belonged to the opposing political party, the Ghibellines, and Dante's family were Guelphs. As is alluded to in this particular canto, Farinata had twice led the Ghibellines against the Guelphs and had twice defeated them. Thus he and Dante should be bitter enemies. However, this is not someone whom Dante hates; instead Farinata was a person whom Dante admired tremendously: one may respect an enemy even while being opposed to him.

Farinata, along with Cavalcanti, is in the circle of the heretics, partly because both he and Cavalcanti were Epicureans. According to Dante's definition, a heretic was one who chose his own opinion rather than following the judgment of the church; Cavalcanti and Farinata followed the Epicurean philosophy. The Epicureans believed that there is no soul, that everything dies with the body. They regarded the pleasures of this life as the highest goal for man. Since Dante knew both Farinata and Cavalcanti as Epicureans, he had fully expected to meet them in this circle of Hell.

Farinata's concerns are those of a warrior; any other sentiments are meaningless to him. He is a citizen: the request he makes to Dante is uttered in the name of their homeland. He is a partisan: the first question he asks the poet is about his ancestors. He is an invincible warrior: he tells of scattering his opponents twice. Farinata's greatest glory was his love for Florence, a love which withstood every hatred and saved his beloved city. The theme of Cavalcanti's paternal love, interwoven with this heroic one, is very effective from the poetic point of view.

Dante has created an image of Farinata as a very proud person, and also an image of power, character, and strength. He describes Farinata as raising himself erect, so that he could be seen only from the waist up, as though his upper body represents his total personality. This suggests that, spiritually, he towers above all of Hell, and creates an image of infinite strength and grandeur.

The remark about Guido (Cavalcanti) holding Virgil in disdain is a puzzling one. Several explanations have been offered. One of the most logical is that Guido was a supporter of the papacy in its struggle against the empire and would therefore oppose the ideas of Virgil, poet of the empire.

The two figures mentioned are Frederick II, the most versatile and enlightened emperor of the Middle Ages, and Ottaviano degli Ubaldini, a fierce Ghibelline cardinal, who is reported to have said: "If there is any soul, I have lost mine for the Ghibellines."

The movements of the poets at the end of the canto may be somewhat confusing. The city of Dis is completely encircled by its own wall; its center is the circular abyss. Dante and Virgil have been following along the base of the wall, and now they turn left onto a path that strikes across the circle at right angles to the wall and reach the edge of a cliff.

CANTOS 11-12

Summary

The two poets reach a bank made of broken rock, and because of the foul odor, take refuge behind a large stone, the tomb of Pope Anastasius. Virgil remarks that they should stay where they are until they get used to the stench, and Dante asks what they can do to pass the time. His guide had intended to instruct him and tells him what lies below them: first there is a circle of three divisions, or rounds, each filled with condemned souls. Next—because all malice ends in injury and is hated in Heaven—are the fraudulent, confined in a lower circle. This is because only man is capable of fraud, and this is particularly offensive to God.

The first circle below, Virgil continues, is for those who have committed violence against God, against themselves, or against their neighbors. The first round of this seventh circle is for those violent against a neighbor's person or his property, and this includes murderers, assailants, and robbers.

In the second round are those violent against themselves: suicides and those who waste their goods. And in the third and smallest round are those who do violence to God through blasphemy and denial.

In the circle below the violent, the fraudulent are confined, and Virgil gives a long list of those condemned. Finally, in the last and smallest circle, at the bottom of the pit, are held the traitors—for all eternity.

Dante now understands what lies below but asks his master why those guilty of incontinence are punished outside the walls of Dis. Virgil reproves him for not remembering Aristotle's *Ethics,* in which it is explained that incontinence is somewhat less offensive to God (because it is without malice). Dante thanks him for the explanation, then asks another question, concerning usury: why does it so anger God?

Virgil replies that Nature follows the divine plan of God; and art (that is, artisanship, the working of natural resources and the product of labor) follows Nature. Art is, in this sense, the grandchild of God; it was God's intention that man should live by nature and his own art—the labors that he performs—and that the man who seeks to evade this labor goes against the plan of God.

Virgil asks Dante to follow him; it is growing late, and they must walk some distance to the next descent.

The beginning of the descent is rocky and broken, as from an earthquake. The only opening is a cleft in the rock, and it is guarded by the Minotaur. He is in a towering rage, and Virgil taunts him, asking if perhaps he thinks Theseus is here. He orders the monster to remove himself, and while the monster is plunging about in helpless anger, Virgil urges Dante to begin the descent quickly.

It is rocky and steep, and Dante notices that the stones move under his feet because of his weight. He is deep in thought, and Virgil tells him how the walls of the abyss came to be broken and fallen as they are. When he had first been sent (by Erichtho) to the lowest circle of Hell, the walls had been solid and unbroken; just before Jesus descended into Hell, a terrible earthquake shook the valley and the rocks fell, and the walls of the abyss became as they are now.

Virgil tells Dante to look into the valley and he will see the river of boiling blood, in which the violent are confined. Dante sees a wide ditch, and along its bank are centaurs armed with arrows. They see the two poets, and three of them come forward carrying bows and spears. One asks where the poets are from, and why they are here, and threatens them with his bow. Virgil replies that he will speak with Chiron, then tells Dante the names of the three: Nessus, Chrion, and Pholus. They are only three among the thousands who go along the bank and keep the tortured spirits in their proper place in the river of blood.

Dante and Virgil approach the centaurs, and Chiron, moving his beard aside with the end of an arrow, speaks first to his companions. He has seen that the rocks move beneath Dante's feet; therefore Dante is alive. Virgil confirms this and tells the centaur that he is guiding Dante and that they are making the journey because they must, not because they are enjoying it. He explains the visit of the blessed lady and tells Chiron they are not robbers, but require one of the centaurs to guide them to the ford across the river, where Dante must be carried, since he is not a spirit. Chiron sends Nessus to guide them and to guard them from the other centaurs, and the three move along the bank.

Dante sees the shrieking spirits sunk in blood, some even to the eyebrows. Nessus explains that those sunk deepest are the tyrants, and he mentions several. Virgil tells Dante to listen carefully to Nessus, and farther on they see spirits sunk to the neck and one standing alone who, Nessus says, is a murderer. Dante recognizes many standing immersed to the chest but does not name them. Again the incessant noise is almost intolerable to him.

The river becomes more and more shallow, until some of the spirits have only their feet covered. The group has reached the ford over the river, and Nessus stops to tell Dante that on the other side of the ford the river again becomes deeper and that Attila and others, including highwaymen, are confined there. Nessus leaves them on the opposite bank of the first round and returns over the ford.

Commentary

Virgil clearly describes the regions below and then in a long moral discourse gives the reasons why each sin is punished in progressively lower circles of Hell.

Note that Dante places the dissipators of their own wealth in the seventh circle, with the suicides and those who "weep where they should be joyous." It is sometimes difficult to see the distinction between the dissipators of wealth below and the prodigal of the fourth circle above; between the joyless of the seventh circle and the sullen confined above in the marsh of Styx. The distinction is in the manner of their sinning: those in the upper circles sinned in carelessness and without thought; the ones confined below sinned deliberately and with malice, which emphasizes Dante's concept of Hell, wherein a deliberate intellectual choice is the worst kind of sin.

Dante makes no distinction between violence to the person and violence to property; they are one and the same. The waning of the feudal system and the rise of commerce had given the citizen of that age, particularly in the great commercial centers, a strong sense of property.

Dante uses the term "usury" in a different sense from the modern one. It did not mean the charging of exorbitant interest for loaning money; it meant the charging of *any* interest at all. Strange as it may seem in our own time, the idea that money makes money was repugnant to Dante, who believed that profits should be fruits of labor. Ironically, his own city of Florence became one of the principal banking centers of Europe during the fourteenth century and continued so for several succeeding centuries.

Fraud may be practiced on men who have no cause for placing confidence in those by whom they are defrauded; in this case only the common bond between man and man is broken. Those who committed this kind of fraud lie in the eighth circle. But the sinners who perpetrated fraud on those bound by natural love – such as traitors to kindred, fatherland, guests, and benefactors – are condemned to the lowest place in Hell, the ninth circle.

With Canto 12, we enter the seventh circle, the circle of violence, with its three rounds. It begins with the violence of the landslide which broke and scattered the stones after the earthquake. The punishment inflicted upon the tyrants and warmakers is clearly related to their faults: because they were bloodthirsty during their lives, they are now condemned to stay in Phlegethon, the river of boiling blood, forever. The motif of the damned gradually immersed in a river—usually of fire—was commonplace in the medieval representation of Hell.

Though Dante usually personifies the particular sin he is discussing, in the first round of the seventh circle, which is the place of punishment for those who have been violent against their neighbors, Dante does not single out any one person. He is content to merely mention the names of various tyrants and violent warriors, particularly those who belong to the Ghibelline party, as though his readers would well understand the meaning behind the names.

The minotaur and the centaurs are much like their figures in mythology. The minotaur is violent and bloodthirsty, a fitting guardian for this seventh circle. The centaurs, half-man and half-horse, were, in mythology, creatures of sudden violence, though the wise Chiron was the legendary teacher of Achilles, Theseus, and other great heroes.

These figures, along with the Harpies in the next canto, are grotesque combinations of human and beast, and are symbolic of the transition from the sins of incontinence in the higher circles to the sins of bestiality in the very pit of Hell.

CANTO 13

Summary

Dante and Virgil enter a wood where there is no path. This is a dismal wood of strange black leaves, misshapen branches, and poison sticks instead of fruit: it is the place where the Harpies nest.

Virgil explains that this is the second round of the seventh circle, where Dante will see things that will cause him to doubt Virgil's words. Dante has already heard cries, but cannot find where they come from and in confusion stops where he is. He believes that Virgil knows his thoughts: the spirits making such an outcry are hiding among the trees. Virgil tells him only to break off any branch, and he will see that he is mistaken in his thought.

Dante pulls a small branch from a large thorn tree, and a voice asks why Dante tears at him. Blood comes from the tree, and with it the voice which asks if Dante has no pity. It continues, saying that all these trees were once men and that Dante should have mercy upon them. Dante drops the branch, and Virgil tells the tree-spirit that if Dante had believed what Virgil had once written, this would not have happened. Since Dante could not believe, Virgil had asked him to pull off the branch, though it grieved Virgil to wound the spirit.

In compensation for this wound, Virgil asks the spirit to tell Dante his story, so that he may repeat it when he returns to earth. The spirit, moved by his words, tells his story: he was minister to Frederick II and absolutely faithful to him, but the envy of the court turned Frederick against him. Because he could not bear to lose this trust, in sorrow he killed himself. He swears he was faithful to the end and asks that Dante tell the true story when he returns to the upper world.

Virgil tells Dante to question the spirit if he wishes, but Dante is too sorrowful and asks Virgil to say the things Dante wishes to know. Virgil therefore asks how the souls are bound into these gnarled trees and if any ever regains freedom.

The imprisoned spirit replies that when the soul is torn from the body (by suicide), it is sent by Minos to the seventh circle, where it falls to the ground, sprouts, and grows. The Harpies eat its leaves, giving it great pain. The spirits will all be called to the Last Judgment, and will reclaim the mortal bodies forsaken by them but will never regain the immortal souls which they took from themselves and will remain forever trapped in this strange wood.

The two poets now hear a noise like a hunt crashing through a forest, and two spirits appear. The second flings himself into a bush, but is quickly caught and torn apart by the pursuing hounds, who carry him off.

Dante and Virgil approach the bush, which is complaining loudly that the fleeing spirit gained nothing by choosing it for a hiding place. Virgil asks this spirit who he was, but in answering, it first asks that they gather up all the leaves which have been torn off in the hunt, then says only that he was a citizen of Florence, who hanged himself in his own house.

Commentary

The meaning of the punishment of the suicides is evident: those who on earth deprived themselves of their bodies, in Hell are deprived of a human form. At the Last Judgment the suicides will rise, like all the other souls, to claim their bodies, but will never wear them. Their bodies will remain suspended on the trees which enclose the spirits of their owners.

One of the greatest changes brought on by the advent of Christianity is the change that took place in judging the suicide. In classical times, when a person could no longer live in freedom, or when he could no longer live heroically, it was considered a stoic virtue for him to die by his own hand. The last great act that a person could perform was to take his own life, which was for him the last free choice he could make.

With the coming of Christianity, however, Jesus preached the concept that a man is free inwardly and no amount of imprisonment, no amount of disgrace could destroy one's spiritual attributes. Thus, where suicide was a virtue in the ancient days, for the Christian it became one of the cardinal sins.

Dante is (naturally) very confused when he arrives at the wood of suicides and hears human sounds but sees no human forms. Consequently Virgil has to do something which seems extremely cruel. He has Dante pick off a branch from one of the trees, which causes the tree to bleed. We have seen before that Dante is a person of infinite pity; therefore the words of the tree evoke from us the expected response – surprise and sympathy.

The entire scene becomes a fantasy as Dante breaks the branch, the tree bleeds, and a voice comes from the tree. It seems almost as though Dante is unconscious of the words; instead it is the startling *fact* that a tree speaks that evokes his feeling of awe and disbelief.

The story of Pier delle Vigne is related so that Dante, on his return to earth, can justify the man's loyalty (though not his suicide). The greatness of the episode comes when Pier delle Vigne says that in order to make himself a just individual, by one stroke of the knife he has made himself forever unjust. Here is a gentleman, a man of honesty, elegance, and breeding, a cultured and intellectual man, who has condemned himself forever to damnation by a single act.

This is one of the great poetic concepts in the *Inferno*. The spirit is not seen as a mean or evil or vicious man; instead he is a man who, in a moment of weakness, has taken his own life. Most of the other characters that we meet in Hell have something despicable about them, but Pier delle Vigne rouses our sympathy in that a man of his obvious greatness should, in a moment of weakness of will, take the irretrievable action, and after a life of service and devotion, be condemned forever.

The naked men pursued and torn to pieces by hounds are spendthrifts, reckless squanderers, who did not actually take their own lives but destroyed themselves by destroying the means of life. The difference between these sinners and the spendthrifts of the fourth circle is that the earlier cases arise from weakness, these later cases from an act of will.

The Harpies were winged creatures with the faces of women and were symbolic of the whirlwind or the violent storm. They stole anything; hence in the wood they symbolize the violence of the suicide and the stealing away of his soul.

CANTO 14

Summary

Dante gathers the leaves and returns them to the bush, and the poets pass to the other edge of the wood. Here is the beginning of a desolate plain, and Dante looks fearfully about him. Many souls are on this plain, some lying down, some crouching, some wandering restlessly. Flakes of fire fall on this desert, making it burn and increasing the pain of these spirits who were violent against God. They try to save themselves from the rain of fire by waving it away with their hands.

Dante's attention turns to one spirit who lies on the sand without moving, paying no attention to the falling flakes. Dante asks Virgil his name, but the spirit himself answers that he is the same dead as he was living (that is, unconquered and blasphemous), and that even if Zeus has thunderbolts to hurl forever, he will never succeed in subduing this shade. This is Capaneus, killed by a thunderbolt from the hand of the angry Zeus. Virgil calls him by name and upbraids him for his pride, in a tone that Dante has never heard him use before.

Virgil tells Dante that this is the spirit of one of the Seven against Thebes, and that for his defiance of the gods, he is confined here.

Virgil asks Dante to follow and not step on the burning sand but stay close to the wood. Walking between the two rounds, they reach a small stream which is so red it disgusts Dante. Its banks are stone, and it quenches the fire even in the desert near it; Dante realizes that this is the path they must follow across the burning sand. Virgil tells him this is the most remarkable thing they have yet seen, and Dante asks him to explain.

His guide begins a long discourse. The island of Crete, he says, was ruled by a great king in the Golden Age. On the island is Mount Ida, once green with trees but now arid. This is the very mountain on which the goddess Rhea, wife of the jealous Cronus, had hidden her son to save him and ordered great noise to be made so the king could not hear his cries. Inside the mountain is a strange and wonderful being, who stands with his shoulders toward Damietta (Egypt), his face toward Rome. His head is made of gold, his arms and chest of silver; his torso is brass, and his legs of iron, except that his right foot is of clay, and he puts more weight upon this foot.

Except for his head, every part of his body has cracks from which tears come forth. These collect in the cavern where he stands, then run down into Hell, forming Acheron, Styx, and Phlegethon; this stream which they now follow; and, at the bottom where it can flow no farther, Cocytus, whose nature Dante will later see for himself.

Dante then asks his master a question: if the stream has flowed such a distance—from Crete to the center of the earth—why are they seeing it only now? Virgil answers that in descending the abyss, which is circular, they have been bearing to the left and have therefore not made a complete circle. If Dante sees new and strange things, this is the reason.

Again Dante has a question. Where can Phlegethon and Lethe be found? Virgil is pleased by this interest, and points out that the boiling red stream (Phlegethon) has already been passed, but that Lethe is not part of this abyss, and flows in another place, where the spirits who have been doing penance may then wash themselves.

The poets leave the wood, and Dante is warned to follow the edge of the stream closely to avoid the fire of the burning desert.

Commentary

The intellectual concept of Capaneus in Canto 14 is one of the great characterizations in the *Inferno*. The character of Capaneus re-emphasizes one concept of Dante's Hell, that is, that the person retains those very qualities which sent him to Hell. In classical times, Capaneus was a figure who thought himself so strong that not even Jove (Zeus, or Jupiter) could destroy him, but he *was* destroyed by the thunderbolts of Jove. For his blasphemy on earth he is condemned to Hell, and his first words to Dante are "Such as I was alive, such am I also in death." This emphasizes that he has *not* changed.

Although Virgil does upbraid Capaneus for his pride, Dante seems to be drawn toward this powerful figure who dared to defy the gods. For example, look at the difference in character between Capaneus and Fucci (Cantos 24-25), who "made figs" at God and blasphemed him. There is a certain power in Capaneus' defiance (certainly lacking in Fucci!), and even in Hell he remains as he was on earth – and has the blind strength to say so. Being condemned to death because of his pride and his blasphemy, in Hell he remains filled with pride and continues to blaspheme against God. Capaneus insults God even yet by saying that Jove himself will grow weary of trying to punish him before he, Capaneus, will give in to Jove's punishment. This is the ultimate defiance.

We have expressed here an idea which is important throughout Hell: that in any particular circle the *degree* of punishment is not always the same. Capaneus is being punished more than anyone else in this circle and, according to Virgil, as Capaneus keeps blaspheming against God, his punishment will increase throughout eternity.

There occurs in the canto one of the longest passages concerning a mythological being. This is the Old Man of Crete, whose flawed figure is symbolic of the imperfect ages of mankind – save for the perfect golden head which is the sign of the golden age. From the flaws come the tears which are the sorrows of man, flowing through Hell and depositing all the filth of sin at the feet of Satan.

Dante apparently makes an error of recollection in this canto. Virgil describes the course of the repulsive little red stream, naming the rivers it has formed as it flowed downward. Dante asks (lines 121-22) why they have not seen it before if it has flowed the long distance from Crete. The point is, of course, that they *have* seen it before, and Dante already knew the names of both the river Acheron and the marsh of Styx (which Virgil has just repeated) and has crossed Phlegethon, although he did not know its name. (Reference to Lethe will be found in the last canto and in the *Purgatorio.*)

CANTO 15

Summary

Dante and Virgil follow the stone bank of the river, which Dante compares to a dike holding back the sea. They walk a long distance across the burning plain, and can no longer see the wood, when they meet a group of spirits. These spirits peer at the two poets as though in darkness, until one of them recognizes Dante and speaks to him.

Dante looks at the spirit's face, so terribly changed by the searing heat, and calls him by name: Ser Brunetto. Brunetto asks if he may walk with them, and Dante of course is delighted to have him, asking if he wishes to sit down and talk. Brunetto explains that whoever stops for an instant must spend a hundred years without fanning himself in the terrible heat. He will walk beside Dante, talking as they go. And so, with Brunetto walking on the plain and Dante on the bank, they continue their journey.

Brunetto asks why Dante has come here and who his guide is. Dante tells the story of his first adventure on the mountain and his rescue by Virgil, though he does not give his name. Brunetto, in symbolic language, foretells the future fame of Dante, a fame which Brunetto would gladly have aided if he had lived. He also prophesies the events of Dante's exile.

Dante speaks with great kindness and gratitude for Brunetto's past help and teaching, and tells him that he thinks of him often. Dante also says he will ask a certain lady about the prophecies and is prepared to accept what Fortune wills for him. Virgil glances back and tells Dante that he is right to listen and remember.

Dante asks Brunetto who is with him on the burning plain, and is told that only a few can be mentioned, since time is short. All the spirits with him were scholars of renown and all are guilty of the same crime (sodomy, though Brunetto does not name it). He sees a new group approaching and he is not allowed to be with them; therefore he recommends his great book, the *Tresor,* to Dante and runs off.

Commentary

Dante meets the spirit of the man who did so much to guide and encourage his work. This was the illustrious scholar, Ser Brunetto Latini, whom Dante finds in the circle of sodomites. Their meeting is full of sorrow, and Dante greets Brunetto with love and deference, addressing him with the plural *you* as a sign of respect.

The meeting and conversation with Latini is one of the high points of the *Inferno*. Even Dante's posture while walking, though imposed by the conditions of their miserable surroundings, reveals the reverence he felt for this great master.

Brunetto gives Dante some fatherly advice about his future and expresses his wish to help, which no doubt he could have done, had he lived, for he was an important man in his time. He also warns Dante against the political division of Florence (which had already happened, of course).

Brunetto Latini was one who understood Dante's genius when others failed to do so; now the poet still finds in his master the support and the encouragement he needs to withstand the attacks that his fellow citizens are going to direct at him. In Brunetto Latini, Dante finds a sympathetic echo of his own disdain and pride. By his master Dante is encouraged to follow his star in order not to miss the glorious fortune for which he is destined.

The exchange of sentiments between the young and the old man is touching and compelling; if Ser Brunetto understands Dante so well, so does the poet understand his master when Brunetto recommends his *Tresor (Li Livres dou Tresor),* hoping that the fame of his great encyclopedic work is still alive in the world.

Dante's tribute to Brunetto is a sincere and moving one. Brunetto was not Dante's teacher in the formal sense, but rather his adviser, who took an interest in Dante, fostered his intellectual development, and served as his inspiration.

The symbolism of the rain of fire and the scorching sand is that of sterility and unproductiveness: the rain should be life-giving, the soil fertile. Instead, symbolically the sex practice of the sodomite is unnatural in that it is not life-giving; the practice of the usurer is unnatural because it is unproductive of anything except more money – a contemptible act in Dante's time.

CANTOS 16-17

Summary

Dante can hear the waterfall ahead, where the stream falls into the next lower circle, but before they reach it, the two poets see three spirits leave a large group and come toward them. The spirits recognize the distinctive Florentine dress (a long gown and folded hood) which Dante wears, and they ask him to wait. Dante is saddened by their wounds, which have been caused by the flakes of fire.

As the spirits approach, Virgil says that these are ones who deserve courtesy. The spirits again are crying out, and as they reach the two poets, they start walking in a circle (for, as Brunetto said, they dare not stop), and telling their stories.

One says they should not be looked upon with contempt because of their present condition, for in life they were famous. They wish to know what a living man is doing in Hell. Before Dante can answer, the spirit continues. The one ahead of him is Guido Guerra, a famous commander, and behind him is Tegghiaio Aldobrandi, a counselor of Guerra. The speaker is Jacopo Rusticucci, whose reputation has been greatly harmed by his own wife.

Dante would have embraced these three, leaders of his own party, but the fire prevents it. He can only tell them that he is indeed a Florentine (as his dress has shown) and that he will not forget their sorrow. He has heard and spoken of their great deeds all his life. He will be leaving Hell behind, but first he must visit the lower circles.

The spirits wish him long life and fame, and ask if Florence is still the same fine city they left, for another spirit lately arrived has told them otherwise. Sorrowfully Dante tells them that Florence is now a proud and sinful city. The spirits ask him to speak of them when he returns to earth, and then run to join their group.

Dante and Virgil have now come so close to the waterfall they can hardly hear each other. Dante has a cord tied around his waist—he had hoped to catch the leopard with it earlier—and Virgil asks him to untie it. Dante hands it to him in a coil, and he flings it far out into the abyss. Dante realizes this is some kind of signal, and Virgil tells him that what he expects will soon be there.

Knowing what what he is about to tell will scarcely be believed, Dante swears it is true: that such a creature as he had never dreamed of came swimming up through the darkness of the pit.

Virgil tells Dante that this wild beast with the pointed tail can go over mountains and destroy walls and weapons; he is the beast that corrupts the world.

Dante sees the figure of Fraud: the pleasant and kindly face of a man, hairy paws and arms, and the body of a snake painted in designs such as Dante has never seen before. It rests its arms upon the edge of the pit, showing only its head and shoulders and the end of its poisonous tail.

Virgil says they must go to him, and they step down onto an empty space which is not burning and see another group of spirits sitting. Virgil directs Dante to talk with them while he persuades the beast to carry them, and Dante walks toward the weeping spirits. They sit on the very edge of the circle, trying to brush off the flakes of fire, and Dante sees that each of them has a crested pouch hanging from his neck. Each spirit looks unmoving at his own pouch, and each crest is different. These are the usurers.

One spirit speaks to Dante, ordering him to leave because he is alive. The spirit continues to talk, however, and tells Dante that Vitaliano shall soon sit on the plain beside him. He is the only Paduan; the rest are of Florence, and they often cry out the name of another Florentine who will soon join them. The spirit sticks out his tongue at Dante, who retreats quickly, to find Virgil already on the back of the monster. Virgil orders him to mount quickly; Dante turns pale but obeys. Virgil holds him and orders the monster Geryon to circle slowly to their landing place.

Dante is terrified by the descent and can see nothing, though he can feel the strong wind and hear the whirlpool below. Finally, he gathers courage and looks down, but the sight and sound are frightening: he sees fires and hears great cries. Geryon sets them down near the bottom of the jagged rocks and flies off like an arrow.

Commentary

Canto 16 holds less interest in comparison to the sincerity and sorrow of the preceding canto. The allusions here are almost entirely political.

Dante's answer to the three Florentines represents his own diagnosis of the swift changes which actually took place in Florence at the end of the thirteenth century because of a rapid transformation in the economy and in the society of the commune. Dante sees in these economic and social changes the origin of the moral decadence of the city and the cause for the disappearance of the old habits that were dear to him. His words hold disdain for the "upstart people" and distrust for the new fashions which he does not understand and, therefore, does not like. The same feelings are expressed repeatedly in the *Divine Comedy*.

The description of the usurers, who try to defend themselves from the rain of fire and the hot soil, is full of contempt and is intended to stress the degradation of those men of noble stock who were in fact ignoble and contemptible. Their faces, scorched as they are by the flakes of fire, have lost all human aspect and are not recognizable; their movements are not those of men, but of animals. All their humanity has been consumed by their thirst for gold; therefore the only signs which distinguish one from the other are the moneybags, which hang from their necks. They are disgusting and despicable in Dante's eyes.

Much of the critical interest in this canto centers on the symbolism of the cord which Dante wears and which Virgil tosses into the pit as a signal. It is believed that the cord may have some connection with the Franciscan order, in which it symbolizes humility. By Dante's own admission he had hoped to catch the leopard with it. If the leopard symbolized incontinence, Dante may be indicating that he had hoped to overcome his errors (pride in his work or perhaps too great a dependence on philosophy?) through humility. This is only one of many interpretations. Whatever the significance of the cord, it serves as a command to the monster which personifies fraud.

The monster Geryon has a kindly face, but the decorations of his body symbolize the twisted dealings of the fraudulent. The scorpion's tail is symbolic of the *coup de grâce* which completes the fraud, the unexpected sting from one who proves unworthy of trust.

Dante has described admirably the swimming motions of Geryon, which carry him like an eel through the dark air, but the clearest image is that of the falcon, deprived of his prey, who wheels and sinks in flight, sullenly ignoring his master. In contrast, when Geryon is relieved of the burden of Dante's weight, the monstrous figure is airborne in an instant.

CANTOS 18-19

Summary

Dante describes Malebolge, the eighth circle, in which increasingly terrible sins are punished. Its walls are made of stone, and exactly in the center is a well which Dante says he will describe later.

Malebolge is round, as the other levels have been, but it is divided into ten deep, concentric valleys, whose banks go down like stairsteps toward the central well. Across these valleys, going from bank to bank, are bridges which lead to the well.

Dante and his guide move away from the place where Geryon has left them and start toward the left. They see the first chasm, or valley, filled with tormented sinners walking in both directions. Demons with horns flog them continuously to keep them moving.

One of the shades looks up at Dante, who recognizes him. Dante goes back a few steps, and although the spirit tries to hide his face, Dante calls him by name. It is Venedico Caccianimico, and the spirit is compelled to tell Dante his ugly story: the spirit arranged the seduction of his own sister Ghisola. As if in his own defense, he says he is not the only one from Bologna in this circle of panderers. A demon strikes him with a whip and orders him on.

Dante rejoins Virgil, and they start across the bridge on the first chasm. They stop in the middle to look down at the circle of sinners going in the direction opposite from the panderers. The first figure they see is that of the proud Jason, who gives no sign of pain; with him are other seducers.

The two cross to the bank of the second chasm and, because they cannot see the bottom, again go to the middle of the bridge. This is the circle of flatterers, whose shades are sunk in excrement.

Dante sees someone he knows, Alessio Interminei of Lucca, who says he is sunk to the top of his head because his tongue could never stop its flattery. Virgil directs Dante to look farther on, at the figure of a woman. He identifies her as Thais, who flattered her lover extravagantly when he sent her a gift. With this, the two poets have seen enough.

Dante now speaks out against those of the third chasm, the simonists, who trade the grace and favor of the church for money. Standing in the middle of the bridge, Dante sees that the bottom of the chasm is full of round holes. From each of these holes protrude the feet and legs of a spirit, with the rest of his body upside down in the hole. The soles of their feet are on fire, and Dante sees one shade who is apparently suffering more torment than others, moving and shaking, his feet burning more fiercely than any others.

Naturally Dante wishes to know who it is, and Virgil replies that if Dante will go with him, he will find out. They descend to the bottom of the chasm and stand next to the pit of the sinner. Dante asks him to speak, if he can; the spirit replies by calling him Boniface and asking if he is here already, before his time.

Startled, Dante cannot answer until Virgil tells him to say simply that he is not Boniface, which he does. The spirit weeps and tells Dante that since he was so curious to know the shade's identity, he will tell him: he was a pope (Nicholas III) who engaged in simony. Below him, in cracks in the rock, are other popes who did the same. When the next pope shall join them, Nicholas, too, will fall down into the stone.

Dante reproaches the shade by asking him how much gold Jesus asked of Peter before he gave him the keys of the kingdom and reminding him that the only requirement was that Peter should follow Jesus. And, he says, Peter and the other disciples asked for no money when they chose Matthias to take the place of Judas. The poet can barely restrain his words; he believes these sinners are receiving the punishment they deserve, and only his respect for the former high office they held keeps him from saying worse things. As it is, he continues his tirade, observing that Virgil is pleased.

At last Virgil picks him up, climbs the side of the chasm, and walks to the center of the next bridge, where Dante sees another valley below him.

Commentary

The poets have entered the circle of Malebolge. There is a certain amount of confusion over the terminology, which can lead to a confusion of images. The word "bolgia" in Italian means both "pit" and "pouch," but neither term seems to be the best translation for the idea Dante wanted to convey. The words "chasm" or "ravine" seem to carry the connotation of depth and ruggedness that Dante would wish, but "moat" would probably be equally acceptable, as Dante implies in an early stanza. The word "well" might be replaced with "crater" or "abyss" in the interests of clarity.

Malebolge is a terrible place, in the real sense of the word. Dante has devoted thirteen cantos to this one circle of Hell. These are the heart of the *Inferno* and contain some of the most dramatic scenes, both in content and in poetic richness. Canto 18 opens with a long descriptive passage unequalled in the *Inferno*.

Dante seems to be drawn to the figures of courageous heroes. Here Jason is described as undaunted by his punishment; earlier the proud

Capaneus captured the imagination of Dante, as will the figure of Ulysses later.

The opening lines of Canto 19 are a bitter denunciation of the simonists, reflecting Dante's preoccupation with the corruption of his church. The sinners are punished in a manner which is a curious reversal of baptismal practices of the time: they are plunged head down in narrow pits and are tortured by fire playing on the soles of their feet, rather than being cleansed and purified by the cool sweetness of holy water.

Dante describes the pits and takes the opportunity to refute publicly a charge (probably of sacrilege) brought against him years earlier. He had broken the baptismal font at San Giovanni, he says, in order to save someone from drowning.

The subject of simony seems to rouse Dante to rage, as any corrupt practice of the church did. It also elevates him to the heights of poetic expression, as he angrily demands an answer to his questions, and he sternly rebukes Pope Nicholas even as he reiterates his reverence for the papal office.

CANTO 20

Summary

Dante views the shades who are walking slowly and weeping. He is amazed to discover that their heads are turned backward on their bodies. They are not simply looking over their shoulders; their heads have been turned around so that they are forced to walk backward in order to see where they are going, and as they weep their tears run down their backs. Dante weeps to see such distortion of the human body.

Virgil reproves him for questioning the judgment of God on the sinners and tells him to look at the shades. They are ones who sinned by trying to foretell the future, which is known only to God. He names several, ending the list with the name of Manto the sorceress, mythical founder of the city of Mantua, Virgil's birthplace. He tells the long story of the founding of the city and asks Dante to promise that, if he ever hears any other version, he will tell this, the true story. Dante promises and asks Virgil to point out more of the spirits by name.

Virgil indicates Eurypylus, who, with Calchas, determined by sorcery the propitious time for the Greek ships to set sail against Troy. Virgil says that Dante surely must remember the story from Virgil's own writings. He then points out Michael Scott, a writer on the occult sciences; Guido Bonatti (an astrologer); and Asdente, who had been a shoemaker before he turned to sorcery. These are followed by many women who left their proper work to become witches.

Virgil urges Dante to hurry on, for the moon is already setting. Virgil reminds Dante that the moon was full and lighted his way while he wandered in the dark wood; then they walk on toward the next circle.

Commentary

There is a definite break in the narrative here. Dante the writer intrudes upon Dante the pilgrim; once before, in Canto 16, he has mentioned his writing, but it was less obtrusive. Then he simply said "I swear by this my Comedy."

If Dante was in the habit of sending several finished cantos to Can Grande della Scala, perhaps Canto 19 marks the end of one of those sections and Canto 20 the beginning of another. There may have been a lapse of time, during which Can Grande read and returned previous cantos, with his comments.

Dante, following the teachings of the church, obviously did not approve of sorcery in any form, and therefore would seek to negate Virgil's reputation as a white magician. In his long discourse on the origins of his native city of Mantua, Virgil denies that its founding was in any way attributed to the influence of Manto, the sorceress. By this devious means Dante seeks to clear Virgil of guilt by association, emphatically declaring that this and only this is the true story of the founding of Mantua.

For the first time, Dante violates his own concept of judging each spirit by the standards of the time in which it lived. Here he condemns the Greek prophets, who were held in high esteem in their own time. One would think Dante would also be forced then to condemn the prophets of the Old Testament, and since he is silent on this point, it is difficult to see the fine line of distinction drawn by Dante. His only argument could be that the gift of prophecy, or the genuine spirit of prophecy, was valid only as a forerunner of Christianity, hence offering, in effect, another excuse for Virgil.

Though he does not approve, Dante can still sympathize with the plight of the sinners and their torment which makes them appear less than human. In life these spirits tried to look ahead into the future; now they are condemned to look behind them. Considering this condemnation, why are all the spirits of Hell given the power to foresee the future? Is it because the knowledge of events and disasters of future times will increase their torments?

CANTOS 21-23

Summary

The travelers cross to the center of the next bridge and view the next chasm, which is extremely dark. Dante compares it with the arsenal in Venice where pitch is boiled to caulk the ships and other repairs are made.

This is indeed a river of boiling pitch, which has splashed up on the banks everywhere. Dante can see nothing except bubbles and some indication of movement beneath its surface. He leans over to look more closely, but Virgil warns him to be careful, not of the bridge, but of another danger. Dante turns to see a black demon approach, carrying a new spirit over his shoulders. He calls to the Malebranche (Evil Claws) of the bridge to push this citizen of Lucca (the city of Saint Zita) under the pitch, while he goes back to the same city for more, for there is a plentiful supply there. He throws the spirit into the circle of barrators, or grafters—those who profit from their position in public office—and hastens back for more.

The shade is tossed into the pitch and comes to the surface, but the demons under the bridge warn him that the will not swim here as he did in the river Serchio, near Lucca. He must stay under the surface or be punished with their hooks, and they strike him to make him plunge downward. Whatever he may steal, they say, he will take in secret, as he did in life.

Virgil now orders Dante to hide himself in the ruins of the bridge and to remain silent no matter what happens, since Virgil has been this way before and can handle matters himself.

Virgil walks calmly to the bank of the sixth chasm. All of the demons of the bridge rush at him, threatening him with their weapons, but Virgil holds them off momentarily by asking to talk with one of their number. Malacoda (Evil Tail) comes forward, asking what good this conference will do.

Virgil tells him firmly that he and Dante are safe from any harm, since their journey was willed in Heaven. Malecoda drops his hook and orders the others not to attack. Virgil then calls to Dante, in somewhat unflattering terms, and tells him to come forward. Dante goes to his side and stands close, fearing that the demons, who have moved closer, may not follow the orders of Malacoda.

The demons do not raise their hooks to threaten Dante, but instead taunt him by talking among themselves, suggesting that he should be tormented with their hooks—just a little.

Malacoda silences them roughly, then turns to Virgil and tells him that the nearest bridge across the sixth chasm is broken (and he gives the exact date and hour when it happened) but that there is another bridge not far ahead. Some of his men (demons) are going to walk along the bank to keep the spirits under the pitch, and the two poets can accompany them in safety. He calls a patrol of ten demons forward, ordering to watch for rebellious shades. He tells them that the two travelers will go with them as far as the unbroken bridge.

Dante is terrified at going with these demons and asks Virgil if they cannot find the way alone. He points out the demons, frowning and gnashing their teeth, but Virgil says this show of fierceness is for the spirits not for them.

The patrol marches away, along the bank, each saluting the captain by sticking out his tongue, and the captain replies by breaking wind with a noise like a trumpet.

Dante is a man of considerable military experience, but he has never before experienced an exchange of salutes like this one! Still shaken by the presence of the demons, he accepts it more or less philosophically, and the two poets follow the demons.

Dante's interest now is not in the demons but in the luckless sinners trapped in the mess of pitch. Occasionally one will rise to the surface like a dolphin and as quickly disappear; others sit near the bank, submerged like frogs with only their muzzles showing. All but one disappear as the demon Barbariccia approaches, and this one is hooked like an otter by the demon Graffiacane and dragged up out of the pitch.

As the demons call out, Dante, who has remembered the name of each one, listens as they shout to Rubicante to claw this sinner and flog him well. Dante asks his master to learn the name and story of this shade. Virgil moves closer, and in reply to his question, the spirit answers that he is from Navarre and was in the service of King Thibaut. He used his position to sell political favors, and that is why he is being tortured here.

As he is speaking, the demon Ciriatto rips at him with one of his long tusks; Barbariccia, who is holding the shade, orders the demons back, then turns to Virgil and tells him to go on with his questions before another demon attacks. Virgil asks if any Latian lies below. The shade replies that he has just now seen one from the other side (Sardinia) and wishes he were down with him now.

Another demon attacks, hooking his arm, and a second tries to jab his legs, but their leader quells them with a look – temporarily. Virgil asks the name of this barrator from Sardinia, and the shade replies that it is Friar Gomita of Gallura, who worked so smoothly he was indeed a king among barrators. Don Michel Zanche is with him, and they never tire of talking about Sardinia.

Another demon threatens and is warned off. The shade offers to call more spirits, these from Tuscany and Lombardy, if the demons can be kept back. One of the demons instantly suspects a trick, which the shade denies, and a second demon threatens the spirit, saying that if he tries to escape, the demon will not run after him but will fly to the very surface of the pitch to catch him.

The demons are beginning to quarrel among themselves when the spirit sees his chance, dives into the pitch, and goes under. Two demons start after him, one pulling up in his flight just before he reaches the river of pitch, the second attacking him because he has let the sinner escape. Like two birds of prey they battle with their claws, only to become mired in the pitch so they cannot fly. The captain sends four more demons to rescue them with their hooks, and Dante and Virgil leave the noisy scene of the quarrel.

The two poets walk in welcome silence, and Dante is lost in thought, recalling Aesop's fable of the frog and the mouse, in which the frog offers to tie the mouse to his leg and carry him over a marsh but dives into the water, drowning the mouse; a hawk then carries off both of them. Following this train of thought, Dante recalls the demons, who may blame the two poets for the whole quarrel, and adding anger to their natural evil, may pursue the travelers.

By now he is thoroughly frightened and begs Virgil to hide them quickly. Virgil has had the same thought and has already decided to climb down into the next chasm. The demons are in fact pursuing them, and Virgil picks Dante up, as a mother would a child, and carries him rapidly to the very bottom of the seventh chasm. This leaves the demons high above them on the bank in impotent rage, for these pursuers can no more leave their own realm than the condemned sinners can.

The travelers see that the chasm is filled with spirits walking very slowly, as with a heavy burden. These shades wear cloaks and hoods that are dazzling with their glitter but lined with lead. Dante and Virgil turn to the left and follow the bed of the chasm but are walking faster than the spirits, so Dante asks Virgil to find someone they might know.

A spirit calls to Dante, recognizing his Tuscan speech, and asks him to wait. Two spirits approach without speaking. Finally one observes that Dante must be alive because his throat moves. Speaking to Dante, they ask why he has come to this valley of hypocrites and who he is.

Dante says he is a Florentine and is indeed alive; in turn, he asks who they are who weep so bitterly and what their punishment is. The answer is given: their bright cloaks are of thick lead and their punishment is to carry them forever. They were of the order of the Jovial Friars and had been named to govern Florence jointly, in order to keep the peace.

Dante angrily begins to speak to the friars of their evil, when he sees a figure on the ground held by three stakes. Friar Catalano explains that this is one (Caiaphas, the high priest) who told the Council that it was better for Jesus to die than for the whole nation to perish. Therefore he lies where each one who passes must step upon him, and his father-in-law (Annas) and all the Council are punished in the same manner. Virgil looks at Caiaphas for some time. Finally he turns and asks the friar if there is a bridge over the chasm. The friar answers that all were destroyed at the same time, but the travelers may climb out on the ruins of one nearby without much difficulty.

Virgil realizes that Malacoda has lied to him about the bridges, as he had about the dependability of the bodyguard. Angrily he walks away from the cloaked spirits, and Dante follows.

Commentary

The opening lines of Canto 21 probably refer to a further discussion between the two poets concerning witchcraft and sorcery. Dante does not care to repeat the conversation, first, because it is not a proper topic for his *Comedy,* and second, because he probably does not wish for any further reflection on Virgil as a white magician.

All three cantos are bright with imagery and description, and lack any trace of that moral concern which is inspired by other scenes of torment. Dante compares the chasm with the arsenal at Venice; he describes the demons and their tortures with gusto, making them seem a bunch of fiendish rascals gleefully applying their hooks. There is not the somber tone of many other cantos, and when Virgil discovers that Malacoda has told two outright lies, he stalks across the floor of the chasm in a very human manner. The flow of the narrative and the poetic unity to the end of the cantos show Dante's art at its best.

The destruction of the bridges, as well as the landslide Virgil has described, was believed to have taken place when Jesus was crucified and an earthquake occurred. (See Canto 12.) One wonders, though, why Caiaphas, who presided at the Council that sentenced Jesus to death, is not in the circle of evil counselors.

Virgil is something less than sympathetic to Dante. Having ordered Dante to hide in the ruins of the bridge, he calls him forth with a suggestion of rebuke for cowering among the stones.

In the circle of hypocrites, Dante is again recognized as being alive, this time because his throat moves as he talks. The cloaks of the hypocrites, which dazzle the eye, actually are instruments of torture. Moreover, the heavy garments they wear force the sinners to adopt a decorous and subdued attitude which is entirely in character with their worldly habit of hiding a vicious nature beneath a virtuous and holy appearance.

Dante has placed the hypocrites far down in the circles of Hell. Their presence is a restatement of Dante's definition of sin as perversion of the intellect; few sins can equal the deliberate cloaking of one's true character and feelings in a false aspect of piety, tolerance, or honesty.

CANTOS 24-25

Summary

Virgil's anger, though not directed at him, has made Dante as downcast and troubled as a shepherd without pasture for his sheep. Dante is dependent upon his master not only for physical help but also for spiritual guidance and moral support, and it now seems to Dante that this has been withdrawn with alarming suddenness. One look from Virgil soon calms his spirit, however, for he wears the same benign expression as when Dante first saw him.

Virgil's plan is clear: he has looked at the ruins of the bridge and knows it can be climbed if they are careful. The ascent presents no problem for Virgil—he is weightless—but he gives careful directions to Dante to test each rock before he puts his weight on it. Holding (and pushing) Dante from behind, Virgil selects the route and they mount from rock to rock. Dante is well aware that, even if Virgil could have climbed it alone, he himself could not have done it without help.

At last they reach the top, and Dante drops exhausted. Virgil somewhat unfeelingly urges him forward, saying he cannot gain the heights if he is lazy. Dante pretends that he has overcome his exhaustion and with false eagerness goes ahead, talking all the time as if he were not out of breath. A voice from the chasm answers; Dante cannot make out the words even though they are now in the middle of the bridge, but the voice speaks in anger.

Dante can see nothing in the darkness of the seventh chasm and tells his master so. They walk to the end of the bridge, where it rests on the wall between the seventh and eighth chasms, and look down on the mass of strange serpents below them. Even the memory of this makes Dante's blood run cold.

The poets see naked people running, with no place to hide, nor, as Dante says, with any hope of invisibility (the heliotrope was a stone supposed to make its wearer invisible). There are strange and terrifying sights: the hands of each shade are tied behind him with a serpent, whose head and tail are thrust through the spirit's body at the loins and tied in coils and knots at the front; another serpent sinks its fangs in the neck of a shade, who immediately takes fire and burns to ashes on the ground, only to resume its shape—and its torment—once again. This shade seems bewildered by what has happened, as one who has been the victim of a seizure of some kind.

Virgil asks who he is, and he answers that he came recently from Tuscany, where he lived the life of a beast. He gives his name as Vanni Fucci of Pistoia. Dante asks what his crime was, for he had seen him once and considered him a man of violence. The spirit, ashamed, confesses that it hurts him more for Dante to see him there than it did to be condemned for his sin. He had robbed the sacristy of a church (San Zeno), and although his crime had gone undetected for a time, he was condemned to this chasm of thieves. He then prophesies, in somewhat obscure language, a future battle involving Pistoia first, then Florence itself, and Dante's party shall suffer greatly from it.

Dante is shocked by the next action of the thief, who makes an obscene gesture with both hands, and shouts blasphemies in the face of God. Dante is gratified when one of the serpents coils around the thief's neck, silencing him, and another binds his arms to his sides. Dante laments the evil of the citizens of Pistoia, saying that in all of Hell he has seen no spirit so blasphemous, not even Capaneus. The shade runs off, and is immediately followed by a monster (mistakenly called a centaur by Dante) who is covered with snakes up to his waist and bears a firebreathing dragon on his back.

Virgil identifies this creature as Cacus, who stole some of Hercules' cattle, for which Hercules killed him with his club. The monster runs off, and Dante and Virgil hear the voices of three shades asking who the travelers are. Dante does not know them but learns their names as they call to one another.

In the most vivid language, Dante tells of the two horrible transformations that take place. One of the shades is grasped tightly by the six legs of a serpent who then sinks his fangs into the spirit's face. Gradually the two shapes become indistinguishable; then that which was the serpent becomes the shade, and the shade is the serpent.

While this is going on, an evil, black little reptile bites the second of the spirits. Smoke issues from both the mouth of the serpent and the wound of the shade, though the shade seems to take no notice of its wound. As the two jets of smoke meet, the legs of the spirit grow together, while the tail of the serpent divides; the skin of the snake softens, that of the shade grows scaly. The monstrous changes continue until the former spirit runs hissing away as a serpent, and the former serpent speaks in the shape of a man.

Dante's pen fails him, his eyes are clouded and his mind numbed, but he recognizes the third spirit, the only one unchanged, as that of Puccio Sciancato.

Commentary

The canto of the thieves begins with a long-drawn image which is couched in obscure phrasing. In the original it is a carefully contrived relief from the scenes Dante has just witnessed and a pause before viewing further torments. It is followed by a humorous passage describing Dante as he clambers with great difficulty up the stony bank of the chasm and trots breathless behind his master, talking to keep up the pretense. This is a very human Dante, poking a little fun at his stodgy self, and proves an effective contrast in style.

The obscene gesture of the thief startles Dante, and the poet's words concerning Pistoia are a curse rather than a lament. Fucci's cynical self-portrait, drawn with a sort of proud satisfaction, dwells on the baseness of his conduct, his origin, and his city. His shame is not born of repentance but rather of resentment and anger at being surprised in such a place and condemned to that horrible metamorphosis. He seeks revenge against Dante and utters the dark prophecy of the triumph of the Blacks only in the cruel hope of hurting the poet.

The transformations of the spirits and the serpents are described at length with terrifying vividness, but not with the tone used in telling about the demons of the fifth bolgia. Watching in horrified fascination, Dante seems to be recalling an evil nightmare, and words fail him at the end—an effective literary device that he will use again. The fifth spirit runs off unchanged, but we may easily guess that he will be next in the succession of dreadful transformations by which men are made beasts, and beasts, men.

CANTOS 26-27

Summary

Dante bitterly addresses his native city, whose fame has spread not only over the earth but also throughout Hell because of the actions of her citizens. He prophesies disaster in the future, and since he knows it will happen eventually, he wishes for it to happen now; his knowledge weighs heavily upon him and he is powerless to stop the disaster.

The travelers are at the eighth chasm, that of the evil counselors, and Dante sees little flames as numerous as fireflies on a summer night. He looks so intently that he nearly falls off the bridge and saves himself by catching hold of the parapet. His guide tells him that each of these flames holds a spirit and that each spirit holds close the fire which torments him. Dante has already observed this and asks the name of the spirit with a divided flame.

Virgil says that this flame holds two spirits, those of Ulysses and of Diomede, who together planned the stratagem of the Trojan horse. They also suffer torment for separating Achilles from Deidamia, who died of a broken heart, and for stealing the statue of Pallas, which guarded the city of Troy. Dante is eager to speak with these two. Virgil is pleased but reminds Dante that, since these spirits speak the Greek language and Dante does not, it might be best for Virgil to talk with them.

Virgil speaks respectfully to the double flame, recalling his own poetry to them and asking if he might know how Ulysses died, and where. The greater part of the flame speaks, flickering with each word. This is the spirit of Ulysses the wanderer, and in comparable language Dante tells the story of his last voyage.

Ulysses had at long last returned home, but neither the love of his wife and son, nor the respect due his father, could conquer the wanderlust that was in him. Once again he sailed the open sea, in one ship with a few trusted companions. He saw all the strange sights of the Mediterranean—Spain, Morocco, Sardinia—and then, because he and his comrades were old and desired to see more before they rested on shore forever, they passed through the Pillars of Hercules and sailed south on the unknown ocean.

For five months they sailed, until they could see the stars of the south pole and the guiding stars of the north were not visible above the horizon. And then one day they saw a mountain, the highest they had ever seen, and a hurricane rose from the land. It struck their ship, and the ship went down, bow first, and the waters closed over them.

The flame becomes silent and is dismissed by Virgil. It is followed by another, which speaks in such confused tones that Dante compares it with the bellowings of a brass bull used as an instrument of torture and death.

Finally the spirit is able to control the flame and speak intelligibly. It asks courteously to speak and wishes to know if the travelers have come recently from his own Latian land. Is there now peace or war? it asks.

Virgil says that Dante is a Latian, and Dante speaks immediately, giving a long discourse on the past and present troubles of that unhappy land: Romagna is at present not at war; Ravenna and Cervia are under the same ruler (whose crest is an eagle); Forli, once victorious over the French, is now ruled by Sinibaldo degli Ordelaffi (whose coat of arms is a green lion); Montagna is ruled by the cruel Rimini, father and son, whose castle is Verucchio; the cities on the Lamone and the Santerno are governed by a lord who tries to support both factions; and, finally, Cesena on the Savio is misruled by its appointed leaders.

Catching his breath, Dante asks the name and story of this spirit. The flame answers that it will tell the truth, since none ever returned to earth from here to tell the story. He was a soldier; then, repenting of his evil ways, he became a brother of the order of St. Francis. He had been famous for his cunning while he was a soldier but sincerely repented and became a monk. Heaven was his goal, and this he would have gained, except that the pope (Boniface VIII), who was making war, not upon infidels but upon other Christians, asked him to devise a plan of cunning and deceit, absolving him of sin in advance, as it were.

The plan was successful, and the pope triumphed. Meanwhile, the monk died and St. Francis descended from Heaven to receive his soul, as he did with every brother of the order, but a demon claimed the spirit, which had fallen into sin and had not repented. Even the absolution of the pope could not save him, and he was sent by Minos to this chasm of evil counselors. The flame moves away, and Dante and his guide go to the bridge that crosses the ninth chasm, that of the sowers of discord.

Commentary

In the realm of the evil counselors, Dante meets the spirits of Ulysses and Diomede in the form of a double flame. Virgil charges them to speak, naming their obligation to him in a kind of conjuration, and Ulysses tells the tale of his last voyage.

Poetically, this is another of the high points of the *Inferno*. The story is apparently an invention by Dante and, while beautiful in itself, serves also to display Dante's increasing sureness of touch in the handling of his material. Ulysses seems to be speaking in his own words, not Dante's, in contrast with the story of Francesca, for example, which was told in Dante's own style. Read the rallying cry of Ulysses to his crew, beginning with "Consider your origin. . . ." Then compare this with any part of Francesca's speech and with the stanza of the cranes, and the difference will be obvious. Francesca and Dante speak with one voice, but the story of Ulysses is the compelling, unembellished yarn of an experienced and courageous sailor. Dante has brought this legendary figure to life to tell its final story, a story that captures the imagination, and Ulysses is a powerful creation of unusual stature and tragic dimension.

Note that the two spirits cannot depart until dismissed by Virgil—the conjuration is ended. Here again, Dante has violated his own concept of the spirits being judged by the standards of their times. The action of Ulysses and Diomede in advising the building of the Trojan horse was, to the Greeks, an acceptable and admirable strategy of war. It is *Dante* who considers it an act of treachery.

Dante speaks with another figure, Guido da Montefeltro, who arouses his sympathy, and its story, like that of Ulysses, is told simply but forcefully. This spirit is not aware that Dante is alive and thus could reveal its sin when he returns to eath (ll.61-66). Only in ignorance does he confess his treachery to Dante. This tale does not have the appeal of the other, but its construction and language are as sound. Dante places the noble figure of the great soldier and repentant friar in opposition to the protagonist, Boniface VIII, for whom Dante reserves his bitterest invective because the pope dares to wage war, not against the Saracens, but against the Christians themselves, and because he is the instrument of the spiritual damnation of one of the sons of the church.

Though Guido is suffering the torture of the flames, he can still speak of the sweetness of his native land, an effective contrast. Boniface VIII, the Black Cherubim with his irrefutable logic, and St. Francis descending for his brother in Christ, are unforgettable images.

CANTO 28

Summary

Dante warns of the horrors to come, more gruesome than even he can describe. This is the place of the sowers of discord and scandal, and the creators of schism within the church.

The first one Dante sees is Mahomet, disembowelled, who tells him that his son-in-law and successor, Ali, is in the same condition and that all the others are horribly mangled in some manner. As they circle the chasm the wounds heal, but when they complete the circle the wounds are renewed by a devil with a sword.

The shade asks Dante's identity, suggesting that perhaps he is trying to delay his punishment. Virgil replies that Dante is alive and is being guided through Hell so that he may know what it is like (and presumably avoid it). A large group of spirits has now gathered to listen. Mahomet bids Dante deliver a message to Fra Dolcino, leader of a schismatic sect within the church, warning him to supply his community with food so that the Novarese will not be victorious because of the winter snow.

Mahomet's place is taken by another mutilated spirit who recognizes Dante. He asks Dante to warn Messer Guido and Angiolello that they will be drowned at sea by the treachery of a one-eyed ruler, who will summon them to a parley. The shade mentions one who wishes he had never seen the land (Rimini) of this treacherous ruler, and Dante asks to see this spirit. It cannot speak, however, and the first shade tells Dante it is Curio, who urged Caesar to cross the Rubicon. For this, his tongue has been slit and he is mute.

Another spirit has had his hands cut off. This is Mosca (de' Lamberti), whose rash counsel was the beginning of the disastrous rivalry between the Guelphs and the Ghibellines in Florence. Dante bitterly wishes death to all of Mosca's kindred, and Mosca, pained by this comment, walks away.

Now Dante sees something which is beyond belief. A headless spirit comes toward them, but in his hand he carries the severed head and swings it like a lantern. When he reaches the bridge, he holds up the head so it can speak, and it identifies the shade as Bertrand de Born. With his evil scandal, he caused father and son to become enemies, and now his brain, inventor of the tales, is parted from his body.

Commentary

Dante, viewing the sowers of scandal and dissension, describes in vivid terms the tortures and the sins of the damned. He views Mohammed as a sinner whose religious beliefs led to discord and schism.

Though he has seen the sowers of religious discord, Dante reserves his bitterest comment for the man whose evil counsel started the quarrel in Florence between the Guelphs and the Ghibellines. This man is Mosca dei Lamberti, and his advice caused the initial feud between two Florentine families, the Donati and the Amidei. A man betrothed to one of the Amidei broke the engagement (which in those days was as binding as marriage) and became engaged to a Donati. Mosca's counsel to the Amidei was brief: "A thing done has an end" (do it and get it over), and the man was murdered. As a consequence the offended Donati, to whom he was now allied by betrothal, began the vendetta which brought so much sorrow to Florence. Dante's words "And death to thy kindred!" cut across the dismal air like a whip.

The punishment of Bertrand de Born, a Provencal poet of some note, escapes the grotesque because of Dante's poetic skill. The spirit carries its head like a lantern because it used vicious scandals to separate father from son, namely Henry II of England and his eldest son. Thus it was aptly punished by having its head separated from its body. Dante expresses his own mystification and the lament of the spirit briefly and lucidly.

CANTOS 29-30

Summary

The sight of the tortured shades of the ninth chasm compels Dante to stay and weep; Virgil reminds him that they have not stayed this long at any other chasm, and that since their time is short, they must be on their way. Dante tells his master, in morose tones, that if he knew why Dante was waiting, he would not wish to hurry on. Following Virgil, Dante continues his lament: he had been looking for one of his own kinsmen in the ninth circle.

Virgil replies that he had seen the spirit just under the bridge; it had shaken its finger threateningly at Dante, and the other shades had called it Geri del Bello. This had happened while Dante was talking with the other spirit. Dante replies sorrowfully that the murder of Geri del Bello has not been avenged by those who plotted with him, and therefore his spirit was angry and went away without speaking. Somewhat defiantly, Dante says he still feels sorry for this kinsman.

While they have been speaking, they have reached the bridge over the tenth and last chasm of the eighth circle, Malebolge. So loud are the wails and weeping that Dante puts his hands over his ears and thinks of the noise of the hospitals of Valdichiana, and of Maremma and Sardinia, during the unhealthful summer season. Ever the experienced soldier, the stench reminds him of rotting human limbs.

They move across the bridge to the lower bank of the chasm, where Dante can have a better view. This dark and stinking place is that of the falsifiers, and Dante finds the air stifling. The diseased shades are lying in heaps, and some are crawling about. Dante sees two sitting together, scratching vigorously at each other and pulling off scabs as one scales a fish.

Virgil asks if there are any Latians among them, and the shades, weeping, reply that they are Latians, but who is it who asks the question? Virgil replies that he is guiding one who lives through the paths of Hell. The shades stop their scratching, and Virgil tells Dante that he may talk with them if he wishes. Dante of course asks them their names and their stories.

The first one says that he is Arezzo and was burned at the request of Albert of Siena when he told Albert, as a joke (he says), that he could teach him to fly; Minos, who knows all things, condemned him to this tenth chasm, not for his lie but because he was an alchemist, another form of falsifying. Dante remarks on the vanity of the Sienese, which makes them gullible subjects for the falsifiers, and the second shade speaks out, naming other Sienese he knew in his lifetime who were still more vain.

This spirit then tells Dante to look closely at him and he will see the shade of Capocchio, also an alchemist and, he says with a touch of vanity, a good one.

Two spirits run through the darkness. One comes to Capocchio, sinks its teeth in his neck and drags him off. The spirit who had first spoken trembles and says this rabid shade is that of Gianni Schicchi. Dante asks who the other one is, and is told that this is Myrrha, who conceived an incestuous passion for her own father and went to his bed disguised. Schicchi had conspired to falsify a will, using a disguise, and in so doing had gained possession of a fine mare known as the Lady of the Troop.

These shades have all gone, and Dante looks around at others, seeing one so swollen out of shape with dropsy that he looks like a lute. He identifies himself as Master Adam, counterfeiter of the gold coin of Florence, and he begs for water. He is unable to move but he would willingly give up even the sight of water if the other conspirators in the counterfeiting plan were here with him.

Dante asks the names of two who lie nearby. They are identified as the wife of Potiphar, who falsely accused Joseph, and Sinon the Greek, who was taken prisoner and then persuaded his Trojan captors to bring the wooden horse inside the walls of the city. One of the shades, insulted by his words, strikes Master Adam in the belly, which sounds like a drum. Master Adam quickly strikes back, hitting the shade in the face. The two begin bickering and insulting each other, and Dante listens intently.

Virgil speaks to him sharply for (apparently) enjoying this verbal exchange, and Dante shows that he is very much ashamed. Virgil smiles and says that so much shame would expiate a greater sin and he only wanted Dante to stop listening because the wish to hear such talk is vulgar.

Commentary

The death of Dante's kinsman had not been avenged at the time Dante was writing his poem. Geri del Bello's death was avenged by his nephews nearly thirty years later, and it required intervention by others, and a formal reconciliation before the feud was ended. To better understand the meaning of this episode as presented by Dante, one must remember that private revenge was, in Dante's time, both a right protected by law and a duty for the kinsmen of the person offended.

Dante enters the realm of the falsifiers, the last round of Malebolge, to describe new horrors with continued clarity. By the use of homely metaphors – pan leaning against pan, bedbugs keeping the sleeper awake – he shows with real impact the terrible punishment of the sinners. The noise of the place simply adds to the torture.

Dante had the gift of describing vividly in a few words, and the stories of the spirits here are excellent examples of this gift. The nostalgic evocation of the cool brooks and green hills of Master Adam's homeland is pathetic, coming as it does from the mouth of the thirsty wretch. His desire for vengeance is highly effective because it is at once so tenacious, and so impotent. The angry exchange between Master Adam and Sinon the Greek is told in terse, clear language, and Dante displays an all-too-human curiosity in what they have to say.

CANTO 31

Summary

Dante and his master climb the bank of the chasm in semi-darkness. Dante hears a horn sounding, as loud as thunder, and certainly louder than the horn of Roland. He looks intently in the direction of the sound and sees what appears to be a number of towers; he asks what town this is.

Virgil says it is too dark for Dante to see the forms properly, and when they arrive at the place where these things are, he will find that his eyes have deceived him. Then taking Dante by the hand, he halts for a moment, saying that it will be better for him to explain now so that Dante will not be startled by what he sees. These are not towers but giants in the pit of Hell (the ninth circle). They are ranged around its bank and sunk to the navel in the bank of the pit.

The travelers come closer, and Dante sees more clearly but is also more frightened, for the giants encircle the pit like the turrets of a castle wall. He sees one of the giants at close range and says that Nature was wise to discontinue the creation of these monsters. There is a place for other creatures of great size, like elephants and whales, but not for these, who because of their powers of reason and their faculty for evil are far more dangerous to man.

The giant which Dante sees has a face as long as the pine of St. Peter's and his body is in proportion, so that the part of his body which shows – from the navel up – is taller than three Frieslanders (a people noted for their great height). Suddenly the great mouth roars gibberish at the two poets, and Virgil calls him stupid, telling him to use his horn to vent his rage – adding insult by pointing out to him that his horn is hanging around his neck.

Virgil tells Dante that this giant is Nimrod, builder of the Tower of Babel, and that speaking to him is useless, for he can no more understand than he can be understood. They approach a second giant, larger and more frightening than Nimrod; he is held with a chain that circles his body five times from the neck down – Dante wonders who was strong enough to do this – with his right arm behind him, his left in front.

This is Ephialtes, one of the giants who made war against the gods. Dante wishes to see Briareus, one of the warring Titans, but Virgil tells him that Briareus is far off and tied like Ephialtes, and they will see only Antaeus, who is not confined and will set them on the bottom of the pit. The chained giant shakes himself until Dante is afraid they will be struck dead; then he remembers that the giant's hands are bound.

They reach a cavern just as Antaeus emerges. Virgil greets him with a recital of the giant's might on earth: he had killed a thousand lions, and if he had joined his brothers against the gods, the giants might have won. Virgil asks him to set them down on the base of the pit (Cocytus), telling him that Dante can give him what he desires: fame on earth.

As Antaeus stoops to lift them, Dante is reminded of Carisenda, the leaning tower of Bologna; he also recalls that Antaeus nearly defeated Hercules in a wrestling match. Dante fears for his life, fervently wishing there had been another way to descend, but Antaeus sets them gently in the pit which holds Lucifer and Judas, and again stands straight as the mast of a ship.

Commentary

Through the gloom of Malebolge, Dante gets his first glimpse of the Titans and giants. Their introduction is a bold one; he hears a horn louder than that of Roland and seems to see towers in the distance. These resolve themselves into gigantic figures: Nimrod, legendary builder of the Tower of Babel (hence his meaningless jabbering); Ephialtes, one of the giants who warred against the gods of Olympus; and Antaeus, who is not bound because he did not attempt revolt against the gods. Dante asks to see Briareus, a Titan who, with his brother Otus, attempted to scale Olympus.

According to legend, Antaeus was the giant who accosted any passing stranger and wrestled him to the death. Since Antaeus drew his strength from the earth, he was invincible as long as he could touch ground. He was slain by Hercules, who lifted him off the ground until he weakened, then crushed him. Antaeus is condemned to Hell for his many murders. Virgil plays upon his vanity – for he was very proud of his prodigious strength – to have him transport the two poets down the chasm.

If Dante erred in the writing of this canto, it was in being too specific about the size of the giants. Their size could have been left to the imagination, but Dante gets out his figurative yardstick and tells us the face of the giant was as tall as the pine of St. Peter's – a pine cone of gilt bronze that originally was probably ten or eleven feet high. He closes with the images of Antaeus as a moving tower and as the tall mast of a ship.

CANTOS 32-33

Summary

This is Cocytus, the frozen pit of Hell, which almost defies description. To Dante, it requires the use of all the coarse language at his command, and describing it is no task for one who uses the language of the jester or the child. Dante invokes the Muses, asking their help in speaking the truth. Angrily he addresses the spirits confined here, saying that it would have been better if they had been born sheep or goats!

A voice from the first round, Caina, warns him not to walk on the heads of his condemned brothers, and looking down he sees a lake of ice as clear as water. In it are spirits sunk to the chin; their teeth chatter as they look down at the ice and they weep bitterly. Near Dante's feet are two who are close together, and Dante asks their names. The spirits weep until their tears freeze, binding them more closely. This does not prevent them from butting at one another, and a third spirit, with both ears frozen off, tells Dante they are brothers. He adds there is none in Cocytus more deserving of punishment than these two. And if Dante is a Tuscan, he says, he should know the speaker, Camicion de' Pazzi.

The two poets have almost reached the center of the lake, when Dante accidentally kicks the face of a spirit. It weeps and asks why Dante should add to its misery. Dante asks Virgil to wait, and as the shade continues its wailing, Dante indignantly asks how it dares to reproach others. The shade angrily asks who Dante is, that he can go through Antenora (this second division of the pit) hitting the shades. Dante replies that he is alive and will give fame to the shade if he can learn its name, but the shade wants no mention of his name on earth and tells Dante to go away and stop bothering him.

A real altercation has begun between these two: Dante grasps the spirit's hair, demanding that he give his name or lose his scalp. The spirit heatedly replies that he will lose every hair a thousand times before he will tell. Dante has in fact pulled out some tufts of hair, and the spirit is still wrangling, when another shade calls out the name Dante seeks – Bocca – and tells the spirit to be quiet.

Dante is satisfied and tells Bocca to speak no more, but Bocca is undaunted and replies to Dante by giving the names of other traitors confined in the ice of Antenora.

Dante sees two more spirits confined close together – so close, in fact, that one is feeding upon the head and neck of the other. Dante asks their names and what their offenses were on earth, so that he may tell their stories.

The first spirit replies: it will cause him much grief to tell his story, but if it exposes the traitor who is confined with him, he will do so gladly, though he weeps as he talks. He knows that Dante is a Florentine; Dante should recall Count Ugolino, who is speaking, and Archbishop Ruggieri, the other shade. Ugolino was captured and put to death by Ruggieri—this Dante already knows—but the manner of his death was so cruel that the world should know the tragic story.

Ugolino had been in prison for several months, when he had a dream of the future. When he woke, he heard his four sons (actually two were grandsons), who were imprisoned with him, asking for food. At the time when their meal was usually brought, they heard the ominous sound of the door of the tower being nailed shut, and they were left to starve. One by one the sons died, and finally Ugolino, blind from hunger, died too.

Here his story ends, and once more the shade begins gnawing on the other's skull. Dante is both sad and indignant because of the tale Ugolino has told. It is true that Ugolino had betrayed certain strongholds of Pisa and deserved to die, but his sons deserved no punishment, and certainly not of that kind.

The poets move on to a place where the spirits are confined in the ice with their faces upraised, which causes their tears to form pools over their eyes and freeze them shut.

Dante has, of course, felt the cold as they crossed the ice; now he seems to feel a wind blowing and asks his master where it comes from. Virgil says they will soon reach the place that is the source of the wind.

One of the shades cries out to Dante to remove the ice from his eyelids, and Dante replies that he will if the shade will tell its name (rashly adding that he will go to the bottom of the ice if he does not keep his promise). The spirit replies that it is Friar Alberigo and gives a cryptic allusion to the murder of his younger brother. Dante is surprised to find him already dead, and he replies that he does not know whether his body on earth is dead or not, but he forfeited his soul by the betrayal of his brother. Therefore it is confined to Ptolomaea, this third division of the pit of Hell, while a demon inhabits his body on earth.

Dante finds this difficult to believe, for the shade has mentioned Ser Branca d'Oria, who is confined just behind him, and Dante is sure d'Oria is still alive. The shade assures him that d'Oria's spirit has been here for many years and that in the circle of the Malebranche above (in the boiling pitch) the spirit of Michel Zanche, whom d'Oria treacherously murdered, had not yet arrived when the soul of d'Oria came here. A devil took the place of his soul, though d'Oria *seems* to be alive.

The shade then asks Dante to remove the frozen tears as he had promised—and Dante refuses, considering rudeness a grace in Hell. Dante lashes out at the Genoese, immoral and corrupt, wishing them gone from the face of the earth, for he has found the soul of one in Hell while the body still walks the earth.

Commentary

At a loss for words, Dante again calls upon the Muses to come to his aid. This is the pit of Hell–the very center of evil, the abyss of Satan–and Dante recognized that the noble art of poetry is not designed to describe the horrors of this dreadful abode. Poetry is not usually devoted to harsh and grating words; therefore, Dante invokes the aid of the Muses to help him describe horror in poetic terms.

There are four rounds in this circle of traitors: Caina, for those treacherous to kin; Antenora, for those treacherous to country; Ptolomea, for those who betrayed guests; and Judecca, for those who betrayed masters. Caina is named for Cain; Antenora for the Trojan Antenor, who is portrayed as an excellent character in the *Iliad,* but who, in the Middle Ages, was universally believed to have betrayed Troy to the Greeks. Ptolomea derives its name from Ptolomey, a captain of Jericho and son-in-law of Simon the high priest. Ptolomey arranged a banquet honoring Simon and his two sons, then treacherously murdered them while they were his guests. Judecca is, of course, named for Judas Iscariot.

All the sins of the upper circles have flowed into this abyss, yet the ice has a startling clarity. Dante must have experienced a harsh winter somewhere, to be able to give this final circle its still, dead, frozen atmosphere.

And in the midst of it, Dante has a typically Dantean argument. With furious temper he attacks one of the frozen spirits, simply for the satisfaction of knowing its name so he can tell its story on earth. The violent anger which inspires his behavior reveals Dante as a man of his times, accustomed to cruelty and barbarity. These spirits, as noted before, want to be forgotten on earth because of their vicious crimes, unlike those in the upper circles, who ask to be remembered.

The story is a tragic one and yet takes only a part of the canto, so swiftly does the action move. Dante does not deny Ugolino's sin, but laments that the count's sons and grandsons shared his terrible fate. He does not discuss whether or not Ugolino's crimes were great enough to deserve death, but with pitiless energy he protests against the injury suffered by innocence and invokes a just revenge upon the ferocious executioners.

Ugolino's feelings are described with masterly gradation: after the warning dream, anguish and fear fill his heart. Soon after, he hears the door of the tower being nailed shut. At the moment when his suspicion becomes certainty, the desperation which takes hold of him is so great that he is denied even the comfort of tears. The man becomes the immortal representation of despair. He longs for death to come and to free him from the torturing sight of his starving sons, but death is slow to come, and he still must undergo a long agony before his final release.

The story of Ugolino is perhaps one of the most shocking in all the poem. Dante asks what hatred, what rage justifies such a horrible and bestial act, promising that if he hears the story he will right the wrong on earth. Thus Dante avoids emphasizing the crime of Ugolino and emphasizes, instead, Ugolino as a victim.

Here, in the pit reserved for traitors, we encounter Dante's intellectual concept of man become beast. In general this bottom part of Hell is the place where man has lost all of the qualities which ever distinguished him as being man. Every aspect of the inner essence of man has been frozen out of him. Ultimately Lucifer himself, at the very bottom of Hell, is nothing but a giant mass of matter, totally devoid of any intellect.

Two of the greatest characters in the *Inferno,* Francesca and Ugolino, are found at the beginning and at the end. There are many parallels that could be drawn. For example, Francesca was bound by love to Paolo at the beginning of Hell; and at the end we find another pair bound together, but Ugolino is bound to Ruggieri by hate. The first words Francesca spoke, "I will tell you my story as one who weeps and tells at the same time," have their counterpart in Ugolino's as he says "I will tell you but it renews the grief which is so desperate in me." Both characters recall the past with great reluctance and with grief. But the difference is also significant, for Francesca remembers a happy time which has brought her to her present damnation, while Ugolino remembers only the hatred and the horror which brought him here.

Ugolino's is the concept of retaliation. This is a masterful stroke on Dante's part, for in the pit of Hell, how else can he evoke pity for someone whose crime is so monstrous as Ugolino's? We note, therefore, that Ugolino is here in Hell as a traitor (which he is, having betrayed his party to Ruggieri), but also that he is here in the poem as the betrayed. Ugolino may be said to be both the victim of divine justice and also the instrument of it, in that he also punishes his betrayor, Ruggieri.

As Ugolino tells his story, we wonder how a man can hate so violently, then we realize that the hatred is so violent because he had loved with such great intensity; that his grief is so desperate because his love was so great; and that no amount of vengeance can ever satisfy his hatred because of all he has suffered.

There are two other striking passages. The first tells of a soul leaving the body after a foul betrayal has been enacted; with the spirit gone, the body still lives – or exists, for Dante describes it as only eating, sleeping, and wearing clothes. Dante violates his own concept of condemnation and repentance for the sake of a vivid poetic image. Even a murderer may repent, but Dante preferred the image of a soul seized at the instant of sinning and flung into Hell while the empty shell of its human form inhabits the earth.

The second is Dante's startling cruelty to Friar Alberigo. Dante fails to remove the ice from the Friar's eyelids, though he had promised to do so.

The friar has told Dante all he wished to know, and more, and Dante's only comment on his own callous act is that to be rude in Hell is a courtesy. Although he has previously shown sympathy and compassion, the increasing degradation of the sinners has forced upon him the conclusion that to feel anything but contempt for these base sinners is to go against the judgment of God. Allegorically, Dante's behavior suggests that treachery and brutality always evoke the responses of violence, for we have seen Dante respond with pity in the upper circles.

Dante closes the canto with an outburst against the city of Genoa, for he has found in Hell the spirit of one who still walks the streets of Genoa. Dante probably suspected that this spirit was not the only one of its kind in Hell.

CANTO 34

Summary

This is the source and the end of all evil, the abode of Satan. Virgil quotes in Latin the beginning of a hymn – The banners of the king go forth – and adds, ironically, *inferni:* the king of Hell. Dante peers ahead and sees a dim shape like a windmill in a mist. The wind is so cold he takes shelter behind his master. At his feet, completely covered with the clear ice, are the spirits of other traitors.

Dante and Virgil have come to a place where they can see Satan (Dis) clearly. Dante stands dazed and shaken in the presence of this hideous being and can only attempt to describe him.

Dis is frozen up to his breast in the ice of Cocytus, and so great is his size that one of his arms seems to be larger than the giants they have just passed. Dante is horrified to see that Dis has three faces: a red one in the middle, a black one on the left, and a yellow one on the right. Below each face is a pair of huge wings in continuous motion, and from them comes the wind which freezes Cocytus. Dis weeps with all six eyes, and from his mouths comes a bloody froth, for he is chewing the worst of traitors. In the red mouth is Judas Iscariot, who is also being clawed by Satan's talons; the black mouth tortures Brutus, and the yellow, Cassius.

Abruptly, Virgil says they must leave, and taking Dante upon his back, he waits until Satan's wings are extended backward, then begins the perilous climb down Satan's hairy side. They descend between Satan's body and the ice until they reach a point where Virgil turns completely around, with his head where his feet had been. Dante thinks they are returning to Hell, and when his guide, after great exertion, lifts him onto a rocky ledge, Dante is startled to see Satan's legs upright in a dismal cave.

Virgil orders Dante to his feet: it is very late, and there is a long, hard road ahead. Dante stands bewildered in this dark cavern. Where are they?

and where is the ice of Hell? Above all, how does Satan come to be upside down in this place?

Virgil explains that, in climbing down Satan's side, they passed the center of the earth and are now beneath the southern hemisphere. Satan has not moved. He is still fixed in the place to which he fell from Heaven; the earth above his head closed again and hid itself beneath the sea, while under his feet it was pushed upward. There is a stream (Lethe) which runs down to this hidden place from the earth above. Dante begins his climb to the living earth, and looking up, sees the stars.

Commentary

Dante has reached the center of the earth, and the climax of the *Inferno:* Judecca, the abode of Satan. Appropriately, Dante has reserved the worst fate in Hell for the traitors to church and empire, and they are in the grasp of the arch-traitor, Satan. This is an image of Satan that is scarcely expected. This is not Lucifer, son of the morning, as in the book of Isaiah; nor is he a fallen angel, nor the prince of darkness. Dante calls him the emperor of the dolorous realm, but the repellent figure with three heads scarcely has the majesty of a ruler.

But perhaps Dante had seen Satan as he really was: ugly, repulsive, abhorrent, the origin of all sin immobilized as a captive in the product of sin, as all the spirits of Hell are. Dante summed it all up in the sentence beginning "If he was once as beautiful as he is ugly now. . . ."

It is characteristic of Dante that he carefully develops parallels in the various sections of the book. The view of Satan at the climax of *Inferno* is matched by the vision of God in *Paradiso,* and the triple nature of Satan, symbolized by his three faces, is a parody of the trinity.

The rest is anticlimax. The poets make a hurried exit, scrambling down Satan's side. A few questions are answered, and the long, laborious climb begins. Only at the last does the magic return, when the poets step out onto the solid earth and for a brief moment look up at the stars.

LIST OF CHARACTERS

The number following each name refers to the canto in which the character *first* appears.

Achilles (12). One of the heroes of the Trojan War.

Adam, Master (30). Falsified the gold coin of Florence.

Alberigo, Friar (33). A Jovial Friar, who had his brother and nephew murdered.

Aldobrandi, Tegghiaio (16). A Florentine Guelph and one of the men Dante asked Ciacco about (Canto 6).

Amidei family (28). Florentines; one of the two feuding families (the other was the Donati) who caused the split between the Guelphs and the Ghibellines.

Anastasius, Pope (11). Called a heretic by Dante, who may have confused him with the Emperor Anastasius.

Annas (23). Father-in-law of Caiaphas, and a member of the Council which sentenced Jesus to death.

Antaeus (31). Giant slain by Hercules.

Arezzo (29). An alchemist, burned at the stake. He had told Albert of Siena that he could teach him to fly.

Argenti, Filippo (8). Florentine, and apparently a bitter enemy of Dante's.

Asdente (20). Soothsayer and prophet from Parma.

Attila (12). Chief of the Huns, called the "Scourge of God."

Barbariccia (22). A demon, leader of the Malebranche.

Beatrice (2). The inspiration for Dante's work, she entreats Virgil, on behalf of the Virgin Mary, to save Dante.

Bertrand de Born (28). One of the most famous of the troubadours of the twelfth century.

Bocca degli Abati (32). Traitor of Florence, and partly responsible for the defeat of the Guelphs at Montaperti.

Bonatti, Guido (20). Astrologer.

Boniface VIII, Pope (27). Bitter enemy of Dante's.

Branco d'Oria (33). Murdered his father-in-law, Michel Zanche.

Briareus (31). A giant who plotted against the gods of Olympus.

Brunetto Latini (15). Distinguished scholar; adviser and friend to Dante.

Brutus (34). One of the conspirators in the murder of Julius Caesar.

Caccianemico, Venedico (18). Guelph of Bologna. Arranged the seduction of his own sister, Ghisola.

Cacus (25). A monster mistakenly called a centaur by Dante.

Caiaphas (23). High priest who influenced the Council to assent to the crucifixion of Jesus.

Calchas (20). Greek soothsayer who allegedly foretold the day of sailing of the Greek fleet from Aulis to Troy.

Camicion de' Pazzi (32). Murdered one of his kinsmen.

Capaneus (14). One of the Seven against Thebes; defied Zeus to stop him from conquering Thebes and was killed by a thunderbolt.

Cappochio (29). An alchemist, probably from Siena. His name means "blockhead."

Cassius (34). Roman general; conspired with Brutus to murder Julius Caesar.

Catalano, Friar (23). *Podestá* of Florence.

Cavalcanti, Cavalcante dei (10). Father of Guido dei Cavalcanti.

Cavalcanti, Guido dei (10). Poet and close friend of Dante's.
Celestine V, Pope (3). Resigned the papal throne after only five months in office, making way for Boniface VIII.
Cerberus (6). The three-headed hound; in mythology, guardian of the gates of Hell.
Charon (3). Ferryman of the river Acheron in Hell.
Chiron (12). A centaur, legendary tutor of the Greek heroes.
Ciacco (6). A notorious glutton; his name means "the hog."
Ciriatto (22). One of the Malebranche; he has tusks like a boar.
Cleopatra (5). Queen of Egypt, mistress of Caesar and of Mark Antony.
Curio (28). Advised Caesar to cross the Rubicon.
Dante (1). Central figure in the *Inferno*.
Deidamia (26). Died of grief when she was abandoned by her lover, Achilles.
Dido (5). Queen of Carthage; killed herself on a funeral pyre when her lover, Aeneas, sailed away.
Diomede (26). Companion of Ulysses in the Trojan War.
Dolcino, Fra (28). Leader of a schismatic Christian sect.
Donati family (28). With the Amidei, originators of the split between the Guelphs and the Ghibellines.
Ephialtes (31). A giant who plotted with his brother Otus against the gods of Olympus.
Erichtho (9). Sorceress who conjured Virgil's spirit and sent him on his first journey through Hell.
Eurypylus (20). A Greek soothsayer, possibly associated with Calchas.
Fallen Angels (8). Oppose Virgil and Dante at the City of Dis as they opposed Jesus at the entrance of Hell.
Farinata degli Uberti (10). A prominent Ghibelline leader who defeated Florence, but averted her destruction.
Francesca da Rimini (5). Wife of Giancotto da Rimini, and lover of his brother Paolo.
Francis of Assisi, Saint (27). Founder of the Franciscan Order.
Frederick II, Emperor (10). Attempted to unite Italy and Sicily, but was defeated by the papacy.
Furies (9). Mythological figures of vengeance.
Geri del Bello (29). Cousin to Dante.
Geryon (17). A monster who represents fraud.
Gianciotto da Rimini (5). Husband of Francesca, and brother of Paolo; murdered both.
Gianni Schicchi (30). Aided Simone Donati in falsifying a will.
Gomita, Friar (22). A Sardinian, he was hanged for abusing the privileges of public office.
Grafficane (22). One of the Malebranche, part of the escort for Dante and Virgil.
Griffolino d'Arezzo (29). An alchemist, he was burned at the stake.

Guerra, Guido (16). A Florentine praised by Rusticucci for his courage and intelligence.

Harpies (13). In mythology, birds with the faces of women, who personify the winds.

Heavenly Messenger (9). Sent to force the admittance of Dante and Virgil to the City of Dis.

Helen (5). Wife of Menelaus, she was kidnaped by Paris, prince of Troy, thereby causing the Trojan War.

Homer (4). Great epic poet of Greece, author of the *Iliad* and the *Odyssey*. According to legend, Homer was blind.

Horace (4). One of the greatest of the Latin poets.

Interminei, Alessio (18). A Florentine, notorious for his flattery.

Jason (18). Leader of the Argonauts in their quest for the Golden Fleece.

Judas Iscariot (34). One of the twelve disciples, he betrayed Jesus for thirty pieces of silver.

Leopard (1). Symbol of incontinence.

Lion (1). Symbol of malice.

Lucan (4). A great Roman poet, he conspired against Nero and killed himself when the plot was discovered.

Lucia, Saint (2). Messenger of the Virgin Mary to Beatrice.

Mahomet; Mohammed (28). Founder of the Islamic religion.

Malebranche (21). Demons who guard and punish the barrators. The name means "evil-claws."

Malecoda (21). One of the Malebranche; his name means "evil-tail."

Manto (20). A sorceress, by legend responsible for the founding of the city of Mantua, Virgil's birthplace.

Medusa (9). One of the Gorgons. The sight of her snake-covered head turned men to stone.

Minos (5). One of the semi-legendary kings of Crete.

Minotaur (12). A monster with the body of a man and the head of a bull. Confined in the Labyrinth on Crete, he was slain by Theseus.

Montefeltro, Guido da (27). Military leader; later joined the Order of Franciscans.

Mosca de' Lamberti (28). A Florentine nobleman who advised the murder which started the feud of the Donati and the Amidei.

Myrrha (30). Princess of Cyprus, who conceived an incestuous passion for her father.

Nessus (12). One of the centaurs, killed in the battle at the wedding feast of Hercules.

Nichoals III, Pope (19). Successor to Pope John XXI; accused of simony by Dante and others.

Nimrod (31). "Mighty hunter before the Lord" (Gen. 10: 9), named as a giant by Dante.

Old Man of Crete (14). An allegorical figure based upon the Book of Daniel, and on Ovid's *Metamorphoses*.

Otus (31). A giant who, with his brother Ephialtes, plotted to scale Mount Olympus in defiance of the gods.

Ovid (4). Roman poet, whose best known work is the *Metamorphoses*.

Paolo da Rimini (5). Lover of Francesca, his brother's wife.

Phlegyas (8). Ferryman of the river Styx in Hell.

Pholus (12). Onc of the centaurs.

Plutus (7). God of riches. Dante may have confused him with Pluto, god of the underworld.

Potiphar's Wife (30). Falsely accused Joseph of attempting to seduce her (Gen. 39). Her name is not known.

Puccio Sciancato (25). Florentine, called a thief by Dante.

Rubicante (22). One of the Malebranche assigned to escort Dante and Virgil.

Ruggieri degli Ubaldini, Archbishop (33). Responsible for the death by starvation of Ugolino and his sons and grandsons.

Rusticucci, Jacopo (16). Wealthy Florentine statesman. His shrewish wife is said to have driven him to homosexual practices.

Satan (34). Also called Beelzebub, Lucifer, and Dis, he is the "Emperor of the Dolorous Realm."

Scala, Can Grande della (1). Dante's friend and protector in exile.

Scott, Michael (20). Scottish magician, often called a "wizard."

She-wolf (1). Symbol of bestiality or fraud.

Sinon the Greek (30). Accused of treachery during the Trojan War.

Socrates (4). One of the greatest of the Greek philosophers, he was condemned to die by drinking hemlock and met his death calmly.

Thais (18). A courtesean who flattered her lover excessively.

Theseus (12). King of Athens, slayer of the Minotaur, and one of the great lovers in Greek legend.

Ubaldini, Ottaviano degli (10). A cardinal of the church, he was overjoyed at the victory of the Ghibellines at Montaperti.

Ugolino della Gherardesca, Count (33). After much treachery on his part, Ugolino was imprisoned by Ruggieri, and consequently starved to death.

Ulysses (26). Legendary hero of Homer's *Odyssey*.

Vanni Fucci (24). Thief from Pistoia, who shocks Dante with his obscenity.

Vigne, Pier delle (13). Minister to Frederick II. He was imprisoned by Frederick (perhaps unjustly), and committed suicide.

Virgil (1). Dante's guide through Hell.

Virgin Mary (2). Alarmed at Dante's wandering, she commands Virgil, through Beatrice, to escort him through Hell.

Vitaliano (17). A usurer, the only one mentioned by name by Dante, but whose identity is not clear.

Zanche, Michel (22). Governor of Logordo in Sardinia. He was murdered by his son-in-law, Branco d'Oria.

REVIEW QUESTIONS AND ESSAY TOPICS

1. The punishment of sinners is usually by analogy or by antithesis. Discuss one canto where Dante follows his plan closely. Where does he depart from it?
2. Punishment is accorded the condemned by the standards of their own society. Where in the *Inferno* does Dante fail to follow this basic concept of Hell?
3. Would you arrange the sins and punishments of Hell in a different order? If so, how? Should some of the sins have punishments other than those Dante has given them?
4. There is a notable absence of women—particularly Dante's contemporaries—in the *Inferno*. How do you account for this?
5. Dante seems particularly attracted to certain types of characters and emphasizes the episodes concerning them. Who are some of these characters? Why, in your opinion, was Dante drawn to them?
6. Virgil is extremely important to the *Inferno,* both symbolically and in his own person. Explain this importance.
7. Mythology plays a large part in the *Inferno*. Compare the mythological characters and places as used by Dante with the same characters and places as understood today.
8. The *Divine Comedy* was written in *terza rima.* Describe this rhyme scheme. Has it been used successfully in English poetry, other than in translations?

Divine Comedy - II. Purgatorio

THE DIVINE COMEDY: PURGATORIO

NOTES

including

- *General Introduction*
- *Synopsis*
- *Summaries and Commentaries*
- *Critical Commentary*
- *List of Characters*
- *Review Questions and Essay Topics*
- *Selected Bibliography*

by
Harold M. Priest, Ph.D.
Department of English
University of Denver

INCORPORATED
LINCOLN, NEBRASKA 68501

Editor

Gary Carey, M.A.
University of Colorado

Consulting Editor

James L. Roberts, Ph.D.
Department of English
University of Nebraska

ISBN 0-8220-0394-5

Printed in U.S.A.

1992 Printing

Cliffs Notes, Inc. Lincoln, Nebraska

CONTENTS

General Introduction

Purgatorio Notes

General Introduction

The story of the *Divine Comedy* is simple: one day Dante finds himself lost in a dark wood; but Virgil appears, rescues him from that savage place, and guides him to a contemplation of Hell and Purgatory. Then, having confessed his faults, and with Beatrice as his guide, he is conducted into Paradise and attains a glimpse of the face of God.

Dante gave the title of *Comedy* to his masterpiece because the word indicated a pleasant or (as Dante himself put it) a "prosperous" ending after a "horrible" beginning. Dante used the humble lowly language "which even women can understand," rather than the sublime language of tragedy. The adjective "divine" was added to the title later, apparently by an editor some time in the sixteenth century.

The *Divine Comedy* is distinctly a product of medieval times. Its view of the universe is the Ptolemaic view; its social setting that of the jealous, warring city-states of Italy, and of the powerful, arrogant, and feuding aristocrats and the political factions which supported them. Over all were the contesting powers of a fading empire and a grasping papacy.

In attempting understanding, one may become so entangled in the complexities of the *Comedy* and its environment that one loses sight of Dante the man. And it was Dante, the man of his times, who wrote the *Divine Comedy*—a man whose lifelong devotion to the figure of Beatrice was in the highest tradition of courtly love; whose political feuds were first with the party of the opposition, then with factions within his own party, until he formed a party of his own; a man who believed firmly in alchemy and astrology, in witchcraft and spells; and finally, an intensely human man, with fierce hatreds and loyalties, with no little vanity, with pity, and with love.

The date of the composition of the *Divine Comedy* is uncertain, but undoubtedly the poem was written during Dante's exile. Even here there is some disagreement, for there is a tradition which insists that the first seven cantos were written before he was banished from Florence. The predominant opinion is that it was begun around 1307; the setting of the poem is the year 1300. There is some evidence that the *Inferno* had been completed and circulated before 1314, and that the *Purgatorio* followed very soon after. The *Paradiso* was completed shortly before Dante's death in 1321 and released posthumously by his sons.

The *Divine Comedy* is a monumental work of imagination, dedicated in spirit to an immortal love; it is mortal to the point of repugnance in its beginning, mystical almost beyond understanding at its close.

DANTE'S LIFE

Dante Alighieri was born in Florence in May, 1265, of an old family, of noble origin but no longer wealthy. His education was probably typical of any youth of his time and station: he studied the *trivium* and *quadrivium,* probably spent a year, or part of a year, at the University of Bologna, and came under the influence of some of the learned men of his day. Most notable of these was Ser Brunetto Latini, whose influence Dante records in his poem (*Inferno* 15).

In accordance with custom, Dante was betrothed in his youth to Gemma Donati, daughter of Manetto Donati. These betrothals and marriages were matters of family alliance, and Gemma's dowry was fixed as early as 1277, when Dante was twelve years old. There were at least three children: sons Pietro and Jacopo, and a daughter Antonia, who later entered a convent at Ravenna and took the name of Sister Beatrice. A third son, Giovanni, is sometimes mentioned.

There can be no doubt that the great love of Dante's life, and the greatest single influence on his work, was his beloved Beatrice. He first met her when he was nine years old and she was eight. The meeting took place in her father's home, probably at a May Day festival. Dante has described this meeting in his *Vita Nuova.* He tells of seeing the child Beatrice, wearing a crimson gown and looking like an angel. From that day on, his life and work was dedicated to her. He mentions no other meeting with her until nine years later, when he saw her on the street, dressed in white, accompanied by two other girls. She greeted him sweetly by name, and he was in raptures. A short time later, having heard gossip linking his name with another young woman, she passed him without speaking, and Dante mourned for days, determining to mend his ways.

If all this seems slightly preposterous, it is necessary to remember two things: that the young women of marriageable age were so strictly chaperoned that it was virtually impossible to have even a speaking acquaintance with them and that Dante's love for Beatrice was in the strictest tradition of courtly love, wherein the lover addressed his beloved as being completely out of his reach, and which viewed marriage between the lovers as impossible, in fact undesirable.

To what extent this was, at first, a true and lasting love cannot be determined. There is little doubt that Dante enjoyed the sweet misery of his situation and the sympathy of other ladies for his plight. After the death of Beatrice, and particularly after his exile, he put away his adolescent fancies, and Beatrice became a true inspiration.

Beatrice was married in about 1287 to Simone de' Bardi, a wealthy banker of Florence, a marriage of alliance of the two houses and one completely immaterial to Dante and his work.

Dante wrote many poems in praise of his lady during her lifetime, and when she died in 1290, at the age of twenty-five, he was inconsolable. He had had a dream of her death, and in her honor collected the poems he had written about her, which are included in the *Vita Nuova*. The later *Comedy* was also inspired by her memory.

Dante's public life began in 1289, when he fought against Arezzo at Campaldino. In 1295 he was one of the council for the election of the priors of Florence, and in May, 1300, went as ambassador to San Gemignano to invite that commune to an assembly of the Guelph cities of Tuscany. From June 15 to August of the same year, he was one of the priors of Florence, and it was during that year that his best friend, Guido Cavalcanti (*Inferno*, Canto 22), caused a street riot on May Day. Guido was exiled to Sarzana by the officers of the city, one of whom was Dante. Sarzana proved so unhealthful that Guido petitioned to return to Florence, and was allowed to do so. He died of malaria, contracted in Sarzana, in August, 1300.

Dante was vigorously opposed to the interference of the pope in secular affairs, and was induced to take a stand with the Whites when the Blacks favored the intrigues of the pope. Charles of Valois was coming to Florence, ostensibly as a peacemaker between the two factions but in reality as a partisan of the Blacks and supporter of the pope. In October, 1301, Dante and two other men were chosen as ambassadors on a mission to Rome, rightly suspecting the motives of Charles as peacemaker. After they had left Florence, the Blacks easily took over control of the city with the help of Charles, and Dante was exiled from his native city, never to return.

The terms of exile were harsh: Dante was charged with graft, with intrigue against the peace of the city, and with hostility against the pope, among other things. The list of charges is so long that it is reminiscent of those brought against the political enemies of any party in power today. In addition, a heavy fine was imposed, and Dante was forbidden to hold public office in Florence for the rest of his life.

Dante did not appear to answer the charges – it probably would not have been safe to do so – and a heavier penalty was imposed: in addition to confiscation of his property, he was sentenced to be burnt alive if caught. Also, his sons, when they reached their legal majority at age fourteen, were compelled to join him in exile.

Thus began Dante's wanderings. At first he joined in the political intrigues of his fellow exiles, but, disgusted by what he considered their wickedness and stupidity, he formed a party by himself. It is not known exactly where he spent the years of his exile, though part of the time he was with the Malaspini, and he also spent time at the court of Can Grande della Scala in Verona, with whom he remained on good terms for the rest of his life.

Once during the years of his banishment his hopes for peace in Italy, and his own return to Florence, were revived. This was in the reign of Henry VII of Luxemburg, who announced his intention of coming to Italy to be crowned. Dante addressed a letter to his fellow citizens urging them to welcome Henry as emperor. When Henry was met by strong opposition, Dante in great bitterness sent a letter to him, urging him to put down the rebellion quickly; he also addressed a letter in similar vein to Florence, using abusive terms which could not be forgiven. When Henry's expedition failed, and the hopes of empire died with him, Dante was not included in the amnesty granted certain exiles. Later, amnesty was extended to him on the condition that he admit his guilt and ask forgiveness publicly, which the poet refused to do. His sentence of death was renewed.

Dante's last years were spent in Ravenna, under the protection of Guido Novello da Polenta. They seem to have been years of relative contentment in compatible company – but Ravenna was not Florence. One final mission was entrusted to Dante: he was sent to Venice in the summer of 1321 by his patron in an unsuccessful attempt to avert a war between Ravenna and Venice. On his return trip, he fell ill, possibly of malaria. He reached Ravenna and died there on the night of September 13, 1321.

He was buried with the honors due him. Several times during the following centuries, the city of Florence sought to have his body interred with honor in the placc of his birth, but even the intercession of popes could not bring this about. His opinion of the citizens of his city was clearly stated in the full title of his great work: *The Comedy of Dante Alighieri, Florentine by Citizenship, Not by Morals.*

Dante still lies in the monastery of the Franciscan friars in Ravenna.

DANTE'S WORLD

Dante's world was threefold: the world of politics, the world of theology, and the world of learning. His *Comedy* encompasses and builds upon all of these, and so interdependent were they that it would be impossible to say that any one was the most important.

Throughout the Middle Ages, politics was dominated by the struggle between the two greatest powers of that age: the papacy and the empire. Each believed itself to be of divine origin and to be indispensable to the welfare of mankind. The cause of this struggle was the papal claim to temporal power, supported and justified by the spurious "Donation of Constantine." This document, which was a forgery of the eighth century, maintained that Emperor Constantine, before leaving for Byzantium, had transferred to the Bishop of Rome, Pope Sylvester I, political dominion over Italy and the western empire.

Dante lived in an era of virtually autonomous communes, ruled by either an autocratic hereditary count or a council elected from an aristocratic—and exclusive—few. The political situation was never stable, and the vendettas went on forever, family against family, party against party, city against city.

The strife began in the tenth century with Otto I, the emperor who laid the foundation for the power which was to transform Germany into the mightiest state in Europe and who dreamed of restoring the Holy Roman Empire. At the beginning of the eleventh century, the situation worsened, with Henry IV humiliated at Canossa by an aggressive opponent, autocratic Pope Gregory VII (Hildebrand).

In the first part of the thirteenth century, the growing conflict was headed by two outstanding antagonists: Innocent III, the most powerful of all the popes, and the brilliant Frederick II, King of Germany, Emperor of Rome, and King of Naples and Sicily, the most gifted of all the monarchs of the Middle Ages. The enmity of the pope, who was firmly resolved to free Italy from German authority, shook the stability of the empire, which was already undermined by the insubordination of the princes in Germany and the rebellion of some of the city-states of northern Italy.

When Frederick died in 1250, he left a very unstable situation to be handled by his successors, especially in Italy. There, in 1266, his illegitimate son Manfred was defeated and killed in the battle fought at Benevento against Charles of Anjou, who had been summoned to Italy by the pope. Two years later, this same Charles defeated Corradino, Frederick's grandson, at Tagliacozzo, and put him to death. Thus the line of the descendants of the great emperor was extinguished, and Italy was lost to the empire.

In reading Dante, indeed throughout medieval history, one hears much about two major political factions, the Guelphs and the Ghibellines. In Italy the party lines were originally drawn over the dispute between the papacy and the emperor for temporal authority. The Ghibellines, representing the feudal aristocracy, wished to retain the power of the emperor in Italy as well as in Germany. The Guelphs were mainly supported by the rising middle-class merchant society, who hoped to rid Italy of foreign influence and maintain the control of governments in their independent communes. They espoused the cause of the papacy in opposition to the emperor.

The rivalry between the two parties not only set one city against another but also divided the same city and the same family into factions. In time the original alliances and allegiances became confused in strange ways. For example, Dante, who was a Guelph, was a passionate supporter of imperial authority all his life.

In Florence the Guelphs and Ghibellines succeeded each other, alternately ruling the city. During the rein of Frederick II, the Ghibellines, supported by the emperor, gained the upper hand and drove the Guelphs out of the city. But at the death of Frederick II, in 1250, the

Guelphs were recalled to Florence for a temporary reconciliation and later gained control of the city.

The Ghibellines again returned to power in 1260, and ruled the city until 1266, but the next year the Guelphs, aided by French forces, gained supremacy in the city, and the Ghibellines left Florence, never to return.

Dante was an ardent White Guelph, putting his hopes for Italy's future in the restoration of the empire, and to the end of his days was politically active, though ultimately he was forced by the violence of his views to form a party "by himself," and, as a White, was actually allied to the Ghibellines.

Not even the supremacy of the Guelphs, however, endowed Florence with a peaceful and stable government, for in 1300 the Guelph party split into two factions: the Whites and the Blacks, led respectively by the families of the Cerchi and the Donati. The basis of this split was the usual blood-feud between two families. In nearby Pistoia, a family quarrel existed between two branches of the Cancellieri family. The first wife of the original Cancelliere was named Bianca, and her descendants called themselves Whites in her honor. The name of the second wife is not known, but her descendants, in opposition to the Whites, called themselves Blacks. The quarrel erupted into open violence after a murder committed by one Foccaccia (mentioned by Dante in Canto 32 of the *Inferno*).

The Guelphs of Florence, in the interests of maintaining the precarious peace of the district, intervened in the hostilities, and in so doing furthered the jealous rivalry of the Cerchi and the Donati families, who naturally took opposite sides. The city was torn by strife; personal ambitions, feuds, and the arrogance of individuals and families further agitated the situation.

At this point, the Blacks secretly enlisted the aid of Pope Boniface VIII, who intervened in the affairs of the city, largely in his own interest. The pope considered the throne of the empire still vacant, since Albert I had not received his crown in Rome. In his assumed capacity as vicar of the emperor, Boniface plotted to extend the rule of the church over the territory of Tuscany. To accomplish this, he first obtained the favor of the Blacks, then dispatched Charles of Valois, brother of the King of France, to Florence, ostensibly as a peacemaker, but actually as a supporter of the Blacks. In 1302, with the help of Charles of Valois, the Blacks gained control of the city. In the list of some six hundred Whites banished from Florence was the name of the citizen Dante Alighieri.

While the rest of Italy, like Florence, was troubled by rivalries between parties, or by wars of city against city, in Germany the emperor's throne was vacant, first because of an interregnum, then because of a conflict between two rival claimants. The emperor's position was still regarded as vacant by the Italians when the two emperors who followed, Rudolph of Hapsburg and Albert I, failed to come to Italy to be crowned and paid no attention to Italian affairs. Therefore when the news came that Henry of Luxemburg, who succeeded Albert I in 1308, was coming to Italy to oppose King Robert of Sicily, many Italians, for whom Dante was the most eloquent and fervent spokesman, welcomed the prospect with feverish enthusiasm. They saw in the figure of Henry the end of all the woes which had wracked the peninsula.

Henry was crowned at Milan early in 1311. Very soon after, he faced the armed hostility of the opposing party, which had Florence as its leader. Henry, nevertheless, was able to reach Rome and be crowned there in 1312. The coronation took place in the church of St. John Lateran rather than in St. Peter's because the latter was being held by the forces of King Robert of Sicily. The emperor was still fighting to unite the empire when he died in the summer of 1313, succumbing to a fever with suspicious suddenness. The death of Henry put an end forever to the expectations of Dante and all other Italians who had longed for the restoration of the imperial power in Italy.

Dante's theological ideas were strictly orthodox, that is, those of medieval Catholicism. He accepted church dogma without reservation. His best authorities for insight into the more complex problems confronting the medieval thinkers were Augustine, Albertus Magnus, and Thomas Aquinas. He followed the Pauline doctrine of predestination and grace as presented by Augustine, but he managed to bring this into a kind of conformity with free will, to which he firmly adhered. Man has inherited sin and death through Adam's fall, but also hope of salvation through Christ's redemption. God in his love created humans with the power of perceiving good and evil and the opportunity of choosing. On the basis of their choice depended their eternal bliss or damnation. Those who set their will against the divine law were sentenced to Inferno and everlasting torment. Those who sinned but confessed and repented were given their reward in heaven after a period of purifying atonement in Purgatory. Thus repentance, the acceptance of divine law, was the crux of judgment in the afterlife.

Among the familiar tenets of medieval theology, we recognize such concepts as the "seven deadly sins" in Purgatory and the corresponding seven virtues in Paradise. The doctrine that only those persons who had been baptized as worshipers of Christ were to be admitted to Paradise is expressed in the treatment of the souls in Limbo (*Inferno* 4). Of the many more complex theological concepts expounded through the *Commedia*, explanations will be offered in the textual commentaries.

In castigating the individual popes (and particularly his bitter enemy, Boniface VIII), he was in no way showing disrespect for the *office* of the papacy, for which he held the greatest reverence. He was, in fact, following the long tradition of critics, many of them in high places in the church, who had not hesitated to recall popes to the duties and responsibilities of the chair of Peter. Dante held to the ideal of the papacy and the empire as the dual guardians of the welfare of man, spiritual and secular, each deriving its separate powers directly from God.

Readers cannot fail to recognize Dante's erudition. He appears to have taken all learning for his province, or what passed for learning then. The fact that much of the scientific teaching was hopelessly in error is not Dante's responsibility. The fact that he displayed extraordinary curiosity and avid interest in all branches of scientific learning (geography, geology, astronomy, astrology, natural history, and optics) reveals something important about the poet's mind.

Among the concepts that influenced the plan of the *Commedia* was the belief that only the northern hemisphere of the earth was inhabited, that the southern hemisphere was covered with water except for the mount of Purgatory. The scheme of the heavens was dictated by the Ptolemaic, or geocentric, system of astronomy, upon which Dante based the entire plan of *Paradiso*.

In addition to his thorough and easy familiarity with the Bible, Dante displays a scholar's acquaintance with not only those great theologians previously mentioned (Augustine, Aquinas, etc.) but with a score of others.

Finally, wide reading and absorption of works of *belles lettres*, especially the Latin classics, was of the greatest importance. (Further details will be given later in the discussion of sources of the *Comedy*.)

DANTE'S MINOR WORKS

LA VITA NUOVA

The *Vita Nuova (New Life)* is a little book consisting of the love poems written in honor of Beatrice from 1283 to 1292. Written in Italian ("the Vulgar Tongue"), they were collected and linked by a commentary in prose, probably in 1292.

The book of memories and confessions presents a proper introduction to the *Divine Comedy,* as it speaks of a love which, in the mature life, through the path of philosophy and the ascendancy of faith, led the poet to his greatest poetical achievement. However, in the *Vita Nuova* the inspiration comes, without doubt, from reality. Beatrice is not an allegorical creature, but a real woman, smiling, weeping, walking in the street, and praying in the church. From the sincerity of its inspiration, the book derives a note of freshness and originality that is remarkable for that age.

The poems, most of them sonnets and canzoni, are arranged in a carefully planned pattern. These lyrics, like all of Dante's early verses show the influence of the new school in Bologna, led by Guido Guinizelli, which was identified as *il dolce stil nuovo* (the sweet new style). This group of poets followed the tradition of the poetry of courtly love in certain respects, but developed techniques of greater refinement than their predecessors and treated love in a lofty, spiritual vein.

The prose passages accompanying each poem include not only an account of the circumstances which suggested the writing of the poem but also some analysis of the techniques employed in the construction of the poem, thus giving a unique character to the work.

CANZONIERE

Canzoniere, also in Italian, comprises the collected lyrics other than those included in the *Vita Nuova* and the *Convivio.* Love poems predominate in the collection, some to Beatrice, some to other ladies. The volume includes a group of poems called the "Pietra" lyrics because they were dedicated to a woman "hard as stone." These poems reveal a violent and sensual passion but demonstrate as well experiments in very complicated artistic techniques. There are also exchange of poems between Dante and other poets, sometimes complimentary and sometimes caustic and satirical. Other poems in the collection, written during exile, deal with moral and civic doctrine.

IL CONVIVIO

The *Convivio* (the *Banquet*) was written during the exile, possibly in the years 1306-07. The name is metaphorical. Dante means to prepare a banquet of learning and science for such people as princes, barons, knights, and women, who are too busy with civil and social affairs to attend schools and familiarize themselves with scholarship. Such being the aim of the work, Dante employs the vernacular, the common speech, which will benefit a greater number of people, in spite of the fact that in those days Latin was generally required for a learned and scholastic commentary.

According to his original plan, the work was to consist of fourteen chapters, each with a *canzone* and an elaborate prose commentary. Actually only four sections were written, one being the introduction and each of the other three presenting a *canzone* with its commentary.

The two ideas of greatest importance discussed in the *Convivio* are the nobility and the empire. Speaking of the first, Dante maintains that true nobility does not derive from heredity or from the possession of wealth but rather from the practice of virtue. The ideas about the empire, of which Dante here speaks only briefly, were further developed in the *De Monarchia* and in the *Divine Comedy*. However, the secular office of the empire is already seen in the perspective of a divine plan ordained by God for the redemption of man and his betterment in the earthly life.

DE VULGARI ELOQUENTIA

After demonstrating the efficacy of the vernacular in the *Convivio*, Dante made it the subject of a treatise which, being addressed to scholarly people, was written in Latin. The treatise was to consist of four books, but only the first book and sixteen chapters of the second were completed.

The work deals with the origin and the history of languages in general, then attempts a classification of the Italian dialects. The ideal language is considered to be the "illustrious, vulgar tongue," a common language for the whole peninsula which would combine the best qualities of the different dialects. To Dante, this ideal seemed to have been attained by the writers of the Sicilian school, and the poets of "the sweet new style" *(il dolce stil nuovo)*.

EPISTLES

All of the *Epistles* were written in Latin, and among the thirteen left to us (one of which may be a forgery), the three written to Henry VII on the occasion of his coming to Italy show the same spirit of prophecy which inspires some of the more eloquent passages of the *Divine Comedy*. Dante strongly desired the unification of Italy under Henry's rule and a peaceful Florence to which he could return from exile.

One of the most interesting is that addressed to the six Italian cardinals after the death of Pope Clement V at Avignon. It exhorts the cardinals to elect an Italian pope who will restore the Holy See to Rome. In this letter, as in the *De Monarchia* and the *Divine Comedy*, political and religious problems are closely related. Dante desires not only the return of the popes to Rome but also their peaceful cooperation with the emperors and the moral reformation of the church, then corrupted by simony and avarice.

His letter to Can Grande della Scala outlining the purpose and ideas of the *Comedy* gives the four levels of its interpretation, and serves as an introduction to the work. This letter accompanied some cantos of the *Paradiso,* which Dante dedicated to Can Grande. Boccaccio, in his biography of Dante, relates that the poet was in the habit of writing several cantos of his work, then sending them to Can Grande, his friend and patron.

DE MONARCHIA

The *De Monarchia* states in the most complete manner Dante's views upon the perfect government of human society. Being of universal interest, it was written in Latin, probably during the time Henry was en route to Italy. It was meant to be a warning to the numerous opponents encountered by the emperor on his way to Rome.

Divided into three parts, the book maintains that the empire is necessary for the welfare of mankind because it is the only means o establishing peace in the world; that the right to exercise this office belongs to the Roman people; that the authority of the emperor, like that of the pope, comes directly from God. Thence derives the independence of the empire from the church because both powers are autonomous and destined to guide mankind, respectively, toward earthly happiness and toward celestial beatitude; the emperor, however, should show the pope the same kind of reverence that a son should show his father.

Dante was convinced that the principal cause of the evils devastating Italy and the world was to be found in the pope's usurpation of the authority assigned by God to the emperor. He was particularly opposed to the policies of Boniface VIII, and strongly condemned the spurious "Donation of Constantine," which was claimed as the authorization of the pope's temporal power.

The claim that Rome should be the seat of the emperor did not conflict with its being the seat of papal authority as well, since the two powers have to coordinate their plans for the welfare of mankind. The emperor, Dante believed, could not be universally recognized as such unless he was crowned by the pope in Rome. In other words, Italy, with Rome as the seat of the empire and of the papacy, had been ordained by God to give the world a universal spiritual and temporal government.

THE DIVINE COMEDY

SOURCES OF THE *COMEDY*

Dante used two main literary sources in the writing of his *Comedy:* the religious and theological works of earlier times, and the classics.

It is evident, of course, that he drew heavily upon the Vulgate Bible, and he refers to it as one thoroughly familiar with it. Probably next in importance, to him, were the writings of St. Thomas Aquinas, and, to a lesser degree, those of other saints and religious philosophers.

The Latin classics had been an important part of Dante's formal training and certainly of his later reading. His eloquence in Latin is evident in his own writing to the end of his life. The study of philosophy, particularly the work of Aristotle, had occupied much of his time—so much, in fact, that it has been suggested by many later scholars that it was philosophy which caused him to wander from the "straig path" and lose himself in the dark wood of his *Inferno*.

He knew well those Latin classics which were available to schola of his time, notably Virgil, Ovid, Cicero, Seneca, Livy, and Boethius. I was familiar with much of Plato and Aristotle through Latin translation His acquaintance with Homer was secondhand, since accounts of t Homeric heroes were circulated in Dante's time only through late Lat or medieval adaptations.

THE FIGURE OF VIRGIL

In the Middle Ages, Virgil had come to be regarded as a sage a necromancer. Virgil's poems were used in the type of divination call *sortes*, in which the book is opened at random and a verse selected the same manner, as an answer to a problem or question. The Bible h been, and still is, used in the same manner.

Virgil's *Aeneid* offered the pattern for the structure of Dante's He but this alone is not the reason why Virgil was chosen as the gui through Hell. Dante himself salutes Virgil as his master and the inspi tion for his poetic style; further, Virgil is revered by Dante as the pc of the Roman Empire, since his *Aeneid* tells the story of the empir founding. Finally, in his fourth eclogue, Virgil writes symbolically the coming of a Wonder Child who will bring the Golden Age to t world, and in the Middle Ages this was interpreted as being prophe of the coming of Christ. Thus, in the figure of Virgil, Dante found sy bolically represented the two institutions, church and empire, destin by God to save mankind.

PLAN OF THE *COMEDY*

Dante lived in a world that believed in mystical correspondences, which numbers—like stars, stones, and even the events of history—h a mystical significance. In planning the structure of the *Divine Come* therefore, Dante had in mind a series of symbolic numbers: three, symbol of the Holy Trinity; nine, three times three; thirty-three, multiple of three; seven, the days of creation; ten, considered duri the Middle Ages a symbol of perfection; and one hundred, the multip of ten.

The plan was carried out with consummate precision. We find three *ıntiche,* each formed by thirty-three cantos, totaling ninety-nine. The ıtroductory first canto of the *Inferno* makes one hundred cantos in all. he entire poem is written in the difficult *terza rima,* a verse form of ıree-line stanzas, or tercets. The first and third lines rhyme, and the cond line rhymes with the beginning line of the next stanza—again, ree, and three.

Hell is divided into nine circles (in three divisions), the vestibule aking the tenth; Purgatory is separated into nine levels, the terrestrial ıradise making ten; and Paradise is formed by nine heavens, plus the mpyrean. The celestial hierarchies are nine and are divided into triads. he sinners in Hell are arranged according to three capital vices: incon-ıence, violence, and fraud. The distribution of the penitents in Purga-ry is based on the threefold nature of their rational love. The partition the blessed in Paradise is made according to the secular, active, or ntemplative nature of their love for God. The very fact that each *ıntica* ends with the word "stars" helps to demonstrate the studied plan the whole work.

STRUCTURE OF INFERNO

Inferno is a huge, funnel-shaped pit located with its center beneath rusalem, its regions arranged in a series of circular stairsteps, or ter-ces, diminishing in circumference as they descend. Each of the nine gions is designated for a particular sin, and the order of the sins is cording to their wickedness, the lightest near the top of the pit and the ost heinous at the bottom.

The punishments in Inferno are regulated by the law of retribution; erefore, they correspond to the sins either by analogy or by antithesis. ıus, for example, the carnal sinners, who abandoned themselves to the mpests of passion, are tossed about incessantly by a fierce storm. The olent, who were bloodthirsty and vicious during their lives, are owned in a river of blood. The sowers of dissension, who promoted cial and domestic separations, are wounded and mutilated according the nature of their crimes.

SPIRIT OF INFERNO

As soon as we enter the gate of Hell we are struck by an unforgettable sion of darkness and terror, stripped of any hope: "Abandon all hope, u who enter here," and even of the sight of the stars. In the dark,

PLAN OF DANTE'S INFERNO

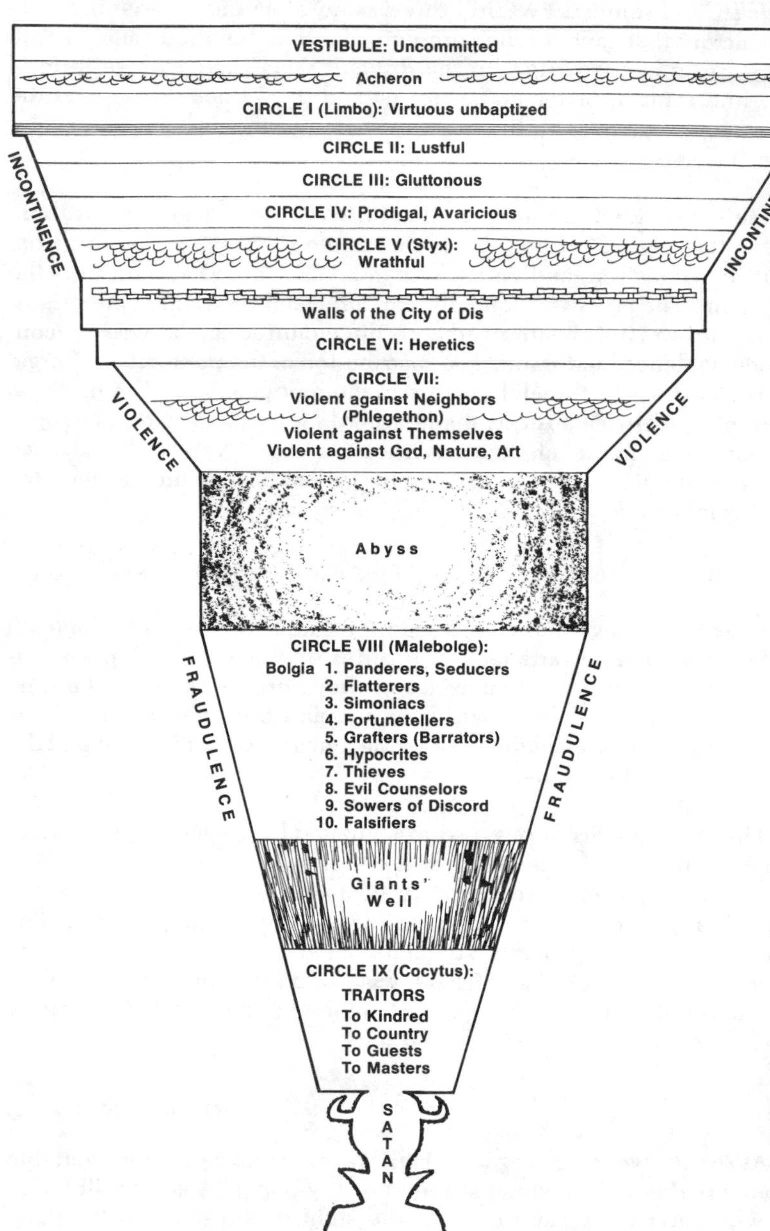

tarless air, we listen to only "strange tongues, horrible outcries, words f wrath, and sounds of blows."

Hell is the reality of sins of the flesh, of chaos, of ugliness. And yet he *Inferno* has long been the most popular and the most widely read, nd by romantic critics, it was exalted as the richest in poetry. The reason or the extraordinary fortune of the *Inferno* must be seen in the fact that his *cantica* is the closest to our world: here earthly passions are still live in all their force, and the human character of the souls is unchanged. Ieaven repudiated these souls; therefore they must remain attached to arth. Their memories, their interests and affections, their miseries, heir turpitudes, their cowardice, their ugliness, seen against that background of eternity, acquire a new tragic dimension and become immortal. There is a real vitality in the *Inferno* that is lacking in the other *antiche,* possibly because the thoughts of the age were turned less to e joys of Heaven than to the eternal damnation of Hell.

Occasionally the condemned souls are redeemed by a kind sentiment or a heroic gesture, as in the case of Paolo and Francesca, or of Ilysses. Nevertheless, Hell remains the kingdom of misery and ugliness, ate, torture, noise, and despair, without pause and without end.

STRUCTURE OF PURGATORY

Purgatory is a huge mountain located on a small island in the middle f the ocean and antipodal to Jersualem. The realm is divided into three ajor sections. Ante-Purgatory, at the foot of the mountain, has two arts: the mountain of Purgatory has seven ascending terraces, each ssigned for one of the "seven deadly sins"; and on the summit of the ount, above Purgatory proper, is the Earthly Paradise. The sufferings ndured in Purgatory are accepted voluntarily by the spirits in their esire to atone for their sins.

Penance corresponding to the sin by antithesis prevails. Thus, the roud are bowed down with heavy burdens, the lazy run without rest, e gluttons are starving. The souls are sustained by examples of the sin unished on each terrace and by its opposite virtue. The examples are arved in the stone of the mountain, chanted by invisible voices, or lled aloud by the sinners themselves.

PLAN OF DANTE'S PURGATORY

SPIRIT OF PURGATORY

Upon entering the realm of Purgatory we feel a sensation of swee and comforting relief. We return to see the sky, while a soft hue o sapphire extends to the horizon, and Venus still makes the whole Eas smile; we see in the distance the living surface of the sea.

Purgatory is the kingdom of peace and affection, of friendliness, of tenderness, and delicacy of feelings, of a resigned expectation. Hope is the keynote of Dante's *Purgatorio*. The souls still retain their affections and remember their earthly lives, but they do so with detachment, having in mind the new life toward which they aspire.

Earthly life and glory, seen with new eyes from the hereafter, is despoiled of all its illusions, its vanity, and its fallacious appearances. If the *Inferno* is the *cantica* richest in poetical contrast, and unforgettable because of its gallery of characters, the *Purgatorio* is certainly the richest in lyricism and nuances of color and sentiment. The souls of Purgatory are very often musical beings; they express their sensations in songs, hymns, and psalms. Purgatory is the realm of hope.

STRUCTURE OF PARADISE

Dante's representation of Paradise takes him into the heavens, heavens corresponding to the Ptolemaic system of astronomy. Circling around the earth are successive concentric spheres, each designated for a heavenly body or bodies. The first seven are the planetary spheres (including the sun and moon), and in each sphere are spirits distinguished for a particular virtue. The eighth sphere is that of the fixed stars; the ninth is outer space, called the Primum Mobile; the tenth region (not a sphere), the Empyrean, the heaven of heavens, a realm where God sits on his throne.

SPIRIT OF PARADISE

When we come to Paradise, we come to a very different world beyond earth and time. Seen from the height of Heaven, the earth has such a pitiful semblance that it makes the poet smile.

Paradise is the realm of the spirit emancipated from the senses and made completely free: the souls have forgotten earthly affections; they live only for the joy of loving and contemplating God. The sole feeling that exists in Paradise is love, the sole sensation is beatitude, the sole act is contemplation, and all these have the form of light. The *Paradiso* has very properly been called the *cantica* of light because light is the whole substance of Heaven. The souls express their thoughts by light: Beatrice shines with light every time she smiles, and the whole of Heaven changes color during the invective of St. Peter; the stages of virtues and the degrees of beatitude are also expressed by light.

PLAN OF DANTE'S PARADISE

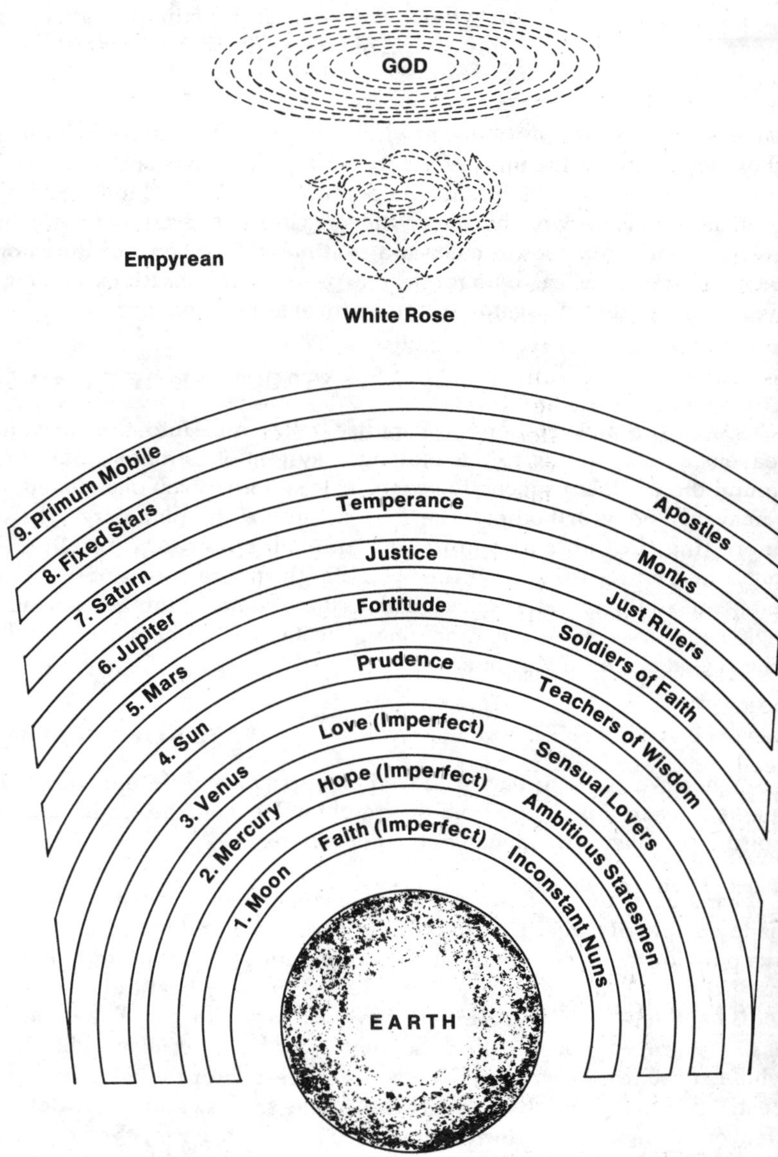

INTERPRETATION

The *Divine Comedy* has had many interpreters. Some have followed Dante's own thought, as outlined so clearly in his letter to Can Grande; others appear to ignore it.

Dante said plainly that the first meaning was the literal one. By this he meant that the cantos tell the story of the state of souls after death, according to the beliefs of medieval Christianity. He did *not* mean, nor intend his readers to infer, that it was a literal story of a trip through Hell, Purgatory, and Paradise; and he was safe in assuming that his audience was familiar with the literature of such journeys, a favorite subject throughout the Middle Ages. (This does not preclude reading the *Comedy* as excellent science fiction.) Hell (or Purgatory, or Paradise) is, therefore, the *condition* of the soul after death, brought to that point by the choices made during life.

Closely allied to its literal and allegorical meaning is the stated moral purpose of the *Comedy:* to point out to those yet living the error of their ways, and to turn them to the path of salvation.

Allegory is, by definition, an extended metaphor, organized in a pattern, and having a meaning separate from the literal story. C. S. Lewis has said "It is an error to suppose that in an allegory the author is 'really' talking about the thing that symbolizes; the very essence of the art is to talk about both." Aristotle believed that for a poet to have a command of metaphor was the mark of genius because it indicated a gift for seeing resemblances. This implies the gift of imagination, the ability to set down not only the images of vision, but, particularly in Dante's case, vivid images of noise and odor.

Dante wanted his reader to experience what he experienced, and from the beginning of the poem to the end he grows in power and mastery. His language is deceptively simple and so is his method. He writes in the vernacular, using all its force and directness; it is not the high poetic language of tragedy, as he said himself.

The imagery is designed to make the world of Dante's Hell intelligible to the reader. His world is the world of the thirteenth-century church, but his Hell is the creation of his mind, an allegory of redemption in which Dante seeks to show the state of the soul after death.

The poem is a demanding one. The reader must enter Dante's world without prejudice, and perhaps T. S. Eliot was right in recommending that the *Comedy* should be read straight through the first time, without giving too much attention to the background of the times, and without examining the more complex symbols.

TRANSLATION

Dante once remarked that he detested translations, thereby giving personal force to the Italian proverb *Tradutori traditori* (the translator is a traitor). To read a translation of Dante is not to read Dante, but the same may be said of Homer or Dumas or Goethe. One of the difficulties with Dante is the verse form that he used, which is not easy to render into English. The *terza rima* is a three-line stanza, as has been explained, its rhyme scheme being *aba, bcb, cdc,* etc. Often a thought will carry over from one stanza to the next. In Italian, the endings tend to be feminine (unstressed); in English they are usually masculine, or stressed. This produces basic differences in the movement and tonal quality of the poetry.

Because the *Comedy* was composed in Italian, the modern reader working with a translation is faced with certain difficulties. Each translator has put something of himself into his work. Some have written in prose, some in verse, and all have in some way interpreted as they transposed the words into English. Different teachers will recommend different versions, and of course one should follow his instructor's advice. However, the student should always remember that no single translation is definitive and that a second reading of the *Comedy*, or parts of it, in a different rendition will diminish the problems caused by the individual views of the translators.

Alice Curtayne, in her *Recall to Dante,* has devoted an entire chapter to comparative translations of the *Comedy*. She favors prose translation and gives convincing arguments for it. Dorothy Sayers, in her "Introduction" to the *Inferno,* has given some insight into the difficulties the translator faces, but unlike Miss Curtayne, believes that the *terza rima* can and should be used in English translations and demonstrates by using it in her translation of the *Comedy,* as does John Ciardi.

Purgatorio Notes

GENERAL SYNOPSIS

Before dawn on Easter, Virgil brings Dante to the shores of the island mountain in the midst of the southern ocean. When they are challenged by Cato, guardian of the realm, Virgil explains Dante's right to pass through Purgatory by heavenly dispensation. Cato instructs Virgil to wash the stains of Inferno from Dante's face and to gird him with a reed from the shore. After performing that ritual, they notice a bright light on the ocean that is swiftly approaching the island. It is a ship bringing a group of souls who are free to undertake the journey through Purgatory. Among them Dante recognizes Casella, a musician who had composed music for some of Dante's early lyrics. Happy at this meeting, Dante asks Casella to sing one of his works, and the group of spirits gather around, charmed by the singing. Cato interrupts their pastime with a stern remonstrance, reminding the spirits of their mission on the island, and they quickly disperse.

By now the sun has risen, and as the poets are searching for a path leading up the mountain, they meet a crowd of spirits who greet them with astonishment because they discover that Dante casts a shadow indicating that he is a living body. This first group of souls in Ante-Purgatory is composed of persons who were under excommunication when they died. Their spokesman, Manfred, the son of Emperor Frederick II, tells Dante that his repentance at the time of his death gained him divine forgiveness but that he must wait in Ante-Purgatory for a time before he can enter Purgatory because of his long-delayed repentance. This is the key to Ante-Purgatory. All of the sinners lingering on the lower slopes must delay their entrance into Purgatory proper because, for one reason or another, they postponed repentance or were unable to receive the final sacrament of the church.

Farther up the mountain, on a second ledge of Ante-Purgatory the "pilgrims" (Dante and Virgil) meet three types of negligent souls. The first is a group of spirits who are listlessly waiting out their time. Dante learns from Belacqua, a former acquaintance from Florence, that these are the indolent, those who neglected their religious obligations until their last moments because of indifference. Another group in this region is the unshriven souls, those who failed to receive extreme unction because they died sudden deaths, having been killed in battle or murdered. Dante talks to three of these, learning something of the circumstances of their deaths. When they realize that Dante is alive, all of the spirits plead with him to speak to their relatives or friends when he returns to earth, asking for their prayers in the hope of shortening the stay of the spirits in Ante-Purgatory. Apart from that group the poets meet a spirit who at first seems aloof, the poet Sordello. When he learns that Virgil was a native of Mantua, his own birthplace, he salutes him cordially; and when he learns that this is Virgil, the great Roman poet, he expresses his indebtedness and devotion in tones of reverence.

The last group of spirits in Ante-Purgatory, the preoccupied, is made up of rulers who were so busy with affairs of state that they found little time for spiritual concerns and made their peace with the church only late in life. Included are some famous emperors, dukes, and magistrates. The section of the mountain where they await their time to ascend to Purgatory is a beautiful valley. At evening two angels come to guard the valley, and when a serpent approaches, it is driven away by them.

The pilgrims have spent the entire day in Ante-Purgatory; since they cannot travel on the mountain at night, they lie down to rest in the Valley of Kings. In the early morning hours Dante dreams that an eagle seizes him and soars up with him into the region of fire. When he wakes it is morning, and he discovers that he and his guide are higher up on the mountain at the gate of Purgatory. While Dante was sleeping, St. Lucia came and carried him up the steep slope.

Admittance to Purgatory proper is attended with some ceremony. An angel, guardian of the entrance, is seated above a flight of three steps which Dante must mount. The steps, symbolic of the three stages of purification, are white, black, and red. Dante mounts the steps and kneels before the angel, who inscribes seven *P*'s on his forehead with the point of his sword, one initial for each of the sins to be purged on the mountain. The angel, satisfied that Dante is qualified, opens the gate with the keys of St. Peter, one of gold and one of silver.

The terraces of Purgatory, one above the other, represent the "seven deadly sins." In each an appropriate type of penance is practiced, and the spirit ascending the mountain must cleanse itself of each sin of which it was guilty.

When the pilgrims reach the first terrace, they observe marble carvings on the side of the path illustrating instances of notable acts of humility. Since the sin atoned for on this terrace is pride, the penitents are shown examples of the virtue opposite to that sin. Comparable examples of virtue, called "goads" or "spurs," are introduced in each terrace as incentives for the penitents.

The souls on this terrace plod slowly around the mountain, bowed double by huge rocks on their backs. Dante converses with one of the penitents, the artist Oderisi, who explains how pride over his achievement in art was his besetting sin; and he reflects bitterly on the futility of that love of fame which possesses men and which is found in the end to be transient. Dante also learns of the other kinds of pride that stained two other spirits, pride of ancestry which led to arrogance, and pride of power.

As the poets are concluding their passage on the first terrace, they discover more scenes carved on the rocky path, this time presenting the tragic effects of excessive pride. These examples, intended as deterrents, are referred to as "checks," "reins," or "bridles." The Angel of Humility salutes Dante, brushes a *P* from his brow, and directs the poets to the path leading up to the next terrace.

Dante is surprised to discover that climbing now seems easier than it did before. The reason, Virgil tells him, is that one of the initials has been removed from his forehead by the angel and that the effort will be increasingly lessened as he climbs higher.

On the second terrace, where envy is atoned for, the goads are instances of love of fellow man, or charity. The penitents are huddled against the wall of the mountain clad in hair shirts and have their eyes sewed shut with iron wires. The first soul to address Dante is Sapia, a lady from Siena. Her envy was such that it surmounted affection for her kindred and loyalty to her city. She now begs Dante to try to restore her good name among her neighbors. Next the poet meets two men from the region of Romagna. The spokesman, Guido del Duca, denounces the inhabitants of the valley of the Arno, calling some of them swine, others curs, wolves, or foxes. He then directs his venom against his own people of Romagna as a corrupt and degenerate lot, greatly inferior to their forebears. In his praise of numerous nobles of Romagna now dead he is offering recompense for his earthly sins, for those were the men he envied during his lifetime.

The Angel of Charity, having brushed away a second *P* from Dante's brow, invites him to mount to the next terrace. While the poets are climbing, Virgil explains a remark of del Duca that has puzzled Dante involving a distinction between those material possessions men set their hearts upon, possessions that incite envy, and spiritual possessions, which increase in worth when shared with others.

On the third terrace, the goads appear to Dante in the form of visions revealing examples of peacemaking and of mildness of manner under provocation. The penitents on this terrace, who had been ruled by anger, must walk in a blinding and irritating cloud of smoke, and Dante is likewise obliged to make his way through the cloud. He cannot see the spirits nor can they see him, but they hear him speaking to Virgil. One of the spirits identifies himself as Marco of Lombardy, someone whom Dante evidently regarded as a person of learning and character. The poet asks him what is the cause of depravity in men: are the stars to blame for their crimes or is the fault in their character? Marco then delivers an impressive discourse on free will, on the necessity for laws to regulate men's lives, and on the division of authority between spiritual and temporal powers.

The curbs or checks of this terrace, showing examples of insane anger, are revealed to Dante in the form of visions. When the visions have passed, the Angel of Peace appears, touches Dante's brow with his wing, and shows the pilgrims the path to the next terrace.

By the time they reach the fourth terrace it is evening and they stop to rest. Virgil explains the plan of Purgatory and the rationale on which it is based. The three lower divisions, which they have already visited represent different forms of love perverted: pride, envy, and wrath. The terrace they have now reached is for the slothful, those who had either defective love or insufficient zeal. The three terraces above this deal with different forms of excessive love for unworthy objects.

In the moonlight the poets see a group of spirits running toward them. The leaders shout reminders of persons who exhibited great zeal. These are the goads for the slothful. As the spirits rush past, Dante engages in a brief conversation with an abbot from Verona, who complains that his monastery is now ruled by an unworthy abbot who attained his post through nepotism. A spirit bringing up the rear of the group calls out sentences recalling tragic instances of sloth.

After that brief encounter Dante falls asleep and dreams that he is visited by a Siren who tries her charms on him until she is exposed by irgil. When he wakes, an angel appears to remove another *P* from his row and direct the pilgrims to the path leading up. Virgil explains that he Siren is symbolic of the love of unworthy objects which are atoned or on the next three terraces.

The spirits on the fifth terrace were guilty of either avarice or rodigality. As in Inferno these two types of sin are treated together ecause they display opposite extremes. The penitents are lying face own in the dust, weeping, and reciting psalms or prayers. The pilgrims re addressed by a spirit who tells them that he was avaricious all his ife until he attained the high throne of the church. He is Pope Adrian . A voice of one of the penitents announces notable examples of digni-ied poverty and of generosity.

Hugh Capet, founder of the dynasty that had ruled France for more han two centuries, pronounces scathing censure of the conduct of his escendants, their treachery, and especially their spirit of acquisitive-ess. He specifically denounces three Charleses and two Philips of ante's time.

As the poets make their way beside the crowd of prostrate figures, hey feel a violent quaking of the mountain, at which the spirits all roclaim *Gloria in excelsis Deo* (Glory to God in the highest). While ante is puzzling over that phenomenon, a spirit comes up behind hem; from him they learn that the quaking signals the completion of ne soul's penance, for which all souls give thanks. It was for the speak-r himself that the recent quake occurred. He tells them he is Statius, a oman poet, author of the epics *Thebaid* and *Achilleid.* When he learns irgil's identity, his greeting to his avowed master displays intense ratitude and affection. From Statius the poets learn that the duration f a soul's penance is determined by that soul.

Statius joins the other two poets for the remainder of the journey in urgatory. While they are climbing to the next terrace, Statius tells how e was first attracted to Christianity through the influence of a passage n Virgil's *Eclogues.*

On the sixth terrace, the first sight is a tree with luscious fruit and fountain gushing from the mountainside watering it. From the tree sues a voice forbidding the tasting of the fruit and then announcing xamples of temperance—the goads of gluttony. As the penitents hurry ast, Dante sees that they are pale, hollow-eyed, and emaciated beyond ecognition. The first spirit to speak to Dante is Forese Donati, a relative of Dante's by marriage and a poet who had exchanged humorously insulting sonnets with Dante. After some discussion of the wasted bodies of the penitents, he reports how his passage through Ante-Purgatory was hastened by his wife's prayers. Other gluttons who are identified for Dante include a pope (Martin IV), an archbishop, and another poet.

Farther along the terrace is a second tree, another offshoot from the tree of forbidden fruit in the Garden of Eden. From it comes a voice declaiming examples of the damaging effects of gluttony.

The seventh terrace, where lust is penalized, is occupied with a river of flames. Examples of chastity are recited by voices in the midst of the flames. Two groups of spirits pass one another going in opposite directions, one group guilty of natural lust, the other of perverted forms of lust. When Dante is addressed by Guido Guinizelli, he expresses his admiration for and indebtedness to Guido, on whose works he patterned his early lyrics. Guido points out another poet famous as one of the Provençal troubadours, Arnaut Daniel. Both Guidio and Arnaut were chiefly known for their amorous lyrics.

When Dante is told he must walk through the fire, he shrinks back in terror; but at Virgil's reminder that Beatrice waits beyond the fire Dante advances eagerly. Though he is not scorched by the flames, he suffers intense pain. At last the poets come out of the fire on the mountainside at the point where the path leads up to the summit.

Night overtakes the pilgrims and they rest on the stairs mounting to the Earthly Paradise. In a dream Dante sees Leah in a flowery field. She tells him that her joy is to walk in the fields, gathering flowers and weaving them into garlands. Her sister Rachel is happy sitting before her mirror all day, contemplating her lovely eyes. The two ladies are allegorical figures for the active and the contemplative life respectively.

At the summit of the mountain Virgil tells Dante that he has completed his mission as Dante's guide. Dante is now his own master.

The Earthly Paradise is compounded of all things beautiful in nature. As Dante explores the garden, he comes to a clear stream across which he sees a beautiful young damsel picking flowers and singing an enchanting song. This is Matilda, who, like Leah, in his dream, represents the active life. She tells Dante that this is the Garden of Eden where Adam and Eve dwelt in their original state of innocence.

The stream that separates Dante and Matilda is Lethe. She leads him along the bank until they meet a marvelous procession symbolizing the Church Militant in its pristine state. At the head of the march are seven lighted candles that leave streamers of rainbow-colored lights. Next come a group of elders representing the books of the Old Testament. After these appear four creatures with wings covered with eyes, representing the Evangelists. They are placed at the four corners of a magnificent chariot drawn by a gryphon, half eagle and half lion. The chariot represents the church; the gryphon, Christ. Beside the right wheel of the chariot are three dancing maidens in white, green, and red—the theological virtues. By the left wheel walk four maidens all in purple, the cardinal virtues. Finally come seven more elders representing the remaining books of the New Testament.

The chariot halts opposite Dante but across the river. Through a shower of roses a lady appears who, though she wears a veil, Dante knows is Beatrice. Her first greeting is a stern reprimand for his wayward life after her death. It is necessary, she says, that he pay the penalty of tears for his errant ways. At the recollection of his sins, Dante weeps bitterly. When Beatrice demands that he confess his guilt, he complies, but in a frightened voice that is scarcely audible. He is so overcome with remorse that he faints. When he revives, Matilda is leading him across Lethe, the river that allows one to forget past sins. Once across, he is conducted to Beatrice and, to Dante's intense joy, she lifts her veil.

The procession, wheeling around, comes to form a circle around a bare tree. When the gryphon binds the shaft of the chariot to its trunk, leaves and blossoms burst forth on the tree. The procession then departs, but Beatrice, Matilda, Dante, and Statius remain and witness a series of attacks on the tree and the chariot by an eagle, a fox, a dragon, a harlot, and a giant. The giant carries off the broken remains of the once beautiful chariot. This drama presents an allegory of the history of the church with its enemies from within and without causing its dissensions and corruption.

The foregoing pageant implies the triumph of evil in the modern world, but Beatrice prophesies that in the near future a great leader will appear to restore the rightful authority of both church and state.

Beatrice, Dante, and their companions approach a fountain that feeds the two rivers, Lethe and Eunoë. Matilda conducts Dante and Statius to Eunoë, which restores the memory of good deeds. The soul must drink of both rivers before rising to Paradise. After drinking from Eunoë, Dante feels an exaltation from his completed purification.

SUMMARIES AND COMMENTARIES

CANTO 1

Summary

Now Dante's little ship of his genius, having come from the cruel sea, will hoist its sails as it enters calmer waters, which is to say he will sing in more gracious language of the second kingdom of the dead where the spirit is purified and becomes worthy to rise to heaven. To attain fitting eloquence he invokes the aid of all the Muses but most particularly Calliope, the Muse of epic poetry.

Having mounted through the passageway that leads from the pit of Inferno up to a point directly opposite (antipodal) to Jerusalem, Dante, guided by Virgil, emerges on an island where the Mountain of Purgatory stands. It is nearing dawn of Easter morning when the travelers, just escaped from the murk and horror of Inferno, come out into the fresh air and see the stars shining in a sapphire sky. Dante sees Venus, the morning star, in the sign of Pisces brightening the eastern horizon; then he discovers a constellation of four bright stars that has never been seen by living man since Adam and Eve were banished from Eden.

The guardian of the region, a sage of ancient Rome, appears and sternly demands to know who the travelers are and by what right they have escaped from Inferno in defiance of the laws of the abyss. Virgil, recognizing the venerable guardian as Cato, directs Dante to kneel and bow his head. He then explains that Dante is still living but that a lady came from Heaven bidding Virgil go to Dante's aid in his dire need. To save Dante's soul, which was almost lost, Virgil has led him through the regions of the damned and now proposes, as he was directed, to show him how other spirits are purged under Cato's charge. It should suffice to say that Dante goes in search of liberty—the liberty for which Cato gave his life. Virgil, hoping to strengthen his appeal, adds a promise to bear news of Cato to Marcia, Cato's wife, who like Virgil is consigned to Limbo.

Cato consents to their admittance, not because of his love for Marcia but because of the intercession of the heavenly lady. He directs Virgil to lead Dante to the water's edge where he can wash the stains of Inferno from Dante's face, and to pluck a reed from the shore to make a girdle for Dante. When the two poets have performed those rituals they are ready to start their ascent of the Mountain of Purgatory, and they begin to search for a path.

Commentary

At the opening of this new division of the poem Dante observes due formality. In addressing his invocation to Calliope and the other Muses he displays his allegiance to the traditions of the classical epic. The allusion to the story of Calliope and the magpies is cryptic and, for many modern readers, incomplete. It is directed to an audience presumably familiar with the myth. This type of indirect reference represents a stylistic device extremely common with Dante. The story, very briefly, is that the nine daughters of King Pierus (hence called the Pierides) arrogantly challenged the Muses to a musical competition. Being vanquished by the music of Calliope, they were punished by being turned into magpies. Part of the aptness of the reference stems from the fact that the cause of the damsels' downfall was their presumption, their pride.

Dante's joy at coming out into the pure air is shown by the lyrical description of the pre-dawn sky. As he so frequently does, he indicates the season and the time of day by quite specific astronomical references to the position of celestial bodies. The introduction of Venus, the planet of love, is appropriate as one of the keys to the realm the travelers are about to enter.

The strange constellation composed of four bright stars is visible only in the southern hemisphere, where Purgatory lies. Consequently, no living man had seen the constellation since Adam and Eve were expelled from the Garden of Eden. According to the concept of geography in the thirteenth century, the southern hemisphere was entirely covered with water. Dante introduces the one exception, the small island on which the Mountain of Purgatory stands. The constellation, which was, to the best of our knowledge, an invention of the poet, symbolizes the cardinal virtues (of special import in Purgatory): prudence, fortitude, justice, and temperance. These are the virtues which were revered by the pagan world as well as by Christians, and it is these stars that illuminate the countenance of Cato.

The designation of Cato as guardian of Purgatory is evidence of the great respect for this ancient figure in the minds of Dante and his contemporaries. It is a testimony to his fame that Cato is never named in the passage. The mention of Utica and Marcia are our surest clues to the identification. This is Cato the Younger, Cato of Utica. He committed suicide to escape capture by Julius Caesar, an act much praised since it was performed to preserve his liberty and since suicide was viewed by the ancients as a courageous action if it was taken to escape dishonor. Virgil urges the point that Dante's journey is a quest to recapture his freedom, hoping that this will gain a sympathetic response from Cato. Actually two kinds of freedom are involved: political freedom in Cato's case, freedom of will or spiritual freedom in Dante's.

The honored role assigned to Cato may surprise the reader, since he is the only person that died before Christ's coming who is admitted to Purgatory. It is clear from Dante's earlier works, the *Convivio* and *Monarchia,* that Cato was regarded as one of the noblest of the ancients but it appears from Virgil's words to Cato that the poet understand Cato is to be received in glory at the Resurrection (". . . where thou dids't put off the cloak that will shine so brightly at the great day") We can only guess at the reason for the special dispensation that was granted Cato alone of all the noble pagans. It is significant that the ligh of the four stars representing the cardinal virtues is reflected in his eye but not the light of the stars representing the special Christian virtues faith, hope, and charity, which appear to Dante higher up on the moun tain. Obviously Dante decided that rather than having an angel at the entrance to Purgatory he should have a man of virtue but still not saint, since the saints were received in Paradise.

There is a marked contrast between Virgil's lengthy reply to Cato' challenge to the travelers and the curt responses that he gave to the guards in Inferno. The fuller answer indicates greater respect for thi questioner than for any of the others below, but it also serves as a re minder to the reader of the circumstances of the journey, matters whic have not been brought to the front for some time.

In response to the mention of Marcia, Cato says that since he wa released from Limbo to take his place in this more exalted region h can no longer be moved by those who were part of his earthly life.

The washing of Dante's face with dew to clear the stains from In ferno and to remove the film from his eyes is clearly a gesture of purif cation, both physical and spiritual. Dew familiarly stands for divin mercy. The reed with which Dante must gird himself is a symbol humility, perhaps the quality most prized in Purgatory since it is th antithesis of pride.

CANTO 2

Summary

The sun is rising in Purgatory. At the same time, Dante notes, would be setting in Jerusalem. Glancing to the west, the poets obser a bright light approaching over the ocean at phenomenal speed. As it draws near they detect a ship, and on either side of the brilliant light are objects of gleaming whiteness. Virgil commands Dante to kneel and fold his hands, for he recognizes an angel guiding the vessel and propelling it with the power of his wings. Dante cannot endure the brightness of the angel's face and must bow his head. In the boat are a hundred spirits singing the psalm *In exitu Israel de Aegypto* (When Israel went out of Egypt). As the ship reaches the shore, the spirits hurry to land; but knowing nothing of their whereabouts, they ask the poets to point out the path up the mountain.

Virgil is explaining that he and his companion are new arrivals when the spirits realize by his breathing that Dante is alive, and they crowd around amazed. One of the spirits recognizes Dante and advances to greet him. Three times they try to embrace and three times Dante's arms close in empty air. The spirit is Casella, a musician who had set to music some of Dante's lyric poems. Dante is curious to know why Casella's arrival in Purgatory was delayed and is told that when the souls of those who are consigned to Purgatory gather at the mouth of the Tiber, the angel-pilot, according to "just will," chooses those he will take first. Dante then begs his friend to sing for him the canzone, *Amor che nella mente mi ragiona* (Love that in my mind discourseth to me). All of the spirits gather around, charmed by the sweet song; but the happy diversion is abruptly ended by Cato, who reminds them of their urgent mission, the ascent of the mountain, whereupon they quickly set off on their journey.

Commentary

The opening lines of the canto present one of those astronomical puzzles which inevitably mystify modern readers but which the poet evidently loved. The essence of this passage is that night is falling in Jerusalem at the same time that day is breaking in Purgatory on the opposite side of the globe.

In the account of the ship ferrying dead souls to Purgatory, Dante must have intended a comparison to the scene at the beginning of *Inferno* where Charon ferries the souls of the damned over Acheron into Inferno. Contrasts between the two scenes are emphasized in every detail.

Any writer—or painter—who undertakes to depict God or an angel has a delicate problem. It will be recalled that the angel who came to the travelers' assistance at the gates of the city of Dis *(Inf.* 9) was not described visually, and in the present instance few particulars are given regarding the appearance of the angel. There is merely reference to the great white wings and the blinding light which we discover comes from the shining face of the angel.

We are given the precise location of the point of embarkation of the souls bound for Purgatory: where the Tiber empties into the sea. The poet, it will be recalled, was equally specific about the location of the entrance to Inferno (both are in Italy). He doesn't like to leave such details to guesswork.

The meeting with the spirit of Casella is one of the well-remembered episodes of Purgatory, conveying, as it does, a feeling of human warmth. This is the first of a series of encounters in Purgatory demonstrating the enduring power of friendship or fraternal bonds of sympathy. (For a detailed treatment of this theme in *Purgatorio,* consult Irma Brandeis, *The Ladder of Vision,* Chapter 3.) The incident concerning the abortive attempts of the friends to embrace serves to make clear to the reader the nature of the spirits in this region. They have visual form but no material substance. The attempted embrace, thrice repeated, echoes two familiar and identical passages in the *Aeneid* (II, 792-4; VI, 700-2).

Upon meeting Casella, Dante recalls their common bond of music and poetry, and he impulsively asks his friend to cheer him by singing one of Dante's best known *canzoni,* which Casella had set to music, the second *canzone* of the *Convivio.* Of all the pleasurable earthly experiences that souls in Purgatory are permitted to recall without guilt, those related to artistic creation are pre-eminent, as we shall see. The entire Casella passage sustains admirably the tone of lyrical serenity introduced in the opening canto of *Purgatorio.*

CANTO 3

Summary

The poets now hurry toward the foot of the mountain. Dante observes his shadow falling in front of him but sees no second shadow beside his, whereupon he experiences a moment of panic, thinking that Virgil has deserted him. Virgil explains that his body which could once cast a shadow is now buried near Naples. The puzzle regarding how it is possible that Virgil and the other spirits of the dead are visible though insubstantial, hence without shadows, is one of God's mysteries which are beyond human comprehension. The wisest men of antiquity such as Aristotle and Plato, who thought to resolve all problems through intellect, failed to unravel the divine mysteries.

Reaching the foot of the mountain, the travelers encounter a steep cliff that appears impassable. Dante sees a band of spirits moving toward them and asks Virgil to inquire the way. Thc spirits are astonished at seeing Dante's shadow until Virgil explains the phenomenon, whereupon the spirits courteously offer the poets directions. Then one, handsome and of dignified bearing, steps forward, showing the wounds on his forehead and breast, and asks Dante if he recognizes him. He is Manfred, illegitimate son of the Emperor Frederick II and grandson of the Empress Constance. He begs that Dante, on returning to the living, will assure his daughter that he died repenting of his sins and delivered his soul "to Him who freely pardons." He regrets that his body was removed from its grave on the battlefield where he was killed and was deposited without proper funeral rites outside of papal territory.

Manfred adds that even those who repent in their last moments are granted forgiveness, but those who die excommunicated are sentenced to linger on the lower slopes of the mountain before they can be admitted to Purgatory proper, the length of their delay being thirty times the period of their contumacy (i.e., their rebellion against church authority). His hope is that if Dante will report his state to his daughter, her prayers may bring him some reprieve.

Commentary

The approach to the mountain and the ascent of the lower stages of the mountain (Cantos 3-9) comprise the scenes of Ante-Purgatory, the region where certain spirits are condemned to linger for a period to compensate for their delayed repentance. There are several types of late-repenters here: the excommunicate and the negligent, a broad classification including the indolent, the unshriven, and the preoccupied.

In the present episode the poets meet the first of those groups, the excommunicate. However, before the encounter, the author introduces certain concepts regarding bodies and spirits as they pertain to the mystery of the limits of human reason. Dante's discovery of his shadow in Purgatory presents one of the numerous devices he employed to emphasize the contrast between Inferno and Purgatory, the one murky and fetid, the other a region of fresh air and glorious sunlight. The means devised for noting the apprehension of his shadow and at the same time noting the absence of any shadow from Virgil is ingenious and dramatic. Virgil, in attempting to clarify the problem, merely declares that many mysteries of creation are beyond human comprehension, as demonstrated by the mystery of the shadowless spirits, and he reminds Dante of the limitations of reason.

The first group of spirits in Ante-Purgatory, seen advancing slowly at the base of the mountain, is composed of those who died excommunicated by the church but who repented before death. Manfred, the spokesman for the group, confirms the doctrine that redemption is possible for all who are truly repentant in heart, even those who have been condemned by the authority of the church and denied its sacraments, an idea which conflicted with church teaching.

The name of Manfred was well known in Dante's time. An illegitimate son of Frederick II and grandson of Empress Constance (*Par.* 3), Manfred named his daughter Constance. His reputation involved sharp contrasts: he was handsome and popular, a soldier adored by his men; he was also an impious reprobate who was excessively fond of the company of "minstrels, courtiers, and harlots." His enemies charged him with incest, and he was suspected of having murdered his father.

Leading the Ghibelline army against the papal forces under the command of Charles of Anjou, Manfred was killed at the Battle of Benevento in 1266. His body, which had been given honorable burial by Charles, was disinterred and cast out of the Kingdom of Naples, which Manfred had ruled but which had since become papal territory. It is noteworthy that Manfred speaks of those abuses without rancor, an attitude characteristic of the souls in Purgatory. Contrast this with the spirit of Ugolino in *Inferno* 33.

By choosing a man of Manfred's impious reputation for this role, Dante presents an extreme example of how even the very wicked are not exempt from salvation. The treatment of such a figure as Manfred in heroic colors is difficult to understand unless we ascribe it to the fact that he, as champion of the anti-papal forces, was a hero figure to Dante in his youth.

CANTO 4

Summary

At the conclusion of Manfred's discourse Dante is surprised to notice that it is midmorning. This leads him to a philosophical comment on how his absorption in the conversation has blotted out all other awareness, and from this incident he draws evidence of the unity of the soul as opposed to the doctrine of the plurality of souls.

The poets are now shown a narrow cleft in the steep rocks, which, they are told, is their path toward the summit. Virgil in the lead, they start the climb which proves extremely strenuous, requiring hands as well as feet. Comparing this to the steep approaches to Italian towns noted for their difficult access – San Leo, Noli, and Bismantova – Dante asserts that this ascent is far more rugged. At last they reach a ledge and sit to rest.

While they are resting, Dante notices to his surprise that though he is facing east the sun is on his left. Virgil explains this phenomenon, pointing out that Purgatory is in the opposite hemisphere to Jerusalem; consequently, when the sun is on one side in Jerusalem it is necessarily on the opposite side for Purgatory. Dante now understands and he adds his own particulars about the positions of Jerusalem and Purgatory relative to the Celestial Equator.

When Dante asks how much higher they must climb, Virgil avoids a direct answer but states that the climbing, which is at first very strenuous, will become increasingly easier until it is finally effortless.

A strange voice says somewhat mockingly, "Perhaps you will need to sit and rest before you get up there." Turning, they discover a group of spirits nearby resting in listless attitudes. The one who spoke sits with head bowed between his knees. Dante calls Virgil's attention to this spirit's supreme indifference, as though Sloth were his own sister. The spirit, raising his head a trace, remarks, "Go on up, since you are so stout." He then asks Dante sarcastically if he has finally figured out about the sun being on his left. Dante, now recognizing him, addresses him as Belacqua and says he will no longer grieve for him. Then he asks him why he is loitering here. Belacqua's answer is that he is bound to linger for as long a time as he lived on earth before he will be admitted to Purgatory because, out of indolence, he neglected repentance until he was on his deathbed. He believes that his only hope of shortening this sentence in Ante-Purgatory will be through the prayers of someone who lives in grace.

Virgil urges Dante to hurry on, noting that it is already noon.

Commentary

It will strike the reader that the amount of didactic matter—expounding problems of science and philosophy—almost equals the number of lines devoted to the narrative in this canto. The narrative passages are treated in a simple style. The two travelers, having been directed to the path they must take, struggle up the rugged cliff to the first ledge. To convey the physical experiences, the author uses homely figures. The width of the cleft in the rock is about equal to a gap in the vineyard fence which a farmer could stop up with one forkful of brambles. The climb up the cliff is described as more difficult than the approaches to known Italian locales. San Leo and Bismantova are perched on precipitous mountains, while Noli, on the coast, is reached only by descending a steep cliff.

The account of the meeting with the indolent spirits is devoted entirely to the conversation with Belacqua, an acquaintance of Dante's who made musical instruments, or parts for them, and who had the reputation of being the laziest man in Florence. His physical attitude and his general lassitude through the encounter with Dante is expressive of his former life and equally appropriate for his status in Ante-Purgatory. His bantering exchange with Dante represents the familiar, good-natured baiting between longstanding friends. The whole episode presents a sharp contrast to the meeting with the vital, courageous Manfred in the foregoing canto. There is no dignity in indolence.

This class of sinners, negligent of repentance, are, like the excommunicate, subject to enforced, dreary delay before they can pass the gates of Purgatory.

The didactic matter of this canto is, typically, in Dante's more obscure style; that is, after it has been translated into English it needs to be further translated into terms intelligible to the modern reader. The first learned discussion, suggested by Dante's intense concentration over the discourse of Manfred, concerns the medieval debate over whether man possesses several souls or a single one. Plato theorized that there are three souls: the vegetative, the sensitive, and the intellective. Dante rejects Plato's doctrine, maintaining, in conformity with church teaching and the beliefs of Aristotle and Aquinas, that man has a single soul possessing separate faculties and that at times the functioning of one faculty can become so intense as to blot out the other faculties. In this instance the sensitive faculty—hearing and seeing—cancelled all of Dante's other functions.

The second instructive discourse concerns the fact that the sun's course runs to the north of Purgatory. Everything is stated indirectly, in accordance with the "dense" style. To paraphrase and translate: if the mirror took its complexion from Castor and Pollux (if the sun were now in the sign of Gemini, i.e., if it were summer), you would see the zodiac closer to the Bears (the sun's course would be closer to the constellations of Ursa Major and Ursa Minor, or the Dippers, i.e., farther north). Now you must bear in mind that Zion (Jerusalem) and this mountain (Purgatory) are in different hemispheres but have the same horizon (are antipodal); wherefore, the road that Phaëthon drove so badly (the sun's path, or the ecliptic) must bring daylight on one side here and on the other side there.

Dante's response amounts to this: I see, and now I understand that since the Celestial Equator (the equatorial line of the Crystalline Heaven) always comes between the sun and the frosty reign (the hemisphere that is in winter), Purgatory is exactly as far south from that equator as the Hebrews' Jerusalem is to the north.

The elaborate discussion of the position of the sun over Purgatory is typical of Dante's studied plan to introduce exact measurements, scientific data, and all manner of concrete details to give to his scenes every appearance of reality.

CANTO 5

Summary

Dante's first notice of the next group of spirits comes when a voice behind him remarks on his casting a shadow. As he turns toward the voice, Virgil admonishes him sharply not to let these interruptions delay his journey. He can talk as he walks along. The poets see a crowd of ghosts approaching them singing the *Miserere;* but when the spirits notice Dante's shadow, in their astonishment they stop singing their psalm. Two spokesmen come forward and inquire about Dante's condition. Virgil tells them that Dante's body is true flesh and that they would therefore do well to respect him. The spirits quickly crowd around Dante beseeching him to report news of their condition when he returns to the world of the living. All of them had been taken by violent deaths and hence could not receive the last sacrament but had repented of their sins in their last moments and forgiven those who had sinned against them.

The first speaker asks that if Dante should go to visit the Marches of Ancona he urge the citizens of Fano to pray for him to speed his entry into Purgatory. He relates how, while traveling near Oriago in the territory of Padua, he was caught and murdered by order of his enemy, a member of the house of Este.

The second spirit to request Dante's aid identifies himself as Buonconte of Montefeltro. He regrets that none of his relatives, not even his wife Giovanna, has offered prayers for him. Dante, knowing that Buonconte was killed at the Battle of Campaldino but that his body was never found, asks him to explain how this came about. Buonconte replies that as he fled from the field mortally wounded he died with Mary's name on his lips. An angel and a demon fought over him, and though the angel took possession of his soul "because of a little tear," the devil took revenge on his corpse, causing a terrible downpour that washed his body into the Archiano River and thence into the Arno.

A final supplication to Dante comes touchingly from a lady, La Pia, whose address is simple and brief: "Remember me when you have returned to the world and are rested from your journey. I was born in Siena, died in Maremma. My husband knows about it."

Commentary

Here once again we encounter the common belief that prayers of the living are efficacious for the relief of souls in Purgatory. The souls that greet Dante in this canto represent a second class of "negligent" spirits. Their type of default is distinctly different from the indolent. These died unshriven only because their lives were cut off by violence without allowing them the opportunity for the final rites of the church. They died, as the Ghost in Hamlet says, "Unhous'led, disappointed, unanel'd." The entire group of the unshriven spirits displays a great eagerness to have their status reported to family or friends in the world.

The chief interest of the canto lies with the identities and the histories of the pleaders for help from Dante, all three tragic figures of recent fame. The first of them is Jacopo del Cassero, who is not identified by name in the text; so we may assume that his story was well enough known to Dante's audience that the mention of his native city, the place of his death, and the name of the enemy who had him killed are sufficient. A native of Fano, Cassero had become a magistrate in Bologna. He had incurred the enmity of Azzo VIII d'Este; and on a journey through the territory of Padua he was pursued by the henchmen of Este. Having chosen a dangerous route to escape, he was trapped in a marsh where he was overtaken and murdered.

The second and principal figure seeking Dante's aid was Buonconte da Montefeltro. He had commanded the Aretine forces against the Florentine Guelfs in the Battle of Campaldino in 1289, a battle in which Dante himself served. The explanation for the mysterious disappearance of Buonconte's body was presumably imagined by thc poet.

This account of the death and redemption of Buonconte presents a striking contrast to his father's deserts. The father, Guido da Montefeltro, recounted his life and tragic death to Dante in *Inferno* 27, in the circle of evil counselors. He had accepted the promise of absolution from a corrupt pope as a guarantee of his salvation. He also told of the struggle for his soul between St. Francis and a black devil; but in his case the devil was victorious for the conditions of Guido's repentance were irregular. His son, on the other hand, was truly contrite, as demonstrated by his prayer to Mary, his "little tear," and the crossing of his arms over his breast in death.

The third suppliant to approach Dante was the lady Pia de' Tolomei. Her husband, wishing to marry another woman, sent her to one of his castles in the Maremma and there had her murdered. She appears to have no living relative whose sympathy she can count on; wherefor she begs Dante to remember her when he returns to the world—"and has rested from his journey." Her entire scene, consisting of only seven lines, is reported with a quiet tenderness. Much of what she tells of her life story is contained in one haunting line:

"Siena made me, Maremma undid me."
(Siena mi fè, disfecemi Maremma.)

CANTO 6

Summary

Dante likens his predicament to that of a gambler who, having won a good sum at dice, is followed by a throng of people all begging for a gift. The spirits of the unshriven trudge beside him, vying for his attention. All died violent deaths; all hope for intercession by their living relatives. Dante identifies six of these, either by name or other means, and sketches each tragedy in two or three lines.

When the poets have finally left the throng, Dante asks Virgil if it is true, as Virgil once wrote, that prayers are futile for diminishing a divine decree. Virgil's answer is that the hopes of these sinners are not vain. Their long penalty may be satisfied in a brief moment through "the fire of love," i.e., the loving intercession of family or friends. The passage referred to in the *Aeneid,* Virgil explains, concerned a pagan and therefore had a different application. This interpretation of prayers, Virgil declares, is according to his best understanding; but the final answer to these problems will be revealed when Dante meets Beatrice above. At the mention of the name of Beatrice, Dante is eager to hurry upward.

They meet a solitary, disdainful figure from whom they hope to get directions; but, ignoring their request, the spirit asks who they are and where they had lived. No sooner has Virgil mentioned Mantua than the spirit responds joyously that he too was a Mantuan, Sordello the poet; whereupon the two greet one another with a spontaneous embrace.

As Dante witnesses this scene displaying the kind of bond that existed in former times between fellow citizens—despite the fact that they were not acquainted, that one lived before Christ and the other in the thirteenth century—he is moved to compare that attitude with the one prevailing in his day. He therefore delivers a bitter diatribe against the people of Italy. Not only is there strife between city and city but even within cities between faction and faction, between family and family, such as the Montagues and Capulets. The fault, he complains, lies in the fact that the clergy has usurped governmental authority plus the fact that a succession of recent Hapsburg emperors has neglected Italy. He specifically mentions Albert and his father Rudolf, and sounds a warning to Albert's successor, Henry VII. Even Christ, he declares, seems to have turned his eyes away from Italy's sad plight.

Finally he directs his invective specifically against Florence, this time employing exaggerated praise which no one could fail to recognize as bitter irony.

Commentary

Among the crowd of spirits besieging Dante with their requests are six whose recent tragedies were probably readily recognized by his contemporaries. The Aretine, Benincasa da Laterina, was killed by the robber Ghin di Tacco because he had sentenced Tacco's brother to death. Another Aretine, Guccio dei Tarlati, was drowned in the Arno while pursuing the enemy. Federico Novello was killed at war. "He of Pisa" was murdered. His father, Marzucco, pardoned the murderer. Count Orso de Mangona was murdered by his cousin. Pierre de la Brosse, chamberlain of Louis IX and Philip III of France, was hanged as a result of the connivance of the queen, Mary of Brabant.

The belief in the efficacy of prayers to shorten the penalty of souls of the dead was mentioned by every type of the negligent sinners in Ante-Purgatory. It is evidently of urgent concern to the unshriven. In this canto Dante poses the question of its validity to Virgil, recalling a passage to the contrary in the *Aeneid.* To explain his statement in the *Aeneid,* which related to the mourning for the pilot Palinurus, Virgil points out that those prayers were from pagans to a pagan god. It is his understanding that the belief is justified for Christians, but he refers Dante to Beatrice for a more definitive explanation.

The figure of Sordello, introduced in this canto and further treated in the following, is impressive. He was a poet of consequence in the thirteenth century who used the Provencal language and followed the Provencal tradition. He traveled extensively in Italy, France, and Spain, and in his later years he become an honored figure at the court of Charles of Anjou. It is unlikely that Dante was familiar with a great deal of his poetry, but evidently one short poem impressed him, a lament on the death of a noble patron of letters in which he satirized the corrupt rulers of his day.

It is interesting that Browning was so captivated by Sordello's story that he treated the subject fancifully in a long early poem.

Though Sordello appears sullen on first meeting the poets, his attitude alters radically when he learns that one of them is from his native Mantua. The affectionate greeting of these two strangers leads Dante to reflect on how the bonds of fellowship and loyalty, once so strong among Italians, have been abandoned. His lament over the state of anarchy in Italy is the bitter declaration of a man who loves his country but finds it in a desperate state. To many generations of Italians, reading this account of their oppressed and strife-torn country, it has seemed that Dante was writing for their own times. His analysis of the basic cause of the present calamities is typical of his long-standing political philosophy. He believed that those evils stemmed primarily from the ambition of the church and the attempts of the papacy to encroach upon the temporal authority of the emperor. Secondly, he condemned the recent Hapsburg emperors for refusal to assert their authority in Italy.

The concluding passage, the ironic tribute to his native Florence, is undoubtedly tinged with personal animosity because of his banishment; nevertheless, it gives a faithful representation of the violent internecine quarrels that were plaguing the city. This subject, it will be noted, recurs throughout the *Comedy (Inf.* 15, 26; *Par.* 16).

CANTO 7

Summary

The story reverts to the scene of greeting between the two fellow-citizens. Sordello, who knows only that Virgil is from Mantua, asks who he is. Virgil, while giving his name, adds that since he lived before souls came to Purgatory—i.e., before the time of Christ—he could not attain heaven, though free from guilt. At the name of Virgil, Sordello is struck with awe, and kneeling before the revered poet he clasps Virgil's knees exclaiming, "O glory of the Latins, . . . who brought eternal honor to our city!" He then asks Virgil where he is consigned to dwell. Virgil explains that his place is with the virtuous pagans, who observed the cardinal virtues but not the "three holy virtues." They are without punishment but also without hope of attaining Paradise.

Virgil now repeats his request for directions. Sordello points out that it is almost dark and explains that they cannot travel at night. He leads them to a valley hollowed out of the hillside where they can rest, a lovely spot, grassy and filled with bright and fragrant flowers. A band of souls lingering there is singing *Salve Regina* (Hail, Queen of Heaven); these are the negligent rulers. From a ridge Sordello points out some of the renowned personages, rulers who, because they were preoccupied with state affairs, neglected their religious duties. From them the region takes its name, Valley of Kings. Seated highest among them is the Emperor Rudolf, and beside him is Ottocar, King of Bohemia. Others surrounding them are: Philip III of France, the Bold; Henry of Navarre, the Fat; Peter III of Aragon, the burly one; Charles I of Anjou, with the manly nose; Alphonse III, Peter's eldest son; Henry III of England; and William VII, Marquis of Montferrat, called Longsword.

Accompanying the identification of these figures is a running commentary, pro and con, on the expectations that the father's virtues will be inherited by the son.

Commentary

The account of the meeting between Sordello and Virgil makes an appealing scene—first, the delighted recognition of fellow citizens, and second, Sordello's excitement at the revelation of Virgil's identity and his spontaneous tribute to the great poet. This is the second of four prominent scenes in Purgatory portraying fraternal love. The first described the meeting between Dante and the musician Casella (Canto 2). Comparing the two scenes, one notes that the two parties showing mutual admiration and warmth of affection are fellow artists. One curious difference is that Virgil and Sordello are able to execute their embrace while Dante and Casella were not, the difference being that in one instance both are spirits and in the other one is a spirit and the other is living flesh.

In the Valley of Kings are numerous rulers who died within Dante's memory. They were good princes who had neglected their religious obligations because of their earnest preoccupation with affairs of state, a mitigating circumstance in Dante's mind. This explains the agreeable surroundings assigned for their durance. Some of them are already familiar to the reader, e.g., the Emperor Rudolf, mentioned in the preceding canto as one who ignored his obligations to Italy, and Charles of Anjou, who defeated Manfred at Benevento (Canto 3). In pairing off the monarchs Dante shows old enemies in amicable association. The Bohemian Ottocar, who was killed in a battle against Rudolf, is comforting him; and Peter of Aragon is singing beside Charles of Anjou, who was once his hated rival.

The most important theme running through the catalogue of rulers concerns the question of whether or not the virtues or faults of the father are passed on to the son. Ottocar, it is said, was worth more in his swaddling clothes than his son Wenceslas as a bearded man. Philip III and Henry of Navarre are shamed by the sins of Philip IV, who was the son of the former and son-in-law of the latter. The successors of Peter and Charles are unkingly. On the other hand, the case of Henry III of England illustrates the reverse. That weakling king begot a son of distinguished virtue, Edward I.

This discussion throws light on the debated theory that nobility of character is a matter of heredity, a belief which Dante refuted elsewhere (*Convivio* 4).

CANTO 8

Summary

As darkness is falling, one of the spirits begins to sing *Te lucis ante* [*terminum*] (Before the ending of the day), an evening devotion, and the others join him. Two angels descend and take stations to guard the valley. In describing them the poet says that their wings and raiment are green, they hold blunted flaming swords, but their features are not discerned because of the dazzling light of their faces.

The poets descend among the crowd of spirits and Dante is recognized by one, Nino Visconti. When Nino learns that Dante is still living, he announces the phenomenon to a companion, Conrad. Nino asks Dante to beg his daughter Giovanna to pray for him. His wife, he says, has made a second marriage to Galeazzo Visconti, a Milanese, and no longer cares for him.

Dante's eyes are directed to the sky where he notices that a group of three stars has replaced the four he saw at dawn.

Sordello calls attention to the approach of a serpent creeping through the grass; but at the sound of the angels' wings, swooping down like falcons, the serpent flees.

Nino's companion, Conrad Malaspina, now addresses Dante, asking if he can report any news from Conrad's native Val di Magra, or Villafranca. Dante replies that he has never visited that region but that its rulers are still famed for "the sword and the purse." Conrad prophesies that before seven springs have passed Dante will confirm this opinion through experience.

Commentary

The mood of evening is marked by a beautiful passage, not a description of the light in the sky but a suggestion of the sense of loneliness that comes over the traveler at that time of day. With the coming of darkness, Dante observes a group of three stars that have replaced the set of four he saw at dawn. As the four stars represented the cardinal virtues recognized by the ancients, these stand for the Christian or theological virtues: faith, hope, and charity.

The appearance of the angels and the serpent is steeped with allegory. The significance is that the souls in Ante-Purgatory are still tempted by their old sins—the attack of the serpent. The appearance of the angels demonstrates how heaven fights to guard those who have determined to take the road of repentance.

Dante engages in conversation with only two of the spirits in the Valley of Kings. The first is Nino (Ugolino) Visconti, who recognizes

Dante at the same time that Dante recognizes him. Originally from Pisa —he was a grandson of the famous Ugolino of the Tower of Famine episode in *Inferno* 33—he became captain general of the Guelph league in Tuscany and later served as a prominent magistrate at Gallura in Sardinia. His chief concern is that Dante beseech his daughter Giovanna for her prayers. He expects no help from his wife, Beatrice d'Este, who has married a scion of the Visconti family of Milan. He remarks sardonically that it would have been better to have as emblem on her tomb the cock of Gallura, his escutcheon, than the viper, the sign of those Visconti of Milan.

The second conversation is with Conrad Malaspina, a former lord of Villafranca. When he asks Dante for news from his home, the poet takes the opportunity to pay handsome tribute to the reputation of the Malaspina family for their courage and liberality. Though Dante had not visited Conrad's territory and knew of it only by reputation in 1300, he would enjoy the hospitality of that family in 1306, i.e., before the writing of *Purgatorio*. Thus this passage is an expression of gratitude to them.

Here ends the story of the first day on the mountain and, simultaneously, the passage through Ante-Purgatory, one more evidence of the careful structuring of the poem.

CANTO 9

Summary

It is near the end of the third hour of night (between 8 and 9 P.M.), when the moon is rising in the sign of Scorpio, that Dante falls asleep. In the early morning hours he has a dream in which he sees an eagle soaring overhead, and it seems to him that he is on Mount Ida, where Ganymede was abducted by Jove's eagle. The eagle in his dream plunges down like lightning and bears him up to the sphere of fire. As he and the eagle seem to catch fire he awakes.

Looking around him, frightened, he discovers Virgil, his comforter, who cheers him with the news that they have arrived at the entrance of Purgatory. Shortly before dawn, Virgil tells him, Saint Lucia came to where he was sleeping in the valley and carried him up the steep ascent to this point.

Approaching the gate in the wall surrounding Purgatory, they see three steps, and on the top step a guardian is seated bearing a naked sword, his countenance too bright for Dante's sight to sustain. In reply to the angel's challenge, Virgil declares that a lady from heaven brought them there and directed them to the gate. The guardian angel bids them approach. The first step they must mount is of gleaming white marble; the second is dark purple, seared and scarred; the third is of blood-red porphyry. On Virgil's advice, Dante pleads humbly for admission. The angel, with his sword's point, marks seven *P*'s on Dante's forehead and admonishes him to have those wounds removed in Purgatory. The angel then produces two keys, one silver and one gold, to open the gate. Those keys, he says, were delegated to him by Peter and both must function before the gate will open for the suppliant. As the poets are about to enter, they are warned never to look back.

Dante's first impression on entering Purgatory is that he can hear voices, through indistinct, singing *Te Deum laudamus* (We praise thee, O God).

Commentary

About halfway through this canto Dante notes that his theme is now more exalted and that his art must become correspondingly more elevated. It is not clear whether this remark concerns the entire canto or only that part which is to follow. Certainly the first half of the canto is full of what Chaucer calls the "figures and colors" of rhetoric. In the opening passage, to refer to the time of the rising of the moon, Dante employs a mythological figure. The "concubine of Tithonus" is the attendant of moonrise, a curious analogy to Tithonus' wife, Aurora, who is the attendant of sunrise. In the next phrase, the beast that smites with his tail is the scorpion. Hence the moon is rising in Scorpio. The steps the night must climb are the hours. Thus the moon is rising in the third hour after sunset. This timing of the moon, incidentally, is accurate for the evening of Easter, 1300, according to astronomical records.

Following the citing of Tithonus are several more allusions to classical letters, suggestive of "stylish" writing. One is the legend of Philomela, transformed into a swallow. In another version of the story Philomela was turned into a nightingale and her sister Procne into the swallow, but apparently Dante identified the swallow with Philomela. Another classical allusion is to Ganymede and Mount Ida in connection with the dream of the eagle. Next comes the reference to Achilles being abducted from his tutor Chiron by his mother and of his awakening amid strange surroundings on Scyros.

In the second half of the canto, devoted to the scene and ceremony at the gate to Purgatory, the artistry is of an entirely different character. With virtually no figurative language or allusions, the section gains its effect through vivid, concrete images—such images as would be automatically suggestive of allegorical values for a medieval audience but which can stand on their own merit for the modern reader.

Dante's dream, that first night on the mountain, is a reflection of what is actually happening to him. While in his dream he is being borne aloft by the eagle, St. Lucia is transporting him up the slope of the mountain. It was this same Lucia who interceded for Dante at the beginning of *Inferno* together with Mary and Beatrice. In allegorical terms she represents illuminating grace. Her assistance at this point in the story signifies that the sinner who is striving toward God will receive help from heavenly grace.

The steps leading to the gate and the guardian angel are associated with the penitent sinner and the power of the church to grant absolution. Clearly the angel is the priest, but the actual interpretation of the meaning of the three steps to the threshold is a matter of some disagreement. The common view is that they represent three steps toward repentance: white for confession, dark and scarred for contrition, and red for satisfaction (Sayers). In a slightly different version, the order is: contrition, confession, satisfaction (Sinclair). Grandgent offers an alternate interpretation, substituting the stages in the career of mankind leading up to the founding of the church: original innocence, sin, and atonement. The appropriateness of the type of rocks for the conditions represented according to this latter interpretation seems particularly effective: white marble for innocence; dark, scorched, and scarred rock for sin; blood-red porphyry for atonement. In any case the three stages represent a progression from sin to purification.

The seven *P*'s inscribed on Dante's brow by the angel, signifying *peccatum* (sin), represent the sins of the seven divisions of Purgatory. At the completion of his passage through each of the divisions, one of the initials will be erased to symbolize his having purged his soul of the sin of that particular region.

The keys of heaven, which Christ gave to Peter—"And I will give unto thee the keys of the kingdom of heaven"—are now in the keeping of the guardian angel at the entrance to Purgatory. This is appropriate because admittance here is a necessary step toward entering heaven, and no one except the saints can enter heaven without passing through

Purgatory. The golden key is the symbol of church authority, the silver key stands for discernment, which must be exercised together with authority in the matter of absolution. Hence both keys must function if the gate is to open.

CANTO 10

Summary

Entering Purgatory, the poets climb by a difficult, zigzag path until they reach a flat ledge, about as wide as "three times a man's height." This is the first terrace. On the side of the terrace next to the mountain the sheer wall is pure white marble carved to represent scenes of humility. The first portrayal Dante sees is of the Annunciation, so life-like that he seems to hear the angel pronounce *Ave* (Hail) and Mary's words, *Ecce ancilla Dei* (Behold the handmaid of the Lord). The second scene depicted is of King David dancing before the Ark of the Covenant with his wife looking on scornfully because of what she considers his undignified behavior. A third relief pictures the Emperor Trajan at the head of his troops confronted by a woman pleading with him to delay his march until he has avenged her son's death.

Soon a group of penitents approach, creeping along at a painfully slow pace and bowed down so low by huge rocks on their shoulders that they are hardly recognizable as human forms. Some are crouched lower than others, depending on the degree of their offense. Dante berates the proud spirits, condemning them for forgetting the true human condition: "that we are worms born to become angelic butterflies."

Commentary

When the poets reach the first terrace of Purgatory, they are first confronted with examples of humility in the form of bas-reliefs carved on the wall of the mountain. On each terrace the opening passage of the canto is devoted to representations of the virtue which is the opposite of the sin of that particular terrace. Since this first terrace is devoted to penance for the sin of pride, scenes of humility are offered as examples, or "goads," for the spirits performing their penance there. The examples of virtue in each terrace always include instances from both Biblical and pagan literature, as in the present passage. The first example given in every case is derived from the life of the Virgin.

The form of atonement that Dante conceives for the proud is that of painfully struggling along the ledge, bowed low under the burden of huge rocks because, in their pride, they held their heads too high. The last line of the canto is impressive: even the most patient sufferer seems to say, "I can endure no more."

It must be understood that in Dante's thinking, as in the doctrine of the church, pride is not only the most heinous of the seven deadly sins, because it is based on a belief that the individual is above the law, but pride is also the source of all other sins. Consequently, every soul passing through Purgatory must do penance on this terrace.

CANTO 11

Summary

The spirits of the proud recite an expanded version of the Lord's Prayer for themselves and for the living. Dante is moved to pity them and believes that the living ought to exert their efforts on behalf of those wretched spirits.

Virgil asks for directions, announcing that Dante is still alive and is eager to speed his climb up the mountain, whereupon a voice answers, though they cannot tell whose because all heads are bent so low. The speaker identifies himself as Omberto of the famous Aldobrandeschi family and relates how his great pride of ancestry and his haughtiness toward others caused the downfall of his kinsmen as well as his own death and his present suffering in Purgatory.

Another spirit twists his neck so he can see the travelers, and Dante, recognizing him, addresses him as Oderisi, celebrated artist of Gubbio. Oderisi disclaims his superiority, saying that his art is surpassed by that of Franco of Bologna, though he would never have admitted that when he was alive. Then deprecating the fame that artists strive for, he emphasizes its transience, noting how the great reputation of Cimabue as a painter has been overshadowed by Giotto's and how one Guido has supplanted the other Guido in poetry. The world's acclaim, he declares, is but a breath of wind, and who can expect to be renowned a thousand years after his time? And yet a thousand years is only the blinking of an eye to eternity.

Oderisi next identifies one of his companions, Provenzan Salvani, a former lord of Siena who is paying the penalty for his pride of power.

Dante expresses his surprise that Salvani has avoided the usual lengthy delay in Ante-Purgatory, and Oderisi explains that because of a notable deed of humility which Salvani performed he was spared that delay despite his late repentance. At the height of his power he stood as a beggar in the central square of Siena to get money for the ransom of a friend.

Commentary

The spirits in each terrace chant a prayer that is appropriate to the attitude of the region. The proud pronounce the Lord's Prayer, adding to each phrase a brief expansion which expresses their spirit of humility.

Three of the spirits in this group are identified, each representing a different source of pride: arrogance based on famous lineage, vainglory arising from artistic attainment, and haughtiness derived from wordly power. The first example is Omberto Aldobrandesco, scion of a famous family in Santafiore. His first remark—". . . the son of a great Tuscan . . ." —suggests that he has not completely eradicated his old habit of mind, but he quickly acknowledges that his fierce pride in his noted ancestry caused his downfall.

The second meeting is with Oderisi of Gubbio, a celebrated illuminator of manuscripts, who quickly demurs when Dante refers to his supremacy in his art. His denunciation of the fame attained through the arts is eloquent. Furthermore, it is interesting because of the names he cites to make his points. Cimabue and his pupil and successor, Giotto, are still familiar, a circumstance that detracts somewhat from the effectiveness of his moral on the insubstantial nature of such fame. In the passage, ". . . one Guido has taken from the other the glory of our language, . . ." the two poets referred to were both closely associated with Dante's career: Guido Guinizelli, leader of the school of *il dolce stil nuovo*, and Guido Cavalcanti, Dante's close friend and fellow poet. The remark following to the effect that another poet may soon unseat them both must surely point to Dante himself.

The third penitent introduced, Salvani, was a mighty Ghibelline lord in Siena who aided in defeating the Florentines at Montaperti in 1260. He was later killed in a battle against the Florentines. His form of pride was pride of power. The act which earned him free passage through Ante-Purgatory was that he humbled himself by begging in public until he had raised the money to pay the ransom for a friend.

CANTO 12

Summary

Virgil urges Dante, who has been walking beside Oderisi, bowing down and keeping pace with him, to move faster. The master then directs Dante's attention to the pavement where there are more scenes carved to edify the proud as they walk stooping. These are scenes illustrating the fatal consequences of pride. The first is the scene of Lucifer being cast down from heaven. Then follow twelve more pictures alternating between classical and Biblical lore: the defeat of the giants by the Olympian gods, Nimrod at the tower of Babel, Niobe all tears for her dead sons and daughters, Saul slain on his own sword, Troy in ruins, and several more.

An angel appears to greet the poets. He brushes Dante's forehead with his wing and invites them to mount a flight of stairs leading to the next terrace. The stairway reminds Dante of the steps mounting from beside the Arno up to the church of San Miniato on a hilltop outside of Florence.

In a parting message as they are leaving the terrace of pride, they hear voices singing *Beati pauperes spiritu* (Blessed are the poor in spirit).

Dante is surprised to find how easy it is for him to climb now. Virgil tells him that as he has more of these initials erased from his brow the mounting will become increasingly easier. Dante then feels his forehead and discovers that the angel has wiped away one of the *P*'s. He compares the stairway to the easy ascent from the Rubiconte, a bridge in Florence, up to the church of San Miniato on a hill overlooking the city.

Commentary

As Dante moves along the terrace conversing with the spirits, he bends down, assuming the attitude of the penitents. This is a symbolic gesture implying that he has some guilt to purge in this region. It is in only three of the terraces that he participates in the form of penance practiced there, indicating his confession of his own weaknesses.

Before leaving the terrace, the travelers are shown other pictures, this time carved in relief on the floor of the terrace. These are scenes showing famous examples of the destruction caused by pride. These warning examples, which are called "checks" or "reins" of sin, become a standard final feature of each terrace just as the "goads" – the examples of the opposite virtue – regularly appear at the beginning of each terrace.

In presenting the examples of how "pride goeth before destruction," the author has developed a curious kind of formal acrostic pattern. Each example is treated in a single tercet (3 lines). The first four examples all begin with *Vedea* (I saw), the next four examples with *O*, and the next four examples with *Mostrava* (It showed). Then for the thirteenth example the three lines begin with those same words in that same order. It has been noted that the initials of those words VOM or UOM – since *V* and *U* were treated interchangeably – spell MAN in Italian. This elaborate technical scheme was obviously carefully worked out, and some translators have tried in some fashion to imitate the pattern in their English versions.

The time of leaving the terrace is indicated as the sixth handmaiden of day, the sixth hour after sunrise, i.e., about noon.

Before leaving the region, Dante has one *P* removed from his brow by an angel, hears the appropriate beatitude, and is shown the ascent to the next terrace. These formalities will be followed in each of the succeeding terraces.

The comparison of the stairway taken by the poets to the flight of steps from the Rubiconte – the bridge now called Ponte alle Grazie – up to San Miniato, obviously a vivid recollection from Dante's youthful experience, is effective because many readers, even to the present time, would recall those broad, easy steps and understand. The steps, he says, were carved before Florence became corrupt. The mention of the stave and the leaf refer to two instances of corruption exposed in Dante's day. Some officials reduced the size of a barrel used as a standard of measurement by leaving out one stave. In the other scandal a leaf was torn from a ledger to remove evidence of embezzlement.

CANTO 13

Summary

When the poets reach the second terrace, they find it apparently deserted. Virgil decides to turn to the right and follow the ledge because that is in the direction of the sun. Soon they hear mystic voices above them, though no speakers are seen. These present the goads for the terrace—the instances of the virtue opposite to the sin of the region. The first voice pronounces *Vinum non habent* (They have no wine). The second voice cries out insistently, "I am Orestes." The third voice admonishes, "Love those who have done you harm." Virgil explains, to resolve Dante's astonishment, that this is the terrace for those doing penance for envy, and the voices present notable instances of the opposite virtue, namely, love of fellow men.

After they have traversed about a mile along the ledge, Virgil directs Dante's attention to a group of spirits huddled against the livid rock wall and almost indistinguishable from it because of the color of their clothing. Their cloaks are of haircloth. They are leaning against the wall, and each is resting his head on his neighbor's shoulder. Their attitude suggests blind beggars, and Dante perceives that their eyelids are sewed shut with iron wires in the manner that captive falcons' eyes are sewed. Tears constantly wet their cheeks.

After addressing the spirits with kind words of encouragement, Dante asks if any of them is Italian, saying that he may be of some help to them. A woman answers, saying that she was from Siena. Though her name is Sapia, she was not wise, for she had taken delight in the misfortunes of others. When the Sienese army fought at Colle, she prayed for their defeat and rejoiced so in seeing them routed that she cried to God, "Now I no longer fear Thee." She repented of her evil ways only at the last, but through the intercession of a pious citizen, Pier Pettinagno she was spared a long stay in Ante-Purgatory.

Sapia now asks Dante who he is and how it is that he can see and is breathing. He replies that he was sent here to look and that when he returns he will not have long to tarry in this region. It is the terrace below that he fears will torment his soul longer. But since he is still alive and will return to the living, he offers to perform any favors he can for her. She begs him to say a prayer for her sometimes; and she asks that if he should visit Tuscany he will restore her name among her people. They are among those foolish citizens who pinned their hopes on Talamone and Diana's well.

Commentary

In the first phase of the sojourn on the second terrace, the introduction of the examples of virtue, there are no pictures but simply voices uttering speeches which, to the initiated, give keys to famous stories,

Biblical or classical. Pictures would be useless here, since the penitents are blind. The first voice, saying "They have no wine," echoes the words of Mary, expressing her sympathy for the guests at the wedding in Cana. It was her speech that brought about Christ's first miracle, turning water into wine. The second voice cries out, "I am Orestes." Aegisthus, the story goes, condemned Orestes to death, but he did not know Orestes by sight. Pylades, Orestes' faithful friend, claimed that he was Orestes, being willing to die in place of his friend. Orestes came forward and said "I am Orestes." The third voice echoes the words Christ spoke in the Sermon on the Mount, "Love those who have done you wrong."

Explaining that this is the terrace of envy, Virgil says that these examples are demonstrations of love, the love of fellow men—*caritas*.

The description of the penitents here is vividly and meticulously detailed. They are blurred against the background of the rock which is the color of their hair cloaks: "livid," i.e., blue-black, as in a bruise. Huddled together and leaning on one another, they sit like beggars and chant their prayer, which is the Litany of the Saints. And then the final touch, their eyes are sewed shut with wires and tears are welling out. Their blindness is appropriate punishment because they sinned through sight; that is, they looked with envy on goods and attainments of their fellow men.

Sapia, the first spirit to talk with Dante, carried her envy to the point of madness. Although she was the aunt of Provenzan Salvani (Canto 11), she was so jealous of his rise to power that she rejoiced over his death and the defeat of his army. Her vindictive spirit had political as well as personal motivation, though Dante does not mention this circumstance. She belonged to the Guelph faction, while Salvani was a leader of the Ghibellines. In any case, she must have been regarded by neighbors with peculiar opprobrium.

Dante's statements about himself lay emphasis on sight. He is traveling this way, under special dispensation while still alive, to observe and to learn. Sapia is impressed with God's special favor to Dante. She asks for prayer, as so many did in Ante-Purgatory; and she begs to have her name restored among her people. To identify her people—the citizens of Siena—she mentions two of their abortive projects. They made futile attempts to develop a harbor at the town of Talamone, hoping to rival the trade of Genoa and Pisa. Also they kept digging all over their city in hope of locating an underground water supply which, according to tradition, was referred to as Diana's well.

These jibes, suggesting that the Sienese were a foolish lot, are spoken by Sapia, but sound suspiciously like Dante's own sentiments.

CANTO 14

Summary

Two other spirits, whose curiosity has been aroused by the conversation with Sapia, ask Dante who he is. He answers that he came from Tuscany on the banks of a river whose source is on Mount Falterona. He explains that he will not mention his name because it is not yet well enough known to be recognized. The spokesman of the pair, deducing that the river mentioned is the Arno, supposes that Dante preferred to avoid speaking that loathsome name. The speaker then delivers a vilification of the river because of those who live along its shores. The inhabitants along the upper reaches he characterizes as hogs; those farther down as cowardly curs; still farther along as wolves; and finally as foxes, masters of fraud. He concludes with a prediction that a grandson of his companion will bring great slaughter to the region of the wolves. The speaker's companion, upon hearing this prediction, appears to be deeply troubled.

Dante asks the two spirits to identify themselves. The spokesman names himself, Guido del Duca, and confesses his former disposition to envy anyone who showed himself to be happy. He then names his companion as Rinieri da Calboli, adding that none of his descendants have inherited his virtues. In fact, the entire province of Romagna, the territory including Bologna, Faenza, Forlì, and Ravenna, has become degenerate. He praises many of the former residents of that land and laments the decay of their offspring.

Leaving the penitents of envy, the poets hear other airy voices reminding them of examples of great envy, which are to serve as checks or bridles. The first voice announces, "Whoever finds me will slay me." Soon after comes a second voice declaiming, "I am Aglauros, who was turned to stone."

Virgil comments that such examples should serve as the "bits" which would hold men in check, but instead men become victims of the lures of Satan. God puts before them the beauties of the heavens, but they look only on the things of earth.

Commentary

When Sapia asked Dante his name (Canto 13), he ignored the question and spoke only of his mission. Now when the question is put to him by a second spirit, he offers only an indication of his birthplace and that in indirect language, excusing his reluctance to give his name on the grounds that it is not yet well enough known to be recognized. "Not yet" is indicative of his attitude toward his prospects for literary celebrity.

The two companion souls who now engage him in talk are both from Romagna: Guido del Duca and Rinieri da Calboli, the one a Ghibelline, the other a Guelph. Of Guido, who was from Brettinoro, in the neighborhood of Ravenna, we know little except that he engaged in a number of campaigns of the local wars. Rinieri, a native of Forlì, held the post of *podestà* in Faenza, Parma, and Ravenna during his distinguished career. Once in trying to recapture Forlì from the Ghibellines, he was defeated by the famous Guido da Montefeltro *(Inf.* 27).

The spokesman, Guido del Duca, assumes that Dante is ashamed to mention the name of the Arno, an attitude that he himself shares. He denounces the inhabitants of the Arno valley systematically, starting with the source and tracing its course to the sea. Its first passage, where the brutish natives resemble swine, is through the Casentino region. Farther along, where the citizens are likened to curs that snarl but are not truly bold, indicates Arezzo. The wolves of the next section are the Florentines, and the foxes at the mouth of the river represent the crafty folk of Pisa. At the end of his diatribe against those natives of Tuscany, he predicts that the wolves will be savagely brought down by a grandson of Rinieri. This is a reference to another of those events falling after 1300 which are treated in the poem as prophecies of things to come. The fact is that in 1303 the grandson referred to, Fulcieri da Calboli, staged wholesale executions among the Florentines.

Having thoroughly castigated the Tuscans of the Arno valley, Guido turns his attack against the present generation of the natives of Romagna, the region lying generally northeasterly from Tuscany between the Reno River and the Po, the Adriatic Sea and the Apennines. The burden of his lament is that the descendants of once noble figures are now corrupt. He then recites the names of the distinguished courtiers of former days that he remembers. The passage has a nostalgic tone as he speaks their names and praises their deeds. The significance of the speech lies in the fact that those same people, whom he knew when he was alive, aroused his envy. He tells Dante that he could not endure to see the happiness of others.

The poets, leaving the spirits and moving along the terrace, hear voices that cry out examples of envy which are to serve as warnings, deterrents, or checks. The term Virgil uses in this passage is "the bit" to hold men in control, i.e., the bit in the horse's mouth. The first voice pronounces the words of Cain, whose envy caused him to murder his brother and made him an outcast: "Whoever finds me will kill me." The second example is taken from the story of Aglauros, an Athenian maiden who envied her sister Herse because Mercury fell in love with her. When Aglauros refused Mercury admittance to her sister's chamber, she was turned to stone.

Virgil comments ironically that these warnings are of little avail against the bait of the old Enemy (Satan), and that despite the offer of eternal beauties, men are ever drawn to earthly goods.

CANTO 15

Summary

It is midafternoon and the travelers are walking westward along the terrace with the sun in their faces. Suddenly a dazzling brightness smites Dante on the brow. He supposes it is caused by the sun; but when he shades his eyes from it the new brightness persists, and he is forced to close his eyes. Virgil reminds him that the approach of an angel is still too powerful for his earthly senses, but says this will not always be so. The angel points their way and invites them to mount the stairs to the next terrace. As they start the ascent, they hear behind them the singing of the beatitude, *Beati misericordes* (Blessed are the merciful).

Dante asks Virgil to clear up a matter that is puzzling him. He recalls a puzzling remark by Guido del Duca to the effect that men direct their desires where sharing is denied. Virgil's interpretation is that material goods can have only one possessor, or their value decreases with sharing, and their ownership is the cause of others' envy. Spiritual possessions, on the other hand, increase the more they are shared with others. As a ray of light striking a bright object increases its brilliance, so the more souls there are loving God, the more his love is poured out to all. A fuller explanation of this subtle matter, Virgil says, will be given by Beatrice.

As that discourse is concluded, they reach the next terrace. Dante experiences a series of visions which present examples of the virtue opposite to the sin of this region. The first vision shows a distracted mother as she finds her lost son in a temple crowded with people. She addresses him in gentle tones, saying, "Son, why hast thou thus dealt with us? Behold thy father and I have sought thee sorrowing." In the second vision a weeping mother urges her husband, Pisistratus, to punish a youth who has embraced their daughter. The father's quiet, conciliatory reply is, "What shall we do to one who wishes to harm us, if we condemn one who loves us?" In a third vision Dante sees a crowd stoning a young man and screaming, "Kill, kill!" As the victim falls dying he prays that his persecutors may be forgiven. When Dante recovers consciousness after the visions, Virgil tells him that what he has been shown is intended to restrain his disposition to anger.

They hurry along the terrace, eager to take full advantage of the remaining daylight. Near evening they encounter a dense, smoky cloud.

Commentary

In the opening lines the author indulges in one of his involved astronomical passages to tell the time of day. The amount of time left before sunset is equal to the period between daybreak and the third hour; in other words, it is three o'clock in the afternoon. The sphere referred to that plays like a child is simply the sun, whose ecliptic course skips from one side of the equator to the other with the changing seasons.

Telling that they are walking toward the west and facing into the sun is a way of noting that they have reached a point on the north side of the mountain, since they started on the east side and have always turned to the right, circling counterclockwise.

Dante is mystified by the intense brightness that strikes his brow. He does not learn until later that it has erased another *P* from his forehead. Here again the style becomes dense. When shading his eyes against the sun fails to reduce the new glare, he explains that the light strikes his eyes as if reflected; whereupon he states the rule for the angle of reflection of light. Thus he introduces the angel of *caritas*, the love of fellow man.

The last formality before their leaving the terrace of envy is the singing of the appropriate beatitude, "Blessed are the merciful."

On the third terrace the goads, examples of the opposite virtue, come to Dante in the form of visions. The first shows the parents of Jesus discovering the lad disputing with the elders in the temple. His mother, overjoyed to find him, tempers her rebuke with gentle words. The second vision presents a scene in which Pisistratus, a ruler of ancient Athens, restraining his angry wife, offers a soft answer that turns away wrath. The third vision shows Dante the martyrdom of St. Stephen, whose extraordinary mildness is revealed in his prayer for the forgiveness of his murderers. When Dante recovers after the visions, dazed and shaky, Virgil bids him profit from the examples of those visions, implying that Dante has been guilty of this same sin of wrath.

CANTO 16

Summary

The poets enter a cloud of smoke which is as black as a cloudy, starless night and irritating to the skin and eyes. Unable to see the way, Dante has to cling to his escort's shoulder. They hear the spirits in that gloom praying to the Lamb of God for forgiveness and peace, chanting *Agnus Dei*. When Dante asks his guide about the voices, Virgil explains that the spirits here are atoning for anger. One of the spirits, having heard the conversation and realizing that Dante is not one of them, asks who he is and how he came there. Dante tells him of his special grace in being permitted to make the journey. The spirit gives his name as Marco of Lombardy and consents to help them find their way.

Dante questions him about the cause of the depravity of mankind: is it the influence of the stars that accounts for their corruption, or are men to be blamed for their evil ways? Marco replies that though the stars undoubtedly exert some influence over men's characters, it is a great mistake to attribute all human actions to their influence. If such were the case, man could not be held responsible for his acts, and any system of rewards for good and punishment for wickedness would be meaningless. Since men are given a knowledge of good and evil, and since through the exercise of free will they can make a choice of good or evil and hence exercise control over their course of life, they have a responsibility for their actions.

The soul, born in innocence, naturally pursues what promises happiness, but because of its inexperience it needs the guidance of laws and rulers to enforce the laws. In earlier and better times Rome had two rulers, one for political, the other for spiritual rule. Now in

Italy there is only one; he who holds the crozier has also adopted the sword. This breech of authority is the principal cause of the deplorable state of mankind.

Until the troubled times late in the reign of Frederick II, valor and courtesy flourished among the Lombards (in the lands watered by the Adige and Po), but now there remain only three men of the old breed: Currado da Palazzo; the good Gherardo (Gherardo da Cammino); and Guido da Castello. Dante asks who is meant by "the good Gherardo." Marco replies that Dante, as a Tuscan, should know about him. The only other designation he can give is that his daughter is named Gaia—joyous.

Commentary

In the smoky cloud of the wrathful, Dante suffers both blindness and smarting. This is one of the regions where he shares to some degree the same form of penance endured by the penitent souls, indicating his disposition to this sin.

The spirit with whom he converses is Marco Lombardo (Mark the Lombard), about whom we have no specific knowledge regarding his birthplace or family. He was obviously regarded by the author as a man of character and wisdom. The complaint he makes about the depravity of his race in recent times is reminiscent of the speech of Guido del Duca in the preceding canto decrying the degeneracy of the natives of Tuscany and Romagna. This time it is the Lombards who are denounced.

The discussion over whether our faults be in our stars or in ourselves makes a positive declaration of the supreme role of free will in man's course of life as opposed to the belief in the deterministic influence of the stars. The judgment is pronounced by Marco, but the doctrine is assuredly subscribed to by Dante. The problem is of great significance to Dante, and he will revert to it several times later.

The discourse on man's responsibility for his conduct leads to an examination of the responsibility of laws and rulers for guidance and control. Marco, again voicing opinions that are Dante's, describes the dual system of rule for mankind: the pope for spiritual life, the emperor for political affairs. In Dante's mind this was God's plan. The depravity of the present generation is attributed to the abrogation of that arrangement. Recent emperors have failed to maintain their control over Italy, and the popes have attempted to exercise that temporal authority in addition to their rightful spiritual powers. In this connection Marco speaks of the shepherd who chews the cud but does not have the cloven hoof, a reference to an Old Testament passage declaring that the Israelites may eat only those animals that chew their cud and have divided hooves. According to Aquinas, chewing the cud allegorically signifies ruminating on the scriptures, the cloven hoof signifies the power to distinguish between good and evil. The passage therefore implies that the pope (the shepherd) possesses the first quality but is wanting in the second, at least in matters of temporal rule. Frederick II, who died in 1250, was the last emperor who had exerted imperial authority in Italy, and even he had lost his power in the later years of his reign.

Marco speaks specifically of the decay of valor and courtesy in his native Lombardy, which he identifies with the valleys of the Po and the Adige rivers. The region of the Adige is no longer considered part of Lombardy but in Dante's time much of northern Italy was encompassed by the term. Only three living Lombards, according to Marco, possess the virtues of earlier times. The first, Currado (Conrad) da Palazzo, had served as vicar general for Charles of Anjou in Florence in 1276. Another in his list, Guido da Castello, of Reggio, had received mention in the *Convivio.* The other figure, whom he refers to simply as "the good Gherardo" (Gerard) has been identified as Gherardo da Cammino, captain general of Treviso, whom Dante had also mentioned in his *Convivio.* Why Marco expects that all Tuscans would recognize him by this simple designation is not clear.

CANTO 17

Summary

The poets issue from the gloomy cloud shortly before sunset. Dante, once again falling into a trance, receives visions that display instances of the excesses of wrath. The first of these shows the sin of Procne – she who was turned into a nightingale. She murdered her little son and served his flesh to her husband in revenge for his having ravaged Philomela. The second vision reveals the execution of Haman, witnessed by Ahasuerus, king of the Persians, and the Jew Mordecai, Haman's intended victim. The third vision shows Lavinia discovering the body of her mother who has hanged herself.

After the visions have passed, an angel greets them. Again the brightness overpowers Dante's sight, but he hears the angel's invitation to mount the next stairs and feels a wing brush his forehead. Then follows the pronouncing of the beatitude, *Beati pacifici* (Blessed are the peacemakers).

When they reach the next terrace, they pause, for it is night, the time when their progress must stop. To pass the time, they engage in a discussion of the plan of Purgatory. To Dante's question as to what sin is represented on this new terrace, Virgil replies that it is a love of good which is not diligently carried out, "a slackening of the oar." Virgil then outlines the arrangement of Purgatory and expounds its rationale. Explaining that all actions, good or evil, stem from some form of love, he then analyzes the diverse aspects of love. There are two principal kinds of love, the natural or instinctive, and that of the mind, or elective love. The natural is without fault, perfect according to God's plan; but elective love, which is a special attribute of man because of his gift of free will, is susceptible to error. Perverted love, which is that directed toward evil ends and aims to harm others, takes one of three forms: pride, envy, or wrath, the sins of the first three terraces of the mountain. The love represented on the fourth terrace, the one the poets have now reached, is defective love; that is, love directed toward a worthy good but pursued with insufficient zeal. The sin is sloth. The three upper terraces involve excessive love of earthly objects. What the three vices of excessive love are, Virgil does not reveal.

Commentary

The presentation of the checks, or bridles – the examples of execrable wrath – like the "goads" that introduced Dante to the terrace, come in the form of visions. The first shows Procne carrying out her vengeance by serving her child to Tereus, the father. According to Dante's version of the myth, Procne was changed by the gods into a nightingale and Philomela to a swallow to spare them from the vengeance of Tereus. Another version of the myth, as was noted earlier (Canto 9), has Philomela transformed into the nightingale and Procne, or Progne, into the swallow. Procne's type of anger caused her to violate the bonds of family.

The second vision, drawn from the Old Testament, shows the execution of Haman for his hatred of the Jews. He was chief minister of King Ahasuerus. In a fit of anger against Mordecai, he ordered the execution of all the Jews in captivity in Persia. Queen Esther, herself a Jew, saved her people, and Haman was executed for his attempted pogrom.

The third vision reveals a scene from the *Aeneid.* Queen Amata committed suicide, having heard a false report that the fiancé of her daughter, Lavinia, had been killed. The object of her anger was Aeneas and his Trojan followers, the founders of the Roman Empire. Any offense against Rome and the empire was serious to Dante; and by the same token, the offense of Haman against God's chosen people was culpable.

Virgil's elaborate explanation of the arrangement of sins in Purgatory presents not simply a listing of sins in their order but a reasoned plan as well. All actions, good or bad, he says, stem from some form of love. This discussion is difficult to follow unless we equate the term "love" with "desire," especially in the interpretation of its evil aspects.

It is no accident that Virgil's exposition on the scheme of Purgatory is presented at a point midway through the ascent. Standing on the fourth terrace, there are three terraces below and three above. Furthermore, the seventeenth canto is the mid-point of this canticle. A similar explanation was given for the arrangement of Inferno in the eleventh canto, as the poets were moving from the sixth circle to the seventh. That passage was obviously not centered with the mathematical precision of the passage in Purgatory.

CANTO 18

Summary

Dante expresses a desire for a fuller clarification of the doctrine of love, whereupon Virgil elaborates on the foregoing discourse, exploring the sensitive and intellective faculties and the function of the will—a kind of medieval lesson in psychology. From the physical object, he declares, the mind creates an image; and as the image is attractive the mind is obsessed with a desire for it. This natural love is as instinctive to man as it is natural for fire to rise heavenward. Not every desire is good, however.

Dante interrupts, puzzled over why, if love comes to us in this natural way, there should be any special merit in either good or bad behavior. Virgil promises to give the best explanation that it is within the province of reason to supply, but that it must be left to Beatrice to treat what can be made clear only through faith. Man, Virgil explains, cannot understand why those natural desires arise in him. They are as instinctive to him as the making of honey is to bees. The crucial point is that man is endowed with the faculty for distinguishing between good loves and evil ones, and when he has exercised his power of judgment, he can choose between the right course and the wrong one. This exercise of choice is called free will.

This discussion is concluded toward midnight as the moon is beginning to mount in the sky. The poets become aware of a crowd of spirits running toward them. Two in the lead cry out, "Mary went into the hill country in haste," and "Caesar, to subjugate Lerida, struck at Marseilles and then hurried into Spain." The other souls call out, "Hurry, hurry; let no time be lost through little love, for zeal in doing good may renew grace."

Virgil asks the penitents to show them the way to ascend. One of the spirits answers, "Follow us. We are so eager to rush on that we cannot delay for you." He informs them briefly as he passes that he was the Abbot of San Zeno at Verona in the time of Barbarossa, and he complains that recently one in authority has placed his own unworthy son as head of the monastery.

The last member of the pack of speeding souls calls, "All of those for whom the seas divided were dead before coming to Jordan," and then, "Those who chose not to follow Aeneas in his last labors gave themselves up to an inglorious life."

Meditating on what he has seen and heard, Dante falls asleep.

Commentary

This second discourse on love repeats the basic concepts of the previous passage but takes a different direction. The former discussion was concerned with the anatomizing of love according to its different types and distinguishing the errors and abuses resulting in perverted love, defective love, and excessive love of unworthy goals. The present discussion deals with the sensory and psychological origins and the obligations imposed upon man to exercise judgment and will in determining those forms which ought to be pursued or shunned.

The first example of virtue is the announcement of Mary's hastening to the hills seeking her cousin Elizabeth to tell her the news of the Annunciation. The second sentence tells of how Julius Caesar hurried his army into Spain to deliver the city of Ilerda, which was in the hands of Pompey's forces. The events came in the civil wars between Caesar and Pompey. Caesar had begun the seige of Marseilles but left the attack under the command of Brutus in order to hasten his campaign in Spain.

The penitents are met rushing along the terrace pell-mell, reminiscent of the ancient Thebans in a Bacchic revel. Ismenus and Asopus are rivers near Thebes. This violent form of animation is to compensate for the former lassitude of the spirits. The word Dante uses for sloth, *accidia*, comprehends both physical and mental laziness or indifference. In the Middle Ages the term was commonly used to describe the attitude of certain monks indicating a laxity of spiritual zeal, a fact which helps the reader understand the desire for haste expressed by the penitents.

The one penitent with whom Dante holds a hasty conversation is a former abbot from Verona. His complaint is against a certain man who placed his crippled illegitimate son at the head of that same monastery. That certain man, who has "one foot in the grave" already and who will soon have cause to regret his action, was Alberto della Scala, Lord of Verona. He died in 1301, hence the "foot in the grave" in 1300. Albert was the father of the famous Can Grande della Scala, whom Dante greatly admired.

The notable examples, the checks of sloth, are again sentences cried out in passing by one of the penitents. The first sentence deals with the Israelites who were led through the Red Sea by Moses but were not permitted to enter the Promised Land because of their wavering in fidelity. The second instance of sloth deals with the followers of Aeneas who gave up their mission and stayed in Sicily when their leader went on to Italy and founded Rome.

Here Dante falls asleep on the mountain. There is no beatitude or benediction pronounced as was the custom on the previous terraces.

CANTO 19

Summary

Shortly before dawn Dante dreams of a woman who at first appears ugly, horribly deformed, and stammering. As he looks at her she is transformed into a beautiful and alluring damsel who sings a fluent, melodious song to him. She declares that she is the Siren who charms men with her singing as she did Ulysses. An angel appears and asks Virgil to tell who the creature is, whereupon Virgil tears off the Siren's garment exposing her ugliness and the stench of her corruption. The dream is broken as Virgil wakens Dante.

An angel appears, invites them to ascend, fans them with his wings, and pronounces the beatitude, *Benedicti qui lugent* (Blessed are they that mourn).

As the poets mount the path, Virgil tells Dante that the Siren has caused the sorrowing of those who are above them on the mountain. The safeguard against her seductions, he says, is to trample upon earthly enticements and turn the eyes toward Heaven.

On the next terrace they find a multitude of spirits lying face down on the path weeping and reciting the psalm, *Adhesit pavimento anima mea* (My soul cleaveth to the dust). Dante questions one of the spirits, who says he was once pope. He had been given to avarice throughout his life; but when he attained the office of pope, he became committed to the holy life. He explains that because he and all of those guilty of avarice had loved earthly goods and had refused to turn their eyes toward Heaven, they were now groveling face down in the dirt in penance. When Dante kneels out of respect, the spirit tells him to stand, saying that in the spirit world all are equal as fellow servants of God. He names a niece, who is still living, Alagia, upon whom he counts for prayers for his soul.

Commentary

The opening lines of the canto indicating the time of night are, as usual, couched in intricate figurative language. The heat of the day is overcome by the natural cooling of the earth plus the influence of the moon and Saturn. This occurs in the early morning hours. The geomancers referred to practiced a pseudo-science of prognostication by the use of dot patterns. One of their familiar figures, called Fortuna Major (Greater Fortune) was patterned upon star arrangements found in sections of Aquarius and Pisces. Since those two constellations would appear shortly before dawn, the geomancer could see Fortuna Major in the sky at that time of night in that season. That time of night, it should be noted, was considered most propitious for prophetic dreams.

Through the dream of the Siren the poet presents a symbolic concept of the sins to be treated in the final three terraces, the sins of the flesh, or, in the language of Virgil, excessive love of earthly objects. Those evil desires, which at first appear disgusting, seem to become attractive if we let our minds dwell on them, as the hag becomes beautified and eloquent under Dante's steady gaze. The cure for escaping the coils of that temptress comes through Reason (Virgil), stirred by divine counsel (the angel), exposing the Siren's true loathsomeness.

The Ulysses reference was probably taken from a passage in Cicero. It is not in accord with the Homeric version, which Dante did not know at first hand in any case.

After awakening from the dream, Dante is visited by the angel of Zeal, who removes another *P* from his brow and dismisses him from the terrace of Sloth. It is noteworthy that for the first time Dante is not stunned by the brightness of the angel so that he has to turn away or shut his eyes.

On the new terrace the poets are directed to turn to the right, as they have done on each preceding terrace. They are still on the north side of the mountain moving westward, and the rising sun is at their backs.

The spirit from whom they received directions identifies himself merely as a successor of Peter and one who came from the country between Sestri and Chiaveri, i.e., east of Genoa on the Levantine coast. He was Pope Adrian V, who held the papal office only a little more than a month. He confesses how he was subject to avarice until he came to the supreme office, after which he strove to keep the mantle of that office clean. The niece of whom he speaks was Alagia de' Fieschi, a woman known for her good works. Dante was probably acquainted with her and may have enjoyed her hospitality.

This is the terrace of both avarice and prodigality (which were punished together in the fourth circle of Inferno), those opposite extremes of incontinence with respect to worldly property. Emphasis here, however, is almost entirely on avarice. The explanation for the kind of penance practiced here is stated explicitly by the pope. Lying motionless, their faces in the dust just as in life they had looked toward earthly objects, they weep and pray.

CANTO 20

Summary

The poets are forced to keep close to the cliff wall as they move along the terrace because of the multitude of souls crowded on the ledge. Dante apostrophizes avarice, the "she-wolf," who has captured more prey than any other beast, and he expresses the hope that soon one will come to drive her away.

A voice announcing examples of virtue first cites the poverty of Mary, who bore her baby in a stable. As a second example, Fabricius, a Roman consul, is honored for rejecting a rich bribe, preferring poverty with virtue to great riches with vice. The third example praised is St. Nicholas, who, by his generosity, furnished dowries for three sisters, saving them from degradation.

Dante addresses the spirit he heard reciting those examples and learns that he is Hugh Capet, founder of the Capetian dynasty of French kings. He denounces the sins of his descendants, particularly the acquisitiveness and treachery of three Charleses and two Philips. In a detailed list of crimes of French royalty he notes the seizure of Normandy by Philip II; of Ponthieu and Gascony by Philip the Fair; and of Provence by Charles of Anjou. Charles of Anjou is also charged with the deaths of Conradin and Thomas Aquinas. Charles of Valois captured Florence through treachery. A third Charles, Charles II of Apulia, sold his daughter in a marriage arrangement. A final and supreme crime, which Capet foresees as a future event, is the act of Philip the Fair in the capture and indignities visited upon a pope which led to his death. He also anticipates the attack on the Order of Templars by that same monarch.

Capet explains that the penitents recite examples of poverty and generosity during the day while at night they rehearse notable instances of avarice. Among other examples, he cites the stories of Pygmalion, Midas, Crassus, Ananias and Sapphira, and Heliodorus.

As the poets advance after leaving Hugh Capet, they feel a violent quaking that shakes the mountain, at which the spirits cry out in chorus, *Gloria in excelsis Deo*. Dante is frightened and greatly puzzled by the experience. The spirits quickly return to their penance with renewed zeal.

Commentary

The reference to avarice as the she-wolf and the expressed hope that a man will come to earth to overcome that beast is clearly reminiscent of a passage at the opening of the *Inferno* (Canto 1), where the poet's path is barred by three beasts: a leopard, a lion, and a she-wolf.

The wolf in that passage is thought by many commentators to represent avarice, an interpretation which seems to be supported by comparison with the passage in *Purgatorio.* In both passages there is a prophetic reference to a coming leader who will overcome the influence of the wolf. In the *Purgatorio* passage the hoped-for leader will free men from the curse of avarice; in the *Inferno* the savior destined to heal the ills of Italy is referred to as "the hound," which scholars have identified with Can Grande della Scala, a leader in whom Dante placed great hopes. The failure to introduce Can Grande in the *Purgatorio* passage does not necessarily indicate a loss of trust in him. Such a connection would not have the same appropriateness in this instance.

The presentation of the instances of virtue for this terrace comes in the form of utterances by the spirits. The example of Mary's poverty is demonstrated through the humble stable where she gave birth to her baby. The virtue of Fabricius is revealed through his refusal of wealth which would be acquired at the expense of his honor. The third example, the story of St. Nicholas and his gift of dowries to the three poor sisters, is a demonstration of generosity.

After the pronouncement of the whips of avarice, Hugh Capet denounces his descendants in the royal house of France. He lived in the latter half of the tenth century, and his heirs ruled France until 1322. Charles of Anjou, Charles of Valois, and Philip the Fair, names that figure prominently in this diatribe, occur frequently in the *Commedia* because of their ruthless interference in recent events in Italy. Charles of Anjou, in supporting the papal cause, killed Manfred and Conradin, the son and grandson respectively of Frederick II. The rumor that he was responsible for the death of Thomas Aquinas, which Dante accepted, was probably unfounded. Charles of Valois entered Florence in 1301 posing as a peacemaker and then condemned and banished all the leaders of the Whites, including Dante. The worst crime of the "Lily" of France, according to Capet, was still to come, the capture and persecution of Pope Boniface VIII by Philip the Fair in 1303. Since this had not yet occurred in 1300, the time of Dante's supposed journey to Purgatory, it is put in the form of a prophecy. Although Dante hated Boniface on several counts, he judged Philip's action reprehensible because it represented a crime against the holy office. The likening of the affair to the treatment of Christ by Pilate constitutes the most severe condemnation imaginable.

The numerous examples of avarice punished are divided about equally between classical lore and Biblical. The Pygmalion mentioned is not the one most readers are familiar with, the sculptor whose statue came to life. This one was Dido's brother, who murdered his brother-in-law, Sichaeus, for his treasure. Sapphira and her husband, Ananias, kept for themselves some of the money belonging to the community of the early church; and when Peter, discovering their crime, rebuked them, they fell dead on the spot. Heliodorus, in the Apocryphal Old Testament, was struck down by a visionary horse when he entered the Temple to rob the treasure.

One of the most dramatic events of the passage through Purgatory is introduced next, the earthquake on the mountain; but the reader, like Dante, is left in suspense for an explanation at the close of the canto.

CANTO 21

Summary

Curiosity about the trembling of the mountain continues to occupy Dante's mind as he and Virgil make their way along the terrace. Soon they hear a voice behind them and are greeted by a spirit who has caught up with them. Since Virgil, in his salutation, indicates that he is not one of the souls destined for Heaven, the stranger wishes to know how they are permitted to climb the mountain; and Virgil tells him that since Dante has been granted this journey though still living, it is necessary that he have a guide. For this purpose he, Virgil, was summoned from Limbo.

In response to Virgil's inquiry about the quake, the spirit informs them that this phenomenon occurs when a soul has completed its penance and is free to advance to Paradise. The termination of the period of penance, he explains, is a matter determined by the soul itself and not by any other sentence. At the signal of the trembling of the mountain all of the penitents shout the praise of the Lord. The spirit tells them he is Statius and that it was for his deliverance that the mountain quaked just now. He was a citizen of Rome in the time of the Emperor Titus and had attained fame for his epic poems on Thebes and Achilles. His chief guide and inspiration, he says, was his great Roman predecessor Virgil. On hearing this remark, Virgil signals Dante to keep silent, but Dante cannot repress a smile that Statius notices. Feeling that he must explain the smile to avoid offending the spirit, Dante announces that his companion is that same Virgil. Statius impulsively kneels and attempts to embrace the master's ankles but is checked by Virgil with the reminder that they are both shades.

Commentary

The quake on the mountain serves as a dramatic introduction to the appearance of Statius. After polite greetings Virgil asks their new companion about the quake. In his reply the spirit discourses on the nature of Purgatory—its changeless character, its freedom from rain, sleet, clouds, lightning, and such earthquakes as come from tormented winds in the bowels of the earth. In Purgatory proper—"above the three steps"—the trembling is an announcement of the completion of one soul's penance. The test of satisfaction rests with the soul itself. When it feels that purification is effected, it rises and moves on its journey to Heaven. The explanation of the will in this operation, which is rather complicated, follows scholastic doctrine. One aspect of the will, "the absolute will," never deviates from directing the soul toward God; but another aspect, "the conditioned will," may waver under the influence of worldly desires. The conditioned will not only leads men into sin but also dictates their undertaking of penance for sins committed. When the two aspects of the will finally come into accord, the soul recognizes that it has become purified.

The reputation of Statius as a classicial epic poet was greater in Dante's time than at present. That Dante knew his works well and admired them is clear. We know also that both Boccaccio and Chaucer knew and made use of the *Thebaid,* Boccaccio in his *Teseida* and Chaucer in *The Knight's Tale.*

The meeting of the two Roman poets adds one more to the list of scenes of fraternal love, following the spirit of the meeting of Dante and Casella (Canto 2) and that of Virgil and Sordello (Cantos 6-7). It is presented with remarkable effectiveness. The admiration in which Statius held Virgil, so admirably expressed before he knows he is talking to Virgil, is a source of delight to Dante and to the reader as well. Then the spontaneous gesture of devotion by the disciple toward the master contributes to a memorable episode.

During the rest of the journey through Purgatory, Statius makes a third in the party, and he shares with Virgil the role of guide. Where Virgil represents human reason, Statius represents reason supported by faith.

CANTO 22

Summary

The angel of the fifth terrace directs the poets to the passage leading to the next region after brushing another *P* from Dante's forehead and pronouncing the Beatitude, "Blessed are they that . . . thirst after righteousness, . . ." omitting the word "hunger."

The two elder poets converse while they climb toward the next ledge. Virgil tells Statius he heard such excellent reports about him from Juvenal when that poet came to Limbo that he is very happy to meet him. He confesses some surprise, however, to learn that so noble a character could have been guilty of avarice. Statius corrects his impression, saying that his sin was prodigality, the opposite of avarice. As is proper, these two extremes opposed to moderation with respect to wordly goods are punished together. Statius tells how he was so affected by a passage in the *Aeneid* condemning hunger for gold that he steered far from that vice, too far, in fact. For his squandering he has paid with a thousand moons of penance.

Virgil remarks that nothing in the *Thebaid* indicates that Statius was a Christian, and he asks how he came to adopt the faith. Statius replies that just as Virgil was the one who led him to Parnassus (symbol of sublime poetry), so too it was Virgil's influence that drew him to the true God. It was a passage in Virgil's *Eclogues* predicting the coming birth of a new progeny and the restoration of the first age of man that first drew his interest in the new faith. He saw Virgil's words as a prophecy of the coming of Christ and the new dispensation and consequently as support for the new religion. He became a convert, but for a long time he kept his conversion secret, a fault for which he had to pay with four hundred years of penance on the terrace of sloth.

Statius asks for a report of the Roman poets who were non-Christians, Plautus, Terrence, and others. Virgil tells him that they, together with famous Greek authors, are in Limbo where they often converse of the Muses. In that same region, he adds, are some of the Thebans whom Statius had honored in his epics: Antigone, Ismene, Hypsipyle, and more.

By this time the group has reached the sixth terrace. Turning to the right, they discover a tree laden with fruit and sweet smelling. It is peculiar in that the branches are widespread at the top but taper toward the bottom. A spring gushing from the cliff waters the branches. A voice issuing from the tree cries, "You shall have dearth of this fruit." Then the voice cites examples of the virtue of temperance: Mary at the marriage in Cana, more concerned for the success of the feast than her own hunger; the women of ancient Rome, who drank only water; Daniel, who because he would not partake of the king's meat and wine was granted the power to interpret dreams; the men and women of the golden age, who relished acorns for food and water for drink; and John the Baptist, who lived on honey and locusts in the wilderness.

Commentary

The Angel of Moderation on the fifth terrace pronounces the Beatitude in an irregular fashion. Instead of ". . . they that hunger and thirst after righteousness, . . ." he says only ". . . they that thirst after righteousness, . . ." *Sitiunt* is Latin for thirst. The reason for the alteration is that the same Beatitude is to be applied in the next region, but using the word "hunger" there because that is the region of gluttony. We learn for the first time from Statius that the fifth terrace includes the souls of the prodigals as well as the avaricious.

Virgil's information about Statius had come through Juvenal, the great satirical poet who was a contemporary of Statius but who, not being a Christian, was consigned to Limbo.

There is no historical basis for the claim that Statius was a Christian. Either Dante invented the idea or he drew upon some traditional source now lost, but at any rate he developed the idea in an elaborate fiction. Statius, according to Dante's presentation, was drawn to Christianity through Virgil's text. Like so many readers in the middle ages, Statius interpreted Virgil's *Fourth Eclogue* as a prophecy of the coming of Christ, and he felt that the forecasting by his great master lent great credibility to the story of the Christians. It is now believed that Virgil was writing about a child of the emperor and empress, whose birth was expected shortly.

A question that many readers of *Purgatorio* want to ask is: how long do souls remain in Purgatory? Obviously the periods must vary according to individual cases. Dante comes closer here to an intimation of the duration of penance, at least for one instance. Statius says at one point he has been doing penance for more than five hundred years. Elsewhere he specifies four hundred years on the third terrace and a thousand moons for prodigality. Actually it is easy to calculate that since he lived in the reign of Titus, i.e., in the first century A.D., he has spent more than twelve centuries in Ante-Purgatory and Purgatory.

Upon reaching the sixth terrace, the poets discover a tree on the path, tempting to the senses but forbidding the enjoyment of the fruit. The instances of virtue, uttered by a voice from the tree repeat the episode of Mary at the marriage in Cana, which was used before in another connection (Canto 13). In this instance she is shown devoting her attention to the pleasure of others rather than to the satisfying of her own appetite. The following examples, some Biblical and some classical, reveal notable examples of abstemious diets such as acorns and water or locusts and honey.

CANTO 23

Summary

After the three poets have passed the tree, they hear someone singing *Labia mea, Domine* (Open Thou my lips, O Lord). Soon spirits pass them hurrying along the terrace, and Dante notices that they are so pale, hollow-eyed, and terribly emaciated that he is reminded of the legend of Erysichthon's curse of hunger and of the scriptural story of the Jewish mother who ate her own baby. It is difficult for Dante to understand how the spirits can be so wasted simply because of the odors from the tree.

When one of the shades speaks to Dante, the poet does not recognize him by his appearance but he remembers the voice. It is Forese Donati, a Florentine and a fellow poet whom Dante had known well. Forese explains that the tree and the stream that waters its leaves have the power to cause their wasting as they purify themselves through hunger and thirst. The scent of the fruit and the smell of the water on the leaves stir their craving for food and drink. They hastily circle around the terrace, always returning to the tree that increases their pain, which is also their solace.

When Dante expresses surprise that Forese, who died so recently (1296), is not still lingering in Ante-Purgatory, Forese tells him that the prayers of his virtuous widow, Nella, have speeded his passage to this point. The mention of his exemplary woman leads him to contrast her character with the majority of Florentine women, whom he brands as more shameless than the barbarians of Sardinia and far more immodest than the Saracen women because of the current style in Florence for women to appear in public with their breasts and paps exposed. For these sinful ways Forese predicts that they will have cause for regret before those who are now babies will grow beards.

Forese and his companions have noticed Dante's shadow and ask for an explanation. In reply Dante reminds Forese of the reckless lives they used to lead and then tells how Virgil came to rescue him from that life, guided him through Inferno and up the mountain, and will remain his guide until he meets Beatrice.

Commentary

It is a peculiarity of the terrace of gluttony that the physical appearance of the spirits is affected by their penance. They actually look like people who have been starving for a long time, whereas in the other regions the penitents appear in their normal human forms. The story of Erysichthon, which comes to Dante's mind when he sees these spirits, is of a man who offended Ceres and was punished by being cursed with insatiable hunger. He ended his life by devouring his own flesh. The second recollection is of the woman who succumbed to such hunger during a siege of Jerusalem that she ate her own child. Her name was given as Mary, or Miriam, in different versions of the episode.

The first words heard coming from the tree are *Labia mea, Domine.* The full quotation is, "Open my lips, O Lord, and my mouth shall pour forth Thy praise." This characterizes the region admirably. The spirits open their mouths, not to eat but to worship.

The spirit with whom Dante converses, Forese Donati, was a member of the prominent Donati clan. His brother Corso, a leader of the Blacks, commanded the Florentines in the Battle of Campaldino, in which Dante fought. A sister, Piccarda, appears in a passage in Paradise *(Par.* 3). Gemma Donati, Dante's wife, was also a relative. The kind of life in which Dante and Forese had been associated was evidently somewhat disreputable, and it was from that way of life, Dante says, that Virgil had rescued him when he led him out of the dark woods. Something of the Dante-Forese association is recorded in a group of sonnets exchanged between them. The poems are coarse and scurrilous, and Dante accuses Forese of gluttony and infidelity and ridicules Forese's wife, Nella, for her perpetual cold. Forese, in return, abuses Dante for beggary and pusillanimity.

It is not clear whether these poems were written with animosity or in a mood of vulgar bantering. Certainly Dante shows pleasure at meeting Forese and presents him in a highly favorable light, crediting him with an impressive statement of how the spirits rejoice in the pain of their penance. Dante also makes amends to Nella, expressing Forese's love for her and crediting her with effecting her husband's speedy passage through Ante-Purgatory by her prayers. In an eloquent diatribe

Forese, no doubt voicing Dante's opinion, severely censures Florentine women in general for their immodesty and forecasts drastic punishment for them in the afterlife.

In explaining his journey Dante says that Virgil has been his guide through Inferno and Purgatory and will lead him to where he is to meet Beatrice. In all other instances where Dante mentions Beatrice to someone he explains who she is, but here he simply mentions her name; this appears to be an interesting piece of evidence of his former close acquaintance with Forese.

CANTO 24

Summary

Dante asks Forese about his sister, Piccarda, and is told that she is in Paradise. Forese then identifies some of his fellow penitents since their emaciation makes them difficult to recognize. First he points out Bonagiunta, a poet of Lucca, and close by a pope who is simply identified as a native of Tours. He is more wrinkled and spare than most of the others because of his fondness for eels cooked in white wine. Others mentioned are Ubaldino dalla Pila, who is gnashing his teeth at the air for hunger; Bonifazio, who entertained lavishly; and Master Marchese, who drank but was never satisfied.

Dante notices that Bonagiunta the poet is muttering something to him about Gentucca and asks him to say what is on his mind. His reply is merely that a certain woman will make Lucca pleasing to Dante. He then asks Dante if he isn't the author of the poem, *Donne ch'avete intelletto d'amore*. Dante answers that when love breathes in him, he writes as love dictates. Bonagiunta acknowledges that it is this doctrine that sets apart the poetry of Dante and the *dolce stil nuovo* from the earlier Italian poets, namely, Jacopo da Lentino, the Sicilian notary; Guittone d'Arezzo; and Bonagiunta himself.

All the spirits who have gathered around to listen to the conversation turn and speed on their way, except Forese, who stays briefly to ask Dante how soon he will return this way. Dante does not know but hopes it will be soon because the city where he lives is rapidly becoming corrupted. Forese agrees, and he predicts that soon the man most responsible for that turmoil will be dragged at the tail of a wild horse until he is battered to death and his soul will be dragged where there is no remission of sins. He then dashes off, saying that time is very precious here and that he must hurry after his companions.

The poets now come to another fruit tree where many spirits are gathered in useless supplication. At length the spirits leave, realizing that their pleadings are in vain. A voice from within the branches tells the poets to pass on. The same voice urges them to bear in mind the fate of the centaurs who, having feasted and become drunk, fought against Theseus and his companions. The second example of the evil consequences of gluttony cited by the voice speaks of the soldiers who were rejected by Gideon because of their manner of drinking.

Dante is now greeted by the Angel of Temperance, whose brightness is like the red glow of molten metal or glass. Showing the passage up the mountain, the angel removes another *P* from Dante's brow with a puff of wind from his wing, and he pronounces the Beatitude in paraphrase: "Blessed are they who are so illumined by grace that the love of food does not kindle their desires beyond what is fitting."

Commentary

Among the penitent gluttons pointed out by Forese are a pope, an archbishop, a mayor, a soldier, and a poet. The pope was Martin IV of Tours (1281-85), who reputedly died from over-indulgence in feasting on eels stewed in sweet white wine. Ubaldino dalla Pila, a leader in the victorious Ghibelline army at Montaperti, was the father of the Archbishop Ruggieri, who figures with Ugolino in the *Inferno* (Canto 33). The Boniface mentioned here was an Archbishop of Ravenna; and Master Marchese degli Orgogliosi was *podestà* of Faenza.

The penitent who talks with Dante at length is Bonagiunta of Lucca. He first speaks about a woman of Lucca, Gentucca, who will endear that city to Dante. This reference appears to be an expression of appreciation for hospitality. Bonagiunta then turns to the subject of poetry, recalling one of Dante's early poems, "*Donne ch'avete . . .*," which was the first *canzone* in *La Vita Nuova*. In acknowledging the authorship of the poem, Dante expresses his credo of lyric poetry succinctly. He writes of love as love dictates; in other words, his poetry was based on his actual emotional experiences rather than on conventional devices. Bonagiunta recognizes in this statement the important distinction between the Dante group and the works of earlier Italian poets. The two names he mentions together with his own, Jacopo da Lentino and Guittone d'Arezzo, are among the few reputable poets who wrote in the vulgar tongue before Guido Guinizelli introduced *il dolce stil nuovo* (the sweet new style).

Dante, returning to his conversation with Forese, speaks bitterly of the decline of virtues in his native Florence. Forese then predicts that the man chiefly responsible for the city's turmoil will soon be dragged to Inferno. The man he is speaking of is none other than his brother, Corso Donati, who was the leader of the Blacks. He was a prime instigator in the massacre and banishment of the Whites, including Dante, in 1301. In 1308 his party turned against him and had him arrested. The circumstances of his death are probably close to the version Dante gives, though there are variations in the reports.

A second tree appears on the terrace from which a voice urges the travelers not to tarry here for this is but a slip of the tree farther up the mountain from which Eve ate the forbidden fruit. The same voice announces the examples of the horrible consequences of gluttony. The first example concerns a battle of the centaurs. After the wedding feast of Pirithous and Hippodamia, the drunken centaurs attempted to kidnap the bride and other ladies present. Theseus led the native men in the defense of their women and defeated the monsters. A second lesson on gluttony refers to the selection of soldiers for Gideon's expedition against the Midianites. Watching the troops crossing a stream, he rejected all of the men who bent down to drink, choosing only those who scooped water in their hands so that their heads were up and their eyes alert.

The angel of the terrace removes the sixth *P* from Dante's forehead with the breath of air from his wing. The Beatitude is similar to that pronounced on the terrace below except for the exchange of "hunger" for "thirst," but in this instance the blessing is given in an elaborate paraphrase.

CANTO 25

Summary

During the afternoon of the third day the poets hurriedly mount the narrow steps leading to the seventh and final terrace. As they climb, Dante asks how it can be that souls can suffer from hunger and can be altered in their appearance though they are only airy substances and have no need of food. Virgil suggests that a consideration of other supernatural phenomena might aid his understanding. One example he uses is that of Meleager, whose body wasted away as a certain branch was being burned, because of a prophecy of the Fates. In another example Virgil reminds Dante of how an image in a mirror simultaneously duplicates every motion of the figure before the mirror. For a more detailed discussion of the problem, Virgil turns to Statius.

The answer Statius offers is long and complicated and typically medieval. To begin at the beginning, he explains the relation of body and soul starting with the act of procreation. A special kind of refined blood, passing from male to female, starts the creation of a human being. The first phase of development is the vegetative faculty, then the sensitive faculty. At the moment of birth God breathes into the infant the intellective faculty, thus forming a complete soul. At the moment of death the soul, leaving the body, retains memory, intelligence, and will in an active state while the vegetative and sensitive faculties become inert. But when the soul reaches "one or the other shore"—Acheron or Tiber—on the way to Inferno or Purgatory, the soul assumes the form of the body in air and not only becomes visible but also takes on the attributes of its former organs. Thus the shades can see, hear, speak, laugh, sigh, and weep. Moreover, they can reflect whatever bodily shapes are dictated by their desires and other affections.

Upon reaching the seventh terrace, the poets discover that much of the passage is taken up with a river of flames running along the cliff wall, so that they find only a narrow strip on the outer edge of the ledge where they can walk and avoid the fire. Within the flames they hear voices chanting *Summae Deus clementiae* (God of clemency supreme). After each singing of the hymn, examples of chastity are recited. The first is a mere quoting of Mary's words to the angel at the Annunciation, *Vinum non cognosco.* (I know not a man.). The second example refers to the banishment of Helice from the woods of Diana after she has desecrated the sacred precincts, having been seduced by Jove and borne him a child. The voices also call the names of women and men who were chaste according to the laws of virtue and marriage.

Commentary

As the poets are mounting the steps, they engage in a learned discussion. As before, the discussion turns upon some quandary in Dante's mind regarding what he has just witnessed. In this instance it is the problem of how shades can become so lean when there is no need for them to eat or drink. Virgil's reply is indirect. He says that thinking about certain other curious phenomena will shed some light on the present problem. The first illustration he uses is the experience of Meleager. At his birth the Fates decreed that his life would last only until a branch of wood in the fire was consumed. His mother, Althaea, snatched the branch out of the fire and hid it. However, when Meleager killed his brothers in anger because they stole the boar's hide he had presented to his wife, Atalanta, Althaea put the branch back in the fire. As the branch burned up, Meleager's life was consumed. The implication is that if a body can be affected by some external object through spiritual influences, the bodily form of an airy figure could be affected by the suffering of the spiritual being within that form.

Virgil's second example calls attention to the reactions of the image in a mirror to the actions of the body that is reflected. This demonstrates how an influence may be transmitted without any physical contacts to effect the transmission.

After offering those suggestions of parallel phenomena, Virgil defers to Statius to give a fuller explanation. It has been suggested that Statius was better qualified to answer this question because he represents reason supported by Christianity. That interpretation appears to be negated by Statius' assertion that Virgil could have answered the question well.

The explanation as given by Statius is long and involved and, for many modern readers, dispensible; but to Dante the clarification of such a profound question as the relationship of the body to the soul and the participation of all the faculties—vegetative, sensitive, and intellective—in the unified soul is of the utmost importance and merits the most careful treatment. And all of that is essential to an understanding of the condition of the aerial shades after death.

Statius makes reference to a certain wise man who was mistaken in concluding that the soul must be separate from the intellect since he could find no organ in which the soul resides. The wise man was Averroes, the Spanish-Arabic philosopher.

On the seventh terrace the punishment for the lustful is walking in a river of fire, a concept peculiarly appropriate since fire was a familiar symbol for lust. The weakness of these sinners was surrender to a burning passion. The hymn that the poets hear as they approach the penitents, *Summae Deus clementiae,* is a fitting one since it includes a prayer for purification by fire.

The examples of chastity, i.e., the whips or goads of lust, are pronounced by the penitents in the fire. The first example merely quotes Mary's words in response to the angels announcement that she will give birth to the Christ child: "I have not known a man." The other example is from classical mythology, citing Diana's indignation over Helice's violation of her vows of chastity – regardless of the ameliorating circumstances – and the punishment of the offending nymph.

CANTO 26

Summary

The three poets have now reached a point west-northwest on the mountain; and as it is the latter part of the afternoon, the sun is striking Dante on the right shoulder, causing his shadow to fall on the flames and make them appear a darker red. The sight of his shadow attracts a group of spirits. Just as he is about to answer their query about his condition, a new band of spirits approaches them from the opposite direction; and the spirits in the two groups salute one another with brief kisses as they pass. The newly arrived group shouts "Sodom and Gomorrah"; those of the first group call out that Pasiphaë has taken the disguise of a cow to draw the lust of the bull. The groups part in opposite directions, and those going Dante's way resort to their former chants, weeping.

The same spirits that first questioned Dante gather, and he assures them that he is living. He asks them to say who they are that he may write of them and perhaps speed them on their journey to Paradise. He also wishes to know about the other group. One of the spirits answers that those going in the opposite direction were guilty of Caesar's vice for which he was called "queen." This is why they reproach themselves with the names of Sodom and Gomorrah. The other spirits, those moving in a clockwise direction, were guilty of natural lust. Their offense was against the laws of man; and since their acts were bestial, they call on the name of one who made herself a beast.

The spokesman for the group of spirits identifies himself as Guido Guinizelli, at which announcement Dante expresses his admiration and indebtedness, for he considers Guido one of the finest of love poets and the model for many other poets. Not daring to go nearer to him because of the flames, Dante gazes at him before speaking, then offers him his services. He tells Guido of his admiration for his verses, at which Guido points to another shade in the flames saying that *he* surpasses all other craftsmen of the mother tongue. Those who rank Giraut of Limoges above the other shade were influenced merely by hearsay. It was in the same fashion that Guittone's reputation as the best of the Italians had prospered until the truth of the matter prevailed. Guido ends by asking Dante to say a paternoster for him.

Dante now addresses the spirit pointed out by Guido as the great artist of words and is answered in Provençal verses, naming himself, Arnaut, and urging Dante to take heed of his pain.

Commentary

The penitents on the terrace of lust are separated into two classes, one moving around the mountain in the normal direction, i.e., following the course of the sun, the same direction taken by the poets. The other class is going in the opposite direction. The latter souls were guilty of unnatural or abnormal sexual practices. This accounts for their cry of "Sodom and Gomorrah," those cities of Old Testament times that the Lord destroyed because of the prevalence of their gross perversions. The reference to Julius Caesar's perversion is based on an account by Suetonius that Caesar was reported to have had abnormal relations with the conquered king of Bithynia and that at a public celebration people greeted him as "queen."

The main group of penitents, those going in the normal direction, were given to normal, heterosexual amours. Their calling to mind the mating of Pasiphaë is a forceful example of the bestial nature of amorous passions. Pasiphaë, the queen of Crete, was smitten with a lascivious passion for a young bull. Concealing herself in an imitation cow devised her desires. As a consequence, she gave birth to the Minotaur, with the head of a bull and a man's body.

The manner of kissing practiced by these penitents as the two groups pass is in conformity with admonitions in the New Testament for Christians to bestow on one another the kiss of brotherly love.

The only two spirits who are identified in this terrace are Guido Guinizelli and Arnaut Daniel, two poets whose works Dante admired. Guinizelli, of Bologna, was the elder leader of the school of *il dolce stil nuovo* and the master whom Dante imitated in his early lyric poetry. He was one of the two Guidos mentioned in Oderisi's discourse on the transience of fame on the terrace of pride (Canto 11). Dante's enthusiastic, almost reverential greeting to Guido is one more example of that type of scene displaying fraternal admiration and affection between artists which is typical of Purgatory. Memorable earlier examples are the encounters of Dante with Casella (Canto 2), Virgil with Sordello (Cantos 6-7), and Virgil with Statius (Canto 21).

Just as Dante was paying tribute to Guido, a poet to whom he was indebted, so Guido in his turn pays his tribute to an earlier master, Arnaut Daniel. It is Guido who refers to Arnaut as a "better craftsman of his mother tongue" *(miglior fabbro del parlar materno),* but it must be understood that this opinion was also Dante's. The phrase *il miglior fabbro* has come to the attention of English readers through T. S. Eliot's use of it in his dedication of *The Wasteland* to Ezra Pound. Modern critics find in Arnaut's work more ingenuity and versatility in forms and techniques than seriousness of purpose or inspiration. His attraction must have been based on that phase of Dante's poetic nature which enjoyed developing complicated forms like the passage presenting examples of pride punished, in which the initial letters spell VOM, "Man" (Canto 12).

Guido refutes the popular claim that Arnaut was surpassed by Giraut de Bornelh, a later Provençal troubadour. Such opinions, he declares, were based on hearsay judgments rather than examination of the poetry. The same custom of hearsay criticism maintained the reputation of Guittone d'Arezzo, even when he had been surpassed by a younger poet—presumably Guido himself. Arnaut's speech to Dante, which is in Provencal, is highly appropriate for the occasion and extremely affecting. The reason for putting Guido and Arnaut in the terrace of lust is not clear, since we have no record of notorious amorous indulgence for either of the men. It must be concluded, then, that Dante assumed some passionate escapades on the basis of their love poems.

The reader would profit greatly by returning to the *Inferno,* Canto 5, to the circle of carnal sinners and to *Inferno* 15, the circle of the sodomites.

CANTO 27

Summary

As evening is coming on, an angel appears on the terrace and sings *Beati mundo corde* (Blessed are the pure in heart). He announces that there is no way to proceed up the mountain but to pass through the fire. Dante is terrified, recalling a scene when he saw persons burned to death. Virgil tries to reassure him with the promise that he will surely survive the ordeal, but still Dante cannot bring himself to take the first step or even to put his hand in the flame for a test as Virgil suggests. But when Virgil reminds him that Beatrice is waiting up the mountain, he quickly overcomes his hesitation and advances into the flames with his companions. Once in the fire, he suffers agonizing pain from the fierce heat. Virgil, meanwhile, continually encourages him with words of Beatrice. Finally the sound of chanting leads them out of the flames on the other side at the point where the ascent to the region above begins. An angelic voice invites them to proceed in haste while there is still a little light. When darkness comes the poets lie down on the steps to rest and wait for daybreak.

Virgil and Statius watch like shepherds while Dante sleeps. In a dream Dante sees a lady, young and beautiful, gathering flowers. She is Leah, she tells him, and her delight is picking flowers that she weaves into a garland, while her sister Rachel prefers always to sit before her mirror and view her beautiful eyes.

On awaking, Dante, with his companions, resumes the climb. Virgil promises him that on this day he will attain the happiness that all men long for. Then, in a final speech, Virgil says that he has brought Dante as high as he (Virgil) can mount, and that Dante, having witnessed the torments of Inferno and having passed through the trials of Purgatory, has now attained freedom of will sufficient to be his own instructor. "Over thyself I crown and mitre thee."

Commentary

In indicating the time on the mountain, the poet writes that the sun is just rising in Jerusalem (where Christ shed his blood) while it is midnight over Spain (the Ebro river) and noon over India (the Ganges). That means the sun is setting in Purgatory.

The river of flames is continuous around the mountain on this terrace; consequently, anyone wishing to reach the cliff side of the terrace in order to climb higher up the mountain must pass through the fire. Dante's fright and hesitation at the command to walk into the fire creates an effective dramatic passage. For the first time Virgil's assurances and persuasion are not sufficient to give Dante the courage for the ordeal, but the mere mention of Beatrice produces the desired result instantaneously. As Virgil promised, the fire does not sear a hair of Dante's head or burn his clothes; nevertheless, he endures such intense heat that, as he says, he would gladly plunge into boiling glass to cool himself. This purification by fire is unquestionably Dante's penalty for certain offenses on his part. It will be recalled that there were only two other instances where Dante participated in the penance of the terrace he was passing through: pride and anger. Lust is the third type of sin that he acknowledges.

During his third night on the mountain, Dante rests on the stairs mounting from Purgatory proper to the Earthly Paradise, and again in the hour before dawn he is visited with a prophetic dream. The two sisters of the dream are Old Testament figures, the two wives of Jacob. Leah was the fertile one, Rachel the barren one. Allegorically they stand respectively for the active and the contemplative life. The dichotomy of those two patterns of life was prominent in medieval thinking and figures repeatedly in passages related to both Earthly Paradise and Paradise proper.

At the top of the steps they reach the Earthly Paradise, the point where Virgil has completed his mission. He declares that Dante has now attained freedom of will and can follow his own inner dictates. He therefore pronounces the pupil his own master.

CANTO 28

Summary

Dante starts to explore the "divine forest" of the Earthly Paradise followed by the ancient poets and is delighted with the sweet odors, gentle breezes, continual singing of the birds, and the accompaniment of the rustling trees. He reaches a river of sparkling water which is in deep shade. Across the river he sees a lady, young and beautiful, who is picking flowers and singing as she goes. He begs her to come closer so that he can hear the words of her song, saying that she reminds him of Proserpine gathering flowers in the fields. The lady comes close to the opposite bank; and when she lifts her eyes, Dante thinks that the eyes of Venus when she was in love could not have shone with such glory. Though the lady and Dante are only three paces apart, he regrets the stream that separates them.

The lady says if it seems strange to him that she is smiling and gay in this sanctified region, the psalm *Delectasti* may help him to understand ("For Thou, Lord, hast made me glad through Thy works"). She then offers to answer any questions that are puzzling him. He asks how it is that there are breezes and flowing streams. He has been led to suppose those phenomena did not belong above the gates of Purgatory. She explains that the light motion of the air is different from the winds below on the earth, for here it is created by the motion of the heavens, specifically the Primum Mobile, around the earth. Consequently, the breezes always blow in the same direction. The flowing of the streams here also differs from those below, which result from the cycle of evaporation, condensation into clouds, mists, and rainfall. Here a fountain, whose source is the will of God, pours its waters into two streams, Lethe, whose waters bring forgetfulness of past sins, and Eunoë, which revives the memory of good deeds performed. The soul is healed only after drinking from both Lethe and Eunoë.

The lady adds that when the poets of old pictured a long-past Golden Age, they were inspired by a vague consciousness of this region where man first lived in innocence enjoying eternal spring and abundant fruits. Virgil and Statius are pleased to learn the origin of those classical visions.

Commentary

As the three poets set out to explore the Earthly Paradise, it is Dante who takes the lead. Virgil's assurance that Dante is now qualified to be his own guide is being demonstrated. In the account of the initial view of the region, they discover all of the conditions characteristic of the other-world gardens of earlier literature: a rich abundance of green grass, great trees, many-colored flowers, crystal streams, lovely singing of birds, and the harmonious rustling of the trees. The language of the passage suits the subject in a delightful manner. The one allusion introduced is the comparison of the sound of the wind in the trees to that of the pine forest at Chiassi, a spot near Ravenna which has made a deep impression on several other writers, among them Boccaccio, Dryden, and Byron.

The picture of the lovely maiden picking flowers presents a charming contrast to the penitents described in Purgatory. She is the living realization of the figure of Leah in his dream of the previous night; and, as the reader recognizes later, she likewise symbolizes the active life while Beatrice represents the contemplative life. There is a tendency, in discussions of these two patterns of life, to choose sides and argue for the supremacy of one against the other. Dante recognizes the importance of both, and he maintains that without the contribution of those engaged in the active business of the world, there would be no possibility for others to practice a life of contemplation. In simplest terms the dichotomy may be stated as the practical in contrast to the spiritual. Viewed in terms of medieval life, one might equate active and contemplative with those engaged in worldly affairs and monks in their cells. But to Dante there must be in every fully developed human being an involvement in both ways of life.

The lady gathering flowers, though not named until later (Canto 33), is Matilda. Naturally there have been numerous attempts to identify her with a real person. Historians who have searched the records for a Matilda that might fit this character have proposed Matilda, Countess of Tuscany, who lived in the eleventh century and was a supporter of Pope Gregory VII in his disputes with Emperor Henry IV. Though this proposal has been passed down through generations of commentators, it is hardly convincing. Grandgent suggests that Matilda may be identified with the young lady mentioned in *La Vita Nuova*, a friend of Beatrice who died young. The lady is not named in the earlier work for reasons of privacy. The association of that lady with Beatrice and the relation of Matilda to Beatrice in the Earthly Paradise lends credence to the theory.

When Dante notices the breezes and running streams at the top of the mountain, he is confused because these features appear to contradict the statement of Statius that above the gates of Purgatory there are no natural disturbances. That would appear to preclude winds, clouds, rain, and rivers supplied by rain and snow. Matilda explains that the winds here are cosmic, so to speak. It is the turning of the universe around the earth that stirs the air. This accounts for the fact that the breeze blows steadily and always in the same direction, from east to west.

The explanation for the rivers of the region is supernatural. God created an ever-flowing fountain which furnishes the headwaters of two rivers with different properties. Lethe, the traditional river of forgetfulness, in Dante's version causes forgetfulness of one's sinful deeds. Eunoë, the companion stream, apparently an original concept with Dante, revives the memory of one's good deeds. A spirit rising to Paradise after purgation must drink from both streams.

Matilda informs Dante further that this spot was man's first abode, the Garden of Eden, where he might have lived blissfully innocent amid abundant fruits in eternal springtime had it not been for Adam's sin. Poets of all ages who have envisioned such an existence in such a garden, calling it the Age of Gold, must have had some mystic consciousness of man's primal state. This reference calls to mind the many literary versions of other-world gardens or earthly paradises, both classical and Christian, of which Dante has made a synthesis in the present scene.

It is worth noting the number of classical allusions in this canto which contribute overtones to the passage: Aeolus, Proserpine, Venus, the Hellespont (associated with Leander and Xerxes), Lethe, Helicon, and the Age of Gold. Eunoë, an invented name, is a compounded Greek word.

CANTO 29

Summary

The lady of the flowers resumes her singing with the psalm *Beati quorum tecta sunt peccata* (Blessed are those whose sins are forgiven), and as she sings she walks along the bank of Lethe moving upstream. Dante, on the opposite bank, matches his steps to hers; and when they have gone some hundred paces, a sharp bend in the river causes them to turn to the east. Here the lady admonishes Dante: "My brother, look and listen well." Suddenly he becomes aware of a brilliant glow, and he hears music of such melting loveliness that he regrets the boldness of Eve which caused mankind the loss of Eden and consequently the loss of such melodies.

The course of the narrative is interrupted at this point by an eloquent invocation to the Muses beseeching their aid to put in verse things hard to understand.

At first Dante sees what appeared from a distance to be golden trees but at closer view are seven lighted candlesticks. In his amazement he turns to Virgil but discovers that the sage is equally awed by what they are witnessing. The flaming candles move slowly forward, and trailing after them are streamers of light in the seven colors of the rainbow. The outermost candles appear to be about ten paces apart. Following them come twenty-four elders walking two by two, crowned with garlands of white lilies and singing a hymn honoring the Virgin. After them appear four creatures crowned with green leaves. Each has six wings and the wings are covered with eyes. The appearance of these creatures, though not described with further details, is a composite, the author states, of those seen by Ezekiel in the sky and those described by St. John in the Book of Revelation.

In the midst of the four winged creatures is a magnificent chariot drawn by a gryphon. The wings of the gryphon, which extend upward out of sight, are lifted up on either side of the central band of the trails of light streaming behind the seven candles. The portions of the gryphon resembling an eagle are of gold, the portions resembling a lion are white and red. The chariot is more splendid than those of a great Roman triumph, more splendid than the chariot of the sun. Beside the right wheel of the chariot are three ladies dancing, one red as fire, one emerald green, and one white as snow. At the left wheel are four ladies clad in purple. The leader of the four has three eyes in her forehead.

Two grave old men follow in the procession, one in the garb of a physician, the other carrying a gleaming sword. Four humble men come after, and, ending the pageant, a solitary figure with keen countenance comes walking as if asleep. These last seven marchers are all dressed in white like the twenty-four elders in front of the chariot, but these are crowned with bright red roses.

When the chariot arrives opposite where Dante stands, a clap of thunder sounds and the procession halts.

Commentary

Matilda's service to Dante, in addition to explaining certain physical phenomena, is to lead him to Beatrice, a circumstance contributing to the symbolic relationship of the active and contemplative life.

The meeting with Beatrice, which is unquestionably the most dramatic event in *Purgatorio* for Dante, is prepared for and accompanied with impressive fanfare. The preparation in the reader's mind started with the first canto of *Inferno* and has been touched upon repeatedly through both *Inferno* and *Purgatorio*, but the immediate signal that an occasion of great moment is about to take place is the introduction of an invocation beseeching the Muses to aid him in reporting what he has to tell.

The solemn and colorful pageant performs a double function. It presents the Church Triumphant in an elaborate allegory and it also serves as a ceremonial device for the apotheosis of Beatrice. The pictorial effect of the pageant, without regard for the allegory, is striking enough to hold the attention. It appears to be based on the kind of religious ceremonies Dante must have seen all through his life, but these have been happily enhanced by his reading of the scriptures, especially the Old Testament prophets and the Book of Revelation.

The allegorical significance of the various elements in the procession obviously requires interpretation for modern readers. The seven golden candles represent the Biblical "gifts of the Spirit of the Lord": wisdom, understanding, counsel, might, knowledge, piety, and fear of the Lord. The candles are borne abreast of one another leaving a trail of seven bands of light streaming back over the rest of the procession, displaying the seven colors of the rainbow. The twenty-four elders following represent the books of the Old Testament. This division of the work into twenty-four books is based on the arrangement by Jerome in the Vulgate Bible. The white robes and garlands of lilies suggest purity of faith. The four "creatures" placed at the four corners of the chariot stand for the first books of the New Testament, the Gospels. In describing them Dante mentions only their crowns of green, the color of hope, and their six wings covered with eyes. Instead of giving other details, he refers the reader to Ezekiel, though he says that their six wings conform to the figures described by St. John. The creatures described by Ezekiel had the bodies of men though with four faces and four wings. The creatures, according to St. John in Revelation, had individual forms. "And the first beast was like a lion, and the second beast like a calf, and the third beast had a face as a man, and the fourth beast was like a flying eagle." (Rev. iv, 7). These different forms came to be accepted in the Middle Ages as familiar symbols for the writers of the Gospels.

The gryphon, with the head and wings of an eagle and the body of a lion, is a symbol for the dual nature of Christ, part divine and part human. The chariot, led by the gryphon, is the church. The three ladies dancing at the right wheel are the theological virtues, Faith in white, Hope in green, and Love in red. The four ladies beside the left wheel, all in purple, are the cardinal virtues, Prudence, Fortitude, Justice, and Temperance. She of the three eyes is Prudence.

Following the chariot are seven men representing the remaining books of the New Testament. The physician is Luke, author of the Acts of the Apostles; the man with the sword is Paul, author of several epistles. Then come four authors of lesser epistles: Peter, James, John, and Jude. Finally a simple old man who appears to be in a trance is John of the Apocalypse (Revelation).

The entire pageant portrays the ideal church as set forth through the Holy Scriptures. Later Dante will depict another pageant showing the actual history of the church with its record of confusion, corruption, and unsanctified divagations.

CANTO 30

Summary

When the seven lighted candles that guide the procession come to a halt, the elders preceding the chariot turn to face it, and one of them cries in a loud voice, *Veni, sponsa, de Libano* (Come with me from Lebanon, my spouse). A host of angels begin to strew flowers over the chariot, singing *Benedictus qui venis* (Blessed is he that cometh). Then like the sun breaking through the mist at dawn, there appears through a curtain of flowers a lady crowned with an olive garland and wearing a white veil. Over her flame-colored gown she wears a mantle of green. Though Dante cannot see her face because of the veil, he begins to tremble, recognizing his lady through some invisible virtue that she imparts to him now as she did in life. Turning to tell Virgil of the stirring of his blood, he discovers that his trusted mentor has left his company. When he starts to weep over the loss of Virgil, the lady chides him, calling him by name and saying that he will soon weep more for another sorrow.

Standing upright and stern in the chariot, the lady fixes Dante with her glance, which he perceives despite her veil. Her next words are, in effect, "I am Beatrice. Look at me and tell me how you deigned to climb the mountain." Dante, bowing his head in shame and seeing his reflection in the stream, recoils from it. The angels show compassion for him as he weeps pitifully. Beatrice pronounces her accusation of Dante, not speaking directly to him but addressing the angels and recounting his errant ways. She declares that this man was endowed with such native power that he gave promise of good works and that her countenance had guided him to a new life and sustained him on the right way, but that after her death and ascent to glory he had turned to other company and the pursuit of false images. Though she strove to bring him inspiration from Heaven, it was of no avail. At last his only help was to bring him where he could see the lost souls; wherefore she had descended to Limbo to send him a guide for his journey. Now if before tasting of Lethe he did not pay his due penalty of remorse and tears, it would be a violation of God's law.

Commentary

The opening lines of the canto present a difficult astronomical figure. The seven-starred constellation (Septentrion) is Ursa Minor or the Little Dipper, containing the North Star, which serves as a guide for mariners. However, the seven stars of the first heaven, the Empyrean, are here identified with the seven candlesticks of the pageant as they represent the seven Spirits of the Lord.

When the elders have turned around at the signal from the candles, all eyes are turned to the chariot. One of the elders pronounces in a loud voice, "Come with me from Lebanon, my spouse," a line from the Song of Solomon. The spouse, in this context, is traditionally interpreted as the church. When at long last Beatrice makes her appearance, it is through a cascade of flowers like the rising sun breaking through mists. The colors she wears, white, green, and red, are those of faith, hope, and love. She appears veiled and does not show her face to Dante until he has suffered her rebuke and undergone his final ordeal of purgation. Despite her veil, Dante knows her at once through a force that she transmits to him which is felt through all his bloodstream.

Beatrice's behavior at their first meeting seems unexpectedly harsh. The reader is apt to be taken by surprise, remembering that it was through her ministrations that Dante was granted the rare dispensation to make his journey. The handling of the episode constitutes Dante's voluntary self-torment as atonement for his dereliction after her death, which amounted to some form of infidelity. He puts his rebuke into her mouth, but it is actually his confession. Her justification for her severity is logical: for his departure from the true path Dante must experience the pain of contrition. The scene, then, is a kind of recapitulation and epitome of the basic concept of Purgatory.

In allegorical terms Beatrice represents revelation, and as such she is enthroned in the chariot of the church. Henceforth revelation is to take the place of reason in interpreting for Dante the most difficult problems of metaphysics in the eternal regions. Nevertheless, allegorical abstractions notwithstanding, the scene derives its striking effect from the highly personal and deeply emotional quality it carries. How is it possible, after this, to regard seriously the theory that Beatrice is really only an idea?

Not the least important element in this canto is the superb effectiveness of some of the figures of speech. The simile of the misty sunrise, for instance, is a notable example. The two mother-and-child similes, which are part of a whole series of figures on this theme occurring in the later cantos of *Purgatorio* and the early section of *Paradiso*, strike notes of love and tenderness.

CANTO 31

Summary

Beatrice asks Dante to say if her accusations are true and declares that a confession is required of him. He is so overcome with shame that he can barely utter a "yes." Then she asks him what lures or hard obstacles he encountered to deter him from the high purpose she had instilled in him, or what pleasures or profits induced him to pay court to others. He answers briefly that after her death the vanities of the world drew him to false pleasures. When he has made this confession, Beatrice tells him that a free confession blunts the sword of justice. Nevertheless, to make certain that he will not repeat his stumbling, she continues, saying that the memory of her ought to have been sufficient to keep him on his appointed course, and that the decay of her mortal beauty should have taught him the fallacy of lesser earthly allurements.

He stands before Beatrice, his head hanging in shame, whereupon she commands him to lift up his face that he may see something that will increase his suffering. With the greatest effort he is able to raise his head. Then looking at Beatrice he perceives, even through her veil, that she is more beautiful than when she surpassed all other women on earth. Overcome by the pain of his guilt, he faints. When he revives, Matilda is standing over him; she leads him across Lethe, at one point submerging his head so that he will drink the water of forgetfulness of sins.

On the opposite shore of Lethe, Dante is greeted by the four ladies in purple, the cardinal virtues, who conduct him to Beatrice. Standing before her, he sees the image of the gryphon reflected in her eyes, first one aspect of him appearing, then the other. The three other attendants of the chariot, the theological virtues, come dancing and urge Beatrice to turn her eyes toward her loyal servant who has come on so hard a journey to meet her and to unveil her face. She complies, and the effect is something beyond the power of the most inspired poet to describe.

Commentary

It is abundantly evident that Dante is contrite when Beatrice charges him with his erring ways. After contrition comes confession. Beatrice reminds him that confession is an essential step toward purification, regardless of the sure knowledge of one's sins in Heaven. Confession, she says, "blunts the sword of justice" so that it cuts less deep, which is to say it diminishes the punishment.

The fact that Beatrice's rebuke and Dante's agonizing ordeal is drawn out to considerable length indicates that he regarded some acts in his past with profound remorse and that he intended to use this passage as an occasion for a public confession. The question naturally arises as to what, exactly, were the sins that he finds so painful to recall. Neither he nor Beatrice is explicit. Commentators have theorized that he was guilty of infidelity to the love for Beatrice, perhaps only in sentiment, perhaps in carnal indulgence. Another quite different interpretation, however, is that he considered his eager pursuit of fame and his devotion to philosophy as constituting an abandonment of the true purpose of life, which is devotion to God. In this debate over interpretation, two words in the Italian text are significant though somewhat ambiguous. Beatrice asks Dante what delights or profits appeared in the face of others that caused him to *passeggiare*. The commonest meanings of the term are "to take a walk" or to "promenade." In the present context it might be taken in a very general meaning "to walk such a path (as you did)." It can also be interpreted "to pay court to." The latter could also mean to become subservient to or to make love to someone. The other word admitting different interpretations is also spoken by Beatrice. The speech, freely rendered, reads, "No young maid *(pargoletta)* or other vanity should have been allowed to weigh down your wings"; i.e., to hold you earthbound. Although the translation as "young maid" makes perfectly good sense, it has been suggested that love of a maiden is a metaphor for devotion to Lady Philosophy, and there is some authority for this interpretation in Dante's earlier works. There was a *pargoletta* that figures in *La Vita Nuova* in the section dealing with events after Beatrice's death. In commenting on that passage in the *Convivio* Dante identifies her with Philosophy. Could it be that at the time he wrote the *Convivio* he was trying to conceal the guilt which, in *Purgatorio,* he felt compelled to confess? The belief that he was referring to an amorous adventure with a live woman seems more plausible.

Beatrice, in making her point that Dante was a mature man and should have known enough to escape attack at the first sign of danger, employs an elaborate figure citing the difference between the young bird that doesn't take flight until it has been shot at two or three times and the older bird that knows how to avoid the hunter's arrows or nets.

Dante's pain of grief is dramatically revealed. It was harder for him to lift his head to face Beatrice than for a great oak to be torn up by the roots. And when he sees how beautiful she is, even through the veil, he is so overcome that he falls unconscious.

Having completed his ordeal of contrition and confession, he is led across Lethe, and with his immersion in the river, he is happily rid of his memories of guilt. He has now reached the side of the river with Beatrice and the pageant.

The dual nature of the gryphon is seen reflected in Beatrice's eyes, a device which indicates that the mystery of Christ's incarnation (God taking human form) is made clear to man only through revelation (Beatrice). The beast remains unchanged and yet the images Dante sees in Beatrice's eyes show one or the other aspect, not both united. This puzzles Dante, but it is not until later, at the climax of Paradise, that he is able to see the two as one.

The ladies representing the cardinal virtues, those virtues practiced before the coming of Christ, conduct Dante to the presence of Beatrice. They were assigned as her handmaidens before she was born. However, it is for the theological virtues, the special Christian virtues, to achieve for Dante the sight of the eyes of Beatrice unveiled. At the climactic moment when Beatrice lifts her veil, the concern for allegorical significances is submerged in the emotional experience of a man long deprived of the sight of his beloved.

CANTO 32

Summary

Dante stands gazing at Beatrice with such absorbed attention that all other sensations are blotted out. Finally his trance is broken by the attendant ladies, and when he turns his eyes away from Beatrice his sight is blurred like that of one who has looked directly at the sun. He discovers that the procession has started to move again and has wheeled to the right so that the sun and the light of the candles are before the marchers. The gryphon is drawing the chariot, and the attendant virtues have resumed their appointed places by the wheels. Dante, with Matilda and Statius, follow the right wheel.

When the procession has advanced three times the length of an arrow's flight, the marchers form a circle around a tree that is bare of any foliage and the branches of which spread wider as it grows taller. Beatrice steps down to the ground. The celebrants exclaim, "Adam!" The gryphon draws the chariot under the tree and binds the shaft to the tree trunk. Suddenly the tree bursts out in foliage and purple blossoms as if it were spring. The attendants shout praises for the gryphon, for he did no damage to the tree. As the marchers start to sing a hymn Dante falls asleep. When he wakes, the gryphon and most of the procession have departed. Beatrice, seated by the tree and surrounded by her handmaidens, guards the chariot. She tells Dante to observe attentively what he is about to witness and to write it down when he returns to earth for the profit of the evil ways of men.

An eagle comes swooping down out of the sky. Attacking the tree, he tears bark, blossoms, and leaves. Then he dives at the chariot, which shakes and rocks from side to side like a ship in a storm. Next a fox climbs into the chariot but is soon driven off by Beatrice. The eagle returns to the chariot and deposits some of its feathers in it. After that a dragon bursts out of the earth between the wheels, strikes the chariot with its venomous tail and breaks off a portion of the floor, which it carries away. Quickly the remains of the chariot become entirely covered over with the eagle's feathers. Seven heads sprout from the chariot, three on the shaft, each with the horns of an ox, and one at each corner of the chariot, each with a single horn. Soon a harlot, loosely dressed, takes her seat in the chariot and looks about haughtily. She is joined by a giant, who kisses her again and again, but when he sees her turn wanton glances toward Dante, he whips her unmercifully. Then in his anger he pulls the chariot away through the woods.

Commentary

The pageant of the church resumes its march with Matilda, Statius, and Dante joining. The column wheels to the right in good military formation and faces toward the seven candles and the sun. The basic significance of the pageant is that for a sinner who has chosen the path of righteousness the church comes to meet him and directs him on his new course of enlightenment and virtue.

The tree represents Law. It was denuded by Adam in his original breach of the law. The coming of the gryphon to the tree is Christ's coming to earth. The shaft of the chariot is the cross. By joining the chariot to the tree and avoiding any damage to the tree, the gryphon brings about a state in which church and state flourish in unison. The color of the blossoms, purple ("less than rose, more than violet"), identifies the tree with empire. The gryphon (Christ) is praised for not harming the tree, i.e., not interfering with the temporal power of the state. The gryphon replies, "Thus is preserved the seed of all justice."

As a choir sings a hymn, Dante falls asleep, and when he is aroused by a command to arise, he compares his awakening to the experience of Peter, James, and John when they witnessed Christ's transfiguration on the mountain. They saw Christ in glory and with him Moses and Elias, and they heard a voice out of a cloud, at which they fell down in a fright. When Christ touched them and said, "Arise, and be not afraid," they looked up and found that Moses and Elias were gone and Christ was alone. When Dante wakes, he sees Beatrice sitting under the tree. The gryphon and the elders have departed. The chariot (the church) is still there, and Beatrice, attended by the handmaidens and the candles, guards it.

What Dante has been seeing is a representation of the church as it was conceived and as it should still be. He is now to be shown a pageant dealing with the real history of the church, a presentation dramatizing major events contributing to its dissentions and corruption. Beatrice instructs him to watch and listen carefully and to write of what he sees for the benefit of the living.

The allegorical significance of this message for the living would be clouded in dark mystery for modern readers without the help of generations of expert annotators. Briefly, the actions are explained as follows: the first descent of the eagle shows the persecution of the early Christians by the Roman emperors; in its attack it damages the tree (the state) as well as the chariot (the church). The fox, representing heresy, a crafty enemy, is put to flight by Beatrice (revealed truth). The second descent of the eagle with the depositing of its feathers concerns the much talked of Donation of Constantine. It was reported that the Emperor Constantine had bestowed all of his possessions in the Western Empire on the church. His intention was said to be good, but the ultimate effect was harmful. Next comes the dragon episode and the breaking apart of the chariot. This refers to a great schism, but it is not certain whether Dante meant the division between the Eastern and Western Church or the split of Mohammedans from Christianity. The spreading of the feathers that covered the chariot shows the increasing fondness for rich possessions on the part of the clergy. The seven heads sprouting from the chariot are the seven deadly sins. Finally, pointing toward contemporary history, indeed to some events in the future, Dante presents as the wanton harlot the corrupt papacy under Boniface VIII. Her loving companion, the giant, stands for the French royal line but particularly Philip IV. These last two figures, Boniface and Philip the Fair, were deep-dyed villains in Dante's view of contemporary affairs, as has appeared before. The whipping of the harlot by the giant evidently points to Philip's betrayal and humiliation of Boniface at Anagni (Canto 20). The giant's dragging off of the chariot marks the transfer of the Papal See from Rome to Avignon.

In the last passage, the chariot is referred to as "the monster" because it has become so deformed by its enemies.

CANTO 33

Summary

After witnessing the despoiling of the chariot, the virtues chant a lament over the supposed triumph of evil. The response from Beatrice seems enigmatic—a promise in the words of Christ "A little while and ye shall not see me: and again, a little while and ye shall see me." Then Beatrice signals Dante, Matilda, and Statius to follow her. Soon she turns to Dante and asks why he doesn't question her about matters that are puzzling him. He replies in a feeble voice that she already knows what he does not understand and what is proper for him to know. At this she tells him that it is now time for him to cast off fear and shame.

Beatrice prophesies that although the chariot has been overthrown, God will appoint an avenger and restorer. Before long, she says, an heir to the eagle will bring back good order, a "Five Hundred Ten and Five" will appear to slay the harlot and the giant. If her words are hard for Dante to understand, she promises that events will soon make them clear. She urges him that when he writes of these things he must tell how he has seen the tree in the garden ravaged twice, which acts are offenses to God. She further cautions him that, though he does not understand everything, since his wits have been dulled, he must nevertheless remember everything he sees and hears so he may report it faithfully. Dante vows to remember all well, but he wonders why she speaks to him in such enigmas. She answers that she wants him to realize how inadequate his philosophical studies are for coping with such matters as she is discoursing about. Dante says he has no recollection of having deserted her for philosophy, and she explains that this lapse is the result of his having drunk from Lethe. She then promises that from now on her speech to him will always be clear and open.

It is now noon. The seven ladies halt near a spring which is feeding two streams. When Dante asks about them, Beatrice tells him to consult Matilda, and Matilda reminds him that she told him about the fountain and the streams before. Beatrice suggests that a greater concern has caused his forgetfulness. She then asks Matilda to lead him to the river Eunoë. She consents and invites Statius to join them. The waters of that river give Dante a new birth, and he feels himself purified and ready to mount to the stars.

Commentary

The theme of this closing canto is found in the words of Jesus: ". . . and again, a little while and ye shall see me." What it amounts to is a promise of the ultimate return of better times. A little farther on, Beatrice renews the discussion. To counteract the impression given by the pageant that the church has been hopelessly defeated, she promises that a new champion will come to restore the rightful authority of both state and church. The reference to an heir to the eagle means a new emperor. The curious phrase about "five hundred ten and five" stands for the Roman numerals *DXV*, which, by a transfer of letters, spells *DUX*, Latin for "leader." (It is no wonder that Dante failed to grasp her meaning immediately.) This passage is one of several expressing Dante's passionate hope that the Emperor Henry VII would restore imperial authority in Italy and return the seat of the papacy to Rome. It is clear that this portion of *Purgatorio* must have been written during the period of Henry's reign as emperor, 1308-13.

When Beatrice asks Dante to remember and write about seeing the sacred tree (the law) twice ravished, this constitutes another way of affirming the belief that the emperor's temporal authority is bestowed by God and that to oppose that authority is a capital crime, even on the part of a pope.

Beatrice, in speaking of how Dante's brain has been stultified, refers to the Elsa river. This was a river in Tuscany, a tributary of the Arno, which was saturated with carbonate of lime. The suggestion is that Dante's brain has been dipped in Elsa's waters and has become petrified. The companion reference is to Pyramus staining the mulberry tree with his blood. Again it means that Dante's brain has been clouded.

The souls that have been purged in Purgatory are restored to a state of perfect innocence by receiving the benefits of Lethe and Eunoë, with the memory of their evil deeds on earth wiped away and with the memory of their good deeds revived. So it is with Dante who, although still living, has passed all of those stages symbolically when he is taken through Eunoë. He is now prepared for the ascent into the heavens.

An interesting phrase appears at the end of this final canto. The author says he must not elaborate upon the present incident because he has come to the end of the pages assigned for this canticle. The bridle of art *(lo fren de l'arte)* restrains him. The way that Dante was controlled by the bridle of art, i.e., by structural design and by restraint of expression, is one of the outstanding qualities of this poem of one hundred cantos and one that the careful reader comes to understand and appreciate.

CRITICAL COMMENTARY

PURGATORIO: BASIC CONCEPT

The central concept of *Purgatorio* is simple and clear. Through divine grace man can attain everlasting beatitude regardless of a wicked life if he is truly repentant; but that does not mean that for his evil deeds he must not be penalized. Repentance involves a desire for purgation, and purgation requires strenuous atonement. Every sin, whether discovered on earth or not, is recorded in Heaven and must be reckoned with for penance. This is Dante's understanding of divine justice.

It goes without saying, then, that Dante urges conformity to law, above all to the laws of God, but also to the laws of the state. Beyond these basic concepts we ought to be able to extract something of a scheme of life from a study of the multitude of scenes and the maze of characters in his hundred cantos. The scheme which is revealed is one which gives primary emphasis to discipline and purpose. Purpose means an active life, the energetic pursuit of self-improvement, learning and judgment, and the high-principled engagement in social and political affairs. His heroes—or, let us say, the characters who attract his special attention—are more often leaders, poets, or artists than ascetics.

This is not to say that he ignores or deprecates the pursuit of the contemplative life. He accepts the medieval dictum that this constitutes the highest state of human existence, but he takes the practical view that a society composed entirely of mystics is not possible. Furthermore, he makes the point that one man's pursuit of the contemplative life in this world is dependent upon the labors of men in active life. The good life for most mortals, apart from the sainted few, may well embody a portion of the active with a portion of the contemplative life.

STYLE

Dante's style has received much praise, and a good many writers have attempted to explain its essential qualities. Obviously, when dealing with a translation, there are certain aspects of style which cannot be appreciated, but there are some features that can be observed and analyzed with considerable accuracy in a good translation.

Dante's simplicity of language and his compact style are qualities that impress themselves on every reader of the original text. The compactness of phraseology is, in many passages, absolutely amazing, and this quality can often be captured in English. The relative simplicity of expression is not always so easily transmitted in English because the cognate of a word that is plain and familiar in Italian may sound rather stylish in English.

Not all passages can be characterized as simple, as we shall see, but even where the plain style predominates Dante introduces numerous artistic and rhetorical devices, the most persistent and effective of them being similes, classical allusions, and Biblical quotations and allusions. There are more than a hundred references to Greek and Roman history, literature, and mythology in *Purgatorio*. Dante uses these allusions with the same easy familiarity that we find among some of the most learned Renaissance authors: Erasmus, Montaigne, or Bacon, for example. These allusions provide a colorful spark to their passage, assuming that the reader is also familiar with the character or myth referred to.

Dante's use of Biblical material is similar to his use of classical material in many instances, comprising allusions to characters and episodes with which the reader is assumed to be familiar. There is, however, another aspect of the employment of Biblical material to be considered: quotations. The introduction of brief passages from the Latin Bible, such as the Beatitudes and phrases from the Psalms, must have struck his contemporaries with the kind of pleasurable recognition that many modern readers derive from those same passages quoted in the English of the King James version of the Bible.

The Dantesque similes are justly famous. One reason that they call themselves to our attention is that they occur twice as frequently as those of any of the other chief epic poets. For the most part they are essentially functional, serving to clarify the text rather than serving a gratuitously ornamental purpose as do so many of the typical epic similes of other poets. Nevertheless, these functional and often unobtrusive figures can be strikingly effective, not only because they contribute to the reader's comprehension and visualization of a scene but also because of their power for emotional coloring of the passage. In *Purgatorio* the subjects and tone of the similes do much to convey the spirit of the canticle.

A few examples will suggest the variety of treatment of these figures. A good many of them are couched in brief phrases.

Like lightning when it sharply rends the air
Seemed a voice that reached us crying out,
"Everyone that findeth me shall slay me";
And it fled like thunder that dissolves
If suddenly the clouds burst into rain.
(Canto 14)

While I was peering into the green leaves,
Eyes fixed, as one is wont who wastes his life
In hunting little birds, . . .
(Canto 23)

I turned me to the left, with all the trust
With which an infant hurries to his mother
When he is frightened or abused,
To say to Virgil: . . .
(Canto 30)

The commonest type of his similes is basically sensuous, illuminating the sight or sound he wishes to describe; and they characteristically depend on familiar, homey, or even homely experiences. In *Inferno* they are sometimes violent or revolting. In *Purgatorio* even the more elaborate examples present familiar comparisons. Describing the actions of a group of spirits, Dante writes:

As sheep that come out straggling from the fold
By ones and twos and threes while others stand,
Their eyes and muzzles lowered to the ground,
And what the leader does the others do,
Pushing up behind her if she stops,
Simple and quiet, and they know not why;
So I saw starting to advance
The leader of that happy flock of souls
With modest mein and bearing dignified.
When those in front . . .
Stopped and then withdrew a pace,
Then all the others who came up behind,
Not knowing what the cause was, did the same.
(Canto 3)

The appearance and postures of the Envious reminds him of the look of a group of beggars.

With vile haircloth they all seemed to be clad,
And one bore up another with his shoulder,
As all of them were leaning 'gainst the wall;

Just so the blind, who in their dire want
Sit crouched at pardons begging for their needs;
And one against another leans his head
To excite pity the more readily,
Not only by the sounding of their words
But by the sight, which no less pity breeds.
And as the sun yields nothing to the blind,
So to the present shades, of whom I speak,
The light of heaven will not bestow its good;
For all have iron threads piercing their lids
To sew them shut, as a wild falcon's lids
Are sewed to keep him quiet.

(Canto 13)

The climactic passage of *Purgatorio,* when Dante first sees Beatrice, is introduced with a simile.

I have sometimes beheld at break of day
The orient region all suffused with rose,
But clear and beautiful the rest of heaven;
The sun's face at its rising clouded o'er
So that through the tempering of mists
The eye could well endure a long-held gaze;
Just so, within a lovely cloud of flowers
Which fell in showers strewn by angel hands,
Appeared a lady decked with olive wreath
Over a white veil, and underneath
Her mantle's green she wore a robe the hue
Of living flame.

(Canto 30)

A careful examination of Dante's use of similes bears out an illuminating observation by Macaulay to the effect that Dante's imagery is to Milton's what picture writing is to Egyptian hieroglyphics. The one simple and universally understood, the other requiring a sophisticated knowledge of the symbols.

The characteristics of plainness and compactness apply to a considerable portion of the text, but occasionally a passage is encountered that is far from simple and anything but compact. The fact is that Dante has two quite distinct styles. (I do not mean that there are *only* two. There are probably a dozen distinguishable styles. What I am pointing out is a radical polarization of two major styles.) The second style may be designated as obscure, involved, allusive, indirect. It depends for the most part on avoidance of calling objects or persons by their familiar designations or of making a clear, direct statement of a fact or an action. Furthermore, its circumlocutions and periphrases depend upon special and often recondite knowledge. They assume an extensive knowledge of astronomy (or astrology) or of classical mythology or Scriptural texts. A notable example of this obscure style is found in the passage where Virgil "enlightens" Dante on the reason why on the Mountain of Purgatory the sun's course lies to the north.

> The poet perceived that I was puzzled
> at the chariot of light where it passed
> between us and the north (wind).
> Whence he to me: 'If Castor and Pollux
> were in company with that mirror
> that conducts its light up and down,
> you would see the ruddy zodiac
> turn yet closer to the Bears,
> if it had not departed from its old path.
> How that may be, if you will think of it,
> consider well Sion and this mountain
> standing so on earth
> that both have the same horizon
> and different hemispheres, whence the road
> that Phaëton could not drive well,
> you will see how it must go
> on one side of this and on the other side
> of that, . . .
>
> (Canto 4)

There are a good many more such passages, but even so they do not occupy a large place in the long poem. It is interesting to note that this kind of writing was revived in the later Renaissance and became a prominent characteristic of Gongora and numerous other Baroque poets.

SELECTED LIST OF CHARACTERS

The number following each name refers to the canto in which the character appears.

Adrian V, Pope (19). His papacy lasted only from July to August of 1276.

Aeneas (18, 21). Son of Anchises and Venus. Trojan warrior who was the legendary founder of Rome. He was the hero of Virgil's *Aeneid.*

Albert I of Austria (6). Emperor 1298-1308. One of those who neglected to enforce his authority in Italy.

Aldobrandesco, Omberto (11). Lord of Santafiora, a Ghibelline leader, enemy of Siena.

Amata (17). Wife of King Latinus and mother of Lavinia, in the *Aeneid*.

Antenor (5). Trojan warrior, legendary founder of Padua.

Aquinas, St. Thomas (20). A Dominican whose works influenced Dante's theological concepts.

Arachne (12). A princess in ancient Lydia. For challenging Minerva to a contest in weaving, she was turned into a spider.

Argus (19, 32). Creature with a hundred eyes, employed by the gods as watchman. He was tricked and slain by Mercury.

Arnaut Daniel (26). One of the best known of the Provençal troubadours.

Averroes (25). An Arabian scholar whose works influenced Western Europe in medicine and other sciences and in the interpretation of Aristotle.

Beatrice (30-33). The Florentine lady who inspired Dante's early poetry. In the *Divine Comedy* she gains for him the privilege of visiting the realms of the dead and, after receiving him in the Earthly Paradise, guides him through Paradise.

Belacqua (4). A maker of musical instruments (or parts for them) in Florence and an acquaintance of Dante's.

Bonagiunta (24). A poet of Lucca, a few years Dante's senior.

Boniface of Ravenna (24). Archbishop, noted for lavish hospitality.

Boniface VIII, Pope (20). During his papacy (1294-1303) the Whites were driven out of Florence through his connivance. Dante regarded Boniface as the epitome of all the corruption and ambition for temporal power that stained the high office of pope.

Calboli, Rinier del (14). Noble from Romagna, a Guelph leader who was defeated by Guido da Montefeltro.

Casella (2). A musician who had set some of Dante's lyrics to music.

Cato of Utica (1). A Roman statesman and philosopher. He is guardian of the approach to Purgatory.

Cavalcanti, Guido (11). A Florentine poet and close friend of Dante.

Charles I of Anjou (7, 11, 20). A member of the French royal family, he was Count of Anjou and Provence and became king of Naples with the help of Pope Clement IV. He defeated Manfred at Benevento in 1265.

Charles II of Anjou (5, 20). Son of Charles I and king of Naples.

Charles of Valois (20). Brother of Philip the Fair. Charles and his army forced the exile of the Florentine Whites in 1301, including Dante.

Cimabue, Giovanni (11). A painter whose fame, according to Oderisi, was surpassed by Giotto's.

Circe (14). A beautiful enchantress who entrapped many of Ulysses' sailors.

Clement IV (3). Pope who excommunicated Manfred and invited Charles of Anjou to Italy to assume the crown of the Kingdom of Naples.

Colonna, Sciarra (20). A member of the famous family in Rome. At the instigation of the French king, he made Pope Boniface VIII a prisoner at Anagni in 1303.

Conrad (Currado) Malaspina II (8). A member of a distinguished family of Villafranca.

Conradin (20). Son of Emperor Conrad IV and heir to the throne of Naples. Manfred usurped the crown but lost it to Charles of Anjou. Conradin fought Charles but he too was defeated and executed.

Corso Donati (24). A member of the prominent Florentine family, brother of Forese Donati and Piccarda. He was the leader of the Blacks at the time of Dante's exile.

Cytheraea (27). An epithet for Venus. The island of Cythera was sacred to Venus. The term applies to either the goddess or the planet Venus.

Dante (Durante) Alighieri. The full name of the poet is not often used or even known by many readers of the *Comedy.*

Diana (25). Goddess of the moon, the hunt, chastity, childbirth, and the underworld in Roman mythology.

Duca, Guido del (14). A Ghibelline from Romagna, companion of Rinier da Calboli, a Guelph.

Erysichthon (23). A Greek punished by Ceres for cutting down a tree in her sacred grove.

Esther (17). A Jewess who became queen of the Assyrians. She saved the captive Jews from a mass slaughter.

Eteocles (22). Son of Oedipus, king of Thebes. He fought against his brother Polynices for the throne.

Forese Donati (23). Brother of Corso and Piccarda Donati, Florentine poet and friend of Dante.

Frederick II, King of Sicily (7). Ruled in Sicily 1296-1337. He is not to be confused with the Emperor Frederick II.

Ganymede (9). Handsome Trojan youth transported by Jove's eagle to Olympus to serve as cupbearer of the gods.

Gentucca (24). A lady of Lucca. Thought to be the wife of Bonaccorse Fondora.

Gideon (24). A commander in the army of Israel (Judges 7).

Giotto di Bondone (11). Most famous painter of the day. A Florentine and an acquaintance of Dante.

Gregory I (10). "Gregory the Great," pope about 600. The music adopted for services during his papacy took his name (Gregorian chant). It was believed that he brought the Emperor Trajan back to life and baptized him.

Guinizelli, Guido (11, 26). Bolognese poet, leader of *il dolce stil nuovo.*

Guittone D'Arezzo (11, 24, 26). Tuscan poet, predecessor of Guinizelli and Dante.

Helice (25). One of Diana's attendant nymphs. She was seduced by Jove.

Henry VII of Luxemburg (7). Emperor 1308-13. Dante's hopes for the restoration of imperial authority in Italy were centered on him.

Holofernes (12). Commander of the army attacking the Israelites. He was tricked and beheaded by the Jewess Judith.

Hugh Capet (20). Duke, founder of the Capetian dynasty of French kings who ruled from the tenth to the fourteenth century.

Hypsipyle (22, 26). Heroine in Greek mythology, betrayed by Jason. She directed the army marching against Thebes to the fountain of Langeia.

Jacopo del Cassero (5). A prominent magistrate of Romagna who was murdered by the henchmen of Azzo VIII d'Este.

John, St. (29, 32). An apostle, author of the Book of John and Book of Revelation.

Jove (29, 32). Ruler of the Olympian gods in Roman mythology. In Latin the nominative of his name is Jupiter; other cases are based on the Jove stem. The Greek counterpart is Zeus.

Justinian (6). Roman emperor in sixth century, famous for his codification of Roman law.

Juvenal (22). Roman satirical poet of the first century A.D.

Lavinia (17). Daughter of Latinus, the one Italian king who was friendly toward Aeneas. Aeneas won the territory of Latium and the king's daughter for his wife.

Leah (27). One of the wives of Jacob. She represents the active life in the allegorical interpretation of Dante's dream.

Leander (28). Lover of Hero in famous mythological tale. He swam across the Hellespont to meet his beloved.

Lentino, Giacomo da (24). Nicknamed "the Notary." A poet of the Sicilian school, he antedated the poets of the *dolce stil nuovo*.

Lucia, St. (9). The heavenly spirit who, with Mary and Beatrice, concerned herself with Dante's welfare.

Manfred (3). Illegitimate son of the Emperor Frederick II. He assumed the crown of the Kingdom of Sicily, was defeated and killed at Benevento by Charles I of Anjou.

Marco Lombardo (16). A Venetian whom Dante respected for his character and highmindedness.

Mary (3, 5, 8, 13, 15, 18, 20, 22, 25). The Blessed Virgin, mother of Christ. One of the goads for each terrace is taken from an episode in her life.

Matilda (Matelda) (28, 33). A lady met in the Earthly Paradise representing the active life. Identification with a real person is uncertain.

Meleager (25). Greek hero. One of the principals in the hunting of the Calydonian boar.

Minos (1). Ancient king of Crete. Dante placed him as a judge in Inferno assigning sinners to their appropriate circles.

Montefeltro, Buonconte da (5). Son of Guido da Montefeltro, the great Ghibelline leader, whom Dante met in Inferno. He was killed at Campaldino fighting against the Florentines.

Nimrod (12). Biblical king whose ambition led him to try to build the tower of Babel.

Nino (Ugolino) Visconti (8). The grandson of Count Ugolino of Pisa (*Inf.* 33) and a prominent Guelph in Dante's early years.

Nogaret, Guillaume (20). One of the functionaries of Philip IV involved in the imprisonment of Pope Boniface VIII.

Oderisi (11). A painter and illuminator who instructs Dante on pride.

Orestes (13). Son of Agamemnon who killed his mother to avenge his father's murder. A prominent figure in the trilogy by Aeschylus, *Oresteia.*

Pasiphaë (26). Wife of King Minos. She was obsessed with an unnatural passion for a bull.

Peter, St. (9, 13, 19, 22). One of the principal apostles of Jesus. He was given the keys to Heaven.

Phaëton (4, 29). Son of Phoebus, the god of the sun. When he tried to drive his father's chariot, he lost control and fell into the sea.

Philip IV (7, 20, 32). King of France, called "the Fair." He betrayed Pope Boniface VIII and transferred the seat of the papacy from Rome to Avignon.

Pia dei Tolomei (5). Referred to in the poem simply as La Pia (Piety) of Siena. She has been identified through the circumstances of her murder.

Pierre de la Brosse (6). Prominent figure at the court of Philip III of France. He was the victim of the queen's enmity.

Pilate, Pontius (20). Roman governor of Judea who sentenced Christ to death.

Polydorus (20). Son of King Priam of Troy. He is the subject of a celebrated passage in Virgil's *Aeneid.*

Polymnestor (20). King of Thrace who murdered Polydorus (above) in order to keep the treasure entrusted to him by Priam.

Proserpine (28). Daughter of Ceres, goddess of harvests. When Pluto abducted Proserpine, nothing would grow on earth because of the grief of Ceres. Pluto allowed her to return to earth six months of the year.

Provenzan Salvani (11). A Ghibelline leader from Siena, victor at Montaperti, loser at Colle di Valterra.

Pygmalion (20). Brother of Dido, murderer of her husband Sichaeus. Not to be confused with the Greek sculptor.

Rachel (27). Wife of Jacob and mother of his two youngest sons, Joseph and Benjamin. In Dante's dream she represents the contemplative life.

Rudolph I (6, 7). Emperor, 1272-92. One of the rulers who had neglected Italy.

Sapia (13). A lady of Siena, a relative of Provenzano Salvani.

Scala, Can Grande della (33). Host to Dante during his exile. Dante hoped that Can Grande ("the great hound") would become a leader of all Italy and restorer of her glory.

Scipio (29). Scipio the Elder, was honored with the title of "Africanus" for his victories over the Carthaginians.

Simon de Brie (24). Became Pope Martin IV. He died after over-indulgence in eels cooked in wine.

Siren (19). Seductive female creatures bent on ruining their victims. The Sirens were the subject of a famous episode in the *Odyssey*.

Sordello (6, 7, 8). Italian poet singled out for an important role in Purgatory. He was apparently proud of his birthplace, Mantua, but he wrote his poetry in Provençal.

Statius (21, 22, 25, 27, 32, 33). Roman epic poet, who, according to Dante, was converted to Christianity.

Theseus (24). One of the great legendary heroes of ancient Greece. One of his exploits involved a fight with the centaurs at the wedding feast of his friend Pirithous.

Tiresias (22). Blind soothsayer of ancient Thebes, father of the sorceress Manto.

Tithonus (9). Husband of Aurora, goddess of the dawn.

Trajan (10). Roman emperor, 98-117 A.D. A successful general and admirable administrator. Was believed to have been made a Christian through miraculous intercession by Pope Gregory I.

Venus (28). Goddess of love and beauty. Her Greek name was Aphrodite. The planet Venus was under her dominion.

Virgil. Roman epic poet, author of the *Aeneid.* He was Dante's guide through Inferno and Purgatory.

William of Monferrato (7). Marquis of Monferrat and Canavese. The rebellious citizens of Alessandria sentenced him to death by exposure in an iron cage.

REVIEW QUESTIONS AND ESSAY TOPICS

1. Specify the location of Purgatory on the globe.

2. Outline or diagram the main divisions and subdivisions on the mountain.

3. Describe the activities of the different groups of spirits in Ante-Purgatory.

4. Identify three or four of the spirits that Dante meets in Ante-Purgatory who receive special attention, and explain why they are given such prominence.

5. Review the details of the passage describing Dante's admission to Purgatory proper, and explain their significance.

6. What is the significance of the initial *P*?

7. What is the basis for the ordering of the sins in Purgatory?

8. Explain the reasons governing the form of atonement (type of suffering) assigned to the different terraces of Purgatory and cite three or four examples.

9. In addition to the description of the spirits undergoing their penance on each terrace and the conversations between the poet and the penitents, what other features are included in the account of the inspection of each of the terraces?

10. How many nights did the poets spend on the mountain? What point had they reached in their ascent each night? Describe the dream for each night.

11. As the poets climb the mountain, their course also takes them around it. In what direction?

12. In which regions does Dante share the penance practiced by the spirits?

13. Name five or six prominent characters in Purgatory, note the terrace in which each is encountered, and relate the nature of the discussion of each with the poet.

14. Who was Statius? What is his role in the poem?

15. What opinions are expressed regarding the moral and spiritual condition of Italy in Dante's time?

16. Name prominent historical personages (rulers and popes) who are mentioned repeatedly, and indicate Dante's interpretation of their roles in recent history for good or evil.

17. What is Dante's doctrine regarding the proper relationship between the empire and the papacy?

18. What are the characteristics of the Earthly Paradise that set it apart from other gardens on earth?

19. Name the two rivers in the Earthly Paradise and designate the properties of each.

20. Explain the role of Matilda.

21. In the pageant of the Church Triumphant what distinction is made between figures representing the books of the Old Testament and those of the New Testament?

22. What is the allegorical interpretation of the gryphon?

23. How are the maidens representing the theological virtues differentiated from those representing the cardinal virtues in appearance?

24. What is the basic difference between the two classes of virtues?

25. Note the position of Beatrice in the procession, and describe her as she first appears to Dante.

26. How is the stern rebuke with which Beatrice first greets Dante explained?

27. What events in Biblical or church history are represented allegorically by the following elements in the second pageant: the tree, the eagle, the dragon, the harlot, the giant, and the carrying off of the broken chariot?

28. Examine Dante's use of similes. Note the distribution of this figure of speech. Study the variety of subject matter in the similes

and their relation to the context of the passages in which they are employed.

29. Examine Dante's use of metaphors, following the directions for similes in question 28.

30. Cite several instances of the use of the obscure style, and analyze the mode of expression in some detail. Note the circumstances under which they commonly appear.

31. Trace the time schedule for the journey up the mountain, the days of the week and the times of day referred to.

SELECTED BIBLIOGRAPHY

BRANDEIS, IRMA (ed.). *Discussions of the Divine Comedy*. Boston: D.C. Heath, 1961. Comments and essays on Dante by writers of various periods, e.g., Boccaccio, Petrarch, Voltaire, Coleridge, Croce, Etienne Gilson, Allen Tate.

CARROLL, JOHN S. *Prisoners of Hope: An Exposition of Dante's Purgatorio*. London: Hodder and Stoughton, 1906. A standard commentary on *Purgatorio*, thorough (500 pages) and in many respects definitive despite its date.

GILBERT, ALLAN. *Dante and His Comedy*. New York: New York University Press, 1963. A valuable study of the *Comedy* that is organized topically, with discussions centered on numerous aspects of structure, style, themes, and problems.

SAYERS, DOROTHY L. (trans. and ed.). *The Comedy of Dante Alighieri: Cantica II, Purgatory*. Baltimore: Penguin Books, 1955. The Introduction, pp. 9-71, is detailed, perceptive, and eminently readable. The notes, diagrams, and appendices are elaborate and extremely valuable.

______."'. . . And Telling You a Story': a Note on *The Divine Comedy*," in *Essays Presented to Charles Williams*. London: Oxford University Press, 1947. An essay treating the story-telling techniques and the careful structural design of the *Comedy*.

Divine Comedy - III. Paradiso

THE DIVINE COMEDY: PARADISO

NOTES

including

- *General Introduction*
- *Introduction to* Paradiso
- *Synopsis*
- *Summaries and Commentaries*
- *List of Characters*
- *Review Questions and Study Projects*
- *Selected Bibliography*

by
Harold M. Priest, Ph.D.
Department of English
University of Denver

INCORPORATED
LINCOLN, NEBRASKA 68501

Editor

Gary Carey, M.A.
University of Colorado

Consulting Editor

James L. Roberts, Ph.D.
Department of English
University of Nebraska

ISBN 0-8220-0396-1

Printed in U.S.A.

1992 Printing

Cliffs Notes, Inc. Lincoln, Nebraska

CONTENTS

Paradiso Notes

General Introduction

The story of the *Divine Comedy* is simple: one day Dante finds himself lost in a dark wood; but Virgil appears, rescues him from that savage place, and guides him to a contemplation of Hell and Purgatory. Then, having confessed his faults, and with Beatrice as his guide, he is conducted into Paradise and attains a glimpse of the face of God.

Dante gave the title of *Comedy* to his masterpiece because the word indicated a pleasant or (as Dante himself put it) a "prosperous" ending after a "horrible" beginning. Dante used the humble lowly language "which even women can understand," rather than the sublime language of tragedy. The adjective "divine" was added to the title later, apparently by an editor some time in the sixteenth century.

The *Divine Comedy* is distinctly a product of medieval times. Its view of the universe is the Ptolemaic view; its social setting that of the jealous, warring city-states of Italy, and of the powerful, arrogant, and feuding aristocrats and the political factions which supported them. Over all were the contesting powers of a fading empire and a grasping papacy.

In attempting understanding, one may become so entangled in the complexities of the *Comedy* and its environment that one loses sight of Dante the man. And it was Dante, the man of his times, who wrote the *Divine Comedy*—a man whose lifelong devotion to the figure of Beatrice was in the highest tradition of courtly love; whose political feuds were first with the party of the opposition, then with factions within his own party, until he formed a party of his own; a man who believed firmly in alchemy and astrology, in witchcraft and spells; and finally, an intensely human man, with fierce hatreds and loyalties, with no little vanity, with pity, and with love.

The date of the composition of the *Divine Comedy* is uncertain, but undoubtedly the poem was written during Dante's exile. Even here there is some disagreement, for there is a tradition which insists that the first seven cantos were written before he was banished from Florence. The predominant opinion is that it was begun around 1307; the setting of the poem is the year 1300. There is some evidence that the *Inferno* had been completed and circulated before 1314, and that the *Purgatorio* followed very soon after. The *Paradiso* was completed shortly before Dante's death in 1321 and released posthumously by his sons.

The *Divine Comedy* is a monumental work of imagination, dedicated in spirit to an immortal love; it is mortal to the point of repugnance in its beginning, mystical almost beyond understanding at its close.

DANTE'S LIFE

Dante Alighieri was born in Florence in May, 1265, of an old family, of noble origin but no longer wealthy. His education was probably typical of any youth of his time and station: he studied the *trivium* and *quadrivium*, probably spent a year, or part of a year, at the University of Bologna, and came under the influence of some of the learned men of his day. Most notable of these was Ser Brunetto Latini, whose influence Dante records in his poem (*Inferno* 15).

In accordance with custom, Dante was betrothed in his youth to Gemma Donati, daughter of Manetto Donati. These betrothals and marriages were matters of family alliance, and Gemma's dowry was fixed as early as 1277, when Dante was twelve years old. There were at least three children: sons Pietro and Jacopo, and a daughter Antonia, who later entered a convent at Ravenna and took the name of Sister Beatrice. A third son, Giovanni, is sometimes mentioned.

There can be no doubt that the great love of Dante's life, and the greatest single influence on his work, was his beloved Beatrice. He first met her when he was nine years old and she was eight. The meeting took place in her father's home, probably at a May Day festival Dante has described this meeting in his *Vita Nuova*. He tells of seeing the child Beatrice, wearing a crimson gown and looking like an angel From that day on, his life and work was dedicated to her. He mentions no other meeting with her until nine years later, when he saw her on the street, dressed in white, accompanied by two other girls. She greeted him sweetly by name, and he was in raptures. A short time later having heard gossip linking his name with another young woman, she passed him without speaking, and Dante mourned for days, determining to mend his ways.

If all this seems slightly preposterous, it is necessary to remember two things: that the young women of marriageable age were so strictly chaperoned that it was virtually impossible to have even a speaking acquaintance with them and that Dante's love for Beatrice was in the strictest tradition of courtly love, wherein the lover addressed his beloved as being completely out of his reach, and which viewed marriage between the lovers as impossible, in fact undesirable.

To what extent this was, at first, a true and lasting love cannot be determined. There is little doubt that Dante enjoyed the sweet misery of his situation and the sympathy of other ladies for his plight. After the death of Beatrice, and particularly after his exile, he put away his adolescent fancies, and Beatrice became a true inspiration.

Beatrice was married in about 1287 to Simone de' Bardi, a wealthy banker of Florence, a marriage of alliance of the two houses and one completely immaterial to Dante and his work.

Dante wrote many poems in praise of his lady during her lifetime, and when she died in 1290, at the age of twenty-five, he was inconsolable. He had had a dream of her death, and in her honor collected the poems he had written about her, which are included in the *Vita Nuova*. The later *Comedy* was also inspired by her memory.

Dante's public life began in 1289, when he fought against Arezzo at Campaldino. In 1295 he was one of the council for the election of the priors of Florence, and in May, 1300, went as ambassador to San Gemignano to invite that commune to an assembly of the Guelph cities of Tuscany. From June 15 to August of the same year, he was one of the priors of Florence, and it was during that year that his best friend, Guido Cavalcanti (*Inferno*, Canto 22), caused a street riot on May Day. Guido was exiled to Sarzana by the officers of the city, one of whom was Dante. Sarzana proved so unhealthful that Guido petitioned to return to Florence, and was allowed to do so. He died of malaria, contracted in Sarzana, in August, 1300.

Dante was vigorously opposed to the interference of the pope in secular affairs, and was induced to take a stand with the Whites when the Blacks favored the intrigues of the pope. Charles of Valois was coming to Florence, ostensibly as a peacemaker between the two factions but in reality as a partisan of the Blacks and supporter of the pope. In October, 1301, Dante and two other men were chosen as ambassadors on a mission to Rome, rightly suspecting the motives of Charles as peacemaker. After they had left Florence, the Blacks easily took over control of the city with the help of Charles, and Dante was exiled from his native city, never to return.

The terms of exile were harsh: Dante was charged with graft, with intrigue against the peace of the city, and with hostility against the pope, among other things. The list of charges is so long that it is reminiscent of those brought against the political enemies of any party in power today. In addition, a heavy fine was imposed, and Dante was forbidden to hold public office in Florence for the rest of his life.

Dante did not appear to answer the charges—it probably would not have been safe to do so—and a heavier penalty was imposed: in addition to confiscation of his property, he was sentenced to be burnt alive if caught. Also, his sons, when they reached their legal majority at age fourteen, were compelled to join him in exile.

Thus began Dante's wanderings. At first he joined in the political intrigues of his fellow exiles, but, disgusted by what he considered their wickedness and stupidity, he formed a party by himself. It is not known exactly where he spent the years of his exile, though part of the time he was with the Malaspini, and he also spent time at the court of Can Grande della Scala in Verona, with whom he remained on good terms for the rest of his life.

Once during the years of his banishment his hopes for peace in Italy, and his own return to Florence, were revived. This was in the reign of Henry VII of Luxemburg, who announced his intention of coming to Italy to be crowned. Dante addressed a letter to his fellow citizens urging them to welcome Henry as emperor. When Henry was met by strong opposition, Dante in great bitterness sent a letter to him, urging him to put down the rebellion quickly; he also addressed a letter in similar vein to Florence, using abusive terms which could not be forgiven. When Henry's expedition failed, and the hopes of empire died with him, Dante was not included in the amnesty granted certain exiles. Later, amnesty was extended to him on the condition that he admit his guilt and ask forgiveness publicly, which the poet refused to do. His sentence of death was renewed.

Dante's last years were spent in Ravenna, under the protection of Guido Novello da Polenta. They seem to have been years of relative contentment in compatible company—but Ravenna was not Florence. One final mission was entrusted to Dante: he was sent to Venice in the summer of 1321 by his patron in an unsuccessful attempt to avert a war between Ravenna and Venice. On his return trip, he fell ill, possibly of malaria. He reached Ravenna and died there on the night of September 13, 1321.

He was buried with the honors due him. Several times during the following centuries, the city of Florence sought to have his body interred with honor in the place of his birth, but even the intercession of popes could not bring this about. His opinion of the citizens of his city was clearly stated in the full title of his great work: *The Comedy of Dante Alighieri, Florentine by Citizenship, Not by Morals.*

Dante still lies in the monastery of the Franciscan friars in Ravenna.

DANTE'S WORLD

Dante's world was threefold: the world of politics, the world of theology, and the world of learning. His *Comedy* encompasses and builds upon all of these, and so interdependent were they that it would be impossible to say that any one was the most important.

Throughout the Middle Ages, politics was dominated by the struggle between the two greatest powers of that age: the papacy and the empire. Each believed itself to be of divine origin and to be indispensable to the welfare of mankind. The cause of this struggle was the papal claim to temporal power, supported and justified by the spurious "Donation of Constantine." This document, which was a forgery of the eighth century, maintained that Emperor Constantine, before leaving for Byzantium, had transferred to the Bishop of Rome, Pope Sylvester I, political dominion over Italy and the western empire.

Dante lived in an era of virtually autonomous communes, ruled by either an autocratic hereditary count or a council elected from an aristocratic—and exclusive—few. The political situation was never stable, and the vendettas went on forever, family against family, party against party, city against city.

The strife began in the tenth century with Otto I, the emperor who laid the foundation for the power which was to transform Germany into the mightiest state in Europe and who dreamed of restoring the Holy Roman Empire. At the beginning of the eleventh century, the situation worsened, with Henry IV humiliated at Canossa by an aggressive opponent, autocratic Pope Gregory VII (Hildebrand).

In the first part of the thirteenth century, the growing conflict was headed by two outstanding antagonists: Innocent III, the most powerful of all the popes, and the brilliant Frederick II, King of Germany, Emperor of Rome, and King of Naples and Sicily, the most gifted of all the monarchs of the Middle Ages. The enmity of the pope, who was firmly resolved to free Italy from German authority, shook the stability of the empire, which was already undermined by the insubordination of the princes in Germany and the rebellion of some of the city-states of northern Italy.

When Frederick died in 1250, he left a very unstable situation to be handled by his successors, especially in Italy. There, in 1266, his illegitimate son Manfred was defeated and killed in the battle fought at Benevento against Charles of Anjou, who had been summoned to Italy by the pope. Two years later, this same Charles defeated Corradino, Frederick's grandson, at Tagliacozzo, and put him to death. Thus the line of the descendants of the great emperor was extinguished, and Italy was lost to the empire.

In reading Dante, indeed throughout medieval history, one hears much about two major political factions, the Guelphs and the Ghibellines. In Italy the party lines were originally drawn over the dispute between the papacy and the emperor for temporal authority. The Ghibellines, representing the feudal aristocracy, wished to retain the power of the emperor in Italy as well as in Germany. The Guelphs were mainly supported by the rising middle-class merchant society, who hoped to rid Italy of foreign influence and maintain the control of governments in their independent communes. They espoused the cause of the papacy in opposition to the emperor.

The rivalry between the two parties not only set one city against another but also divided the same city and the same family into factions. In time the original alliances and allegiances became confused in strange ways. For example, Dante, who was a Guelph, was a passionate supporter of imperial authority all his life.

In Florence the Guelphs and Ghibellines succeeded each other, alternately ruling the city. During the rein of Frederick II, the Ghibellines, supported by the emperor, gained the upper hand and drove the Guelphs out of the city. But at the death of Frederick II, in 1250, the

Guelphs were recalled to Florence for a temporary reconciliation and later gained control of the city.

The Ghibellines again returned to power in 1260, and ruled the city until 1266, but the next year the Guelphs, aided by French forces, gained supremacy in the city, and the Ghibellines left Florence, never to return.

Dante was an ardent White Guelph, putting his hopes for Italy's future in the restoration of the empire, and to the end of his days was politically active, though ultimately he was forced by the violence of his views to form a party "by himself," and, as a White, was actually allied to the Ghibellines.

Not even the supremacy of the Guelphs, however, endowed Florence with a peaceful and stable government, for in 1300 the Guelph party split into two factions: the Whites and the Blacks, led respectively by the families of the Cerchi and the Donati. The basis of this split was the usual blood-feud between two families. In nearby Pistoia, a family quarrel existed between two branches of the Cancellieri family. The first wife of the original Cancelliere was named Bianca, and her descendants called themselves Whites in her honor. The name of the second wife is not known, but her descendants, in opposition to the Whites, called themselves Blacks. The quarrel erupted into open violence after a murder committed by one Foccaccia (mentioned by Dante in Canto 32 of the *Inferno*).

The Guelphs of Florence, in the interests of maintaining the precarious peace of the district, intervened in the hostilities, and in so doing furthered the jealous rivalry of the Cerchi and the Donati families, who naturally took opposite sides. The city was torn by strife; personal ambitions, feuds, and the arrogance of individuals and families further agitated the situation.

At this point, the Blacks secretly enlisted the aid of Pope Boniface VIII, who intervened in the affairs of the city, largely in his own interest. The pope considered the throne of the empire still vacant, since Albert I had not received his crown in Rome. In his assumed capacity as vicar of the emperor, Boniface plotted to extend the rule of the church over the territory of Tuscany. To accomplish this, he first obtained the favor of the Blacks, then dispatched Charles of Valois, brother of the King of France, to Florence, ostensibly as a peacemaker, but actually as a supporter of the Blacks. In 1302, with the help of Charles of Valois, the Blacks gained control of the city. In the list of some six hundred Whites banished from Florence was the name of the citizen Dante Alighieri.

While the rest of Italy, like Florence, was troubled by rivalries between parties, or by wars of city against city, in Germany the emperor's throne was vacant, first because of an interregnum, then because of a conflict between two rival claimants. The emperor's position was still regarded as vacant by the Italians when the two emperors who followed, Rudolph of Hapsburg and Albert I, failed to come to Italy to be crowned and paid no attention to Italian affairs. Therefore when the news came that Henry of Luxemburg, who succeeded Albert I in 1308, was coming to Italy to oppose King Robert of Sicily, many Italians, for whom Dante was the most eloquent and fervent spokesman, welcomed the prospect with feverish enthusiasm. They saw in the figure of Henry the end of all the woes which had wracked the peninsula.

Henry was crowned at Milan early in 1311. Very soon after, he faced the armed hostility of the opposing party, which had Florence as its leader. Henry, nevertheless, was able to reach Rome and be crowned there in 1312. The coronation took place in the church of St. John Lateran rather than in St. Peter's because the latter was being held by the forces of King Robert of Sicily. The emperor was still fighting to unite the empire when he died in the summer of 1313, succumbing to a fever with suspicious suddenness. The death of Henry put an end forever to the expectations of Dante and all other Italians who had longed for the restoration of the imperial power in Italy.

Dante's theological ideas were strictly orthodox, that is, those of medieval Catholicism. He accepted church dogma without reservation. His best authorities for insight into the more complex problems confronting the medieval thinkers were Augustine, Albertus Magnus, and Thomas Aquinas. He followed the Pauline doctrine of predestination and grace as presented by Augustine, but he managed to bring this into a kind of conformity with free will, to which he firmly adhered. Man has inherited sin and death through Adam's fall, but also hope of salvation through Christ's redemption. God in his love created humans with the power of perceiving good and evil and the opportunity of choosing. On the basis of their choice depended their eternal bliss or damnation. Those who set their will against the divine law were sentenced to Inferno and everlasting torment. Those who sinned but confessed and repented were given their reward in heaven after a period of purifying atonement in Purgatory. Thus repentance, the acceptance of divine law, was the crux of judgment in the afterlife.

Among the familiar tenets of medieval theology, we recognize such concepts as the "seven deadly sins" in Purgatory and the corresponding seven virtues in Paradise. The doctrine that only those persons who had been baptized as worshipers of Christ were to be admitted to Paradise is expressed in the treatment of the souls in Limbo (*Inferno* 4). Of the many more complex theological concepts expounded through the *Commedia*, explanations will be offered in the textual commentaries.

In castigating the individual popes (and particularly his bitter enemy, Boniface VIII), he was in no way showing disrespect for the *office* of the papacy, for which he held the greatest reverence. He was, in fact, following the long tradition of critics, many of them in high places in the church, who had not hesitated to recall popes to the duties and responsibilities of the chair of Peter. Dante held to the ideal of the papacy and the empire as the dual guardians of the welfare of man, spiritual and secular, each deriving its separate powers directly from God.

Readers cannot fail to recognize Dante's erudition. He appears to have taken all learning for his province, or what passed for learning then. The fact that much of the scientific teaching was hopelessly in error is not Dante's responsibility. The fact that he displayed extraordinary curiosity and avid interest in all branches of scientific learning (geography, geology, astronomy, astrology, natural history, and optics) reveals something important about the poet's mind.

Among the concepts that influenced the plan of the *Commedia* was the belief that only the northern hemisphere of the earth was inhabited, that the southern hemisphere was covered with water except for the mount of Purgatory. The scheme of the heavens was dictated by the Ptolemaic, or geocentric, system of astronomy, upon which Dante based the entire plan of *Paradiso*.

In addition to his thorough and easy familiarity with the Bible, Dante displays a scholar's acquaintance with not only those great theologians previously mentioned (Augustine, Aquinas, etc.) but with a score of others.

Finally, wide reading and absorption of works of *belles lettres*, especially the Latin classics, was of the greatest importance. (Further details will be given later in the discussion of sources of the *Comedy*.)

DANTE'S MINOR WORKS

LA VITA NUOVA

The *Vita Nuova (New Life)* is a little book consisting of the love poems written in honor of Beatrice from 1283 to 1292. Written in Italian ("the Vulgar Tongue"), they were collected and linked by a commentary in prose, probably in 1292.

The book of memories and confessions presents a proper introduction to the *Divine Comedy,* as it speaks of a love which, in the mature life, through the path of philosophy and the ascendancy of faith, led the poet to his greatest poetical achievement. However, in the *Vita Nuova* the inspiration comes, without doubt, from reality. Beatrice is not an allegorical creature, but a real woman, smiling, weeping, walking in the street, and praying in the church. From the sincerity of its inspiration, the book derives a note of freshness and originality that is remarkable for that age.

The poems, most of them sonnets and canzoni, are arranged in a carefully planned pattern. These lyrics, like all of Dante's early verses, show the influence of the new school in Bologna, led by Guido Guinizelli, which was identified as *il dolce stil nuovo* (the sweet new style). This group of poets followed the tradition of the poetry of courtly love in certain respects, but developed techniques of greater refinement than their predecessors and treated love in a lofty, spiritual vein.

The prose passages accompanying each poem include not only an account of the circumstances which suggested the writing of the poem but also some analysis of the techniques employed in the construction of the poem, thus giving a unique character to the work.

CANZONIERE

Canzoniere, also in Italian, comprises the collected lyrics other than those included in the *Vita Nuova* and the *Convivio*. Love poems predominate in the collection, some to Beatrice, some to other ladies. The volume includes a group of poems called the "Pietra" lyrics because they were dedicated to a woman "hard as stone." These poems reveal a violent and sensual passion but demonstrate as well experiments in very complicated artistic techniques. There are also exchanges of poems between Dante and other poets, sometimes complimentary and sometimes caustic and satirical. Other poems in the collection, written during exile, deal with moral and civic doctrine.

IL CONVIVIO

The *Convivio* (the *Banquet*) was written during the exile, possibly in the years 1306-07. The name is metaphorical. Dante means to prepare a banquet of learning and science for such people as princes, barons, knights, and women, who are too busy with civil and social affairs to attend schools and familiarize themselves with scholarship. Such being the aim of the work, Dante employs the vernacular, the common speech, which will benefit a greater number of people, in spite of the fact that in those days Latin was generally required for a learned and scholastic commentary.

According to his original plan, the work was to consist of fourteen chapters, each with a *canzone* and an elaborate prose commentary. Actually only four sections were written, one being the introduction and each of the other three presenting a *canzone* with its commentary.

The two ideas of greatest importance discussed in the *Convivio* are the nobility and the empire. Speaking of the first, Dante maintains that true nobility does not derive from heredity or from the possession of wealth but rather from the practice of virtue. The ideas about the empire, of which Dante here speaks only briefly, were further developed in the *De Monarchia* and in the *Divine Comedy*. However, the secular office of the empire is already seen in the perspective of a divine plan ordained by God for the redemption of man and his betterment in the earthly life.

DE VULGARI ELOQUENTIA

After demonstrating the efficacy of the vernacular in the *Convivio*, Dante made it the subject of a treatise which, being addressed to scholarly people, was written in Latin. The treatise was to consist of four books, but only the first book and sixteen chapters of the second were completed.

The work deals with the origin and the history of languages in general, then attempts a classification of the Italian dialects. The ideal language is considered to be the "illustrious, vulgar tongue," a common language for the whole peninsula which would combine the best qualities of the different dialects. To Dante, this ideal seemed to have been attained by the writers of the Sicilian school, and the poets of "the sweet new style" *(il dolce stil nuovo).*

EPISTLES

All of the *Epistles* were written in Latin, and among the thirteen left to us (one of which may be a forgery), the three written to Henry VII on the occasion of his coming to Italy show the same spirit of prophecy which inspires some of the more eloquent passages of the *Divine Comedy*. Dante strongly desired the unification of Italy under Henry's rule and a peaceful Florence to which he could return from exile.

One of the most interesting is that addressed to the six Italian cardinals after the death of Pope Clement V at Avignon. It exhorts the cardinals to elect an Italian pope who will restore the Holy See to Rome. In this letter, as in the *De Monarchia* and the *Divine Comedy*, political and religious problems are closely related. Dante desires not only the return of the popes to Rome but also their peaceful cooperation with the emperors and the moral reformation of the church, then corrupted by simony and avarice.

His letter to Can Grande della Scala outlining the purpose and ideas of the *Comedy* gives the four levels of its interpretation, and serves as an introduction to the work. This letter accompanied some cantos of the *Paradiso,* which Dante dedicated to Can Grande. Boccaccio, in his biography of Dante, relates that the poet was in the habit of writing several cantos of his work, then sending them to Can Grande, his friend and patron.

DE MONARCHIA

The *De Monarchia* states in the most complete manner Dante's views upon the perfect government of human society. Being of universal interest, it was written in Latin, probably during the time Henry was en route to Italy. It was meant to be a warning to the numerous opponents encountered by the emperor on his way to Rome.

Divided into three parts, the book maintains that the empire is necessary for the welfare of mankind because it is the only means of establishing peace in the world; that the right to exercise this office belongs to the Roman people; that the authority of the emperor, like that of the pope, comes directly from God. Thence derives the independence of the empire from the church because both powers are autonomous and destined to guide mankind, respectively, toward earthly happiness and toward celestial beatitude; the emperor, however, should show the pope the same kind of reverence that a son should show his father.

Dante was convinced that the principal cause of the evils devastating Italy and the world was to be found in the pope's usurpation of the authority assigned by God to the emperor. He was particularly opposed to the policies of Boniface VIII, and strongly condemned the spurious "Donation of Constantine," which was claimed as the authorization of the pope's temporal power.

The claim that Rome should be the seat of the emperor did not conflict with its being the seat of papal authority as well, since the two powers have to coordinate their plans for the welfare of mankind. The emperor, Dante believed, could not be universally recognized as such unless he was crowned by the pope in Rome. In other words, Italy, with Rome as the seat of the empire and of the papacy, had been ordained by God to give the world a universal spiritual and temporal government.

THE DIVINE COMEDY

SOURCES OF THE *COMEDY*

Dante used two main literary sources in the writing of his *Comedy:* The religious and theological works of earlier times, and the classics.

It is evident, of course, that he drew heavily upon the Vulgate Bible, and he refers to it as one thoroughly familiar with it. Probably next in importance, to him, were the writings of St. Thomas Aquinas, and, to a lesser degree, those of other saints and religious philosophers.

The Latin classics had been an important part of Dante's formal training and certainly of his later reading. His eloquence in Latin is evident in his own writing to the end of his life. The study of philosophy, particularly the work of Aristotle, had occupied much of his time—so much, in fact, that it has been suggested by many later scholars that it was philosophy which caused him to wander from the "straigh path" and lose himself in the dark wood of his *Inferno*.

He knew well those Latin classics which were available to scholar of his time, notably Virgil, Ovid, Cicero, Seneca, Livy, and Boethius. H was familiar with much of Plato and Aristotle through Latin translations His acquaintance with Homer was secondhand, since accounts of th Homeric heroes were circulated in Dante's time only through late Lati or medieval adaptations.

THE FIGURE OF VIRGIL

In the Middle Ages, Virgil had come to be regarded as a sage an necromancer. Virgil's poems were used in the type of divination calle *sortes,* in which the book is opened at random and a verse selected i the same manner, as an answer to a problem or question. The Bible ha been, and still is, used in the same manner.

Virgil's *Aeneid* offered the pattern for the structure of Dante's Hell but this alone is not the reason why Virgil was chosen as the guid through Hell. Dante himself salutes Virgil as his master and the inspira- tion for his poetic style; further, Virgil is revered by Dante as the poe of the Roman Empire, since his *Aeneid* tells the story of the empire' founding. Finally, in his fourth eclogue, Virgil writes symbolically o the coming of a Wonder Child who will bring the Golden Age to th world, and in the Middle Ages this was interpreted as being propheti of the coming of Christ. Thus, in the figure of Virgil, Dante found sym- bolically represented the two institutions, church and empire, destine by God to save mankind.

PLAN OF THE *COMEDY*

Dante lived in a world that believed in mystical correspondences, i which numbers—like stars, stones, and even the events of history—ha a mystical significance. In planning the structure of the *Divine Comed* therefore, Dante had in mind a series of symbolic numbers: three, symbol of the Holy Trinity; nine, three times three; thirty-three, multiple of three; seven, the days of creation; ten, considered durin the Middle Ages a symbol of perfection; and one hundred, the multipl of ten.

The plan was carried out with consummate precision. We find three *cantiche*, each formed by thirty-three cantos, totaling ninety-nine. The introductory first canto of the *Inferno* makes one hundred cantos in all. The entire poem is written in the difficult *terza rima*, a verse form of three-line stanzas, or tercets. The first and third lines rhyme, and the second line rhymes with the beginning line of the next stanza—again, three, and three.

Hell is divided into nine circles (in three divisions), the vestibule making the tenth; Purgatory is separated into nine levels, the terrestrial paradise making ten; and Paradise is formed by nine heavens, plus the Empyrean. The celestial hierarchies are nine and are divided into triads. The sinners in Hell are arranged according to three capital vices: incontinence, violence, and fraud. The distribution of the penitents in Purgatory is based on the threefold nature of their rational love. The partition of the blessed in Paradise is made according to the secular, active, or contemplative nature of their love for God. The very fact that each *cantica* ends with the word "stars" helps to demonstrate the studied plan of the whole work.

STRUCTURE OF INFERNO

Inferno is a huge, funnel-shaped pit located with its center beneath Jerusalem, its regions arranged in a series of circular stairsteps, or terraces, diminishing in circumference as they descend. Each of the nine regions is designated for a particular sin, and the order of the sins is according to their wickedness, the lightest near the top of the pit and the most heinous at the bottom.

The punishments in Inferno are regulated by the law of retribution; therefore, they correspond to the sins either by analogy or by antithesis. Thus, for example, the carnal sinners, who abandoned themselves to the tempests of passion, are tossed about incessantly by a fierce storm. The violent, who were bloodthirsty and vicious during their lives, are drowned in a river of blood. The sowers of dissension, who promoted social and domestic separations, are wounded and mutilated according to the nature of their crimes.

SPIRIT OF INFERNO

As soon as we enter the gate of Hell we are struck by an unforgettable vision of darkness and terror, stripped of any hope: "Abandon all hope, you who enter here," and even of the sight of the stars. In the dark,

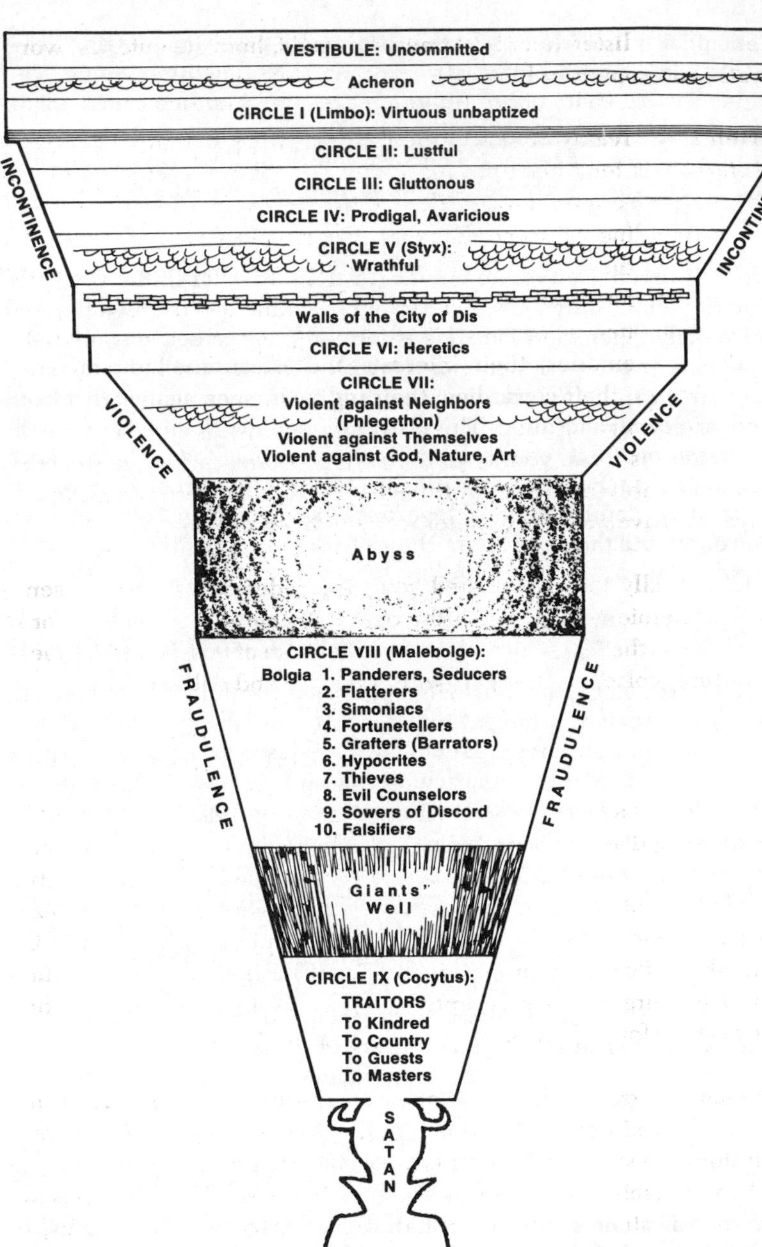

PLAN OF DANTE'S INFERNO

starless air, we listen to only "strange tongues, horrible outcries, words of wrath, and sounds of blows."

Hell is the reality of sins of the flesh, of chaos, of ugliness. And yet the *Inferno* has long been the most popular and the most widely read, and by romantic critics, it was exalted as the richest in poetry. The reason for the extraordinary fortune of the *Inferno* must be seen in the fact that this *cantica* is the closest to our world: here earthly passions are still alive in all their force, and the human character of the souls is unchanged. Heaven repudiated these souls; therefore they must remain attached to earth. Their memories, their interests and affections, their miseries, their turpitudes, their cowardice, their ugliness, seen against that background of eternity, acquire a new tragic dimension and become immortal. There is a real vitality in the *Inferno* that is lacking in the other *cantiche*, possibly because the thoughts of the age were turned less to the joys of Heaven than to the eternal damnation of Hell.

Occasionally the condemned souls are redeemed by a kind sentiment or a heroic gesture, as in the case of Paolo and Francesca, or of Ulysses. Nevertheless, Hell remains the kingdom of misery and ugliness, hate, torture, noise, and despair, without pause and without end.

STRUCTURE OF PURGATORY

Purgatory is a huge mountain located on a small island in the middle of the ocean and antipodal to Jersualem. The realm is divided into three major sections. Ante-Purgatory, at the foot of the mountain, has two parts: the mountain of Purgatory has seven ascending terraces, each assigned for one of the "seven deadly sins"; and on the summit of the mount, above Purgatory proper, is the Earthly Paradise. The sufferings endured in Purgatory are accepted voluntarily by the spirits in their desire to atone for their sins.

Penance corresponding to the sin by antithesis prevails. Thus, the proud are bowed down with heavy burdens, the lazy run without rest, the gluttons are starving. The souls are sustained by examples of the sin punished on each terrace and by its opposite virtue. The examples are carved in the stone of the mountain, chanted by invisible voices, or called aloud by the sinners themselves.

PLAN OF DANTE'S PURGATORY

SPIRIT OF PURGATORY

Upon entering the realm of Purgatory we feel a sensation of sweet and comforting relief. We return to see the sky, while a soft hue of sapphire extends to the horizon, and Venus still makes the whole East smile; we see in the distance the living surface of the sea.

Purgatory is the kingdom of peace and affection, of friendliness, of tenderness, and delicacy of feelings, of a resigned expectation. Hope is the keynote of Dante's *Purgatorio.* The souls still retain their affections and remember their earthly lives, but they do so with detachment, having in mind the new life toward which they aspire.

Earthly life and glory, seen with new eyes from the hereafter, is despoiled of all its illusions, its vanity, and its fallacious appearances. If the *Inferno* is the *cantica* richest in poetical contrast, and unforgettable because of its gallery of characters, the *Purgatorio* is certainly the richest in lyricism and nuances of color and sentiment. The souls of Purgatory are very often musical beings; they express their sensations in songs, hymns, and psalms. Purgatory is the realm of hope.

STRUCTURE OF PARADISE

Dante's representation of Paradise takes him into the heavens, heavens corresponding to the Ptolemaic system of astronomy. Circling around the earth are successive concentric spheres, each designated for a heavenly body or bodies. The first seven are the planetary spheres (including the sun and moon), and in each sphere are spirits distinguished for a particular virtue. The eighth sphere is that of the fixed stars; the ninth is outer space, called the Primum Mobile; the tenth region (not a sphere), the Empyrean, the heaven of heavens, a realm where God sits on his throne.

SPIRIT OF PARADISE

When we come to Paradise, we come to a very different world beyond earth and time. Seen from the height of Heaven, the earth has such a pitiful semblance that it makes the poet smile.

Paradise is the realm of the spirit emancipated from the senses and made completely free: the souls have forgotten earthly affections; they live only for the joy of loving and contemplating God. The sole feeling that exists in Paradise is love, the sole sensation is beatitude, the sole act is contemplation, and all these have the form of light. The *Paradiso* has very properly been called the *cantica* of light because light is the whole substance of Heaven. The souls express their thoughts by light: Beatrice shines with light every time she smiles, and the whole of Heaven changes color during the invective of St. Peter; the stages of virtues and the degrees of beatitude are also expressed by light.

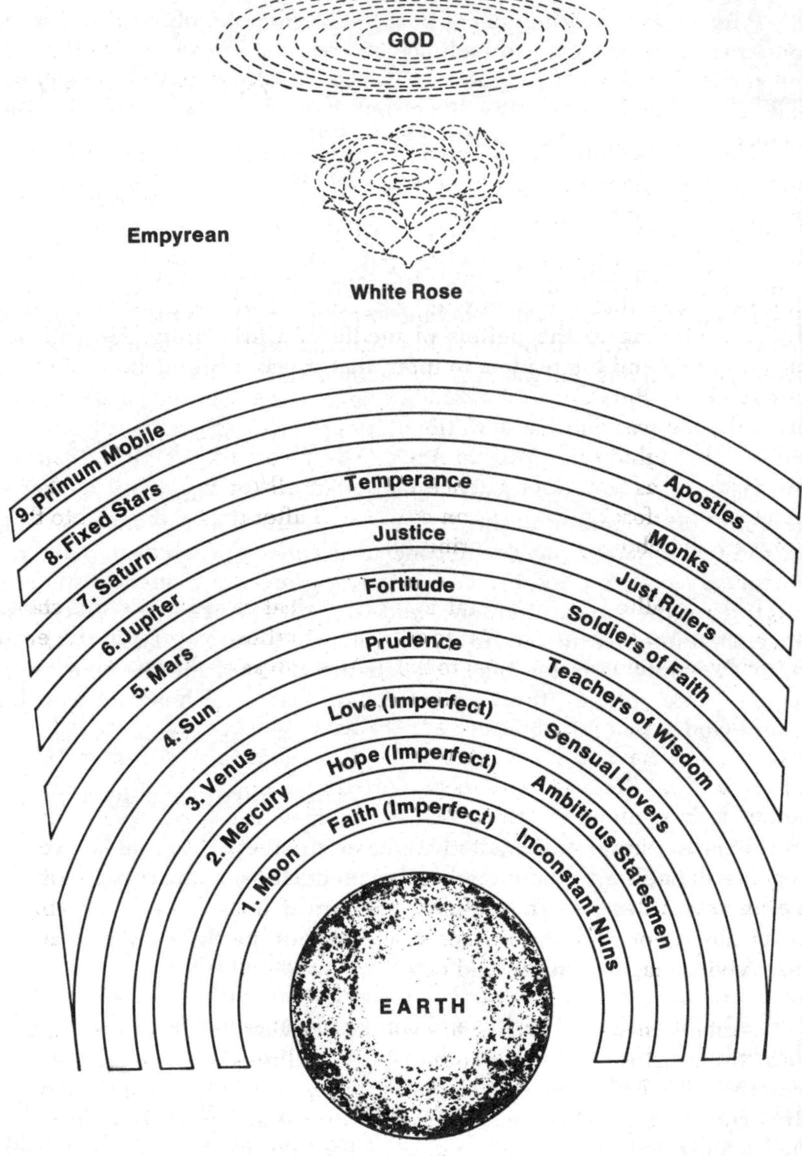

PLAN OF DANTE'S PARADISE

INTERPRETATION

The *Divine Comedy* has had many interpreters. Some have followed Dante's own thought, as outlined so clearly in his letter to Can Grande; others appear to ignore it.

Dante said plainly that the first meaning was the literal one. By this he meant that the cantos tell the story of the state of souls after death, according to the beliefs of medieval Christianity. He did *not* mean, nor intend his readers to infer, that it was a literal story of a trip through Hell, Purgatory, and Paradise; and he was safe in assuming that his audience was familiar with the literature of such journeys, a favorite subject throughout the Middle Ages. (This does not preclude reading the *Comedy* as excellent science fiction.) Hell (or Purgatory, or Paradise) is, therefore, the *condition* of the soul after death, brought to that point by the choices made during life.

Closely allied to its literal and allegorical meaning is the stated moral purpose of the *Comedy:* to point out to those yet living the error of their ways, and to turn them to the path of salvation.

Allegory is, by definition, an extended metaphor, organized in a pattern, and having a meaning separate from the literal story. C. S. Lewis has said "It is an error to suppose that in an allegory the author is 'really' talking about the thing that symbolizes; the very essence of the art is to talk about both." Aristotle believed that for a poet to have a command of metaphor was the mark of genius because it indicated a gift for seeing resemblances. This implies the gift of imagination, the ability to set down not only the images of vision, but, particularly in Dante's case, vivid images of noise and odor.

Dante wanted his reader to experience what he experienced, and from the beginning of the poem to the end he grows in power and mastery. His language is deceptively simple and so is his method. He writes in the vernacular, using all its force and directness; it is not the high poetic language of tragedy, as he said himself.

The imagery is designed to make the world of Dante's Hell intelligible to the reader. His world is the world of the thirteenth-century church, but his Hell is the creation of his mind, an allegory of redemption in which Dante seeks to show the state of the soul after death.

The poem is a demanding one. The reader must enter Dante's world without prejudice, and perhaps T. S. Eliot was right in recommending that the *Comedy* should be read straight through the first time, without giving too much attention to the background of the times, and without examining the more complex symbols.

TRANSLATION

Dante once remarked that he detested translations, thereby giving personal force to the Italian proverb *Tradutori traditori* (the translator is a traitor). To read a translation of Dante is not to read Dante, but the same may be said of Homer or Dumas or Goethe. One of the difficulties with Dante is the verse form that he used, which is not easy to render into English. The *terza rima* is a three-line stanza, as has been explained, its rhyme scheme being *aba, bcb, cdc,* etc. Often a thought will carry over from one stanza to the next. In Italian, the endings tend to be feminine (unstressed); in English they are usually masculine, or stressed. This produces basic differences in the movement and tonal quality of the poetry.

Because the *Comedy* was composed in Italian, the modern reader working with a translation is faced with certain difficulties. Each translator has put something of himself into his work. Some have written in prose, some in verse, and all have in some way interpreted as they transposed the words into English. Different teachers will recommend different versions, and of course one should follow his instructor's advice. However, the student should always remember that no single translation is definitive and that a second reading of the *Comedy,* or parts of it, in a different rendition will diminish the problems caused by the individual views of the translators.

Alice Curtayne, in her *Recall to Dante,* has devoted an entire chapter to comparative translations of the *Comedy.* She favors prose translation and gives convincing arguments for it. Dorothy Sayers, in her "Introduction" to the *Inferno,* has given some insight into the difficulties the translator faces, but unlike Miss Curtayne, believes that the *terza rima* can and should be used in English translations and demonstrates by using it in her translation of the *Comedy,* as does John Ciardi.

Paradiso Notes

INTRODUCTION TO *PARADISO*

Paradiso is the least read and, to many readers, the least successful canticle of the *Divine Comedy;* and yet it is evident that for its author it was the most important part of the poem, the capstone of the work and its greatest glory. In this respect, the final portion of the epic has suffered a fate similar to that of Goethe's *Faust, Part II,* or the second part of *Don Quixote,* and for some of the same reasons. All three are the products of the author's mature years and the receptacles of his most profound philosophy.

Although these sequels are clearly less popular and less earthy in their appeal than their antecedent works, they are esteemed superior by some serious critics; but whether one prefers the early or the later section of the work in question, all are agreed that it is impossible to deal intelligently and fairly with any of these major authors without surveying his work as a whole.

If we are to be honest in our claims for *Paradiso,* we must admit at the outset that there are difficulties for the modern reader. Certain discussions are tedious for most of us; for example, the cause of spots on the moon, the language Adam spoke, and the many Florentine families that have lost their prestige are beyond our comprehension without elaborate notes. Furthermore, the total concept of this medieval Christian heaven is quite foreign to our thought patterns.

To begin with, the student should consider the basic problem Dante faced in depicting a heaven of joy. What manner of heaven would have a universal appeal? What kinds of pleasures are suitable for a heaven that is to have a spiritual character? Earthy, sensual delights, such as the heavenly fishfry of *Green Pastures* or the refreshing Mohammedan paradise with its rich repasts and its amiable houris, are not admissible. The sensory experiences on which Dante builds his heaven are sights and sounds. The sights consist mainly of brilliant lights with their varied colors, their symbolic formations, and their gyrations. If one reverts to his own experiences in calling up imagined scenes—marching bands on a football field or the garish lights of Broadway by night—

Dante's conceptions may seem tame and amateurish. Perhaps, the best modern conceit would be a brilliant Fourth of July fireworks display. The most sensitive readers, however, come to recognize that just as Keats' unheard melodies are sweeter than those heard on earth, scenes presented to our imagination through the language of poetry may surpass the scenes of our experience.

A further problem Dante had to contend with is the fact that in our experience there are no pleasures that would not become commonplace, even boring, if prolonged indefinitely. Joy is a thing of high moments. Even the calm feeling of well-being, which has a better reputation for duration, must pass through periods of highs and lows. For this reason, the perpetual joy of Dante's saints in heaven does not call to us in compelling tones.

What we are promised in Paradise is summed up in these terms: beauty (light and music), joy, peace, and love. For Dante, the greatest of these is love, and the highest form of love is the love for God. The reward of peace, though not so positively enunciated as those other features, is woven into the entire poem. It is interesting to compare this with the final scene of Goethe's *Faust,* where the hero is elevated into heaven, and with the closing lines of the "Cantos on Mutability" at the end of Spenser's *Faerie Queene.* In both of these long and powerful works the author has demonstrated how life on earth must be a continual struggle, which is only justified, only endurable, if there is the goal of peace in victory at the end.

Ruskin declared that if *Paradiso* is less read than *Inferno* it is because "it requires far greater attention, and, perhaps for its full enjoyment, a holier heart." One may well add that it calls for greater patience but also for a deep intellectual concern and a type of imagination that goes out to meet Dante's.

PROBLEMS OF CHRONOLOGY

It is important for the reader to be alert to certain ramifications concerning the presumed date of Dante's journey through the realms of the dead, the year 1300. When he was actually engaged in writing *Paradiso,* which was between ten and twenty years after that date, people had come on the world scene and events had transpired that he felt compelled to write about. Consequently, to maintain a consistent stance, he was obliged to present everything postdating 1300 as predictions which the spirits in heaven foresee through their power to read future events.

DANTE VENTING HIS SPLEEN

A survey of *Paradiso* leaves no doubt in anyone's mind about Dante's attitude toward his contemporaries and toward the parties and institutions of his day. Those he disliked were roundly and frequently castigated through the speeches of the saints. Accordingly, Leigh Hunt maintained that the work seems more angry than celestial.

Inescapable features of the work are the poet's resentment of the papacy, with its political ambitions, and of the clergy, for their greed, stupidity, and general worldliness. Certain popes—Boniface VIII, Clement V, and John XXII—are presented as archenemies of God's kingdom on earth. So too are political leaders who struggled to obstruct the fulfillment of Dante's hope for a revival of imperial rule in Italy. Among the most hated of those figures was Philip IV, "the Fair," of France.

The explanation is simple. Dante held his convictions with passionate intensity. Moreover, he considered that it was his mission to write a poem that would benefit men of the present and future, and he believed that this could be accomplished through diverse approaches. One was to guide them through a vivid vision of penalties for sin and future glory as a reward for righteousness, but another was to sound the alarm through direct criticism of the laxity, the misdirection, and the viciousness running rife not only among leaders but even among whole nations. Obviously, the vehemence of his criticism is a calculated and important part of his message.

BEATRICE

The glorification of Beatrice—the girl Dante first saw when he was nine years old, the woman who was the object of his idealized love and the source of his inspiration during her life and after her death—is the fulfillment of the promise Dante made at the end of *La Vita Nuova:* "to write of her what has never yet been said of mortal woman." No other woman in literature has been given such a magnificent apotheosis as Beatrice here.

In her role as guide and lecturer, Beatrice stirs little enthusiasm in the reader, but neither does she provoke our antipathy because we ascribe her lectures to the Voice of Theology and accept them as expositions necessary for the unravelling of certain perplexing phenomena. The other aspect of her role in the poem is the personal treatment of a lady whom Dante loved virtually all of his life, a lady who had such love for Dante that she relinquished her seat in the Celestial Rose and descended into Hell in order to save him from his wandering in the dark wood and from the assaults of bestiality.

The passages treating Beatrice's beauty, brightness, and love constitute a tour de force of mounting intensity. Corresponding to that is the sequence expressing Dante's ever increasing feeling of love for her. The scores of passages that treat the human and personal aspect of Beatrice's role constitute a major feature of the work. Those passages, occurring in introductory or climactic situations are the most appealing, the most memorable, and the most poetic passages in the epic.

The major theme of the *Comedy* is the rich reward that is attained by a mortal through his love of God. But how can the poet make us understand that kind of love? The ladder on which we must mount to that understanding is the love of a fellow human being. Thus we recognize how vital the role of Beatrice is to this great poem.

SYNOPSIS

The poet announces the theme of this climactic canticle as the ineffable vision of heaven, whereupon he invokes the aid of the muses and Apollo for inspiration and eloquence.

The time is high noon on the Mountain of Purgatory and the season is the vernal equinox, the most propitious time of the year. Dante, having been instructed and purified in Purgatory, is prepared for his journey to Paradise. Seeing Beatrice lift her glance toward the sun, he follows her example and is at that moment transformed ("transhumanized") in preparation for his great adventure. He is surprised to discover a new brightness and wonderful music around them, until Beatrice explains that they have flown, swifter than thought, up to the *Sphere of Fire,* and that his new state (transhumanized) permits him to hear the music of the spheres.

After a flight of incredible speed, the travelers arrive in the first heaven, the *Sphere of the Moon*. Because the sphere is composed of matter, Dante has difficulty understanding how he can penetrate that body, and he speculates on whether or not he is in his corporeal state.

The age-old question of the cause of the spots on the moon is treated at length. Beatrice asks Dante for his conjecture regarding the puzzle, but she refutes his theory and then proceeds to expound the real cause of the appearance of those apparent blemishes.

Through the pearly, diaphanous substance of the sphere, the poet perceives the faces of spirits. One of these identifies herself as Piccarda Donati, a former acquaintance. She tells him that she is in this region because she was forced to violate her vow of chastity and to marry a man she hated. Consequently, she has been consigned to this, the lowest stage of blessedness; but she assures him that all the souls in Paradise are perfectly contented with whatever degree of blessedness God has willed for them. A companion of Piccarda is then introduced, the Empress Constance, mother of Frederick II. Like Piccarda, she was withdrawn from her convent and forced into marriage.

In answer to a problem worrying Dante, Beatrice explains that all the heavenly spirits have their permanent abode in the Empyrean, the highest heaven; but for Dante's instruction different categories of spirits will descend and appear for him in one of the planetary spheres with which they are associated through their distinguishing virtue.

Several problems concerning vows, about which Dante has some doubts, are explained at length for him by his instructress, questions concerning the responsibility for vows broken under duress, and the possibility of substituting new acts of righteousness for the one originally pledged.

Suddenly Dante becomes aware that they have arrived in a new region, the *Sphere of Mercury*. Beatrice's countenance has acquired a new radiance, which is a sign of her increased delight, the result of the ascension. The souls in this region appear as glowing lights; neither their faces nor other physical features are recognizable. (This is a condition of all the remaining spirits in the heavenly spheres except those in the Empyrean.)

In response to Dante's query, a spirit identifies himself as Justinian, the emperor who was the author and sponsor of the Roman legal code.

He proudly surveys the history of the Roman Empire, citing great figures and major events with an emphasis on the important role of imperial rule as part of the divine plan for mankind.

He further explains that the company of spirits assembled in Mercury are those who were so absorbed in their pursuit of fame and honor that they neglected their religious duties. He then identifies one of his companion spirits as Romeo da Villanova, a devoted minister of a count of Provence, who unjustly suffered disgrace and exile.

Justinian's discourse leaves Dante with certain questions about the Crucifixion which Beatrice undertakes to explain for him. She distinguishes two aspects of the Crucifixion based on the dual nature of Christ. She further expounds upon the nature of redemption and affirms the final resurrection of the body.

Seeing Beatrice become yet more lovely, Dante realizes that they have soared into a new heaven, the *Sphere of Venus*. One spirit, advancing from the dancing lights, addresses Dante as a former acquaintance. He is Charles Martel of the Anjou dynasty. A discussion of heredity follows, which, in turn, leads to a treatment of the problem of celestial influences that endow individuals with diverse dispositions and capabilities.

Other persons who are identified among the spirits in Venus (Cunizza, Folco, and Rahab the Harlot) are all persons who in early life "burned with amorous fire" but later were converted to true *caritas*, or divine love. Their discourse, however, is chiefly aimed at the degeneracy of contemporary political and religious life—Cunizza's against her native Treviso, Folco's against Florence and the papacy.

The arrival of the pilgrims in the *Sphere of the Sun*, the heaven of wisdom, is marked by a surrounding light of indescribable brilliance. At first they are circled by a ring of twelve dancing lights singing in harmonious tones. One spirit offers to name the members of the circle. He is St. Thomas Aquinas, and his companions include some of the great sages, teachers, and theologians—among them, Albertus Magnus, Solomon, Boethius, the Venerable Bede, Orosius, and Dionysius the Areopagite.

As the circle of saints pauses, Aquinas relates the story of St. Francis of Assisi: how he foreswore his wealthy heritage and took a strict vow of poverty, how he founded the order of Franciscan friars, how he preached to the Sultan, and how he received the stigmata. Aquinas then speaks disparagingly of his own order, the Dominicans, many of whom, he bitterly reports, have forsaken the high purpose of their leader.

As Aquinas ends his speech, a second circle of twelve lights appears outside the first. Their spokesman, Bonaventura, who was a prominent Franciscan leader, relates the story of the life of St. Dominic: his Spanish birth, his eloquent preaching, his battles against heresy, and his powerful influence on Christianity through the foundation of his order. Bonaventura then denounces his own brother Franciscans for their laxity and degeneracy.

The second circle of sages includes, in addition to Bonaventura, Nathan the Prophet, Hugh of St. Victor, Chrysostom, Anselm, and Donatus, as well as the earliest disciples of St. Francis.

Aquinas, discussing a point about the superior wisdom of Solomon, explains that Christ and Adam are exempt from comparison with other men because they were created by God, whereas all other humans are created by God's ministers, the Intelligences in the stars. Solomon then resolves one further problem puzzling Dante concerning the reuniting of bodies and souls at the Resurrection. Suddenly, a third circle of light appears surrounding the other two. No spirits of this circle are named, but the emblem of the three rings stands for the Trinity and foreshadows the climactic vision in the Empyrean.

Arriving in a new realm, the *Sphere of Mars*, the voyagers perceive two streams of light that intersect to form a great cross, within which they momentarily see a vision of Christ. The lights composing the cross sing a martial hymn which at first Dante does not fully understand.

One spirit descends to the foot of the cross to speak to the poet. It is Cacciaguida, his great-great-grandfather, who fought and died as a crusader under the Emperor Conrad. He praises Florence as she was in his day, a city which was distinguished for its plain and sober living and reverence for moral customs. When pressed for more details by the poet, Cacciaguida gives the time of his birth (about 1100) but refuses to discuss his ancestry. He notes that the population of Florence, which has increased five times, has deteriorated in the character of its citizens because of the incursion of inferior stock from surrounding towns and farms; and he cites numerous families once prominent in Florence but now of little note.

To satisfy Dante's question regarding the misfortunes that he has been told are in store for him, Cacciaguida, in a moving speech, describes the conditions of Dante's life in exile, but he also promises some relief through the generous patronage of the della Scala family, and he further predicts punishment for those responsible for Dante's exile.

Finally, the old crusader identifies a few of the distinguished warriors who are among his companions in this sphere: Joshua, Judas Maccabeus, Charlemagne, Roland, and Godfrey of Bouillon.

A glance toward Beatrice, whose features show an added brightness, tells Dante that they have risen to a new region, the *Sphere of Jupiter.* A series of swimming lights spells out, letter by letter, a biblical message on justice: DILIGITE IUSTICIAM . . . TERRAM ("Love justice, ye that judge the earth"). The final letter of the message, M, lingers but is then transformed, first to the emblem of a lily and then to an eagle, the symbol of the Empire. Contemplating the relationship between heavenly and earthly justice, Dante inveighs against the reigning pope for his abuse of earthly justice.

The band of spirits forming the eagle addresses Dante in unison. When he asks for an explanation of divine justice, he is told that its nature is beyond human comprehension. One issue which especially worries Dante concerns the fate of virtuous heathens. He is told that these souls may attain a better place in glory than factitious worshipers of Christianity.

The eagle denounces numerous sovereigns who have perverted justice: Emperor Albert of Austria, Philip the Fair of France, Edward I of England, and most of the other living rulers.

An interval of glorious song follows. Then the eagle designates some of the noblest souls in its formation—those marking its eye and brow. In the pupil of the eye is King David; the five souls forming the eyebrow are: the Emperor Trajan, Hezekiah, the Emperor Constantine, William II of Sicily, and Ripheus the Trojan. It has to be explained to Dante how two of those persons were included, since he supposed that they were not Christians. Trajan, he is informed, was miraculously restored to life through Pope Gregory I's intercession and converted to the faith. Ripheus was granted foreknowledge of Christ and believed.

Upon arrival in the *Sphere of Saturn,* Dante sees a golden ladder upon which angel lights are mounting and descending. These are spirits who devoted their lives to contemplation.

A spirit descends to greet Dante, identifying himself as Peter Damian, a monk renowned for asceticism. He dismisses predestination as beyond man's comprehension and he castigates the present-day clergy for having grown fat and rich. All of the spirits present join him in a thunderous shout of approval.

A second light approaches and addresses the poet. It is St. Benedict, who founded the order of Benedictine monks and the famous monastery at Monte Cassino. He decries the decay of the true monastic spirit among his living followers, whom he labels "a den of thieves." They ignore the path of contemplation, which, like the golden ladder, leads upward toward God.

As Benedict and the host of lights mount the golden ladder, Dante is directed by Beatrice to follow. Thus the pilgrims attain the *Sphere of Fixed Stars*. From their new height Dante looks back down to earth; and, noting how tiny and inconsequential it appears from that distance, he is led to reflect upon the vanity of all worldly goals.

Following Beatrice's example of gazing heavenward, Dante is greeted with a vision of Christ. The brilliance of Christ's image is too great for him to bear, and he is forced to lower his eyes. Beatrice bids him to look at her, then she smiles and he looks up again. Christ has soared to heaven and now Mary appears surrounded by a host of the blessed—the prophets and the apostles. Gabriel leads the host in paying solemn tribute to her.

When Mary has followed her Son toward the Empyrean, St. Peter detaches himself from the throng of lights and proceeds to examine Dante on his understanding of faith. Finding the responses wholly satisfactory, the saint expresses his delight. A second light, St. James, descends to examine the candidate on hope, and Dante discourses on hope to the eminent satisfaction of St. James and the attendant host. A third spirit approaches, St. John, who examines Dante on love. Dante explains that his understanding of love is based on both reason and revelation. The greatest bond of his love of God is Christ's sacrifice. The assembly of spirits greets his responses with "Holy, holy, holy!"

Finally Adam appears before Dante and answers questions that have long puzzled biblical students: how long did Adam dwell in the Garden before his banishment? how long did he live on earth? how long was he in Limbo? and, finally, what language did he speak?

Before the departure of the apostles, St. Peter delivers a vehement denunciation of his recent successors in the papal seat (Clement V and John XXII), who have turned his tomb into "a sewer of blood and filth."

As Dante and Beatrice enter the ninth sphere, the *Primum Mobile,* Beatrice explains that it is this sphere that drives the motion of all the lower spheres. Here the poet will witness a vision of God and His relation to the angels. Dante sees a dot of intense brilliance surrounded by a series of concentric rings of light. Beatrice explains that the circles represent the classes of angels and that they receive their light and force in proportion to their nearness to God, the central light. The classes of angels are named in the order of their virtue, from greatest to least: Seraphim, Cherubim, Thrones, Dominations, Virtues, Powers, Principalities, Archangels, and Angels. The angels are also designated as Intelligences, and each order sheds its influence on one of the spheres below.

Beatrice answers two questions concerning angels: whether they existed before the Creation, and whether they possess memory as well as understanding and will.

Dante again turns to Beatrice, and he tells us that if all he has ever said of her beauty could be compounded it could not express the beauty she has now attained. She announces their arrival in the *Empyrean,* the region of pure light; and she informs Dante that he will be privileged to see the saints in their corporeal forms as they will appear on the day of the Resurrection.

At first he sees a river of light between flowery banks, but as he dips his eyes in that river, it is transformed into a great rose at whose center is a wonderful source of light. The petals are formed with row on row of saints in glory. Beatrice points out to him that there are few unfilled places. She then calls his attention to the throne reserved for the Emperor Henry VII.

The blessed souls clad in white raiment fill the great rose. Angels fly, like a swarm of bees, up from the heart of the rose to the petals, their faces of living flame, their wings of gold, their bodies white as purest snow.

After gazing at the mystic scene, Dante turns to speak to Beatrice but discovers that she is no longer beside him. In her place is a saintly elder, St. Bernard, who points out Beatrice where now she has resumed her honored place in the rose. Bernard then enjoins Dante to look up to the highest tier where Mary sits enthroned, surrounded by a thousand joyful angels.

The arrangement of the principal souls in the Celestial Rose is explained by Bernard. Directly below the Virgin are heroines of the Old Testament: Eve, Rachel (beside her is Beatrice), Sarah, Rebecca, Judith, and Ruth. On the opposite side of the rose in a similar vertical arrangement are the male figures of the Christian era: John the Baptist, St. Francis, St. Benedict, and St. Augustine. Seated to one side or the other of Mary are: Adam, Peter, Moses and John the Apostle; flanking John the Baptist are St. Anne and St. Lucy. All of the upper rows of petals are occupied by adult figures, whereas the lower tiers are filled with infants.

St. Bernard now delivers a memorable apostrophe and prayer to the Virgin, praising her for her benign spirit, then pleading for her intercession on Dante's behalf that he may be permitted the Beatific Vision. With a gracious smile she signals her consent, and Dante lifts his eyes toward the light at the heart of the rose. What he saw he can report only in faintly recollected form, so potent was the experience. Within one blinding light he recognized three separate lights in the form of interlocking circles (a symbol of the Trinity), and within one circle he perceived the dim image of a human face, a reminder that God, through Christ, lived—and still lives—as man on earth.

At this point the poet comprehended the oneness of the manifold pages in the book of the universe; he felt desire and will brought into conformity.

SUMMARIES AND COMMENTARIES

CANTO 1

Summary

God's glory, which is resplendent through all the universe, shines more brightly in one part and less brightly in another. In the part of heaven that receives His brightest light, Dante has stood, but it is impossible for one who has returned from there to tell the wonder of it fully. Still, what his memory retains of that treasured experience will be the theme of his song.

He solemnly invokes Apollo to give him power to speak of that blessed realm in fitting terms. Now he needs the support of both peaks of Parnassus; now he needs the eloquence which gave Apollo victory in his contest with Marsyas. He pledges to strive for the crown of laurel, which is too seldom sought in his time.

The sun, which has risen in its most beneficent position—that is, in the sign of Aries and about the time of the vernal (spring) equinox—is lighting all the hemisphere of Purgatory, where Dante stands with Beatrice. When he sees Beatrice look directly at the sun, Dante follows her example and is able to endure the brightness better than mortal eyes can normally do. Sparks like hot iron boil out of the sun's fire. Then suddenly the day seems doubly bright. Dante turns and fixes his gaze on Beatrice, and as he looks at her he becomes transhumanized—like Glaucus, who was transformed into a sea god after eating a certain herb. He cannot say if in that state he existed physically or was only "that part of me created first," the rational human soul.

The sounds of harmony and the intense brightness that surround them bewilder the poet, whereupon Beatrice offers an explanation. His confusion is caused by his failure to realize that they have left the earth and have risen to the Sphere of Fire; his soul has sped swifter than lightning toward "its home." It is the law of the universe, she declares, that all things, animate and inanimate, move by instinct toward their natural abode. As fire rises toward heaven, so the pure soul rises to God. For Dante, now that he has been purified, it should not be a surprise that he is soaring heavenward.

Commentary

In opening the account of his journey through Paradise, Dante leaves no doubt that the adventure he is about to relate transcends all other experiences. God's glory shines more radiantly in the Empyrean, the heaven of heavens, than in any other part of the universe, and Dante says, "I was there." To reveal that glory fully is beyond human power, but he will tell as much of that experience as his memory holds. To aid him in this endeavor, he invokes Apollo and the muses for the gift of eloquence. Whereas in *Inferno* and *Purgatorio* he called upon the muses only, he now adds his appeal to Apollo. The twin peaks of Mount Parnassus to which he refers were sacred to those divinities, one to Apollo and the other to the muses. He made the distinction earlier *(La Vita Nuova)* between the muses as directors of the poet's science, or art, and Apollo as the giver of divine inspiration. In his invocation to Apollo,

Dante recalls the contest in which Apollo defeated the satyr Marsyas in a musical contest; and he also refers to the legend of Daphne, who was turned into a laurel tree; because the tree was henceforth sacred to Apollo, wreaths of laurel were used to crown both poets and victorious generals.

If the reader is surprised or shocked to discover that in a poem of such intense Christian dedication the author should call upon a pagan god for inspiration, he must remember that for Dante the model for noble poetry was the classical epic and thus the formalities of epic poetry were prized props for him, as indeed they were for many later Christian poets.

The time for the beginning of the flight toward heaven, the poet notes, is most propitious. The sun is lighting all of the hemisphere of Purgatory, which is to say that it is noon there. Furthermore, it is the best time of the year, the vernal equinox (the time of year when God, it was believed, created the world) and the time when the sun exerts its greatest influence on earth—"stamps the wax of the world with its temper." The reference to the four circles joined to three crosses specifies that the line of the equator, the ecliptic (of the zodiac), and the horizon intersect at the equinoctial colure (the great circle traversing the two poles). Their intersecting forms the crosses.

When Dante sees Beatrice turn her face up toward the sun, he does the same and discovers that his eyes can now sustain its brightness. He soon perceives that they are surrounded by a double brightness (the Sphere of Fire that is between the Sphere of the Earth and the Sphere of the Moon) and that harmonious sounds fill the air (the music of the spheres); still, however, he does not understand that they have risen high into the heavens. Beatrice explains how it is that he has soared swifter than lightning. Since his soul was purified in Purgatory and all sin was cast off, it is free to obey a basic law of the universe which dictates that the pure soul is drawn by instinct toward God.

CANTO 2

Summary

The poet addresses his readers and, using a striking nautical metaphor, warns all who have been following his ship to turn back, for his journey will now take him far out over the unknown, dangerous deep; but he invites those who have been striving for "the bread of angels" to follow, keeping close in his wake, and he promises that they will see much to amaze them.

Dante and Beatrice, borne upward as swiftly as a glance by their thirst for heaven, arrive in a new region of heaven with the speed of an arrow from a crossbow. They have entered the Sphere of the Moon. Dante wonders how his body can enter into that pearly, solid substance that surrounds them – if indeed he is a body now – for that appears to contradict the laws of science. After serious consideration, he discovers that the phenomenon helps to illuminate the mystery of Christ's incarnation.

When he asks Beatrice the cause of the dark spots on the moon, she asks what his opinion is. He advances the theory that different portions of the planet are of different density. Beatrice, in refuting that theory, reasons that the light from the Sphere of Fixed Stars is affected by something far different than the magnitude or density of various stars. Different stars possess different virtues, hence their differences in intensity and color. Against Dante's variable density theory, she further suggests that if the areas of rarified matter extended clear through the moon, the sun's light ought to show through at the time of an eclipse. She also refutes another theory which had been proposed to the effect that the rarified regions were of variable depths and that light rays were reflected from the bottom of those depressions and consequently were dimmer than those reflected from the planet's surface because they came from a greater distance. To show the fallacy of that concept, Beatrice proposes a simple experiment: place two mirrors equidistant from an observer and place a third mirror farther away, then have a light held behind him so that he can observe the reflection in the mirrors. He will discover that the image in the farther mirror is as bright as the other images.

The explanation of the true cause of the spots involves an account of the manner in which energy and light are transmitted throughout the universe, deriving from God and carried from the Primum Mobile down through the lower spheres. The energy and light transmitted are uniform, but the results of their impact on various heavenly bodies differ in accordance with the nature or essence of the body. The differences, then, are not differences of quantity but of quality; by the same reasoning, the differences found in the light on the moon are caused by variations in the essences of different regions.

Commentary

The ship mentioned at the opening of this canto is a counterpart to one at the beginning of *Purgatorio* (Canto 1). Since the basis of Dante's narrative is a journey, it is to be expected that he will draw many similes and metaphors from different modes of travel: pilgrimages, riding, climbing, swimming, sailing, and even flying. In this passage, he tries to discourage the majority of readers—those in small boats—from reading further. Only those who have cultivated a love for "the bread of angels"—a biblical phrase meaning spiritual understanding (Psalms 78)—are encouraged to venture out on this ocean. The reference to the men who crossed the sea to Colchis, the Argonauts, and their surprise at Jason's turning plowman is apt in its context, and it is also interesting for its associative juxtaposition to the nautical metaphor just mentioned.

The substance of the sphere of the first planet, the moon, is solid and pearl-like. The puzzle as to how two bodies can occupy the same space causes Dante to speculate. "If I was then a body," he says, "how could that body enter the solid body of the moon's sphere?" He manages to turn this speculation into a revelation of the mystery of Christ's being God and man in one.

A lengthy discussion now follows about the spots on the moon. This was a subject of serious concern to astronomers and philosophers before Galileo's dramatic view through his telescope, three centuries after Dante, revealed mountains and valleys, craters and fissures on its surface. The theory of varying densities was one that had been espoused by such scholars as Averroes and Albertus Magnus and which Dante had sanctioned in his *Convivio*. The refutation of that theory and the presentation of a new theory, although propounded by Beatrice, represents Dante's more mature judgment on the question.

To understand the argument about the different essences in the various stars, planets, and constellations, we must recall that scientists believed then in the diverse influences exerted on men's lives by the individual heavenly bodies. The discussion of the problem of the moon's spots, which must seem to modern readers not only tedious but even silly, serves Dante as the occasion for introducing a much more important concept—that is, the design of the force that drives and animates the universe.

The long and, to us, theoretical discourse of this canto is the beginning of that hard and dangerous intellectual voyage about which we were warned, the voyage that will explore the mysteries of God's universal plan.

CANTO 3

Summary

In the pearly atmosphere of the moon, Dante notices seven faces that seem eager to speak to him. The faces appear so diaphanous that at first he supposes that he is looking at hazy reflections, but Beatrice assures him that they are true substances, spirits whose status is represented by this sphere. She encourages Dante to speak to them.

When Dante addresses one of the spirits asking who she is, she replies that she is Piccarda, whom he should recognize even though she is more beautiful than she was on earth. She explains that all of the spirits in this region are in this lowest sphere because they broke their vows to God or failed in complete fulfillment of them, but she assures Dante of their contentment. He asks if they aspire to rise eventually to a higher station, at which Piccarda and her companions smile, declaring that their happiness is complete because they occupy the status chosen for them by divine love. "In His will is our peace." Through this revelation, Dante comes to understand that though God's grace is bestowed on different souls in different degrees, all of the blessed spirits are perfectly happy in their various degree of blessedness.

Piccarda relates that after she had taken religious vows and entered the order of St. Clare, she was taken from her convent against her will and forced by one of her brothers to marry Rossellino della Tosa.

Beside Piccarda is another spirit, whom she identifies as "the great Constance." The experience of Constance was much the same as Piccarda's; she was forced to leave her holy order and to enter into marriage. Her husband is referred to as one of those representing "the wind out of Swabia" (the Swabian dynasty of the Empire). Although the veil was snatched from Constance's brow, Piccarda declares, she always wore it in her heart.

As Piccarda sings an *Ave Maria,* her image fades as though she were sinking ever deeper into water. Losing sight of her, Dante turns to Beatrice, but now her face appears so glowing that he cannot at first endure its brightness.

Commentary

In Dante's journey through the heavens he will meet groups of spirits in each successive sphere; thus the narrative of the journey through Paradise parallels the narrative structures of *Inferno* and *Purgatorio,* in which he passed from circle to circle and terrace to terrace meeting special groups of spirits. The classification of the groups in Paradise is governed by the virtue associated with the sphere involved, the virtues being arranged in an ascending order of holiness. The spirits in the first three spheres are the least sanctified because their virtues include some taint of earthliness, just as those planets nearest the earth —the Moon, Mercury, and Venus—sometimes come under the shadow of the earth in an eclipse.

The spirits who appear to Dante here seem like indistinct reflections or images seen dimly underwater. In the higher regions of heaven, the bodily forms of the spirits are entirely indistinguishable and they are seen only as bright lights.

The virtue associated with the moon is faith. The spirits consigned to this sphere were distinguished by that virtue on earth, but failed to achieve perfection. They were guilty of broken vows. The fact that they were victims of violent enforcement and did not willingly betray their faith must, however, be considered as a mitigating circumstance in judging their merits. Their degree of blessedness is the least of all the heavenly spirits, but to them it constitutes perfect contentment and they aspire to no higher condition. Their will is identical with the will of God, and their happiness is summed up in the famous speech, "In His will is our peace" *(E'n la sua volontade è nostra pace).*

The first spirit to converse with Dante is Piccarda Donati, whom Dante knew in her lifetime. She was a relative of his wife and the sister of his friend Forese (cf. *Purg.* 23, 24). It was Piccarda's other brother, the notorious Corso Donati, who acted the villain in this adventure, invading Piccarda's convent and forcing her into a marriage of convenience. Dante's deep-seated animosity toward Corso may have no particular bearing on this episode, but it will be recalled that Corso was a leader of the "Black" party in the revolt that brought about Dante's exile.

A second spirit, appearing beside Piccarda, is introduced to Dante as "the great Constance," an empress of the Holy Roman Empire (mentioned in *Purg.* 3). In identifying Constance, Piccarda speaks of the second and third winds that came out of Swabia, a reference to the Swabian dynasty—Frederick I (Barbarossa), Henry VI, and Frederick II. She calls them "winds" because of their reputations for extraordinary energy. The story of the life of Constance is similar to Piccarda's since she was said to have been abducted from her convent to be married to the prince who later became Emperor Henry VI – "the second wind" – and she was the mother of Frederick II.

It is no accident that an empress stands beside a woman of citizen status without regard for the regal or aristocratic rank of earthly life. In heaven, such earthly distinctions no longer have validity. This same kind of abrogation of social rank is demonstrated in almost every one of the regions of Paradise.

The canto closes, as it opened, with a reference to the radiance of Beatrice in Dante's sight.

CANTO 4

Summary

At the end of his meeting with Piccarda and Constance, Dante is perplexed by two questions, but unable to decide which to broach first, he stands mute. Beatrice, knowing his thoughts, offers to resolve his problems. The first concern she treats is whether all of the souls in heaven inhabit a sphere from which they came to earth and from which they derived their character, as Plato maintained, or whether all have their heavenly abodes in the Empyrean. Beatrice declares that those spirits they have just seen and, indeed, *all* of the blessed dwell in the Empyrean together with the Seraphim and the saints, and with Moses, Samuel, the two Johns, and Mary. They are shown to Dante in the sphere with which they are associated spiritually in order to make clear to Dante the different kinds and degrees of blessedness among the heavenly spirits. This method for instructing Dante is adopted, Beatrice explains, because in dealing with the human intellect, perception through the senses is necessary for understanding. She says that Plato expressed the belief that souls return to the stars from which they came before their earthly existence, but he was in error in this matter, unless his words were intended to convey a hidden meaning; that is, Plato's theories were always taken literally. Beatrice comments that Plato *may* have been speaking symbolically. Since, however, no one considered this possibility, the result was that most nations named the planets for false gods – Jupiter, Mercury, and Mars.

The second problem worrying Dante concerns whether or not it is just to blame someone for an action that is forced upon him against his will. Beatrice points out that the "perfect will" does not die in a person; if one accepts a condition under duress, he will return to his true position at the first opportunity. The fault lies *not* in the original act but in the ultimate *acceptance* of the new role, as in the case of those ladies who, when forced to break their religious vows, failed to return to the convent when they were free to do so. This seems to bring into question Piccarda's remark that Constance kept her love for the veil always in her heart. Beatrice points out that one must recognize the distinction between the will that is checked by fear or some other counterforce and the type of will which surmounts all fear or pain, as that of St. Lawrence, for example.

Dante expresses his keen gratitude to Beatrice for her instruction and then asks one more question: can one pay the debt for the breaking of vows by performing virtuous deeds? Thereupon, Beatrice looks at Dante with eyes so bright that he is forced to turn his glance away.

Commentary

The present canto is wholly didactic, being concerned with matters of interpretation regarding what was seen and heard in the previous canto. Dante's indecision as to which question he should ask first, described by a series of figures of speech, represents what medieval logicians called the dilemma of Buridan's ass, the ass that stands between two bales of hay, debating which to eat first.

Beatrice, reading Dante's mind, proceeds to answer the questions, taking up the more dangerous problem first: do certain souls in heaven inhabit certain spheres or do all dwell in the Empyrean before the throne of God? Plato, in his dialogue *Timaeus*, maintained that before birth every soul inhabits a star that casts its influence over the individual temperament and the soul returns to that star after death if its earthly life was well ordered. Since the doctrine had so notable an author, and since it was supported by Cicero, Dante evidently felt that it had to be taken into account. Beatrice says that *all* souls dwell in the Empyrean and that Plato's doctrine is in error if interpreted literally; but she suggests that Plato may have intended his statement in an allegorical sense. In any case, she points out, many people have been misguided by it; and, attaching stellar influence to souls at birth, they named the planets for pagan gods and goddesses.

The reason given for having certain spirits show themselves to Dante in a particular sphere is that this presentation will make more readily understandable the hierarchy of the souls in Paradise. Human intellect requires sensory demonstration. By this arrangement, the poet has, in fact, applied Plato's concept of souls residing in their proper spheres although he rejected it for theological purposes.

Dante's second perplexity, which Beatrice now offers to resolve, concerns the problem of justice for those who are forced to abandon a way of life to which they were dedicated and are nevertheless held guilty. Their guilt, she explains, lies in their resigning themselves to the new way of life and failing to return to their former life when they are free to do so. Concerning Piccarda and Constance, she says that their absolute will dictated that they should return to the veil; but their "conditioned will" permitted them to make concessions to external pressures which threatened distasteful or disastrous consequences. These ladies chose the easier way, the compromise, in contrast to St. Lawrence, who, through adherence to his absolute will, accepted martyrdom.

Piccarda spoke the truth, Beatrice says, when she declared that the love of the veil was always in Constance's heart. This love in her heart was a response to her absolute will, but her conditioned will allowed her to accept her new role throughout the rest of her life.

After expressing his intense gratitude to Beatrice for her elucidations, Dante proposes one further question, the answer to which is delayed until the following canto.

CANTO 5

Summary

Beatrice first explains the increase in her brightness, which has momentarily blinded Dante. As joy increases, it is expressed in greater light; therefore, as she perceives his growth in spiritual insight, she is pleased and so gives forth a greater brilliance. She then proceeds to answer his latest question about the possibility of compensating for broken vows by performing good works. She reminds him that man's most precious possession is his free will, and she explains that a vow to God constitutes one's sacrifice of that free will, and that nothing can equal that most precious possession. Therefore, good deeds can never compensate fully for breaking one's vow. But to go into the matter more deeply, she explains that there are two parts to the vow, the act of promising and the things promised. The promise itself cannot be withdrawn, but the things promised, the deeds one pledges, can be replaced by other deeds; but when such a substitution is performed, it requires formal sanction through Church authority (the turning of the white key and the yellow). Furthermore, the deeds offered in compensation must be in a ratio to the original pledge of six to four.

A further distinction, according to Beatrice, must be drawn between the vow which is acceptable to God and one that is unacceptable, for the vow must be regarded as a compact between two parties. If a vow is unreasonable, God would reject it; hence, it should not be fulfilled. Jephthah the Israelite should have realized the fallacy of his pledge and retracted it rather than executing it. The same reasoning can be applied in the case of Agamemnon, who sacrificed his daughter Iphigenia because of his ill-considered vow.

Beatrice then exhorts all Christians to be cautious in the making of vows and urges obedience to both the Old and the New Testaments. Follow your Good Shepherd, she says, and avoid the tempter who may lead you astray like foolish sheep.

Suddenly the poet and his guide are transported to the second planetary sphere. The joy of Beatrice creates such radiance that she causes the sphere to glow more brightly, and Dante's delight is likewise responsive to her radiance. He sees crowding toward them more than a thousand bright souls, "a thousand splendors," and hears them say, "Behold one who will increase our loves." One of the leading spirits addresses Dante as someone granted exceptional grace to visit heaven while still alive and invites him to question them. Dante replies that he understands how they are concealed in their own brightness and that he detects their smiles by the added sparks from their eyes, but he cannot recognize them. He begs them to tell who they are and how they come to be associated with this sphere. The spirit to whom Dante spoke begins to glow more brightly than before as he prepares to address the poet.

Commentary

The explanation of Beatrice's brightness involves a spiritual law. Joy, which depends on love, increases with one's understanding or spiritual vision, and that increase in joy is expressed in added brightness. Beatrice has grown brighter because of her apprehension of Dante's growing insight into divine truth.

The discourse that follows concerning religious vows has been judged by some critics to be more thorough than the subject deserves.

The reason for Dante's giving it so much attention may be, as Grandgent has suggested, that the subject was of particular interest to the poet because, according to an old tradition, he at one time seriously considered entering the Franciscan order.

It is to be noted that Dante has seasoned the abstract discourse with concrete examples and literary allusions. To illustrate the distinction between the act of promising and the things promised, Beatrice introduces the comparison with the Hebrew sacrifices. The Hebrews were bound to perform the sacrifice, but the thing sacrificed could be changed. So with respect to Christian vows, the vow may not be retracted but the deeds promised may be substituted, though only under ecclesiastical dispensation. The reference to the authority of dispensations delegated to the Church is couched in the phrase "the turning of the white key and the yellow" (the silver and gold keys). The allusion is to the keys held by the angel guarding the gate to Purgatory *(Purg.* 9).

As examples of vows that ought not to have been binding because they were not accepted by God, Beatrice produces one biblical and one classical instance. Jephthah vowed that if God granted his army victory he would sacrifice the first living creature that came out to greet him upon his return home. When his daughter met him, he was painfully grieved but he considered his vow to be binding. Under somewhat similar circumstances, Agamemnon sacrificed his daughter Iphigenia to Artemis to obtain favoring winds to blow the Greek fleet to Troy.

In Beatrice's warning to mankind, "If you are tempted by greed to stray from the guidance of your Shepherd, . . ." the suggested interpretation is, "If you are tempted by fake pardoners to take your vows lightly because you can buy pardons for a fee, don't be led astray like silly sheep."

Dante again notes the phenomenon of the increasing of Beatrice's brightness and his own as they advance to the new region. The second sphere, that of Mercury, is not directly named in this passage, an instance of the type of intellectual game that Dante plays with his readers. Those who can will be pleased to supply the name themselves.

The spirits here appear simply as spots of light, no features or bodily forms being recognizable, and such is the case throughout the remaining regions of Paradise, with the exception of the Empyrean.

The first words spoken by the spirits, "Behold one who will increase our love," is an echo of the doctrine concerning spiritual possessions, which was expounded in *Purgatorio* 15, to the effect that the more souls there are loving God, the more His love is poured out to all.

The spirit, not yet identified, who first spoke to Dante, increases in splendor at the poet's address to him. And thus the canto ends on the theme with which it opened, the instance of a spirit gaining in brightness with increase of love – love that is derived from increased spiritual sight.

CANTO 6

Summary

The spirit addressing Dante identifies himself as Justinian, the sixth-century emperor. Justinian's greatest achievement, the codification of Roman law, was accomplished, he explains, only after he was freed from heresy by the pope and instructed in the dual nature (human and divine) of Christ. To enlighten Dante further, he reviews the high points in the history of the empire, basing his history on the movements of the Roman eagle as the symbol of the empire. He cites the westward voyage of Aeneas to establish the new Troy in Italy, the adventures of the Horatii, the defeat of Hannibal, the wars of Caesar and Pompey, Augustus as first emperor, Tiberius as third emperor in whose reign Christ was crucified, the vengeance under Titus against the Jews for the Crucifixion, and the defense of Rome by Charlemagne against the barbarian Lombards. Concluding his report of the past glories of the Roman eagle, Justinian points out the evil course of present factions within the empire tending toward the weakening or even tearing down of the eagle. The Guelfs under "the new Charles" are hoping to substitute the lilies of France for the eagle, and the Ghibellines wish to claim the eagle as the emblem of their faction exclusively.

To answer Dante's second question regarding the character of the spirits consigned to the sphere of Mercury, Justinian explains that these were virtuous persons who became so absorbed in gaining fame and honor that they neglected their devotion and service to God. He expresses their contentment with their degree of blessedness, which they recognize as fitting for their natures.

One of the spirits is identified by Justinian as Romèo, a man who rose from a humble station to the post of minister to the Count of Provence, Raymond Berengar. Romèo served his lord exceedingly well but was defamed by jealous courtiers and subsequently driven to a life of exile and privation in his old age.

Commentary

The chief purpose of Justinian's discourse is to expound upon the sanctity of the empire as a prominent feature of God's plan for human society. Justinian, as an emperor confirmed in the Christian faith, was not only well qualified to establish the great Roman code of secular law but also to assert the eternal role of the empire.

Justinian recognizes that the main facts of Roman history are familiar to Dante. Note how often he introduces an episode with "You know that. . . ." Similarly Dante, in composing the passage, assumes that his audience is also well versed in the history. The purpose of the discourse is to interpret the facts. For instance, Constantine, in transferring the capital from Rome to Constantinople, was turning the eagle backwards, in a direction contrary to that initially taken by Aeneas in moving from Troy to Italy. The significance of Rome as the capital of the empire is all-important in Dante's thinking.

Certain details in the historical sketch may require explanation for readers of our generation. In the opening lines of the canto, the man "who took Lavinia to wife" was Aeneas. The mention of three who fought against three refers to the duel of the Horatii, three brothers defending Rome, versus the Curiatii, three champions of Alba. The "hill beneath which you were born" is the hill just north of Florence on which Fiesole is situated. It was captured by the Romans when Cataline took refuge there. The Rhine, Seine, Rubicon, Spain, Pharsalia, and several other places are cited because of their association with the campaigns of Julius Caesar. The establishment of a (brief) period of world peace under Augustus is symbolized by the closing of the temple of Janus. The crucifixion of Christ, which occurred in the reign of Tiberius, is declared a noble act of vengeance. Then the subsequent destruction of Jerusalem under the Emperor Titus is described as a fitting vengeance against that vengeance. The apparent conflict or contradiction of terms introduced here is not explained until the following canto.

The historical survey of the "everlasting empire" prepares the reader for Dante's warning of present threats to the empire. While the Ghibellines are asserting their proprietary claim to the eagle for their emblem, the Guelfs are attempting to supplant the emblem of the eagle with the French fleur-de-lis. A leader of the movement, "the new

Charles," was Charles II of Apulia, a son of the famous Charles of Anjou *(Purg.* 20).

The souls in the Sphere of Mercury, Dante is informed, devoted their lives to honor and glory, aims which in themselves are laudable, but they allowed their ambitions to overshadow their devotion to the worship of their creator. The only individual introduced from this host of spirits, other than Justinian, is the politician Romèo, about whom a legend had been circulated which Dante accepted. As minister to Raymond Berengar, Romèo had succeeded in arranging marriages with kings for all of the count's four daughters. The circumstances of his undeserved dismissal and the miserable conditions of his exile obviously struck a sympathetic chord for Dante because of his own troubled life in exile.

CANTO 7

Summary

Justinian's spirit, singing praises to God, rejoins the other lights, who appear to be swiftly dancing sparks. Dante stands pondering over a question that Justinian's discourse has raised in his mind but left unanswered, and he yearns to ask Beatrice for an answer but hesitates because of his great reverence for her. She, knowing his unspoken thoughts, offers to expound the complex matter. He fails to understand how one act of vengeance that is just deserves punishment through another act of vengeance. In other words, if the Crucifixion was a just vengeance for Adam's sin, why was it just that Jerusalem should be destroyed in an act of vengeance? To understand the first vengeance, Beatrice declares, one must remember that through Adam's original sin all of his seed were condemned and all men suffered under that sentence until Christ came to earth assuming the nature of man, and so the punishment of Christ (as man) was justified to atone for Adam's sin inasmuch as it was an act against the human side of His nature. At the same time, however, His executioners were committing an act of sacrilege against the divine side of His nature; hence the vengeance which Titus worked against the Jews in destroying Jerusalem was due punishment for that sacrilege.

A second problem puzzling Dante which Beatrice anticipates and expounds is why God chose this particular mode of redemption for mankind. God in his bounty, Beatrice explains, creates objects and beings pure, free from all taint. Such purity was in man's soul when it was created, but its perfection was soiled by Adam's sin. The soul's redemption could only be achieved either through man's atoning or through divine mercy. Divine mercy was revealed when Christ offered Himself as a sacrifice, and atonement was performed through the crucifixion of Christ, the man.

One further aspect of those matters treated by Justinian requires the illumination of Beatrice. We detect in earthly objects the workings of corruption and the brief span of endurance. How can this be reconciled with what was said about the perfection of God's creations? Beatrice explains that what God Himself creates, such as angels and the heavenly bodies, is incorruptible; but earthly elements and objects formed from those elements are created by secondary powers—"informing powers" that reside in the stars. This rule of corruption, then, applies to plants and beasts; but man is of God's own creation, both body and soul, and therefore incorruptible. Remembering that God breathed life into human flesh in Adam and Eve confirms the incorruptibility of man's body as well as his soul, and in this we find justification for the doctrine of the resurrection of body and soul at Judgment Day.

Commentary

In the present canto, which concludes the account of the Sphere of Mercury, the author, through Beatrice, presents solutions to serious problems which arose as a result of the discourse of Justinian, spokesman for the spirits of the region. This passage revealing Dante's confusion and Beatrice's instruction follows the pattern of treatment established in the previous sphere and generally followed through the poem: first, a description of the new scene with its cluster of glowing spirits; then, an introduction of one of the spirits, who converses with the poet, discussing the nature of the sphere and the characters assembled there, and identifying one or more of the spirits of the group; finally, the conversation ended, a discussion with Beatrice to resolve questions left unanswered through the encounter. The questions, as we shall see, are sometimes concerned with astronomy or physics but more frequently with philosophy or theology. In this passage the answers offered by Beatrice are expressed in terms sufficiently clear—if somewhat scholastic in subtlety—so that they scarcely need repeating here.

The reader may find it strange that after listening to Justinian's historical treatise, the main purpose of which was the glorification of the empire, Dante's thoughts should be absorbed with problems centered on redemption. The explanation for this may be that all of the issues raised in the emperor's discourse were resolved except for the seeming paradox of the two vengeances, hence the detailed explanations revolving around that issue.

The role of Beatrice as all-knowing lecturer does her much credit and conforms to her allegorical representation of Divine Wisdom or Revelation, but it is not calculated to endear her to the reader in a personal way. To confirm her in the role of Dante's beloved, the poet introduces many striking passages praising her beauty and her tenderness toward him. One such passage occurs early in this canto:

> Beatrice suffered me to stand thus a little,
> And then, beaming on me with a smile
> Such as would make a man in the fire happy, . . .

CANTO 8

Summary

The planet in the third heavenly sphere, called the Sphere of Venus, was thought by the ancient pagans to be the propagator of love-madness, but in this belief they erred, Dante declares.

The poet, seeing Beatrice become more lovely, suddenly becomes aware of their arrival in a new sphere. He now perceives within the bright light of the planet separate lights like sparks or torches circling as in a dance. Those lights approach swiftly, singing *Hosanna* in such beautiful tones that Dante has longed ever since to hear that sound again.

One spirit, advancing before the rest, declares that all here are prepared to give Dante pleasure, as well as the angelic spirits of the sphere whom Dante addressed in one of his early poems, *"Voi ch' ntendendo il terzo ciel movete"* ("Ye who by intelligence move the Third Heaven"). Dante, much moved, asks the spirit who he is. The speaker replies that Dante loved him on earth and that, had his life not been cut short, much evil might have been avoided. Then without giving his name (Charles Martel), he identifies himself by saying that he had the rule of the Danube region below the German borders and that he should have become lord of the land on the left bank of the Rhone as well as ruler of southern Italy. His heirs would still be ruling in Sicily had it not been for a rebellion brought on by his family's ruthless government. Later, the excessive parsimony of his brother ruling in Naples and the greed of the Spanish troops that served him brought further disaster to the family.

Dante expresses great pleasure in recognizing a former beloved acquaintance and gratification in finding that his noble friend has attained Paradise. Then, pursuing the thought of how different Charles' miserly brother was from their liberal father, he asks Charles to explain why it is that sons do not always inherit the virtues of their parents.

Charles explains how God has ordained that power to exert influence over individual characters shall be vested in the celestial bodies, and that these influences, however differing from one another, are right and in accord with the universal scheme. If God's influence of the heavens were to be imperfect, subject to error, that would imply a possible fault in the Creator. Charles then points out that in a society there must be diversity of characters for the various trades and offices; hence one is born a judge, one a general, one a mechanic. The circling planets imprint characteristics on man's nature in such fashion that Esau differed from his twin brother, Jacob, and a noble son like Romulus was the product of a base father. These apparent irregularities in families are thus to be attributed to Providence (the stars). When it occurs that the dispositions of Providence are overturned by men, as when one born for the sword is made a leader of the Church or when one who is apt for the pulpit is crowned a king, then it is bad for society.

Commentary

The eighth and ninth cantos are devoted to encounters in the Sphere of Venus where Dante meets spirits assigned there because of their too great devotion to a love that was primarily earthly. Oddly enough, however, the eighth canto does not appear to be primarily concerned with the subject of love but rather with problems of heredity.

The opening lines reject the belief of the ancient pagans that the third planet (Venus) drove men into love-madness and degeneracy. The remainder of the canto is concerned more or less directly with the refutation of that belief. The reference to Venus as the planet that woos the sun sometimes from the front, sometimes behind, points to the fact that Venus is sometimes the morning star, sometimes the evening star.

The spirit that comes forward first to greet Dante is Charles Martel, son of Charles II of Apulia and grandson of Charles of Anjou, not to be confused with an earlier and more famous Charles Martel, the grandfather of Charlemagne. Dante's Martel was married to a daughter of the Emperor Rudolph I; his brother was Robert, King of Naples, whose misrule is referred to. The titles and family connections of Charles are all alluded to by indirect references which the poet assumes would be readily recognized by his contemporaries. The land of Provence is indicated as the region on the left bank of the Rhone River below its juncture with the Sorgue; Ausonia is the ancient name for southern Italy, the Kingdom of Naples and Apulia. The lands lying along the Danube below the boundaries of Germany refer to Hungary; Trinacria was the Roman designation for Sicily. Had it not been for the misrule of certain members of the Anjou dynasty, Sicily, Charles says, would still be ruled by the seed of Charles (of Anjou) and of Emperor Rudolph, the grandfather and the father-in-law respectively of Charles Martel. The rebellion in which the Sicilian populace cried "Death to the French" and overthrew the rule of the House of Anjou occurred in 1282 and has become known in history as the "Sicilian Vespers."

The friendly greeting accorded Dante by Charles Martel clearly implies a past acquaintanceship. Charles paid a formal state visit of several weeks to Florence in 1294, at which time Dante had attained a considerable reputation as the leader of a prominent group of poets. It is fair to assume that Dante presented some of his verses to the young king, quite possibly the very poem referred to here, which, coincidentally, speaks of the "Intelligences of the Third Heaven." The poem appeared later as the first canzone of the *Convivio*.

The remark about the miserliness of Robert which contrasted with his father's liberality leads into the discussion of differences of temperament often found within a family. Clearly children do not always inherit the traits of their parents, and brother can differ from brother. Differences in dispositions and aptitudes among men are necessary to the development of society, which needs persons of diverse talents for diverse occupations. The force which governs the assignment of various talents is Providence; that is, the power which exerts its influence through the stars at one's birth. The lengthy discussion of astronomical influences points toward what might be called predestination or determinism and suggests a contradiction of the doctrine of free will set forth in *Purgatorio*. The distinction that Dante would draw to admit the efficacy of both Providence and free will is that though a man's temperament is determined by the stars at birth, he is nevertheless endowed with free will to make choices and is therefore responsible for the disposition he makes of his talents and the control he exercises over his native weaknesses.

Providence endows individuals with diverse capabilities in order to give society generals, justices, artisans, and ministers. It is a calamity for society when a man suited for the cloth becomes a monarch or when a military type becomes pope.

CANTO 9

Summary

Dante, praising Clemence (possibly Charles Martel's wife, possibly his daughter), cites Charles' prediction of ill to befall his family but adds that those wrongs will be effectively chastised.

A second spirit approaches Dante and, like Charles, is happy to give him satisfaction. She identifies herself as Cunizza, who lived in the region between the Rialto and the headwaters of the Piave and the Brenta rivers. She confesses that her character was formed under the influence of Venus, but she declares that here she is not troubled by regrets for her amorous misdeeds. Pointing to another spirit beside her, she predicts that his fame will live for five hundred years; the reader is not informed of the spirit's identity until later.

Cunizza censures the viciousness that prevails among the people of her native district, Treviso, and she predicts future evils that will befall her neighbors. The "waters of Vicenza" will run red with the blood of Padua's soldiers; a cruel tyrant of the region will meet calamity; and a bishop of Feltro will betray a group of Ghibellines from Ferrara who will seek refuge under his protection.

With the departure of Cunizza, another glowing spirit approaches, the one that she had spoken of as a precious jewel whose fame would last through the centuries. Dante asks why the spirit delays answering the question in Dante's mind, since Dante knows that the spirit can read his thoughts. The spirit then gives his name as Folco (Folquet of Marseilles) and indicates his birthplace—in indirect phrasing—as lying on the Mediterranean coast between Spain and Italy. In his early years, he says, he burned with amorous desires, being under the stamp of Venus, as much as did Dido, Phyllis, or Hercules. Now, however, he reports, as did Cunizza, the memory of those wayward years causes him no remorse.

He points to a spirit whom he identifies as Rahab, a harlot of Jericho who was transported to heaven by Christ in the Harrowing of Hell. Her salvation was earned, despite her sinful life, because she aided Joshua in the capture of Jericho. Folco then denounces Florence because it is the source of "that cursed flower" (the florin) which has corrupted churchmen, causing them to devote themselves to profit, to the neglect of the true spirit of Christianity. Soon, however, he declares, Rome will be delivered from that vice.

Commentary

The identity of the lady named Clemence, addressed in the opening of the canto, is in some doubt. It could have been Charles Martel's wife or his daughter, both of that name. The wife was still living in 1300, the date of Dante's supposed journey through Paradise. She died in 1301. The daughter was Queen of France at the time he was writing the *Paradiso*.

The first spirit to converse with the poet in this canto is Cunizza da Romano, a sister of the notorious tyrant Ezzelino, who is referred to simply as "the fiery brand" (cf. *Inf.* 12). She acknowledges having been dominated by "this burning star"—Venus—for she was known for her amorous adventures in her early life. Later she won acclaim for her charities. Her speech dwells chiefly on the wicked inhabitants of her native province of Treviso and predicts numerous miseries to be visited on them in the near future. Treviso lies mainly to the north of Venice, which is here referred to as the Rialto, the chief island of the city. The battle she speaks of in which the blood of the Paduans will stain the river was one in which Can Grande della Scala defeated the Paduan Guelfs outside Vicenza in 1314. The unnamed tyrant whose downfall Cunizza predicts was a lord of Treviso, a city which stands at the juncture of the two rivers named, the Silë and the Cagnano. The final calamity that Cunizza predicts is the heinous betrayal of thirteen Ghibellines of Ferrara by the Bishop of Feltro. All of these events were accomplished facts when Dante was writing, but were naturally treated as predictions, since they were purported to have been spoken in 1300.

Dante next meets Folco (*Folquet* in French), the spirit whose enduring fame Cunizza predicted. He was a troubadour with a reputation for amorous exploits, but in his later years he entered a Cistercian monastery and eventually became a bishop. His reputation is now clouded because of the cruel role he played in the persecution of the Albigensian heretics, but in Dante's day his name was honored through numerous legends extolling his piety.

Folco's designation of his birthplace is given in a roundabout fashion. On the shores of the great valley flooded with water (the Mediterranean Sea) between the Ebro and the Magra (a river in Spain, a river in Italy) and opposite Bugia (a city on the African coast) is discovered to be Marseilles. This circuitous method of identification is a familiar feature of Dante's style, but in this instance there seems to be more than a testing of the reader's acuteness. One gets the impression that the speaker and his audience are looking down on the face of the earth from an exceedingly great height where large features appear greatly reduced.

Folco compares his former obsessive desires to the wantonness of several characters from pagan antiquity. Dido, the daughter of Belus, causes a double breach of fidelity by her passion for Aeneas—her unfaithfulness to her dead husband, Sichaëus, and Aeneas' unfaithfulness to his dead wife, Creusa. The maiden of Rhodope was Phyllis, who fell in love with Demophoön but was abandoned by him. Alcides (Hercules) met his death through his passion for Iole. Folco repeats Cunizza's assertion that there is no remorse for misconduct here. The souls in heaven are wholly absorbed in joy for their present state and in wonder at God's power and mercy.

To strengthen his point that the lowliest sinners may enjoy God's grace, Folco points to a radiant light who was known as Rahab the Harlot. The story of how she concealed Joshua's spies and thus aided in the taking of Jericho is related in 2 Joshua. The subtle remark about "the cursed flower" from Florence that has corrupted the clergy refers to the florin, the gold coin with the stamp of the Florentine lily that was standard currency throughout Europe. Pope Boniface VIII, Folco adds, has put aside his obligation to liberate the Holy Land, and his clergy are concerned only with the pursuit of profit. He predicts that Rome will soon be rid of the degenerate churchmen, a possible forecast of the removal of the papal seat from Rome to Avignon, which was accomplished in 1305.

CANTO 10

Summary

The reader is urged to contemplate the marvels of the universal plan, in which the various circlings of the sun and the planets provide for the changing of the seasons on earth, without which life could not survive. Furthermore, if the revolutions were greater or lesser, the effects on earth would be disastrous.

Dante suddenly becomes aware that he has now entered the Sphere of the Sun, "the greatest minister of nature," one of indescribable brightness. His mind is so filled with the love of God that it eclipses his feeling for Beatrice. Next, he and Beatrice find themselves surrounded by many individual lights forming a circle similar to the corona that sometimes encircles the moon. Three times the crown of lights circles about the voyagers as in a dance, singing a glorious melody. Then one voice from the group speaks out, offering to answer Dante's unspoken question about the identity of those jewels of light in the crown. He first names the one on his right, Albert of Cologne, then names himself, St. Thomas Aquinas, a Dominican friar. As he goes around the circle, he next names Gratian and Peter Lombard. Then he designates several figures by mentioning their achievements without giving their names; one spirit ranked above all others for his supreme wisdom; another expounded the nature of angels; a third proved that the world had not deteriorated since Christian times, a theory used by Augustine. Continuing around the circle, Aquinas then calls by name: Isidore of Seville, "the Venerable Bede," Richard of St. Victor, and Sigier of Brabant. The circle of spirits, like a clock with its twelve figures, again begins to wheel as they resume their singing in exquisite harmony.

Commentary

Dante and Beatrice have traversed the three spheres which constitute the lower division of Paradise, those which fall within the shadow of the earth, and correspondingly the nature of the spirits associated with those spheres partake of some earthly weakness or imperfection. Marking the transition from the lower to the higher division of Paradise, Dante opens the present canto with a tribute to the wonders of the universal plan. That the earth's polar axis is tilted and that the resultant angle between the equator and the ecliptic is precisely calculated to produce the cycle of the seasons are cited as evidence of the perfection of God. Whoever contemplates this scheme must have his mind lifted to renewed reverence for the Creator.

This new heaven is the Sphere of the Sun, the region of spirits distinguished for their wisdom. The location of the sun below Mars, Jupiter, and Saturn and the assignment of the great teachers and theologians to a position below warriors, rulers, and those devoted to contemplation is not the result of value judgments but rather the consequence of Dante's following the Ptolemaic scheme of the heavens, which placed the sun in the fourth sphere. Dante's enthusiasm for this virtue and for the figures represented in this sphere is indicated by the space allotted to the region and the eloquence of his treatment of the subject.

The first spokesman for the region is St. Thomas Aquinas, who was the chief authority for Dante's theological doctrines, as, in fact, he has been for Roman Catholicism up to the present.

Among the twelve jewels of light in the crown surrounding Dante and Beatrice, some are named, but others not named are identified in terms that would assure their recognition by informed readers of Dante's day. The one whose wisdom has never been equalled is Solomon. One described as the authority on the nature and classification of angels is Dionysius the Areopagite. The author whose work Augustine drew upon is Orosius. The trenchant writer who was martyred for "stripping the world's hypocrisies" is Boethius, author of *On the Consolation of Philosophy*.

Among those in the circle who were named by Aquinas were: Albert of Cologne, "Albertus Magnus," who was Aquinas' teacher; Gratian, whose *Decretum* did much to bring ecclesiastical laws and civil laws into conformity; Peter Lombard, who referred to his voluminous *Sententiae* as his "widow's mite." The Isidore mentioned is St. Isidore of Seville, a seventh-century author. The Venerable Bede is the well-known author of the *Ecclesiastical History of the English Nation*. Richard of St. Victor was the author of an important treatise on contemplation. Sigier of Brabant lectured in Paris in Aquinas' time. Aquinas' remark that Sigier "hammered home invidious truths" is paradoxical; Sigier and Aquinas were enemies at the University of Paris in the thirteenth century. Sigier taught truths according to logic; Aquinas, according to Church doctrine.

CANTO 11

Summary

In an introductory passage the poet reflects upon the vanity of men's pursuits on earth, one person devoting his energies to the law, one to medicine, one to the priesthood, others to power, wealth, or carnal pleasures. How trivial all those activities seem when compared to the state which Dante enjoys in heaven with Beatrice.

The crown of heavenly lights again stops its circling, and Aquinas again addresses Dante. He declares that Providence, to insure the perfect marriage of the Church with Christ, appointed two pious leaders —one a man of great heart, the other of keen mind. He then gives a laudatory account of the career of the first of these men, St. Francis of Assisi. He relates how Francis, in his youth, though born of a wealthy family, declared his devotion to a "Lady" (Poverty), the same lady beloved by Christ. Soon he attracted disciples to his cause—Bernard, Giles, and Sylvester, who adopted their leader's practice of going barefoot, dressed in coarse cloth, and girded with a humble cord. When the number of his followers multiplied, his rule and order received the sanction of Pope Innocent III and later confirmation from Honorius III. During the fifth crusade, Francis journeyed to Egypt, where he boldly preached Christianity to the Sultan. His great sanctity was marked by his receiving the stigmata. At his death he left with his followers the injunction to remain faithful to Lady Poverty.

Continuing his discourse, St. Thomas observes that the second of the great leaders, St. Dominic, also offered admirable instructions to his followers, but, sad to tell, many have become obsessed by greed, and now few of the members of his order remain faithful to his rules of life.

Commentary

The present canto and the one following are devoted to two of the greatest medieval religious leaders, St. Francis of Assisi and St. Dominic, and to the orders of friars that they founded. Both orders were founded early in the thirteenth century. As the geniuses of the leaders differed, so did the aims of the two orders differ. The Franciscans were dedicated primarily to poverty and humble, selfless service to the weak and unfortunate; the Dominicans were devoted chiefly to learning. A century after the founding of those orders, Dante notes that many of their members neglect to follow the principles of their leaders and have become lazy or corrupt (a judgment which, incidentally, was strongly seconded by Chaucer in *The Canterbury Tales*). Furthermore, bitter rivalry and animosity had developed between the Franciscans and the Dominicans in Dante's time.

In heaven we find the chief representatives of these orders fraternizing and praising one another. To honor the name of St. Francis, Dante chooses St. Thomas Aquinas, a Dominican; and, later, the life of St. Dominic is related by a distinguished Franciscan, St. Bonaventura.

In the account of the career of St. Francis, Dante, through Aquinas, indicates his birthplace by first naming rivers and towns in the vicinity of Assisi, and in the same fashion he withholds the name of the saint until he is well into the account. Assisi is perched on a hill between two rivers, the Tupino and the Chiascio (where St. Ubaldo had his hermitage), and lies to the north of Perugia. There is a play on the word *Ascesi,* which was the old Tuscan form of Assisi, but which also means "I have risen" and is here referring to the sun and daybreak.

Of the numerous rules of conduct set down by St. Francis for his disciples, Dante emphasizes one, the dedication to a life of poverty, a feature of the life of Francis which invited comparison with the life of Christ, and a guiding principle that Dante believed to be a keystone for the restoration of true Christianity. Similarly Dante selected from the many accounts of miracles in the life of the saint only one to recite, the receiving of the stigmata, which further emphasizes the resemblance of St. Francis to Christ.

The censure of those followers of St. Dominic who have neglected his rule of life is pronounced, it should be noted, by a Dominican.

CANTO 12

Summary

As the circle of lights again starts its wheeling dance, a second circle approaches and surrounds the first, moving in unison and singing in rapturous harmony with it. A voice from one of the lights in the new circle addresses Dante, saying that it is impelled to extol the greatness of St. Dominic, since he and St. Francis strove together in a common cause. When Christians had strayed from the path, Christ appointed those two men as champions to succor His bride and lead the stragglers back to the true path.

In a land to the west, beyond which the sun sets for all men, in Calahorra, which is under the ensign of two lions, was born this champion of the faith. His mother had a prophetic dream of his greatness before his birth, and his godmother was also visited by a favoring dream before his baptism. He was named Dominic, "of the Lord." In his infancy he was often found by his nurse awake upon the ground, looking as if he would say, "For this end am I come." It was no accident that his father was named Felix (happy) and his mother Giovanna (the grace of God). As Christ's minister he held to the Master's chief counsels. Early he became renowned as a brilliant teacher, and he traveled widely preaching his message. When he appealed to papal authority, it was not for personal profit or advancement but for sanction to combat the doctrines of the heretics; and he struck his best blows where resistance was most stubborn. In his long career he did much to cultivate the "Catholic garden," the fruits of which have prospered ever since.

The speaker next reverts to St. Francis, the comrade with St. Dominic in the struggle to restore the true Christian life. He complains that now many of the followers of Francis have turned from the path of their leader, either neglecting or twisting the interpretation of the rules. There are still a few who are faithful, but leaders of contending factions, one from Casale and one from Acquasparta, are causing a grevious division in the ranks of the order.

The speaker now announces that he is Bonaventura (a Franciscan). He names the spirits in the second circle of shining lights. The first two, Illuminato and Austen (Agostino), were among the early converts of St. Francis. Others named around the circle are: Hugh of St. Victor, Peter Mangiadore, Peter of Spain, Nathan the Prophet, St. John Chrysostom, St. Anselm, Donatus, Rabanus, and Joachim the Calabrian abbot.

Bonaventura repeats that his eulogy for St. Dominic is a response to the generous praise accorded St. Francis by Aquinas.

Commentary

The appearance of the second circle of spirits, its conformity to the motion of the first circle, and the harmonious choiring of the two are symbolic of the harmony that reigns among the various religious orders in heaven.

St. Bonaventura, who acts as spokesman for the newly arrived spirits, was appointed General of the Franciscan Order and was the author of a work on the life of St. Francis. His account of St. Dominic's career obviously counterpoints that of St. Francis, reported by Aquinas. That Dominic was ordained by heaven for his great mission was revealed by his mother's vision before his birth. It is reported that she dreamed she gave birth to a dog with a flaming torch in its mouth. The godmother's dream was of a baby with a bright star shining in his forehead.

Dominic's birthplace is revealed through references to a western land (Spain), the city of Callaroga (or Calahorra) in old Castile, which is indicated by the reference to its coat of arms: a shield quartered with two lions and two castles, one lion above a castle and one beneath the other castle. The saint's religious aims are contrasted with the worldly goals of "him of Ostia" and Thaddeus. The former, Enrico of Susa, was typical of the scholars devoted to studying the *Decretals* (canon law); the latter, a physician bent on serving for profit. Dominic did not apply for permission to withhold part of the money due for charity ("for leave to dispense two or three for six"), as many clergy did; nor did he seek benefices. His one request was for permission to combat heresy. The remark "where opposition was most stubborn" appears to be a reference to his mission in Provence preaching against the Albigensian heresy. Bonaventura's concluding observation that from the saint sprang "streams that watered the garden of the Church" is more than justified by the great services of the Dominicans in educational and intellectual fields.

The bitter commentary delivered by Bonaventura on the quarreling factions within the Franciscan order matches the complaint of Aquinas over the defection of his fellow Dominicans. The citation of the schools of Casale and Acquasparta has reference to factions within the Franciscan order known as "the Spiritualists," led by Ubertino of Casale, and "the Conventuals," headed by Matteo of Acquasparta, who advocated relaxing the old rules.

The lights of the second ring, who are named by Bonaventura, are as follows: Illuminato and Agostino, early converts to the teachings of St. Francis; Hugh of St. Victor, a famous theologian of Paris; Peter Mangiadore of Troyes and later of St. Victor in Paris; Peter of Spain, who became Pope John XXI; Nathan, the Old Testament character who rebuked David (II Samuel, 12); St. Chrysostom, who was made patriarch of Constantinople; St. Anselm, an archbishop of Canterbury; Donatus, a famous Roman grammarian; Rabanus, an archbishop of Mayence and a prominent theologian; and Joachim of Flora, an abbot of Calabria who propounded the theory of the coming dispensation of the Holy Ghost.

CANTO 13

Summary

In attempting to convey an impression of the brilliance of those spinning circles of light, Dante tells the reader to imagine twenty-four of the brightest stars he knows—including the Great and Little Dippers

—and imagine them arranged as a double crown; then realize that that image would be exceeded greatly by the lights that surround him and Beatrice. The circles are wheeling in opposite directions in their dance, and all the while they sing of the glory of the Trinity and Christ's dual nature (human and divine).

St. Thomas Aquinas speaks again, offering to resolve one of the problems in Dante's mind concerning the superior wisdom of Solomon. How can it be that Solomon has had no equal for wisdom? Dante believes that both Adam and Christ were endowed with perfect wisdom, hence would be placed above Solomon. The complex explanation involves a restatement of the differences between those beings created directly by God and those created by God's ministers, "the nine contingencies (or subsistences)." The former, God's original creations, include the angels and also Adam and Christ (in His human aspect); they are naturally exempted from the comparison with Solomon. When God asked Solomon what gift he desired, Solomon asked for wisdom to rule well; consequently, Solomon's wisdom is the subject of comparison with the wisdom of other earthly rulers.

Aquinas concludes his discourse with an admonition against making uninformed judgments and coming to hasty conclusions. To illustrate such errors, he cites certain misguided philosophers, Parmenides, etc., and heretical teachers, such as Arius and Sabellius.

Commentary

The discourse resumed at this point by Aquinas is concerned with a remark that he made earlier which puzzled Dante—namely, that Solomon's wisdom was never equalled by another human being. The explanation given involves a distinction between those beings created by God and those created by His agents, the basis for exempting Christ and Adam from comparison with other men. This discussion relates to the theory regarding the cause of imperfections and individual differences among men that was propounded by Charles Martel in the Sphere of Venus (Canto 8).

The basis for the high regard for Solomon's wisdom is the biblical passage relating a dream of Solomon in which the Lord appeared to him and asked what gift he would choose. Solomon's answer was: ". . . an understanding heart to judge Thy people, that I may discern between good and bad. . . ." The Lord was pleased with his choice and replied: ". . . I have given thee a wise and understanding heart; so that there was none like thee before thee, neither after thee shall any arise like unto thee" (I Kings, 3).

In his parting words of counsel to Dante, Aquinas cautions him against making hasty conclusions or building up systems upon misinformation or insufficient evidence. Among those cited for faulty judgment are early philosophers who were criticized by Aristotle—Parmenides, Melissus, and Bryson—and promoters of heretical doctrines—Sabellius and Arius. This speech of admonition (112-142), though neither profound nor original, is surely appropriate to the Sphere of the Sun. Furthermore, it is elevated by the introduction of several striking figurative passages.

CANTO 14

Summary

Beatrice speaks to the angelic spirits asking for a clarification of one more problem in Dante's mind. The question is whether or not the souls will retain their present brilliance after the Resurrection, when the bodies will be joined to their souls; and if such brightness will remain, how the eyes will endure it? The spirits join in singing a hymn to the Trinity three times, and then a voice from one of the spirits in the inner circle (Solomon) offers an explanation. The souls will indeed retain their brilliance, which is an outward expression of their ardor. The eyes, and all the organs of the body, will grow in strength to endure that excessive brightness. The final reunion of body and soul is destined to restore the individual's completeness in the final stage of everlasting glory.

A third ring of lights appears and takes its place surrounding the other circles, and it intensifies in brightness until Dante has to lower his gaze. Beatrice restores Dante's confidence with a smile, and when he lifts his glance he discovers that they have entered a new sphere, the Sphere of Mars. He expresses the intense joy he feels in the presence of the ruddy planet by offering a silent prayer to God. Within the new sphere he perceives two enormous beams of light which intersect to form a cross, the symbol for Christ. Within those beams flash many smaller lights, the spirits of this sphere, moving to and fro in the intricate patterns of a dance; as they dance, they sing a marvelous hymn which ravishes Dante's soul although he does not fully comprehend its meaning. He declares that the sweetness of that encounter—the sight of the dancing lights and the beauty of their song—surpassed any pleasure he had yet known. Then, not to detract from the thrilling presence of Beatrice, he explains that he had not yet turned his glance to her since they arrived in this sphere.

Commentary

The problem under discussion here has to do with the doctrine that our bodies will be joined to our souls at the Judgment Day, which was a commonly accepted belief. The argument runs that man was created with a body and a soul and that he will attain perfection in heaven only when body and soul are joined to restore the completeness of the individual. Dante does not question the belief in that reunion, but he wonders how the human body, with its limited sensibilities, will be capable of enduring the brilliant radiance which the souls have acquired in their present heavenly state. Solomon's answer is, of course, that the sensory organs will develop to the point of tolerating the intensified sensations. At the conclusion of Solomon's speech, the spirits all cry "Amen," showing that they look forward with pleasure to the recovery of their bodies.

The appearance of the third circle of lights is treated with surprising brevity. No names are mentioned and no special significance is hinted at in the passage. The best explanation for the introduction of this third, outer circle is that it completes the symbol of the Trinity and that it foreshadows the scene at the climax of Paradise where the vision of God is represented in three circles of dazzling brilliance.

The Sphere of Mars, into which Dante is now transported, is characterized first by its reddish cast of light, for this is known to astronomers as the red planet. His expression of thanks to God, "a burnt offering in the language common to all," means simply a silent prayer. The sign of this sphere is a cross, a familiar symbol for Christ and also for the crusaders who populate the sphere, soldiers of the cross. The great beams forming the cross are likened to the Milky Way. Here the dance of the spirits and the harmony of their singing are more glorious than any sights and sounds Dante has yet encountered; for, as he explains, each higher stage of heaven intensifies the beauty and brilliance of its spirits. Correspondingly, Beatrice appears more luminous at each advancing state of the journey and inspires in Dante a more thrilling joy.

CANTO 15

Summary

The music stops, as if by command, and a light from the right arm of the cross descends to its foot, blazing like a shooting star. The spirit in the light welcomes Dante to the sphere, calling him one "of my own blood" and praising him for the gift of grace that has permitted him to journey through Paradise while still alive. After speaking for a time of things too profound for Dante's comprehension, he tells Dante that he has been eagerly awaiting his coming, of which he read in the Book of Fate. He urges Dante to utter the questions that are in his mind, for even though the spirits can read those unexpressed thoughts, it will be pleasing for him to hear them voiced by Dante. In Dante's response, he apologizes for not being capable of expressing adequately in words his gratitude for the paternal greeting of the spirit, and he humbly asks the spirit's name. The spirit answers that his son was Dante's great-grandfather, the ancestor from whom Dante's family derived its name.

Florence, the spirit tells Dante, was in his lifetime a city of peace, sobriety, and modesty. She shunned the use of showy adornments; she had no ostentatious mansions and her customs did not admit lascivious indulgences. She had not come to the point of surpassing Rome in splendor. Men went in plain dress and women did not paint their faces but attended to their household duties faithfully. He tells how fortunate he was to be born at such a time in such a city. In the city's ancient baptistry, he was christened Cacciaguida. His wife, who came from the valley of the Po, brought the surname of Alighiero into the family. Cacciaguida joined the Emperor Conrad III on a crusade and was knighted by him for good service. He died in battle against the Saracens and was thus martyred and transported to "this peace."

Commentary

The crusader who first addresses Dante in the Sphere of Mars is introduced with considerable fanfare. Evidently the poet wishes to make his entrance impressive. He is Cacciaguida, Dante's great-great-grandfather. His first words, spoken in Latin, claim a blood relationship and express his delight at Dante's arrival and his admiration for the special grace bestowed on the poet. Altogether his reception of Dante is exceedingly cordial, and Dante's reply is humble and grateful.

Cacciaguida says that his son, Alighiero, the family namesake, has been on the Terrace of Pride in Purgatory for a hundred years and that

Dante would do well to offer prayers for some remission of his further penalty.

Cacciaguida then delivers a lengthy eulogy to the Florence of the twelfth century, when the citizens lived simple, virtuous lives. Corruption and excesses of luxury had not become prevalent. The portrait he draws of that earlier way of life is similar to accounts of life among the Romans in the early days of the Republic or of life in colonial America. It is obviously intended to serve as a contrast to what Florence had become in Dante's time.

CANTO 16

Summary

Dante observes that it is not surprising if men on earth pride themselves on nobility of birth, because even in heaven he was infected with that same kind of pride as he talked with his noble ancestor. He now recognizes that nobility of blood is something that quickly diminishes unless it is constantly renewed and strengthened.

He humbly begs Cacciaguida to tell him when he lived, who his ancestors were, and what worthy families were in Florence in his time. The elder indicates the date of his birth by saying that this planet (Mars) had made 553 revolutions since the Annunciation of Christ's birth, which tells us that he was born about 1100 A.D. He designates the neighborhood where his family lived but prefers not to give further information about his forebears. The population of Florence then, he says, was only one-fifth of its present population, not having yet been swollen by inroads from surrounding villages and farms. Had it not been for the conspiring of the Church against the Empire, Florence would not have become involved in capturing towns in Tuscany, victories which flooded Florence with refugees.

Since cities rise and fall, says Cacciaguida, it should be no matter for surprise that families follow the same pattern, even as the tides ebb and flow. He then recites a long list of families that were prominent in his day but have lost their distinction by Dante's time, noting in certain instances the causes for dissension among feuding families or parties.

Commentary

Dante's philosophical observations regarding the fallacy of taking pride in the nobility of blood repeats a sentiment that he expressed on earlier occasions (the third *canzone* of *Convivo* and in *Purg.* 11). By addressing Cacciaguida with the plural form *voi*, a mark of dignified formality, Dante gives Beatrice a clue to his feelings about his distinguished ancestry, at which she shows him by her smile her awareness of his weakness.

In response to Dante's questioning, Cacciaguida continues his account of Florence as he knew it two centuries earlier. The way he indicates the date of his birth has led to a variety of interpretations. In the first place, there is a difference in the reading of manuscripts and early texts, some using the figure 553 (550 and 3), some using 580 (550 and 30). Then, too, there is the debate over whether the time for the circuit of Mars' orbit should be computed roughly as two years or more precisely as 687 days. Different commentators have dated his birth between 1090 and 1106.

Since Cacciaguida's day the city's population has increased, but the character of its citizens has degenerated through the influx of country folk and people from the outlying villages that have come under Florentine domination. Much of the trouble has stemmed from the interference of the Church ("the people most degenerate in all the world") against the authority of the Empire (Caesar). He cites the names of numerous leading families of his time that are now of slight consequence, most of them names carrying no meaning or interest for modern readers but surely holding more interest for Dante's contemporaries. Among the families mentioned that have risen to prominence since those early days, a few deserve special notice because they move in and out of the scenes in Florentine history. The Buondelmonti and the Amidei developed a bitter feud over a jilted bride that led to the Guelf-Ghibelline split among the Florentines. The Cerchi tribe, immigrants from Pistoia, became leaders of the Whites in a second intra-city feud.

CANTO 17

Summary

Encouraged by Beatrice, Dante asks his ancestor to tell him what the misfortunes are that have been intimated to him by several of the spirits he has talked to on his journey. Cacciaguida first explains that events of the future are seen in the mind of God, as in a mirror, but do not interfere with man's free will. He then proceeds to relate the imminent exile of Dante from Florence, the outcome of a plot involving the pope. He forecasts the privations, humiliation, and isolation in store for the poet in his wandering among strangers, and how, after becoming disappointed with his fellow exiles, he will break with them and take his own way, literally and figuratively.

Dante's first true refuge, Cacciaguida tells him, will be with a Lombard (Bartolommeo della Scala, of Verona) whose family crest shows an eagle above a ladder. Della Scala will receive him with honor and anticipate his needs and desires. At della Scala's court Dante will meet a youth of exceeding promise whose later deeds will win him great renown (Can Grande della Scala). What great deeds he will perform are related to Dante but he is instructed not to report them in advance.

As Cacciaguida concludes his moving forecast of Dante's future calamities, he promises that the poet will live to witness the avenging of the perfidies of those Florentines who will sentence him.

Dante believes the warning he has received will aid him in facing the approaching trials. He then asks pointedly if it will be wise for him to reveal all that he has learned on his journey when he returns to earth, considering how many persons would be embittered by things he could tell. He recognizes that, on the other hand, by timidly withholding the truth he will lose credit with future generations ("those who will call these times ancient"). Cacciaguida urges him to "make his whole vision manifest," no matter who is displeased by it: "Let them scratch where it itches." If Dante's words at first seem harsh, Cacciaguida says, they will nevertheless provide good nourishment for those who will digest them; it was for this that Dante was conducted through these regions, where he was shown chiefly persons of renown in order that his hearers might be more impressed by what he has to report than they would be with accounts of humble individuals.

Commentary

It has been made clear earlier in the narrative that the spirits of the dead can foretell future events, a fact which might lead us to suppose that all our actions are foreordained. Cacciaguida denies this supposition categorically, stating that God's foreknowledge does not rule our acts.

Since Dante has heard indefinite prophecies of misfortunes that are in store for him, he urges his great ancestor to tell him more precisely what he may expect so that he can prepare himself for those misfortunes. The prophecy given by Cacciaguida of Dante's exile and the resulting misery and degradation was written, as we know, after Dante had experienced twelve or fifteen years of wandering in exile. Though written in simple, quiet language, it is one of the most moving and memorable passages in the *Comedy*. Dante's relationship with the Whites who were exiled at the same time is indicated only briefly. Contemporary records confirm the fact that he joined with other Florentine outcasts for a time, but they give us no certain explanation for his break with them. Certainly, by deciding to go his own way he could maintain his integrity, but at the same time he increased the loneliness of his wanderings.

In identifying the della Scala family, Dante paid grateful tribute to one of his best patrons. There is more in his relations with them than appreciation for shelter and kindness; there is also the link with his lifelong hope for the restoration of imperial rule in Italy, which was centered in part on Henry VII and in part on Can Grande della Scala (cf. notes to *Inf.* 1 and *Purg.* 33), the member of the family referred to by Cacciaguida as a youth who was destined to perform great deeds.

One last point on which Dante wishes to consult his honored ancestor is the question of whether or not he ought to relate everything he has seen and heard on his journey when he returns to his earthly life. He faces the choice of stirring up great bitterness among certain of his contemporaries or losing the respect of posterity. In that speech he reveals his hopes that "his fame will live on through his book." The sentiment is similar to that expressed by Brunetto Latini (*Inf.* 15). Cacciaguida's reply amounts to a command to Dante to reveal all his experiences for the profit of those who will hear and digest them. It is to be noted that the word "vision" is here used to refer to Dante's journey.

CANTO 18

Summary

While Cacciaguida appears to be absorbed with his own reflections, Dante looks toward Beatrice and finds in her eyes such a shining expression of love that he doubts his power to describe it. His gaze is soon interrupted, however, by Beatrice, who notices Cacciaguida's changed expression and directs Dante's attention back to him.

Cacciaguida declares that it would not be proper for Dante to leave the Sphere of Mars without being shown some of the great soldiers who shine in the cross. He names Joshua, Judas Maccabaeus, Charlemagne, Roland, William of Orange, Renouard, Godfrey of Bouillon, and Robert Guiscard; and as each hero is named, his light gleams with added brightness and stirs with additional motion.

Turning his gaze again to Beatrice, Dante observes her features becoming ever brighter; whereupon he realizes that they have been transported into a new sphere. The light around them is white, in contrast to the reddish cast in Mars, a sign to Dante that they have arrived at the "temperate star," Jupiter.

The lights of the souls here, soaring and wheeling like a great flock of birds, change their formations to spell the letters of a message: first *D*, then *I*, then *L*, and so on. The full message reads DILIGITE IUSTITIAM QUI IUDICATIS TERRAM ("love justice, ye that judge the earth"). At the end of the message the *M* remains. Soon new lights come to rest above it, and the figure of the *M* is transformed, first to the emblem of the lily, and then finally to complete the figure of an eagle.

In an apostrophe to the planet, Dante declares how he came to understand that justice on earth is the reflection of heavenly justice. He then inveighs against the papacy, which ought to be the seat of earthly justice but which instead has come to be the mercenary perverter of justice through abuses of excommunication. He concludes with a warning to the reigning pope, who has replaced the ideals of Peter and Paul with the image of John the Baptist (imprinted on the florin) as the object of his devotion.

Commentary

Dante's recording of his apprehension of Beatrice's increasing beauty and of his mounting joy in her company is one of the most effective devices he employs to register the ascending scale of the glories he is witnessing and the soaring of his feelings.

Several of the great warriors who are pointed out to Dante are well known to every reader—Joshua, Charlemagne, and Roland—but others are less universally recognized. Judas Maccabaeus was a general who led the Jewish army against Syria in the second century B.C. His deeds are recorded in the Vulgate Bible. William of Orange—not to be confused with later figures in the history of the Netherlands and England—was a ninth-century French hero who fought against the Saracens in southern France. Rainouart was a converted Saracen who fought with

William. Godfrey of Bouillon was commander-in-chief of the First Crusade. Robert Guiscard was the leader who established Norman rule in Sicily and Southern Italy in the eleventh century by defeating the Saracens there.

Upon arrival in the sixth heavenly sphere, Jupiter, Dante is greeted with a new series of figured formations that spell out, letter by letter, a scriptural message. The literal English translation is "Love justice, ye who judge the earth."

Before completing the description of the emblem formed by the lights of Jupiter, the poet invokes one of the muses for aid in setting forth worthily what he saw there. He does not name the muse but he uses the term "Pegasean divinity," suggesting Pegasus, the winged horse associated with the muses. It is generally assumed that he was invoking Calliope, the Greek muse of epic poetry.

The step-by-step transformation of the final *M* into an eagle introduces a series of symbolic renderings. *M* signifies monarchy. The eagle was the emblem of Rome and, consequently, stands for imperial unity and dominion. The figure of the lily, an intermediate stage in the transformation of the *M* into the eagle, is presumably the emblem of Florence and its ruling Guelf party, the suggestion being that the Guelfs must eventually yield to the ideal of a unified empire.

The invectives pronounced against the papacy may be taken, in general, as directed against several of the recent popes. It is their "smoke" that has dimmed the beams of Jupiter through their "buying and selling in the temple." The attack, however, becomes more directly personal with the charge of withholding the bread of mercy—a reference to the abuse of recommunications. The particular object of this attack was Pope John XXII, who was accused of excommunicating numbers of people in order to collect heavy fees for their reinstatement. Here Dante has left the pretense that he is speaking in 1300 about affairs as they stood at that time. John XXII's papacy lasted from 1316 until 1334, the period in which this passage was composed.

The allusion to Peter and Paul, with their examples of miracles and martyrdom, are clear enough, but in the suggestion that the incumbent pope is more devoted to John the Baptist lies the implication that he is greedy for money. Here, as on several other occasions, the poet has let the figure of the Baptist symbolize the love of money because of his image on the florin.

CANTO 19

Summary

The many spirits making up the great emblem of the eagle, each one shining like a brilliant ruby, address Dante, all speaking in unison and using the pronouns "I" and "my" as if one spirit spoke, the voice of justice. It first declares that it has left a name on earth for justice and piety. Then Dante begs for some clarification of the mysteries of divine justice, which he could never learn on earth. The eagle responds by saying that creation is of such infinite complexity that not even the highest of the created beings, the archangel Lucifer, could comprehend it. It follows that the lesser beings cannot hope to comprehend even the finite portion of creation that concerns them. Man's understanding can no more read the riddles of the universe than can his vision penetrate the depths of the ocean.

The eagle detects a question distressing Dante; that is, where is the justice of condemning a native of India who has never heard of Christ and who is therefore denied a place in Paradise, even though he has led a blameless life? The answer is that for such inscrutable questions man's only recourse is to accept the authority of the Scriptures.

In further speech the eagle declares that on Judgment Day those who did not know Christ may be closer to Him than some who proclaim themselves Christians but commit heinous sins. It then denounces numerous sovereigns whose crimes will bring them to damnation when the recording angel reads the records of their acts.

Commentary

Each spirit in the emblem shines with its own light, and yet all speak in unison as a demonstration of the unity of justice. The voice of the eagle declares that man cannot expect to grasp the complex scope of the plan of the Creator, hence can little fathom the workings of divine justice. He therefore must put his faith in the word of the Bible. Dante is, nevertheless, consumed with desire to understand why virtuous heathens must be denied the blessings awarded to good Christians. This is an echo of the concern he expressed upon meeting the noble spirits of antiquity in Limbo *(Inf.* 4). The eagle responds, like the Voice out of the Whirlwind addressing Job, with a question: "Who are you to judge such a case, you who are so limited in view?" One does best to trust in authority and, above all, remember that whatever is good comes from God and that nothing that comes from God can be evil.

The voice of the eagle further explains that virtuous heathens will be closer to Christ on Judgment Day than many professed Christians. By way of examples, it names contemporary or near contemporary rulers and potentates, all of whom were guilty of crimes unworthy of their noble stations. The Emperor Albert of Austria is blamed for his invasion of Prague's kingdom (Bohemia); Philip IV, "the Fair," who was killed by a wild boar, is blamed for his corruption of French currency; Edward I of England and the Scottish Wallace, for their border feuds; Ferdinand IV of Castile and Wenceslas IV of Bohemia for their vicious lives; and Charles II of Naples, the titular King of Jerusalem, who neglected his responsibility to lead a crusade and restore the Holy City to Christian rule. His good deeds are marked with *1*, his errant deeds with *M*, the Roman numeral for 1,000. Other renegade rulers mentioned nearly complete the list of living sovereigns: Frederick II of Sicily; his uncle, King of the Balearic Islands; and Frederick's brother, King of Aragon; Dionysius of Portugal; Haakon of Norway; Stephen of Rascia, who counterfeited Venetian coins; and Henry II of Lusignano, who kept the French reign over Cyprus (Nicosia and Famagusta, cities on Cyprus).

CANTO 20

Summary

After an interval of exquisite song, the eagle resumes its discourse with Dante, pointing out that the noblest of the souls in that emblem form its eye. At the very center, the pupil of the eye, stands David, the author of the Psalms and the king who brought the Ark of the Covenant back to Jerusalem. Above the pupil are five other lights forming the eyebrow, identified as the Emperor Trajan; Hezekiah, a King of the Jews; the Emperor Constantine; William II of Sicily; and Ripheus, a Trojan hero.

Dante is so surprised at learning that certain of these personages are included in this honored company that he blurts out a question: "How can this be?" The eagle recognizes that Dante's confusion concerns two of the figures who he supposed were pagans, Trajan and Ripheus. Trajan, the eagle explains, was brought back to life from Limbo through the intercession of St. Gregory's prayers so that he might be converted to the faith and die a second time a Christian. The case of Ripheus is perhaps even stranger. He was granted the foreknowledge of Christ's coming to earth and suffering for mankind; and, believing, he was baptized through the ministrations of those three ladies of the three Christian virtues, faith, hope, and love.

The eagle concludes its discourse with an admonition to mortals to refrain from hasty judgments, considering that not even the souls in heaven know what souls are among the elect. At the conclusion of the meeting, the two souls in question, Trajan and Ripheus, intensify in brightness as a sign of their pleasure.

Commentary

As a counterpart to the list of reprobate monarchs given in the preceding canto, Dante now offers a list of some of the noblest spirits among the lights of Jupiter. The identifications of these personages given by the eagle are indirect in most instances, only two of them being called by name. The "singer of the Holy Ghost" who brought the Ark from house to house is, of course, King David. The ruler who consoled the poor widow for her son is Trajan, the emperor whose act of humility was depicted in *Purgatorio* among the "goads" on the Terrace of Pride *(Purg.* 10). Though Trajan lived after the time of Christ, he was not a Christian during his natural lifetime; but, according to a legend, he was later redeemed, having been granted a special dispensation through the prayers of St. Gregory (Pope Gregory I, known familiarly as Gregory the Great).

The next to be mentioned, the Hebrew king who, through his own prayers, was allowed to delay his death long enough to rectify his way of life, is Hezekiah. The incident is related in II Kings, 20. The ruler who "became a Greek," that is, who transferred the capital of the empire to Constantinople, was Constantine. His well-intentioned action resulted in evil consequences but Dante condones the "high purpose" of the act, regardless of its consequences.

The only contemporary figure included in this distinguished group is William II, "the Good," of Naples and Sicily, a twelfth-century ruler in that land which now, the Eagle says, mourns under the tyranny of Charles, "the King of Jerusalem," and Frederick II of Sicily, two of those evil modern sovereigns cited in the preceding canto.

The last of those named in this special group, and one who caused Dante's special perplexity, is Ripheus the Trojan, a character who is briefly mentioned in the *Aeneid* as one who loved justice. By representing this ancient pagan as one of the blessed spirits in heaven, Dante is declaring his stand on the much debated question of whether or not baptism is an absolute requirement for attaining paradise. At the same time, he is also illuminating the question of divine justice raised in the preceding canto regarding the chance for salvation of an Indian on the banks of the Ganges who has led a blameless life but who has never heard of Christ.

This canto contains a curious passage of formal rhetorical construction similar to the passage in *Purgatorio* 12 with its repetition of initial words at regular intervals. In the present canto, the six notables are presented in a series of double tercets or six-line passages; and in each instance the second tercet begins with the words "*Ora conosce . . .*" ("Now he knows"). The repeated phrase serves to point up the structural pattern, but it also effectively emphasizes the state of blessedness which is the reward of these virtuous rulers.

CANTO 21

Summary

The scene opens with yet another ecstatic expression of the glory of Beatrice's beauty, a signal that the two have arrived at a new sphere. Beatrice instructs Dante to turn his gaze to this new region which is ruled by Saturn, the god who, according to pagan mythology, reigned over the world in the Golden Age. There Dante discovers a golden ladder mounting upward out of sight; on the ladder, the bright lights of spirits are seen ascending and descending.

When one of the spirits draws near, Dante, encouraged by Beatrice, asks why he has come down the ladder to approach the visitors and also why it is that there is no singing here as there was in each of the spheres below. The spirit's answer to the second question is that the absence of singing is to spare Dante's mortal ears. He says further that he has come down the ladder to greet Dante and to "make him glad." Dante then asks the spirit why he, of all those lights, was elected for this service. At that, the spirit begins to express his ecstasy by spinning around swiftly like a cartwheel and replies that he has been touched by a divine beam from heaven that enables him to contemplate the Supreme Being; but as to the reason for his selection—or predestination—for this role, he cannot fathom it, nor can any created being. He then admonishes Dante to take the message back to earth that men should abstain from attempting to resolve this problem of predestination and other mysteries of creation.

Dante then asks the spirit his name. He announces that he is Peter Damian, and he relates that in his early years he lived a holy life in a monastery on Mt. Catria, but later he was appointed to offices in the active service of the Church, finally attaining the rank of cardinal. He concludes his discourse with a severe censure of the present clergy, who, so unlike St. Peter and St. Paul, have grown exceedingly fat and rich.

Other spinning lights descend the ladder to join Peter Damian and unite in a thunderous shout that robs Dante of his senses.

Commentary

The arrival of Dante and Beatrice in the seventh planetary sphere is marked by the increased radiance of Beatrice, which is such that she dares not smile at Dante lest that would increase her glory to a point beyond the power of Dante's mortal senses.

The Sphere of Saturn is consecrated to the fourth cardinal virtue, temperance. The souls assigned to the region are those devoted to contemplation, which in medieval doctrine was held to be the highest form of Christian virtue. An indication of the prominence given to the contemplative life was shown in *Purgatorio* (Cantos 27, 30-33) in its allegorical representation of the figures of Rachel and Beatrice. A life devoted to contemplation could be achieved only in monastic isolation.

Dante is surprised that there is no singing here, but it should be recognized that quiet surroundings are appropriate for contemplation. A further reason offered for the absence of song is the necessity of sparing Dante's mortal senses, "the same reason that Beatrice has no smile."

As in the lower spheres, each planet has its emblem—the crown for the Sphere of the Sun, the cross for Mars, the eagle for Jupiter—so Saturn has the emblem of the golden ladder. It symbolizes the means for the soul's ascent through divine contemplation. The source for this familiar medieval emblem was the biblical account of Jacob's vision: "Behold a ladder set up on earth, and the top of it reached to heaven, and behold the angels of God ascending and descending on it" (Gen. 28).

The spokesman for the spirits here is Peter Damian, a notable church figure of the eleventh century. Much of his life was passed in a monastery in the Apennines, where he became known as an effective reformer of Church discipline. In his mature years he served as papal legate on several important missions. On one of his missions to the imperial court, he succeeded in persuading the young Emperor Henry

IV to abandon his plan to divorce Bertha of Savoy. At length he was permitted to return to the quiet of monastic life, much to his joy.

Dante, in questioning Peter Damian regarding his selection for this assistance to Dante, is really trying to fathom the puzzle of predestination. The saint not only does not offer an explanation but he urges the poet to take the message back to men on earth that they are not to pry into this inscrutable question.

Damian concludes his discourse with a complaint about the decline of the modern clergy from the models of St. Peter (Cephas) and St. Paul (the Vessel of the Holy Ghost), who went barefoot and lean. *Cephas* is the Aramaic word for *stone*, the equivalent of the Latin *Petrus*.

CANTO 22

Summary

The thunderous roar uttered by the host of spirits fills Dante with fright, whereupon Beatrice explains that it expresses a denunciation of the deterioration of clerical life as designated by Peter Damian and a prayer for the punishment of the offenders.

Another brilliant light from among the spirits on the ladder speaks to Dante; it is St. Benedict, who relates how he brought Christianity to the pagans in the neighborhood of Monte Cassino, where he founded a famous monastery. He then points to two other spirits among the crowd of those devoted to this contemplative life, St. Maccarius and St. Romualdus.

Dante begs for the privilege of seeing Benedict in his bodily form. The saint replies that the request can be gratified only when Dante arrives in the highest heaven. St. Benedict then pronounces a bitter censure of monastic life at present, calling the religious houses dens of thieves. He particularly denounces usury and the misdirection of monies that should be spent for the relief of the poor. None, he declares, now lifts his feet to mount up Jacob's Ladder. Then, having sounded his condemnation of his living followers, he returns to his companion lights who together ascend the golden ladder.

At a sign from Beatrice, Dante follows the saints up the ladder; in a twinkling, he discovers himself in the House of Gemini, the sign of the Zodiac under which he was born. From that height Dante pauses to turn his gaze downward, and he smiles to see how small and insignificant the earth appears; he thinks how vain are the earthly goals men strive for and how much wiser are the persons who strive for spiritual goals. Next he observes and admires the seven planets beneath him, marveling at their circling and the great distances that separate them. Then after one more glance at "that little threshing floor that makes men fierce," he turns his eyes to the eyes of Beatrice.

Commentary

The second speaker to address Dante from among the lights on the golden ladder is, appropriately, St. Benedict, founder of the first great order of monks in western Europe. Early in the sixth century he founded the famous monastery on Monte Cassino in what had been a pagan temple, and he set down rigid rules for the monks of his order. His realization of the neglect and the abuse of those rules among his living followers provokes his bitter diatribe. This attack on the monastic orders, much in the spirit of that pronounced by Peter Damian in the previous canto, is also reminiscent of the denunciations of the Dominicans by St. Thomas *(Par.* 11) and the Franciscans by St. Bonaventura *(Par.* 12).

The speed of Dante's ascent to the next region is described as quicker than one would pull his finger out of a fire. His arrival in the eighth sphere is described with his customary attention to astronomical details. He is in the House of Gemini, which is a significant choice not only because it was the sign of his birth date but also because it was under the influence of Gemini that he derived his love of learning. For this, he expresses his gratitude.

At this transitional point in his journey, the poet looks back to survey the territory he has passed through. From his lofty vantage point, he sees the earth as a miniscule dot in the universe, and he reflects on the vanity of all the worldly hopes men set their hearts upon. Such a view of earth and the concomitant scornful reflections belong to a literary tradition stemming from Cicero's *Dream of Scipio* and Boethius' *On the Consolation of Philosophy* and recurring in Chaucer's *House of Fame* and *Troilus and Criseyde,* as well as in the epics of Ariosto and Tasso and a good many other poets long before the development of aviation or the space flights of the astronauts.

In his sweeping survey of the circling spheres, Dante indicates the various planets by indirect references rather than by their familiar names for the benefit of his educated audience. Thus the moon is "Latona's daughter" and Mercury and Venus are designated as the children of Maia and Dione, respectively. Jupiter stands between, and is tempered by, the heat from his son Mars and the chill of his father Saturn.

CANTO 23

Summary

As Beatrice stands looking upward expectantly, Dante follows her example and is soon rewarded with a scene of intense splendor. Beatrice, her countenance aflame, announces the approach of Christ in triumph, and Dante sees many lights surrounding one great light, a scene resembling the moon surrounded by the stars. This great light, however, is of such brilliance that the poet is forced to lower his eyes. Beatrice tells him to open his eyes and look at her, for now he has gained the power to behold her smiling. The beauty of that smile is such that it induces in him a state of ecstasy that he cannot adequately describe.

After Dante's brief glance at her, Beatrice bids him turn his view once again to the heavenly scene. The light of Christ is soaring far above, and now he perceives the Rose "in whom God's word was made flesh" (Mary) and the lilies "whose fragrance led men to the good pathway" (the apostles). A flaming light, shaped like a diadem and spinning like a wheel (Gabriel), descends and circles the Rose, surrounding it with such sweet music that it would make earth's finest harmonies sound like a thunderclap. As the circling diadem of light hymns in Mary's honor, all the company of spirits sound her name.

Mary, following the course of her Son, rises toward the Empyrean, which is so high above where Dante stands that his sight cannot follow her. As she rises, the surrounding lights, reaching upward to express their affection, become pointed flames, as they sing *Regina coeli*.

What a rich reward, the poet exclaims, is reserved for those devout apostles who lived their earthly lives in righteousness!

Commentary

In this new region of heaven, Dante looks upward and is greeted with a special vision, the triumph of Christ and Mary, who have descended from the Empyrean to greet the soul as it rises toward the highest heaven. The fact that Dante cannot endure the brilliance of the divine Christ is in accordance with Church teaching. The triumph of Mary, which Dante is able to view after Christ's ascent, is spectacularly accompanied by Gabriel's circling light and the sweet music of the choiring saints.

The many lights surrounding Christ and Mary in this scene represent a special band among the blessed, the apostles and the prophets.

> Here triumphs, under the great Son
> Of God and Mary, in his victory,
> With both the ancient council and the new,
> He who holds the keys to so great glory.

The ancient council refers to the prophets of the Old Testament; the new council is composed of the apostles. "He who holds the keys" is St. Peter. The glorious reward for those spirits who "wept in exile in Babylon" (suffered on earth) is hailed by the poet.

To impress the reader with the splendor of this scene, Dante has introduced an abundance of delightful figures that enrich the passage.

CANTO 24

Summary

Beatrice, addressing the band of spirits there as those invited to the supper of the Lamb of God, begs that they will favor her companion with some crumbs from their table. In response, they form themselves into spheres that turn in varied motion, some swift, some slow. Then one bright light detaches itself from its group and offers to satisfy her request. She recognizes the spirit as that great man "to whom the Savior bequeathed the keys" and requests him to test Dante on his conception of faith.

Like a doctoral candidate preparing for an oral examination, Dante braces his mind. To the initial question, "What is faith?" he answers that the essence of it is summed up in Paul's words: " . . . the substance of things hoped for, the evidence of things not seen" (Heb. 11). His examiner then asks how he understands "substance" and "evidence" in that definition. In his response Dante states that those subjects of mystery that are hidden from those on earth are revealed in heaven and their existence in heaven constitutes the substance of belief for men;

in dealing with theological questions—the mysteries—one is obliged to reason from beliefs, in syllogistic manner. Thus do beliefs serve as our evidence.

The examiner declares his satisfaction with the answer, then asks Dante how he came to this understanding. He answers that it came to him through the Holy Scriptures concerned with miracles. The next question is: "How do you know that you can believe the accounts of the miracles?" The answer is that the success of Christianity in converting the world, had it come about without miracles, would have been the greatest of miracles.

Finally Dante pronounces the basis of his credo: "I believe in one God, sole and eternal, who, unmoved, moves all heaven with love and desire. . . . I believe in the Trinity. . . ." The saint, well pleased with all of Dante's responses, expresses his joy by circling around the candidate three times.

Commentary

In the eighth heaven Dante is subjected to a series of examinations in preparation for his ascent to the two higher heavens. The examinations are concerned with his understanding of the three Christian virtues, faith, hope, and love; the examiners are to be the three favorite apostles, Peter, James, and John. The present canto records the examination on faith conducted by St. Peter. Peter is an appropriate figure to speak on the subject of faith because of his part in the incident of walking on the water and his being the first to enter the tomb of Christ on Easter morning.

The procedure for the examination is reminiscent of that of a candidate for the doctorate in philosophy. The answers of the candidate, being derived from the Scriptures or from Augustine and Aquinas and wholly orthodox, are received by St. Peter not only with approbation but with delight. The tone of this passage, that of sober dialectic discourse, is in striking and deliberate contrast with the rapturous, poetic style of the preceding canto.

CANTO 25

Summary

In the opening lines Dante states that if the fame of his poem opens the way for him to return to Florence, he will enter proudly to receive the poet's crown in the Baptistry because he first entered into the Christian faith there, the faith that has now been hailed by Peter.

A new light now approaches which Beatrice recognizes as the apostle whose shrine in Galicia attracts so many pilgrims (St. James). She asks the saint to discourse on hope, since he was the apostle distinguished for that virtue. The saint reminds them that Dante's journey to heaven before his death is for the purpose of confirming his hope of heavenly reward and that of others still alive. He then asks Dante, "What is hope?"

Before Dante can reply, Beatrice speaks, declaring that there is no man living more confirmed in hope than Dante, the proof of which is his dispensation to journey to Paradise while still alive. She then defers to Dante to discuss matters concerning hope which will not give occasion for boasting on his part.

Dante defines hope as the certain expectation of future glory which is attained through divine grace and precedent merit. How did he learn of this? Through many inspiring guides, he says, first through David in the Psalms and also from the Epistle of James. What does hope promise? Both the Old and New Testaments promise hope for all those that God wills to dwell with Him. Isaiah promises that each shall be clad in a double garment "in his own promised land" (heaven); and John (James' brother) expresses that same hope in Revelations. At the conclusion of the interrogation there is heard singing from above, *Sperent in te* ("They hope in Thee").

A third shining light now descends from a sphere of lights and joins the two apostles with whom the poet has conversed, and the three lights dance joyfully together. Beatrice introduces the third as ". . . he that lay on the breast of [Christ] our Pelican" and received the great charge from the cross (St. John). Dante, following Beatrice's gaze, stares at the new light until he is blinded. The spirit chides Dante for staring at him so intently as if he expected to see his bodily form, for it lies buried in the earth.

Abruptly all is hushed, and Dante turns to Beatrice only to discover that he cannot see her though she is close beside him.

Commentary

The canto dedicated to hope opens with lines suggesting what Dante may do if his poetry wins him reinstatement as a citizen of his native Florence, pathetic evidence that such was a fond hope that he cherished until his last years.

The apostle chosen to conduct the examination on hope is St. James. Typically, he is not named in the text but is identified through reference to his famous shrine in Galicia, Spain, at Campostella. As James opens the questioning in the customary manner, Beatrice intercedes to spare Dante an occasion for self-praise, assuring the saint that Dante is as sound in hope as any living man, a fact confirmed by his journey to heaven before his natural death. This last is stated in allusive language: ". . . therefore it is granted that he come from Egypt (earth) to Jerusalem (heaven) before his warfare is finished."

From the definition that Dante offers of hope, it is clear that he is treating the specific concept of a theological virtue, not the broader general concept of the term. Hope is the certain expectation of *heavenly reward.* It depends on two requirements, heavenly grace and past performance of good deeds. The sources of this knowledge, he says, are many, of which he cites two: a passage in the Psalms and one in the Epistle of James. The passage from James that he has in mind is in Chapter 1, verse 12. This, however, involves a confusion of Jameses, for in Dante's day James of the Epistle and the apostle James were thought to be the same person.

In answer to the question concerning the promise of hope, Dante cites a passage from Isaiah to the effect that the blessed one shall wear a double garment in his own country. The standard interpretation of the passage is that the body and soul would be joined in heaven. A second biblical reference is to the promise of white robes in St. John's Revelations. Again Dante is mistaken in believing that John, the brother of James, and John of Revelations are the same person.

The third apostle makes his appearance, John, "the beloved disciple." Beatrice introduces him as "he who rested on the breast of our Pelican. . . ." The pelican was a familiar symbol for Christ. The great charge which John received from the cross was to care for Mary.

John assures Dante that he does not have his bodily form here, that only two humans have their bodily forms in heaven, Christ and Mary, and that John must wait like all other souls until the Resurrection for the reunion of body and soul. The point here is that there was a belief current that John had been transported to heaven while living.

The effulgence of John's light is such that Dante is struck blind by looking at it intently; this blindness will last throughout the remainder of his conversation with John.

CANTO 26

Summary

John assures the fearful Dante that his blindness is not permanent and that Beatrice has the power to heal him. Dante is content, for it was through his eyes, through his seeing her, that she first brought the fire that kindles him. He declares that whatever good pleases heaven is all the direction that his love requires. The saint then asks who inspired him to so high a goal. This, Dante answers, came to him through philosophic argument and through authority, that is to say, through reason and revelation. Some of his understanding he owes to Aristotle, some to God's words to Moses, and some to John's writings in his gospel.

When asked to explain what has bound him so firmly to the love of God, Dante states that of the many forces inclining his heart to God, the foremost is the sacrifice of Christ through his death. Then, by way of a conclusion, he declares his love for all of God's creatures in proportion to the degree of blessedness God has bestowed on them.

Dante's pronouncements are greeted with lovely singing by the spirits and with "Holy, holy, holy!" from Beatrice. His sight is then restored, by means of Beatrice's brightness so that his vision is better than before. He first sees a new light, the fourth to greet him. The new spirit, whom Beatrice identifies as Adam, excites Dante's curiosity; but he waits for Adam to speak, knowing that he knows what is in Dante's mind. Adam's first revelation is that his exile from the Garden was not in punishment for eating the apple but for his disobedience. He then says that he spent 4,302 years in Limbo after his life on earth that lasted 930 years. To the question of what language he spoke in the Garden of Eden, he says it was lost even before the Tower of Babel episode. It is natural for men's languages to change because they are the inventions of human reason. Adam's final revelation is that the duration of his stay in the Garden was only six hours.

Commentary

The poet's first intimation of what love means to him lies in the remark concerning Beatrice, who first opened his eyes to "the fire that kindles me still." He then avers that for him the object and center of love is the will of heaven, which is to say love for God. Questioned about the source of his assurance concerning love, he credits philosophy and revelation, first citing Aristotle—who discusses the attributes of the First Mover, *Metaphysics XI*—and then the Bible. In his biblical citations, he refers to passages in both the Old and the New Testaments, a practice he has observed consistently through all his discussions in the eighth sphere.

In asking Dante what has bound him so firmly in his love for God, John uses a striking, unconventional figure of speech: "With what teeth does this love bite thee?" The answer Dante gives is that Christ's sacrifice for mankind is the chief binding force for him. Then, as his final statement, he likens a gardener to the Creator and the leaves in the garden as the expression of His love for all His creatures.

The discourse with St. John on love being concluded, Dante's sight is restored stronger than before. He then is greeted by Adam, who answers many of the questions that men of Dante's age puzzled over: how much time did he spend in the Garden? How long was his life on earth? How long was he in Limbo before Christ released him? And what language did he speak? The figures Adàms gives are as precise as one could wish. However the short period in the Garden before the banishment, six hours, may come as a surprise to modern readers. Adam's long life after the Fall is supported by a passage in Genesis. He was 930 years old when he died, and he spent 4,302 years in Limbo before Christ rescued him. It may be supposed that Dante understood Christ's age at the time of his descent into Hell as thirty-two, which would put the creation of Adam exactly 5,200 years before the birth of Christ.

When Adam says that the language he spoke was lost before the affair of the Tower of Babel brought about the confusion of tongues, this represents a change of opinion on Dante's part; in his *De Vulgari Eloquentia* he expressed the opinion that Adam spoke Hebrew. Evidently his later study of languages led him to realize that a language without a written literature could not continue long without change.

CANTO 27

Summary

As the heavenly host sings to the Father, Son, and Holy Ghost, the whole universe seems to smile and Dante experiences a moment of inebriate rapture. The four brightest lights stand shining before Dante, but now the light of St. Peter takes on an intense and fiery glow. The saint proceeds to deliver a scathing denunciation of the modern papacy for its degeneracy and corruption. Recent popes have turned his tomb into a sewer choked with blood and filth. The founding of the Church through the blood and sacrifices of the early popes (Linus, Sixtus, Urban, etc.) was not for gain of gold, nor was it intended that the keys of the office should be an emblem in battle against fellow Christians, as it is now. Let these recent popes (Cahorsines and Gascons) beware, for vengeance is not far off. Peter now admonishes Dante to speak out boldly against these vices when he returns to earth.

The scene in the Sphere of Fixed Stars closes with the ascent of all the apostles and prophets, resembling a sparkling snowstorm disappearing into the heavens. Dante takes one last look downward at the earth, discovering that his position has changed during his discourse here. He is now over Gibraltar, and the eastern half of the Mediterranean is in shadow because of the position of the sun. Turning his gaze back to Beatrice, he is entranced with the sight of her radiant countenance; and as he gazes, they are transported to "the swiftest of the heavens."

Beatrice informs Dante that the sphere they have reached, the Primum Mobile or Crystalline Sphere, is the base from which all of the lower spheres receive the impetus for their motion and that this sphere is powered by the force of God's love. Now, she says, it should be clear to Dante how time has its roots in this sphere and its leaves in the other spheres. She then complains that covetousness has taken control over mankind. It is not that men are vicious by nature, for in childhood they display innocence and faith; but as they grow older, they turn to evil ways and, especially now, no one in the world governs well. There is a promise, however, that the future will bring a light from heaven that will guide men on an altered course.

Commentary

St. Peter speaks again but in a different role from that of an examiner on faith. Here he speaks as the founder of the papacy, voicing his disgust over the conduct of the recent popes. He singles out the pope reigning at the time Dante was writing *Paradiso,* Pope John XXII, and John's immediate predecessor, Clement V, both of whom Dante attacked in earlier passages. The Gascon pope, Clement V, was responsible for transferring the papal seat from Rome to Avignon *(Par.* 17). The native of Cahors, John XXII, got rich through his practice of excommunicating kings and nobles who would pay generously for their reinstatement.

As the author looks down on the little globe of earth, he indicates with utmost precision his position with reference to the earth, the sun, and the zodiac, though his references are in oblique language. He is still in the sign of Gemini, and he can see where Ulysses ventured on his last voyage. The sun is ahead of him by about 40°, so that a part of the earth's surface within his view is shaded from the sun, that is, the Phoenician coast, where Europa started her journey mounted on the bull.

The physical nature of the ninth heaven is presented in vague terms. It is called crystalline because it is colorless as well as transparent. Dante must have thought of it as extending into virtually limitless space, for there is nothing beyond it save that it is embraced by the Empyrean, which is the Mind of God. Its influence on the other spheres as their driving force is a familiar concept that has been mentioned in several earlier passages.

Time is compared to a plant: its roots in the Primum Mobile are not visible to man, but the leaves of the plant are the planets, by which our time is measured.

Beatrice inveighs against the present decay of morals, which she attributes to the dominance of covetousness. Dante's embittered view of the state of the world, here expressed in the words of Beatrice, is countered, as it invariably has been throughout the *Comedy*, by a prophecy of a better time to come under the rule of a heaven-sent leader. God will not allow such viciousness to endure. In this instance the promised time for the coming of the brave new world is rather more remote than usual. The date when January would be advanced to spring would be far removed from Dante's age. According to the Julian calendar then in use, the year was computed a small fraction of a day longer than the true sidereal year, with the result that January started a little later in the season every year. To wait until January would be in the spring season would have required almost ninety centuries.

CANTO 28

Summary

Dante is given a sight that reveals God in relation to the orders of angels, but his first awareness of the vision comes to him through the reflected light in the eyes of Beatrice. When he discovers the extraordinary light in her eyes, he turns to see a tiny dot of intense brightness that is surrounded by nine concentric circles of light. The brightness of the circles is in proportion to their closeness to the central dot of light; similarly, the closer the circles are to the center, the more swiftly they move. Dante is puzzled by this pattern, since it is contrary to the condition and movement of the planetary spheres. The explanation given by his guide is that these spheres derive their light and energy from God, who is the central light of the system, and their benefits are in ratio to their proximity. God is beyond the planetary spheres; consequently, the outer ones move at greater speeds.

The circles of light are composed of showers of sparks. Beatrice, responding to Dante's unspoken question, begins to identify the orders of angels in the circling spheres. Starting with the innermost, the swiftest and brightest, and progressing outward, she names the first triad as the Seraphim, the Cherubim, and the Thrones. These are especially blessed by their intimate sight of the Creator and are graced with superior powers of intelligence. In the second triad are the Dominations, the Virtues, and the Powers, creating harmonious descants with their Hosannas. The last triad is composed of the Principalities, the Archangels, and the Angels. All of these angelic orders gaze upward; at the same time, their influences are impelled downward toward their appropriate spheres in the physical universe.

Citing the principal authors who have treated the subject of angelic orders, Beatrice mentions first Dionysius and then Pope Gregory I. The latter's theories differed somewhat with the former but, she declares, Dionysius was correct.

Commentary

The scene, or vision, that is presented to Dante here reveals the relation of the Godhead to the angels. The fact that this image is first revealed as a reflection in Beatrice's eyes is meant to suggest that it is a truth transmitted through revelation, which Beatrice symbolizes.

The angels, classified in nine separate orders, are described as spheres, ranged according to their degrees of holiness and, consequently, of influence. Each of them acts on one of the nine heavenly spheres and is identified as the "Intelligence" controlling that sphere. The highest order in rank, the Seraphim (Hebrew plural of seraph), dominate the Primum Mobile. The Cherubim control the Fixed Stars; the Thrones control Saturn, and so on down in order.

The number of sparks in the spheres is compared to the progressive doubling of the numbers of squares on a chessboard. The reference is to an ancient Eastern legend: a king, wishing to reward the man who invented chess, asked what he wanted for a reward. The man said he would like a grain of wheat doubled for every square on the chessboard. The count proved to be astronomical.

The idea that angels should be classified and ranked according to their virtues and powers was universally taught in the Middle Ages and considerably later (See Milton, for example). It was in conformity with the general idea that every aspect of the scheme of creation was hierarchical, the basis for "the Great Chain of Being." The author who first announced the number and arrangement of the classes of angels was Dionysius the Areopagite, who was said to have received his information from St. Paul. Pope Gregory I, "the Great," proposed some modifications of Dionysius' plan, but as he was to learn when he reached heaven himself, he was mistaken.

CANTO 29

Summary

Beatrice pauses briefly, gazing toward the shining dot which is God. She then begins to resolve several questions regarding angels that she knows Dante would wish to have answered. God, with whom there is no *where* and no *when*, created the angels as a reflection of his splendor. Their creation and the combining of form and matter came about in a single moment. "Pure form (or act)," the summit of creation, is the angels; "pure matter (or potency)" signifies matter without form; the combining of form and matter (act and potency) produced the heavenly bodies. St. Jerome was mistaken in his conjecture that the angels existed long before the universe of spirit and matter.

Not long after the creation of the angels, Beatrice reports, a band of rebel angels was cast out of heaven, creating a great disturbance on earth. The rest of the angels have remained in heaven ever circling and reflecting the Divine Presence. The faculties ascribed to the angels by various mortals are confused, some claiming that they possess understanding, memory, and will. Beatrice explains that they have no use for memory since they are perpetually occupied in one activity.

Beatrice now comments on some of the foibles and abuses practiced by theologians and preachers. The kind of idle speculation just spoken of would be considered relatively harmless were it not practiced at the expense of serious teaching and preaching of the Gospel. Preachers who devote their sermons to fantastic tales and to "getting a laugh" are culpable and are courting Satan.

To give some impression of the vast number of angels in those spheres, Beatrice refers to a passage in the Book of Daniel, which is not specific in its thousands. The prime light from the Godhead is sent back by the angels in different fashion, reflecting in diverse colors the variations in the sweetness of love as from a multitude of mirrors.

Commentary

The "children of Latona" cited in the opening passage of the canto are Apollo and Diana, the sun and the moon. This astronomical figure speaks of a brief moment at the vernal equinox when the sun and moon are exactly opposite, one rising and one setting. The sun is in the sign of Aries and the moon is in the sign of Libra. This situation lasts only a fleeting moment.

Through much of this canto, Beatrice continues her instruction concerning the nature of angels, a subject that fascinated medieval audiences. She settles unequivocally the question of whether the angels were created before, or at the same time, that form and matter were united. She mentions, though only briefly, the revolt of the angels, reminding Dante of the condition in which he saw Satan in the pit of Inferno.

Speaking of some of the fanciful speculations engaged in concerning angels, Beatrice takes the occasion to condemn certain preachers who devote their sermons to ingenious imaginings about such matters as whether or not angels have memory or whether the entire earth was darkened at the time of the Crucifixion. Meanwhile they neglect preaching the Gospel to their congregations. Her censure of such errant preachers includes a disparaging association between them and pigs. Because a pig was associated with St. Anthony, swine belonging to monks were treated as sacred and were permitted to feed anywhere. The monks, in gratitude, gave out pardons freely, which pardons, Beatrice maintains, are invalid and will give their recipients a false sense of security.

CANTO 30

Summary

The gradual fading and final disappearance of the lights in the angelic orders is compared to the dimming of stars, first near the horizon, and then over the whole sky just before sunrise.

With the vision gone, Dante turns to Beatrice again. If all that he has previously said of her beauty were added together, it could not express what beauty he now sees in her; he confesses himself hopelessly defeated in the attempt. Since he first saw her on earth, her beauty has been the constant theme of his verse, but henceforth he must forego that theme as beyond his powers.

Beatrice announces that they have risen to the region of pure light, the heaven of heavens, where Dante will see both angels and saints assembled. By special dispensation he will be permitted to see the saints clothed in their corporeal forms as they will appear at the Resurrection.

A bright light blinds the poet but only for a moment, and when he regains his sight, it has been strengthened so that he can endure any brightness. He now sees a great river of light flowing between two flowery banks. Sparks rise out of the river, fly to the flowers, and then—as if intoxicated—return to the river. At Beatrice's bidding, Dante "drinks" from the river by touching his eyes to it, whereupon the river is transformed into a sea, and the sparks and flowers assume a new pattern. The form is that of a great rose whose center is a wonderful light, whose petals are in more than a thousand tiers, and whose expanse would more than girdle the sun. Beatrice calls attention to the immense throng of spirits and to the few unfilled places in the tiers. She then directs his attention to one empty seat marked with a crown which is reserved for the Emperor Henry VII, who, she says, will come to free Italy, though his attempt is doomed to failure. The pope who will contribute to that failure by his underhanded opposition will not rule long and will be punished in Inferno in the company of Simon Magus and Boniface VIII.

Commentary

Here again a canto opens with an elaborate astronomical image describing the dimming of the stars just before dawn. A man located

6,000 miles west of where the sun is shining at noon would be more than 90 degrees from the sun and thus in darkness. Ninety degrees of the earth's circumference, according to Dante's information, would be 5,100 miles. The observer would be within the shadow of the earth but near sunrise. However, there is a time before the sunlight reaches the man when it touches the sky on the eastern horizon because the shadow of the earth is conical. This complex image serves to describe the fading of the angelic lights as the pilgrims soar to the Empyrean.

One of the phenomenal achievements in *Paradiso* is the glorification of Beatrice's ever increasing beauty, which reaches its climax in this magnificent passage. It is interesting that in this moment Dante remembers his first sight of Beatrice in his childhood. It is also characteristic that she quickly resumes her role as guide and teacher.

The sense of sight has played a major role throughout the poem. Here it is given very special prominence. Dante is blinded so that he may attain a new faculty of vision. The river of light is symbolic of divine grace; the sparks from the river are angels; and the flowers to which they are ministering are the souls of the blessed. Dante is granted an entire new vision of heaven through dipping his eyelids in the stream of light. The heart of the Rose is the omnipotent light of God, and surrounding it are rows on rows of the angels and the saints. Of the thousands upon thousands of "seats" in the Rose, most are filled, signifying that Dante did not expect the world to last much longer. In the *Convivio* (II, xv) he had said, "We are already in the last age of the world."

Emperor Henry VII is awarded a singular tribute in this scene. This and earlier references to Henry are necessarily treated as prophecies because of the supposed date of Dante's journey. Henry did not come to the throne until 1308. It should be recalled that Dante had pinned his hopes of the restoration of imperial authority in Italy on Henry. Even though Henry died before he could accomplish his mission, Dante honors him with a high station in Paradise in contrast with the fate assigned to the pope who opposed Henry, Clement V ("prefect of the divine forum"). Beatrice reminds Dante that a place is reserved for that pope in Malebolgia along with Simon Magus and Clement's predecessor, Boniface VIII ("him of Anagni"). Thus the cause of the empire against the papacy is recognized again in heaven.

The reminder of a passage far, far back among the scenes of *Inferno*, together with the reference in the preceding canto to Satan in *Inferno*, is a remarkably effective means of calling to our minds the long journey we have taken and consequently helping to unify the total pattern of this extremely complex poem.

CANTO 31

Summary

The souls of the redeemed, clad in white raiment, fill the great Rose. Angels, like a swarm of bees, fly about, dipping down into the heart of the Rose and soaring up to touch its petals. Their faces are of living flame, their wings of gold, their clothing whiter than the purest snow. All eyes are turned toward a star that gleams with a triple light. Dante, who has recently come from the corrupt world to the heavenly city, is filled with a wonderful joy; silently he views the faces of the blessed.

When he wishes to question Beatrice, he turns only to find that she is gone and in her place stands a saintly elder, who points to Beatrice in her seat among the blessed. Dante eloquently expresses his gratitude to her; and though they are separated by a great distance, she hears him and she turns and smiles. The new guide tells him to gaze on "this garden" in order to prepare his eyes for God's luminance. He tells Dante that he is St. Bernard, and he assures Dante that the Queen of Heaven will grant him grace. He then tells Dante to look up to the highest tier where sits the Queen, enthroned in brilliant light and surrounded by more than a thousand angels flying and singing joyfully. Her light is of a beauty that brings joy to the other saints. St. Bernard's expression in looking at her shines with such love that it inspires Dante with greater eagerness.

Commentary

The climactic effect that the poet is building toward depends on the same sensory characteristics that we have seen thoughout *Paradiso*, light in moving patterns and music. In order to dramatize effects, he often resorts to reporting his emotional responses. One detail that adds to the psychological appeal in this scene is that saints and angels are no longer spots of light but appear in their individual incarnate forms.

Concrete visual images, conveyed through similes, contribute to the effectiveness of the scene. Dante's amazement at the spectacle of the Rose is compared to that of the Goths upon first entering Rome. (The reference to Helice is to the maiden transformed into the Great

Bear or Dipper, her son being the Little Bear. Saying that the barbarians came from the region spanned by Helice and her son is Dante's way of saying they came from the far north.) In another figure, the poet compares his concentrated gaze with that of a pilgrim from Croatia who has come to see the Veronica in Rome and cannot take his eyes away as long as the relic is being shown.

The most dramatic feature of the narrative in this canto is that there is a transfer of guides. Beatrice leaves her pupil to take her place in the Rose, and St. Bernard replaces her as final instructor and intermediary. The departure of Beatrice is without warning and without farewells, a circumstance reminiscent of the departure of Virgil in the Earthly Paradise. Beatrice has a place of high honor in the upper third row of the Rose.

In her role as Dante's guide Beatrice represents Revelation, the kind of intelligence necessary for direction through Paradise, as distinct from Reason, the intelligence of Virgil. Now that Dante has been brought to the heaven of heavens with the aid of Reason and Revelation, a new mentor is assigned before his vision of the Divine Presence. This guide, St. Bernard, represents Intuition. He is chosen for this role because he is peculiarly qualified to intercede with Mary, who is the final intercessor to the Trinity. Bernard of Clairvaux, a twelfth-century French monk, was especially known for his devotion to the Virgin. In fact, it was he, probably more than any other man, who was responsible for the great upsurge in the veneration of Mary which marked the later Middle Ages. The role of Mary in Christianity during this period, so beautifully demonstrated through the dedication of the great Gothic cathedrals (Notre Dame, for example), is nowhere more clearly revealed in literature than in the *Divine Comedy*. This canto gives us a dramatic sight of her in all her glory on the highest tier of the great Rose.

CANTO 32

Summary

St. Bernard explains the arrangement of the spirits within the celestial assembly and identifies certain saints who occupy places of honor. On the second tier from the top and seated just at the feet of Mary is Eve. On the third tier is Rachel and beside her is Beatrice. Then in descending tiers are Sarah, Rebecca, Judith, and Ruth. These and many more Old Testament women in a vertical row form a dividing line between those who believed in Christ though He was yet unborn and those who believed after His coming. Among the former group, the seats are all occupied, but amid the latter there are places still unfilled.

Directly opposite Mary and the line of Hebrew women is St. John the Baptist and a row of male saints, headed by St. Francis, St. Benedict, and St. Augustine. Thus we see that the basic pattern separates the men from the women, though the plan is not entirely consistent in this respect.

The upper sections of the Rose are for adults; the lower sections are taken by infants who died before they attained the age of moral responsibility. Their salvation is won for them through the faith of others. Bernard points out that God has decreed various degrees of blessedness among the infants, citing the marked differences between Jacob and Esau although they were twins. He explains that in addition to the faith of the child's parents, a ceremonial act is called for. In the case of ancient Hebrew children, it was circumcision; in the case of Christians, baptism.

At St. Bernard's bidding, Dante again lifts his eyes toward Mary, whose brightness can prepare him for the refulgence of Christ. The joy expressed on the faces of the angels surrounding her is beyond anything he has yet seen. Gabriel spreads his great wings before her, and to the hymn *Ave Maria, gratia plena*, the entire court of heaven sings responses.

Dante asks who the angel is that is gazing at the Queen with such rapture and is told that he is the one who brought Mary the news that she would bear the Christ-child. Then his instructor identifies other figures closest to Mary, Adam on one side, Peter on the other; beside Peter, John the Apostle, and beside Adam, Moses. Opposite St. Peter is St. Anne, and opposite Adam sits St. Lucy.

St. Bernard, reminding Dante that his time in Paradise is limited, advises him that to penetrate the Divine Image he must obtain grace from Christ's mother.

Commentary

The blessed who are singled out for mention in the heavenly court are those we should expect in the conception of a medieval Christian. If anything surprises the reader, it is the restraint exercised by the author, for there must have been a strong temptation to mention many more holy names. Many readers must wonder why their favorite saint was not cited, but a longer list would certainly have become tedious. Most of the honored figures are simply mentioned by name; a few are introduced through characterizing phrases. Eve is indicated as she who opened the wound that Mary healed, the wound caused by eating the apple. She not only caused the wound but deepened it by feeding the apple to Adam. Ruth is mentioned simply as the great-grandmother of the singer (David) who sang *Miserere mei* (Psalms 51). "The great John" who dwelt in the wilderness and spent two years in Limbo is St. John the Baptist. He died two years before the Harrowing of Hell.

When Dante is directed to look at the face that bears the greatest resemblance to Christ's, that face is Mary's. The angel who came down to greet Mary, singing *Ave Maria, gratia plena* is, of course, Gabriel. Of Mary's immediate companions, the one whose "rash tasting" caused mankind such bitterness is Adam. The "Father of Holy Church" to whom Christ entrusted the keys to this glorious flower (the heavenly Rose) is St. Peter.

The presence of infants in heaven is based on accepted doctrine. For their admission what is necessary is the faith of their parents plus the performance of a ceremonial act, baptism for Christians or circumcision for pre-Christians. The question of whether all children enjoy equal blessedness or whether there are degrees of blessedness bestowed by God is settled by Dante in favor of the latter concept. On this point he differs from St. Thomas. He finds support for his position in the story of Jacob and Esau, who fought in their mother's womb and who were born with radically different physical and temperamental characteristics.

CANTO 33

Summary

The final canto opens with a prayer to the Virgin on Dante's behalf spoken by St. Bernard. He commences with an invocation which recites the magnificent attributes of the mother of Christ, to whom men pray for blessings from heaven because of her motherly tenderness toward mankind and her influential voice before the Almighty. He then beseeches grace for Dante that he may be granted the vision of God and that he may have the skill to report his vision for future generations.

The Virgin's eyes reveal how she is gratified by devout prayers; she lifts her gaze toward the Eternal Light, at which sign Bernard indicates to Dante that his wish has been granted, and Dante looks up into the Light.

The glorious vision that comes to the poet is almost wholly lost to his memory. His experience was like that of a dreamer who on waking cannot recall the substance of his dream but still feels the emotion it stirred in him. He invokes the Almighty to grant him power to recall at least a spark of the glory of it so that he will be able to transmit it to his fellow men.

He tells us that he gazed steadily into the Light until his sight was united with the Infinite Good, and within that Light he saw bound together all of the various pages of the volume of the universe. There he perceived all the world's substance joined in such a way that it appeared a simple unity. So much was comprehended in that vision that what he forgot after its passing exceeded all that was forgotten of the enterprise of the Argonauts in twenty-five centuries. But this he knows, that he saw there the Good which is the object of the Will.

For that small part of the vision which he holds in remembrance, his language is no more adequate than the speech of a suckling babe. The fullness of that experience was made possible because his faculties were transfigured. Within that single Light he saw three circles of different colors mutually reflecting one another. Finally, within one circle he saw the human image, a sight which fascinates and at the same time perplexes him deeply. Then there came a flash of revelation; his desires and will were brought into perfect conformity, incited by the power of Love, "the Love that moves the sun and the other stars."

Commentary

Bernard's prayer to Mary, spoken on Dante's behalf, compresses into thirty-nine lines the full spirit of Mariolatry which plays so great a role in the Christianity of the age. A prayer to Mary was believed to win a sympathetic ear and hence an influential advocate with Christ. The sweetness and gentleness, the mother-child relationship of Mary to mankind, was ultimately related to the new attitude toward women that so greatly transformed Western culture in the later Middle Ages.

As the final and climactic scene of the *Comedy,* Dante wishes to report his mystic experience, coming into the presence of God, yet he knows that he dare not present the episode in terms wholly explicit. He ascribes the vagueness of his remembrance to the overwhelming power of the moment in which his human faculties were miraculously transfigured. If he cannot relate *in toto* the physical aspects of the revelation, he can still retain the emotional impact that it made on him. He knows that in the moment of revelation he saw the complex universe as a unified whole and that his will was merged with the World-Will. This is in conformity with a familiar definition of mysticism: "to recognize unity in diversity and permanence in change."

What he can recapture of the vision is the image of the Trinity, for within that single Light were visible three circles, coexistent, of different colors; and within one of the circles, wonderful to tell, the image of man. That circle, of course, represents the Son, who took on mortality; but it will not escape the reader that the image carries the implication that there is some spark of divinity in man himself.

When Milton announces in *Paradise Lost* that he proposes to "assert Eternal Providence," he is expressing Dante's precise intention, for this scene in Paradise is his way of expressing his belief in God. The rest of Milton's claimer helps further to describe the *Divine Comedy*.

> That to the highth of this great Argument
> I may assert Eternal Providence,
> And justify the ways of God to men.

SELECTED LIST OF CHARACTERS

The number in parentheses following the name refers to the canto in which the character appears or is cited.

Albert I of Austria (19). Emperor 1298-1308. Censured by Dante for his invasion of Bohemia. Cf. *Purg.* 6.

Albert of Cologne (10). "Albertus Magnus," famous theologian and teacher of Aquinas.

Alighiero (15). Dante's ancestor from whom the family name was derived.

Anchises (15, 19). Father of Aeneas.

Anne, St. (32). Mother of Mary.

Anselm (12). Archbishop of Canterbury, author and teacher.

Aquinas, St. Thomas (10-13). Theologian who wrote prolifically, who influenced Dante's religious thought more than anyone else, and whose authority over Catholic doctrine is still profound. A Dominican, he praises St. Francis, founder of the rival order of friars.

Ariadne (13). In Greek mythology, she was the daughter of Minos; with her sister Phaedra she helped Theseus kill the Minotaur and escape from Crete. After being deserted by Theseus, she was married to Dionysus. At her death she was transported to heaven as a constellation, the Corona Borealis.

Aristotle (24, 26). Ancient Greek philosopher whose work was widely studied and much admired during the later Middle Ages, especially through the influence of Thomas Aquinas. Cf. *Inf.* 4; *Purg.* 3.

Arius (13). Early Christian leader responsible for the Arian heresy which was condemned by the Council of Nicaea.

Augustine, St. (10, 32). One of the most powerful early Church fathers, author of *Confessions* and *Civitas Dei*. He became Bishop of Hippo in North Africa.

Beatrice Portinari. A Florentine lady whom Dante knew and loved in his youth. She inspired his *Vita Nuova* and became his spiritual guide on his journey through Paradise.

Bede (10). Anglo-Saxon monk who wrote the *Ecclesiastical History of the English Nation.*

Benedict, St. (22, 32). Founder of the first monastic order in western Europe, the Benedictines. Their first monastery was established at Monte Cassino.

Bernard, St. (31-33). Religious leader in France in the twelfth century. He was a strong advocate of the Second Crusade. He did much to stimulate the rise of Mariolatry.

Boethius (10). A prominent sixth-century Roman statesman who was unjustly condemned to prison and death. In prison he wrote *On the Consolation of Philosophy.*

Bonaventura, St. (12). A prominent Franciscan. In the Sphere of the Sun he delivers a eulogy on St. Dominic.

Boniface VIII (9, 12, 27, 30). The reigning pope in 1300. Through his influence Dante and his party were exiled. He figures throughout the *Comedy* as the archenemy of the religious and political well-being of Europe. Cf. *Inf.* 15, 19, 27; *Purg.* 20.

Buondelmonti (16). A member of this family was murdered for jilting a girl of the Amidei family. The feud resulting developed into the Guelf and Ghibelline parties in Florence.

Cacciaguida (15-17). Dante's great-great-grandfather, who was killed in the second crusade. He greets Dante in the Sphere of Mars and predicts the miseries in store for the poet as an exile.

Caesar, Caius Julius (6, 11). Brilliant general and head of the Roman state under the Republic. Cf. *Inf.* 1, 4, 28; *Purg.* 18.

Caesar, Octavianus (6). The great-nephew of Julius Caesar. He was the first emperor of Rome, was given the title of Augustus.

Caesar, Tiberius (6). Successor of Augustus, emperor at the time of the Crucifixion.

Can Grande della Scala (Cf. **Scala**).

Charlemagne (6, 18). King of France who became the first emperor of the Holy Roman Empire, receiving the crown from Pope Leo III in 800.

Charles I of Anjou (8). He seized the crown of Naples and Sicily in 1265 with the support of the pope, defeating Manfred, leader of the Ghibelline faction. Cf. *Purg.* 7, 11, 20.

Charles II of Naples (6, 19). Son of Charles I of Anjou and the father of Charles Martel.

Charles Martel (8-9). Son of Charles II of Naples. He inherited the title of King of Hungary. He had visited Florence in 1294, and on meeting Dante in the Third Heaven he greets him as a friend.

Chrysostom, St. (12). Patriarch of Constantinople in the fourth century. He was sent into exile for his public rebuke of the Empress Theodosia for her wanton conduct.

Clement V, Pope (17, 27, 30). It was during his papacy (1305-14) that the Papal See was transferred to Avignon under pressure from Philip IV of France. Dante despised him for this action.

Clymene (17). Maiden loved by Apollo; the mother of Phaëthon.

Conrad III, Emperor (15). One of the leaders of the second crusade, by whom Cacciaguida, Dante's ancestor, was knighted.

Constance, Empress (3). Lady taken out of her convent to marry the Emperor Henry VI. She was the mother of Frederick II.

Constantine, Emperor (6, 20). Roman emperor who was the first Christian emperor and who established a second capital at Byzantium, renaming it Constantinople.

Creusa (9). First wife of Aeneas. She was lost during the flight of the family from burning Troy.

Cunizza (9). A lady of Treviso, north of Venice, sister of the notorious Ezzelino da Romano. Given to passionate amours in her early life, she turned to charity in her later years.

Damian, Peter (Cf. **Peter Damian**).

Demophoon (9). Greek warrior for whom Phillis committed suicide, imagining that he had deserted her.

Dido (9). Queen of Carthage, widow of Sycheus; she fell in love with her guest Aeneas. She killed herself when he sailed for Italy at the command of the gods. Cf. *Inf.* 6.

Dionysius the Areopagite (10, 28). A Greek who was converted to Christianity by St. Paul. He was regarded as an authority on the hierarchy of angels.

Dominic, St. (11-12). As founder of the Dominican order of friars, he was one of the most effective religious leaders of the Middle Ages.

Donati, Piccarda (Cf. **Piccarda Donati**).

Donatus (12). A church scholar of the fourth century, an authority on grammar.

Europa (28). Daughter of the King of Phoenicia; she was abducted by Jupiter in the form of a bull and carried to Crete.

Folco (Foulquet) (9). A troubadour who, after a life devoted to worldly pleasures, turned to the religious life and became Abbot of Torronet.

Francis, St. (11, 13, 22, 32). Founder of the order of Franciscan friars at the beginning of the thirteenth century. A Christlike figure who is one of the most revered saints of the Church.

Frederick II, Emperor (3). A sovereign whom Dante admired. He ruled the empire from Italy in the first half of the thirteenth century. Barbarossa was his grandfather, Constance his mother, and Manfred his bastard son.

Frederick II, King of Sicily (19). A descendant of the royal house of Aragon, rivals of the house of Anjou in Sicily, he ruled the kingdom from 1296 to 1337.

Gabriel (4, 9, 14, 23, 32). The archangel chiefly remembered as the angel of the Annunciation.

Glaucus (1). A fisherman who, after eating a certain plant, was transformed into a sea god, thus "transhumanized."

Godfrey of Bouillon (18). Commander-in-chief of the First Crusade. He liberated Jerusalem in five weeks.

Gratian (10). Twelfth-century Church scholar who was credited with bringing canon law and civil law into conformity.

Gregory I, Pope (Gregory the Great) (28). His papacy, 590-604. He sent missionaries to the Anglo-Saxons under St. Augustine of Canterbury. He was responsible for the adoption of the Gregorian chant as the official form of church music.

Hannibal (6). Great Carthaginian general who dealt the Romans many severe defeats but was finally defeated by Scipio.

Henry VII, Emperor (17, 30). The emperor (1308-1313) on whom Dante pinned his hopes of re-establishing imperial rule in Italy in opposition to papal secular control.

Hippolytus (17). Son of Theseus who was unjustly accused by his stepmother, Phaedra, and banished with his father's curse.

Hugh of St. Victor (12). A twelfth-century theologian who became prior of St. Victor's in Paris.

Innocent III, Pope (11). The pope who first gave official sanction to the order of Franciscans.

Isidore of Seville, St. (10). An ecclesiastical scholar of the late sixth and early seventh centuries, who wrote an encyclopedia of science.

James the Apostle, St. (25). One of the apostles closest to Christ. There was a famous shrine to him in Campostella, Spain.

Jason (2). Greek legendary hero who led the expedition of the Argonauts in quest of the Golden Fleece. According to tradition he was the first sailor. Medea, who helped him gain the Golden Fleece, became his wife but was later abandoned by him.

Jephthah (5). A leader of Israel who vowed that if God would give him victory in battle he would sacrifice the first living thing that greeted him. It was his daughter who came out first.

Jerome, St. (29). One of the great Church fathers. His translation of the Bible into Latin, known as the Vulgate, was the official text for the Church.

Joachim of Flora (12). An abbot of Calabria whose influence among spiritual Franciscans was considerable.

John the Baptist, St. (4, 31-33). Elder cousin of Jesus who preached the coming of the Messiah. Patron saint of Florence, his figure was on their gold coin, the florin.

John the Apostle, St. (4, 24, 25, 26, 32). Brother of St. James the Apostle, John was called the "beloved disciple." Dante apparently believed that the author of the Gospel of John and John the Evangelist, the author of Revelations, was the same person.

John XXII, Pope (27). Born in Cahors, France, he succeeded Clement V to the papacy in 1316. It was during his reign that Dante was writing the latter part of *Paradiso*.

Justinian, Emperor (5-6). Ruling the tottering Roman empire from Constantinople in the sixth century, he repelled barbarian invaders. He is renowned for his codification of Roman law.

Lavinia (6). Second wife of Aeneas. Her father, Latinus, was an Italian king who formed an alliance with Aeneas.

Lawrence, St. (4). He was martyred by being roasted over a grill and is always so represented in religious art. During his ordeal he refused to reveal the hidden treasures of the Church.

Leda (27). Disguised as a swan, Jupiter made love to her. She gave birth to Helen and the twins, Castor and Pollux, the Gemini.

Lucy, St. (32). One of the "Three Blessed Ladies" (with Mary and Beatrice) responsible for Dante's journey. Cf. *Inf.* 2, *Purg.* 9.

Maccabaeus, Judas (18). A general who was greatly honored in Jewish history; he delivered his people from the tyranny of the Syrians in the second century B.C.

Marsyas (1). A satyr who challenged Apollo to a musical duel. He was defeated and as punishment he was bound to a tree and flayed.

Michael, St. (4). An archangel, often referred to as the warrior angel and depicted in armor.

Minos (13). A legendary king of Crete who, after his death, became a judge in Hades. Cf. *Inf.* 5.

Mucius (4). Caius Mucius Scaevola, without flinching, held his hand in the fire until it was consumed. This was his self-inflicted punishment for having failed to kill Lars Porsena.

Nathan the Prophet (12). He rebuked King David for having sent Uriah to his death because he lusted after Uriah's wife.

Nebuchadnezzar (4). King of Babylon whose dreams were interpreted by Daniel.

Nimrod (26). King of Babylon whose people attempted to build the tower of Babel. The result of that experiment was that people began speaking a diversity of languages.

Orosius (10). A Spanish priest of the fifth century who is famous for his *Compendious History of the World.* This was one of the books translated in King Alfred's Anglo-Saxon library.

Pallas (6). A youthful Trojan follower of Aeneas who was killed in battle by Turnus.

Parmenides (12). An ancient Greek philosopher whose work was criticized by Aristotle.

Paul, St. (18, 21, 24, 26, 28). An early convert to Christianity, he was the author of Acts and several of the Epistles of the New Testament. A fountainhead of Christian doctrine and the greatest early missionary.

Peter, St. (9, 18, 21, 22, 24, 27, 32). A leader among Christ's disciples, he was given the keys to heaven to admit or exclude souls. As first Bishop of Rome, he was the source of papal authority.

Peter Damian (21). A monk of the eleventh century who worked for monastic reform. From abbot he rose to cardinal and served as papal legate on important missions.

Peter Lombard (10). Having studied under Abelard and Hugh of St. Victor, he taught theology at the Universities of Bologna and Paris. He is most famous for his collection of the sayings of the Church fathers.

Peter Mangiadore (12). A twelfth-century scholar of St. Victor; author of commentaries on the Bible.

Peter of Spain (12). A Spanish priest who was elected Pope John XXI in 1276; he died the following year.

Phaedra (17). Second wife of Theseus, she fell in love with her stepson Hippolytus. When he rejected her advances, she falsely accused him and forced his banishment.

Philip IV ("the Fair") (19). King of France who ruled from 1285 to 1314. He quarreled with Pope Boniface VIII, and he persuaded Pope Clement V to transfer the papal seat from Rome to Avignon.

Piccarda Donati (3). Sister of Forese (Cf. *Purg.* 23) and Corso (Cf. *Purg.* 24, *Par.* 17). They were cousins of Dante's wife.

Pius I, Bishop of Rome (27). Second-century exemplar of the virtuous early popes.

Pompey (6). A member of the "First Triumvirate" with Julius Caesar and Crassus. His rivalry with Caesar later led to civil war, and he was defeated at Pharsalia.

Quintius (15). Lucius Quintius Cincinnatus, better known as Cincinnatus, Dictator of Rome in 458 B.C. He was regarded as an exemplar of the highest virtues of the early Romans.

Rabanus Maurus (12). Archbishop of Mayence in the eighth and ninth centuries; a poet and a biblical commentator.

Rachel (32). Second wife of Jacob; mother of Joseph and Benjamin. She figured in Dante's symbolic dream in Purgatory. Cf. *Purg.* 27.

Rahab (9). The harlot of Jericho whose aid to Joshua in his capture of the city (Hebrews 11) won her salvation.

Rebecca (32). Wife of Isaac, mother of Esau and Jacob.

Renouard (18). A gigantic warrior who fought with William of Orange against the Moors. He was a Saracen who had been converted to Christianity.

Richard of St. Victor (10). A twelfth-century theologian, pupil of Hugh of St. Victor.

Ripheus (20). Trojan warrior mentioned briefly in the *Aeneid* for his love of justice.

Robert Guiscard (18). Distinguished general in the wars of the Normans against the Saracens in southern Italy and Sicily in the eleventh century.

Roland (18). Nephew of Charlemagne; hero of the great medieval French epic, *Le Chanson de Roland.*

Romeo (6). Seneschal of Raymond Berengar, Count of Provence, in the early thirteenth century.

Romualdus (22). Founder of the Order of Reformed Benedictines.

Rudolph I of Hapsburg (8). Emperor from 1272-92. One of the emperors censured by Dante for neglect of Italy. Cf. *Purg*. 6-7.

Ruth (32). Heroine of the Book of Ruth, great-grandmother of David.

Sarah (32). Wife of Abraham.

Sardanapalus (15). King of Assyria, cited by Dante as an example of one living a life of luxury and depravity.

Scala, Bartolommeo della (17). Lord of Verona and one of Dante's patrons during his exile.

Scala, Can Grande della (17). Son of Bartolommeo. Dante placed his hopes in him as the future savior of Italy. He dedicated *Paradiso* to Can Grande and submitted the MS to him. Cf. *Inf*. 1, *Purg*. 20, 33.

Scipio (6). Roman general, victor in the Carthaginian campaign in 202 B.C. Given the title of "Africanus."

Sigier of Brabant (10). A professor at Paris who engaged in a violent debate with Thomas Aquinas over the teachings of Averroes.

Sixtus I, Bishop of Rome (27). A second-century exemplar of the virtuous early popes.

Solon (8). Famous judge in ancient Greece.

Sychaeus (9). Husband of Dido. When he was murdered in their homeland, Phoenicia, Dido escaped and founded the new colony of Carthage.

Tiberius. Cf. Caesar, Tiberius.

Titus, Emperor (6). The Roman commander who captured and destroyed Jerusalem in 70 A.D.

Tobit (4). Principal character in the Book of Tobit (in the Apocrypha) whose blindness was cured by the archangel Raphael.

Torquatus (6). A Roman leader of the fourth century B.C.

Trajan, Emperor (20). One of the best of all the Roman emperors; he reigned from 98-117 A.D.

Typhoeus (8). Monster overthrown by Jupiter and buried under Mt. Aetna.

Ubaldo, St. (11). He lived in a hermitage near Gubbio (in the vicinity of Assisi) before he became Bishop of Gubbio in the early twelfth century.

Ulysses (27). One of the Greek leaders in the Trojan War. He played a prominent role in the *Iliad* and was the central figure in the *Odyssey*. Cf. *Inf.* 26; *Purg.* 19.

Urban I (27). Bishop of Rome in the early third century who was martyred.

Veronica, St. (31). Lady whose veil bore the imprint of Christ's features. It was revered as one of the most precious of all holy relics.

Virgil (15, 17, 26). Roman poet, first century B.C., author of the *Aeneid.* He was called "master" by Dante and served as the poet's guide through Inferno and Purgatory.

Wenceslas IV, King of Bohemia (19). Contemporary of Dante who ruled from 1278-1305. Cf. *Purg.* 7.

William, Count of Orange (18). Hero of several *chansons de geste,* he fought against the Saracens.

William II, King of Sicily and Naples (20). Called "the Good," he ruled in the second half of the twelfth century.

Xerxes, King of Persia (8). The Persian king who led an invasion of Greece, c. 480 B.C. The war involved famous battles at Thermopole, Marathon, and Salamis.

REVIEW QUESTIONS AND STUDY PROJECTS

1. What scheme is employed to give *Paradiso* a structural pattern that parallels the plans of *Inferno* and *Purgatorio?*

2. What are the basic differences between the Ptolemaic astronomy and Copernican astronomy?

3. Do the spirits in Paradise have their permanent abodes in the planetary spheres where Dante meets them or in the Empyrean?

4. In what spheres are the spirits seen only as bright spots of light?

5. What is the astronomical peculiarity of the three lowest planets that marks them with "the taint of earth"?

6. Why are the spirits in those three lowest spheres held to enjoy degrees of blessedness inferior to those above?

7. Name the regions of Paradise in order, and specify the characteristics or vocations of the spirits encountered in each.

8. Specify the emblems formed by the lights in the several spheres and explain the significance of each.

9. Identify each of the following characters, designate his or her sphere, and report the substance of Dante's discourse with each: Cacciaguida, Cunizza, Justinian, Peter Damian, Piccarda Donati, St. Benedict, St. Bernard of Clairvaux, St. Bonaventura, St. Peter, and St. Thomas Aquinas.

10. Give an account of the life of Beatrice and of Dante's association with her.

11. What is the allegorical concept that Beatrice stands for in the *Comedy*?

12. Cite several puzzling subjects which Beatrice expounds for Dante in her role as guide and instructress.

13. What means does Dante employ to impress the reader with his personal adoration of Beatrice?

14. What types of sensations and emotions are introduced into Dante's heaven, and what types are excluded?

15. What type of passages has led some of Dante's detractors to accuse him of venting his spleen on persons and institutions against whom he bore a grudge?

16. Cite several contemporary political figures mentioned, and determine from their treatment what the author's views on national and international affairs were.

17. Cite several contemporary ecclesiastical figures and discuss the author's stand on Church politics.

18. Describe the Celestial Rose and indicate the arrangement of spirits there.

19. Paraphrase Dante's account of the Vision of God (the Beatific Vision).

20. Compare the use of similes in *Paradiso* with their use in *Inferno* and *Purgatorio:* that is, frequency, subjects, tone.

21. Give several examples of the employment of the obscure or indirect style in *Paradiso*. Consider the nature of the context of the passages, and explain what kind of appeal they held for Dante's more erudite contemporaries.

SELECTED BIBLIOGRAPHY

BRANDEIS, IRMA (ed.). *Discussions of the Divine Comedy*. Boston: D. C. Heath, 1961. Comments and essays on Dante by writers of various periods, such as Boccaccio, Petrarch, Voltaire, Coleridge, Croce, Etienne Gilson, Allen Tate.

———. *The Ladder of Vision, A Study of Dante's Comedy*. Garden City, N. Y.: Anchor Books, 1962. Topical essays on several aspects of the *Comedy*. For the study of *Paradiso*, chapters III, IV, and V are especially pertinent.

CHANDLER, S. BERNARD, and MOLINARO, J. A. (eds.). *The World of Dante. Six Studies in Language and Thought*. Toronto: University of Toronto Press, 1965. Essays by Glauco Cambon, John Freccero, Joseph A. Mazzeo, et al.

CIARDI, JOHN (trans. and ed.). *Dante Alighieri, The Paradiso*. Introduction by John Freccero. New York and Toronto: The New American Library, 1970. An excellent verse translation, with extensive and valuable notes.

COSMO, UMBERTO. *A Handbook to Dante Studies,* translated by David Moore. Oxford: Basil Blackwell, 1950. New York: Barnes and Noble. Excellent source of information on the author's life and times and his early works as well as the *Comedy.*

DINSMORE, CHARLES A. *Aids to the Study of Dante.* Boston: Houghton Mifflin, 1903. Elaborate handbook information and valuable commentary.

ELIOT, T. S. "Dante," *Selected Essays, 1917-1932.* New York: Harcourt Brace, 1932. Part II of this celebrated essay is devoted specifically to *Purgatorio* and *Paradiso.*

FRECCERO, JOHN (ed.). *Dante, A Collection of Critical Essays.* Englewood Cliffs, N.J.: Prentice-Hall, 1965. A collection of articles treating various aspects of Dante studies by such writers as Erich Auerbach, T. S. Eliot, Charles S. Singleton, and Charles Williams.

GILBERT, ALLAN. *Dante and His Comedy.* New York: New York University Press, 1963. A valuable study of the *Comedy* that is organized topically, with discussions centered on numerous aspects of structure, style, themes, and problems.

GRANDGENT, C. H. (ed.). *La Divina Commedia di Dante Alighieri.* Boston, New York, et al.: D. C. Heath, 1933. The text is in Italian. The English introduction and notes have become indispensable for Dante scholarship.

SAYERS, DOROTHY L. "'. . . And Telling You a Story': a Note on *The Divine Comedy,*" *Essays Presented to Charles Williams.* London: Oxford University Press, 1947. An essay treating the story-telling techniques and the careful structural design of the *Comedy.*

SAYERS, DOROTHY L., and REYNOLDS, BARBARA (trans. and eds.). *The Comedy of Dante Alighieri the Florentine: Cantica III, Paradise.* Baltimore: Penguin Books, 1962. Introduction, pp. 13-52, is detailed, perceptive, and eminently readable. The notes, diagrams, and appendices are elaborate and extremely valuable, especially for advanced students.

SINCLAIR, JOHN D. (trans. and ed.). *The Divine Comedy of Dante Alighieri, Vol. III, Paradiso.* New York: Oxford University Press, 1961. A bilingual edition which offers an excellent literal prose translation. At the end of each canto the editor supplies brief factual notes plus an analytical-critical essay.

WILLIAMS, CHARLES. *The Figure of Beatrice*. London: Faber and Faber Ltd., 1943. A classic study of the life of Beatrice and her role in the works of Dante. Some of its interpretations are subject to controversy.

NOTES

NOTES

NOTES

NOTES

NOTES

Doctor Faustus

DOCTOR FAUSTUS

NOTES

including

- *Life of Christopher Marlowe*
- *The Faust Legend*
- *Brief Synopsis*
- *List of Characters*
- *Summaries and Commentaries*
- *Critical Notes*
- *Review Questions*
- *Selected Bibliography*

by
Eva Fitzwater, Ph.D.
Department of English
Midland College

INCORPORATED
LINCOLN, NEBRASKA 68501

ISBN 0-8220-0406-2

Printed in U.S.A.

1993 Printing

Cliffs Notes, Inc. Lincoln, Nebraska

CONTENTS

Doctor Faustus

LIFE OF CHRISTOPHER MARLOWE

Christopher Marlowe was the son of a wealthy Canterbury shoemaker who was an influential citizen in his community. Marlowe was born on February 6, 1564, and was baptized at Saint George's church in Canterbury on February 26. After attending King's School in Canterbury, Marlowe went to Corpus Christi College in Cambridge in December, 1580. He attended on a scholarship founded by Archbishop Parker which was granted for six years to those who were studying for a career in the church. From this fact, it appears that it was Marlowe's intention to go into the church, even though in the college records he first appears as a student of dialectics.

Marlowe received his B.A. in 1584, and three years later he received his M.A. degree. His academic career was fairly conventional except for some long periods of absences during his second year. The only trouble which Marlowe had was just before he was granted his M.A. degree. Because of the prevalence of certain rumors, the college was going to hold up his degree. The Privy Council of the queen wrote a letter to the university assuring the college about Marlowe's character and asserting that he had been of service to her majesty. The purpose of this letter was to allay rumors that Marlowe planned to join the English Catholics at Reims in France.

Marlowe appears to have performed services for the government during these years, such as carrying dispatches overseas or else acting as a spy in the service of Sir Francis Walsingham, who was the head of Queen Elizabeth's secret service. No direct evidence, however, remains as to what his specific tasks or assignments were in the service of the queen.

After receiving his M.A. from the university, he moved to London, where he was a part of a brilliant circle of young men which included Rawley, Nashe, and Kyd. Before the end of the year 1587, both parts of his first play, *Tamburlaine the Great,* had been performed on the stage. At this time, Marlowe was a young man of only twenty-three and already established as a known dramatist as a result of the success of this first play.

In the remaining six years of his life after he had left the university, he lived chiefly in the theatrical district of Shoreditch in London. Although he traveled a great deal for the government during this time, he always retained this London address. For a time, he had as his roommate Thomas Kyd, who is also the author of a very popular Elizabethan play, *The Spanish Tragedy*. Kyd later made the statement that Marlowe had a violent temper and a cruel heart.

In September of 1589, Marlowe was imprisoned in Newgate for his part in a street fight in which William Bradley, the son of a Holborn innkeeper, was killed. One of Marlowe's friends named Watson had actually killed the man with his sword; so Marlowe was not charged with murder himself. He was released on October 1, on a bail of forty pounds, and was discharged with a warning to keep the peace.

Three years later, in 1592, Marlowe became involved in a court action as he was summoned to court for assaulting two constables in the Shoreditch district. The officers said that they had been in fear of their lives because of Marlowe's threats. He was fined and released.

In the spring of 1593, Marlowe again found himself in difficulty with the Privy Council on the charge of atheism and blasphemy. Thomas Kyd had been arrested for having in his possession certain heretical papers denying the deity of Christ. Kyd denied that they belonged to him and maintained that they were Marlowe's. Marlowe was then summoned to the Privy Council, which decreed that he must appear daily before them until he was licensed to the contrary.

Then, twelve days later he was killed in a tavern in Deptford, a dockyard adjacent to Greenwich. On that day, Marlowe had accepted an invitation from Ingram Frizer to feast at the tavern with several other young men of dubious reputation who had been mixed up in confidence games, swindles, and spy work. After supper Marlowe got into an argument with Frizer over the tavern bill. When Marlowe struck Frizer on the head with a dagger, Frizer twisted around somehow and thrust the dagger back at Marlowe, striking him on the forehead and killing him.

During his short career as a dramatist, Marlowe gained a significant reputation on the basis of four dramas. Other than his first play, *Tamburlaine,* he was also the author of *Faustus* in 1589 or 1592, *The Jew of Malta* in 1589, and *Edward II* in 1592. In addition to his dramatic pieces, he translated Lucan's *Pharsalia* and Ovid's *Amores*. He also wrote poems, among which his most famous are "The Massacre of Paris" and "Hero and Leander."

THE FAUST LEGEND

The Faust legend had its inception during the medieval period in Europe and has since become one of the world's most famous and oft-handled myths. The story is thought to have its earliest roots in the New Testament story of the magician Simon Magus (Acts 8:9-24). Other references to witchcraft and magic in the Bible have always caused people to look upon the practice of magic as inviting eternal damnation for the soul.

During the early part of the fifteenth century in Germany, the story of a man who sold his soul to the devil to procure supernatural powers captured the popular imagination and spread rapidly. The original Faust has probably been lost forever. In various legends, he was named Heinrich Faust, Johann Faustus, or Georg Faust. But whatever his first name really was, this Faust was apparently a practitioner of various magical arts. A cycle of legends, including some from ancient and medieval sources that were originally told about other magicians, began to collect around him. One of the most widely read magic texts of the period was attributed to Faust and many other books referred to him as an authority.

Later in the fifteenth century, around 1480, another German magician gave further credence to the legend by calling himself

"Faustus the Younger," thus capitalizing on the existing cycle of legends about the older Faust. This later Faust was a famous German sage and adventurer who was thought by many of his contemporaries to be a magician and probably did practice some sort of black magic. After a sensational career, this Faust died during a mysterious demonstration of flying which he put on for a royal audience in 1525. It was generally believed that he had been carried away by the devil. Owing to his fame and mysterious disappearance, popular superstition prompted many more stories to grow up around the name of Faust, thus solidifying the myth and occult reputation of the legendary character of Faust.

During the sixteenth century, additional stories of magical feats began to attach themselves to the Faust lore, and eventually these stories were collected and published as a *Faust-Book*. A biography of Faust, the *Historia von D. Johann Fausten,* based upon the shadowy life of Faust the Younger, but including many of the fanciful legendary stories, was published in Frankfurt, Germany, in 1587. That same year it was translated into English as *The Historie of the damnable life and deserved death of Doctor John Faustus*. In both these popular editions of the *Faust-Book,* the famed magician's deeds and pact with the devil are recounted, along with much pious moralizing about his sinfulness and final damnation. In fact, the moral of the story is emphasized in the title of the English translation. It was in these versions that the legend took on a permanent form.

When the Renaissance came to northern Europe, Faust was made into a symbol of free thought, anticlericalism, and opposition to church dogma. The first important literary treatment of the legend was that of the English dramatist Christopher Marlowe.

Marlowe, unfortunately, allowed the structure of his drama to follow the basic structure of the *Faust-Book,* thus introducing one of the structural difficulties of the play. The first part of the book (through Chapter 5) showed Faustus' determination to make a pact with the devil, and after this is accomplished, the large middle portion of the *Faust-Book* handles individual and unrelated scenes showing Faustus using his magic to perform all types of nonsensical pranks. Finally, the *Faust-Book* ends with Faustus awaiting the final hour of his life before he is carried off to eternal damnation by the agents of the underworld.

Marlowe's rendition of the legend was popular in England and Germany until the mid-seventeenth century, but eventually the Faust story lost much of its appeal. The legend was kept alive in folk traditions in Germany, though, and was the popular subject of pantomimes and marionette shows for many years.

The close of the eighteenth century in Germany was a time very much like the Renaissance. Before long the old Faust story with its unique approach to the problems of period was remembered. The German dramatist Lessing (1729-81) wrote a play based on the legend, but the manuscript was lost many generations ago and its contents are hardly known.

Perhaps the most familiar treatment of the Faust legend is by the celebrated German poet, Johann Wolfgang von Goethe, one of the rare giants of world literature. A brief outline of Goethe's *Faust* will show both similarities and differences in the handling of this famous theme.

Heinrich Faust, a learned scholar, feels that none of his many achievements has provided him with satisfaction or a sense of fulfillment. He yearns to gain knowledge of truth and the meaning of existence. Faust turns to magic in the hope of finding a way to transcend human limitations. When Mephistophilis appears to him, Faust is willing to make a pact with the devil, but includes many conditions in his agreement. He will yield his soul only if the devil can provide him with an experience so rewarding that he will want the moment to linger forever. But this experience will have to combine extreme opposite emotions such as love and hate at the same time. Furthermore, Faust knows that his essential nature is one of upward striving, and if the devil can help him strive upward enough, then Faust will be at one with God. There is no mention of the traditional twenty-four years of servitude.

In Part I of the drama, Faust attempts, with the devil's help, to find happiness through emotional involvement. He has an exciting but tragic relationship with the beautiful and chaste Gretchen which ends in her disgrace and death, but Faust is much chastened by this experience. In Part II, he tries to satisfy his craving through temporal accomplishments and exposure to all that the world can offer in terms of ideas and externalized gratifications. He attains an important position at the Imperial Court, learns much from the figures of classical antiquity, woos Helen of Troy, wins great victories, and is renowned for his public works, but none of these things gives him that complete satisfaction which transcends human limitations.

When Faust's death approaches, the devil is there to claim his soul, but a band of heavenly angels descend and carry him off triumphantly to heaven.

The chief philosophical difference between Marlowe's and Goethe's treatments lies in the final scene of the drama, where Marlowe's Faustus is dragged off to the horrors of hell but Goethe's Faust is admitted to heaven by God's grace in reward for his endless striving after knowledge of goodness and truth and his courageous resolution to believe in the existence of something higher than himself.

Furthermore, Goethe introduced the figure of Gretchen. The Faust-Gretchen love story occupies most of Part I of the drama, whereas Marlowe confined himself to showing tricks performed by Doctor Faustus.

Goethe's great tragedy struck a responsive chord throughout Europe and reinforced the new interest in the Faust story. Since his time it has stimulated many creative thinkers and has been the central theme of notable works in all fields of expression. In art, for instance, the Faust legend has provided fruitful subjects for such painters as Ferdinand Delacroix (1798-1863). Musical works based on the Faust story include Hector Berlioz' cantata, *The Damnation of Faust* (1846), Charles Gounod's opera, *Faust* (1859), Arrigo Boito's opera, *Mefistofele* (1868), and Franz Lizt's *Faust Symphony* (1857). Even the newest of art forms, the motion picture, has made use of the ancient story, for a film version of Goethe's *Faust* was produced in Germany in 1925. But most important, the legend has continued to be the subject of many poems, novels, and dramatic works. Among the more recent of these are the novel *Doctor Faustus* (1948) by Thomas Mann and the poetic morality play, *An Irish Faustus* (1964) by Lawrence Durell.

Each succeeding artist has recast the rich Faust legend in terms of the intellectual and emotional climate of his own time, and over the past few centuries this tale has matured into an archetypal myth of man's aspirations and the dilemmas he faces in the effort to understand his place in the universe. Like all myths, the Faust story has much to teach the reader in all its forms, for the tale has retained its pertinence in the modern world. The history of the legend's development and its expansion into broader moral and philosophical spheres is also an intellectual history of mankind.

BRIEF SYNOPSIS

Faustus becomes dissatisfied with his studies of medicine, law, logic and theology; therefore, he decides to turn to the dangerous practice of necromancy, or magic. He has his servant Wagner summon Valdes and Cornelius, two German experts in magic. Faustus tells them that he has decided to experiment in necromancy and needs them to teach him some of the fundamentals.

When he is alone in his study, Faustus begins experimenting with magical incantations and suddenly Mephistophilis appears, in the form of an ugly devil. Faustus sends him away, telling him to reappear in the form of a friar. Faustus discovers that it is not his conjuring which brings forth Mephistophilis but, instead, that when anyone curses the trinity, the devils automatically appear. Faustus sends Mephistophilis back to hell with the bargain that if Faustus is given twenty-four years of absolute power, he will then sell his soul to Lucifer.

Later, in his study, when Faustus begins to despair a Good Angel and a Bad Angel appear to him; each encourages Faustus to follow his advice. Mephistophilis appears and Faust agrees to sign a contract in blood with the devil even though several omens appear which warn him not to make this bond.

Faustus begins to repent of his bargain as the voice of the Good Angel continues to urge him to repent. To divert Faustus, Mephistophilis and Lucifer both appear and parade the seven deadly sins before Faustus. After this, Mephistophilis takes Faustus to Rome and leads him into the Pope's private chambers, where the two become invisible and play pranks on the Pope and some unsuspecting friars.

After this episode, Faustus and Mephistophilis go to the German emperor's court, where they conjure up Alexander the Great. At this time, Faustus also makes a pair of horns suddenly appear on one of the knights who had been skeptical about Faustus' powers. After this episode, Faustus is next seen selling his horse to a horse-courser with the advice that the man must not ride the horse into the water. Later the horse-courser enters Faustus' study and accuses Faustus of false dealings because the horse had turned into a bundle of hay in the middle of a pond.

After performing other magical tricks such as bringing forth fresh grapes in the dead of winter, Faustus returns to his study, where at the request of his fellow scholars, he conjures up the apparition of Helen of Troy. An old man appears and tries to get Faustus to hope for salvation and yet Faustus cannot. He knows it is now too late to turn away from the evil and ask for forgiveness. When the scholars leave, the clock strikes eleven and Faustus realizes that he must give up his soul within an hour.

As the clock marks each passing segment of time, Faustus sinks deeper and deeper into despair. When the clock strikes twelve, devils appear amid thunder and lightning and carry Faustus off to his eternal damnation.

LIST OF CHARACTERS

Doctor John Faustus

A learned scholar in Germany during the fifteenth century who becomes dissatisfied with the limitations of knowledge and pledges his soul to Lucifer in exchange for unlimited power.

Wagner

Faustus' servant, who tries to imitate Faustus' methods of reasoning and fails in a ridiculous and comic manner.

Valdes and Cornelius

Two German scholars who are versed in the practice of magic and who teach Faustus about the art of conjuring.

Lucifer

King of the underworld and a fallen angel who had rebelled against God and thereafter tries desperately to win souls away from the Lord.

Mephistophilis

A prince of the underworld who appears to Faustus and becomes his servant for twenty-four years.

Good Angel and Evil Angel

Two figures who appear to Faustus and attempt to influence him.

The Clown

The clown who becomes a servant of Wagner as Mephistophilis becomes a servant to Faustus.

Horse-Courser

A gullible man who buys Faustus' horse, which disappears when it is ridden into a pond.

The Pope

The head of the Roman Catholic church, whom Faustus and Mephistophilis use as a butt of their practical jokes.

Charles V, Emperor of Germany

The emperor who holds a feast for Faustus and at whose court Faustus illustrates his magical powers.

Knight

A haughty and disdainful knight who insults Faustus. In revenge, Faustus makes a pair of horns appear on the knight.

Duke and Duchess of Vanholt

A couple whom Faustus visits and for whom he conjures up some grapes.

Robin

An ostler who steals some of Dr. Faustus' books and tries to conjure up some devils.

Rafe (Ralph)

A friend of Robin's who is present with Robin during the attempt to conjure up devils.

Vintner

A man who appears and tries to get payment for a goblet from Robin.

Old Man

He appears to Faustus during the last scene and tries to tell Faustus that there is still time to repent.

Seven Deadly Sins, Alexander, Helen of Troy, and Alexander's Paramour

Spirits or apparitions which appear during the course of the play.

Chorus

A device used to comment upon the action of the play or to provide exposition.

SUMMARIES AND COMMENTARIES

CHORUS

Summary

The chorus announces that this play will not be concerned with war, love, or proud deeds. Instead, it will present the good and bad fortunes of Dr. John Faustus, who is born of base stock in Germany and who goes to the University of Wittenberg, where he studies philosophy and divinity. He so excels in matters of theology that he eventually becomes swollen with pride, which leads to his downfall. Ultimately, Faustus turns to a study of necromancy, or magic.

Commentary

The technique of the chorus is adapted from the traditions of classic Greek drama. The chorus functions in several ways throughout the play. It stands outside the direct action of the play and comments upon various parts of the drama. The chorus speaks directly to the audience and tells the basic background history of Faustus and explains that the play is to concern his downfall. The chorus is also used to express the author's views and to remind the audience of the proper moral to be learned from the play itself. The opening speech of the chorus functions as a prologue to define the scope of the play.

The chorus speaks in very formal, rhetorical language and explains that the subject of this play will not be that which is usually depicted in dramas. Instead of a subject dealing with love or war, the play will present the history of a scholar. The purpose of this explanation is that, traditionally, tragedy had dealt with such grand subjects as the history of kings, great wars, or powerful love affairs. Consequently, Marlowe is preparing the audience for a departure in subject matter. Most frequently, tragedy is concerned with the downfall of kings, and Marlowe's tragedy does not fit into this formula, since this drama deals with the downfall of a man of common birth.

The Icarus image is used in the opening passage to characterize the fall of Faustus. Icarus was a figure in classical mythology who because of his pride had soared too high in the sky, had melted his wax wings, and subsequently had fallen to his death. This classical image of the fall of Icarus reinforces the Christian images of the fall of Lucifer brought out in Scene 3. Both images set the scene for the fall of Dr. Faustus during the course of the drama.

Another image used by the chorus to describe the situation of Faustus is that of glutting an appetite by overindulgence. Throughout the play, Faustus is seen as a person of uncontrolled appetites. His thirst for knowledge and power lead him to make the pact with the devil which brings about his downfall. The chorus points out the dangers involved in resorting to magic. It makes clear that Faustus is choosing magic at the danger of his own soul.

SCENE 1

Summary

Faustus is alone in his study reviewing his achievements. He concludes that he has attained preeminence in all fields of intellectual endeavor. He disputes superbly and has mastered all treatises of logic. He is such a skilled physician that he has saved whole cities from the plague. He knows all the petty cavils of law but he finds them drudgery. In theology, he takes two scriptual passages which indicate that all men must eventually die and dismisses them. After reviewing his achievements, he decides that necromancy is the only world of profit, delight, power, honor, and omnipotence. He then has Wagner summon Valdes and Cornelius, who will help him conjure up spirits.

While Faustus is waiting for the two German scholars, the Good Angel and the Evil Angel appear. The Good Angel advises him to lay aside the "damned book" of magic and read the scriptures. The Evil Angel appeals to Faustus' ambitions. Faustus becomes absorbed in a vision of what he will be able to do by the power of magic.

When Valdes and Cornelius appear, Faustus welcomes them and tells them that he has decided to practice magic because he has found philosophy, law, medicine, and divinity to be unsatisfactory. Valdes assures Faustus that if they work together the whole world will soon be at their feet. Faustus agrees and tells the two men that he plans to conjure that very night.

Commentary

The first question to be faced in connection with the entire drama is the reason for Faustus' yielding to the practicing of magic. In the opening of the scene, Faustus reviews the most important intellectual fields of endeavor and feels that he has mastered these areas so completely that there is nothing left for him. Not only is he learned in philosophy but his medical skill is the best that can be attained by human knowledge. His mastery of law only serves to show him the drudgery involved in the practice. Finally, theology has not provided him with any final or satisfactory answers.

Faustus reads from the Bible that the reward of sin is death and then he reads another statement that if any man thinks he is not a sinner, he is deceived. For Faustus, this appears to doom man from the beginning. Disgusted with the hopelessness of theological study, he turns to the practice of magic. But Faustus' reasoning is very ironic for he has read both passages out of context. Although he is a learned man in divinity, he overlooks the obvious meaning of the passage. For instance, Faustus ignores the second part of the passage; he reads "the wages of sin is death" but does not finish it with "but the gift of God is eternal life."

Since Faustus thinks that he has achieved the end of all the various studies of the university, he is dissatisfied with the powers that he has gained from them. Although Faustus is a most learned man, he finds himself confined by mere human knowledge. In other words, he feels the limitations of human knowledge and decides to turn to magic to discover greater powers.

According to traditional Christian cosmology, the universe is viewed as a hierarchy which descends from God, through the angels, then man, the animals, and finally to inanimate nature. Everything has been put in its proper place by God and each should be content to remain there. According to this view, it is dangerous for a man to attempt to rise above the station assigned to human beings and it is also forbidden to descend to the animal level. Ambition to go beyond one's natural place in the hierarchy is considered a sin of pride. Consequently, Faustus' desire to rise above his position as a man by resorting to supernatural powers places his soul in dire jeopardy.

Marlowe indicates this in the line "Here, Faustus, try thy brains to gain a deity." Consequently, the first scene sets up the conflict between the limitation of man's knowledge and his desire to go beyond his position in the universe.

The biblical quotations Faustus mentions refer to the concept of sin and death. The entire drama deals with the problems of sin and death and immortality. One of the things Faustus is trying to escape is the limitation of death. On the one hand, he alleges that he does not believe in death and at the same time he spends all his time finding ways to escape it, especially by resorting to necromancy. At the end of the scene, he makes the statement that "this night I'll conjure though I die therefore." What he does not realize is that by resorting to necromancy, he will die a spiritual death also.

The appearance of the Good Angel and the Evil Angel is a holdover from the earlier morality plays. The medieval plays often use abstractions as main characters. The appearance of these allegorical abstractions functions to externalize the internal conflict that Faustus is undergoing; they symbolize the two forces struggling for the soul of Faustus. Throughout the play, these angels appear at the moments when Faustus critically examines the decision that he has made.

After the departure of the Good Angel and the Evil Angel, Faustus has a vision of what he will accomplish with his new magical powers. Some of his dreams demonstrate his desire for greater insight into the workings of the universe, and others suggest the noble ends for which he will use his power. Those desires should later be contrasted with what Faustus actually does accomplish. After receiving his powers from Mephistophilis, Faustus never does anything but trivial and insignificant acts; he resorts to petty tricks and never accomplishes any of the more powerful or noble deeds.

This first scene is filled with ironies. Basically, Faustus is so confident that his new powers will bring about his salvation, he never realizes that, quite to the contrary, they will bring about his damnation. He even refers to the books of necromancy as being "heavenly," whereas in reality they are satanic. He asks Valdes and Cornelius to make him "blest" with their knowledge. Throughout the scene, Faustus uses religious imagery and language to apply to matters which will finally bring about his own damnation.

SCENE 2

Summary

Two scholars come to Wagner to inquire about Faustus. Instead of giving a direct answer, Wagner uses superficial scholastic logic in order to prove to the two scholars that they should not have asked the question. After he displays a ridiculous knowledge of disputation, he finally reveals that Faustus is inside with Valdes and Cornelius. The two scholars then fear that Faustus has fallen into the practice of magic. They plan to see the Rector to "see if he by his grave counsel can reclaim" Faustus.

Commentary

Essentially this scene functions as a comic interlude. This type of scene is often called an "echo scene" because Wagner's actions parody those of Faustus in the previous scene. The scene also functions as a contrast to the earlier scene in that the same subject is being presented—the use and misuse of knowledge. Earlier we had seen Faustus alone in his study displaying his knowledge of logic in order to justify his resorting to black magic. Now we have a contrast in which Wagner tries to use logic for no other purpose than to try to tell two scholars where Faustus is at the time.

Not only is the scene a comic interlude, but it is also a comment on the actions performed by Faustus. By the end of the second scene, we realize that Faustus' choice affects more people than just himself. First, we see that Faustus has had a direct influence upon Wagner, who tries in his silly ways to imitate his master. Furthermore, in the end of the scene, we see that many more people are concerned over Faustus' choice than just Faustus alone. The two scholars indicate their desire to reclaim Faustus. The use of the word "reclaim" keeps in view the idea that Faustus' choice to use magic has already damned him. Essentially, the concern of the scholars heightens Faustus' error. Finally, this scene functions technically to allow a certain amount of time to pass.

It is characteristic of Elizabethan dramatists to have the dramatic persona speak in a language that is appropriate to their characters. The higher or nobler characters speak in an elevated and formal language. The lower characters usually speak in prose. Faustus speaks in "Marlowe's Mighty Line," while Wagner speaks in a simple prose. Shakespeare also uses this same technique in many of his comedies. For instance in *A Midsummer Night's Dream,* the noble characters speak in dignified language while the rustic characters use a more common idiom and speech.

SCENE 3

Summary

Faustus decides to try incantation for the first time. He mutters a long passage in Latin which is composed of passages abjuring the trinity and invoking the aid of the powers of the underworld. Mephistophilis then appears in a hideous shape, and Faustus tells him that he is too ugly. He demands that Mephistophilis disappear and return in the shape of a Franciscan friar. Faustus is elated that he has the power to call up this devil. As soon as Mephistophilis reappears, Faustus finds that it is not his conjuration which brings forth a devil; a devil will appear any time that a person abjures the name of the trinity.

Faustus asks Mephistophilis several questions about Lucifer and learns that he is a fallen angel who, because of pride and insolence, revolted against God and was cast into hell. When Faustus begins to inquire about the nature of hell, Mephistophilis answers that hell is wherever God is not present. Faustus chides Mephistophilis for being so passionate about being deprived of the joys of heaven, and then sends him back to Lucifer with the proposal that Faustus will exchange his soul for twenty-four years of unlimited power. After Mephistophilis leaves, Faustus dreams of all the glorious deeds he will perform with his new power.

Commentary

In this scene, Faustus takes the first definite and inexorable steps toward his own damnation as he abjures the trinity and appeals to the black powers of hell. The incantation, the abjuring of the trinity, and the spectacle of the sudden appearance of a horrible looking devil on the stage are very effective dramatically. The mere fact that a man abjures the trinity and invokes the powers of hell carries an awesome significance. According to the amount of stage machinery available, the appearance of Mephistophilis could be accompanied by dreadful noises, bursts of lightning, smoke, or any combination of the above. In the following comic scenes, the appearance of a devil is accompanied by the explosion of firecrackers.

Mephistophilis' first appearance is also dramatically effective because he appears so suddenly and in a horrifying shape. The symbolic significance of his appearance is obvious – hell is a place of horror and damnation and anything emanating from there would appear extremely ugly. This physical detail alone should function as a portentous warning to Faustus, who, however, ignores the implication and simply orders Mephistophilis to reappear in a more favorable shape.

Faustus' command to Mephistophilis to reappear as a Franciscan friar satirizes the religious order which had been the subject of various literary attacks since the times of Chaucer. The satire on friars also reflects the English rejection of the Roman Catholic church which is also demonstrated in a later scene in the Pope's chamber.

Faustus' first reaction to Mephistophilis' appearance is one of pride in his power to evoke a devil. He thinks that Mephistophilis is completely obedient to his will and feels that he is a "conjuror laureate." Instead, Faustus learns that a devil will appear to anyone who curses the name of God. Faustus is foolish to think that a devil is obedient to anyone except Lucifer. Thus, even at the beginning of the play, Faustus is greatly deceived about his own powers and deceived about his relationship with Mephistophilis.

Faustus acts as if he believes he has complete power and is completely free. But Mephistophilis' condition indicates that no person who deals with the devil is free. Even Mephistophilis is bound over to the devil, and as soon as Faustus enters into a contract he will no longer be free either.

At first, Faustus retains part of his old nobility as he begins to question Mephistophilis about Lucifer. Faustus is now intent upon gaining more knowledge; he wants to know something about the character of Lucifer. Mephistophilis reveals that Lucifer had once been a favorite angel until his fall. The story of Lucifer re-establishes the imagery of a fall which had first been referred to in the classical fall of Icarus.

Lucifer fell because of "aspiring pride and insolence." This image may be applied to the fall of Faustus because in his pride he is trying to discover more than is allowed to man.

Faustus' next question involves the nature of hell and the nature of damnation. The reader should remember that at the time of this play, the Anglican church had been separated from the Roman Catholic church for only a short time. This passage emphasizes the newly established view of hell as advocated by the Anglican church. Rather than being an established or definite physical place, hell is seen as a state or condition. Any place that is deprived of the presence of God is hell.

> Why this is hell, nor am I out of it.
> Think'st thou that I who saw the face of God,
> And tasted the eternal joys of heaven,
> Am not tormented with ten thousand hells,
> In being deprived of everlasting bliss?

Thus, the greatest punishment man can endure is not a physical torment but, more directly, exclusion from the presence of God.

It is highly ironic that Mephistophilis, in remembering the bliss of heaven, suddenly tells Faustus to "leave these frivolous demands, which strike a terror to my fainting soul." Even with this definite warning from an authority of hell, Faustus does not modify his intent to carry out his plans. Instead, Faustus scolds Mephistophilis for not being resolute. Later these roles will be reversed and Mephistophilis will have to urge Faustus to be more resolute.

Faustus sends Mephistophilis back to Lucifer, naming the demands in exchange for his soul. The terms are rather broad in intent but later Faustus makes little use of the powers he now demands. After Mephistophilis leaves, Faustus revels in his sense of omnipotence. He becomes completely absorbed in dreams of what he will do with his newly gained power. Unfortunately for Faustus, he never achieves the things he is now dreaming of even though he has the potential. Instead, he will do no more than play insignificant and paltry tricks. Part of his tragedy is that he received this power but failed to utilize it in any significant manner.

In the Renaissance view, man lived in an ordered universe which was governed by principles of law. Even Mephistophilis recognizes that the universe is governed by law, but Faustus is working under the mistaken belief that he has been able to abrogate divine law by his conjuration.

SCENE 4

Summary

Wagner accosts the clown and tells him that he realizes that the clown is out of work. He accuses him of being so desperate that he would sell his soul to the devil for a shoulder of raw mutton. The clown insists that if he were to make so dangerous a bargain, he would require that his mutton at least be roasted in a fine sauce. Wagner asks the clown to serve him for seven years. If the clown refuses, Wagner threatens to have lice tear him to pieces.

Wagner gives the clown some French money and warns him that he will have a devil fetch him within an hour if he doesn't agree to become his servant. Wagner summons Baliol and Belcher —two devils—who come and frighten the poor clown. Wagner promises the clown that he will instruct him in how to summon up these devils. The clown agrees to the bargain but wants to be taught how to turn himself into a flea on a pretty wench.

Commentary

This scene re-echoes in a comic fashion various parts of the preceding scene between Faustus and Mephistophilis. In the largest view, both scenes involve a promise of servitude in exchange for certain benefits. Whereas Faustus is willing to sell his soul to the devil for complete power, Wagner accuses the clown of being willing to sell his soul to the devil for a leg of mutton. The clown modifies the condition by comically insisting upon a rich sauce to accompany the leg of mutton. In contrast to the servitude of Mephistophilis to Faustus, the clown agrees to serve Wagner. And instead of twenty-four years, the clown is only to serve for seven years.

In both scenes, supernatural devils appear; in the first scene their appearance is dramatically terrifying but in the latter scene it is purely comic. In the Wagner scene, even the names of the devils are comic; the clown mispronounces the devils' names as Banto and Belcheo. Wagner promises the clown that he can teach a person how to raise up devils and how to change people into dogs, cats, or mice. This is a deflation of the grandiose powers discussed in the preceding scene.

As noted earlier, there is a notable contrast between the language used in the third and fourth scenes. Faustus delivers his sentiments in lofty and noble language. In contrast the clown speaks in a low and vulgar manner. The scene contains obscene puns which would be highly amusing to an Elizabethan audience but are little understood by a modern audience. Marlowe also parodies several biblical passages in the lines of Wagner and the clown.

Finally, the comic scene develops in a different manner, another of the contrasting servant-master relationships.

SCENE 5

Summary

Faustus, alone in his study, tries to bolster his own resolution to forget God and dedicate himself solely to Lucifer. The Good Angel and the Evil Angel appear. The Good Angel admonishes Faustus to think on heavenly things, while the Evil Angel emphasizes the value of power and wealth. Faustus decides to think on wealth and summons Mephistophilis, who then tells him that Lucifer will agree to the bargain but it must be signed with Faustus' blood. Faustus stabs his arm, but as he begins to write, the blood congeals. Mephistophilis rushes to get some fire in order to make the blood flow. As Faustus begins to write again, an inscription—"Homo, fuge!"—appears on his arm. Faustus finishes signing the bond and orders Mephistophilis to deliver it to Lucifer.

After the bargain has been completed, Faustus begins to ask again about the nature of hell. But while Mephistophilis is describing hell, Faustus becomes skeptical and refuses to believe in hell. Then, all of a sudden, Faustus changes the topic of the conversation and tells Mephistophilis that he wants a wife because he feels wanton and lascivious. Mephistophilis convinces him that he does not want a wife, and offers to bring him any courtesan or paramour that he desires. Before Mephistophilis leaves, Faustus demands three books—one for incantations and spells, one for knowledge of the planets and the heavens, and one for understanding plants and animals.

Commentary

In the first part of this scene, Faustus' mind begins to waver. There is a conflict within Faustus as to whether he should carry out his plan. This inner conflict is then externalized by the appearance of the Good Angel and the Evil Angel. The advice of the Good Angel and the Evil Angel serves to keep constantly before us the struggle which Faustus is facing and reminds the reader that Faustus is in severe danger of eternal damnation. The problem of salvation and damnation is now central to Faustus' conflict. He is deeply concerned over his own fate. In each appearance, Faustus is more influenced by the advice of the Evil Angel, and thus Faustus centers his thinking on the wealth and power that he is about to receive.

In the contract scene, the bond is presented in legal terms. Lucifer demands the security of having the contract written in blood. There is an old superstition that a contract signed in blood is eternally binding. As soon as Faustus signs with his own blood, he commits himself to eternal damnation. He later realizes that only the blood of Christ could release him from such a bond.

During this scene, two omens appear to indicate to Faustus that he is in dire danger of damnation. The first is the fact that his own blood congeals, the second is the inscription—"Homo, fuge!" —which appears on his arm. The inscription warns Faustus to flee. He ignores both of these warnings and continues blindly on his way to damnation by insisting on signing the pact. Faustus even believes that his senses are deceived by the signs, but it is not his senses but his reason which is deceived in signing the contract.

At the crucial time in this scene and all through the rest of the play, whenever Faustus begins to ask questions about essential things, the devil or Mephistophilis brings forth something to delight Faustus' mind. Mephistophilis constantly tries to discover things which would divert Faustus' attention away from his search for knowledge. Consequently, however noble Faustus' original plans were, he obviously loses part of his nobility simply by dealing with evil forces. Any association with evil forces causes a man to deteriorate as a result of the association.

Immediately after signing the contract, Faustus begins to question Mephistophilis about hell. Again the view of hell is essentially the same as expressed in Scene 3:

> Hell hath no limits, nor is circumscribed
> In one self place; for where we are is hell
> And where hell is there must we ever be.

And, to conclude, when all the world dissolves,
And every creature shall be purified,
All places shall be hell that is not heaven.

Basically, Mephistophilis explains that hell is simply absence from the presence of God. As Mephistophilis tries to describe that he is now in hell because he is away from the presence of God, Faustus is in a state of complete skepticism. Consequently, we see how rapidly Faustus has degenerated. His intellect is so topsy-turvy that Faustus is unable to believe in anything. He does not even believe that death exists. This is paradoxical, since the pact was originally made to escape death. Even though his aim was to conquer death, he also maintains that death does not exist. Marlowe is using this paradoxical situation to show that Faustus' logical or reasoning powers are rapidly dwindling into insignificance as a result of his pact with the devil.

Although Faustus asserts that he wants a godlike power over the world, he spends all of his time satisfying his senses. Instead of noble discussions about the nature of heaven and hell, Faustus suddenly begins to feel lascivious and wants a wife. He now wants to yield to coarse physical desires rather than search for ultimate knowledge.

Faustus does not realize that he is being cheated out of all that he was promised. He is unable to have a wife as he demands, for marriage is a condition sanctified by God. Later in the scene he is also denied knowledge that he was promised. He expected to have all of his questions about the universe answered, but when he asks who made the world, he is refused an answer.

SCENE 6

Summary

Faustus begins to repent that he has made a contract with the devil. Mephistophilis tries to console Faustus by telling him that heaven is not such a glorious place and that man is more wonderful than anything in heaven. The Good Angel and the Evil Angel appear and each tries to influence Faustus' decision. Faustus is haunted by the thought that he is damned. He thinks that he would have killed himself by now if he had not been able to conjure up Homer to sing and soothe him. Now he asks Mephistophilis to argue about theoretical matters. Faustus is not satisfied with the things that Mephistophilis is able to tell him and maintains that even Wagner knows the answers to such questions. He now wants to know about the power behind the universe and who made the world. Mephistophilis tries to get him to think of hell and other things rather than about these heavier philosophical matters.

Faustus cries out for Christ to save him, and at this moment, Lucifer himself appears. Lucifer reminds him that he is breaking his promise by thinking on Christ. He tells Faustus that he has brought some entertainment to divert him.

The seven deadly sins – pride, covetousness, wrath, envy, gluttony, sloth, and lechery – appear before Faustus in the representation of their individual sin or nature. Faustus is delighted with the show and Lucifer hands him a book and promises to return at midnight. After everyone leaves, Wagner appears and says that Faustus has gone to Rome to see the Pope.

Commentary

In this scene we see for the first time a definite change in Faustus. He begins to repent of his pact with the devil. In a reversal of their roles, Mephistophilis now chides Faustus for his lack of resolution, whereas in a previous scene, Faustus had to reprimand Mephistophilis for not being resolute enough. The manner in which Mephistophilis tries to convince Faustus is an instance of logic. He says that man is better than heaven because earth "'twas made for man, therefore is man more excellent."

Note again that the Good Angel and the Evil Angel appear to Faustus at this point – that is, when he is once again in doubt about his decision. As previously, Faustus follows the path of the Evil Angel.

Faustus is torn between two poles of belief which attract him. First he desires to have the beauty of the classical world as represented by Homer and in a later scene by Helen, but at the same time he also wants to keep the best of the Christian tradition. Consequently, we have Christianity and classicism juxtaposed in these scenes and this is part of the tension in Faustus' mind. This tension also existed in the Renaissance world which was interested both in the Hellenistic (Greek) world and the Christian world. The Renaissance man tried to unify his divergent interests in these two worlds.

According to the traditional Christian view, Faustus is now tempted by another sin—that of suicide. Faustus' first sin had been to deny God. Then he also fell into the sin of despair, wherein he lost hope for redemption. In this scene, he considers suicide, which is another cardinal sin.

As Faustus begins to demand deeper knowledge from Mephistophilis, he desires to know about the primary cause of the world but Mephistophilis is unable to answer him. At every point when Faustus begins to question the universe or whenever Faustus begins to think about heavenly things, Mephistophilis tells him to "think on hell." Originally, Faustus made the pact in order to learn about the primal causes of the world; therefore, Mephistophilis is unable to fulfill his part of the bargain. Second, whenever Faustus brings up these questions, Mephistophilis tries to divert him, because he possibly knows that thoughts of heaven would allow Faustus to break his contract with Lucifer.

It is a highly dramatic moment when Lucifer himself appears on the stage. Faustus maintains that Lucifer looks extremely ugly, and again the implication is that hell is ugly.

At the crucial moments when Faustus wavers, the devils always try to divert him in some sensual manner. When Faustus begins to question Mephistophilis about primeval causes, the devils try to take his mind off these noble questions and force him to think about carnal matters. Consequently, in this scene the powers of hell divert Faustus by bringing forth the seven deadly sins to entertain Faustus and to remove all these troublesome questions from his mind.

The appearance of the seven deadly sins is a holdover from the morality plays and becomes another type of interlude in the play. Furthermore, the manner in which they describe themselves is somewhat comic. Whereas in a morality play the seven deadly sins would be paraded before the main character as a warning to abstain from evil, in *Doctor Faustus* they are presented to Faustus only to delight and distract him from heavenly thoughts.

The seven deadly sins do have a philosophical significance and do carry forward the intellectual meaning of the plot. But they also function to appeal to the general audience who would find entertainment in the grotesque physical appearance of these awesome creatures.

Immediately after the appearance of these seven deadly sins, Faustus says "O, this feeds my soul!" Previous to this scene, Faustus had used the same metaphor of eating to express his great hunger for knowledge and power, and now this metaphor is used to show how low Faustus has fallen when the dreadful show of the sins can satisfy his soul.

At the end of the scene, Wagner enters and takes over the function of the chorus by making expository explanations, filling in background material, and letting the audience know that Faustus has now flown to Rome, where he will meet with the Pope.

SCENE 7

Summary

Faustus describes the trip over the Alps and the various cities on the way to Rome. After Mephistophilis tells Faustus that he has arranged to enter the Pope's private chamber, he describes the city of Rome. They prepare to go into the Pope's chambers and Mephistophilis makes Faustus invisible. When the Pope and a group of friars enter, Faustus plays tricks on them by snatching plates and cups from them. Finally, he boxes the Pope on the ear. When the friars who are accompanying the Pope begin to sing a dirge to remove the evil spirit that seems to be present, Mephistophilis and Faustus begin to beat the friars and fling some fireworks among them.

The chorus enters and reviews Faustus' career. When Faustus has seen all the royal courts, he returns home, where many of his friends seek him out and ask him difficult questions concerning astrology and the universe. Faustus' knowledge makes him famous all through the land. Finally the Emperor, Carolus the Fifth, asks him to come to his court.

Commentary

The opening of this scene shows the excellent use of Marlowe's mighty blank verse. The first speech does not make any significant thematic statements, but it resounds with the beautiful poetry. The passage establishes the feeling that Faustus has seen the world and has traveled over mighty expanses of land. We feel then the scope of his travels into the mysterious lands of the known world.

By the time the reader reaches this scene, he should be aware that Marlowe is not adhering to the classical unities of time and place. The scenes now move quickly about the world and there is little indication of the exact place where each scene occurs. Even in some of the earlier scenes, the exact setting was not important. In these short scenes, Marlowe is concerned with sketching in some of the activities of the twenty-four years of Faustus' life and trying to indicate both the passage of time and the manner in which Faustus uses his power.

We must constantly keep in mind that originally Faustus had made his contract with the devil in order to learn more about the essential nature of the universe. In this scene, we must constantly observe how Faustus uses his power. Instead of discussing and learning more about the intelligence behind the universe, Faustus is now misusing his power in order to perform cheap tricks. This indicates that Faustus or any person who begins to make deals with the devil cannot keep a nobility of purpose in mind. Any bargain with the devil will automatically degrade the individual.

The setting of this scene in Rome reminds us again that Faustus is anxious to see the places of great antiquity. He becomes excited about the splendor that was Rome. This is another part of the classical tradition that intrigues him.

> I do long to see monuments
> And situation of bright-splendent Rome.

The scene with the Pope must be viewed as "slapstick" comedy which would appeal to the lowly element in the audience in Marlowe's day. As Faustus snatches cups away and boxes the Pope on the ear, the audience in Marlowe's day would be delighted by this satire against the Pope and the friars. The dirge that the friars sing is also ridiculous and parodies a Roman Catholic chant.

At the end of the scene, we find out that Faustus has attained a certain amount of fame in the field of astrology. He has also experienced a measure of enjoyment. He is now more concerned with satisfying his immediate pleasure and is no longer interested in being instructed in the good life. By describing Faustus' return to Germany, the chorus also fills in the transition between scenes and prepares us for the next scene, which will take place in Germany.

SCENE 8

Summary

Robin the ostler enters with a book in his hand and reveals that he has stolen a volume from Faustus' library. He intends to learn how to conjure in order to make all the maidens in the village appear before him and dance naked. Rafe (Ralph) enters and tells him that there is a gentleman waiting to have his horse taken care of. Robin ignores him, saying that he has more important things to do: he is going to conjure up a devil with his newly stolen book. He promises to procure the kitchen maid for Ralph and then they both leave to clean their boots and continue with the conjuring.

Commentary

This is another low comic scene on conjuring. We see that Robin intends to use Faustus' books for his own pleasure also. The first thing that he intends to do is to make the maidens dance before him stark naked. This is similar to the first thing that Faustus wanted. As soon as he got his new powers, Faustus also began to feel wanton and desired a wife or a whore.

In one sense, the tricks that Robin wants to perform are not much different from the tricks that Faustus has just been playing on the Pope in Rome. Similar to the earlier comic scenes, this scene contrasts with the preceding scene of the main plot. The language is common and filled with obscene puns. Again a servant-master relationship is established; Robin promises Rafe powers for a condition of service in the same way that Mephistophilis promised Faustus power.

SCENE 9

Summary

Robin and Ralph appear with a silver goblet that Robin has apparently taken from a vintner. Robin is very pleased with this new acquisition, but immediately the vintner appears and demands that the goblet be returned to him. Robin insists that he does not have the goblet and allows himself to be searched. The vintner cannot find the goblet. Meanwhile, Robin begins to read incantations from Faustus' book. These incantations summon Mephistophilis, who appears and puts some firecrackers at their backs and then momentarily disappears. In fright, Robin gives the vintner back his goblet. Mephistophilis reappears and complains that he has had to come all the way from Constantinople because these irresponsible servants used incantations without understanding them. He threatens to change them into an ape and a dog, and then leaves. Robin and Ralph can only think about how much fun and how much food they might have if transformed into these animals.

Commentary

This comic interlude actually contributes very little to the development of the play. This is the second scene in a row between Ralph and Robin. The two scenes belong together in showing the result of the men's desire to practice conjuring. Some critics believe that these scenes were later inserted by another author, and there is some dispute whether Marlowe is the author of any of the comic scenes. Generally, in the present condition of the text, the safest thing to assume is that these scenes filled in the time element and provided a type of low comedy which appealed to the less intelligent members of the audience.

SCENE 10

Summary

Later at the German court, the Emperor Carolus tells Faustus that he has heard reports of his magical powers and he would like to see some proof of Faustus' skill. Faustus responds humbly that he is not as skilled as the rumors report him to be, but he will try to please the emperor. The emperor wonders if anyone will ever attain the stature of Alexander the Great, and he asks Faustus to bring Alexander and Alexander's paramour back to life. As the emperor makes this request, a knight in the court makes several skeptical and sarcastic remarks about Faustus' powers. At Faustus' request, Mephistophilis leaves and returns with two spirits in the shape of Alexander and his paramour. After the emperor inspects a mole on the paramour's neck, he declares the two spirits are real. Faustus asks that the sarcastic knight be requested to return. When the knight appears, he has a pair of horns on his head. The knight is furious about his situation and abuses Faustus. Then at the emperor's request, Faustus releases the knight from the spell and the horns are removed. The emperor thanks Faustus for the conjuration and promises to reward him bounteously.

Commentary

This scene shows no significant development or change in the nature of Dr. Faustus. He is still pleasing himself with his new powers, and is still using these powers to satisfy the most trivial demands of other people. This does not imply that summoning two people from the past is trivial, but rather, that Faustus is trying to impress people with his feats rather than striving to use the powers for noble purposes. Before Faustus made the pact, he had anticipated benefiting mankind and Germany with his newly acquired capabilities. Instead of probing into the mystery of the universe, he simply makes horns appear on the head of a knight.

In the time that has elapsed since the first part of the play, Faustus has gained fame and reputation. Because of his reputation, the emperor himself expresses an interest in Faustus and invites him to the imperial court. But the point, as noted above, is that he does not use his advantage to instruct the emperor, but only to entertain him by simple magical tricks and illusions.

It is ironic that Faustus summons up Alexander the Great—a man who conquered the entire world and performed almost impossible tasks. Faustus has at his command the means to surpass the deeds of Alexander, but fails to take advantage of them. Whereas Alexander had sovereignty over the entire known world, Faustus has power to hold dominion over the unknown world. Alexander accomplished the feats he performed only by means of human power, whereas Faustus has had to pay dearly for superhuman capacities.

The incident with the knight demonstrates how Faustus has become increasingly proud of his occult powers. The knight is presented at first as the unbeliever. Because he is sarcastic and insulting to Faustus, he becomes a type of foil for Faustus. Thus Faustus makes a pair of horns grow on his head. For Marlowe's audience, a man whose wife was unfaithful to him was known as a cuckold and was represented as having a pair of horns growing out of his head. Therefore, besides the comic physical appearance of the knight, there was the added comedy of his being the cuckold or foolish man.

SCENE 11

Summary

Faustus begins to be concerned that the end of his allotted time is drawing near. Suddenly, a horse-courser enters and wants to know if Faustus will sell his horse for forty dollars. Faustus willingly agrees to sell his horse but warns the horse-courser that he must never ride the horse into water.

When the horse-courser departs, Faustus resumes contemplating that he is condemned to die, and then falls asleep. The horse-courser returns in a great fluster and accuses Faustus of cheating him. He thought the horse had some magical quality, so he proceeded to ride the animal into a pond. When the horse disappeared under him, he found himself sitting on a bundle of hay and he almost drowned.

Mephistophilis cautions the horse-courser to be quiet because Faustus has just fallen asleep for the first time in eight days. The horse-courser pulls on Faustus' legs, awakens him, and demands that Faustus pay him back his money. He is astounded when Faustus' entire leg comes off. He is so frightened that he promises to pay Faustus forty more dollars.

Wagner enters to tell Faustus that the Duke of Vanholt desires his company, and Faustus agrees to see the noble gentleman.

Commentary

For the first time in many scenes, we see Faustus pondering his ultimate fate. He becomes very aware that time is running out and that his magical powers will soon end. Faustus' consciousness of the passing of time is later dramatized at greater length in the final devastating scene of the play when Faustus watches the minutes and seconds pass.

In his second period of contemplation, Faustus returns to the idea of death itself. Earlier he had spurned the idea of death and thought of ways to escape it. Now he is fully aware of the reality of death that quickly approaches him. At this moment, Faustus also recognizes that he is still a man. In earlier scenes he had lamented that he was only a man and not a God. In his dealings with Lucifer, he had hoped to acquire a godlike position. But at this period of inward meditation, he realizes he is nothing "but a *man* condemned to die."

This scene is constructed differently from other scenes in the play. In many other Elizabethan plays a comic scene is alternated with a serious scene. In this scene both comic and tragic elements occur together. Scenes of Faustus contemplating the idea of his death are interspersed with scenes of low comedy involving the horse-courser.

The comic scenes again show the tragic waste of Faustus' powers. Whereas earlier he had thought in terms of large and vast sums of wealth and power, here he is concerned with the insignificant sum of forty dollars. Faustus blackmails the horse-courser for an additional forty dollars for attempting to awake him.

Another indication that Faustus is beginning to be conscious of his approaching fate is the fact that he has not slept for eight days. To an Elizabethan, this would indicate the spiritual and mental condition of a person. For example, in Shakespeare's *Macbeth,* Lady Macbeth is not able to sleep when her conscience begins to bother her. Thus, the audience would automatically know that Faustus is deeply troubled by his condition.

SCENE 12

Summary

At the court of the Duke of Vanholt, Faustus asks the duchess, who is with child, if she has a desire for any special dainties. Although it is January, she desires to have a dish of ripe grapes. Faustus sends Mephistophilis after them, and when he returns with them, the duke wonders how this could be accomplished. Faustus explains that he sent his spirit to India for them. The duchess exclaims that the grapes are the best she has ever tasted. The duke promises Faustus that he will reward him greatly for this favor.

Commentary

Once again this scene shows what insignificant feats Faustus accomplishes with his powers. Faustus performs a magical trick of obtaining fresh grapes at the request of the nobility. The learned doctor spends some of his last fleeting moments providing "merriment" and "delight" for the duke and duchess. Faustus succeeds in temporarily diverting himself and others from important concerns of life.

SCENE 13

Summary

Wagner enters with the news that Faustus is soon to die because he has given all of his goods and properties to his servants. He doesn't understand why Faustus continues to feast and to carouse if he is so near death.

Faustus enters with scholars discussing who is the most beautiful woman in the world. The scholars think it is Helen of Troy. Because of their friendship for him, Faustus promises to raise her from the dead and let the scholars see her in all her pomp and majesty. Music sounds and Helen passes across the stage. The scholars exclaim wildly about her beauty and thank Faustus for allowing them to see this "paragon of excellence."

As an old man enters, the scholars leave. The old man prevails upon Faustus to repent of "thy most vile and loathsome filthiness," so he could come under the grace and mercy of God and be saved. Faustus fears that hell has him trapped but asks the old man to leave him alone for a while and he ponders his sins.

Mephistophilis then threatens Faustus for disobedience to Lucifer, and Faustus agrees to reaffirm his contract to the devil in blood again. After he writes the second deed, he tells Mephistophilis that he desires Helen for his own paramour. When she appears, Faustus decides that Helen's beauty shall make him immortal and thus, he will not need salvation:

> Was this the face that launched a thousand ships,
> And burnt the topless towers of Ilium?
> Sweet Helen, make me immortal with a kiss.
> Her lips suck forth my soul; see where it flies!–
> Come, Helen, come, give me my soul again.
> Here will I dwell, for heaven be in these lips,
> And all is dross that is not Helen.

After Faustus exits with Helen, the old man re-enters and expresses his disappointment in Faustus, but also sympathizes with him because he too has been tempted but has won victory by turning to God.

Commentary

For the first time since Faustus made his compact with Lucifer, this scene returns us to the central idea of the blood bond in which Faustus bartered his soul. Wagner's opening speech indicates that the time is shortly coming when Faustus will have to face death. At the beginning of the play, Faustus had believed that death did not exist but now he must face not only physical death but eternal death.

Wagner also comments on the manner in which Faustus faces his forthcoming death. Faustus spends his time in banquets and other physical pleasures. He acts as though he does not know that the final feast is about to come to him.

In this scene we see that Faustus performs his last act of conjuring. Again at the request of a friend, Faustus conjures up the image of Helen of Troy.

Note the manner in which Marlowe handles the two appearances of Helen of Troy. During the first appearance, Faustus says nothing about her and only after the three scholars have left do we hear what Faustus' impression is. The comments of the scholars indicate something of her beauty; one calls her the majesty of the world, another refers to her as a paragon of excellence, and the third calls her a "heavenly beauty." Faustus gives the most complete and memorable description of her later in the scene.

The appearance of the old man again brings back into focus the conflict between good and evil that was expressed earlier by the Good Angel and the Evil Angel. Just before the old man's appearance Helen, who represents the beauty of the classical world, appeared upon the stage. The old man comes to remind Faustus of the faith of the Christian world. The old man offers himself as a type of guide who will conduct Faustus to a celestial happiness. The old man is constantly referring to the blood of Christ, which has saved him. This contrasts with the blood which was used earlier to sign the contract with Lucifer and the blood which Faustus will use in a few minutes to renew the pact.

The old man appears at this point because he, along with Faustus, is approaching death. Faustus at this time still has the body of a young person, owing to the magical incantations, but has a blackened soul. The old man is ugly physically but has a beautiful soul and faith in Christ. As Mephistophilis says of the old man:

> His faith is great, I cannot touch his soul;
> But what I may afflict his body with
> I will attempt, which is but little worth.

After a wavering in his soul, Faustus firmly resolves to keep his contract with Lucifer and offers to sign another bond in blood. We must remember that Faustus has just seen the most beautiful woman in the world and desires her. Thus, he makes the second contract to assure himself of getting Helen as his paramour. Originally, he had wanted power and knowledge, but now he is only interested in satisfying his baser appetites. Furthermore, by having Helen, he thinks that her "sweet embracings may extinguish clean/ These thoughts that do dissuade me from my vow." Furthermore, in his moments of despair, there has always been something to divert him so that he will never have to think about his damnation. As the old man tempts him to turn to the paths of righteousness, the memory of the beautiful and desirable Helen intrudes upon his consciousness and causes him to think only of possessing her.

Through the poetic descriptions of Helen, we are convinced that she is the epitome of beauty and the most desirable woman in the world. It is ironic that Faustus thinks that this classical beauty can make him immortal through a kiss more readily than he could achieve immortality through belief in Christ. He thinks that she will be a paradise for him and ironically he gives up all hope of eternal paradise.

The ending of the scene is a contrast to the final scene. The old man re-enters and announces that he has undergone great temptations during life and has overcome his temptations. He notes that he feels that he has triumphed over Mephistophilis and the fiends. In the final scene, Faustus, who has the same opportunity, fails to triumph over the satanic powers and is carried away to damnation. Thus, the appearance of the old man, who announces his triumph, reminds the audience that Faustus could have repented at almost any point and achieved salvation. The fact that Faustus never does repent suggests that Faustus intellectually wills his own damnation.

SCENE 14

Summary

Faustus declares to the three scholars who accompany him that he is in a dejected state because of what is about to happen to him. He admits that he has sinned so greatly that he cannot be forgiven. The scholars urge him to call on God, but Faustus feels that he is unable to call on the God whom he has abjured and blasphemed. He says: "Ah, my God, I would weep, but the devil draws in my tears! . . . I would lift up my hands but, see, they hold them, they hold them!" Faustus tells the scholars that he has done the very things that God most forbids man to do: "for vain pleasure of twenty-four years hath Faustus lost eternal joy and felicity."

One of the scholars volunteers to stay with Faustus until the last minute, But Faustus and the others admit that no one will be able to help him. He must face the final moments alone.

After the scholars leave, the clock strikes eleven, and Faustus realizes that he has only an hour left before eternal damnation. He suffers because he realizes that he will be deprived of eternal bliss and will have to suffer eternal damnation. As the clock strikes half past eleven, he pleads that his doom not be everlasting. He would suffer a hundred thousand years if at last he could be saved. As the clock strikes twelve, he cries out for God not to look so fierce upon him. Thunder and lightning flash across the stage and the devils arrive to take him away.

Commentary

The basic situation in this final scene evokes many literary parallels. For example, we are immediately reminded of Job, who had his friends with him to comfort him during his suffering, but the friends were no help to him. Likewise, in the play *Everyman,* Everyman wants to take all his friends with him to the grave. In *Doctor Faustus,* the doctor has his friends with him and one of the scholars wants to stay with him, but Faustus realizes that he must face death alone.

It is in this scene that Faustus completely realizes what he has done. Because he wanted to live for vain joys, he has lost eternal life. There is a constant interplay throughout the scene between living and dying. Faustus makes a statement to one of the scholars that "had I lived with them then had I lived still, but now I die eternally." In spite of all the admonitions, Faustus even at the end makes no real effort to turn to God. As he realizes the magnitude of his sin, he is almost afraid to turn to the God whom he has abjured. He knows that he has committed those very things which God most strictly forbids. Faustus' only excuse for not turning to God is that "the devil threatened to tear me in pieces if I named God, to fetch both body and soul if I once gave ear to divinity." This is not a rational excuse. In the previous scene, Marlowe demonstrated the example of the old man who abjured the devil and turned to God.

Consequently, Faustus' explanation is false and empty. All he can finally do is to ask the scholars to pray for him.

Man's limitation is that he lives in time, and in his final speech, we see Faustus fighting against this very limitation. As the clock strikes eleven, he realizes that he has only one hour left to live. He suddenly understands that one power he does not possess is the ability to make time stop; he desires to have more time to live and thus repent of his sins.

> Stand still, you ever-moving spheres of heaven,
> That time may cease and midnight never come;
> Fair Nature's eye, rise, rise again, and make
> Perpetual day; or let this hour be but
> A year, a month, a week, a natural day,
> That Faustus may repent and save his soul!

The drama of the scene is heightened by this constant awareness of the passing of time. Faustus is almost frantic as his end approaches. But even in this final scene, Faustus cannot remain resolute and call on God or Christ. He tries at one point to invoke the aid of Christ but ends up by asking Lucifer to spare him. He pleads then that his body suffer punishment but that his soul be spared.

As the clock strikes half past, Faustus then asks that he be punished for a hundred thousand years, but finally he requests that his soul be spared from eternal punishment. Furthermore, he begins to question the existing order of things. He wonders why man must have an eternal soul. It would be better to accept some other theological system where a man's soul could return to the earth in the form of an animal or simply cease to exist. But Faustus is a man with an immortal soul and this soul is damned.

As the clock strikes the final hour, we have one of the most dramatic scenes in all of Elizabethan drama. During thunder and lightning, horrible-looking devils appear to take Faustus off to his eternal damnation. His last pleading words are an effective statement of the horror of trafficking in the black arts. His final speech is incoherent and incomplete, as though he were suddenly dragged off in the middle of his plea.

The chorus makes the final and closing comment on the fall of Faustus. They comment that he had tried to go beyond the limitations of man and had thus fallen into eternal damnation. The chorus admonishes the audience to take note of Faustus' example and not go beyond the boundary of lawful things. The chorus expresses the medieval view that Faustus' fall resulted from his pride and ambition.

FAUSTUS – MEDIEVAL OR RENAISSANCE HERO

Certain aspects of the drama can be used to support an interpretation of Faustus as a Renaissance hero and other aspects suggest he is the medieval hero. According to the medieval view of the universe, man was placed in his position by God and should remain content with his station in life. Any attempt or ambition to go beyond his assigned place was considered a great sin of pride. For the medieval man, pride was one of the greatest sins that man could commit. This concept was based upon the fact that Lucifer's fall was the result of his pride when he tried to revolt against God. Thus, for the medieval man, aspiring pride became one of the cardinal sins.

According to the medieval view, Faustus has a desire for forbidden knowledge. In order to gain more knowledge than man is entitled to, Faustus makes a contract with Lucifer, which brings about his damnation. Faustus then learns at the end of the play that supernatural powers are reserved for the gods and that the man who attempts to handle or deal in magical powers must face eternal damnation. When we examine the drama from this standpoint, Faustus deserves his punishment; then the play is not so much a tragedy as it is a morality play. The ending is an act of justice, when the man who has transgressed against the natural laws of the universe is justifiably punished. The chorus at the end of the drama re-emphasizes this position when it admonishes the audience to learn from Faustus' damnation and not attempt to go beyond the restrictions placed on man.

The character of Faustus can also be interpreted from the Renaissance point of view. At the time of this play, there was a conflict in many people's minds, including Marlowe's, as to whether or not to accept the medieval or the Renaissance view. The Renaissance had been disappointed in the effectiveness of medieval knowledge because many scholastic disputations were merely verbal nonsense. For example, arguments such as how many angels could stand on the head of a pin dominated many medieval theses. The Renaissance scholars, however, revived an interest in the classical knowledge of Greece and the humanism of the past. They became absorbed in the great potential and possibility of man.

According to the Renaissance view, Faustus rebels against the limitations of medieval knowledge and the restriction put upon mankind decreeing that he must accept his place in the universe without challenging it. Because of his universal desire for enlightenment, Faustus makes a contract for knowledge and power. His desire, according to the Renaissance, is to transcend the limitations of individual man and rise to greater achievements and heights. In the purest sense, Faustus wants to prove that man can become greater than he presently is. Because of his desire to go beyond human limitations, Faustus is willing to chance damnation in order to achieve his goals. The tragedy results when a man is condemned to damnation for his noble attempts to go beyond the petty limitations of man.

FAUSTUS AS DRAMATIC CHARACTER

When we first meet Faustus, he is a man who is dissatisfied with his studies in dialectics, law, medicine, and divinity. Even though he is the most brilliant scholar in the world, his studies have not brought him satisfaction, and he is depressed about the limitations of human knowledge. In order to satisfy his thirst for greater knowledge, he decides to experiment in necromancy. He wants to transcend the bonds of normal human life and discover the heights beyond. One might say that he wants to have godlike qualities.

Faustus is willing to sell his soul to the devil under the terms of a contract by which he will receive twenty-four years of service from Mephistophilis and, at the end of this time, he will relinquish his soul to Lucifer. At first he is potentially a great man who desires to perform beneficial acts for mankind. But as a result of his willingness to exchange his soul for a few years of pleasure, he begins to sink toward destruction. He allows his powers to be reduced to performing nonsensical tricks and to satisfying his physical appetites.

At various times throughout the drama, Faustus does stop and consider his dilemma and comes to the verge of repentance. He often thinks about repentance, but he consciously remains aligned with Mephistophilis and Lucifer, and never takes the first steps to obtain forgiveness.

By the end of the drama when he is waiting for his damnation, he rationalizes his refusal to turn to God. Throughout the drama internal and external forces suggest that Faustus could have turned to God and could have been forgiven. In the final scene, the scholars want Faustus to make an attempt to seek the forgiveness of God. But Faustus rationalizes that he has lived against the dictates of God, and he makes no effort to invoke God's forgiveness until the appearance of the devils. But by then, he can only scream out in agony and horror at his final fate.

THE CHARACTER OF MEPHISTOPHILIS AND THE CONCEPT OF HELL

Mephistophilis is the second most important dramatic personage in the drama. He appears in most of the scenes with Faustus. When he is first seen by Faustus, he is horrendously ugly. Faustus immediately sends him away and has him reappear in the form of a Franciscan friar. The mere physical appearance of Mephistophilis suggests the ugliness of hell itself. Throughout the play, Faustus seems to have forgotten how ugly the devils are in their natural shape. Only at the very end of the drama when devils come to carry Faustus off to his eternal damnation does he once again understand the terrible significance of their ugly physical appearance. As Faustus exclaims when he sees the devils at the end of the drama: "Adders and serpents, let me breathe awhile! / Ugly hell, gape not. . . ."

In his first appearance, we discover that Mephistophilis is bound to Lucifer in a manner similar to Faustus' later servitude. Mephistophilis is not free to serve Faustus unless he has Lucifer's permission. Then after the pact, he will be Faustus' servant for twenty-four years. Consequently, the concept of freedom and bondage is an important idea connected with Mephistophilis and Faustus. In other words, no person in the entire order of the universe is entirely free, and what Faustus is hoping for in his contract is a complete and total physical, not moral, freedom. It is paradoxical that the brilliant Dr. Faustus does not see this contradiction in his views about freedom and bondage.

In most of the scenes, Mephistophilis functions as the representative of hell and Lucifer. Only in a few fleeting moments do we see that Mephistophilis is also experiencing both suffering and damnation because of his status as a fallen angel. In the third scene, he admits that he is also tormented by ten thousand hells because he had once tasted the bliss of heaven and now is in hell with Lucifer and the other fallen angels.

Upon Faustus' insistence to know about the nature of hell, Mephistophilis reveals that it is not a place, but a condition or state of being. Any place where God is not, is hell. Being deprived of everlasting bliss is also hell. In other words, heaven is being admitted into the presence of God, and hell, therefore, is deprivation of the presence of God. This definition of hell corresponds to the newly founded doctrine of the Anglican church, which had just recently broken with the Roman Catholic church. But Marlowe also uses a medieval concept of hell for dramatic purposes. As the devils appear in the final scene and as Faustus contemplates his eternal damnation, there are strong suggestions and images of a hell consisting of severe punishment and torment, where ugly devils swarm about and punish the unrepentant sinner.

SERVANT-MASTER RELATIONSHIP IN *DOCTOR FAUSTUS*

One of the basic character relationships and one of the dominant ideas throughout *Doctor Faustus* is that of the relationship between the servant and the master. Faustus' basic desire is that he will never be a slave to anything but that he will be master over the entire world. For this desire he sells his soul. Mephistophilis then becomes Faustus' servant for twenty-four years and has to carry out every wish and command that Faustus makes. The paradox of the situation is that in order to achieve this mastery for these few years, Faustus must sell his soul and thus is, in fact, no longer a free man but, instead, is actually the slave to his desires. Furthermore, when Mephistophilis first appears, he lets Faustus know that there is no such thing as complete freedom. He acknowledges that he now serves Lucifer and that everything in the universe is subjected to something else.

Faustus also is involved in another servant-master relationship with his pupil Wagner. Wagner, the inferior student of the masterful doctor, represents the servant who does not understand either his master or what is happening to him. Wagner tries to emulate Faustus in many things, and tries to take upon himself all the power that his master displays. In his failure, he becomes one of the comic devices in the drama. He tries to use the magical powers to get the clown to serve him, thus establishing another servant-master relationship. On the comic level then, there is even a greater misuse of power. The comic actions of Wagner show that Faustus' essential relationship with Mephistophilis carries a more universal significance. Faustus' actions affects other people, for Wagner tries to imitate his master and only bungles whatever he does.

This master-servant relationship is carried to further comic extremes in the relationship between Robin and Ralph in the comic interludes. Robin gets one of Faustus' conjuring books and tries to force Ralph to become his servant.

Thus, the comic episodes are loosely related to the serious aspects of the drama by this servant-master relationship in which the actions of the master influence the behavior and destiny of the servant.

MOTIFS

MOTIF OF THE FALL

The fall motif in the drama results from two sources, one Christian and one classical. The classical motif is presented in the beginning of the play by the image of Icarus and his fall. Icarus was trapped in a labyrinth and his father made him a pair of wax wings so that he might escape by flying over the confusing maze. In his pride at being able to fly, he flew too close to the sun, melted his wax wings, and fell to his death in the ocean. Thus, the image or allusion to Icarus should evoke the idea of pride bringing about a man's fall and ultimate death.

In conjunction with this classical image is the Christian image of the fall of Lucifer. Lucifer, because of his pride, revolted against God and fell from heaven. In both images the emphasis is upon pride bringing about a fall. The images comment also upon Faustus' situation in that he is likewise a man of pride who aspires to rise above his human limitation and as a result plunges to destruction. His descent from a possible state of salvation into one of eternal damnation is prepared for by the many illusions to a "fall" throughout the drama.

THE APPETITES

At the beginning of the play, Marlowe establishes the image that Faustus has a great hunger for knowledge. When the devil brings various apparitions before him, Faustus comments that these things feed his soul. Each time that Faustus wants to enter into a discussion of the noble things of the world, Mephistophilis shows him something which would appeal to his baser nature and thus satisfy his physical desires. Mephistophilis and Lucifer even parade the seven deadly sins before Faustus and the appearances of these loathsome apparitions evokes from Faustus the comment: "O, this feeds my soul."

During the course of the drama, the manner in which Faustus satisfies his appetites brings about his damnation. Even at the end of his twenty-four years, he signs a second contract in order to satisfy his carnal appetites by having Helen of Troy as his paramour.

Finally in the last scene, he comes to the realization that his appetites have been directly responsible for his downfall. The manner in which he has fulfilled his desires has brought damnation upon himself. "A surfeit of deadly sin that hath damned both body and soul."

STYLE – MARLOWE'S MIGHTY LINE

Before Marlowe, blank verse had not been the accepted verse form for drama. Many earlier plays had used rhymed verse; there are a few examples, such as *Gorboduc,* which had used blank verse, but the poetry in *Gorboduc* was stiff and formal. Marlowe was the first to free the drama from the stiff traditions and prove that blank verse was an effective and expressive vehicle for Elizabethan drama.

One of Marlowe's accomplishments was to capture in blank verse the music inherent in the English language. When Faustus sees Helen of Troy, he exclaims:

> Oh, thou art fairer than the evening air
> Clad in the beauty of a thousand stars!
> Brighter art thou than flaming Jupiter
> When he appeared to hapless Semele. . . .

Earlier blank verse had been metrically precise and regular which, in long passages, could become rhythmically boring. Marlowe alternated the regular stresses and created a more varied, sincere, and beautiful verse. Shakespeare was later to follow Marlowe's example and use the natural rhythm of blank verse.

Ofttimes, instead of using a rhyme, Marlowe uses other poetic techniques to give unity to a passage. As in the ending of the first two lines of the above passage, the assonance of "air" and "stars" imparts a controlled unity to the lines.

In one construction of his poetry, Marlowe did not end each line with a heavy and distinct pause. He often varied the caesuras within a line and he also continued a thought from one line to another. Marlowe used the run-on line so as to give continuity to the poetry. For example, observe Faustus' opening speech.

> Settle thy studies, Faustus, and begin
> To sound the depth of that thou will profess.

Frequently, Marlowe will use geographical names and classical names merely for the resonant quality of the words themselves. In the following lines,

> More lovely than the monarch of the sky
> In wanton Arethusa's azured arms,

note the use of the repetition of the "a" sound and the "r" sounds. The reference to Arethusa, who was embraced by Jupiter, also has a more specific relationship to Faustus' desire to embrace Helen of Troy. But basically, the name does carry heavy alliterative and resonant qualities. Throughout the drama, the student should be aware of the highly ornamental language that Marlowe uses. His speeches are rich in allusions to classical myths. The style, however, has a musical quality about it which appeals to the ear even when the listener does not know the exact nature of the allusions.

The combination of the above qualities influenced the trend of blank verse in Elizabethan drama and earned for Marlowe's verse the term "Marlowe's Mighty Line."

THE RENAISSANCE THEATER

The medieval drama had been an amateur endeavor presented either by the clergy or members of the various trade guilds. The performers were not professional actors, but ordinary citizens who acted only in their spare time. With the centralization of the population in the cities during the later part of the Middle Ages, the interest in secular drama began to increase.

At the end of the medieval period when there were still some guild productions, a rivalry developed between the amateur actor and the new professional actor which stimulated interest in the art of acting. In the sixteenth century, the Elizabethan stage became almost wholly professional and public. Professional groups were formed which charged admission fees to allow audiences to witness their performances. The new theater groups devoted their entire time to the art and craft of play producing. The art of acting became a profession during the Elizabethan period which would furnish a good livelihood for the actor. Likewise, the production of plays at this time was a good financial venture.

Because of the Act of 1545 which classed any person not a member of a guild as a vagabond and subject to arrest, the groups of actors were exposed to a new danger, since many of them were no longer members of a guild and were devoting themselves to traveling about the country and acting. In order to save themselves from being arrested, many of the actors put themselves under the patronage of an important person. Then they could be called a servant of this person and would be free of the charge of being a vagabond. Although many times the relationship between actors and patrons was only nominal, there were a few of these patrons who did give some financial assistance to the actors.

Late in the century, Queen Elizabeth gave permission for a group of actors to perform in London in spite of local rules against actors. Elizabeth stipulated that they could act in London as long as their performances met the approval of the Master of the Revels. By the end of the century, there were always a number of groups of companies playing in London and also others touring the outlying districts.

The actors, usually young males, organized themselves into companies in which each of them would own a certain number of shares. These companies were cooperative and self-governing and divided the profit from the performances. The company would either lease or build its own theater in which to perform, hire men to play the minor parts, and get young apprentice boys to play the female parts in the plays. The important members of the company usually played definite types of characters. For example, Richard Burbage would always play the leading tragic roles, whereas such actors as William Kempe and Robert Armin would play the comic roles.

Plays were often written for a particular troupe or company, and often at their direction. For example, a playwright might read the first act to the members of the company and then accept their criticism and suggestions for changes. Consequently, many plays might be considered as the combined effort of dramatists and actors.

The method of acting was peculiar to the Elizabethan period. The actors expressed themselves in a highly operatic manner with flamboyant expressions. The gestures were stylized according to certain rhetorical traditions. Rhetoric books of the time told exactly how to use one's hands to express fear or anger or other emotional states.

The Elizabethan stage was a "presentational theater" in that there was no attempt to persuade the audience that they were not in a theater and no attempt was made to create any dramatic illusions because there was very little scenery. Also, the actors could speak directly to the audience; the soliloquy, a speech spoken directly to the audience, was a typical characteristic of Elizabethan drama. Since the stage was relatively unadorned, the actors depended upon the visual color and pageantry of their elaborate costumes to give color to the play. Sometimes there was an attempt to wear historical costumes, but most often the actors wore decorative and elaborate Elizabethan dress.

The Elizabethan stage also was a repertory stage; that is, an actor would have memorized certain roles for a limited number of plays. Therefore, each company would present only a given number of plays at prescribed intervals. An incomparable record of the repertory system is Henslowe's diaries. Henslowe kept valuable records of the plays which were performed by the Admiral's company, with which he was associated from 1592 to 1597.

From Henslowe's records we have derived the following information about the repertory season. The plays were performed almost daily throughout the year except when the companies observed a Lenten suspension. Then oftentimes there was a summer break from mid-July to the beginning of October. In any two-week period, there would be eleven performances and only one would repeat a play. A play would never be presented on two consecutive days. Six out of the ten plays would be new works for that season, two would be carry-overs from the previous year, and two others would be older plays which had been revised. The alteration of plays was generally irregular. But with a new play, there seems to have been a general pattern of presentation. The play would be repeated several times after it had been first staged, then it would be acted two times a month for the first months and gradually would be repeated less frequently until in a year and a half it would generally fade from the repertory.

The Elizabethan theater building evolved from constructions that had previously been used for public entertainments – the bear-baiting ring, the innyard. The first plays were given in inns, where tables would be put together to function as a platform or stage. Then the guests would watch from the balcony of their rooms or from the innyard.

The first regular theater was constructed in 1576 by James Burbage and was called "The Theater." In the next thirty years, eight new theaters were built around London, mostly in the district of Shoreditch or Bankside. They were located in these districts because they were just outside the city limits and thus were not under the jurisdiction of the city council, which opposed the opening of theaters because of fire, sedition, and plague. The most important theaters which were built in this period were the "Curtain" in 1577, the "Rose" in 1587, the "Swan" in 1595, the "Globe" (Shakespeare's theater) in 1599, the "Fortune" in 1600, and the "Red Bull" in 1605.

A few records have survived showing the architecture of the Elizabethan theater. There is one drawing by DeWitt showing the construction of the "Swan" theater. From this sketch, we know that the "Swan" was a three-tiered circular building with a large protruding platform extending out into the center of the enclosure.

It was an open structure so that natural light entered through the top. The spectators sat in either the gallery around the sides or down in the "pit."

Considerable information has also been preserved concerning the design of the Globe theater. The "Globe" was octagonal in shape with a platform extending to the center of the theater. The stage had an inner stage which was used for special scenes. There was also a trapdoor in the platform (and sometimes another one in the concealed stage) which was used for the sudden appearance of ghosts and specters. Most of the action of a play would take place on this platform, which contained virtually no scenery.

The Elizabethan theater was an "intimate" theater, since the actor was seldom farther away than forty feet from the audience. This close physical proximity provided for the maximum communication. The spectators were not only sitting in front of the stage but on three sides as well.

STAGE PERFORMANCE

The first recorded stage performance of *Doctor Faustus* took place at the Rose Theater on September 30, 1594, under the direction of the Admiral's Men. No records of performance before 1594 have remained, but the play probably had been produced a number of times before the 1594 production, for Henslowe, the owner of the Rose Theater, did not list it as a new play in his records. The date of the original production has been speculated to be either 1589 or 1592.

Henslowe, who kept a diary and record of all the plays he bought and produced, indicates that the play was frequently produced and that it brought in a sizable profit each time it was performed. It was produced twenty-four times between 1594 and 1597, at which time it diminished in popularity. The next revival of the play was in 1602, when Henslowe paid Bird and Rowley four pounds to write additions to the play (see section on Textual Problems).

Because of all the frequent contemporary allusions to the play in many works of this period, it is evident that *Doctor Faustus* was one of the most popular plays staged during this period. The drama has had frequent revivals in each century since the Elizabethan age and is considered one of the world's most famous plays today.

There are many stories connected with the productions of *Faustus*. One of the tales concerns the great Elizabethan actor Edward Alleyn, who portrayed Faustus. The legend tells that his retirement from the stage was the result of having a real devil appear during one of the conjurations scenes while performing the role of Dr. Faustus.

TEXTUAL PROBLEMS

One of the difficulties in studying *Doctor Faustus* lies in establishing the authoritative text. In 1601, the stationer Thomas Bushell registered a publication entitled "A book called the play of Doctor Faustus." A quarto of the play may have been printed that year, but there is no existing copy to be found.

The play which we now have has been handed down in two widely different versions: the 1604 or *A* quarto and the 1616 or *B* quarto. The *A* quarto was also reprinted in 1609 and 1611. Since there is a record in Henslowe's diary in 1602 that he paid four pounds to William Bird and Samuel Rowley for writing additions to *Doctor Faustus,* this earlier quarto probably contains some of these interpolations and additions which Marlowe did not write. Since the *A* text is so short and does not have any traditional divisions into scenes or acts, W. W. Gregg speculates that the *A* text represents a report from memory by some of the actors in the original acting company.

The 1616 or *B* quarto is a greatly expanded edition of the play and contains some six hundred lines more, making it about the normal length of an Elizabethan play. The *B* quarto was also reprinted in 1619, 1620, 1624, 1628, and 1631. Several scholars think that this text is of composite origin, being from several original drafts with certain revisions.

Although several scholars, including Greg and Boas, argue that the 1616 text is the more authoritative of the two, most editors have used the 1604 quarto, which had apparently been cut for acting. Most of the editors, while using the 1604 quarto, have added corrections from the 1616 editions. Thus any text that is now used will be a combination of these two texts according to the views of the individual editor.

Because the text of *Doctor Faustus* is so corrupt, it is impossible to determine whether or not Marlowe wrote the complete play as it now appears in any of the texts. The problems of structure and also the unrelated comic scenes suggest that the clown or comic scenes were inserted by other writers. However, without these comic scenes the play would have been exceptionally short. It is probably safe to assume that Marlowe intended to have a certain amount of comic scenes in the play, and judging from the structure of the early scenes, he probably intended Wagner to appear in most of these. However, this is only speculation and cannot at present be settled definitely.

REVIEW QUESTIONS

1. Is Faustus' damnation tragic or an act of justice? Discuss in detail.
2. Compare the master-servant relationship in the drama.
3. What is the function of the Good Angel and the Evil Angel in the drama?
4. How are the Good Angel and the Evil Angel related to earlier morality plays? What else in the drama is a holdover from the morality plays?
5. How are the comic interludes related to the main plot?
6. What is the role of the old man in Scene 13?

7. How does Faustus' use of his magical powers correlate with his earlier desires and plans?

8. Write a description of hell as it is variously described and presented in this drama.

9. Comment on the weaknesses found in the structure of the drama.

10. How does Greek classical imagery function in the drama?

11. After the original contract with Lucifer, is there a possibility for Dr. Faustus to repent?

12. How is the image of the "fall" used throughout the drama?

13. Explain the satire against the Roman Catholic church and describe its purpose.

14. How does Marlowe use the classical concept of the chorus during the play?

15. How does Faustus' relationship with Helen of Troy epitomize the activities of the twenty-four years?

SELECTED BIBLIOGRAPHY

BOOKS

Bakeless, John. *Christopher Marlowe: The Man in His Time*. New York, 1937. A biography which attempts to deal with Marlowe's life and works as a whole rather than concentrating on an isolated aspect of his career.

Boas, F. S. *Christopher Marlowe*. Oxford, 1940. A comprehensive study of both the biographical and critical aspects of Marlowe. The critical interpretation discusses the plays and poems according to an analysis of the plots in relation to their sources. Boas also analyzes the classical influences on Marlowe's works.

Cole, Douglas, *Suffering and Evil in the Plays of Christopher Marlowe*. Princeton, 1962.

Ellis-Fermor, U. M. *Christopher Marlowe*. London, 1927. An attempt to trace the development of Marlowe's mind and art as revealed in his works and then to portray the personality they reveal.

Greg, Sir W. W. *Marlowe's Doctor Faustus, 1604 and 1616: Parallel Texts*. Oxford, 1950. A comparison of the two folio versions of *Doctor Faustus*.

Henderson, P. *Christopher Marlowe*. London, 1952. A brief survey of Marlowe's life and short critical interpretations of the plays and poems.

Knights, L. C. *Drama and Society in the Age of Jonson*. London, 1937. A study of the economic environment in the late sixteenth century and the social significance of this environment in the plays of Elizabethan dramatists.

Kocher, P. H. *Christopher Marlowe*. Chapel Hill, 1946. A study of the different phases of Marlowe's learning—his religious thought and his secular thought.

Levin, Harry. *The Overreacher*. Cambridge, 1952. A critical study of Marlowe's plays with an emphasis on recurring motifs and themes.

Marlowe, Christopher. *The Works and Life of Christopher Marlowe*, ed. R. N. Case. 6 vols. London, 1930-33. The definitive edition of the complete works of Marlowe.

Norman, Charles. *The Muse's Darling: The Life of Christopher Marlowe*. New York, 1946. A biography which focuses on Marlowe and his friends and enemies as (1) men and (2) Elizabethans against the background of their time.

Poirier, M. *Christopher Marlowe*. London, 1951.

Röhrman, H. *Marlowe and Shakespeare*. Arnheim, 1952. A thematic exposition of *Tamburlaine, Doctor Faustus, Hamlet, Troilus and Cressida* and *Macbeth*.

Smith, Marion Bodwell. *Marlowe's Imagery and the Marlowe Canon*. Philadelphia, 1940. A catalogue of the images in Marlowe's works. The imagery is used as an indication of the author's personality and also as a means of determining the authorship of plays attributed to Marlowe.

Wilson, F. P. *Marlowe and the Early Shakespeare*. Oxford, 1954. A collection of five lectures which discuss five of Marlowe's plays and then compare Marlowe's history plays with those of Shakespeare.

ARTICLES

Campbell, Lily B. "*Doctor Faustus:* A Case of Conscience," *PMLA*, LXVII (1952), 219-239. A study of the nature of Faustus' sin. The author's premise is that the dramatic suspense of the play results from the fact that Faustus could have repented up until the final minute. She also compares the nature of Faustus' sin to a contemporary case involving a man named Francis Spira.

Greg, W. W. "The Damnation of Faustus," *MLR*, XLI (1946), 97-107. This is a study of the fall of Faustus in terms of his physical transformation into a devilish spirit as compared to his spiritual fall.

Kocher, Paul H. "The Early Date for Marlowe's *Faustus*," *MLN*, LVIII (1943), 539-542. This is an attempt to establish the date of the play as 1589 instead of 1592. The arguments for the earlier date are based upon contemporary references to the play in 1589.

Kocher, Paul H. "Nashe's authorship of the Prose Scenes in *Faustus*," *MLQ*, III (1942), 17-40. Kocher tries to give evidence and proof that Nashe is the author of the comic prose scenes in *Doctor Faustus*.

McCloskey, J. C. "The Theme of Despair in Marlowe's Faustus," *CE,* IV (1942), 110-113. McCloskey maintains that Faustus embodies the medieval concept of despair and that it is the sin of despair which damns him.

NOTES

NOTES

NOTES

Don Quixote

DON QUIXOTE

NOTES

including

- *Life and Background of Cervantes*
- *Chapter Summaries and Critical Commentaries*
- *Purpose of the Novel*
- *Technique and Style*
- *Characterization*
- *Themes*
- *Questions for Discussion*
- *Selected Bibliography*

by
Marianne Sturman

INCORPORATED

LINCOLN, NEBRASKA 68501

ISBN 0-8220-0415-1

Printed in U.S.A.

1993 Printing

Cliffs Notes, Inc. Lincoln, Nebraska

CONTENTS

DON QUIXOTE

INTRODUCTION

Don Quixote is a work that has universal and contemporary appeal.

These notes are designed to introduce you to this novel, to suggest a few interpretations of Cervantes' work in particular instances, and to remark on the author's technique in order to familiarize you with the material itself. Short chapter summaries, however, cannot include the gentle ironies, the ridiculous comic situations, the rollicking dialogues, and above all, the memorable characterizations of Don Quixote and his squire Sancho Panza. To fully appreciate *Don Quixote*—the delightful details of episode and dialogue, character and ideas—one must go to the novel itself.

Don Quixote, although considered a great classic today—indeed the first modern novel—was a best seller the first year it appeared. Today it is still a best seller, and although Cervantists have filled libraries with critical commentaries and erudite analyses for fifteen generations, the book can be enjoyed by readers of all intellectual levels. *Don Quixote* includes drolleries of the sort that silent film audiences expect, characterizations that are spontaneous and untouched by the kind of heavy-handed artist who tries to make his readers weep or guffaw. It etches such strong images that the hack-mounted knight and the fatbodied squire on his ass will remain impressed in the mind of the reader throughout his life, enabling him to recognize and admire other windmill-tilting Quixotes and comic men of practical affairs who are the Sancho Panzas today.

Regard these notes only as an incomplete approach to *Don Quixote*; then turn to the novel itself for true illumination. After you have read the book, then review these notes once more. Hopefully, you will discover further rich meanings in the novel.

BIOGRAPHICAL SKETCH AND BACKGROUND OF CERVANTES

Miguel de Cervantes Saavedra lived from 1547 until 1616 in a period that spanned the climax and decline of Spain's golden age. All his life he shared the ideals of an idealistic national purpose that led to Spain's glory and downfall at a time when the nation was the Catholic bulwark against a reformation-torn Europe and against the ravishing advances of the aggressive Turkish power.

Imbued with heroic exploits, Spain was proud of her epic heroes, Cortez and Pizarro, who subdued entire populations in the New World and released a stream of gold that supported the military might of Charles V and Phillip II. Despite the rich American source of treasure, the defense of Spain exhausted the resources of her peasants and of her colonies, until, at the defeat of the Armada, the country was too impoverished to recover. With the decline of Spanish power, England and the reformation countries of Europe began their ascendancy.

Born into penurious circumstances, Miguel Cervantes was the fourth son in a family of seven children. His father, Rodrigo, was a surgeon, one of the salaried employees of the university of Alcala de Henares, the birthplace of Miguel, and he earned very little to feed his family. Little is known of Cervantes' early life, but it is doubtful if he received much formal education.

When he was twenty, Miguel was in the retinue of the Cardinal Nuncio Acquaviva and spent his service in Rome. Joining the army with his brother Rodrigo, he participated in the battle of Lepanto where the Spanish established superiority of seapower against the Turks. Sick below decks, Cervantes insisted on joining the battle in a most exposed position. He fought bravely, receiving two shots in his chest and a wound which rendered his left hand useless the rest of his life. This lacerated hand was his glory, and the bravery he showed at Lepanto earned him a document of recommendation from Don Juan himself, the Austrian half brother of Phillip who commanded the Spanish forces. After a long convalescence, Cervantes rejoined the army to fight in the famous battle of La Goleta (mentioned in the Captive's story). He also campaigned in Tunis, Sardinia, Naples, Sicily, and Genoa, learning much about Italian culture during this period of service. Returning with Rodrigo to Spain, their ship was captured by pirates and both brothers were sold as slaves in Algiers.

The story of his incredible bravery during those five years is almost legendary, for Cervantes schemed again and again, not only for his own escape, but for the liberation of numerous fellow slaves. Each time he failed, he declared he alone, and not his countrymen, was to blame, knowing full well the atrocities reserved for punishing escaped Christians. The bloodthirsty Dey of Algiers, Hassan Pacha, however, was impressed by the audacity of the maimed Spaniard and always spared him. Although Rodrigo was eventually ransomed, it was not until much later that Miguel's ransom was negotiated.

In 1580 Cervantes returned to Spain, maimed, without any means of livelihood. Don Juan was dead and hated by the king, so Miguel could not hope for any preferment through his recommendations. Out of desperation, he began to write for the theater, but of as many as thirty or forty plays only a few have survived. During this period, Cervantes had an affair with a Portugese girl who eventually deserted him, leaving their daughter Isabel de Saavedra for him to raise.

Still an unsuccessful playwright at the age of forty, Cervantes married the daughter of a well-to-do farmer, Catalina Salaza y Vozmediano. Little is known of his wife, but the marriage was not a successful one. At this time of life, Cervantes had to support, besides his wife and natural daughter Isabel, his mother, two sisters and the widowed mother-in-law. He applied for many civil service posts and eventually was granted a job as commissary collecting foodstuffs for the Invincible Armada. It is during this period that Cervantes learned to know the Spanish peasant, and his stored-up knowledge was to result in the creation of Sancho Panza.

Bookkeeping was a complicated and arduous procedure, and Cervantes was twice imprisoned for owing money to the treasury from a shortage in his accounts. Cervantists disagree whether or not the Seville prison was where he began to write *Don Quixote*. In the preface, the author hints to the reader that "You may suppose it [*Don Quixote*] the Child of Disturbance, engendered in some dismal prison..."; this line is the basis for controversy among biographers.

Misfortune continued to dog him when he was out of prison, as if to impede the composition of his masterpiece. Finally completed in 1604 the *Quixote* was an immediate best seller. Running into six editions a year after that, Cervantes derived no further profit from the book, other than the money originally paid him by his publisher. The success of his work, however, interested the Count of Lemos and the Cardinal Archbishop of Toledo who became his patrons, although they did not do much to improve Cervantes' miserable circumstances.

Sixty-seven years old, still dogged by poverty and with his health failing, Cervantes began the sequel to *Don Quixote* only to find that a pirate edition of his idea had become popular. As if to retort to this underhanded publication, Cervantes quickly completed Part II.

During this brief span of his life—between the ages of 57 and 69—Cervantes published his *Exemplary Novels,* twelve stories of Spain which survive as perceptive accounts of the local life of that time. He also published some plays, *Eight Interludes and Eight Comedies,* which manifest a dramatic talent that his earlier pieces never quite achieved. His last work, *The Troubles of Persiles and Sigismunda,* is notable mainly for its prologue dedicated to the ungrateful Count of Lemos. Aubrey Bell, an outstanding Cervantist, considers this work to be "the most pathetic and magnificent farewell in all literature." Cervantes, writing from his deathbed, began the prologue: "With one foot already in the stirrup and with the agony of death upon me, great lord, I write to you." Cervantes died in April, 1616, the same month that marks the death of William Shakespeare.

Although *Don Quixote* is one of the most read novels in the world, as well as one of the longest, and continues to be a best-seller, the life of Spain's greatest author is less known than the lives of lesser literary figures. What is outstanding in the scanty biographical date available about Cervantes, is the energy and warmth which radiated from the personality of this penurious, ill-fated figure. A product of the proud Catholic-inspired Spanish heritage, Cervantes believed implicitly in religious orthodoxy and military heroism. Like Don Quixote, Cervantes traveled through life with a strong sense of purpose. Meeting with misfortune and disillusion like his hero, Cervantes contributed to civilization, possibly as a result of his own life's experiences, the people and the values of *Don Quixote*.

THE AUTHOR'S PREFACE TO THE READER

Unable to recommend his "stepchild" to his readers with laudations or apologies, Cervantes writes that "though I bestowed some time in writing the book, yet it cost me not half so much labor as this very preface." Stalemated at this task of preface-writing, he welcomes the intrusion of a friend and complains to him of his difficulty. The friend laughs at such a simple problem, and Cervantes transcribes the wise counsel he receives. To make the work appear scholarly, his friend advises him to insert random Latin phrases among his sentences in the most appropriate contexts. Cervantes must provide footnotes as well, phrasing these in glib, pseudo-scientific language. Finally, for an impressive bibliography, he should copy the entire alphabetical index of authors out of some book that has such a list and incorporate it as part of his own.

On the other hand, continues the friend, *Don Quixote* requires slightly different treatment, being a profane history. "Nothing but pure nature is your business,...and the closer you can imitate your picture is the better," he counsels. Furthermore, no outside sources have to be cited since the aim of *Don Quixote* is merely to "destroy the authority and acceptance the books of chivalry have had in the world." Though you wish to "challenge attention from the ignorant and admiration from the judicious," he tells the author, keep your attention riveted to the main purpose of this writing—"the fall and destruction of that monstrous heap of ill-contrived romances, which, though abhorred by man, have so strangely infatuated the greater part of mankind." Cervantes reports that his friend's arguments were so convincing that he was moved to write the whole story by way of preface.

COMMENTARY

The preface itself functions to show the readers what a good storyteller the author is, cleverly inviting them to seek the main body of the book for even better stories. Furthermore, the reader can instantly notice the utter candor of this author who not only admits his dullness at preface-writing, but transcribes an entire conversation to show the development of his thoughts. The reader also learns that there appears no false scholarship in this "profane history" of the famous knight of La Mancha, so that the story must be a truthful one.

Thus by example, as well as by direct explanation, Cervantes sets forth his main qualities as a writer: felicity to natural happenings, realistic detail portrayed as if in a painting, and purposeful writing in order to destroy the pernicious influence of books of chivalry. Besides amusing the reader in his preface, promising him a didactic, truthful history, Cervantes also suggests that *Don Quixote* is not superficial and that the "judicious" will find much to think about in the course of the reading.

PART ONE

BOOK ONE

CHAPTER I

The Quality and Manner of Life of the Renowned Don Quixote de La Mancha.

Alonso Quixano, a middle-aged gentleman of La Mancha, lives with a housekeeper and a young niece. He has sacrificed his usual pastime of hunting and caring for his estate for the all-consuming passion of reading books of chivalry. Cervantes shows that the books are so illogically written that it is no wonder a poor gentleman loses his reason when he feeds this faculty with such fabulous tales day and night. To the dismay of his household members, as well as engaging the concern of the Don's friends, the curate and the barber, the respected citizen of La Mancha feels himself inspired to become a knight-errant and systematically collects the effects necessary to his calling. He shines his great-grandfather's armor, devises a visor and cap after working on them more than a week, and renames his skinny stable horse Rosinante, which means that before having a knight-errant for a master, this steed was once an ordinary horse. Now thought Don Quixote, after renaming himself, his horse, his ambitions, he must name the lady of his pure heart, for a knight-errant "without a mistress, was a tree without fruit or leaves, and a body without a soul." He selects a young country lass named Aldonza Lorenza for his own Dulcinea del Toboso although she is all but a complete stranger to him.

Commentary

The first chapter of any great novel deserves careful perusal, for it introduces the tone of the author, the main characters, and provides quiet hints for the further development of the story.

Cervantes carefully describes his hero, a middle-aged hidalgo, idle and quite poor, who lives with prosaic people, housekeeper, niece, and handy man. Because Don Quixote has literary arguments with the curate and barber about happenings in books of chivalry, the reader gets the first inkling that the hero takes knight-errantry very seriously. A few sentences later, Cervantes shows that his hidalgo is strong-willed enough about this matter to take up this profession himself. By another act of will, his jaded hack becomes a noble steed, and his secret love for a peasant lass becomes his chaste ideal of beauty, for every knight must serve an ideal mistress.

Don Quixote spends much time in thinking and talking, rather than quietly accomplishing valorous deeds. One can argue that he approaches knight-errantry not like a madman who believes that he is someone else, but rather like an actor who memorizes and practices a role. This is a reasonable viewpoint and Cervantes provides ample evidence to justify either the madman theory or the actor theory, just as Shakespeare has done for Hamlet. Whichever critical approach is used, it is necessary to consider Cervantes' interest in telling the truth. Whatever exaggeration appears in the novel is the result of Don Quixote's imagination, not that of the author. The madman hero, or actor hero, is always trying to do justice in the world, to find truth, and he therefore follows a knightly code that demands truthful behavior under any circumstances. By describing how the strong-willed Don Quixote makes up his own truths, Cervantes displays a keynote of his humor. For instance, the author depicts the scene when the knight, testing his handiwork after the homemade visor and cap are completed, swings his sword as hard as he can, completely cleaving the pasteboard helmet. Don Quixote again sets to work to remake the article, and when this one is finished, he prudently refrains from testing its strength. To have faith in strength is enough, thinks the hero, for reality is always weaker. Willpower—the power to see absolute truths—admits no doubt, whereas material truths are never trustworthy.

CHAPTER II

Of Don Quixote's First Sally.

Attired now to his satisfaction, Don Quixote sets out for his first adventure. He travels all day until he comes to an inn at dusk. Disappointed at having found no adventure at all, he pleases himself by considering the inn a great castle with buttresses, moat, and lofty pinnacles. The innkeeper has no food for his strange guest other than salt fish (it is Friday) and moldy bread, but the Don's madness turns his repast into delicate trout and most excellent bread. The two prostitutes who wait on him are lovely damsels in his fancied world, and he addresses them as great ladies. The wenches help the knight undo his armor, but he does not allow them to cut the green ribbons that secure the headpiece. Despite their help, Don Quixote has great difficulty in eating and drinking with his helmet on; he is also obliged to sleep with it on.

Commentary

Regarding the inn as a castle, the prostitutes as highborn maidens, Don Quixote embraces his first adventure. Again his will conquers the everyday situation, for the innkeeper is forced to respond to his strange guest as a castellan must respond when receiving a knight-errant. And the two strumpets administer to Don Quixote with as much consideration and kindness as if they really were courteous ladies of quality. The realistic author writes the chapter so that the reader is amused at the knight's extravagance. Despite the burlesque, despite the objectivity of Cervantes, Don Quixote transforms the scene until even the reader can believe that the inn is a castle, and the wenches are highborn maidens. The innkeeper is even glad to allow his guest to depart without paying for his lodging, just as if he were a castellan entertaining a knight.

CHAPTER III

An Account of the Pleasant Method Taken by Don Quixote to Be Dubbed a Knight.

Don Quixote's great problem is to get himself dubbed a knight, preferably by some powerful lord in a castle. He begs this boon of his landlord, a sharp man who has himself read many books of chivalry, and who also knows that one must humor a madman's fantasies. The innkeeper agrees to perform the ceremony at dawn, and Don Quixote goes about the ritual of watching his arms and meditating throughout the night. He sets his weapons in a horse trough, and when a carrier approaches to water his mules, after laying aside the sacred armor, Don Quixote rushes to attack the poor man. As soon as the fancied enemy is dispatched, another carrier approaches to water his animals, and he too is laid low next to his companion. Don Quixote now fancies that the place is infested with his enemies, and he prepares to defend himself against anyone who approaches. The clever innkeeper wishes only to preserve the peace of his courtyard and begs the knight to make ready for the dubbing—"two hours watch is all that is needed"—which he accomplishes after the manner described in books of chivalry.

CHAPTER IV

What Befell the Knight After He Left the Inn.

The newly-dubbed knight leaves the inn at dawn in search of adventure. The first injustice he comes across concerns the plight of a young apprentice tied to a tree. The master is whipping the boy with great determination. Don Quixote thunders his chivalrous challenge, and the countryman, with great humility, explains himself to the knight. "This boy," he says, "Whom I hire to guard my flocks is so heedless that he loses some sheep every day. When I scold him he says I am angry because I do not want to pay his wages. He belies me."

"What! The lie in my presence!" the knight exclaims. "You scoundrel! Untie this tender youth and pay him all that you owe. Then let him go free. If you do not pay him fairly, I shall return to settle with you once and for all." The countryman promises, and the self-righteous knight continues proudly down the road, pleased to have redressed a serious grievance. As soon as Rosinante and his rider disappear from sight, the angry master lashes the boy to the tree once more, and again and again gives him "what he owes and more besides!" with a heavy strap.

As the brave knight rides in search of more adventure, he breathes a brief dedication to his mistress, the peerless Dulcinea del Toboso. In this mood Don Quixote stops a group of merchants. "No man continue further," he cries, lance couched threateningly, "unless he acknowledge that no lady is more perfect or more beautiful than the Empress of La Mancha, the peerless Dulcinea del Toboso." Naturally, the men perceive that he is mad, and one of them asks Don Quixote for a bit of portraiture of the lady so they can honestly assess her charms. Angered at the doubt, Don Quixote charges the man, but Rosinante stumbles, and his thrown rider rolls over and over on the ground. At this opportunity, one of the muleteers takes up the broken lance, and begins to beat the hapless knight until he wearies his arm. Too bruised to get up, Don Quixote can only watch the caravan as it disappears down the road.

Commentary

The adventure with poor Andrew is one incident – not the last – where the Don's meddlesomeness results in the undoing of those he would wish to help. Critics infer from this adventure that Cervantes wishes to show the futility of impetuously intruding into people's lives without considering all facets of the situation. Don Quixote's intrusions stem from his will to impose his faith on everyday situations. As he is certain that the rich countryman will faithfully remunerate his servant, because he has promised to do so, his job as a knight-errant is finished. This same faith impels Don Quixote to challenge the silk merchants in order to force them to acknowledge a pure abstraction, the perfection of his ideal mistress Dulcinea. Traders, however, used to bargaining and haggling, do so even in matters of faith. The spokesman asks for a bit of portraiture "though it were no bigger than a grain of wheat," a blasphemy which deserves instant punishment. Don Quixote gets beaten, however, not only by the unconvinced merchants, but by an ignorant muleteer. Here Cervantes shows that, although the basic beliefs of common men are tenets of faith, yet their imaginations are so circumscribed that they cannot admit any other faith. Don Quixote, on the other hand, is prepared to defend not only his own faith and sense of truth, but that of others as well. This will be shown in future adventures.

CHAPTER V

A Further Account of Our Knight's Misfortunes.

Still unable to rise, Don Quixote searches his memory for passages from books of chivalry that would give him comfort. He recites appropriate verses from an epic he has memorized, declaiming so loudly that the noise attracts the attention of a passerby who rushes to the spot. The kind peasant, a neighbor of his, examines him gently for injury, helps him up and heaves Don Quixote onto his donkey. Leading Rosinante by the bridle, he takes the knight home. Don Quixote's housekeeper and niece and his friends gather around the hero asking many questions. Aside from saying that he fell heavily off his horse while fighting ten giants, Don Quixote is silent and desires repose above all.

CHAPTER VI

Of the Pleasant and Curious Scrutiny Which the Curate and the Barber Made of the Library of Our Ingenious Gentleman.

The curate and barber, accompanied by the housekeeper, venture into Don Quixote's library. They have decided to burn the books of knight-errantry, the cause of the poor gentleman's madness. Before committing the volumes to the fire, however, the two learned friends examine the title pages of the books, remarking and exchanging critical comments on the value of the volumes, all of which are very familiar to them.

Commentary

Cervantes writes this scene as if it were an inquisition, with the curate and barber putting the books on trial and then passing sentence. This device serves to show not only how extensive Don Quixote's readings are, but how familiar these volumes are to everyone who has the ability to read. The curate and the barber, speaking of the merits of each book, show themselves to be almost as extravagant as Don Quixote. They take the literature very seriously in order to accuse books as being the cause of the Don's madness in the first place. The inquisitors are, however, interested in saving a few of the works from the fire, and these innocents are put aside in another pile.

CHAPTER VII

Don Quixote's Second Sally in Quest of Adventures.

Don Quixote awakens in a raving fit and his friends grab hold and force him back into bed. At this, the simple housekeeper is fully convinced that all books are bedeviled. She collects even those volumes which have been reprieved and burns them all. Meanwhile, the barber and the curate are equally fearful for Don Quixote's health. They arrange to have the entrance to his study walled up, and instruct the niece and housekeeper to tell the knight that an evil conjurer, mounted on a fiery dragon, has removed not only the books, but the entire library.

The knight accepts the explanation, and while he seems to be recovering his senses, quietly schemes to continue his profession of chivalry. Sancho Panza comes now into the scene, for Don Quixote manages to convince this poor, honest, and ignorant peasant to serve as his squire.

Promising many rewards, especially mentioning that he might conquer some island and make his squire governor of the place, he induces Sancho to steal quietly from the village in the middle of the night in order to outwit possible pursuers.

Commentary

This chapter also bears another example of the reality of Don Quixote's imaginings. The knight believes that an evil enchanter works constantly for his undoing. His real nemesis, however, is the prosaic unimaginative world, and the individuals of the prosaic world work as tirelessly for his overthrow as if they were hirelings of his evil enemy. The sooner the knight-errant can adventure in the world, then the sooner will evil enchanters, like the ones in the minds of the curate and barber who wall up the library entranceway, be banished.

As soon as possible then, Don Quixote followed by Sancho Panza leaves the village. Although the credulous peasant follows his master in hopes of material gain, he is led on by an ideal of glory—governor of an island—almost as compelling as the ideal of Dulcinea del Toboso. His actual quest, then, is not one of greed, but one of faith. Poor Sancho is destined to struggle with this tension throughout the many adventures which follow.

CHAPTER VIII

Of the Good Success Which the Valorous Don Quixote Had in the Most Terrifying and Never-to-Be-Imagined Adventure of the Windmills, with Other Transactions Worthy to Be Transmitted to Posterity.

At daybreak the two travelers find themselves on a plain dotted with thirty or forty windmills. Don Quixote is jubilant. "Look yonder, friend Sancho," he cries, "Fortune has provided me with thirty or forty giants to encounter. When they are dead we may claim the lawful spoils of our conquest." The naive squire asks, "What giants?" but Don Quixote covered with his shield, lance couched, has already spurred Rosinante forward. He drives his weapon into the revolving sail of the first windmill, but the motion breaks the lance and roughly hurls horse and rider a good distance away. "Did I not tell you they are windmills!" cries Sancho, rushing to his aid. Don Quixote says that he is truly unlucky, for the same accursed necromancer who carried away his books and study now deprived him of victory by changing these giants into windmills.

Finally finding a place to rest for the night, Sancho falls into deep sleep while Don Quixote remains wakeful, meditating until dawn on his mistress Dulcinea del Toboso, in imitation of what he has read in books of chivalry. Another adventure presents itself the next morning. Two monks on muleback approach, followed by a carriage, which is followed by a mounted escort and some muleteers. Telling Sancho that these are two black necromancers carrying off some distressed princess, the knight challenges and attacks the first monk. He escapes death by diving from his mule, while his companion flees as fast as his beast can go. Sancho, newly learned in chivalry, eagerly begins to despoil the fallen monk, but the two muleteers prevent this and give him a sound beating as well. Don Quixote is busy at this time presenting himself to the lady in the carriage. Her gentleman-squire, a man from Biscay, takes offense, and the two men begin an epic struggle.

Commentary

Quickly, with many adventures, Don Quixote is launched on his career of faith as a knight-errant. Sancho is likewise launched, for if he can withstand the adventure of the windmills and still remain attached to his madman master, then he can be loyal throughout even more extravagant adventures.

The combat with the windmill is rich in symbolism. It does not matter whether the ponderous machine stands for stultified human insitutions that need attacking, or ancient traditions that must be newly questioned, or totalitarian government requiring renewal by revolution, or bureaucracy being attacked by individual demands. What matters is that only a positive act of will is capable of attacking anything, and the success or failure is unimportant. "Thy triumph, my Don Quixote," writes Unamuno, "Was ever a triumph of daring, not of succeeding." Not only is Don Quixote victorious because he dares, but he is always spiritually triumphant as well. He has a stoical ability to disregard his physical failures and is willing to follow his adventures after a slight recovery.

BOOK TWO

CHAPTER I

The Event of the Most Stupendous Combat Between the Brave Biscainer and the Valorous Don Quixote.

The author intercedes here, explaining that the history of the famed knight of La Mancha has been vexedly cut off at this point where the two combatants are about to deliver each other a mortal blow. In his Moorish travels, however, the author has discovered an old manuscript written in Arabic by a historian named Cid Hamet Benegali. By mere coincidence it happens to be the history of Don Quixote and the second book of the manuscript begins with the fight between the knight and the Biscainer, which he sets down exactly as Cid Hamet has written it.

By fortunate mistakes, the Don wins the duel, stunning his adversary with a tremendous blow. He spares the Biscainer's life, though only after he promises to present himself to the Lady Dulcinea del Toboso who shall dispose of him as she desires.

Commentary

Cervantes depicts the struggle between Don Quixote and the Basque squire as an epic combat between equals. The Biscainer has a quixotic idea of his gentility which the rest of the world would disagree with. "What me no gentleman?" he cries and is ready to kill Don Quixote to defend his honor.

In this chapter Cervantes introduces the device of a narrator who steps in and out of his story as it it were a piece of stagecraft. To insure the objectivity of the storyteller, the author is a Moor, for an infidel would try very hard to understate the achievements of a Spaniard. This assures the reader that the history of Don Quixote is true and unexaggerated.

CHAPTER II

Of the Pleasant Discourses Which Passed Between Don Quixote and Sancho Panza, his Squire.

The chapter consists of a long, earnest conversation between the knight and his ignorant squire who wishes to learn as much as possible about knight-errantry. Don Quixote instructs Sancho that although there are plenty of islands to conquer, they must also accept the many poor and unfortunate situations that knights-errant encounter on the road. Sancho, however, is mainly impressed by the rich prospects following the fortunate encounters. Don Quixote then tells him about a wonderful balm whose recipe he has learned in books of chivalry. This balm can heal a man even though he is sliced in two pieces. "Never mind about the island," Sancho decides right away, "Just supply me with the ointment and I shall sell it for three reals an ounce and be forever content." When night falls they take shelter among the huts of goatherds who are courteous and share supper and wine with the travelers.

CHAPTER III

What Passed Between Don Quixote and the Goatherds.

Don Quixote is so delighted to find himself in humble surroundings that, instead of eating, he makes an eloquent speech about the virtues of the Golden Age when men lived in close communion with nature. When human nature lost this purity and innocence, then the order of knighthood was established in order to oppose the torrent of violence. The goatherds do not understand a word of the talk but they stare attentively and listen while they eat. As if to return the respect of the knight who so sincerely expressed his ideas, one of the goatherds introduces a young boy whose beautiful singing and playing entertains the company. Sancho, who had been gorging himself with meat and wine while Don Quixote made his speech, promptly falls asleep when the music begins.

CHAPTER IV

The Story Which a Young Goatherd Told to Those That Were with Don Quixote.

A new arrival brings them news of a recent death. A young man of the village, Chrysostom, has died for love of Marcella, a coy and beautiful daughter of a rich merchant who has dressed herself in the garb of a shepherdess and pastured her sheep in the hills. So desirable is she that many suitors have dressed themselves as shepherds, driving their flocks into the hills in hopes of gaining Marcella's attention. While shepherds all over the hills are thus pining, sighing, lamenting, Marcella remains deaf to all words of love and refuses to hear suits for marriage.

CHAPTER V

A Continuation of the Story of Marcella.

Don Quixote sets out the next morning with the goatherds to attend Chrysostom's funeral. They meet a party of shepherds dressed in black, and two gentlemen on horseback who are traveling in that direction. The knight and one of the horsemen, Vivaldo, enter into conversation about knight-errantry while they travel to their destination. At the burial service, one of Chrysostom's friends speaks. This young man, he says, so well-favored in appearance, talents, and person, has died for the love of a cruel and hard mistress. With him are to be buried the beautiful verses he wrote to immortalize the ungrateful Marcella. Vivaldo interrupts to beg that the verses be rescued from oblivion to serve as a warning to others to avoid "such tempting snares and enchanting destructions."

CHAPTER VI

The Unfortunate Shepherd's Verses and Other Unexpected Matters.

The poem is read to the company. Entitled "The Despairing Lover," it expresses the grief and pain of a rejected love. The murderess herself suddenly appears at the top of the rock and answers the accusations of the entire company. "Just because I am beautiful," Marcella says, "I am not obliged to love everyone who loves me. I have never encouraged, promised, or deceived any of these importunate young men, but rather I have warned and admonished them. Thus you can see that she who has never pretended to love, cannot cause wilful mischief, and a free and generous declaration of my fixed resolution not to marry cannot be considered as hate or disdain." Marcella disappears after her speech, causing everyone to admire not only her beauty but her discretion and honesty. Don Quixote now resolves to search for the shepherdess and offer his services to protect her to the utmost of his power.

Commentary

In this chapter Cervantes portrays another character whose strong will emboldens her to seek an independent way of life. Marcella lives as if she were in the Golden Age that Don Quixote tries to reëstablish in the world. Therefore the knight is committed to protect the girl's way of life against any intrusions from those who wish to involve her in a more realistic way of life, that of being bound to a husband and family. Marcella's life as a shepherdess is parallel to Don Quixote's life as a knight-errant. Both individuals exemplify the nobility of free will overcoming society-dictated reality.

BOOK THREE

CHAPTER I

Giving an Account of Don Quixote's Unfortunate Rencounter with Certain Bloody-Minded and Wicked Yanguesian Carriers.

During the search for Marcella, Don Quixote and Sancho rest and eat in a pleasant meadow. Their beasts graze nearby. Meanwhile some Galician (Yanguesian) carriers have rested their herd of mares in the same grazing area, and Rosinante, usually so chaste and modest, begins to pay gallant court within the herd. The carriers are furious and with their staves and poles beat the poor horse until he sinks to the ground. Don Quixote rushes to the rescue and Sancho, despite his better judgment, fights at his side. The odds are two against twenty. The carriers have soon beaten the knight and squire so badly that they (the carriers) flee with their mares rather than be accused of murder.

Still too sore to move, Don Quixote and Sancho have a long discussion, the squire maintaining a position of absolute pacifism, while his master upholds the nobility of violent defense. They manage at last, however, to limp their way toward an inn, which the knight declares is a castle.

CHAPTER II

What Happened to Don Quixote in the Inn Which He Took for a Castle

The night spent in this unaccommodating inn climaxes their misfortunes. A lusty mule carrier who sleeps in a nearby chamber, wakefully awaits the visit of the deformed servant of the innkeeper, Maritornes. Too sore to sleep, Don Quixote has imagined that the daughter of the powerful lord who owns this castle has fallen in love with him and has arranged a tryst. Maritornes is punctual but must pass by the knight's couch on her way to the mule carrier. Don Quixote grabs her, whispering that despite her loveliness, charm, and generous heart, his affections belong to his beloved mistress, Dulcinea. The muleteer, enraged, grabs a cudgel and smacks Don Quixote first on the jaw, then tramples him with his great feet. The bed falls in with such a noise that the innkeeper awakens. Blaming Maritornes, he rushes upstairs to punish her. The servant hides next to the sleeping Sancho who is terrified to find a lump in his bed. He flails around as if in a nightmare, and Maritornes begins to hit him in return. With the aid of the innkeeper's light, the mule carrier now beats Sancho, while the landlord attacks Maritornes. Then, when the lamp goes out, a police officer, lodging at the inn, charges into the fray. He grabs the senseless Don Quixote and discovering no response shouts "Murder!" At this, everyone quietly desists, and each slinks back into his own bed.

CHAPTER III

A Further Account of the Innumerable Hardships Which the Brave Don Quixote, and His Worthy Squire Sancho, Underwent in the Inn, Which the Knight Unluckily Took for a Castle.

When the police officer returns with a light, he finds Don Quixote conscious, but bruised. The knight insults him, mistaking him for the cause of all the trouble, and the officer gets so angry that he hits him over the head with the lamp. To relieve his pains, the Don orders the ingredients for his special balm, and swallows the preparation. After violent nausea he feels quite restored and Sancho then drinks what is left in the pot. He, on the other hand, suffers such dreadful reactions that he is weaker and more miserable than ever when the attack is over. His master is ready to leave, however, and saddles their beasts, giving the innkeeper a gracious speech of thanks for his hospitality. "Where is my payment?" asks the landlord, but the distracted knight cannot understand that he is anything but a guest at whichever castle he stops at. He marches off, leaving Sancho to continue arguing with the innkeeper. At this point, some stout jolly fellows in the courtyard seize this opportunity for a jest. They lay Sancho in a blanket and toss him high in the air many times before allowing him at last to rejoin his master outside the gate.

CHAPTER IV

Of the Discourse Between the Knight and the Squire, with Other Matters Worth Relating.

Sancho is so unhappy about the blanketing that he would like to go home. Just then Don Quixote spies a large cloud of dust in the distance. "A prodigious army is approaching," he says, "And this day shall not only see a change in our fortunes, but shall see exploits of mine that shall be forever part of history." But Sancho sees two dust clouds which his master interprets as two armies about to attack one another. He describes giants and crests and heraldic symbols which Sancho cannot discern for the dust. As the two armies approach, however, Sancho hears the bleating of sheep and warns his master—too late—that the hosts are but separate flocks crossing the path. Don Quixote charges into the midst, scattering, trampling, and wounding many animals. The shepherds respond to the attack by expertly using their slingshots. Don Quixote is hit by so many rocks that he is quite unconscious when Sancho arrives to help him. Toothless and sore all over, the knight curses the necromancer who has robbed him of victory by changing the armies into a flock of sheep.

CHAPTER V

Of the Wise Discourse Between Sancho and His Master; as Also of the Adventure of the Dead Corpse, and Other Famous Occurrences.

Very weary, very hungry, they continue to plod along after nightfall. Sancho shakes with fright as they see a great number of lights moving toward them in the blackness. They soon distinguish about twenty white-clad horsemen carrying torches, followed by a hearse and six men in deep mourning. Don Quixote addresses the group, asks their business and destination. To further impose himself, he grabs the bridle of the first mule. The animal rears, throwing its rider. Then Don Quixote attacks someone who shouts rudely at him, and the whole funeral party scatters into the night, leaving only the man whose mule has unseated him. Begging for his life, the stranger says he is but a clergyman accompanying the hearse to town for a burial service. Don Quixote apologizes and helps the man back on his mule. Sancho in the meantime, has collected all the food the procession has carried. They eat a most excellent meal from these provisions, but still remain thirsty.

Commentary

This adventure shows that Don Quixote, intrepid when in a real situation is full of fear when ghosts approach. But again, his tremendous will overcomes even the dead as he rallies his courage and puts the funeral party to flight.

CHAPTER VI

Of a Wonderful Adventure Achieved by the Valorous Don Quixote de la Mancha; the Like Never Compassed with Less Danger by Any of the Most Famous Knights in the World.

Continuing their thirsty traveling through the night, Sancho and Don Quixote hear the cheering sounds of a waterfall nearby, but they are filled with horror when they hear accompanying thuds of heavy, regular blows. Sancho begs his master to investigate the strange noises only in the daylight, but Don Quixote is brave and firm, charging his squire to tighten Rosinante's girth in readiness for the attack. Sancho, however, ties the horse's back legs together so that he leaps forward at the spur but cannot move further. "Heaven is on my side," declares Sancho, "So you must have patience until it is light." At dawn, Sancho quietly unties Rosinante's legs, and they ride closer to the noise. Don Quixote is "ready to drop from his horse with shame and confusion" for the heavy thuds are merely the noises of six fulling-mill hammers pounding out the cloth. Sancho laughs so hard that Don Quixote strikes him in anger. "See here, Mr. Jester," he says, "If these, instead of fulling hammers had been some perilous adventure, have I not, think you, shown the courage required for the attempt and achievement." Sancho begs pardon and swears to "always stand in awe of you and honor you as my Lord and Master."

Commentary

This chapter not only describes again how the imaginative weapons of Don Quixote overcome obstacles, but how the relationship between master and squire develops. Sancho, anxious to imitate his master, thinks that tying Rosinante's legs and then saying it is the will of Providence to keep them in one place, is a typical Don Quixote rationalization. At this point, however, Sancho is merely an imitative clown, transforming reality by tricks, and not by the force of faith. Until he becomes a bit "quixotized" he will still have a muddled notion of the difference between truth and illusion.

Don Quixote, on the other hand, uses no tricks at all. Understanding everything with his imagination, he is capable of overcoming any danger because the appearance of the obstacle is inconsequential. Fulling-mills and giants are conquered by efforts of the imagination, by a strong-willed attack of ideals and ideas. Sancho, fearful and anxious in the dark, huddles close to his visionary master because he cannot see the danger, but he is ready to mock the hero when there is nothing to fear. In other words, Sancho and the rest of common men, depend on men of ideas when they are threatened with something their senses cannot grasp. The heroes and leaders of men are always those who impose their will on reality, who bend events according to the idea. Reality, to Don Quixote, is therefore an internal quality, and he renounces this strength of perspective only when at the point of death.

CHAPTER VII

Of the High Adventure and Conquest of Mambrino's Helmet, with Other Events Relating to Our Invincible Knight.

From a distance, Don Quixote sees a knight on a dappled steed wearing a golden, glistening helmet. As they approach Sancho remarks that it is indeed a person on a grey ass wearing something like a barber's basin on his head. "Nonsense," says the Don, "That is a knight wearing Mambrino's helmet [Mambrino was a Saracen deprived by Don Rinaldo of his golden helmet] and I shall deal with him while you wait here." Sancho is right, of course, for the traveling barber has placed his bronze basin over his new hat to protect it from the rain. Don Quixote charges his adversary, and the poor barber throws himself to the ground to avoid being speared by the lance. He then runs through the fields as fast as possible. Don Quixote wins the helmet and Sancho exchanges the trappings of his ass for the superior packsaddle of the barber's mule. Pleasantly discoursing, the two well furnished companions ride contentedly along.

CHAPTER VIII

How Don Quixote Set Free Many Miserable Creatures, Who Were Carried, Much Against Their Wills, to a Place They Did Not Like.

The next adventure begins when Don Quixote stops some guards who are taking twelve prisoners in a chain gang to the place where they will serve as galley slaves. After listening to the story of each prisoner, the knight demands that the guards set them free for " 'tis a hard case to make slaves of men whom God and nature made free." The guard refuses, and while Don Quixote fights with him, the prisoners use the opportunity to struggle out of their chains. When the guards are all subdued, Don Quixote demands of each prisoner that he present himself before the Lady Dulcinea and describe how he gained his freedom. The ringleader, a notorious rogue named Gines de Passamonte, realizes that the knight is mad, and he signals to his companions. All the prisoners throw stones at their liberator until he is knocked down. Stealing whatever they can find, they swiftly scatter and disappear along their separate ways.

CHAPTER IX

What Befell the Renowned Don Quixote in the Sierra Morena (Black Mountains). Being One of the Rarest Adventures in This Authentic History.

Sancho, afraid that the police force of the Holy Brotherhood would search for the man who freed the king's prisoners, suggests they go through the Sierra Morena to discourage pursuit. The ringleader of the prisoners, Gines de Passamonte, is also hiding out in these mountains. When he sees his chance, he steals Sancho's beloved ass Dapple, leaving the squire brokenhearted. Sancho is cheered, however, when his master finds a portmanteau lying on the path which contains 200 gold crowns; he gives it all to his squire, taking sole interest in the poem enclosed in the briefcase. Further along, they see a discarded saddle and then the corpse of a mule. Some goatherds tell them the story which clears up the mystery. A well-born youth has come to do penance for a number of sins. He wanders around in the wilderness, alternating moods of lucidity with fits of insanity, gaining nourishment from the woods or from the kindness of the goatherds. Don Quixote vows to find the young man and assist him in his distress. Cardenio himself appears, and the knight greets him with an earnest embrace, as if the stranger were long familiar to him.

CHAPTER X

The Adventure in the Sierra Morena Continued.

The young man, or the Knight of the Wood, as Cervantes calls him, tells Don Quixote of his misfortunes. The son of an Andalusian gentleman, he was about to become betrothed to his beloved Lucinda, a beautiful, discreet maiden of similar background to himself. His father, however, sent Cardenio to live at the Duke's house and become a companion to Ferdinand, the grandee's amorous son. Ferdinand had just had a brief affair with the daughter of a rich farmer, a rank too far below his own to warrant marriage, and to cool his passion, agreed to visit Cardenio's family. During his stay, Ferdinand made the acquaintance of Lucinda, and, much to Cardenio's discomfiture, was very impressed with her charms. At this point in the narrative, the narrator mentions the chivalric book, "Amadis of Gaul," and Don Quixote cannot resist interrupting. Then the youth and the knight begin a heated argument about the virtue of one of the novel's heroines, and Cardenio flings a huge stone at the Don. During the general fight which follows, he disappears into the woods.

CHAPTER XI

Of the Strange Things That Happened to the Valiant Knight of La Mancha in the Black Mountain: and of the Penance He Did There, in Imitation of Beltenbros, or the Lovely Obscure.

As Sancho and Don Quixote ride further into the mountains, the knight reveals his plans. Sancho must go to Toboso and deliver a letter to the Lady Dulcinea. In the meantime, Don Quixote will do penance in the wilderness, after the manner of knights-errant who have been too long absent from their mistresses. He describes to Sancho how he will express his madness and despair: "Thou wilt see me throw away my armor, tear my clothes, knock my head against the rocks, and do a thousand other things of that kind which will fill thee with astonishment." His squire begs that he be less harsh with himself, but the Don is adamant. Writing the letter, Don Quixote confesses that he hardly knows Dulcinea. Sancho is surprised that his master's ideal mistress is none other than the daughter of Lorenzo Corchuleo, a neighbor of his. He chatters about the wench's virtues, her peasant habits, and Don Quixote stops him by relating a short parable. "It does not matter what her background is," the knight concludes. "Dulcinea del Toboso, as to the use I make of her, is equal to the greatest princess in the world." He continues by saying that none of the ladies whose praises resound in ballads, novels, poems, or prayers have ever been made of flesh and blood—"The greatest part of them were nothing but the mere imaginations of the poets for a groundwork to exercise their wits upon...." Sancho with tears at the parting, prepares to commence his journey.

Commentary

Don Quixote explains to Sancho the real identity of his peerless mistress, informing the ignorant squire that the sublimity of a ladylove has little to do with her actual person. At the same time, the madman reveals the consciousness of Alonso Quixano who bore a twelve-year long love for a pretty peasant lass whom he saw on only four occasions. This unsatisfactory love may well have caused the hero to satisfy his romantic notions through books of chivalry. With his head full of "disordered notions," it follows that the hidalgo's humble—and frustrated—quest for immortality through fathering Aldonza Lorenzo's children, can be sublimated into a knight's search for glory in the name of Dulcinea. Cervantes thus draws a relationship between the buried spirit of Alonso Quixano the Good and the militant Don Quixote; between the knight's knowledge of real identities and the idealizations he consciously forms; between, finally, the madness of the inspired knight and the feigned madness of the disappointed lover.

Just as religious fanatics strive to purify their souls of sinfulness by undergoing severe hardships, so may Don Quixote undergo penance to refine the common soul of Alonso Quixano. Another reason for the madness in the wilderness is Don Quixote's desire to prepare himself, like the fasting knights of old, for further adventures. Cervantes, in fact, has finished with the hero's burlesque adventures proving his character, and after this breathing spell the pattern of the knight's encounters changes. The hero is set in the role of laughingstock, not merely to the author, but to the world at large, and it is this theme that dominates in the second part of the history of the Manchegan knight.

At the same time he provides hints of Don Quixote's deeper nature, Cervantes also develops the relationship between master and squire. More than ever do they depend on each other, and they weep at the separation. Not only is the penance a period of loneliness for the hero, but he misses Sancho's office of securing food and gets quite thin from poor nourishment. On the other hand, Sancho has so much relied on his master's intellect that he is more foolish than ever when alone. Completely forgetting to carry with him the carefully written letter and the order for three ass-colts—absences symbolic of the literary Don himself—Sancho is so helpless that the curate and the barber take advantage of him to play a trick on Don Quixote in order to bring him home for a rest cure.

CHAPTER XII

A Continuation of the Refined Extravagances by Which the Gallant Knight of La Mancha Chose to Express His Love in the Sierra Morena.

Don Quixote has decided to imitate the penance suffered by his hero, Amadis of Gaul, who spent his time of distraction passively and pensively. He writes verses to his Dulcinea and does a great deal of lamenting and sighing. Sancho, meanwhile, making his way toward Toboso, encounters the curate and barber who are stopping at the very inn where he had been tossed in a blanket. They inquire after Don Quixote, and Sancho presently tells them of all the adventures and of his present mission to Dulcinea. He now discovers that he has forgotten to take the letter, but the curate and the barber promise to rewrite it from his dictation. They remind him too, that in order for his master to reward his services with an earldom, he must first be made to give up "this unprofitable penance." Sancho then is willingly instructed in a strategem to bring Don Quixote out of the wilderness.

CHAPTER XIII

How the Curate and the Barber Put Their Design in Execution with Other Things Worthy to be Recorded in this Important History.

Dressed in their disguises, that of a distressed damsel and her gentleman-usher, the barber and the curate and the squire reach the foot of the

Sierra Morena. Sancho goes ahead in order to give Don Quixote the fictional message from Dulcinea, which is, that he must put an end to his penance and repair immediately to her side. In the meantime, the barber and the curate meet Cardenio who tells them the entire story of his misfortunes, Cerventes continuing the narrative at the point he left it.

Ferdinand fell in love with Lucinda and plotted to get rid of his friend in order to marry her. Sending Cardenio on a bogus errand to his brother, Ferdinand gains the father's persmission to wed Lucinda, and the wedding takes place. Cardenio returns just in time to witness secretly the marriage vows of his promised bride. Saddened that Lucinda would rather marry Ferdinand than commit suicide as she promised, Cardenio plans to live his life in the wilderness, mournful and almost insane.

BOOK FOUR

CHAPTER I

The Pleasant New Adventure the Curate and Barber Meet with in Sierra Moreno, or Black Mountain.

As Cardenio concludes his story, their attention is attracted to a new sound of lamenting. They discover a young girl dressed in boy's clothing and in order to excuse her appearance, the beautiful damsel tells them this story: She, Dorothea, is the daughter of a very rich Andalusian farmer, a vassal of one of the grandees of Spain. The Duke's son, Don Ferdinand, paid great court to her, which she tried to ignore because of the inequality of their parentage. Ferdinand, promising marriage and eternal loyalty, seduced Dorothea after having gained access to her bedroom by bribing the maid. After that night, his affections cooled, and the next news that Dorthea received, was that Ferdinand was to marry. She followed her false lover to Lucinda's village, and there heard the startling result of the wedding. The bride, fainting right after she spoke the vow, had a letter hidden in her dress, saying that she could not marry Ferdinand because she was already betrothed to Cardenio. Dorothea concludes her narrative by explaining how she arrived at the Sierra Morena.

CHAPTER II

An Account of the Beautiful Dorothea's Discretion, with Other Pleasant Passages.

Cardenio identifies himself as Lucinda's betrothed, and he vows to protect Dorothea and to brave any hazard in order to see her righted by Don Ferdinand. The curate now tells them why he and the barber happen to be in the mountains, and all agree that Don Quixote should be cured of his strange madness. Dorothea offers to play the part of the distressed damsel, saying she is familiar with books of chivalry and understands how to act.

Sancho returns, delighted to find that the maiden in distress is a princess who will, no doubt, marry his master. Don Quixote, who will rule her kingdom, will then reward his squire with an earldom. They soon arrive at the knight's retreat, and Dorothea throws herself at his feet and begs his services. The knight promises immediately to help her, and not engage in any other adventures until he has rescued her kingdom. The entire party, including Cardenio, the curate, the barber, and Dorothea, now leads the knight and squire in the direction of Don Quixote's village.

CHAPTER III

The Pleasant Stratagems Used to Free the Enamoured Knight from the Rigorous Penance Which He Had Undertaken.

Now Dorothea, calling herself the Princess Micomicona, tells of the fictional misfortunes that have driven her to seek aid. A cruel invader, a giant named Pandafilando, has usurped her father's crown after his death, forcing her to flee the country to save herself. Only with the help of Don Quixote does she have any chance of regaining her country. She also mentions that her father, before he died, counseled her to marry the hero after he killed the giant. Don Quixote says that he cannot consider marriage since his affections belong only to Dulcinea, but he will certainly slay the giant. Drawing his squire aside, Don Quixote begs Sancho to give him the full details of his interview with Dulcinea. Sancho makes up an amusing narrative, plausible to his master, but then stops short when he sights a gypsy, still far off, riding on what appears to be his stolen ass. Hearing Sancho's voice, the gypsy—who is Gines de Passamonte in disguise—jumps down and dashes away as fast as he can. The squire weeps with joy to have Dapple back again.

Commentary

With Dorothea's fictional story, Cervantes again indicates that the world of truth is the province of a knight-errant; illusion belongs to those unenlightened by the spirit of chivalry. Especially unenlightened are the curate and barber, as well as Cardenio who is as chivalric and noble as Don Quixote himself. They are delighted by the convincing manner in which the clever Dorothea plays her role of distressed princess Micomicona. What they do not recognize, and what Don Quixote believes immediately, is that the beautiful farmer's daughter is really a dispossessed aristocrat, victim of a usurper. Dorothea is a princess by virtue of her beauty and personality; she is dispossessed, not of her lands, but of her virtue, with Don Ferdinand, a giant in rank if not in character, as the faithless usurper. And the fictionalized Micomicona who has traveled across half the world to seek redress from a knight, is truly the ravished Dorothea, who, after much journeying, discovers Cardenio, a knight who swears to aid her in relieving her distress.

CHAPTER IV

The Pleasant Discourse Between Don Quixote and His Squire Continued, with Other Adventures.

Sancho continues to answer the persistent questions of Don Quixote, regarding the appearance, dress, activities, remarkings of Dulcinea when she received the letter. Sancho is exceedingly relieved when the curate calls for a rest and refreshment at a roadside fountain. While they are eating, a youth stops before the knight. "Do you not remember poor Andrew," he says, "whom you had caused to be untied from a tree?" Don Quixote loudly recounts his valor in the affair and charges the boy to tell everyone the story and its successful aftermath. "Yes, my master repaid me," sadly and bitterly answers the youth. "No sooner had you gone, than he lashed me to the tree and gave me so many cuts with the strap that I have been in a hospital ever since. Had you not meddled and so insulted my master, my poor back would not have received the brunt of his anger." The company can hardly suppress laughter, and poor Andrew continues on his way, hungrily seizing the crust of bread and slice of cheese that Sancho offers him.

CHAPTER V

What Befell Don Quixote and His Company at the Inn.

After another day of riding, the company arrives again at the inn where Sancho received his blanketing. Don Quixote goes to take a rest, while the others sit down to dine, served by the landlord, his wife and daughter, and Maritornes the scullery maid. The innkeeper, in the course of conversation, confesses himself such a lover of chivalric romances that "I could sit and read them from morning to night." He says, too, that he has "half a mind to be a knight myself." The curate, as he used to do with Don Quixote, begins an argument with the landord about books of chivalry, and they heatedly compare the merits of two famous knights. Dorothea admits that the ignorant innkeeper is close to becoming another Don Quixote for his belief in the truth of history of certain fabled knights. The curate is curious to read a manuscript left at the inn by a previous lodger, and for the diversion of the company, reads aloud from the papers.

Commentary

Although the parallel between the innkeeper and Don Quixote is clear with regard to their implicit belief in the most extravagant fables found in books of chivalry, as well as their inspiration from deeds of knights, the differences in their characters are more outstanding. The innkeeper remains at home, perfectly sane, because he is content to let the world run as it is, so long as he can continue cheating it. Don Quixote, on the other hand, wishes to play a more noble and heroic role in the world and reform it. Thus the madness of the knight is a direct consequence of his nobility of character, whereas the utter sanity of the innkeeper is due to his being perfectly commonplace.

CHAPTER VI

The Novel of the Curious Impertinent.

Anselmo and Lothario, well-born young gentlemen of Florence who are known to all as The Two Friends, maintain their close relationship even after Anselmo's marriage to Camilla, a beautiful, rich, devoted and virtuous maiden. Having such successful relationships with wife and friend, Anselmo is discontented with a malaise that increases each day. "I have an immense desire," he tells the shocked Lothario, "to test Camilla's virtue. I can never value one who owes her virtue to lack of opportunity, rather than to a vigorous denial of an aggressive and persistent lover." Anselmo begs his friend to act as Camilla's tempter, promising to ask someone else to do the job if Lothario should refuse. The husband then takes an out-of-town business trip in order to provide the opportunity for the plan. Despite his reserved behavior, Lothario falls so much in love with Camilla that he begins a sincere courtship. Camilla repulses him immediately and writes a letter to her husband.

CHAPTER VII

In Which the History of the Curious Impertinent is Pursued.

Camilla's letter, urging her husband to return home and protect for himself what his best friend now pursues, receives a cool reply. She resolves to trouble her husband no longer and to face the matter herself. Unable to withstand the ardent Lothario, Camilla surrenders with all her heart, sharing the secret only with her maid Leonela. When Anselmo returns home a few days later, he begs his friend for the news of his fate. Lothario assures him that no wife is more virtuous or more resolute than Camilla. Still dissatisfied, the husband asks his friend to continue acting as seducer just to make sure, and he continues to provide ample opportunity for the test.

Meanwhile Leonela has been getting bolder about the conduct of her own affair with a young man from town. One day Lothario sees this unknown fellow leave the house. Imagining that Camilla entertains another lover, he jealously seeks out Anselmo, telling him that his wife is now ready to surrender her virtue and that the husband must come to witness secretly her faithlessness. For her part, Camilla is so upset with her maid's indiscretion that she asks Lothario for advice, and the young man is remorseful for his jealousy and explains what he has done. But Camilla assures him that she has an excellent plan. Knowing full well that her husband is a secret witness, Camilla and Leonela stage a mock tragedy. The wife would rather die than stain Anselmo's honor. Stabbing herself, though in a place where the wound will do no harm, Camilla makes her husband believe in her unimpeachable virtue, in the faith of his friend, and he is again a satisfied and happy man.

CHAPTER VII

The Conclusion of "The Novel of the Curious Impertinent"; with the Dreadful Battle Betwixt Don Quixote and Certain Wineskins.

At this point in the curate's reading, Sancho rushes in. "Help, help!" he yells, "My master is fighting with the giant, that foe of Princess Micomicona." The innkeeper and the rest discover Don Quixote in his room, wearing only a shirt and nightcap. Fast asleep, he has hacked the wineskins to pieces, considering them in his fevered dreams to be parts of a conquered giant. Don Quixote is put back to bed, while the landlord rages over his spilled wine. The curate reads on.

Eventually the indiscretion of Leonela shatters the paradise in which illusive state Anselmo and Camilla and Lothario frolic. Anselmo goes one night to investigate a noise coming from the maid's room. At his entry, a strange man leaps from the window and runs off. Leonela promises her angry master that she will explain everything if he waits until morning, and Anselmo complies. Camilla, hearing of the incident and fearing that the maid will disclose everything, hastens to Lothario and begs him to find a haven for her. After conveying Camilla to a nunnery, Lothario enlists in the army. Meanwhile Anselmo, rising at dawn, discovers that Leonela has fled. After finding his wife and best friend gone as well, he unhappily leaves his home, and from the gossip of a passing townsman learns the whole truth of his cuckolding. So melancholy does he become that Anselmo prepares himself for death. His last words are in writing: "...a foolish and ill-advised curiosity has robbed me of my life." Lothario is slain in battle soon afterward, while Camilla dies a few months later.

Commentary

The *novella* of the "Man too Curious for His Own Good" (entitled according to Putnam's translation of *Don Quixote*) has been a controversial subject among critics. Many argue that the story has no place in the novel as a whole; many consider it integral. Cervantes himself writes in Part Two of *Don Quixote* that he has been criticized for inserting many extraneous stories in his history of the renowned knight, and he does not repeat this device when he writes the second part.

The story of the Curious Impertinent tells of a man who depends entirely on tested experience as a way to determine truth. Anselmo is so persistent in demanding proof of his wife's virtue that he succeeds, despite his deepest desires, in making her unfaithful. Don Quixote, on the other hand, would never submit his ideals to a test of the senses. He knows that an attitude of "seeing is believing" uncovers, not truths, but lies, and the experience of Anselmo illustrates this point. Once blessed with a virtuous wife and loyal friend, the unfortunate cuckold dies, a victim to a faith which could not free itself from depending on tangible proofs.

Besides posing and solving an interesting problem, the story also serves as a point of comparison between the flesh-and-blood creations of the knight and squire and these cardboard figures in the curate's manuscript. When Sancho interrupts the reading, we are made to feel that reality has now intruded upon a fictional situation, even though we discover Don Quixote in the middle of a fantastic and ridiculous battle against some wineskins. Thus after the formal, stylized narrative of the lives of Lothario, Camilla, and Anselmo is completed, the reader can, with refreshed understanding, follow the more complex, unpredictable adventures of Don Quixote and Sancho Panza.

CHAPTER IX

Containing an Account of Many Surprising Accidents in the Inn.

The innkeeper who is standing at the door, greets some newly-arrived strangers. The man and woman, heavily veiled for traveling, are accompanied by two retainers. The lady does not say a word; she seems overcome by a profound grief. Dorothea strives to comfort her, and she is struck by the beauty of the maiden, although her face is pale and sad. The gentleman also removes his veil, and with a cry, Dorothea recognizes her husband, Don Ferdinand. The lady, of course, is Lucinda, and she and Cardenio are tenderly reunited. Don Ferdinand, so moved by lovely Dorothea's love for him, claims her as his true wife and swears to be faithful. Everyone who witnesses these tender scenes weeps with joy.

CHAPTER X

The History of the Famous Princess Micomicona Continued, with Other Pleasant Adventures.

Sancho Panza is horrified to discover that Princess Micomicona is now merely called Dorothea. He fears that he will never gain his earldom. Running straight to his master, Sancho informs him of the trick, but Don Quixote merely cautions his squire against being taken in by all the enchantments that occur in this castle. Ferdinand, meanwhile, encourages Dorothea to continue with her deception until the curate and barber have safely conducted the madman to his home. More newcomers arrive at the inn now. The man, having returned from imprisonment in Barbary, is still in Moorish dress. Accompanying him is his betrothed, a beautiful "Morisca" named Zoraida who wishes to become a Christian. As they all sit down to dine, a mood of expansive oratory overcomes Don Quixote, just as happened among the goatherds. His speech this time compares the professions of arms and learning, and he discusses the privations and rewards of soldiers and scholars.

CHAPTER XI

A Continuation of Don Quixote's Curious Discourse upon Arms and Learning.

Don Quixote shows that it is the soldier who suffers the most privations, receiving in return lesser compensation, especially when one considers that he may not live to enjoy the rewards of his service. The man of letters, on the other hand, is guaranteed of life, and his scholarship will gain him a career with professional status. The more noble following, Don Quixote concludes, is, however, that of the soldier. Dinner being over, the entire company begs the captive for his life story.

CHAPTER XII

Where the Captive Relates His Life and Adventures.

He tells them of his father, a ne'er do well whose extravagance almost left his children without any means. He and his brother joined the army and fought victoriously in a great naval battle against the Turks. He relates how he was captured by the captain of a corsair, thus beginning a long imprisonment. The captive goes on to describe the battles he witnessed and the particular bravery of a man named Pedro de Aguilar, who Don Ferdinand recognizes as his brother.

CHAPTER XIII

The Story of the Captive Continued.

The fleet for which he was a galley slave returned victorious to Algiers, and his work was changed. Upon the death of his master, the captive became the property of the most bloodthirsty Dey of Algiers, a renegade named Hussan Aga. He was placed in a special prison house, called a *bagnio,* reserved for Christians whose rich connections will soon provide a ransom, although he had no claim to this distinction other than having the title of captain. Overlooking the bagnio's courtyard were the windows of a high-ranking Moor, whose beautiful daughter, secretly a Christian, made clandestine communication with him. She sent the captive money, enclosed in a note which told him of her desire to escape to a Christian land, if he would arrange to free himself and take her to Spain. The letter was written in Arabic, and the captain engaged a renegade to translate it. Many other messages were exchanged between Zoraida and the captive until enough money was collected to furnish a ship and ransom other bagnio captives besides himself.

CHAPTER XIV

The Adventures of the Captive Continued.

Two weeks later the renegade purchased a ship and promptly the captive sought a way to apprise Zoraida of their progress. At the moment of departure, Zoraida's father made such an outcry when he saw his daughter flee that the Christians were forced to capture him and some of his servants and imprison them on board the ship. At a convenient inlet, Zoraida's grieving father and the other Moors were set ashore, while a favoring wind bore the escapees out of earshot of the father's curses and imprecations. Captured by pirates, despoiled of all their possessions, the prisoners finally landed in a small boat at the coast of Spain. The captive concludes his tale by telling how cheerfully Zoraida endured the sufferings of the journey. He pities his lovely fiancée who faces a bleak future attached to a man without any means.

Commentary

The story of the captive is not so fantastic as may be imagined, for Cervantes has included a great deal of his own biography in this narrative. Like the captive, Cervantes was a bagnio prisoner, awaiting ransom which his impoverished family could hardly hope to provide; Cervantes, as well, had attempted to escape many times, perhaps even by the same method described by the captive, Ruy Perez de Viedma.

The captive himself represents a noble follower of the profession of arms, according to the virtues which Don Quixote expressed in his speech. The captain's brother (arriving in the next chapter) represents the successful man of letters. Zoraida, on the other hand, can be considered as the peerless Dulcinea del Toboso of the captive's life, for it is she who has inspired his heroism just as Don Quixote's mistress inspires his.

CHAPTER XV

An Account of What Happened Afterwards in the Inn, with Several Other Occurrences Worth Notice.

The company sympathizes with the captive and Zoraida, and each wishes to help them. Suddenly more guests appear at the inn, although there is hardly any space to accommodate them. The newcomer, accompanied by his young daughter Clara, is a rich and influential judge, on his way to a new appointment in the Indies. The captive recognizes that the guest is his brother, and everyone sheds new tears to witness the tender reunion. The judge and Clara embrace Zoraida warmly and tenderly. When at last everyone retires, the ladies agree to share the garret, the men find sleeping space without, while Don Quixote stands guard outside the castle. He wishes to protect the ladies "lest they be attacked by some giant or wandering rogue of evil intent who might be covetous of the great treasure of feminine beauty within these walls." In the middle of a peaceful night, everyone awakens to listen to the beautiful singing of a mule driver.

CHAPTER XVI

The Pleasant Story of the Young Muleteer with Other Strange Adventures That Happened at the Inn.

Dorothea awakens Clara so that she too can hear the music. The young girl is overcome by sobbing. She explains that the singer is not a muleteer, but a young man of rich background who follows wherever she and her father travel. Because they are both so young—sixteen years—and because Don Luis' father is so wealthly and influential, the couple cannot marry, no matter how deeply they love each other. Dorothea soothes the sobbing Clara until she falls asleep.

Meanwhile Maritornes and the landlord's daughter play a trick on Don Quixote as he stands guard on horseback. The girl softly calls him, and the knight, assuming as before that she is in love with him, bids her to withdraw her attentions because his heart already belongs to Dulcinea. Maritornes begs him merely to extend his hand so that her mistress might satisfy her passion a small amount. Don Quixote complies, standing on the saddle to reach the loft window. Maritornes quietly slips a knot over his wrist, tying the other end of the strap to the bolt on the door. Thus imprisoned, Don Quixote can only assume that he has been enchanted. Rosinante, remaining as immobile as a statue, reinforces his judgment; the knight fervently hopes that his horse remains still. At dawn, however, four horsemen arrive at the inn, and Rosinante gently turns to sniff at one of the mounts. His foot slipping from the saddle, Don Quixote is left dangling by the arm in a most painful manner.

CHAPTER XVII

A Continuation of the Strange and Unheard-of Adventures in the Inn.

The bellowing of the poor knight awakens the innkeeper. Quietly Maritornes unties the sufferer and he drops to the ground. The four horsemen identify themselves. They are sent by Don Luis' father to find the son at all costs. The youth remains defiant, and the judge, recognizing his neighbor's child, draws Don Luis into earnest conversation. Meanwhile the landlord's daughter begs Don Quixote's assistance for her father is fighting with some guests who wish to leave without paying. Surprisingly, the knight settles the argument by his persuasive reasoning rather than with violence. Suddenly the very barber whose basin and donkey-trappings had been despoiled by knight and squire enters the gate. Recognizing Sancho, the barber grabs his packsaddle, and Sancho offers him a punch in the nose. Don Quixote intervenes explaining that the trophy which looks like a basin is Mambrino's helmet, but as to the steed's trappings—lawful spoils for Sancho—he says they have somehow been transformed into a mere packsaddle for an ass.

CHAPTER XVIII

The Controversy About Mambrino's Helmet and the Pack Saddle Disputed and Decided; with Other Accidents, Not More Strange than True.

Master Nicholas, the barber from La Mancha, now decides to maintain the joke. But because of his long professional experience, he says, and because he served in the army, he is an expert on all pieces of barber equipment and knows very well what a helmet looks like. Beyond a doubt, Don Quixote holds a helmet—although with its beaver missing—and not a barber's basin. The curate chimes in with a similar opinion. But as to whether the packsaddle is a packsaddle or indeed a horse's trappings, the curate continues, let the matter be secretly voted on by the entire company. Everyone is amused at these remarks; the barber thinks that they are all madmen. At this point, some troopers of the Holy Brotherhood who have just entered the courtyard participate in the dispute. "This is as much a packsaddle as my father is my father!" shouts one man. Don Quixote attacks him for the lie, and a mad scene of fighting and disputing involves everyone in the courtyard. After everyone is somewhat calmed down, the troopers read aloud their warrant for the arrest of the man who freed the galley slaves. Don Quixote scoffs at their simplicity to imagine a knight-errant bounded by the rules of common jurisprudence.

Commentary

This is another situation in which Don Quixote's vigorous and creative imaginings transform the mockers into true believers, though they do not recognize the occurrence. During the fray in the inn's courtyard, Don Ferdinand, Cardenio, the curate and the barber all defend Don Quixote's notion that what appears to be a packsaddle for an ass are really the trappings for a knight's steed. Although the knight himself is not too sure what to call the equipment, his followers, not recognizing the ambiguities of truth and illusion, choose an opinion and defend it. Though they are merely making fun of the madman's fancies, Don Quixote's friends are actually fighting for the right to be imaginative against those symbols of commonplace realism, the troopers of the Holy Brotherhood.

CHAPTER XIX

The Notable Adventure of the Officers of the Holy Brotherhood with Don Quixote's Great Ferocity and Enchantment

The curate convinces the troopers that they cannot detain a madman. They should rather allow himself and the barber to conduct Don Quixote back to his village where he might be cured, accompanied by a couple of the police officers. Meanwhile the separate members of the inn's company prepare to leave, happy at the new prospects that the reunions and chance meetings have revealed. The curate pays the barber for the basin, the dispute of the packsaddle being settled; he compensates the innkeeper for the loss of his wineskins and the wine, and hires a wagoner to convey Don Quixote in an oxcart. Constructing a kind of cage with wooden bars and a straw floor, the curate and the barber quietly convey the sleeping knight to this vehicle which is then placed on the oxcart. The Don is too amazed to resist or cry out. In a disguised voice the barber explains that the "Manchegan lion," the flower of knight-errantry, is now to be conveyed to La Mancha where he will unite with the "Tobosan dove" and produce brave cubs after the knight's own image.

CHAPTER XX

Prosecuting the Course of Don Quixote's Enchantment with Other Memorable Occurrences

Don Quixote wonders at his enchantment, for knights-errant, he says, are usually swiftly carried in a sky chariot or on the back of a flying beast. At one point in the slow journey, they are overtaken by horsemen heading for a nearby inn. The newcomers, a group of clergymen, wonder at the strange manner of conveying a prisoner of the Holy Brotherhood, and the canon listens attentively as the curate relates the strange history of Don Quixote and his madness. The canon responds by discoursing on the evils of reading books of romances, for, he says, they neither instruct nor provide their readers with a sense of beauty. For all that, he continues, they have one grace, for they are unlimited vehicles for an author to try his skill at depicting various imaginative happenings and fantastic characters.

CHAPTER XXI

Containing a Continuation of the Canon's Discourse upon Books of Knight-Errantry and Other Curious Matters.

The canon now includes a critical appraisal of drama in his discussion with the curate. He says that the plays written for the modern theater are devoid of graceful writing or dramatic development because the public is only interested in spectacle and fast action. Furthermore, he says, the comedies that are played are loosely constructed in terms of historical accuracy, chronological sequence, or moral truth.

CHAPTER XXII

A Relation of the Wise Conference Between Sancho and His Master.

While the curate and canon are so engaged, Sancho has a shrewd talk with his encaged master. He declares that the town curate and barber are playing a shameful trick, and that if Don Quixote were truly enchanted the natural functions of his body would be suspended. The knight admits that he is in need of physical relief because his bodily functions are operating, but he counsels his squire to understand that enchantments always take different forms, according to circumstance. The curate may appear to be a familiar person, but he is in fact a powerful necromancer. Sancho seeks permission for his master to be uncaged in order to relieve himself, and while Don Quixote is gratefully relaxing on the grass, he engages with the canon in conversation about books of chivalry. To all the clergyman's accusations, that the novels are untruthful and therefore pernicious, Don Quixote declares that every incident therein depicted and each person discussed is in the image of truth and is documented in history.

CHAPTER XXIII

The Notable Dispute Between the Canon and Don Quixote, with Other Matters.

To prove his point, Don Quixote describes for the canon an imaginative incident from his readings, where a knight dives into a burning, creature-filled lake, only to find himself on a rich estate and served by lovely damsels in a magnificent castle. Furthermore, declares Don Quixote, in a few days, I shall myself expect to be made a king of some realm or other by grace of my valorous arm, and shall reward my squire "who is the best little man in the world" with an earldom. The canon can only marvel at the extravagant fancies of the madman. Suddenly a fugitive she-goat bursts through the underbrush and joins them. The goatherd follows, talking and scolding the beast as if it were human. To explain this manner of speaking, he prettily tells a story.

CHAPTER XXIV

The Goatherd's Entertaining Tale.

The goatherd says he has fallen in love with a lovely young damsel named Leandra. He is not the only suitor, however, for a rival named Anselmo also wishes to marry the maiden. Unfortunately, Leandra allowed herself to be abducted by a boasting braggart who has turned her head with his dandyism and tales of heroic deeds in the army. When a search party finds Leandra, she is in a cave by the road, abandoned by her false lover, despoiled of all her material goods, though with her virtue intact. Leandra is shipped off to a nunnery by her doting father, while the two rivals, Eugenio and Anselmo, have become goatherds, cynical and mournful for the weaknesses of femininity.

CHAPTER XXV

Of the Combat Between Don Quixote and the Goatherd: the Rare Adventure of the Penitents, Which the Knight Happily Accomplished with the Sweat of His Brow.

Because it is his obligation to relieve the oppressed, Don Quixote announces he will rescue the damsel from her confinement and return her to the arms of Eugenio. Ungratefully, the goatherd says he is crazy, and they begin to fight. The scuffle is interrupted by the appearance of a procession of penitents carrying a hooded effigy of the Virgin Mary. Assuming that they are abductors detaining a lady against her will, Don Quixote mounts Rosinante and challenges the procession. One of the group is so offended that he strikes the knight and the Don falls motionless to the ground. Sancho's weeping and wailing returns the knight to consciousness, and once more imprisoned in the oxcart, Don Quixote and the rest of the strange procession continue to the home village, where they arrive six days later. Teresa Panza greets her husband affectionately. "Is the ass in good health?" she asks. "Have you brought me a gown or a petticoat? Or shoes for my children?" Sancho answers somewhat quixotically: "Nothing in the 'varsal world is better for an honest man, than to be Squire to a Knight-Errant while he's hunting of adventures."

Commentary

In this conversation between Sancho and his wife, Cervantes shows his ability to depict the Spanish peasant with sympathy, accurate dialogue, and warm humor. Teresa is characterized as a shrewd and practical wife, characteristics shared by Sancho as well. The husband, however, has changed from his association with Don Quixote, and now expresses his inclination to sally forth again as an unpaid squire to his master. Sancho is becoming quixotized.

PART TWO

BOOK THREE

THE AUTHOR'S PREFACE

Cervantes writes bitterly against the author who published a book which purported to be a sequel to *Don Quixote*. Assuming an attitude of forgiveness, Cervantes writes that he has no desire to call the writer names and he would rather "let his Folly be its own punishment." He expresses outrage, however, in some parables whose moral is that the writer should be cautious how he exercises his wit in the future.

Commentary

The pirated version of *Don Quixote,* written by a man who called himself Alonso Fernandez de Avellaneda, would not excite much commentary if it did not include such a slanderous, spiteful Preface. It was not unusual for an author to capitalize on a book's popularity by writing a sequel to it, but Avellaneda, in his Preface, made fun of Cervantes' old age, his poverty, his heroically-maimed hand, and wrote that he wished to usurp the market of *Don Quixote* and ruin Cervantes' own chances at selling a true sequel.

Cervantes, in fact, allowed so much time to pass before he brought the second part of *Don Quixote* to his publisher that we may assume he might never have completed the work at all were it not for the spurious Preface that stung him into activity.

CHAPTER I

What Passed Between the Curate, the Barber, and Don Quixote Concerning His Indisposition.

The curate and the barber allow Don Quixote a month of complete retirement before they pay him a visit. Curious to see whether he is truly cured, they soon begin to converse about knight-errantry. The barber is now certain that Don Quixote is as crazy as ever, and tells a story about a madman in a Seville institution who convinced everyone that he was cured until he declared that he was Neptune. Despite the dull barber's expectations, the knight understands the story and is offended. "Ah, Master Shaver, Master Shaver, only the blind cannot see through a sieve," he says. "I am not Neptune; neither do I pretend to set up for a wise man when I am not so. All I aim at, is only to make the world sensible how much they are to blame, in not laboring to revive those most happy times, in which the order of knight-errantry was in its full glory." The three of them now get involved in another of those discussions with the knight once more defending the truth of everything contained in books of chivalry.

Commentary

The serious tone of Part Two is immediately apparent as the barber relates the story of the lunatic in the madhouse. Master Nicholas is shown to be gross and dull of understanding to consider Don Quixote too withdrawn from the real world to comprehend his story. The knight, on the other hand, must now realize that the common people of the world will make fun of him because they think he is too dull-witted to understand. As Part Two progresses, Don Quixote develops more and more as the tragic hero in a world of fools, with Cervantes leading his protagonist, not through a career of drubbings and burlesque, but through incidents of psychological complexity and opportunities for character development.

CHAPTER II

Of the Memorable Quarrel Between Sancho Panza and Don Quixote's Niece and Housekeeper; with Other Pleasant Passages.

The niece and housekeeper refuse to allow Sancho to see his master, saying that he is the cause of his distraction. Don Quixote orders them to desist and eagerly questions Sancho. The squire first informs his master that all their adventures are written down in a history written by Cid Hamet Benengali and that the young student, Samson Carrasco, has read the book. Don Quixote marvels, and surmises that the author must be a powerful enchanter in order to command such universal knowledge. He is eager to talk with Samson and find out the world's opinion.

CHAPTER III

The Pleasant Discussion Between Don Quixote, Sancho Panza, and the Bachelor Samson Carrasco.

The twenty-four-year-old student, carefully described as "one that would delight in nothing more than in making sport for himself by ridiculing others," reassures the knight and squire that their history has been told with great fidelity to the truth. Not only is the book popular in Spain, he says, but it is available to readers as far as Antwerp. The bachelor and knight now discuss how difficult it is for an author to iron out all the small errors he may have committed in the course of writing, how unjust critics can be, themselves devoid of creative talents. Sancho now takes his leave while Don Quixote and Samson Carrasco begin to dine.

CHAPTER IV

Sancho Panza Satisfies the Bachelor Samson Carrasco in His Doubts and Queries: with Other Passages Fit to Be Known and Related.

Samson Carrasco asks that Don Quixote and Sancho supply him with certain missing information that Cid Hamet neglected to include in his history. Sancho is more than eager to oblige, especially describing how his ass was stolen while he was yet sitting on it. Concluding his humorous discourse, Sancho declares, "...that if my master be ruled by me, we had been in the field by this time, undoing of misdeeds and righting of wrongs, as good knights-errant used to do." Rosinante loudly neighs at this moment. A good omen, exclaims Don Quixote, and he immediately sets plans for sallying forth once more. Carrasco kindly volunteers the news of a splendid tournament to be held at Sargossa, and were Don Quixote to outtilt all rivals, he would be famous as the greatest living knight.

CHAPTER V

The Wise and Pleasant Dialogue Between Sancho Panza, and Teresa Panza, His Wife: Together with Other Passages Worthy of Happy Memory.

Cervantes intrudes once more, saying that this chapter is apocryphal because it shows Sancho speaking with an understanding and elegance foreign to his peasant upbringing. The squire tells his wife that he is glad to seek for adventures because he shall soon be rewarded with the government of an island. Teresa is afraid that she and her daughter would never be happy or comfortable in the role of finely-costumed gentlewomen, and the people would laugh at their rusticity. Sancho insists that respect is paid to persons of wealth and fine appearance with no heed to former circumstances. "All those things which we see before our eyes do appear, hold, and exist in our memories much better and with greater stress than things past," he says. Teresa, at last, asks that Sancho send for his son and train him to be a gentleman as soon as he gains his position. But the daughter must try to avoid the false royalty as long as possible.

Commentary

Part Two also introduces a Sancho who amazes his master with his intelligent observations and aptness for the profession of knight-errantry even as he amazes his creator, for Cervantes insists that Sancho's awakened intellect must be "apocryphal." The squire, however, is a quick student of his master and shows his wife that he is imbued with Don Quixote's ambition. He of the "let not the cobbler look beyond his last," and "every sheep to her mate," now wishes that the future Panzas of the world be counts and countesses. Teresa, on the other hand, prefers the status quo, looking forward only to sufficient food and clothing for her family.

CHAPTER VI

What Passed Between Don Quixote, His Niece, and the Housekeeper: Being One of the Most Important Chapters in the Whole History.

Realizing that Don Quixote is preparing for a third sally, his niece Antonia pleads passionately for him to stay home and not engage in such extravagant activities. "You know so much," she cries, "and yet are so grossly blind of understanding as to fancy a man of your years and infirmity can be strong and valiant...and yet what's more odd, that you are a knight, and 'tis well known that poor gentlemen are none." Don Quixote refutes these commonplace, all-too-sensible arguments. "That a young baggage, who scarce knows her bobbins from a bodkin should presume to put in her oar," he begins angrily, and then explains, eloquently and kindly, the character and duties of those professing knight-errantry. It is not necessary to be highborn to have endowments of fine character, pleasant disposition, and bravery, he says. When Sancho arrives, he and Don Quixote closet themselves to make their plans privately.

Commentary

The niece expresses the universal social realities; that a man must stay home and keep his responsibilities confined to his domestic life. Narrow domestication is the basis, not only for family stability, but for mediocrity, and men who wish for glory and immortality – creativity and freedom, that is – must oppose themselves to these restrictions and profess some form of knight-errantry. Perhaps the niece's voice is an echo of Cervantes' personal troubles, for he tried for long, frustrated years to provide for his own household of women, who doubtless never understood his own quixotic temperament as he labored at unsuccessful manuscripts and never achieved reward for his brave sacrifices for Spain.

CHAPTER VII

An Account of Don Quixote's Conference with His Squire, and Other Most Famous Passages.

The housekeeper, in desperation, begs the bachelor Samson to dissuade the señor from his preparations. Instead, the sly student encourages the knight, and bids him make haste on his journey. Meanwhile, Sancho has added his voice of dissent to that of the niece. He requests his master to guarantee him a monthly wage. Don Quixote declares that no squire in history has received anything in payment except what fortunes the knight wins during his travels. He dismisses Sancho, saying that he shall find a squire – perhaps Samson Carrasco – who accepts these terms. The squire is "struck dumb with disappointment; 'twas cloudy weather with him in an instant," and Sancho begs forgiveness and, after a fond embrace, the two friends agree to remain together. They now continue preparations for the journey; Samson offers the Don an intact helmet which he can borrow from a friend. Well-provisioned, Sancho and his master, equally filled with hope for what the future will provide, ride to their first destination, Toboso.

CHAPTER VIII

Don Quixote's Success in His Journey to Visit the Lady Dulcinea del Toboso.

While they travel, Don Quixote and Sancho discourse on the qualities and deeds that purchase immortality. As Sancho points out, more reverence is shown to barefooted, flagellating friars who become sainted, than to many a bolder and more daring knight. Says Sancho, "...a dozen or two of sound lashes, well meant and as well laid on, will obtain more of Heaven than two thousand thrusts with a lance, though they be given to giants, or dragons, or hobgoblins." That is true, says his master, but "all men cannot be friars; we have different paths allotted us to mount to the high seat of Eternal Felicity. Chivalry is a religious order, and there are knights in the fraternity of saints in heaven." At evening of the second day, they arrive at Toboso. Don Quixote will not enter the city until late at night, however, and they rest among some trees outside the town.

Commentary

More serious in this Second Part, Cervantes firmly states his hero's conviction that his way of life is a religious order, respectful of Catholic orthodoxy in his belief that the works of man on earth are rewarded in heaven. Knighthood is no longer a burlesque to the author, and Don Quixote, suggestively characterized with saintliness in Part One, begins to fulfill his spiritual potential. It seems as if Cervantes has become more and more convinced of the depth of character of Don Quixote as he has continued to work with him.

CHAPTER IX

That Gives an Account of Things Which You'll Know When You Read It.

Halfway toward dawn, Don Quixote and Sancho descend the hill and enter the silent, sleeping village. The knight heads for Dulcinea's palace, but the lofty building turns out to be a church. Sancho offers no help for, he says, it is too dark for him to recognize their whereabouts. "You that have seen it a thousand times should locate the place," he tells the Don, but his master says that he admires the Lady only by hearsay and never saw where she lives. "To be plain with you," Sancho confesses, "I saw her but by hearsay, too, and the answer [to the letter] I brought you was by hearsay as well as the rest, and I know the Lady Dulcinea no more than the man in the moon." Before Don Quixote can digest this astounding news, a ploughman suddenly appears, but is unable to give them directions.

Sancho now offers a welcome suggestion: that his master remain in a nearby wood, while he seeks Dulcinea. He will tell her that Don Quixote attends her and will then report back to his master what her instructions are.

CHAPTER X

How Sancho Cunningly Found a Way Out to Enchant the Lady Dulcinea; with Other Passages No Less Certain than Ridiculous.

Leaving his master meditating in the wood, Sancho rides out of sight and then lies down under a tree to think. He decides to tell Don Quixote that Dulcinea has been horribly enchanted into a rustic peasant lass. As he remounts Dapple, he sees three country wenches riding towards him, each on a she-ass. Hastening to Don Quixote he cries, "If you will clap spurs to Rosinante you will yourself meet Lady Dulcinea with a brace of her damsels in the open field." Bewildered, Don Quixote kneels beside his squire who has thrown himself in front of one of the girls recommending her ladyship to the Knight of the Woeful Countenance, her willing slave. Thinking that they are mocked, the wenches attempt to ride off, but one of them is thrown when her donkey rears. The knight hastens to help his Dulcinea remount, but she avoids him by vaulting into the saddle and riding swiftly away. Stunned, disappointed, confused, the poor knight begs Sancho to describe the rich trappings of the princesses' palfreys, the beautiful visage of his Lady and the ornate clothing she wears which the evil enchantment has prevented him from enjoying. Sancho relates the loveliness of the ladies, their apparel, their perfume, their fine-bred mounts, while Don Quixote can only wonder at the vulgar wenches he had beheld.

Commentary

This is a low point in Don Quixote's career, for his most faithful follower, Sancho, has joined the mockers by enacting a cruel comedy at his master's expense, grotesquely exchanging roles by declaring a vision contrary to the knight's observations. Cervantes declares, as well, that his hero's madness in this scene "outstrips all imaginable credulity," for Don Quixote, believing what Sancho tells him, is forced to accept the cruel reality that the peasant girl of the garlic breath is his Dulcinea. Shocking as is this scene to the knight, we may also imagine that the shy lover Alonso Quixano, that tender distracted soul hoping against hope for a chance to confront his Aldonza for the first time, is even more deeply wounded, more confused and doubtful than his knightly other self. On the other hand, those who maintain that Don Quixote is an actor, rather than a madman, may discover that the hero is well equipped to digest this turn of events and go along with the act which Sancho has set up.

This chapter investigates the nature of Sancho a little further. The squire considers his master foolish and easy to fool, "so very mad as to mistake black for white, white for black." But, says he, "I am the greatest cod's-head of the two, to serve and follow him as I do." Without really believing in his master's fancies, yet, by following along, he does believe. Sancho, who sees black for black, who recognizes windmills, not giants, and sheep, not armies, slowly surrenders himself to quixotic faith, tenaciously clinging to a fantastic hope that he will govern an island. Furthermore, Sancho himself is later to be deceived about this very deception, as his patron the duchess convinces him that Dulcinea is truly enchanted. Miguel de Unamuno points to this two-faceted quality as "the mystery of faith sanchopanchesque, which, without believing, believes."

CHAPTER XI

Of the Stupendous Adventure That Befell the Valorous Don Quixote with the Chariot or Cart of the Court or Parliament of Death.

Don Quixote is so melancholy that Sancho tries to cheer him as they ride along. While speaking of enchantments that change the appearance of familiar persons to uglified creatures, they encounter a cart driven by a devil, whose passengers include Death, a winged angel, and a plumed knight. In response to Don Quixote's challenge, the driver introduces them all as a group of strolling players. Having just enacted a tragedy called the "Parliament of Death" in one town, they have remained costumed for a performance at the next. Don Quixote lets them pass, but the fool of the players, with jingling bells and thumping cow's-bladders frightens Rosinante so that the horse throws his master. The fool plays the same game with Dapple, who returns to Sancho after having thrown his tormentor. Sancho persuades his master to desist from revenging himself—"though they seem to be Kings, Princes, and Emperors, yet there's not so much as one Knight-Errant among them"—and Don Quixote yields to the sensible advice.

Commentary

Don Quixote is so sad at this point, shocked as it were into sanity, that he sees the players for what they are. Sancho reminds him that a true knight cannot challenge sham knights, and the sane Don Quixote agrees to leave "these idle apparitions" and search for more "substantial and honorable adventures." It is interesting to note, however, that Don Quixote, finding so many adventures in commonplace incidents, accepts these costumed actors as unworthy opponents.

CHAPTER XII

The Valorous Don Quixote's Strange Adventure with the Bold Knight of the Mirrors.

While Don Quixote and Sancho spend the night under some trees, another knight and another squire stop to rest in the same place. The stranger sighs and laments about his mistress, Casildea de Vandalia. Desirous to learn more about Dulcinea's rival, Don Quixote begins to converse with the newcomer. Meanwhile the two squires have retired to a separate place where they can discuss their common interests.

CHAPTER XIII

The Adventure with the Knight of the Wood Continued; with the Wise, Rare and Pleasant Discourse That Passed Between the Two Squires.

The two squires compare the foolishness of their masters. The stranger says his knight is more of a knave than a fool, and Sancho says, "Mine is not like yours then; he has not one grain of knavery in him...he does all the good he can to everybody; a child may persuade him it is night at noonday, and he is so simple I can't help loving him." After eating and drinking together and chatting amiably, the two squires fall asleep.

CHAPTER XIV

A Continuation of the Adventure of the Knight of the Wood.

The strange knight boasts of having conquered even the great Don Quixote de La Mancha, of having wrung from him a confession that no one excels the beauty of his mistress Casildea. At this, the amiable conversation becomes a parley for a duel. The newcomer dresses himself in a glittering coat set with mirrors, the squires are roused, and the combatants mount and begin to fight. The Knight of the Mirrors loses the battle, and reveals under his visor the visage of the bachelor Samson Carrasco. His squire (after a fake nose fell off) looks exactly like Thomas Cecial, Sancho's neighbor. Don Quixote assures the bewildered Sancho that some enchanter has transformed the faces of their opponents in order to gain mercy from his anger.

CHAPTER XV

Giving an Account Who the Knight of the Mirrors and His Squire Were.

The curate, the barber, and Samson Carrasco decided to overcome Don Quixote according to his own code. In the guise of a knight, Samson would vanquish the Don and order him to return to his own village for a period of two years, departing from town only with the victor's permission. Engaging Thomas Cecial as a squire, Samson followed along the road taken by Don Quixote and Sancho.

Now that the fight is over, Thomas Cecial insists on going home, while the bruised and vengeful Samson insists on continuing his quest until he has the satisfaction of vanquishing Don Quixote.

Commentary

This portrait of Samson, angry and sore from his fall, shows a sane man in a fit of passion—a dangerous, if temporary, madman. Cervantes plays further with this sketch of play-acting and genuineness, of truth and fantasy, as he costumes Samson in a coat of mirrors. The newcomers are mirror images of Don Quixote and Sancho, but like most reflections, are backwards. The squire Cecial is unfaithful to his master; the knight

Carrasco pursues his chivalry for personal revenge. According to these events, then, it is the true madman who wins; the noble visionary is the one who inspires a faithful follower.

CHAPTER XVI

What Happened to Don Quixote with a Sober Gentleman of La Mancha.

Overthrowing the Knight of the Mirrors restores Don Quixote's faith in himself. He would be the happiest knight in the world, he thinks, if he could only find a way to disenchant Dulcinea. A green-clad gentleman on a fine mare overtakes them, at this point, and Don Quixote introduces himself. In his turn, the gentleman describes his own manner of life – sober, pious, intelligent – and tells the knight about his young son, a student at Salamanca. The boy has chosen to study poetry, although his father wishes he would select a useful scientific discipline. Don Quixote delivers himself of an eloquent speech on the virtues and delights of poetry; the sciences are adornments and enrichments and polish for the center, poesy. The gentleman is amazed at the madman's sensible opinions.

CHAPTER XVII

Where You Will Find Set Forth the Highest and Utmost Proof That the Great Don Quixote Ever Gave, or Could Give, of His Incredible Courage, with the Successful Issue of the Adventure of the Lions.

Having spied a wagon, decorated with flags, Don Quixote investigates this new source of adventure. In answer to his questions, the wagoner replies that he is conveying two huge lions to the king, a present from the general of Oran. Don Quixote insists he must fight with the beasts for they undoubtedly are sent here by enchanters. Threatening the carter with instant death, Don Quixote has him open the lion's cage, ordering everyone to clear the field. Bravely, the knight stands and stares at the beast. The lion, however, after getting to his feet to look out of the cage at his opponent, turns his back to the opening and lies down once more. Quickly the wagoner closes the cage door, hitches up his mules again, while Sancho and the gentleman in green return. Don Quixote, now the Knight of the Lions, accepts the gentleman's offer of hospitality, and they repair to his house.

Commentary

Heroes of epic adventures have always sought glory at the risk of their lives, and Don Quixote is no exception. His challenge to the lion is an example of pure courage, and the victory was an important one for it completely restored his self-confidence, so bruised at seeing his Dulcinea so vulgarly enchanted.

Furthermore, in challenging the lion, Don Quixote personifies a favorite Spanish knight, Rodrigo Diaz de Vivar, known as the Cid. In *Poema de*

Mio Cid (written in 1140) the hero confronts a loosed lion, and the beast turns away in shame before the proud bearing of his challenger. With this precedent in mind, then we must consider that the lion turned from Don Quixote because he was ashamed before the imposing courage of the valorous knight.

CHAPTER XVIII

How Don Quixote Was Entertained at the Castle or House of the Knight of the Green Coat, with Other Extravagant Passages.

The knight and squire remain four days as guests of Don Diego de Miranda (the gentleman in green). Don Quixote has pleasant discussions with the student son, Don Lorenzo, and is delighted to discover the boy is truly a poet. Because of the young man's virtuous and sensitive temperament, the knight all but invites Don Lorenzo to become his disciple. When it is time to depart, Sancho is sad to leave such comfortable circumstances.

CHAPTER XIX

The Adventure of the Armorous Shepherd, and Other Truly Comical Passages.

Riding along once more, Don Quixote exchanges greetings with two farmers and two students. After introductions are over, the students invite the knight and squire to attend a wedding to which they are going. Comacho, the wealthy yeoman groom, is sparing no expense on the celebration. Another man also loves the beautiful bride, Quiteria. Well-favored, talented, skilled at fencing, the disappointed lover Basil is too poor to gain Quiteria's hand. The students say that Basil is so melancholy and distracted that this wedding day might prove to be the day of his death. Don Quixote declares that his sympathies go with the poor lover.

CHAPTER XX

An Account of Rich Comacho's Wedding, and What Befell Poor Basil.

Sancho is impressed by the lavish feast prepared for the celebration. A cook casually thrusts three chickens and a couple of geese in his hands, and he immediately gorges himself on these viands, while songs, dances, and a pageant are performed for the wedding guests. Discoursing together, Sancho declares to his master that he is all in favor for the bridegroom: "Comacho has filled my belly and therefore has won my heart." He strings such a long series of proverbs to prove his point that Don Quixote refrains from answering him.

CHAPTER XXI

The Progress of Camacho's Wedding, with Other Delightful Incidents.

When Quiteria appears, Don Quixote decides she is more lovely than anyone except Dulcinea. Suddenly Basil appears and addresses the bride.

Disheveled in appearance, distracted in attitude, he reproaches her for spurning his love and breaking her promise to him. He stabs himself with a dagger, and, as a dying wish, asks the curate to marry him to Quiteria, who can then, in a few minutes, wed Comacho as an honorable widow. The bride agrees. As soon as the curate has performed the ceremony, Basil leaps briskly to his feet and embraces his new wife. Fighting begins immediately but is interrupted by Don Quixote's intervention. He concludes his speech with "those whom heaven has joined let no man put asunder," reinforcing the words with thrusts of his lance. The new bridal party leaves the scene, although Comancho holds the feast as before.

CHAPTER XXII

An Account of the Great Adventure of Montesino's Cave, Situated in the Heart of La Mancha, Which the Valorous Don Quixote Successfully Achieved.

Don Quixote spends three days with the newlyweds, Basil and Quiteria. After lecturing the bridegroom to find some provident employment in order to support his beautiful wife, Don Quixote, with one of Basil's student friends as guide, departs for Montesinos' Cave. The entrance to the pit is all overgrown with weeds and roots, but the knight clears the hole, ties a rope around his waist, and descends to the accompaniment of Sancho's prayers and lamentations. After half an hour, the scholar and squire pull on the rope but find no weight on it. Sancho, panic stricken, hauls in the line as fast as he can, and finally feels the drag. They draw Don Quixote to the ground. He opens his eyes, as if awakening from a deep sleep. After a refreshing meal, Don Quixote proceeds to relate to them the wonders of Montesinos' Cave.

CHAPTER XXIII.

Of the Wonderful Things Which the Unparallelled Don Quixote Declared He Had Seen in the Deep Cave of Montesinos, the Greatness and Impossibility of Which Makes This Adventure Pass for Apocryphal.

Don Quixote tells his friends that, weary of hanging from the rope, he took rest on a spacious ledge about sixty feet down. Sleep overcame him, and he awoke to discover himself in the midst of a beautiful sun-flooded meadow. Before him stood a "royal and sumptuous palace" built of transparent crystal whose guardian is none other than Montesinos himself. Greeting Don Quixote by name, the old man told him that the enchanted knights and ladies who live here have long awaited his arrival. Montesinos showed him the still-living Durandarte, a knight whose dying wish was for Montesinos to deliver his heart as a present to his mistress Belerma. Belerma herself with her waiting women also passed before Don Quixote's eyes. More surprising, however, were the presence of the three country wenches, mounted on she-asses, who again ran away as the knight approached. One of them returned, begging Don Quixote to lend her six reals, for her mistress,

Dulcinea, required money. At this amazing request, the knight gave her all he had, about four reals.

While the narrative continues, Sancho constantly interrupts. Impertinently refusing to believe what his master says, he suggests that this all took place in his head. Unruffled, Don Quixote says that there will come a time to prove to him of the reality of what he has seen, "the truth of which admits of no dispute."

Commentary

Montesinos, a historic character, is a knight who figures in a number of Spanish ballads dealing with Carolingian legends. He is described as having followed the bloody trail of his friend and cousin, the knight Durandarte, after the battle at Roncesvalles. When Montesinos finds his friend, Durandarte's last breath is expelled in asking that his heart be cut out and carried to his lady Belerma, whom he served for seven years; Montesinos fulfils this request. This extravagant story achieved great popularity and was later turned into a parody by Gongora. Actually, a cave in La Mancha nearby a ruined castle was known as Montesinos' Cave, and it is hardly more fitting than to have Don Quixote descend into this gorge.

In this underworld dream sequence, Don Quixote allows himself to express qualities of common sense and prosaic reasonableness which are parts of his inner consciousness. He questions Montesinos, first of all, to confirm some parts of the ballad. The old man corrects certain details. It was with a sharp poniard, not a dagger, he says, that he cut out the heart of Durandarte. Don Quixote also inquires why the supposedly beautiful Belerma has such yellow skin, as well as other blemishes. In another part of the dream, one of the wenches returns to the knight to ask for some money for Dulcinea. Cervantes' gentle suggestion, or Don Quixote's subconscious cynicism, is a quiet insinuation that beautiful ladies of Madrid and Seville must often be in the habit of asking money from their elderly gallants. Perhaps in this dreamy moment of truth, Don Quixote expresses his skepticism that a young girl like Dulcinea would only reply to his advances for mercenary reasons. Thus, in a situation completely freed of reality, Don Quixote reveals his subconscious Alonso Quixano qualities: matter-of-factness, prosaic interest in concrete details, vulgarization of his relation to Aldonza-Dulcinea. To continue even further, perhaps this inherent dullness in the brave hidalgo's character was in itself an impetus which led to his extravagant life of fantasy and escapism.

Cervantes, however, knew nothing of psychoanalysis, but it can be argued that his love of innuendo and double meanings and his general traits of suggestiveness and vagueness led him into working his materials into as many levels as possible.

CHAPTER XXIV

Which Gives an Account of a Thousand Flim-Flams and Stories, As Impertinent as Necessary to the Right Understanding of This Grand History.

Don Quixote, Sancho, and the scholar now seek a lodging. They are overtaken by a briskly walking man leading a mule laden with weapons. Barely greeting them the man hurries past, but says that if they meet at the same inn, he shall relate strange news. The next person they meet is a threadbare page who entertains them with his brief account of how he has been an ill-paid servant and is now ready to join a foot regiment and make his fortune as a soldier. Don Quixote makes a small speech at this point, again expressing his (and Cervantes) ideas of the virtue, nobility, and bright future of the life of a soldier. The young page accepts the knight's invitation to supper, and they arrive at the inn at nightfall.

CHAPTER XXV

Where You Find the Grounds of the Braying Adventure, That of the Puppet-Player, and the Memorable Divining of the Fortune-Telling Ape.

Once at the inn, Don Quixote seeks out the man with the lances and halberds and listens to his tale of the braying adventure. Two aldermen of his village, he says, went to search in the hills for an ass which one of them had lost. They agreed to stand on opposite sides of the hill and bray in order to attract the lost animal. So naturally did they each bray, that they met, not with the ass, but with each other. After exchanging compliments on their mimicry, they separated again to call the ass as before. Once more they brayed so perfectly that they met with each other, and, on their way home, found the corpse of the ass half eaten by wolves. The entire village took up the story, and that night the whole town resounded with braying as the idle fellows played the joke. Neighboring towns carried on the jest; individuals from other villages greeted their friends of the aldermen's town by braying. The stranger concludes his story by saying that he is bringing these weapons to the place where members of his village, the Brayers, will be in the field against jokesters of a rival town.

Now Maestro Pedro, a puppeteer, arrives with his fortunetelling ape who will answer all questions about past and present. The newcomer calls Don Quixote by name, addressing him as the "glorious restorer of knight-errantry," and recognizing Sancho as well. The knight wishes to question the ape. He asks whether what he saw in Montesinos' Cave were dreams or realities. Maestro Pedro, interpreting the ape's whispers, says that some things were dreams, some realities. The puppeteer and his assistant now prepare the puppet show and the spectators take their places.

CHAPTER XXVI

A Pleasant Account of the Puppet-Play, with Other Very Good Things Truly.

The puppet play, "Melisandra's Deliverance," is narrated by a young boy who interprets the action of the puppets and identifies the characters. At the point where the brave knight, Don Gayferos, gallops off with his wife, Melisandra, whom he has just freed from cruel imprisonment, and an angry horde of armed Moors chase him, Don Quixote decides he must aid the brave Christians. Swinging his sword, he hacks at all the Moorish puppets until they are completely dismembered. He cuts the strings and wires in his fury and barely misses slicing the head of the puppeteer himself. When Maestro Pedro laments his losses, Don Quixote slowly realizes his mistake, and, cursing the necromancers for clouding his perspective, pays handsomely for each ruined puppet.

Commentary

This suggestive incident of a puppet play underlines Cervantes' theme of relating truth and fantasy so that they are almost interchangeable. It is not difficult for Don Quixote to accept the adventure happening in the puppet play as a real incident, but he admits his mistake and offers to pay for the ruined puppets. Cervantes, creator of Don Quixote, also offers us a puppet play, and intrudes the remarks of Cid Hamet Benengali's translator to enlarge the action of his stage, just as the boy narrates Maestro Pedro's little show. Like Don Quixote, the ideal reader of this history alternates moments of complete involvement with the novel to be then startled by an editorial chapter into a state of detachment. Cervantes, however, insists that his *Quixote* is a historic account, whereas Maestro Pedro admits that his characters are merely puppets. Thus Don Quixote's action can be interpreted as another incident where the intuitive knight hacks away at lies and deception, the very means of livelihood of rogues like Gines de Passamonte. However one interprets this incident of the puppets, the important point is to show the plastic relationship between reality and stagecraft. This is one of the outstanding themes of the novel and perhaps is one of the most important investigations in the entire *Quixote*.

CHAPTER XXVII

Wherein Is Discovered Who Master Peter Was and His Ape; as Also Don Quixote's Ill Success in the Braying Adventure, Which Did Not End So Happily As He Desired and Expected.

Revealing that the puppeteer is Gines de Passamonte in disguise and with a new profession, the author tells somewhat of how the rogue earns his livelihood; in fact, the description is that of a classic Spanish *picaro*. Back to Don Quixote, the author tells of the battle that the brayers are awaiting. The assembled fighters greet Don Quixote, assuming he is a champion for their cause, and listen to his oration. The knight declares that men should go to war, not for small causes, but for large ones, such as the defense of the Catholic faith, or the defense of Spain or the defense of one's good name. While he pauses, Sancho takes up the speech. It is a silly fancy, he says, to be ashamed of being able to bray. As a child he himself was an excellent brayer. The foolish Sancho, then, opening his mouth, holding his nose, makes such a loud braying that the townsmen think he is mocking them. As they begin to collect stones, Don Quixote sensibly spurs Rosinante and gallops out of danger, but Sancho receives a good beating. After this the villagers leave the field of battle, relieved that the opposing townsmen did not show up.

CHAPTER XXVIII

Of Some Things Which Benengali Tells Us He That Reads Shall Know, if He Reads Them with Attention.

This chapter faithfully transcribes a conversation between Don Quixote and Sancho Panza regarding salary. As the squire pursues his request, the Don politely asks how many months of a monthly wage is owing. Sancho replies that twenty years have passed since he has been promised a government of an island. Gladly will he pay, says Don Quixote, the better to get rid of such a mercenary varlet. Furthermore, he says, "Thou perverter of the laws of chivalry that pertain to squires, where didst thou ever see or read that any squire to a knight-errant stood capitulating with his master, as thou hast done with me, for so and so much a month?" He continues to scold, until tears well up in Sancho's eyes, he begs humble pardon, and the two friends are once more amicably settled in their differences.

CHAPTER XXIX

The Famous Adventure of the Enchanted Bark.

At the banks of the River Ebro, where they have now arrived, Don Quixote spies a little boat moored to the shore. He is convinced that "this boat lies here for no other reason but to invite me to embark in it," and, with Sancho trembling with fear, they enter the boat and begin to drift. Exclaiming at the distances they travel, Don Quixote tells his squire that they are approaching the "equinoctal line" but Sancho points out he can still see Dapple and Rosinante tied to the tree on shore. Slowly they drift toward a water mill, and Sancho is fearful that they will be sucked into the rapids and flung down the falls. But the millers, all covered with flour, rush out with poles to arrest the drift of the boat. Don Quixote slashes at these goblins with his sword. The boat overturns; knight and squire are rescued from the water by some millers. Don Quixote offers the angry fisherman payment for the ruined boat, provided that the evil company release the prisoner in the castle dungeons. The millers are mystified, and the knight, assuming it is a task for some other brave paladin to free the captive, returns with Sancho to their beasts.

CHAPTER XXX

What Happened to Don Quixote with the Fair Huntress.

As knight and squire emerge from the wood, they see a noble hunting party. Leading her attendants, the lovely lady with a goshawk appears to be a person of high quality. Don Quixote dispatches Sancho to greet the fair huntress in the name of the Knight of the Lions. Receiving his embassy courteously, the duchess begs them both to be guests in her castle nearby. Meanwhile she sends a message to her husband the duke to inform him of their strange visitors. Since both have read the first part of the History of the Ingenious Knight, they are eager to find diversion from their guests. The duke and duchess are as much entertained by the impertinences of Sancho as by the extravagances of the knight.

CHAPTER XXXI

Which Treats of Many and Great Matters.

Entering the castle courtyard, Don Quixote is welcomed by all the servants with burlesque pomp and goes into the dining room with his shoulders draped in a red mantle. Recovering quickly from this royal attendance, Sancho's first consideration is his ass, Dapple, and he insults a waiting-woman by asking her to make sure that the beast is comfortably settled. The duchess overhears the argument and chides Sancho gently, promising to take as good care for the ass as for the master. While they prepare for dinner, Don Quixote scolds Sancho for his impertinence and orders him to be more discreet in further conversations. The knight marches in to dinner and accepts the place of honor at the duke's table. The ducal clergyman, when he realizes that the knight is none other than the hero of the famous history, sternly lectures him. "Hark ye, Goodman Addlepate, who has put it into your head that you are a knight-errant, that you vanquish knights and robbers? Go, get you home again, and look after your children if you have any, and what honest business you have to do, and leave wandering about the world, building castles in the air and making yourself a laughing-stock to all that know you, or know you not."

CHAPTER XXXII

Don Quixote's Answer to His Reprover, with Other Grave and Merry Incidents.

Eloquently, nobly, Don Quixote answers the uncivil parson, whose words echo the sentiments of the hidalgo's niece, Antonia. "A fine world 'tis truly," he says, "when a poor pedant, who has seen no more of it than lies within twenty of thirty leagues about him, shall take upon him to prescribe laws to Knight-Errantry and judge of those who profess it." He goes on to say that his only wish is to right wrongs and do good in the world, and surely no one can denigrate these motives. When the clergyman turns his anger to Sancho, the loyal squire replies, using proverbs, of course: "Keep with good men and thou shalt be one of them. I am also one of those of whom it is said, 'Not with whom thou wert bred, but with whom thou hast fed;' as also 'lean against a good tree, and it will shelter thee.' I have leaned and stuck close to my good master, and...now he and I are one; and I must be as he is...and so he live and I live, he shall not want kingdoms to rule, nor shall I want islands to govern." The parson leaves the dining room in anger, and after dinner, the mischievous servants play their own trick on Don Quixote by inventing a washing ritual to make him look ridiculous. To prevent insult to his guest, the duke also demands a washing, although he can barely repress his laughter. While Don Quixote now goes for an afternoon sleep, Sancho agrees to entertain the duchess until the heat of the day has passed.

CHAPTER XXXIII

The Savoury Conference Which the Duchess and Her Women Held with Sancho Panza, Worth Your Reading and Observation.

Punctuating his conversation with proverbs, Sancho relates the truth about Dulcinea's enchantment, describing the whole incident with the three country wenches. The duchess suggests, however, that Dulcinea is truly enchanted, and that the magicians who persecute Don Quixote have put this story into Sancho's head. When they shall all see Dulcinea in her true shape, Sancho shall see how mistaken he is. Believing everything she says, Sancho is very confused. The duchess now begs him to tell her the story of Montesinos' Cave, which he does. She further confounds Sancho by pointing out that if his master saw the country wench in the cave, then doubtless Dulcinea is victim to a powerful enchantment. Then the conversation turns to a discussion of Sancho's governorship, which the duke had previously promised him, and the duchess, very much amused, finally dismisses the bewildered squire.

CHAPTER XXXIV

Containing Ways and Means for Disenchanting the Peerless Dulcinea del Toboso, Being one of the Most Famous Adventures in the Whole Book.

The duke and duchess resolve to further entertain themselves with Don Quixote's extravagances by devising adventures for him. On an appointed day, they organize a boar hunt, presenting Sancho with a green hunting suit for the occasion. When the wild beast actually appears, Sancho is so terrified that he climbs a tree, and later is found by the rest of the party as he hangs upside down with his shirt caught on an overhanging bough. It is now getting dark in the woods, and all are amazed to hear tremendous noises of battle, trumpets, Moorish cries, drums. A costumed rider gallops past, declaring that he is the devil in search of Don Quixote de La Mancha. Six bands of necromancers are coming this way, he says, conducting the peerless Dulcinea enchanted in a triumphant chariot.

Montesinos, her attendant, comes along to give information how she may be freed. More dreadful noises resound through the woods, lights flicker, and Sancho faints from fear. Finally a procession of oxcarts appears, each draped as in mourning, each carrying an old man bearing the name of an ancient sage. The carts stop, while sweet music is heard advancing from the distance.

CHAPTER XXXV

Wherein is Continued the Information Given to Don Quixote How to Disenchant Dulcinea, with Other Wonderful Passages.

The music heralds the arrival of a wagon. On a platform in the rear sits a lovely young girl with a veil over her face, while a black-gowned figure who says he is Merlin, stands next to her. If Sancho Panza would voluntarily bestow three thousand three hundred lashes upon his "bare brawny buttocks" the enchantment would be broken. Sancho starts violently at these words of Merlin, and with a hundred objections, refuses to work this task. Threatened by Don Quixote, begged by Dulcinea, Sancho finally gives in, after the duke promises to bestow his government on a more compassionate ruler. The squire makes some conditions, however, on his task of self-lashing, to which Merlin agrees. Don Quixote hugs his squire now, kissing him again and again in gratitude. The duke and duchess are also pleased and resolve to continue with other such pleasant diversions.

Commentary

For such an unusual, and apparently cruel joke, one must conclude that there is no joke intended at all, and that Sancho's flogging satisfies certain conditions of his squire's life.

Religious penitents flog themselves in order to purify their souls by humiliating their bodies, and thus to gain grace and heavenly reward after death. Sancho, squire to a knight-errant imbued with a slightly more profane mission, but nonetheless holy, must flog himself in order to deserve serving Dulcinea. Only through faith in this ideal can Sancho gain immortality.

Don Quixote, who has already done his penance, is already in his mistress' service and cheerfully endures suffering for her sake. But not so Sancho, and although his "Dulcinea" is his island, he must nonetheless do penance to gain his reward. The duke even threatens the squire by telling him, "No flogging, no government," and at this final straw, Sancho gives in. In other words, Sancho must now serve Dulcinea. Since he has created her enchantment, he has, in a sense, created Dulcinea, although in a way quite opposite to the way that Don Quixote has created her. Sancho must now, through his past mistakes, commit himself entirely to the quixotic ideal.

CHAPTER XXXVI

The Strange and Never-Thought-of Adventure of the Disconsolate Matron, Alias, the Countess Trifaldi, with Sancho Panza's Letter to His Wife Teresa Panza.

Sancho, who, with the help of a scribe, has just written to his wife, shows the letter to the duchess. In the style of Sancho himself, the letter tells Teresa that her husband is a governor and that he is obliged to disenchant Dulcinea by lashing himself three thousand three hundred times. The duchess inquires if Sancho has begun the task. Yes, he says, for I've slapped myself with my hand five times this morning. After dinner is over, Sancho having dominated the entire conversation, the company hears sounds of fife and muffled drums. A huge man in black livery, with pages attending him, steps into the courtyard, and introduces himself as the squire to the Countess Trifaldi, known as the Disconsolate Matron. His mistress has traveled a great distance to seek Don Quixote. The knight steps forward and declares that the lady shall be redressed by "the force of my arm, the intrepid resolution of my soul."

CHAPTER XXXVII

The Famous Adventure of the Disconsolate Matron Continued.

Sancho is not pleased about this new adventure for he fears that serving an old waiting-woman is a source of bad luck. The duchess reassures him that Countess Trifaldi is waiting-woman to a sovereign. At this, the duchess's own waiting-woman, Donna Rodriguez, speaks up in defense of her colleagues, and she and Sancho debate until the duchess begs them to continue at a fitter time.

CHAPTER XXXVIII

The Account Which the Disconsolate Matron Gives of Her Misfortunes.

The lady Trifaldi stands before Don Quixote, her face covered with a heavy veil, twelve heavily-veiled waiting-women attend her. Her native land, she says, is the kingdom of Candaya, and her personal charge has been the care and education of the heiress to the crown, Princess Antonomasia. At the age of fourteen, the beautiful girl was courted by many foreign princes, but she favored a young knight, Don Clavijo. Melting the heart of the guardian Trifaldi, the handsome lover gained access to the princess' chambers, and when it was found that Antonomasia was pregnant, the happy couple were married at once.

CHAPTER XXXIX

Where Trifaldi Continues Her Stupendous and Memorable Story.

When she heard of the unequal match, the poor queen mother died, and the daughter and Don Clavijo accompanied the body to its grave.

Suddenly Malambruno the giant, cousin to the queen, appeared at the grave, mounted on a wooden horse. In revenge, he changed the princess and her lover into statues, placing a plaque between them which said that these presumptuous lovers would remain enchanted until Don Quixote de La Mancha engaged in single combat with the giant. Inflicting a lasting mortification on Trifaldi, the giant planted a beard on her face and on the faces of all her women. At this, the countess and all her attendants tear off their veils, shocking Sancho and Don Quixote by the sight of their bearded visages.

CHAPTER XL

Of Some Things That Relate to This Adventure, and Appertain to This Memorable History.

Don Quixote repeats his vow to aid the distressed ladies. Trifaldi says that Malambruno will send his wooden horse, Clavileno, which flies in the air and is guided by a wooden peg in its forehead. Sancho swears that he will not suffer the discomfort of straddling a wooden steed, nor engage in such a dangerous expedition. Trifaldi begs him with tears.

CHAPTER XLI

Of Clavileno's (Alias Wooden Peg's) Arrival, with the Conclusion of This Tedious Adventure.

When the horse arrives, Sancho remains adamant in his refusal to join his master. The duke then demands that the squire participate as a condition to become a governor of his island, and Sancho, trembling with fear, mounts blindfolded behind Don Quixote who is also blindfolded. The company shouts that they are riding in the air, and knight and squire feel a rush of wind (from bellows strongly pumped behind them) and are sure they have reached the "middle region of the air." The tail of Clavileno is now fired by one of the duke's servants, and, being filled with firecrackers, the horse explodes and its riders are tossed to the ground. A scroll is placed near Don Quixote, and it says that the knight has accomplished the adventure of the Disconsolate Matron. The giant Malambruno is satisfied; the lovers Antonomasia and Don Clavijo are disenchanted, and the Countess Trifaldi and her waiting-women are de-bearded. Now Sancho spins a long story of the sights he had seen while riding in the skies, but nobody believes him although he insists that a powerful enchantment has enabled him to witness all these wonders. As they leave the garden, Don Quixote whispers: "Sancho, since thou would'st have us believe what thou hast seen in Heaven, I desire thee to believe what I saw in Montesinos' Cave."

Commentary

Sancho is depicted here as the fearful, cowardly common man who saves face by imitating his master's Montesinos Cave adventure. Unlike Sancho, Don Quixote actually saw visions in the cave for he had voluntarily descended into the strange sphere to investigate into another world. Sancho, bribed by the duke's promise of a governship to ride on Clavileno, merely made up lies, and unlike his master, is unable to believe in visions sufficiently to make them come true. Thus valor is the source of the Don's visions; cowardice the cause of Sancho's lies. Always tolerant for other people's perceptions, Don Quixote whispers the golden rule of human relationships: if you would have me believe you, you must believe me. This statement serves as a gentle reprimand to all the Sancho Panzas of the world who judge others by their own crookedness, reminding these cowards that communication between human beings must be based on mutual trust.

CHAPTER XLII

The Instructions Which Don Quixote Gave Sancho Panza, Before He Went to the Government of His Island, with Other Matters of Moment.

The duke now tells Sancho to prepare to take possession of his government. Sancho, however, is no longer so eager to have the office, but finally agrees to take it "not out of covetousness...but merely to know what kind of thing it is to be a governor." Don Quixote takes Sancho aside to give him good instructions for his conduct in the discharge of his office. Solemnly the knight intones his advice: Sancho must be honest, compassionate in his judgments, mindful of relatives and friends, and above all, he must remember with pride and humility that he has sprung from peasants. His other injunctions remind Sancho to adjudicate with objectivity and never be tempted into corruption or vice.

CHAPTER XLIII

The Second Part of Don Quixote's Advice to Sancho Panza.

Having advised his squire regarding mental and spiritual traits, Don Quixote now turns to directives for Sancho's physical condition. First of all is cleanliness, the master warns, and Sancho must pare his nails regularly and avoid eating onions and garlic so that his breath remains sweet. He must eat moderately and drink never so much as to get drunk. He must ride a horse with grace and wear trim, neat clothes. With many other injunctions, Don Quixote shows how his squire can discharge his duties as an exemplary governor. They then attend the duke and duchess at dinner.

CHAPTER XLIV

How Sancho Panza Was Carried to His Government, and of the Strange Adventure That Befell Don Quixote in the Castle.

The duke had ordered the management of Sancho's governorship to a clever steward, the same who had impersonated the Countess Trifaldi. As the steward prepares the equipage to accompany Sancho to his island, the squire notes that this man and Trifaldi "have the same face," but Don

Quixote says, "Nonsense." After an exchange of tearful embraces, Sancho is ushered off to his new office, while a disconsolate Don Quixote retires to his chamber after dinner. His misery is complete when he tears his silk stocking—the only pair he owns—and has no matching thread for mending. Overhearing two ladies in the courtyard, the knight opens his window. One of the speakers, Altisidora, bitterly complains to her companion that she is so much in love with Don Quixote that she can hardly sing. Altisidora, knowing that the knight listens, tunes her lute and begins a mocking serenade of love, while the tenderhearted Quixote repeats his vows to serve the peerless Dulcinea del Toboso.

CHAPTER XLV

How the Great Sancho Panza Took Possession of His Island, and in What Manner He Began to Govern.

Entering the town of Baratario (on the Island of Barataria) Sancho and his equipage are welcomed by the whole town, each of whose thousand people is curious to see the new governor. After ridiculous pomp and ritual, Sancho sits in the seat of justice for, says the clever and facetious steward, it is an ancient custom to test each new governor by asking him "some difficult and intricate question." The first dispute Sancho experiences is between a farmer and a tailor. The tradesman says he agreed to make five caps out of the cloth provided by the peasant, but his customer refuses to pay or to accept the merchandise. The tailor shows Sancho the caps, which are so tiny that they fit on each finger of the hand. The verdict of the Court, says the governor, is that "the tailor shall lose his making, and the countryman his cloth, and the caps go to the poor prisoners." The next dispute is between a borrower who says he has returned the twelve crowns, and the lender, who says he did not. In order to swear on the Rod of Justice, the borrower asks his disputant to hold his cane while he makes his vow. The creditor is satisfied, but as the plaintiffs turn to leave, Sancho asks to see the cane. He breaks the stick in two, and twelve crowns drop from the hollow cane, while the borrower is overcome with shame and disgrace. The third test of Sancho's sagacity involves a hefty woman who says she has been raped by the hog driver who accompanies her. Sancho first orders the man to give her his entire purse and, when the wench has left, instructs the man to wrest the money from her. Worn out with scuffling, they both return, and the woman announces she still holds the purse. "Hark you, mistress," thunders Sancho, "Had you shown yourself as stout and valiant to defend your body as your purse, the strength of Hercules could not have forced you." Returning the money to the hog driver, he sends the wench out of the Court in disgrace. The scribe who has been ordered to record all of Sancho's words and actions for the duke is amazed anew at the squire's sagacity.

CHAPTER XLVI

Of the Dreadful Alarms Given to Don Quixote by the Bells and Cats, During the Course of Altisidora's Amours.

Don Quixote, while walking in the hall, meets Altisidora with her maid. The girl feigns a swoon, while the maid scolds all knights-errant who are so ungrateful as to reject pure love. Accompanying himself on a lute, Don Quixote composes a song which he sings from his window that evening. The lyric counsels maids to retain their modesty and virtue and tells of a heart and soul faithful forever to the "Divine Tobosan, fair Dulcinea." When the song is over, a rope hung with more than a hundred tinkling bells descends over the knight's window. Furthermore, a sackful of frightened cats is emptied, and the noise made by yawling cats and tinkling bells is frightening. Some cats find their way into the Don's room, and scrambling about, they put out the candles. The knight slashes with his sword at the necromancers who have invaded his privacy, and one cat attaches itself to his nose and is loosed only by great effort. The ducal couple regret their joke, for Don Quixote is forced to stay in his room for five days in order to recuperate.

CHAPTER XLVII

A Further Account of Sancho Panza's Behaviour in His Government.

Sancho now seats himself at a sumptuous dinner table set with delectable fruits and viands. Every time that a dish is placed in front of him, however, the watchful physician at his side motions it away. He tells Sancho that the fruit is too damp, the meat too seasoned, and suggests that the governor eat only some wafers with a bit of jam. Sancho is furious at the doctor, crying out that to shorten his victuals is to shorten his life, not prolong it. The terrified physician is about to slink from the room, when the governor receives an urgent message from the duke. The note tells Sancho that some enemies intend to attack his land and that spies have already been sent out to murder him.

CHAPTER XLVIII

What Happened to Don Quixote with Donna Rodriguez, the Duchess' Woman; as Also Other Passages Worthy to be Recorded, and Had in Eternal Remembrance.

As Don Quixote lies in his chamber that night, out of temper because of his cat-scratched nose, the duchess' waiting-woman Rodriguez enters. Asking for succor, she proceeds to narrate the story of her life, detailing the death of her husband, and the problems of her sixteen-year-old daughter. The son of a rich farmer, a vassal of the duke who lends him money, has closely courted the child. Offering marriage, the young man seduced the daughter and now refuses to make good his promise. At this point, Donna Rodriguez, as with most aging gouvernantes, relates some gossip. She speaks of Altisidora's strong breath and says that the duchess has open sores on each leg which drain the ill humours from her body. Suddenly someone grabs the waiting-woman, spanks her with a slipper and pulls her out of the room. Don Quixote gets thoroughly pinched, and when the silent phantoms vanish, can only wonder who this new enchanter is.

CHAPTER XLIX

What Happened to Sancho Panza as He Went the Rounds in His Island.

Again Sancho has three experiences which try his abilities as governor. Accompanied by the steward and other attendants as he walks the rounds of his island, he stops two men fighting and demands to know the cause. One tells him that he is a "gentleman in decay," brought up to no useful employment. Frequenting gaming tables, he advises gamblers how to play and earns his living by receiving tips for his service. This gambler, he says, after winning a large sum of money, has given him merely a pittance. Sancho, after ordering the gambler to give the man 100 reals, banishes the parasite from the island. The watchman now brings a suspicious young man to the governor for questioning, but Sancho's queries receive impertinent, but witty, answers. Instead of punishing him, Sancho sends the young wag good humoredly to his home. The third encounter deals with a young girl, dressed in boy's clothing, and her brother. The charming maiden tells the governor that she has been so closely kept at home that she has conceived a great longing to see the world. Dismissing both youngsters, Sancho advises the maiden to act more prudently and with less curiosity in the future. "An honest maid," he says, "Should be still at home as if she had one leg broken."

CHAPTER L

Who the Enchanter and Executioners Were That Whipped the Duenna, and Pinched and Scratched Don Quixote; with the Success of the Page That Carried Sancho's Letter to His Wife Teresa Panza.

It seems that the roommate of Donna Rodriguez, a fellow waiting-woman, followed her colleague down the hall and saw the duenna enter the bedchamber of Don Quixote. Quickly rousing the duchess and Altisidora, the three ladies listened outside the chamber door and became very angry to overhear the secrets disclosed about themselves. They took revenge by mauling and pinching. The duchess diverts her husband, the duke, with this story, and then sends the clever page who impersonated Dulcinea to deliver Sancho's letter to his wife. Enclosing a friendly note of her own, the duchess also sends along Sancho's green hunting suit and a costly coral necklace. When they receive the gifts, Teresa Panza and her daughter are so delighted that they tell the entire village of their good fortune. The curate, the barber and Samson Carrasco can scarcely believe the tale of Sancho's government, but the page assures them it is true. Teresa now writes a letter, with the help of a scribe, to the duchess, and one to her husband.

CHAPTER LI

A Continuation of Sancho Panza's Government, with Other Passages, Such as They Are.

Hard work and scanty diet make Sancho sick of being a governor. One problem he solves as he sits in judgment is a classic paradox: there is an ancient law regarding the crossing of a bridge. If a man swears he tells the truth, he is allowed to pass, but if he lies, then he is to be hanged on the gallows. This time, the man in question tells the judges that his only object in crossing, is to die on the gallows; but since he tells the truth he cannot be hanged, yet if he does not die, the statement is a lie. Sancho orders that the man be passed freely, for he says, my master Don Quixote has always said, "When justice is in doubt, lean on the side of mercy." The duke's steward is truly impressed by Sancho's wise decision. Now the governor reads a letter from Don Quixote in which his master has advised him to protect the poor, to protect the consumers, and establish laws wise, just, and merciful. Immediately Sancho dictates a comical, but sincere, reply. The rest of the governor's busy day is taken up with making excellent regulations, in accord with the knight's counsels, that to this day, writes the author, they are promulgated and called "the Constitutions of the Great Governor Sancho Panza."

CHAPTER LII

A Relation of the Adventure of the Second Disconsolate or Distressed Matron, Otherwise Called Donna Rodriguez.

Just as Don Quixote wishes to inform the duke and duchess of his plans to take up his active life as a knight-errant, he is interrupted by the appearance of Donna Rodriguez and her daughter, both dressed in black. The duke and duchess are also surprised for they realize that the duenna is seriously asking the knight for assistance. In answer, Don Quixote vows to challenge the daughter's false lover, either slaying the offender or forcing him to marry the betrayed maiden. Promptly the duke accepts the challenge, in the name of his vassal and announces the time and place of combat. The page now returns from his visit to Teresa Panza, and with great amusement, the duchess reads Teresa's letter out loud. Don Quixote now reads to them Teresa's letter to Sancho, and the company enjoys the homely style, the gossip from town, and the expressed joy of the wife at her husband's exalted position. Lastly, Don Quixote reads Sancho's letter, and the hearers are startled to discover such wisdom in the governor whom all took for a fool.

Commentary

The clever steward best expresses the theme of these chapters of Don Quixote's "martyrdom," when he tells Governor Sancho: "Every day produces some new wonder, jests are turned into earnest, and those who designed to laugh at others, happen to be laughed at themselves." As the duke and duchess continue with their extravagant entertainments, the knight seems to increase in stature, while they themselves appear fools. Instead of making Don Quixote ridiculous, his humiliating experiences enhance his nobility and exalt his purity of purpose. Sancho is given the opportunity to practice a responsible ethic he never realized he possessed, while Teresa Panza, with her spontaneous and genuine feelings, is favorably contrasted with the duchess. Closing the full cycle, Cervantes shows that the perpetrators of the joke are themselves the subject of ridicule, that madmen are sane in contrast to normal people, and that fools are best capable of great wisdom.

CHAPTER LIII

The Toilsome End and Conclusion of Sancho Panza's Government.

In the dead of night, Sancho awakens to a great noise of bells and outcries and trumpets and drums. Twenty men rush into his chamber shouting that the enemy has overrun the island. "Arm, my Lord Governor," they cry, and clap Sancho between two huge shields so that he can hardly move. Trying to lead his men in a march, he takes one step and falls, helpless as a turtle. The men douse their lights and trample all over him, making as much fuss and noise as if a tremendous combat were in progress. The joke finally concludes with shouts of victory and poor Sancho is raised and returned to bed. Wordlessly, the governor dons his clothes and greets Dapple in his stable with a kiss. Sancho now bids farewell to all his aides, and with some bread, cheese, and provender for the ass, sets off for the ducal castle.

CHAPTER LIV

Which Treats of Matters That Relate to This History, and No Other.

Don Quixote looks forward to the joust with the duenna's daughter's false lover. The author relates that the young man has left the country "to avoid having Donna Rodriguez for a mother-in-law" and the duke substitutes his footman, Tosilos, to act the role. Meanwhile Sancho is on the road to the castle. He meets some pilgrims and recognizes his old friend and neighbor Ricote, a Moorish shopkeeper, among the foreigners. Over a huge meal, Ricote tells Sancho that he is exiled from Spain because he is a Moor, and his wife and daughter live in Algiers. Wishing to recover some gold which he buried near his house, Ricote is returning to the town, and asks Sancho to help him carry the money away. Sancho is covetous, he says, of nothing but his own freedom, and tells the incredulous Ricote the story of his recent governorship. Exchanging some town gossip, especially talking of Don Gregorio, the lover of Ricote's daughter, who has disappeared, the two friends embrace and go their separate ways.

CHAPTER LV

What Happened to Sancho by the Way, with Other Matters Which You Will Have No More to Do than to See.

Darkness coming upon them, Sancho cannot see where he is going, and he and Dapple tumble into a deep pit. Discovering a narrow passageway, Sancho and his ass walk further into the cave. The squire remarks how delighted Don Quixote would be in this same situation: "He would look upon these caves and dungeons as lovely gardens, and glorious palaces, and hope to be led out of these dark narrow cells into some fine meadow." Meanwhile, Don Quixote, exercising Rosinante in preparation for the joust, almost falls in the same pit when the horse stumbles. Believing finally, that the cries and brays of man and beast from the cave are not voices from purgatory, the knight returns to the castle for help. Restored to the upper ground, Sancho is delighted to be reunited with his master.

Commentary

The use of a pit as a symbolic device, suggesting death and birth, end and beginning, deserves some discussion. That part of Sancho which is mercenary, power-hungry, and small-minded has died, while the uncovetous, contented, and faithful squire has emerged refreshed and reborn from the pit. Escaping from the cave – the "dungeon" – Sancho discovers his real freedom which is, not to rule an island, but to serve Don Quixote. Only through his master can he glimpse idealistically, for Sancho can see no visions in a cave and can partake of imaginative words only if Don Quixote shows them to him. Cervantes furthermore uses this device of a pit to show the reader that the series of adventures with the duke and duchess is all but terminated, and that the knight and squire, firmly united, will go on to new encounters.

CHAPTER LVI

Of the Extraordinary and Unaccountable Combat Between Don Quixote de La Mancha, and the Lacquey Tosilos, in Vindication of the Matron Rodriguez's Daughter.

The day of the tournament arrives. The duke instructs Tosilos how to vanquish Don Quixote without injuring him, and the field is prepared for the combat, as spectators from far and near gather to witness the event. Tosilos, resplendent in his armor, mounted on a spirited charger, accepts the terms of the challenge, which are to marry the daughter if he loses, or to be released of obligation if he wins. Tosilos, however, suddenly gazes in admiration at Rodriguez's daughter, and while Don Quixote begins to charge, calls to the marshall of the field that he has decided not to fight and will marry the lady right away. The joust is called off, and even though Tosilos is recognized as the wrong man when he removes his helmet, the mother and daughter accept the marriage proposal. Seeing the duke so astonished, Don Quixote assures him that enchanters always transform the faces of their opponents, and if he would wait two weeks, the footman will change back into the original lover.

CHAPTER LVII

How Don Quixote Took His Leave, and What Passed Between Him and the Witty Wanton Altisidora, the Duchess' Damsel.

While Don Quixote prepares to leave the castle in search of adventure, the duke's steward presents Sancho with a purse of 200 crowns. At the moment of departure, Altisidora steps up to Don Quixote and sings him a mock farewell. Accusing him of hardheartedness in love, she goes even further and suggests that he has stolen her three handkerchiefs and two garters. Completely unruffled, the knight assures the angry duke that Altisidora is taking petty revenge for her unrequited love. Sancho says that the handkerchiefs were given him and then the maiden remembers that she is wearing the garters. Dignified despite this latest jest, Don Quixote departs for Saragossa.

CHAPTER LVIII

How Adventures Crowded so Thick and Threefold on Don Quixote, That They Trod upon One Another's Heels.

First the knight and squire encounter some workmen seated at the roadside eating their lunch. They say they are delivering the figures of various saints for the altarpiece of a village church, and the Don asks if he could look at them. As he scrutinizes the figures of St. George, St. Martin, and San Diego the Moor-Slayer, he eloquently remarks on the virtues of each one, reinforcing Sancho's impression that his master knows all there is to know. Their next adventure begins when Don Quixote gets entangled in some bird snares. Thinking the green netting is again the work of his wicked enchanter, he is ready to burst the cords, when two lovely, richly-dressed shepherdesses appear. The maidens explain that they are part of a company of villagers who are setting up a new pastoral Arcadia. They invite the Don and Sancho to join them, and after dinner, the knight expresses his gratitude. He swears to post himself in the middle of the highway for two days defending the assertion that these maids of the new Arcadia are the most beautiful and courteous maidens in the universe, excepting for Dulcinea of course. Shouting his challenge to the highway, he and Sancho spy a swift-moving company of horsemen, armed with lances. "Stand off!" shouts one man, "Or the bulls will tread thee to pieces!" Even against fierce cattle, however, the knight stands fast, and the herd runs over them all, trampling Dapple, Rosinante, Sancho, as well as the valorous knight. So embarrassed at the outcome of this incident, Don Quixote departs without even saying goodbye to his new friends.

Commentary

Don Quixote feels great gratitude for the hospitality of the new Arcadians, who, notably, do not mock the valorous knight whose history they have all read. At last Don Quixote has found a group of people who are as eager as he to re-establish the "Golden Age," a peaceful, high-idealed society. Thus Don Quixote stands boldly at the highway crossing and challenges the world to disagree with this new society. Wild cattle, however, trample the brave challenger, and when Don Quixote recognizes that they are vile beasts, not enchanters, it is obvious that Cervantes is leading his hero further into disillusionment. With the beginning of sanity, Don Quixote unconsciously prepares himself for death.

CHAPTER LIX

Of an Extraordinary Accident That Happened to Don Quixote Which May Well Pass for an Adventure.

The knight is so melancholy after the rude encounter with the bulls, that he refuses to eat, whereas Sancho eagerly stuffs himself with as much food as he can cram. "I was born, Sancho, to live dying," cries Don Quixote, "And thou to die eating." The squire begs his master to take heart, to rather partake of a good meal and a good sleep than to despair, and the knight then accepts some food. At the inn where they find lodging, which Don Quixote calls an inn, not a castle, the knight must face another source of ridicule. Here they meet with some gentlemen who are discussing a book written by Avellenada which purports to be the continuation of The History of the Knight of La Mancha and Sancho Panza. Don Quixote convinces the gentlemen that he and his squire are the true heroes, and that those individuals described in the book are fictional ones. In order to give the lie to Avellenada's statement which says that Don Quixote is on the road to Saragossa, the knight and squire take the direction of Barcelona, after taking kind leave of their new friends.

CHAPTER LX

What Happened to Don Quixote Going to Barcelona.

While they are resting on the road, Don Quixote thinks so much about Dulcinea's disenchantment that he cannot sleep. He decides to whip Sancho himself, and begins to undo the sleeping squire's breeches. Waking up in a fright, Sancho wrestles with his master, and sitting on top of him, forces him to forswear all notions of lashing. Without defending himself, Don Quixote agrees. Suddenly Sancho is unnerved by the sight of numerous corpses dangling from the trees; his master is tranquil seeing all these dead bandits, for this means they are near Barcelona. Forty live bandits, however, surround them soon after this, and their leader, Rogue Guinart, is a courteous outlaw after the fashion of Robin Hood. Ordering his men to treat Sancho and the knight courteously, Roque discourses with Don Quixote and soon discovers his "blind side." Suddenly a beautiful girl gallops up to the bandit chief, begging his protection, for she has just shot and killed her lover having heard he was to marry someone else. Following the bloody trail, Roque and his men come upon the sad procession which bears the wounded youth, Don Vicente. Breathing his last, the young lover tells the damsel that he has always remained faithful to her. The grief-stricken Claudia wishes to spend the rest of her life in a nunnery. Roque now shows what a chivalrous highwayman he is. Holding up a coach, his men despoil two infantry captains, a gentlewoman, and two pilgrims on foot. Wishing not to pillage women or soldiers, Rogue "borrows" enough money from the captives to pay each of his men two crowns, then bestows ten on each pilgrim, with another ten crowns for Sancho. Then, with a letter of safe passage, he allows the coach to continue on its journey. Now Roque writes a letter to a friend of his in Barcelona, recommending to his diversion the unique and pleasant Don Quixote and Sancho Panza. He dispatches the letter with one of his henchmen.

Commentary

After facing the ridicule of a pirate-author, Don Quixote must now face the humiliation of Sancho's revolt. Accepting his fate, however, he agrees to the squire's conditions, and the rebellion finished, Sancho immediately seeks his master's protection when he is scared by the sight of all the bandit corpses. Sancho's fight with his master, however, is a sign that he is maturing under Don Quixote's tutelage and that he shall soon be able to take up a life independent of serving the knight. Don Quixote's gentle acceptance of Sancho's victory, his passivity in the wrestling match, shows his feeling for the imminence of death.

Roque Guinart is a sympathetic character, very similar to Don Quixote in his eagerness to aid the poor and redress the sufferings of damsels. Roque, however, unlike the Don, leads an anxious, insecure life. Though their chivalrous ideals are the same, the bandit does not have the advantage of a distracted mind to help him transform the realities of his life. His unsuccessful quixotism makes him a pitiful character compared to the freedom from reality which the Don enjoys and which Roque has the misunderstanding to ridicule.

CHAPTER LXI

Don Quixote's Entry into Barcelona, with Other Accidents That Have Less Ingenuity than Truth in Them.

After traveling three days with Roque and his band, Don Quixote and Sancho take fond leave of the bandits right outside Barcelona. A tumultuous greeting by a group of horsemen welcomes the arrivals to the town. The gentleman who received Roque's letter shouts out, "Welcome valorous Don Quixote de La Mancha, not the counterfeit and apocryphal shown us lately by false histories, but the true, legitimate, and identick he, described by Cid Hamet, the flower of historiographers." Thus the knight and squire, surrounded by admiring townspeople, make a grand entry into Barcelona, and are conducted to the house of their host, Don Antonio Moreno.

CHAPTER LXII

The Adventure of the Enchanted Head, with Other Impertinences Not to Be Omitted.

Don Antonio plans a jest at Don Quixote's expense. He draws the knight into a room containing only a table, set with a bronze bust. "This head," whispers Don Antonio, "Is manufactured by one of the greatest necromancers in the world. It has the ability to answer all questions put to it." He promises that Don Quixote shall see for himself the virtues of this head on the following day. Meanwhile he takes his guest on a tour of Barcelona, pinning to his back a sign which says, "This is Don Quixote de La Mancha." Everyone they pass repeats the words of the sign, and the knight marvels that his fame is so widespread. That evening, Don Antonio's wife honors her guest with a ball. So many ladies dance with the valorous knight that he finally sinks with fatigue right in the middle of the dance floor and has to be carried to bed with Sancho's help. His dancing, as well as his peculiar exit, has afforded everyone at the ball immense entertainment. The next day the magical head performs, answering all questions put to it, though providing minimal information each time. The author now discovers for the reader the source of the head's powers. Through a tin pipe connected to the room below, Cid Hamet explains, the voice of Don Antonio's nephew is piped through the hollow table legs and hollow breast and head of the bronze bust.

After this diversion, Don Quixote takes a walking tour through the city. Delighted to discover a printing house, he investigates the entire plant, receiving explanations from the workmen on its operation. This occasion, furthermore, gives Cervantes (through the words of Don Quixote) an opportunity to expound the ruthless practices of booksellers, publishers, and printers.

Commentary

The torments endured by Don Quixote in Barcelona exceed those he suffered at the ducal castle. Paraded through the streets with a sign on his back so that passersby can gape at him, and then forced to dance for the idle amusement of spectators until utterly exhausted, represents the saddest ignominy that he has thus far suffered. Cervantes also shows in these incidents that city life is more of a source of decadence and mockery than country life.

CHAPTER LXIII

Of Sancho's Misfortune on Board the Gallies, with the Strange Adventures of the Beautiful Morisca (Moorish Lady).

Don Antonio takes his guests on board the admiral's galley. Sancho, never having been on a ship before, is both impressed and frightened. One of the rowers, so instructed, hoists Sancho, tosses him to the man behind him, and the poor squire is tossed the whole length of the ship by the slaves. Don Quixote, however, receives the sort of welcome accorded to persons of quality. The courtesies are interrupted, however, for the captain gives chase to an Algerian brigantine, urging the galley slaves to row as fast as possible. As they are alongside the Moorish vessel, however, two drunken Turkish sailors fire into the Spanish ship, killing two soldiers. The General resolves to hang each prisoner when they are all brought to land. Everyone present, even the Viceroy, is amazed when the handsome young captain of the vessel confesses himself to be a "poor Christian woman," a

Catholic-educated native of Spain who was forced to flee to Barbary with her family. The girl, Anna Felix, continues with her story, telling them that her lover, Don Gaspar Gregorio, emigrated to Algiers with them. The Dey of Algiers, she says, was very interested in her for her wealth as well as her beauty. When he heard that a handsome youth was captured as well, his thoughts turned to the newcomer, and realizing that Turks prefer youths to maidens, Anna Felix arranged a strategem. She arranged that Don Gaspar appear before the Dey as a woman, and the king decided to reserve this lovely newcomer as a gift to the Grand Seignior. Meanwhile, the Dey had given Anna Felix instructions to return home to fetch the buried jewels and gold from her house, and thus she and the insolent Turks were found on board the brigantine. Suddenly a pilgrim with the Viceroy's company throws himself at the girl's feet. "Anna Felix, my dear unfortunate daughter! Behold thy father Ricote, that returned to seek thee." The Viceroy is so moved at the tender reunion between father and daughter that he revokes his death sentence even from the guilty Turks. Don Antonio Morena offers hospitality to Anna Felix and Ricote, who in his turn, has a friendly reunion with his neighbor Sancho Panza.

CHAPTER LXIV

Of an Unlucky Adventure, Which Don Quixote Laid Most to Heart of Any That Had Yet Befallen Him.

Ricote offers a handsome ransom for the release of Don Gaspar, and the galley, with the money, is sent, under care of a trustworthy renegade, to return to Spain with the young man. If the renegade fails, then everyone agrees that Don Quixote himself must effect the rescue.

One morning, while Don Quixote is walking on the seashore, as usual fully armed, another armed knight rides toward him. "I am the Knight of the White Moon," the rider tells him, "Lo, I am come to enter into combat with thee." They parley, and agree to the conditions: if vanquished, Don Quixote must give up his arms and remain at home for one year. If he wins, the life and properties of his opponent are his. Hastening to witness the strange event, Don Antonio, the Viceroy, and some others arrive to see the two knights begin their charge. In a moment, the hero of La Mancha lies on the ground, Rosinante stretched beside him. Don Quixote's voice, "as if he had spoke out of a tomb" faintly says that he cannot allow Dulcinea's perfection to suffer through his weakness. "No, pierce my body with thy lance, Knight, and let my life expire with my honor." The conqueror says that he chooses to let Dulcinea's fame remain "entire and unblemished." He would rather that her protector return home upon his faith as a true knight. Don Quixote is taken up in a sad condition; Sancho is so shocked he cannot believe what had just happened.

Commentary

Don Quixote's immense inner strength remains to him even at the moment of his worst defeat; he remains faithful to his ideal love, to his inspiration, to Dulcinea, and does not despair his purpose. Though Dulcinea's perfections are products of his own fancy, Don Quixote has, by strength of faith, given his creation independent life. Even though he dies, the faith in Dulcinea will always remain. In this way, Sancho can be considered as his creation, for Sancho will soon be able to live by himself. Don Quixote has also affected Samson Carrasco, for it can be supposed, that the young man, disguised as the conquering knight, was so persistent in his attempts to "cure" Don Quixote because he wanted to share the glory and renown of the heroic knight by somehow linking their names. Samson, it must be noted, was able to conquer Don Quixote only in that location of lies and malicious amusements, the city of Barcelona.

CHAPTER LXV

An Account of the Knight of the White Moon, Don Gregorio's Enlargement, and Other Passages.

Curious to learn more about the Knight of the White Moon, Don Antonio follows him to his lodging. "I am the bachelor Carrasco," answers the knight. "I live in the same town with Don Quixote." He tells of his first attempt to vanquish the knight, and says Samson, to retrieve my credit, I made this second attempt and have now succeeded. He packs his armor on a mule, and slowly rides homeward. Don Quixote, meanwhile, melancholy and out of humor, keeps to his bed, with Sancho trying to comfort him. The knight says that after a year's retirement he shall again take up his profession. Don Antonio now enters the room, telling them of the Don Gaspar's successful escape from prison. The lovers are reunited, and the Viceroy now promises Ricote to petition the king and gain permission for him and his family to remain in Spain. Two days after this joyful scene, Don Quixote, his armor piled on Dapple, rides Rosinante slowly homeward, Sancho walking beside him.

CHAPTER LXVI

Which Treats of That Which Shall Be Seen by Him That Reads It, and Heard by Him That Listens When 'Tis Read.

On their fourth day of travel they encounter a group of peasants disputing in front of an inn. The argument is between a fat and a skinny rival who intend to run a race. The three-hundred pound challenger insists that the other man carry a heavy load in order to equalize their weights during the race. Sancho is asked to render judgment. Being experienced at this he decides: "The challenger, so big and fat, must cut, pare, slice, or shave off a hundred and fifty pounds of his flesh," and then they can run an equal race. The peasants approve the judgment, and Don Quixote and his wise squire continue on their way. The next person they meet is Tosilos, the duke's footman. For his desire to marry Rodriguez's daughter, the duke had him flogged, packed off the girl to a nunnery and released the duenna from his service. So terminated one of Don Quixote's most successful adventures.

CHAPTER LXVII

How Don Quixote Resolved to Turn Shepherd, and Lead a Rural Life for the Year's Time He Was Not Obliged to Bear Arms; with Other Passages Truly Good and Diverting.

Don Quixote asks Sancho if Tosilos gave out any news about Altisidora. They discourse until they arrive at the place where the bulls had trampled them. Don Quixote reveals to Sancho how he will live a pastoral life. He shall buy a flock of sheep and call himself the Shepherd Quixotis, Sancho the Shepherd Pansino, with suitable names for the curate, the barber, and the bachelor. Sancho is agreeable to try this new way of life, and they converse in this manner for a while. As it is getting late, however, they make shift with a slender meal and prepare to sleep in a field by the roadside.

CHAPTER LXVIII

The Adventure of the Hogs.

Don Quixote again suffers a restless night from thinking of Dulcinea's enchantment. He awakens Sancho and suggests the squire give himself three or four hundred lashes toward the disenchantment of his peerless mistress. While they are arguing, they suddenly hear grunts and squeals resounding through the valley. More than six hundred swine come rushing out of the darkness, trampling the men and their beasts. While Sancho is full of curses, Don Quixote passively accepts the occurrence as a just disgrace for a vanquished knight-errant. They resume their journey and encounter some armed horsemen who take them as prisoners in a different direction. As night falls, the knight and squire are really frightened, but after an hour or so of riding in the dark, the company arrives at the ducal castle.

CHAPTER LXIX

Of the Most Singular and Strangest Adventure That Befell Don Quixote in the Whole Course of This Famous History.

A carefully constructed tableau greets the startled gaze of knight and squire. Lit with flickering tapers, the stage centers on a huge tomb covered with black velvet on which lies the body of a beautiful damsel. Nearby are enthroned two theatrically-attired kings whom Don Quixote recognizes as the duke and duchess. With a closer look, he also sees that the maiden is none other than Altisidora, dead of a broken heart. Now a young lad steps to the side of the tomb, singing a dirge which tells of Altisidora's hopeless passion and her sad end. Two other actors speak lines which tell that Sancho alone has the power to restore the maiden back to life, if he accept the penance of being twitched and pinched on the face by six waiting-women, and pricked by pins in his arms and backside. Overruled in all his panicked objections, poor Sancho suffers the duennas to come solemnly forth. After a few pinches, Altisidora finally stirs, awakens, and steps down from her tomb.

CHAPTER LXX

Which Comes after the Sixty-Ninth, and Contains Several Particulars Necessary for the Illustration of This History.

Cid Hamet now relates to the reader the background of these strange events. After his defeat as the Knight of the Mirrors, Samson Carrasco followed Don Quixote, thinking to find him at the duke's castle where he learned that the knight just left for Saragossa. The duke asked Samson to stop by on his way home and give him the news of his encounter with Don Quixote. This Samson did, and the duke posted his servants on all the roads that Don Quixote would be liable to take. Funeral preparations were made as soon as the duke received word that his servants were returning with the knight. Returning to Don Quixote, the author describes how the knight awakens to find Altisidora in his room. Seating herself next to his bed (he covers his head with the blankets) she sighs and speaks of her desperate love for the hero. She also describes a fanciful scene which Altisidora says happened while she was in Hell. The devils were playing tennis, with books instead of tennis balls, especially abusing a shameful volume called the Second Part of the History of Don Quixote which the fiends thought even they could have written better. Some musicians and a poet come to talk with Don Quixote, and then the duke and duchess enter his chamber. Don Quixote advises the duke that Altisidora has not enough to occupy her, and that is why she wastes her time worrying about an unsuccessful love. After a dinner with their noble hosts, Don Quixote and Sancho take their leave.

CHAPTER LXXI

What Happened to Don Quixote and His Squire on Their Way Home.

Don Quixote, more convinced then ever at Sancho's natural talents for disenchanting and resurrecting, asks his squire to begin the lashings at a certain price per lash. Sancho, reckoning a reasonable fee, immediately and eagerly whips himself. After a few smarts, however, he retires out of sight and whips the trees instead, moaning at every few strokes. Don Quixote, who keeps count, can bear his squire's sufferings no longer, and begs him to stop. The next inn they find lodging at is recognized by the Don to be an inn, not a castle.

CHAPTER LXXII

How Don Quixote and Sancho Got Home.

At the inn they meet a man named Don Alvaro Tarfe whom the knight recognizes as a character in Avellaneda's book. Don Alvaro tells him that he accompanied Don Quixote to the tournament at Saragossa. The true hero convinces him that he accompanied two pretenders, and he asks Don Alvaro to make a deposition to this effect: "That the said Don Quixote was not the same person as the one mentioned in a certain printed history written by Avellaneda." That night, Sancho ends his penance among some other trees while Don Quixote scans the face of every woman he passes in order to find the disenchanted Dulcinea. Without realizing it, they suddenly discover themselves on a hilltop overlooking their native valley.

CHAPTER LXXIII

Of the Ominous Accidents That Crossed Don Quixote as He Entered His Village, with Other Transactions That Illustrate and Adorn This Memorable History.

As they descend into the village, Don Quixote overhears a remark of one boy to another: "Thou shalt never see her while thy hast breath in thy body." He is certain that the significance of the phrase is reserved for him. Then a hare, closely pursued, rests in the shelter of Dapple's legs. Don Quixote says of this new omen: "A hare runs away, hounds pursue her, and Dulcinea is not started." Sancho tries to dispel his fear. "See," he says, "If this hunted hare is Dulcinea threatened by enchanters, I hand her now safely into your keeping." Questioning the two boys, Sancho finds that one refuses to return to the other a cage of crickets, and Don Quixote appears quieted. Arriving in the village, they first meet the bachelor Carrasco and the curate. Teresa and her daughter meet Sancho and happily lead him home. Don Quixote informs his listeners about his defeat, and how he shall now pass the year's retirement as a shepherd, inviting them to join his pastoral life. Humoring this new mad fancy, the curate and Samson applaud the project. Samson says, "As everybody knows, I am a most celebrated poet, and I'll write pastorals in abundance." Don Quixote now greets his niece and housekeeper who are glad again to care for him.

Commentary

Don Quixote, by seeing such dark omens, begins to despair of discovering his Dulcinea in her true form. This despair is the expression of the same Alonso Quixano who now prepares to die, having given up the fantasy of embracing either the real Aldonza or achieving the unblemished vision of Dulcinea with his knightly gaze. As Don Quixote tells the curate and bachelor his plans for a shepherd's life, Samson confesses his own basic quixotism and searching-for-Dulcinea: everybody knows I am a celebrated poet. By these words, Samson confesses his envy of Don Quixote as well as the unconscious desire to cause the downfall of his superior rival.

CHAPTER LXXIV

How Don Quixote Fell Sick, Made His Last Will, and Died.

As Don Quixote languishes, the household imagined he is sick from the regret of defeat and disappointment in Dulcinea's disenchantment. The curate, the bachelor Samson Carrasco, and Sancho try to cheer up the sick man. Nothing helps; Don Quixote makes his will, gets confessed by the curate. Gathering his friends, the hidalgo tells them, "My good friends, I have happy news for you; I am no longer Don Quixote de La Mancha, but Alonso Quixano, the same who the world for his fair behavior has been pleased to call the Good. I now declare myself an enemy to Amadis de Gaul and his whole generation." Then Sancho, weeping, begs his master not to die, for there are chivalric deeds yet to accomplish. No more of that nonsense, says the Don sadly, "There are no birds in last year's nests." In his will, Don Quixote dictates that his niece, if she chooses to marry, must select a man who has no knowledge of books of chivalry. If she insists on the contrary marriage, she shall forfeit her inheritance. Don Quixote dies. Among "sagacious Cid Hamet's" words addressed to his pen, Cervantes writes: "For me alone was the great Quixote born, and I alone for him; it was for him to act, for me to write, and we two are one in spite of that Tordesillesque pretender [Avellaneda] who had, and may have, the audacity to write with a coarse and ill-trimmed ostrich quill of the deeds of my valiant knight."

Commentary

Now that Don Quixote is about to die, Sancho is at the top of his madness. Imploring his master to rise and go forth again as a knight-errant, Sancho expresses his quixotism: to deny death, deny sanity, and once more serve Dulcinea who grants immortality. But he cannot revitalize Don Quixote's disillusioned faith, and he, Sancho, is left as heir to quixotism.

The author's address to his pen underlines again Cervantes' fancy of calling his created characters his "stepchildren." The greatness of *Don Quixote* has been nowhere manifested in his earlier works, and it is not hard to imagine that Cervantes believed himself to be merely the incidental medium of some creative spirit that fathered the visionary knight. "I alone," writes Cervantes, was born for Don Quixote, and, he should add, his spirit transcends my art.

PURPOSE OF DON QUIXOTE

Cervantes himself states that he wrote *Don Quixote* in order to undermine the influence of those "vain and empty books of chivalry" as well as to provide some merry, original, and sometimes prudent material for his readers' entertainment. Whether or not the author truly believed the superficiality of his own purpose is immaterial; in fact, Cervantes did make a complete end to further publications of chivalric romances. Despite the harmful extravagances of these novels, this form of writing has one advantage over more truthful literary forms, Cervantes writes in the latter section of Part I, for chivalry "offers a wide and spacious meadow through which the pen may run without any hindrance." Perhaps Don Quixote owes his genesis to these notions of his author. But as Cervantes launches his idealistic and possessed hero on a career open to public contempt, the possibilities of a many-leveled, kaleidoscopic theme must have become apparent very early.

TECHNIQUE AND STYLE

Relation of Novelist to His Characters

Each author has a "point of view" from which he invents and constructs his characters and incidents. Some novels may be written in first person narrative to expose subjectively society's evils, other forms of writing stem from an omniscient author who can see into each person and recount past and future history at each point in the narrative. Dickens is an example of such a writer.

Cervantes, on the other hand, chooses to write a "history" and thus gives himself certain limitations and advantages. He must journalistically give facts of what clearly occurs at each part of the action; he cannot invent attributes of his characters without documenting these qualities by actions. As a responsible historian, he cannot impose any opinions on his reader, but must present each character with as many details of description and action so that his readers can draw their own conclusions. To further this ideal of objectivity, Cervantes invents the eminent historian, Cid Hamet Benengali, for only a Moor would try to underrate any Spanish achievement, and this guarantees the verisimilitude of all details in the life of Don Quixote.

Further reading into the life of the Manchegan knight, however, reinforces a growing suspicion that provides another reason for the invention of Cid Hamet. Perhaps Cervantes felt that Don Quixote was too quickly outgrowing his artifacted existence, becoming more than just a lampoon out of a chivalric romance, to be, as Byron has termed him, a character created to "smile Spain's chivalry away." Like a Pinocchio animated while Gepetto lay sleeping, Don Quixote seems to wrest himself from his creator's pen and live an independent life. Furthermore, as he lives on and on in world literature, it becomes even clearer today that his organic growth defied restriction and circumvention by a mere author.

Sancho Panza, as well, possesses this quality of self-determination. Don Quixote, returning from his first sally at the inn to obtain fresh linen, some money, and a squire, solicits "one of his neighbors, a country-laborer, and good honest fellow, for he was poor indeed: poor in purse and poor in brains." From this modest introduction of what would become one of the funniest characters in literature—an ignorant, unwilling, gold-seeking squire who eventually becomes wise and quixotic—we may assume that Cervantes had not at first realized the possibilities of Sancho.

Consequently, *Don Quixote* presents this interesting aspect of a novelist who learns and grows in coincidence with his own characters. As he lives with them and loves them, Cervantes investigates with them the fundamentals of human understanding. This notion of an objective creator, set apart from his characters yet integrally consistent with everything they do, began with Cervantes. His organic artist-creation relationship is as complex and plastic as that found in Shakespeare and has become a condition of the modern esthetic for the art of the novel.

Relation of Novelist to Reader

Following the character-artist relationship, there remains the important and often unnoticed relation of the writer to his reader. Just as Cervantean characters seem to "write themselves" we have in this novel the aspect of the reader "writing himself" as well.

Because a reader is forced to think about each invented episode after it occurs, and because he suspects that Cervantes is not saying all there is to say about each incident, *Don Quixote* is sometimes difficult and frustrating for a modern reader to comprehend. He is obliged to wonder for himself why the hero does not lose his illusions sooner, why Sancho insists on remaining with his master to face more and more drubbings, why one feels a sympathy for the ridiculous knight who somehow remains dignified in the most humiliating circumstances. Like Sancho and Don Quixote, the reader is forced to reconsider the meaning of what has transpired each time the knight, bruised and weary, rises to remount Rosinante and continue his errant mission. We slowly come to conclude the final organic nature of this elusive book—to educate and mature the reader himself in the same way as Don Quixote and Sancho increase in self-awareness.

This is the extension of Cervantes' art of objectifying life's experiences. Standing aside from his "stepchildren" he allows them to impress each reader who encounters their careers in his own way. His novelistic realism, unlimited by supplying a given point of view of his creations, presents protagonists to the reader as one presents any human being to another, forcing the reader to understand, sympathize, or deny according to his own nature. Setting each character free in his invented world without guiding murmurs of approval or disapproval, Cervantes, the prime-mover novelist, also sets the reader free. This is another unique quality which makes *Don Quixote* one of the most lasting and elusive books in the world, and what makes Cervantes one of the most consummate novelists that western literature has produced.

Vitality of the Novel

The richness and interest of Cervantes stems, then, not from the profuseness of character types, nor from the variety in his constant inventiveness, nor from the philosophical conclusions we may make from his material, but from an emanation of life that lends vivacity and fascination and dynamism to every part of his huge narrative. This essential quality of *Don Quixote,* eluding more specific appellation, can roughly be called organic. A vital force animates each episode, and it gives even a bony horse and fat donkey immemorable personalities.

In essence, *Don Quixote* shows us that the reality of existence consists in receiving all the impact of experience, which, transformed through the medium of a special awareness, is synthesized as part of the character. The prosaic Alonso Quixano, after an impact on his imagination from books of chivalry, transforms himself into the Knight of La Mancha. Reading of pastoral tales is the impact which causes Marcella to become a shepherdess, Samson Carrasco receives his impetus from trying to conquer the madness of his rival once and for all. All these characters have changed their lives from internalizing essentially external influences. As Don Quixote and Sancho continue their journeys, they change and develop under the impact of each new episode. Having internalized one experience—by their constant discourse—they go on to face another, and once more retrench themselves under this new influence.

The emanation of life is seen whenever any character encounters experience. Dorothea, bathing her feet in a running brook, is a figure out of a pastoral tableau. As soon as she describes how Ferdinand wrought havoc on her normal rustic life, her intelligence awakens and she gains flesh and blood before our eyes. Under these new circumstances, she is able to play the exacting role of Princess Micomicona, although still ignorant as ever about things like geography. People like Don Diego de Miranda (the gentleman in the green coat), the priest at the duke's castle, and the niece Antonia Quixana are inured against external influences and remain static.

Chosen not alone for their comic attributes, episodes provide a testing ground to stimulate all areas of the personalities of Don Quixote, Sancho, and all others. Thus we see the virtuous wife Camilla put to a literal "test," and she quickly emerges as an accomplished adulteress. Whenever Sancho's loyalties are put to a test, on the other hand (his defense of his master at the priest's scolding, the instant when he is "fired" by Don Quixote, his constant desire to quit his squirehood when dissatisfied, for instance), he remains faithful. The whole sequence of the adventures with the duke and duchess provides a testing ground for the values Don Quixote holds dear as a knight-errant. His final test is when, with Samson's lance poised at his throat, he chooses rather to die than to give up the idea of Dulcinea's perfection.

In other words, Cervantes makes things happen in order to reveal latent possibilities. Even the weather is forced into service, for the one time it does rain, it is so the barber can don his basin to protect his new hat; hence the adventure of Mambrino's helmet. The vividness of the rocky wilderness of the Sierra Morena serves only to isolate the various scenes that take place there—Don Quixote's penance, Cardenio's meeting with the curate and barber, Dorothea's story—and it provides, as well, a safe refuge from the police force. The scorched July morning shows what a madman it takes to begin knight-errantry when it is so hot; the dusty road serves to obscure the two flocks of sheep which the hero thinks are armies; and a verdant meadow, the scene of Rosinante's frolic with the mares, provides the adventure of the Yanguesian carriers.

This utilitarian dynamism of every part of the novel is further maintained as episodes interweave with each other like motives in a symphony. Recurring with some variation, these themes are picked up again and again. Sancho, for instance, never forgoes a chance to rue his blanketing; the disenchantment of Dulcinea haunts Don Quixote until his death. Altisidora never gives up her game of courting the knight. Alonso Quixano is always in the shadow of Don Quixote's mad career, and Sancho's wished-for island held out to him like a carrot to a mule finally becomes his prize. Tosilos reappears, Andrew reappears, Gines de Passamonte thrice returns to cross Don Quixote. The ideal of pastoral life weaves in and out of the novel in many variations: Marcella, the New Arcadians, Don Quixote's secondary fantasy. Nothing happens without repercussions, and characters or episodes are invariably picked up again.

The descriptive style is another source of Cervantes' dynamism. Terse, yet elegant, he sketches images that make illustrations in the book seem anticlimactic. Sancho, starved for some good food, is with his master, at the goatherds' huts. "Sancho presently repaired to the attractive smell of goat's flesh which stood boiling in a kettle over the fire...The goatherds took them off the fire, and spread some sheepskins on the ground and soon got their rustic feast ready; and cheerfully invited his master and him to partake of what they had." Introducing Marcella: "'Twas Marcella herself who appeared at the top of the rock, at the foot of which they were digging the grave; but so beautiful that fame seemed rather to have lessened than to have magnified her charms: Those who had never seen her before, gazed on her with silent wonder and delight; nay, those who used to see her every day seemed no less lost in admiration than the rest." The immortal tilt with the windmills occupies a mere forty or fifty lines. "'I tell thee they are giants and I am resolved to engage in a dreadful unequal combat against them all.' This said, he clapped spurs to Rosinante...At the same time the wind rising, the great sails began turning...Well covered with his shield, with his lance at rest, he bore down upon the first mill that stood in his way, giving a thrust at the wing which was whirling at such a speed that his lance was broken into bits and both horse and horseman went rolling over the plain, very much battered indeed."

The overall success of the book lies, therefore, in the vitality and organic development of the characters themselves. The descriptions are vivid, not merely for the prose style, but because they give physical fulfillment to the dynamic image of the personalities. Setting, which Cervantes rarely details, is unforgettably and briefly etched only if it is integral to the development of the corresponding episode. Thus, with a technique of subordinating every other literary ornament to animate and discover all parts of an active character, Cervantes has created a strong unity of episode, setting, dialogue, and characterization which lends this book its protean nature. It is as if the author, considering his creation a great darkness at first, sweeps across its surface beams of light in the form of incident, dialogue, description, background, until the entire configuration of human personality is revealed.

CHARACTERIZATION

The dynamics of characterization in *Don Quixote* has been discussed in the previous section. After considering something of the generalized processes of development, it is useful to consider some of the characters themselves.

Don Quixote and Sancho Panza

To characterize roughly Don Quixote, one can call him the idealist, although, as shown in specific discussions, the prosaic nature of Alonso Quixano is often glimpsed under the veneer of the knight's posturings. Don Quixote is a madman, or rather, an "idealist," only in matters of knight-errantry. He discourses practically on matters of literature, as shown when he discusses poetry with Don Diego de Miranda. He is capable of sincere gratitude (standing at the road crossing to recommend the maidens of the New Arcadians), and he is the mirror of courtesy itself. Giving advice to the penurious Basil on how to keep his new wife, counseling Sancho on how to be a good governor, Don Quixote's common sense and ethical standards resemble those of Polonius advising Laertes in the famous scene in *Hamlet*. He persuades a couple of wily lodgers to pay their innkeeper; he is honest and chaste, and in general, is loved by the people in his village who know him.

An interesting tension of his personality is between these virtuous sane qualities and those developed through his peculiar madness. Imperious, he is stung quickly to anger when he suspects that the institution of knight-errantry is questioned. His sense of duty results in a sometimes-disastrous meddlesomeness. Poetic and sensitive, according to the ideals of the age of chivalry, Don Quixote sings well, composes verse, and is helpful to the distressed. Beyond that, of course, loom the visions and ideals and the seeking for absolute truth and justice which a quixotic faith entails.

Viewed through his quixotism, however, the world casts images as from a rarified plateau whose very clarity is a distortion of the commonly accepted viewpoint. The knight, for instance, sees the goatherds primarily as fellow human beings. Though he would notice their ignorance and poverty if he were not mad, he addresses them as if they were his equals in refinement and erudition. The goatherds respond to his oration by paying elegant homage to his sincerity and directness: they bring forth, for his entertainment, a shepherd who sings verses and accompanies himself on a rebeck. A more appropriate and tactful response could not have been devised. Another example, one mentioned before, is that of the wily innkeeper who, despite himself, acts the part of a gracious castellan receiving a guest of quality. The duke and duchess, however, cannot reach the heights of nobility and the reader sees them as mere fools compared with the knight's high-minded sobriety. The quixotism he inspires in the followers of the ducal pair—in Tosilos, disobeying his lord, in Donna Rodriguez's striving to make her betrayed daughter respectable, as well as in Samson Carrasco's perverted attempt to depose the quixotic madman himself, is finally and definitively developed in his closest disciple, Sancho Panza.

Sancho's struggle between his love for his master upon whom he depends so completely and between his own sense of reality (he constantly recalls the severe blanketing he felt on all his bones and sinews) continues throughout his squire's career. He believes nothing, for the Spanish peasant is skeptical of all but his own experience, yet, by virtue of his unlettered ignorance, is infinitely credulous. It is through this credulity that Sancho follows his master and eventually believes fully in him.

At first, when he tries to imitate Don Quixote by words and trickery, not by emotion and faith, he is unsuccessful and succeeds only in confusing himself. Lying that he has seen visions on Clavileno's back, his attempts to prevent the knight from attacking the fulling-mills, his invention of Dulcinea's enchantment are examples of this failure. Nevertheless he shares his master's desire for immortality, for he dreams he will govern an island.

Sancho finally rises to quixotic heights, when, at the bedside of the moribund Quixote, he begs the Don to leave off this nonsense of dying when there are so many deeds of valor yet to be done. At the summit of his faith, Sancho implores the now-sane madman to "come to his senses" and take up knight-errantry once again. His confusions at an end, Sancho realizes that the madman he served pointed the way to clearheaded truth.

In his relationship with his master, Sancho Panza represents the practical realist. He is the "corrective lens" for what the world would consider Don Quixote's distorted vision. Their separate reactions to the same episode provide the reader with a sort of stereoscope through which to view the world of Cervantes with two lenses focused to produce a three-dimensional image. Sancho says that flocks of sheep approach—Don Quixote declares it is an army; the truth is somewhere in between, because the shepherds give battle. Sancho tells his master how Dorothea demeans herself by kissing Ferdinand; Don Quixote says he lies, for she is a highborn princess. Again, they are both correct. With their constant discourse—Sancho says he must burst if he cannot express himself—the reader has the impression of a single man who talks to himself, arguing first one way, then the other. Perhaps Sancho Panza is really the eternalized Alonso Quixano who provides for Don Quixote his inner core of tranquillity and reasonableness.

The tension of their opposing personalities, however, is resolved on their separate paths to glory. Sancho has his island to dream of, while Don Quixote envisions his valorous deeds. The two are furthermore bound by the same sort of ties that link father to son, teacher to pupil, husband to wife. Cervantes amplifies these dependencies in many ways. A novice in the practice of chivalry, Sancho learns and imitates his master as a student would of his tutor. With their conversations and the I-told-you-so recriminations of Sancho, as well as their division (of tasks) in working together, the squire and knight seem to be married to each other. Sometimes called "my son" by Don Quixote, Sancho actually is the child of quixotism, even maturing within the relationship to revolt against his master. Another need that the relationship satisfies is the need for a leader to have followers, and Don Quixote depends on Sancho for his own self-awareness. Conversely, Sancho demands to follow. After having experienced the responsibility of governing an island, he recognizes that he can only follow a quixotic ideal but not himself initiate the quixotic spirit.

Integral though their relationship is, Sancho and Don Quixote are universal because each is the ultimate in their own character types. The way they develop in their relationship, however, and their thoughtful responses to life's experiences is also universal. They provide a realistic model of how human beings become educated, and this process of learning and reacting to life is part of the psychological maturation of everyone.

Minor Characters

Between the reality-fantasy tension of Sancho's great dilemma, and the fixed ideals of Don Quixote's guiding principles, Cervantes focuses all the characters in his novel. More than four hundred characters appear in *Don Quixote.* Some are sketched in a few words, like the description of Don Antonio Morena: he is "a gentleman of good parts and plentiful fortune loving all those diversions that may innocently be obtained without prejudice to his neighbors, and not of the humor of those who would rather lose their friend than their jest." Some characters, like the duke and duchess, fulfill their characterizations without any description at all.

Most of *Don Quixote's* characters are developed in their relationship to the protagonist. The curate and barber, for example, try so hard to cure the madman that they themselves seem to become the evil magicians who do him the most harm, especially when they disguise themselves as necromancers in order to deliver the hero home in an oxcart. Samson Carrasco, the sophomoric bachelor from the university, has such a shallow understanding of the knight and of himself that he is at best only a false Quixote. The gentleman in green, Don Diego de Miranda, parallels the prosaic character of Alonso Quixano had the hidalgo not become a madman. Completely conventional, a half-hearted huntsman ("I keep neither falcon nor hounds but only a tame partridge and a bold ferret or two") Don Diego has a son gifted in poetry with whom he is dissatisfied because the boy should study something more useful. The various goatherds encountered in the novel incline to be kind and generous, for they supply food to the half-insane "knight of the wood," and they treat the knight and squire with courtesy and hospitality. Chrysostom, the broken hearted lover of Marcella, has pined to death for her favor, whereas Don Quixote, equally unsuccessful in love, sublimates his frustration and is inspired to accomplish immortal deeds. Gines de Passamonte, briefly but unforgettably sketched, is a perfect study of a typical Spanish picaroon. Living by his wits, he has many disguises and practices a variety of deceptions to gain his livelihood.

The majority of women who appear in *Don Quixote* are shallow. Dorothea, outstanding for her intelligence and wit, has perhaps the most personality of any woman in the novel. Maritornes, the scullery wench, is a vivid exception. Grotesque in appearance, she is so kind that she gives herself freely and generously to all muleteers. She kindly offers Sancho a glass of wine, paid out of her pocket, to comfort him after he is bounced in a blanket. Teresa Panza, perfect helpmeet for Sancho, has great integrity as a peasant. But like her husband, she abandons all her reservations as soon as she has proof that he has become a governor. Though unable to become fully quixotized, Teresa does not mock and is ready to believe what she sees. Altisidora, arch, mischievous damsel in the duchess' household, feigns to have a great love for Don Quixote. Still unsuccessful, even after staging her death, Altisidora becomes vengeful like any scorned woman. One suspects that she has eventually come to admire the madman for his constancy to Dulcinea and in her rage to conquer his will, she would even make love to him in order to lower his nobility to her level.

Dulcinea del Toboso remains merely a symbol, although Don Quixote has created her as a personified ideal more valuable than his own life. She symbolizes his immortality, his notion of perfection, and the source of all inspiration for love, bravery, faith. From a profane longing to marry Aldonza Lorenzo and raise children through her, Don Quixote sublimates his fantasy by accomplishing great deeds in order to deserve serving his Dulcinea and gain immortality through his perfect behavior as a knight-errant in her name.

The category of Cervantean characters furnishes an endless list. Each one, however, juxtaposed against the image of the Knight of the Woeful Figure, expresses a part of the real world where ideas and ideals must make their impressions on the human consciousness.

THEMES

Quixotism

Quixotism is the universal quality characteristic of any visionary action. Acts of rebellion or reform are always quixotic for the reformer aims at undermining the existing institution in order to change it. Often held up to ridicule, frequently destroyed, the quixotic individual has been responsible for many great deeds in history, and conversely, for many misdeeds, even as Cervantes shows Don Quixote being responsible for the sufferings of poor Andrew.

Many outstanding madmen in the world, trying to move lethargic populations to better themselves, have been isolated in history. Ignatius de Loyola, founder of the Jesuits, has a career as fanatic and visionary as the mission of Don Quixote. St. Teresa, Joan of Arc, Martin Luther, Moses, and above all, Jesus of Nazareth, have lived and suffered and conquered by their quixotic visions. Against all the imposing odds of majority feeling—strength of established institutions, belief in existing customs—the quixotic heroes have pitted only the integrity of their faith and their will power.

Seeking only "truth" or "justice," the truly quixotic heroes have an internal vision so strong as to see through the illusion of external appearances. Don Quixote, for example, defies ubiquitous institutions so taken for granted that everyone thinks they are harmless windmills, though they may be threatening giants, inexorable machines destructive of the individual. In much the same way, a handful of ridiculous-appearing women attacked the political status quo to gain universal suffrage.

The clarity of the quixotic vision is further exemplified when Don Quixote, instead of seeing two dowdy prostitutes, sees ladies of quality, who respond kindly to his courteous greetings. Helping the knight to undress, assisting him at his meal, one can only conclude that his will power has transformed their outward identities to agree with the ideal image. This notion agrees with a psychological truism: if a man anticipates inferior performance from another, he will receive what he expects. The converse is also true.

Quixotism, then, is a will power defying materiality. It is the attempt to make a utopian vision a reality, but like all utopias, it is unacceptable in a world where absolute values cannot survive. Don Quixote, though he often triumphs over disillusions, must eventually face it, and die.

Although the gentle knight yearned for immortality through his deeds, he leaves us only his history to immortalize his life principle. Succeeding generations of readers, ungifted with imaginative powers and strength of will to be themselves quixotic, can read the biography of the valorous knight of La Mancha and, like Sancho Panza, partake of his visions and his fanaticism. Only once does a book about Don Quixote have to appear, for then the glorious ability to quixotize becomes the common heritage for every man to enjoy and understand.

In expressing and developing the quixotic individual, Cervantes has discovered and defined another avenue of exaltation and self-expression of the human soul. Thus it does not matter whether *Don Quixote* is a burlesque of chivalry, or whether the hero is a madman or an actor. What matters is that he is indelibly set free in our imaginations, and discovers for us a new quality about the human spirit.

Truth and Justice

Connected integrally with the notion of quixotism, Cervantes explores the complexities of fact and fantasy, truth and lies, justice and injustice. Cervantes, with olympian detachment and dynamic character development, considers the problem relatively. The general proposition can be expressed as follows: if a madman sees truth in its most extreme clarity, and his bewildered assistant sees some truths and some illusions, then those individuals most attached to everyday experiences are capable only of seeing the greatest number of distortions.

The guards of the galley slaves, the troopers of the Holy Brotherhood, are able to see justice merely as it is given in the lawbooks of society. Don Quixote, of course, scorns such limitations and declares that knights-errant are not bound by such imperfect doctrines. Gines de Passamonte and other prisoners liberated by the knight are equally disillusioned with the justice of society that has sentenced them. Because of this, they are ready to stone this liberator who hands them new laws to follow ("It is my will and desire," says Don Quixote, "That you...present yourselves to the Lady Dulcinea del Toboso...and then you will relate to her...the whole of this famous adventure which has won you your longed-for freedom..."). The prisoners declare the full extent of their freedom by violently rejecting their champion.

In the story of poor Andrew whose master beats him because he is careless of the sheep, while the shepherd says that his master just looks for an excuse to get out of paying his wages, it is obvious that one of them is a liar. The lie which shocks Don Quixote, however, is the lie that the winner must give an excuse to the loser for beating him. The question of justice becomes farcical in disputes between a physically superior power and his weaker adversary. As the justice – wrong or right – is administered by the farmer's strong lash, dispute is eliminated; thus might makes right.

On a more abstract level, Cervantes includes some little exercises to investigate further the nature of truth and justice. The parodistic problems Sancho solves during his government – the judgments regarding the man crossing the bridge, the woman who says she is raped, the dispute between the tailor and the farmer – are all examples of this application.

Another instance of Cervantes' scrutiny of relativity in truth and justice is his lack of moral judgment on the promiscuous activities of Maritornes. Physically unappealing, she takes lovers out of the promptings of her generous nature. Considering her impulse, the comfort she provides to weary and lusty muleteers is the essence of virtue and charity.

Reality and Fantasy

A discussion of the many facets of this reality-fantasy investigation throughout *Don Quixote* would fill many books, but some suggestions follow. The hero, as has been said, has the ability to change reality with the force of an idea. Fantasy and reality to the madman are aspects of a continuum which he does not have to lower himself to question; not so for Sancho who is always in the throes of trying to understand the difference between the two qualities. The complete cynic, like Gines de Passamonte, is the supreme realist and can play upon the fantasy-reality confusions of others. It is, in fact, one source of his livelihood.

Gines' puppet-play is a suggestive device exposing another facet of this problem of truth-illusion. Don Quixote, his volatile imagination quickly fired, sees the play as reality, and enters into the depicted fray. He easily realizes his mistake, however, and makes amends for the ruined puppets. The knight is just extending the possibilities of an ideal spectator, for the whole delight in stagecraft is this quality that illusion appears as life.

Once a work is identified as a play, the audience readily enters into the fantasy world, and as easily, retreats when the play is over. The difficulty arises, however, when the stagecraft goes unrecognized and is taken seriously, as when entire populations swallow the propaganda of their puppeteer leaders. Frequently throughout the novel, Don Quixote is made the puppet, with people like the duke and duchess or Don Antonio de Morena pulling strings to make him dance. These puppeteers, not having the control over their stagecraft as Gines de Passamonte who does this for a living, are often themselves part of a larger jest set for the entertainment of the reader-spectator.

Altisidora is an example of a puppeteer who loses control. After pretending to sue for Don Quixote's love, she is genuinely piqued and vengeful when he remains unmoved. Perhaps she has been acting out a private fantasy all this time in order to gain for herself the love of such a constant and noble lover, although consciously she deems him ridiculous.

Dorothea, acting the part of Princess Micomicona has been previously cited as an instance when an actress does not realize the reality of her performance. Samson Carrasco, attempting to usurp Don Quixote's immortality, provides a similar example. The puppet-governor Sancho, acting with sincerity, turns the joke to the jester's expense. Many other incidents can be cited to show "things are not what they seem."

To complete the plotting of the fantasy-reality continuum, Cervantes explores the truths of dreams, as in the adventure of Montesinos Cave. The crowing illusion, perhaps the most fitting, is when the dying hero renounces his mad life of knight-errantry, telling the weeping household that he is no longer Don Quixote de La Mancha, but Alonso Quixano the Good. At this moment of utter sanity, the hero expresses the wish that his past acts be consigned to oblivion. So zestful of life that he idealized human possibilities by trying to initiate a new Golden Age of innocence and contentment, Don Quixote now expresses the ironic futility of quixotism and underscores that fantasy and reality are phases on a continuum. The sane hero denies his past madness in a final affirmation that life is a dream, death the moment of reality. Sancho's inheritance is the stored-up spirit of quixotism which enables him to recognize the truth of ideals and either become a knight-errant himself, or imbue his children with the imaginative spirit.

Minor Themes

Cervantes expresses other ideas in *Don Quixote,* and though these are of secondary importance, they at least deserve mention.

Romantic love is often depicted in the novel. Among all the various courtships that take place, their common quality is a love between the two people despite parental disapproval or unequal birth. Cervantes obviously disliked "arranged marriages" and idealizes a wedding of a mutually-affected couple with the blessings of their families.

Sympathy for the Moorish population of Spain is another of the author's inclinations. Cervantes, who has lived as a prisoner in Algiers, understands the Moorish people who lived as a sometimes-hostile and unassimilated subculture of Spain. Among deservedly banished Moors, many families contributive to Spanish cultural life and orthodox in their Catholicism were exiled as well.

Outstanding too is Cervantes' knowledge of the underworld culture of Spain. In a short novel, *Rinconete and Cortadillo,* he shows even more detailed knowledge of the thieves' government that ruled Barcelona. In *Don Quixote,* however, the author limits himself to sketches of Gines de Passamonte and to the outlaw community of Roque Guinart. The chain gang prisoners speak in the slang dialect used by rogues and gypsies.

Subordinate to the theme of law and justice, Cervantes introduces the bold theory, implicit in the story of Sancho's government, that a man of the people who knows and understands their problems, can become a better governor than a man born to authority. Sancho became loved and respected by the citizens of his island, and they begged him to remain. To this day, Cervantes adds, laws are promulgated today which are called "The Constitutions of the Great Governor Sancho Panza."

The author also mentions his esthetic standards of literature. Cervantes believes that the main business in art is "verisimilitude and the imitation of nature" which he expresses in Part I. Since everyone understands what he sees through the senses, or what is "true," it is thus the job of the artist to make the impossible appear possible without straining a reader's credibility. From this esthetically-oriented beginning, Cervantes constructs the delightful fusion of fantasy and reality that is the medium of *Don Quixote*.

Cervantes indulges in literary criticism as well, remarking on the place of poetry, criticizing his famous contemporary, Lope de Vega, for overdone plays, referring to the perniciousness of books of chivalry, expressing himself on the inadequacies of translated works, and extending his comments to denounce the malpractices of booksellers and publishers. Conscious of his trade, Cervantes' remarks are those of a professional who maintains his vigilance over the world of letters as much as possible.

QUESTIONS FOR DISCUSSION

1. What is the function of the invention of Cid Hamet Benengali? (Analysis: Technique and Style; Commentary to Preface and Part II)

2. Why does Don Quixote undergo penance and voluntarily become insane? (Commentary in Part I)

3. What is the significance of Sancho's self-lashing? (Commentary in Part II)

4. What is the significance of Dulcinea del Toboso? (Analysis: Characterization; Commentary in Part I)

5. What is the relationship between the intercalated novel of "The Curious Impertinent" and the main body of *Don Quixote?* (Commentary in Part I; Analysis: Technique and Style)

6. What qualities does Cervantes consider most important in literary art? (Analysis: Secondary Themes; also in Preface and Commentary in Part I)

7. Discuss the types of comedy that Cervantes uses. (To be discussed after reading the novel itself)

8. In your own words, discuss the nature of quixotism.

9. Give examples to show how Sancho unsuccessfully imitates Don Quixote. (Analysis: Characterization; Commentary in Part I)

10. How does Sancho become quixotized? (Analysis: Characterization; Commentary Part II)

11. Describe Sancho's great dilemma in terms of his greed versus his ideals, or in terms of any opposing pair of words you choose. (Analysis: Characterization; Commentary in Part I)

12. Why does Don Quixote fight with the lion? (Commentary in Part II; suggestions of your own)

13. Consider whether you prefer Part I or Part II and why? (To be discussed after reading the novel itself)

14. How is Dorothea related to her role of Princess Micomicona? (Commentary in Part I)

15. What is the function of characters like Don Diego de Miranda, Antonia Quixana, and the scolding priest at the duke's castle? (Analysis: Minor characters)

16. Describe the qualities of Alonso Quixano that remain part of Don Quixote. (Analysis: Characterization; Commentary in Part I and Part II)

17. Why does the barber tell the story of the Seville lunatic? What does this show about the barber? About Don Quixote? (Commentary in Part II)

18. Discuss the importance of reading books in the lives of the following characters: Don Quixote, Cardenio, Marcella, the New Arcadians, the curate and barber, innkeeper. (Commentaries in Part I and Part II)

19. Discuss Samson Carrasco's character to indicate (or deny) that he is a "false Quixote." (Analysis: Characterization; Commentaries in Part I and II)

20. Critics point to Cervantes' free thinking religious ideas as shown in the Don's Adventure with the Penitents, his mistreatment of clergymen. Can you refute this notion by showing examples of Cervantes' religious orthodoxy? (Commentary Part I; suggestions of your own)

21. Discuss some differences in Cervantes' treatment of Part I and Part II. (To be discussed after reading the novel itself; some suggestions appear throughout commentaries of Part I and II)

22. How is the cave used as a symbolic device in *Don Quixote?* (Commentary in Part II)

23. Discuss, if you are familiar with Shakespeare's plays, some qualities or episodes or characters that the art of Cervantes and the art of Shakespeare have in common. (Some suggestions in Analysis)

24. Aubrey Bell writes that *Don Quixote* should be read at least three times in the course of a lifetime: in youth, maturity, and old age. Discuss the appeal of the novel to each of the periods. (Ideas implied in Notes, but not directly discussed)

25. Why does Cervantes write: "For me alone was the great Quixote born, and I alone for him. Deeds were his task, and to record them mine, and we two, like tallies for each other struck, are nothing when apart." Discuss this in your own words. (Commentary in Part II, throughout book)

26. *Don Quixote* has affected the work of many artists of all nations. Discuss a novel you are familiar with by relating it, or its hero, to Don Quixote. Suggestions: Dostoevsky's *Idiot,* Flaubert's *Madame Bovary,* Melville's *Moby Dick,* Fielding's *Joseph Andrews,* Bellow's *Adventures of Augie March.*

BIBLIOGRAPHY

Aubrey F. G. Bell, *Cervantes,* Norman: University of Oklahoma Press, 1947.

Angel Flores and M. J. Benardete (editors), *Cervantes Across the Centuries;* A Quadricentennial Volume; New York: Dryden Press, 1947.

Bruno Frank, *A Man Called Cervantes*; translated by Helen T. Lowe-Porter; New York: Viking Press, 1935.

Jose Ortega y Gasset, *Mediations on Quixote*; translated by Evelyn Rugg and Diego Marin; New York: The Norton Library, 1963 (paperback).

Joseph Wood Krutch, "Miguel de Cervantes," *Five Masters: A Study in the Mutations of the Novel*; New York: Jonathan Cape and Harrison Smith, 1930.

Miguel de Unamuno y Jugo, *The Life of Don Quixote and Sancho According to Miguel de Cervantes Saavedra*; translated by Homer P. Earle; New York: Alfred A. Knopf, 1927.

Mark VanDoren, *Don Quixote's Profession;* New York: Columbia University Press.

OTHER WORKS BY CERVANTES

Journey to Parnassus; translated into English tercets, with Preface and Illustrative Notes by James Y. Gibson; London: Keegan Paul, Trench and Company, 1883.

Numantia: A Tragedy; translated with Introduction and notes by James Y. Gibson; London: Keegan Paul, Trench and Company, 1885.

The Exemplary Novels of Cervantes; translated by N. Maccoll, edited by James Fitzmaurice-Kelly; Glasgow: Gowans and Gray, 1902.

The Exemplary Novels of Cervantes; translated by N. Maccoll, edited by Walter K. Kelly; London: Henry G. Bohn, 1846.

The Interludes of Cervantes; translated by S. Griswold Morley; Princeton: Princeton University Press, 1948.

The Poetry of the Don Quixote of Miguel de Cervantes Saavedra. Done into English by James Y. Gibson (The Cid Ballads, vol. II.) London: Keegan Paul, Trench and Company, 1887.

NOTES

TITLE INDEX

This is the TITLE INDEX, indexing the over 200 titles available by Series, by Library and by Volume Number for both the BASIC LIBRARY SERIES and the AUTHORS LIBRARY SERIES.

TITLE	SERIES	LIBRARY	Vol
Absalom, Absalom!	Basic	American Lit	4
	Authors	Faulkner	3
Adonais (in Keats & Shelley)	Basic	English Lit	1
Aeneid, The	Basic	Classics	1
Aeschylus' Oresteia (in Agamemnon)	Basic	Classics	1
Agamemnon	Basic	Classics	1
Alice in Wonderland	Basic	English Lit	3
All That Fall (in Waiting for Godot)	Basic	European Lit	1
All the King's Men	Basic	American Lit	6
All Quiet on the Western Front	Basic	European Lit	2
All's Well That Ends Well	Basic	Shakespeare	1
	Authors	Shakespeare	8
American, The	Basic	American Lit	2
	Authors	James	6
American Tragedy, An	Basic	American Lit	3
Animal Farm	Basic	English Lit	5
Anna Karenina	Basic	European Lit	3
Antigone (in Oedipus Trilogy)	Basic	Classics	1
Antony and Cleopatra	Basic	Shakespeare	2
	Authors	Shakespeare	9
Apology (in Plato's Euthyphro....)	Basic	Classics	1
Aristotle's Ethics	Basic	Classics	1
Arms and the Man (in Shaw's Pygmalion....)	Basic	English Lit	6
	Authors	Shaw	11
"Artificial Nigger, The" (in O'Connor's Short Stories)	Basic	American Lit	7
As I Lay Dying	Basic	American Lit	4
	Authors	Faulkner	3
Assistant, The	Basic	American Lit	6
As You Like It	Basic	Shakespeare	1
	Authors	Shakespeare	8
Autobiography of Benjamin Franklin	Basic	American Lit	1
Autobiography of Malcolm X, The	Basic	American Lit	6
	Special	Black Studies	
Awakening, The	Basic	American Lit	2
Babbitt	Basic	American Lit	3
	Authors	Lewis	7
"Bear, The" (in Go Down, Moses)	Basic	American Lit	4
	Authors	Faulkner	3
Bear, The	Basic	American Lit	4
	Authors	Faulkner	3
Bell Jar, The	Basic	American Lit	6
Beowulf	Basic	Classics	3
Billy Budd	Basic	American Lit	1
Birds, The (in Lysistrata....)	Basic	Classics	1

TITLE INDEX (cont'd)

TITLE	SERIES	LIBRARY	Vol
Black Boy	Basic	American Lit	4
	Special	Black Studies	
Black Like Me	Basic	American Lit	6
	Special	Black Studies	
Bleak House	Basic	English Lit	3
	Authors	Dickens	1
Bourgeois Gentleman, The (in Tartuffe....)	Basic	European Lit	1
Brave New World	Basic	English Lit	5
Brave New World Revisited (in Brave New World)	Basic	English Lit	5
Brothers Karamozov, The	Basic	European Lit	3
	Authors	Dostoevsky	2
Caesar and Cleopatra (in Shaw's Man and Superman....)	Basic	English Lit	6
	Authors	Shaw	11
Call of the Wild, The	Basic	American Lit	3
Candide	Basic	European Lit	1
Canterbury Tales, The	Basic	Classics	3
"Cask of Amontillado, The" (in Poe's Short Stories)	Basic	American Lit	1
Catch-22	Basic	American Lit	6
Catcher in the Rye, The	Basic	American Lit	6
Choephori (in Agamemnon)	Basic	Classics	1
Clouds, The (in Lysistrata....)	Basic	Classics	1
Color Purple, The	Basic	American Lit	6
	Special	Black Studies	
Comedy of Errors, The	Basic	Shakespeare	1
	Authors	Shakespeare	8
Connecticut Yankee in King Arthur's Court, A	Basic	American Lit	2
	Authors	Twain	13
Count of Monte Cristo, The	Basic	European Lit	1
Crime and Punishment	Basic	European Lit	3
	Authors	Dostoevsky	2
Crito (in Plato's Euthyphro....)	Basic	Classics	1
Crucible, The	Basic	American Lit	6
Cry, the Beloved Country	Basic	English Lit	5
Cyrano de Bergerac	Basic	European Lit	1
Daisy Miller	Basic	American Lit	2
	Authors	James	6
David Copperfield	Basic	English Lit	3
	Authors	Dickens	1
Day of the Locust, The (in Miss Lonelyhearts....)	Basic	American Lit	5
Death of a Salesman	Basic	American Lit	6
Deerslayer, The	Basic	American Lit	1
"Delta Autumn" (in Go Down, Moses)	Basic	American Lit	4
Demian	Basic	European Lit	2
Diary of Anne Frank, The	Basic	European Lit	2
"Displaced Person, The" (in O'Connor's Short Stories	Basic	American Lit	7
Divine Comedy I: Inferno	Basic	Classics	3
Divine Comedy II: Purgatorio	Basic	Classics	3
Divine Comedy III: Paradiso	Basic	Classics	3

TITLE INDEX (cont'd)

TITLE INDEX (cont'd)

TITLE	SERIES	LIBRARY	Vol
Light in August	Basic	American Lit	4
	Authors	Faulkner	3
Lord Jim	Basic	English Lit	5
Lord of the Flies	Basic	English Lit	5
Lord of the Rings, The	Basic	English Lit	5
Lost Horizon	Basic	English Lit	5
"Love Song of J. Alfred Prufrock, The" (in *T.S. Eliot's Major Poems and Plays*)	Basic	English Lit	6
Love's Labour's Lost (in *Comedy of Errors....*)	Basic	Shakespeare	1
	Authors	Shakespeare	8
Lysistrata & Other Comedies	Basic	Classics	1
Macbeth	Basic	Shakespeare	2
	Authors	Shakespeare	9
Madame Bovary	Basic	European Lit	1
Main Street	Basic	American Lit	3
	Authors	Lewis	7
Man and Superman (in *Shaw's Man and Superman*)	Basic	English Lit	6
	Authors	Shaw	11
Manchild in the Promised Land	Basic	American Lit	7
	Special	Black Studies	
Mayor of Casterbridge, The	Basic	English Lit	3
	Authors	Hardy	4
Measure for Measure	Basic	Shakespeare	1
	Authors	Shakespeare	8
Medea (in *Euripides' Electra & Medea*)	Basic	Classics	1
Merchant of Venice, The	Basic	Shakespeare	1
	Authors	Shakespeare	8
Merry Wives of Windsor, The (in *All's Well....*)	Basic	Shakespeare	1
	Authors	Shakespeare	8
"Metamorphosis, The" (in *Kafka's Short Stories*)	Basic	European Lit	2
Middlemarch	Basic	English Lit	4
Midsummer Night's Dream, A	Basic	Shakespeare	1
	Authors	Shakespeare	8
Mill on the Floss, The	Basic	The English Lit	4
Misanthrope (in *Tartuffe....*)	Basic	European Lit	1
Miss Lonelyhearts	Basic	American Lit	5
Moby Dick	Basic	American Lit	1
Moll Flanders	Basic	English Lit	1
Mother Night (in *Vonnegut's Major Works*)	Basic	American Lit	7
Mrs. Dalloway	Basic	English Lit	5
Much Ado About Nothing	Basic	Shakespeare	1
	Authors	Shakespeare	8
"Murder in the Cathedral" (*in T.S. Eliot's Major Poems and Plays*)	Basic	English Lit	6
My Antonia	Basic	American Lit	3
Mythology	Basic	Classics	1
Native Son	Basic	American Lit	5
	Special	Black Studies	
New Testament	Basic	Classics	4
Nichomachean Ethics (in *Aristotle's Ethics*)	Basic	Classics	1

TITLE INDEX (cont'd)

TITLE	SERIES	LIBRARY	Vol
Tender is the Night	Basic	American Lit	5
Tess of the D'Urbervilles	Basic	English Lit	4
	Authors	Hardy	4
Three Musketeers, The	Basic	European Lit	1
To Kill a Mockingbird	Basic	American Lit	7
Tom Jones	Basic	English Lit	2
Tom Sawyer	Basic	American Lit	2
	Authors	Twain	13
Treasure Island	Basic	English Lit	4
Trial, The	Basic	European Lit	2
Tristram Shandy	Basic	English Lit	2
Troilus and Cressida	Basic	Shakespeare	1
	Authors	Shakespeare	8
Turn of the Screw, The (in Daisy Miller....)	Basic	American Lit	2
	Authors	James	6
Twelfth Night	Basic	Shakespeare	1
	Authors	Shakespeare	8
Two Gentlemen of Verona, The (in Comedy of Errors...)	Basic	Shakespeare	1
	Authors	Shakespeare	8
Typee (in Billy Budd & Typee)	Basic	American Lit	1
Ulysses	Basic	English Lit	6
Uncle Tom's Cabin	Basic	American Lit	2
Unvanquished, The	Basic	American Lit	5
	Authors	Faulkner	3
Utopia	Basic	Classics	4
Vanity Fair	Basic	English Lit	4
Vonnegut's Major Works	Basic	American Lit	7
Waiting for Godot	Basic	European Lit	1
Walden	Basic	American Lit	1
Walden Two	Basic	American Lit	7
War and Peace	Basic	European Lit	3
"Was" (in Go Down, Moses)	Basic	American Lit	4
"Waste Land, The" (in T.S. Eliot's Major Poems and Plays)	Basic	English Lit	6
White Fang (in Call of the Wild & White Fang)	Basic	American Lit	3
Who's Afraid of Virginia Woolf?	Basic	American Lit	7
Wild Duck, The (in Ibsen's Plays II)	Basic	European Lit	4
Winesburg, Ohio	Basic	American Lit	3
Winter's Tale, The	Basic	Shakespeare	1
	Authors	Shakespeare	8
Wuthering Heights	Basic	English Lit	4

AUTHOR INDEX

This is the AUTHOR INDEX, listing the over 200 titles available by author and indexing them by Series, by Library and by Volume Number for both the BASIC LIBRARY SERIES and the AUTHORS LIBRARY SERIES.

AUTHOR	TITLE(S)	SERIES	LIBRARY	Vol
Aeschylus	Agamemnon, The Choephori, & The Eumenides	Basic	Classics	1
Albee, Edward	Who's Afraid of Virginia Woolf?	Basic	American Lit	7
Anderson, Sherwood	Winesburg, Ohio	Basic	American Lit	3
Aristophanes	Lysistrata * The Birds * Clouds * The Frogs	Basic	Classics	1
Aristotle	Aristotle's Ethics	Basic	Classics	1
Austen, Jane	Emma	Basic	English Lit	1
	Pride and Prejudice	Basic	English Lit	2
Beckett, Samuel	Waiting for Godot	Basic	European Lit	1
Beowulf	Beowulf	Basic	Classics	3
Beyle, Henri	see Stendhal			
Bronte, Charlotte	Jane Eyre	Basic	English Lit	3
Bronte, Emily	Wuthering Heights	Basic	English Lit	4
Brown, Claude	Manchild in the Promised Land	Basic	American Lit	7
	Manchild in the Promised Land	Special	Black Studies	
Buck, Pearl	The Good Earth	Basic	American Lit	4
Bunyan, John	The Pilgrim's Progress	Basic	English Lit	2
Camus, Albert	The Plague * The Stranger	Basic	European Lit	1
Carroll, Lewis	Alice in Wonderland	Basic	English Lit	3
Cather, Willa	My Antonia	Basic	American Lit	3
Cervantes, Miguel de	Don Quixote	Basic	Classics	3
Chaucer, Geoffrey	The Canterbury Tales	Basic	Classics	3
Chopin, Kate	The Awakening	Basic	American Lit	2
Clark, Walter	The Ox-Bow Incident	Basic	American Lit	7
Conrad, Joseph	Heart of Darkness & The Secret Sharer * Lord Jim	Basic	English Lit	5
Cooper, James F.	The Deerslayer * The Last of the Mohicans	Basic	American Lit	1
Crane, Stephen	The Red Badge of Courage	Basic	American Lit	2
Dante	Divine Comedy I: Inferno * Divine Comedy II: Purgatorio * Divine Comedy III: Paradiso	Basic	Classics	3
Defoe, Daniel	Moll Flanders	Basic	English Lit	1
	Robinson Crusoe	Basic	English Lit	2
Dickens, Charles	Bleak House * David Copperfield * Great Expectations * Hard Times	Basic	English Lit	3
	Oliver Twist * A Tale of Two Cities	Basic	English Lit	4
	Bleak House * David Copperfield * Great Expectations * Hard Times * Oliver Twist * A Tale of Two Cities	Authors	Dickens	1

AUTHOR INDEX (cont'd)

AUTHOR	TITLE(S)	SERIES	LIBRARY	Vol
Dickinson, Emily	Emily Dickinson: Selected Poems	Basic	American Lit	2
Dostoevsky, Feodor	The Brothers Karamazov * Crime and Punishment * Notes from the Underground	Basic	European Lit	3
	The Brothers Karamazov * Crime and Punishment * Notes from the Underground	Authors	Dostoevsky	2
Dreiser, Theodore	An American Tragedy * Sister Carrie	Basic	American Lit	3
Dumas, Alexandre	The Count of Monte Cristo * The Three Musketeers	Basic	European Lit	1
Eliot, George	Middlemarch * The Mill on the Floss * Silas Marner	Basic	English Lit	4
Eliot, T.S.	T.S. Eliot's Major Poets and Plays: "The Wasteland," "The Love Song of J. Alfred Prufrock," & Other Works	Basic	English Lit	6
Ellison, Ralph	The Invisible Man	Basic	American Lit	7
	The Invisible Man	Special	Black Studies	
Emerson, Ralph Waldo	Emerson's Essays	Basic	American Lit	1
Euripides	Electra * Medea	Basic	Classics	1
Faulkner, William	Absalom, Absalom! * As I Lay Dying * The Bear * Go Down, Moses * Light in August	Basic	American Lit	4
	The Sound and the Fury * The Unvanquished	Basic	American Lit	5
	Absalom, Absalom! * As I Lay Dying * The Bear * Go Down, Moses * Light in August The Sound and the Fury * The Unvanquished	Authors	Faulkner	3
Fielding, Henry	Joseph Andrews	Basic	English Lit	1
	Tom Jones	Basic	English Lit	2
Fitzgerald, F. Scott	The Great Gatsby	Basic	American Lit	4
	Tender is the Night	Basic	American Lit	5
Flaubert, Gustave	Madame Bovary	Basic	European Lit	1
Forster, E.M.	A Passage to India	Basic	English Lit	6
Fowles, John	The French Lieutenant's Woman	Basic	English Lit	5
Frank, Anne	The Diary of Anne Frank	Basic	European Lit	2
Franklin, Benjamin	The Autobiography of Benjamin Franklin	Basic	American Lit	1
Gawain Poet	Sir Gawain and the Green Night	Basic	Classics	4
Goethe, Johann Wolfgang von	Faust - Parts I & II	Basic	European Lit	2
Golding, William	Lord of the Flies	Basic	English Lit	5
Greene, Graham	The Power and the Glory	Basic	English Lit	6
Griffin, John H.	Black Like Me	Basic	American Lit	6
	Black Like Me	Special	Black Studies	

AUTHOR INDEX (cont'd)

AUTHOR INDEX (cont'd)

AUTHOR	TITLE(S)	SERIES	LIBRARY	Vol
Knowles, John	A Separate Peace	Basic	American Lit	7
Lawrence, D.H.	Sons and Lovers	Basic	English Lit	6
Lee, Harper	To Kill a Mockingbird	Basic	American Lit	7
Lewis, Sinclair	Babbit * Main Street	Basic	American Lit	3
	Babbit * Main Street	Authors	Lewis	7
Little, Malcolm	The Autobiography of Malcolm X	Basic	American Lit	6
	The Autobiography of Malcolm X	Special	Black Studies	
see also Haley, Alex				
London, Jack	Call of the Wild & White Fang	Basic	American Lit	3
Machiavelli, Niccolo	The Prince	Basic	Classics	4
Malamud, Bernard	The Assistant	Basic	American Lit	6
Malcolm X	see Little, Malcolm			
Malory, Thomas	Le Morte d'Arthur	Basic	Classics	4
Marlowe, Christopher	Doctor Faustus	Basic	Classics	3
Marquez, Gabriel Garcia	One Hundred Years of Solitude	Basic	American Lit	6
Maugham, Somerset	Of Human Bondage	Basic	English Lit	6
Melville, Herman	Billy Budd & Typee * Moby Dick	Basic	American Lit	1
Miller, Arthur	The Crucible * Death of a Salesman	Basic	Amerịcan Lit	6
Milton, John	Paradise Lost	Basic	English Lit	2
Moliere, Jean Baptiste	Tartuffe, Misanthrope & Bourgeois Gentleman	Basic	European Lit	1
More, Thomas	Utopia	Basic	Classics	4
O'Connor, Flannery	O'Connor's Short Stories	Basic	American Lit	7
Orwell, George	Animal Farm	Basic	English Lit	5
	Nineteen Eighty-Four	Basic	English Lit	6
Paton, Alan	Cry, The Beloved Country	Basic	English Lit	5
Plath, Sylvia	The Bell Jar	Basic	American Lit	6
Plato	Plato's Euthyphro, Apology, Crito & Phaedo * Plato's The Republic	Basic	Classics	1
Poe, Edgar Allen	Poe's Short Stories	Basic	American Lit	1
Remarque, Erich	All Quiet on the Western Front	Basic	European Lit	2
Rolvaag, Ole	Giants in the Earth	Basic	European Lit	4
Rostand, Edmond	Cyrano de Bergerac	Basic	European Lit	1
Salinger, J.D.	The Catcher in the Rye	Basic	American Lit	6
Sartre, Jean Paul	No Exit & The Flies	Basic	European Lit	1
Scott, Walter	Ivanhoe	Basic	English Lit	1
Shaefer, Jack	Shane	Basic	American Lit	7
Shakespeare, William	All's Well that Ends Well & The Merry Wives of Windsor * As You Like It * The Comedy of Errors, Love's Labour's Lost, & The Two Gentlemen of Verona * Measure for Measure * The Merchant of Venice * Midsummer Night's Dream *	Basic	Shakespeare	1

AUTHOR INDEX (cont'd)

AUTHOR	TITLE(S)	SERIES	LIBRARY	Vol
Steinbeck, John	The Grapes of Wrath *	Basic	American Lit	4
	Of Mice and Men * The Pearl * The Red Pony	Basic	American Lit	5
	The Grapes of Wrath * Of Mice and Men * The Pearl * The Red Pony	Authors	Steinbeck	12
Stendhal	The Red and the Black	Basic	European Lit	1
Sterne, Lawrence	Tristram Shandy	Basic	English Lit	2
Stevenson, Robert Louis	Dr. Jekyll and Mr. Hyde *	Basic	English Lit	3
	Treasure Island & Kidnapped	Basic	English Lit	4
Stoker, Bram	Dracula	Basic	English Lit	3
Stowe, Harriet Beecher	Uncle Tom's Cabin	Basic	American Lit	2
Swift, Jonathan	Gulliver's Travels	Basic	English Lit	1
Thackeray, William Makepeace	Vanity Fair	Basic	English Lit	4
Thoreau, Henry David	Walden	Basic	American Lit	1
Tolkien, J.R.R.	The Lord of the Rings & The Hobbit	Basic	English Lit	5
Tolstoy, Leo	Anna Karenina * War and Peace	Basic	European Lit	3
Turgenev, Ivan Sergeyevich	Fathers and Sons	Basic	European Lit	3
Twain, Mark	A Connecticut Yankee * Huckleberry Finn * The Prince and the Pauper * Tom Sawyer	Basic	American Lit	2
	A Connecticut Yankee * Huckleberry Finn * The Prince and the Pauper * Tom Sawyer	Authors	Twain	13
Virgil	The Aeneid	Basic	Classics	1
Voltaire, Francois	Candide	Basic	European Lit	2
Vonnegut, Kurt	Vonnegut's Major Works	Basic	American Lit	7
Walker, Alice	The Color Purple	Basic	American Lit	7
	The Color Purple	Special	Black Studies	
Warren, Robert Penn	All the King's Men	Basic	American Lit	6
West, Nathanael	Miss Lonelyhearts & The Day of the Locust	Basic	American Lit	5
Wharton, Edith	Ethan Frome	Basic	American Lit	3
Whitman, Walt	Leaves of Grass	Basic	American Lit	1
Wilder, Thornton	Our Town	Basic	American Lit	5
Williams, Tennessee	The Glass Menagerie & A Streetcar Named Desire	Basic	American Lit	6
Woolf, Virginia	Mrs. Dalloway	Basic	English Lit	5
Wordsworth, William	The Prelude	Basic	English Lit	2
Wright, Richard	Black Boy	Basic	American Lit	4
	Native Son	Basic	American Lit	5
	Black Boy	Special	Black Studies	
	Native Son	Special	Black Studies	

INDEX OF SERIES

BASIC LIBRARY (24-0)

THE SHAKESPEARE LIBRARY: 3 Volumes, 26 Titles (25-9)
- V. 1 - The Comedies 12 titles (00-3)
- V. 2 - The Tragedies, 7 titles (01-1)
- V. 3 - The Histories; The Sonnets, 7 titles (02-X)

THE CLASSICS LIBRARY: 4 Volumes, 27 Titles (26-7)
- V. 1 - Greek & Roman Classics, 11 titles (03-8)
- V. 2 - Greek & Roman Classics, 2 titles (04-6)
- V. 3 - Early Christian/European Classics, 7 titles (05-4)
- V. 4 - Early Christian/European Classics, 7 titles (06-2)

ENGLISH LITERATURE LIBRARY: 6 Volumes, 55 Titles (29-1)
- V. 1 - 17th Century & Romantic Period Classics, 7 titles (07-0)
- V. 2 - 17th Century & Romantic Period Classics, 7 titles (08-9)
- V. 3 - Victorian Age, 11 titles (09-7)
- V. 4 - Victorian Age, 10 titles (10-0)
- V. 5 - 20th Century, 10 titles (11-9)
- V. 6 - 20th Century, 10 titles (12-7)

AMERICAN LITERATURE LIBRARY: 7 Volumes, 77 Titles (33-X)
- V. 1 - Early U.S. & Romantic Period, 11 titles (13-5)
- V. 2 - Civil War to 1900, 11 titles (14-3)
- V. 3 - Early 20th Century, 9 titles (15-1)
- V. 4 - The Jazz Age to W.W.II, 11 titles (16-X)
- V. 5 - The Jazz Age to W.W.II, 10 titles (17-8)
- V. 6 - Post-War American Literature, 13 titles (18-6)
- V. 7 - Post-War American Literature, 12 titles (19-4)

EUROPEAN LITERATURE LIBRARY: 4 Volumes, 29 Titles (36-4)
- V. 1 - French Literature, 12 titles (20-8)
- V. 2 - German Literature, 7 titles (21-6)
- V. 3 - Russian Literature, 7 titles (22-4)
- V. 4 - Scandinavian Literature, 3 titles (23-2)

AUTHORS LIBRARY (65-8)

- V. 1 - **Charles Dickens** Library, 6 titles (66-6)
- V. 2 - **Feodor Dostoevsky** Library, 3 titles (67-4)
- V. 3 - **William Faulkner** Library, 7 titles (68-2)
- V. 4 - **Thomas Hardy** Library, 5 titles (69-0)
- V. 5 - **Ernest Hemingway** Library, 4 titles (70-4)
- V. 6 - **Henry James** Library, 3 titles (71-2)
- V. 7 - **Sinclair Lewis** Library, 2 titles (72-0)
- V. 8 - **Shakespeare** Library, Part 1 - The Comedies, 12 titles (73-9)
- V. 9 - **Shakespeare** Library, Part 2 - The Tragedies, 7 titles (74-7)
- V. 10 - **Shakespeare** Library, Part 3 - The Histories; Sonnets, 7 titles (75-5)
- V. 11 - **George Bernard Shaw** Library, 2 titles (76-3)
- V. 12 - **John Steinbeck** Library, 4 titles (77-1)
- V. 13 - **Mark Twain** Library, 4 titles (78-X)

SPECIAL LIBRARY

Black Studies Volume, 7 titles (90-9)

Moonbeam Publications ISBN Prefix: 0-931013-

CLIFFS NOTES
HARDBOUND LITERARY LIBRARIES
INDEX OF LIBRARIES

This is the INDEX OF LIBRARIES, listing the volumes and the individual titles within the volumes for both the BASIC LIBRARY SERIES (24 Volumes, starting below) and the AUTHORS LIBRARY SERIES (13 Volumes, see Page 6).

BASIC LIBRARY SERIES (24 Volumes)

THE SHAKESPEARE LIBRARY: 3 Volumes, 26 Titles

Vol 1 - The Comedies (12 titles)

All's Well that Ends Well & The Merry Wives of Windsor
As You Like It
The Comedy of Errors, Love's Labour's Lost, & The Two Gentlemen of Verona
Measure for Measure
The Merchant of Venice
A Midsummer Night's Dream
Much Ado About Nothing
The Taming of the Shrew
The Tempest
Troilus and Cressida
Twelfth Night
The Winter's Tale

Vol 2 - The Tragedies (7 titles)

Antony and Cleopatra
Hamlet
Julius Caesar
King Lear
Macbeth
Othello
Romeo and Juliet

Vol 3 - The Histories; The Sonnets (7 titles)

Henry IV Part 1
Henry IV Part 2
Henry V
Henry VI Parts 1,2,3
Richard II
Richard III
Shakespeare's Sonnets

INDEX OF LIBRARIES (cont'd)
BASIC LIBRARY SERIES

THE CLASSICS LIBRARY: 4 Volumes, 27 Titles

Vol 1 - Greek & Roman Classics Part 1 (11 titles)

The Aeneid
Agamemnon
Aristotle's Ethics
Euripides' Electra & Medea
The Iliad
Lysistrata & Other Comedies
Mythology
The Odyssey
Oedipus Trilogy
Plato's Euthyphro, Apology, Crito & Phaedo
Plato's The Republic

Vol 2 - Greek & Roman Classics Part 2 (2 titles)

Greek Classics
Roman Classics

Vol 3 - Early Christian/European Classics Part 1 (7 titles)

Beowulf
Canterbury Tales
Divine Comedy - I. Inferno
Divine Comedy - II. Purgatorio
Divine Comedy - III. Paradiso
Doctor Faustus
Don Quixote

Vol 4 - Early Christian/European Classics Part 2 (7 titles)

The Faerie Queene
Le Morte D'Arthur
New Testament
Old Testament
The Prince
Sir Gawain and the Green Knight
Utopia

INDEX OF LIBRARIES (cont'd)
BASIC LIBRARY SERIES

ENGLISH LITERATURE LIBRARY: 6 Volumes, 55 Titles

Vol 1 - 17th Century & Romantic Period Classics
Part 1 (7 titles)

Emma
Frankenstein
Gulliver's Travels
Ivanhoe
Joseph Andrews
Keats & Shelley
Moll Flanders

Vol 2 - 17th Century & Romantic Period Classics
Part 2 (7 titles)

Paradise Lost
Pilgrim's Progress
The Prelude
Pride and Prejudice
Robinson Crusoe
Tom Jones
Tristram Shandy

Vol 3 - Victorian Age Part 1 (11 titles)

Alice in Wonderland
Bleak House
David Copperfield
Dr. Jekyll and Mr. Hyde
Dracula
Far from the Madding Crowd
Great Expectations
Hard Times
Jane Eyre
Jude the Obscure
The Mayor of Casterbridge

Vol 4 - Victorian Age Part 2 (10 titles)

Middlemarch
The Mill on the Floss
Oliver Twist
The Return of the Native
Silas Marner
A Tale of Two Cities
Tess of the D'Urbervilles
Treasure Island & Kidnapped
Vanity Fair
Wuthering Heights

INDEX OF LIBRARIES (cont'd)
BASIC LIBRARY SERIES

ENGLISH LITERATURE LIBRARY (cont'd)

Vol 5 - 20th Century Part 1 (10 titles)

Animal Farm
Brave New World
Cry, The Beloved Country
The French Lieutenant's Woman
Heart of Darkness & The Secret Sharer
Lord Jim
Lord of the Flies
The Lord of the Rings
Lost Horizon
Mrs. Dalloway

Vol 6 - 20th Century Part 2 (10 titles)

Nineteen Eighty-Four
Of Human Bondage
A Passage to India
A Portrait of the Artist as a Young Man
The Power and the Glory
Shaw's Man and Superman & Caesar and Cleopatra
Shaw's Pygmalion & Arms and the Man
Sons and Lovers
T.S. Eliot's Major Poems and Plays
Ulysses

AMERICAN LITERATURE LIBRARY: 7 Volumes, 77 Titles

Vol 1 - Early U.S. & Romantic Period (11 titles)

Autobiography of Ben Franklin
Billy Budd & Typee
The Deerslayer
Emerson's Essays
The House of Seven Gables
The Last of the Mohicans
Leaves of Grass
Moby Dick
Poe's Short Stories
The Scarlet Letter
Walden

INDEX OF LIBRARIES (cont'd)
BASIC LIBRARY SERIES

AMERICAN LITERATURE LIBRARY (cont'd)

Vol 2 - Civil War to 1900 (11 titles)

The American
The Awakening
A Connecticut Yankee in King Arthur's Court
Daisy Miller & The Turn of the Screw
Emily Dickinson: Selected Poems
Huckleberry Finn
The Portrait of a Lady
The Prince and the Pauper
Red Badge of Courage
Tom Sawyer
Uncle Tom's Cabin

Vol 3 - Early 20th Century (9 titles)

An American Tragedy
Babbitt
Call of the Wild & White Fang
Ethan Frome
The Jungle
Main Street
My Antonia
Sister Carrie
Winesburg, Ohio

Vol 4 - The Jazz Age to W.W.II Part 1 (11 titles)

Absalom, Absalom!
As I Lay Dying
The Bear
Black Boy
A Farewell to Arms
For Whom the Bell Tolls
Go Down, Moses
The Good Earth
The Grapes of Wrath
The Great Gatsby
Light in August

INDEX OF LIBRARIES (cont'd)
BASIC LIBRARY SERIES

AMERICAN LITERATURE LIBRARY (cont'd)

Vol 5 - The Jazz Age to W.W.II Part 2 (10 titles)

Miss Lonelyhearts & The Day of the Locust
Native Son
Of Mice and Men
Our Town
The Pearl
The Red Pony
The Sound and the Fury
The Sun Also Rises
Tender is the Night
Unvanquished

Vol 6 - Post-War American Literature Part 1 (13 titles)

100 Years of Solitude
All the King's Men
The Assistant
The Autobiography of Malcolm X
The Bell Jar
Black Like Me
Catch-22
The Catcher in the Rye
The Color Purple
The Crucible
Death of a Salesman
Dune and Other Works
The Glass Menagerie & A Streetcar Named Desire

Vol 7 - Post-War American Literature Part 2 (12 titles)

The Invisible Man
Manchild in the Promised Land
O'Connor's Short Stories
The Old Man and the Sea
One Flew Over the Cuckoo's Nest
The Ox-Bow Incident
A Separate Peace
Shane
To Kill a Mockingbird
Vonnegut's Major Works
Walden Two
Who's Afraid of Virginia Woolf?

INDEX OF LIBRARIES (cont'd)
BASIC LIBRARY SERIES

EUROPEAN LITERATURE LIBRARY: 4 Volumes, 29 Titles

Vol 1 - French Literature (12 titles)

Candide
The Count of Monte Cristo
Cyrano de Bergerac
Les Miserables
Madame Bovary
No Exit & The Flies
The Plague
The Red and the Black
The Stranger
Tartuffe, Misanthrope & Bourgeois Gentlemen
The Three Musketeers
Waiting for Godot

Vol 2 - German Literature (7 titles)

All Quiet on the Western Front
Demian
The Diary of Anne Frank
Faust Pt. I & Pt. II
Kafka's Short Stories
Steppenwolf & Siddhartha
The Trial

Vol 3 - Russian Literature (7 titles)

Anna Karenina
The Brothers Karamozov
Crime and Punishment
Fathers and Sons
Notes from the Underground
One Day in the Life of Ivan Denisovich
War and Peace

Vol 4 - Scandinavian Literature (3 titles)

Giants in the Earth
Ibsen's Plays I: A Doll's House & Hedda Gabler
Ibsen's Plays II: Ghosts, An Enemy of the People & The Wild Duck

INDEX OF LIBRARIES (cont'd)

AUTHORS LIBRARY SERIES (13 Volumes)

AUTHORS LIBRARY

Vol 1 -Charles Dickens Library (6 titles)

Bleak House
David Copperfield
Great Expectations
Hard Times
Oliver Twist
A Tale of Two Cities

Vol 2 - Feodor Dostoevsky Library (3 titles)

The Brothers Karamazov
Crime and Punishment
Notes from the Underground

Vol 3 - William Faulkner Library (7 titles)

Absalom, Absalom!
As I Lay Dying
The Bear
Go Down, Moses
Light in August
The Sound and the Fury
The Unvanquished

Vol 4 - Thomas Hardy Library (5 titles)

Far from the Madding Crowd
Jude the Obscure
The Major of Casterbridge
The Return of the Native
Tess of the D'Urbervilles

Vol 5 - Ernest Hemingway Library (4 titles)

A Farewell to Arms
For Whom the Bell Tolls
The Old Man and the Sea
The Sun Also Rises

Vol 6 - Henry James Library (3 titles)

The American
Daisy Miller & The Turn of the Screw
The Portrait of a Lady

Vol 7 - Sinclair Lewis Library (2 titles)

*Babbitt * Main Street*

INDEX OF LIBRARIES (cont'd)
AUTHORS LIBRARY SERIES

Vol 8 - Shakespeare Library, Part 1 - The Comedies (12 titles)

All's Well that Ends Well & The Merry Wives of Windsor
As You Like It
The Comedy of Errors, Love's Labour's Lost & The Two Gentlemen of Verona
Measure for Measure
The Merchant of Venice
A Midsummer Night's Dream
Much Ado About Nothing
The Taming of the Shrew
The Tempest
Troilus and Cressida
Twelfth Night
The Winter's Tale

Vol 9 - Shakespeare Library, Part 2 - The Tragedies (7 Titles)

Antony and Cleopatra
Hamlet
Julius Caesar
King Lear
Macbeth
Othello
Romeo and Juliet

Vol 10 - Shakespeare Library, Part 3 - The Histories; The Sonnets (7 titles)

Henry IV Part 1
Henry IV Part 2
Henry V
Henry VI Parts 1,2,3
Richard II
Richard III
Shakespeare's The Sonnets

Vol 11 - George Bernard Shaw Library (2 titles)

Pygnalion & Arms and the Man
Man and Superman & Caesar and Cleopatra

Vol 12 - John Steinbeck Library (4 titles)

The Grapes of Wrath
Of Mice and Men
The Pearl
The Red Pony

Vol 13 - Mark Twain Library (4 titles)

A Connecticut Yankee in King Arthur's Court
Huckleberry Finn
The Prince and the Pauper
Tom Sawyer